Professional Examinations

Paper P6

Advanced Taxation
(Finance Act 2015)
For September 2016 to March 2017
examination sittings

EXAM KIT

British Library Cataloguing-in-Publication Data

A catalogue record for this book is available from the British Library.

Published by:

Kaplan Publishing UK

Unit 2 The Business Centre

Molly Millar's Lane

Wokingham

Berkshire

RG41 2QZ

ISBN: 978-1-78415-237-6

© Kaplan Financial Limited, 2016

Printed and bound in Great Britain.

The text in this material and any others made available by any Kaplan Group company does not amount to advice on a particular matter and should not be taken as such. No reliance should be placed on the content as the basis for any investment or other decision or in connection with any advice given to third parties. Please consult your appropriate professional adviser as necessary. Kaplan Publishing Limited and all other Kaplan group companies expressly disclaim all liability to any person in respect of any losses or other claims, whether direct, indirect, incidental, consequential or otherwise arising in relation to the use of such materials.

All rights reserved. No part of this examination may be reproduced or transmitted in any form or by any means, electronic or mechanical, including photocopying, recording, or by any information storage and retrieval system, without prior permission from Kaplan Publishing.

Acknowledgements

The past ACCA examination questions are the copyright of the Association of Chartered Certified Accountants. The original answers to the questions from June 1994 onwards were produced by the ACCA and have been adapted by Kaplan Publishing.

Kaplan Publishing are constantly finding new ways to make a difference to your studies and our exciting online resources really do offer something different to students looking for exam success.

This book comes with free MyKaplan online resources so that you can study anytime, anywhere. This free online resource is not sold separately and is included in the price of the book.

Having purchased this book, you have access to the following online study materials:

CONTENT	ACCA (including FFA, FAB, FMA)		FIA (excluding FFA, FAB, FMA)	
	Text	Kit	Text	Kit
iPaper version of the book	✓	✓	✓	✓
Interactive electronic version of the book	✓			
Check Your Understanding Test with instant answers	✓			
Material updates	✓	✓	✓	✓
Latest official ACCA exam questions*		✓		
Extra question assistance using the signpost icon**		✓		
Timed questions with an online tutor debrief using clock icon*		✓		
Interim assessment including questions and answers	✓		✓	
Technical answers	✓	✓	✓	✓

* Excludes F1, F2, F3, F4, FAB, FMA and FFA; for all other papers includes a selection of questions, as released by ACCA
** For ACCA P1–P7 only

How to access your online resources

Kaplan Financial students will already have a MyKaplan account and these extra resources will be available to you online. You do not need to register again, as this process was completed when you enrolled. If you are having problems accessing online materials, please ask your course administrator.

If you are already a registered MyKaplan user go to www.MyKaplan.co.uk and log in. Select the 'add a book' feature and enter the ISBN number of this book and the unique pass key at the bottom of this card. Then click 'finished' or 'add another book'. You may add as many books as you have purchased from this screen.

If you purchased through Kaplan Flexible Learning or via the Kaplan Publishing website you will automatically receive an e-mail invitation to MyKaplan. Please register your details using this email to gain access to your content. If you do not receive the e-mail or book content, please contact Kaplan Flexible Learning.

If you are a new MyKaplan user register at www.MyKaplan.co.uk and click on the link contained in the email we sent you to activate your account. Then select the 'add a book' feature, enter the ISBN number of this book and the unique pass key at the bottom of this card. Then click 'finished' or 'add another book'.

Your Code and Information

This code can only be used once for the registration of one book online. This registration and your online content will expire when the final sittings for the examinations covered by this book have taken place. Please allow one hour from the time you submit your book details for us to process your request.

Please scratch the film to access your MyKaplan code.

Please be aware that this code is case-sensitive and you will need to include the dashes within the passcode, but not when entering the ISBN. For further technical support, please visit www.MyKaplan.co.uk

CONTENTS

	Page
Index to questions and answers	P5
Analysis of past papers	P11
Exam technique	P13
Paper specific information	P15
Kaplan's recommended revision approach	P19
Kaplan's detailed revision plan	P23
Tax rates and allowances	P33
Time limits and election dates	P39

Section

1	Practice questions	1
2	Answers to practice questions	149
3	Pilot paper exam questions	681
4	Answers to pilot paper exam questions	691

Key features in this edition

In addition to providing a wide ranging bank of real past exam questions, we have also included in this edition:

- An analysis of all of the recent examination papers.
- Paper specific information and advice on exam technique.
- Our recommended approach to make your revision for this particular subject as effective as possible.

  This includes step by step guidance on how best to use our Kaplan material (Complete text, pocket notes and exam kit) at this stage in your studies.

- An increased number of enhanced tutorial answers packed with specific key answer tips, technical tutorial notes and exam technique tips from our experienced tutors.

- Complementary online resources including full tutor debriefs and question assistance to point you in the right direction when you get stuck.

KAPLAN PUBLISHING

March and June 2016 – Real examination questions

The real March and June 2016 examination questions released by the ACCA are available on **My**Kaplan at:

www.mykaplan.co.uk

You will find a wealth of other resources to help you with your studies on the following sites:

www.mykaplan.co.uk

www.accaglobal.com/en/student.html

Quality and accuracy are of the utmost importance to us so if you spot an error in any of our products, please send an email to mykaplanreporting@kaplan.com with full details, or follow the link to the feedback form in MyKaplan.

Our Quality Co-ordinator will work with our technical team to verify the error and take action to ensure it is corrected in future editions.

INDEX TO QUESTIONS AND ANSWERS

INTRODUCTION

The style of current Paper P6 exam questions changed fairly recently and significant changes have had to be made to questions in light of the legislative changes in recent Finance Acts.

Accordingly, many of the old ACCA questions within this kit have been adapted to reflect the new style of paper and the new rules. If changed in any way from the original version, this is indicated in the end column of the index below with the mark *(A)*.

Also included are the marking schemes for past ACCA real examination questions to assist you in understanding where marks are earned and the amount of time to spend on particular tasks. Note that if a question has been changed from the original version, it will have also been necessary to change the original ACCA marking scheme. Therefore if a question is marked as adapted (A) you should assume that this also applies to the marking scheme.

Note that the majority of the questions within the kit are past ACCA exam questions, the more recent questions are labelled as such in the index.

The pilot paper is included at the end of the kit.

KEY TO THE INDEX

PAPER ENHANCEMENTS

We have added the following enhancements to the answers in this exam kit:

Key answer tips

All answers include key answer tips to help your understanding of each question.

Tutorial note

All answers include more tutorial notes to explain some of the technical points in more detail.

Top tutor tips

For selected questions, we 'walk through the answer' giving guidance on how to approach the questions with helpful 'tips from a top tutor', together with technical tutor notes.

These answers are indicated with the 'footsteps' icon in the index.

PAPER P6: ADVANCED TAXATION (FA2015)

ONLINE ENHANCEMENTS

 Timed question with Online tutor debrief

For selected questions, we recommend that they are to be completed in full exam conditions (i.e. properly timed in a closed book environment).

In addition to theACCA's technical answer, enhanced with key answer tips and tutorial notes in this exam kit, online you can find an answer debrief by a top tutor that:

- works through the question in full
- points out how to approach the question
- how to ensure that the easy marks are obtained as quickly as possible, and
- emphasises how to tackle exam questions and exam technique.
- These questions are indicated with the 'clock' icon in the index.

 Online question assistance

Have you ever looked at a question and not known where to start, or got stuck part way through?

For selected questions, we have produced 'Online question assistance' offering different levels of guidance, such as:

- ensuring that you understand the question requirements fully, highlighting key terms and the meaning of the verbs used
- how to read the question proactively, with knowledge of the requirements, to identify the topic areas covered
- assessing the detail content of the question body, pointing out key information and explaining why it is important
- help in devising a plan of attack

With this assistance, you should then be able to attempt your answer confident that you know what is expected of you.

These questions are indicated with the 'signpost' icon in the index.

Online question enhancements and answer debriefs will be available on **My**Kaplan at:

www.mykaplan.co.uk

INDEX TO QUESTIONS AND ANSWERS

TAXATION OF INDIVIDUALS

		Page number		Past exam
		Question	Answer	(Adapted)
Employment				
1	Clifford and Amanda	1	149	*Jun 07 (A)*
2	Dokham	4	154	*Jun 10*
3	Morice and Babine plc	6	159	*Dec 11*
4	Pita plc	7	165	*Jun 14*
5	Hyssop Ltd	8	171	*Sept/Dec 15*
Unincorporated businesses				
6	Gloria Seaford	10	178	*Dec 06 (A)*
7	Ellroy	12	185	*Dec 09 (A)*
8	Dana	14	190	*Dec 12*
9	Spike	16	196	*Jun 13*
10	Kantar	17	202	*Dec 14*
11	Piquet and Buraco	20	211	*Dec 14*
Changing business scenarios				
12	The Stiletto Partnership	21	217	*Jun 07 (A)*
13	Desiree	24	221	*Jun 10 (A)*
14	Vine	25	226	*Jun 10 (A)*
15	Faure	27	232	*Jun 11*
16	Jerome and Tricycle Ltd	28	237	*Jun 12*
17	Farina and Lauda	30	244	*Dec 13*
18	Ziti	32	256	*Jun 14*
19	Jonny	35	269	*Sept/Dec 15*

KAPLAN PUBLISHING

PAPER P6: ADVANCED TAXATION (FA2015)

			Page number		
			Question	Answer	Past exam (Adapted)
Capital taxes					
20	Joan Ark		39	277	
21	Alex		40	284	Pilot 05 (A)
22	Mabel Porter		42	290	Dec 06
23	Alvaro Pelorus		43	297	Jun 07 (A)
24	Kepler		45	306	Jun 08 (A)
25	Ernest and Georgina		47	312	Dec 08 (A)
26	Fitzgerald and Morrison		49	317	Jun 09 (A)
27	Capstan		50	323	Jun 11
28	Surfe		51	330	Dec 11
29	Una		53	337	Jun 12
30	Ash		56	349	Dec 12
31	Cuthbert		57	354	Dec 12
32	Brad		58	360	Jun 13 (A)
33	Pescara		61	366	Dec 13 (A)
34	Cada		62	373	Dec 14
35	King		64	380	Jun 15
Multi tax personal including overseas					
36	Nucleus Resources		66	386	Dec 08 (A)
37	Boson		69	396	Dec 08 (A)
38	Poblano		70	402	Jun 10 (A)

INDEX TO QUESTIONS AND ANSWERS

			Page number		Past exam
			Question	Answer	(Adapted)
Multi tax personal including overseas					
39	Sushi		73	413	*Dec 10 (A)*
40	Mirtoon		75	420	*Dec 11 (A)*
41	Shuttelle		78	432	*Jun 13 (A)*
42	Kesme and Soba		79	439	*Jun 14*
43	Jodie		81	445	*Jun 15*
44	Cate and Ravi		84	454	*Jun 15*
Personal finance, business finance and investments					
45	Adam Snook		85	460	*Dec 07 (A)*
46	Gagarin		88	470	*Jun 08 (A)*
47	Calisia		89	474	*Jun 11*
48	Tetra		92	486	*Jun 12*
49	Monisha and Horner		93	493	*Dec 13*
50	Stella and Maris		95	501	*Sept/Dec 15 (A)*

TAXATION OF CORPORATE BUSINESSES

Family company issues					
51	Banda Ross		96	505	*Dec 07 (A)*
52	Spica		99	515	*Jun 08 (A)*
53	James		100	519	*Dec 08 (A)*
54	Fedora and Smoke Ltd		101	527	*Dec 09 (A)*
55	Trifles Ltd, Victoria and Melba		103	533	*Dec 10 (A)*
56	Sank Ltd and Kurt Ltd		104	539	*Jun 12 (A)*
57	Banger Ltd and Candle Ltd		106	546	*Dec 12 (A)*

PAPER P6: ADVANCED TAXATION (FA2015)

		Page number		
		Question	Answer	*Past exam (Adapted)*
Family company issues				
58	Bamburg Ltd	107	553	*Jun 14*
59	Nocturne Ltd	109	559	*Jun 15*
Groups, consortia and overseas company aspects				
60	Palm plc	110	565	*Dec 07 (A)*
61	Particle Ltd Group	112	570	*Dec 08 (A)*
62	Cacao Ltd Group	115	579	*Jun 10 (A)*
63	Daube Group	118	588	*Dec 10 (A)*
64	Loriod plc Group	121	600	*Jun 11*
65	Drench, Hail Ltd and Rain Ltd	122	604	*Dec 11 (A)*
66	Janus plc Group	125	614	*Jun 12*
67	Flame plc Group	127	622	*Dec 12*
68	Liza	130	632	*Jun 13*
69	Spetz Ltd Group	132	637	*Dec 13*
70	Opus Ltd Group	134	642	*Jun 14*
71	Bond Ltd	136	650	*Dec 14*
72	Klubb plc	139	657	*Dec 14*
73	Helm Ltd Group	141	662	*Jun 15*
74	Sprint Ltd and Iron Ltd	143	668	*Sept/Dec 15*
75	Cinnabar Ltd	145	674	*Sept/Dec 15*

ANALYSIS OF PAST PAPERS

The table below summarises the key topics that have been tested in recent examinations.

Note that the references are to the number of the question in this edition of the exam kit.

In addition, the Pilot Paper is produced in its original form at the end of the kit.

	Dec 2012	Jun 2013	Dec 2013	Jun 2014	Dec 2014	Jun 2015	Sept/Dec 2015
IHT							
Lifetime gifts	Q8, Q31	Q32	Q17, Q33	Q18	Q10	Q35	Q50
Death estate	Q31			Q42			Q19
Diminution in value		Q32					
BPR/APR		Q32		Q18			
Gift with reservation			Q33				
Consequences of lifetime giving	Q8	Q32	Q33		Q10, Q34	Q35	
Overseas aspects	Q31			Q42		Q43	
Trusts							
Description							
Tax treatment	Q8		Q17			Q35	
CGT							
Basic computations	Q67, Q30	Q32, Q68	Q17, Q49	Q18	Q10	Q35, Q43	
Shares	Q30		Q33				
Reorganisations			Q33				
Liquidations	Q57						
Capital gains tax reliefs:							
Incorporation relief			Q17				
Entrepreneurs' relief	Q30		Q17, Q49	Q18, Q4		Q43	
Gift relief	Q8		Q17			Q35, Q43	
PPR relief				Q42		Q43	
Overseas aspects of CGT		Q32			Q11	Q43, Q44	
Income Tax							
Personal tax computations	Q8	Q41	Q49	Q18, Q42	Q10	Q43, Q44	Q19, Q50
Redundancy payments				Q4			
Share options and share incentives	Q67	Q9		Q4	Q72		
Calculation/discussion of benefits		Q41, Q9	Q69	Q4, Q58		Q44	Q5
Employed v self employed							Q19
Property business profits			Q49	Q42			
Overseas aspects of income		Q41	Q69		Q11	Q43	
NICs			Q49			Q44	Q5

PAPER P6: ADVANCED TAXATION (FA2015)

	Dec 2012	Jun 2013	Dec 2013	Jun 2014	Dec 2014	Jun 2015	Sept/Dec 2015
Self Employed Income							
– Opening year rules	Q8						Q19
– Change a/c date					Q11		
– Closing year rules		Q9		Q18		Q43	
– Capital allowances			Q17	Q18, Q58			
– Trading losses	Q8	Q9			Q10	Q43	Q19
– Partnerships							
Badges of trade						Q44	
Self-assessment	Q30, Q31				Q10		
Sole trader v company							
Corporation Tax							
Anti-avoidance – trading losses					Q71		
Loan relationships	Q57					Q73	
Research and development							Q75
Intangible assets					Q71		Q75
Close Companies	Q57			Q58		Q59	
Purchase of own shares							
Personal service company			Q49				
Groups	Q67			Q70	Q71	Q73	Q74, Q75
Consortium Relief				Q70			Q75
Capital gains implications including Rollover	Q67	Q68		Q58	Q71	Q73	Q5, Q74
Pre entry cap loss						Q73	
Substantial shareholding exemption				Q70		Q73	Q74, Q75
Overseas Aspects	Q57		Q69		Q72		
Extraction of profits (salary vs. dividend)				Q58			
Reorganisations	Q57						
Transfer pricing							
Sale of shares vs. assets	Q67						
Administration					Q72		
Financial planning							
Investments							
Pensions		Q41					Q50
EIS/SEIS/VCT			Q33				
Stamp Duty/SDLT						Q73	
VAT							
Registration/deregistration	Q30				Q10	Q43	Q74
Schemes				Q58			
Partial exemption			Q69			Q59	
Groups		Q68					Q74
Overseas aspects							
Land and buildings	Q67			Q18	Q71		Q5
Transfer of going concern				Q18			
Ethical issues	Q67		Q17	Q70	Q10	Q73	Q19

EXAM TECHNIQUE

- We recommend that you spend **15 minutes reading the paper** at the beginning of the exam:
  - read the questions and examination requirements carefully, and
  - begin planning your answers.

  See the Paper Specific Information for advice on how to use this time for this paper.

- If 15 minutes are spent reading the examination paper, this leaves three hours to attempt the questions.

- **Divide the time** you spend on questions in proportion to the marks on offer:
  - one suggestion for this examination is to allocate 1.8 minutes to each mark available (180 minutes/100 marks), so a 10 mark question should be completed in approximately 18 minutes. If you plan to spend more or less time than 15 minutes reading the paper, your time allocation per mark will be different.
  - within that, try to allow time at the end of each question to review your answer and address any obvious issues

  Whatever happens, always keep your eye on the clock and **do not over run on any part of any question!**

- If you **get completely stuck** with a question:
  - leave space in your answer book, and
  - **return to it later.**

- Stick to the question and **tailor your answer** to what you are asked.
  - Pay particular attention to the verbs in the question.
  - Try to apply your comments to the scenario where possible.

- If you do not understand what a question is asking, **state your assumptions**.

  Even if you do not answer in precisely the way the examining team hoped, you should be given some credit, if your assumptions are reasonable.

- You should do everything you can to make things easy for the marker.

  The marker will find it easier to identify the points you have made if your **answers are legible**.

- **Written questions**:

  Your answer should have:
  - a clear structure
  - a brief introduction, a main section and a conclusion.

  Be concise. It is better to write a little about a lot of different points than a great deal about one or two points.

- **Computations**:

  It is essential to include all your workings in your answers.

  Although computations may be prepared using standard formats, you should always think about whether there is an easier way to arrive at the answer by working in the margin, say.

- **Reports, memos and other documents**:

  Some questions ask you to present your answer in the form of a report, a memo, a letter or other document.

  Make sure that you use the correct format – there could be easy marks to gain here.

KAPLAN PUBLISHING

PAPER P6: ADVANCED TAXATION (FA2015)

PAPER SPECIFIC INFORMATION

THE EXAM

FORMAT OF THE EXAM

Number of marks

Section A: 2 compulsory scenario-based questions:
- Question 1 — 35
- Question 2 — 25

Section B: 3 20 mark questions, 2 only to be answered — 40 marks in total

Total: 100

Total time allowed: 3 and 15 minutes.

Note that:

- Questions will be scenario based and will normally involve consideration of more than one tax, together with some elements of planning and the interaction of taxes. Computations will normally only be required in support of explanations or advice and not in isolation

- There will be four marks for professional skills in question one.

- Every Paper P6 (UK) exam will include an ethical component for approximately five marks. The questions on ethics will be confined to one of the following areas:
    - prospective clients
    - conflicts of interest
    - disclosure of information to HM Revenue & Customs
    - money laundering
    - tax irregularities
    - tax avoidance
    - tax evasion.

  The ethical component of the exam will appear in section A.

- Apart from the above, any subject may be tested anywhere in the exam for any number of marks.

- The exam will not just test P6 knowledge: F6 knowledge is still highly examinable, but will be tested in a more advanced way.

- The requirements of a section A question may be presented in one of two different ways:
    - given in full at the end of the question, or
    - a brief overview can be provided at the end of the question with a reference to the detailed requirements in the body of the question.

PASS MARK

The pass mark for all ACCA Qualification examination papers is 50%.

PAPER P6: ADVANCED TAXATION (FA2015)

SUGGESTED APPROACH TO THIS PAPER

From the September 2016 sitting, the P6 examination will be 3 hours and 15 minutes long, with no separate time allocated for reading and planning. However, reading and planning remain crucial elements of your examination technique and is important that you allocate time in the examination to this.

Spend time reading the examination paper carefully. As stated earlier, we recommend that 15 minutes should be spent reading the paper.

As there is some choice in section B, there is a decision regarding which one of the optional questions to drop, together with the decision of which order you should attempt the questions.

Therefore, in relation to P6, we recommend that you take the following approach with your reading and planning:

- **Skim through the whole paper**, assessing the level of difficulty of each question.

- **Write down** on the question paper next to the mark allocation **the amount of time you should spend on each part.** Do this for each part of every question.

- **Decide which optional question to drop and the order** in which you think you will attempt each question:

    This is a personal choice and you have time on the revision phase to try out different approaches, for example, if you sit mock exams.

    A common approach is to tackle the question you think is the easiest and you are most comfortable with first.

    Others may prefer to tackle the longest questions first, or conversely leave them to the last.

    Psychologists believe that you usually perform at your best on the second and third question you attempt, once you have settled into the exam, so not tackling the bigger Section A questions first may be advisable.

    It is usual however that student tackle their least favourite topic and/or the most difficult question in their opinion last.

    Whatever your approach, you must make sure that you leave enough time to attempt all questions fully and be very strict with yourself in timing each question.

PAPER SPECIFIC INFORMATION

- **For each question** in turn, read the requirements and then the detail of the question carefully.

  Always read the requirement first as this enables you to **focus on the detail of the question with the specific task in mind**.

  For computational questions:

  Highlight key numbers/information and key words in the question, scribble notes to yourself on the question paper to remember key points in your answer.

  Jot down pro formas required if applicable.

  For written questions:

  Take notice of the format required (e.g. letter, memo, notes) and identify the recipient of the answer. You need to do this to judge the level of sophistication required in your answer and whether the use of a formal reply or informal bullet points would be satisfactory.

  Plan your beginning, middle and end and the key areas to be addressed and your use of titles and sub-titles to enhance your answer.

  For all questions:

  Spot the easy marks to be gained in a question and parts which can be performed independently of the rest of the question. For example, tax payment dates, ethical issues, laying out the answer in the correct format etc.

  Make sure that you do these parts first when you tackle the question.

  Don't go overboard in terms of planning time on any one question – you need a good measure of the whole paper and a plan for all of the questions at the end of the 15 minutes.

  By covering all questions you can often help yourself as you may find that facts in one question may remind you of things you should put into your answer relating to a different question.

- With your plan of attack in mind, **start answering your chosen question** with your plan to hand, as soon as you are ready to start.

 Always keep your eye on the clock and do not over run on any part of any question!

DETAILED SYLLABUS

The detailed syllabus and study guide written by the ACCA can be found at:

www.accaglobal.com/en/student.html

KAPLAN'S RECOMMENDED REVISION APPROACH

QUESTION PRACTICE IS THE KEY TO SUCCESS

Success in professional examinations relies upon you acquiring a firm grasp of the required knowledge at the tuition phase. In order to be able to do the questions, knowledge is essential.

However, the difference between success and failure often hinges on your exam technique on the day and making the most of the revision phase of your studies.

The **Kaplan complete text** is the starting point, designed to provide the underpinning knowledge to tackle all questions. However, in the revision phase, pouring over text books is not the answer.

Kaplan Online knowledge checks help you consolidate your knowledge and understanding and are a useful tool to check whether you can remember key topic areas.

Kaplan pocket notes are designed to help you quickly revise a topic area, however you then need to practice questions. There is a need to progress to full exam standard questions as soon as possible, and to tie your exam technique and technical knowledge together.

The importance of question practice cannot be over-emphasised.

The recommended approach below is designed by expert tutors in the field, in conjunction with their knowledge of the examining team and their recent real exams.

The approach taken for the fundamental papers is to revise by topic area. However, with the professional stage papers, a multi topic approach is required to answer the scenario based questions.

You need to practise as many questions as possible in the time you have left.

OUR AIM

Our aim is to get you to the stage where you can attempt exam standard questions confidently, to time, in a closed book environment, with no supplementary help (i.e. to simulate the real examination experience).

Practising your exam technique on real past examination questions, in timed conditions, is also vitally important for you to assess your progress and identify areas of weakness that may need more attention in the final run up to the examination.

In order to achieve this we recognise that initially you may feel the need to practise some questions with open book help and exceed the required time.

The approach below shows you which questions you should use to build up to coping with exam standard question practice, and references to the sources of information available should you need to revisit a topic area in more detail.

PAPER P6: ADVANCED TAXATION (FA2015)

Remember that in the real examination, all you have to do is:

- attempt all questions required by the exam
- only spend the allotted time on each question, and
- get them at least 50% right!

Try and practise this approach on every question you attempt from now to the real exam.

EXAMINER COMMENTS

We have included the examiner's comments to the specific new syllabus examination questions in this kit for you to see the main pitfalls that students fall into with regard to technical content.

However, too many times in the general section of the report, the examiner comments that students had failed due to:

- 'misallocation of time'
- 'running out of time' and
- showing signs of 'spending too much time on an earlier question and clearly rushing the answer to a subsequent question'.

Good exam technique is vital.

THE KAPLAN PAPER P6 REVISION PLAN

Stage 1: Assess areas of strengths and weaknesses

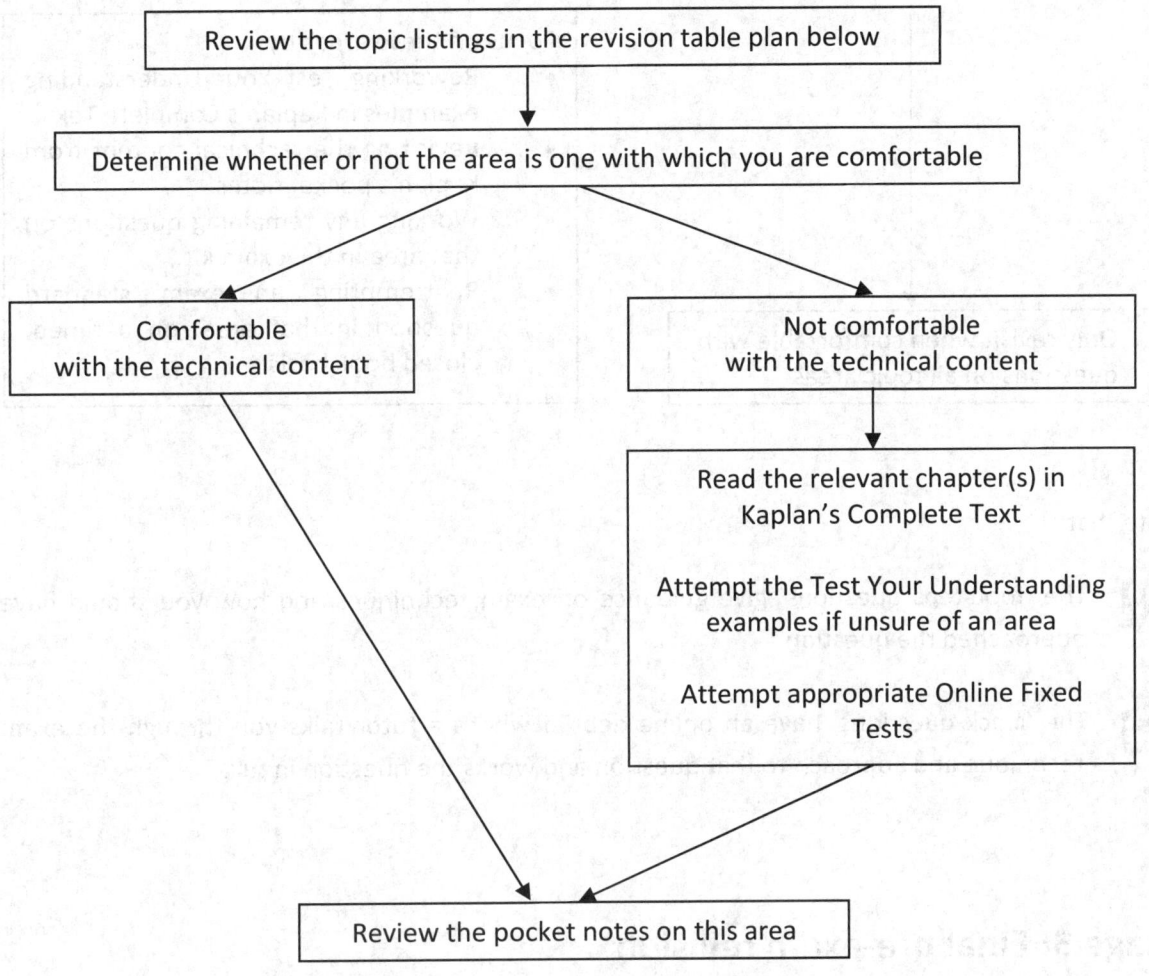

Stage 2: Practice questions

Follow the order of revision of topics as recommended in the revision table plan below and attempt the questions in the order suggested.

Try to avoid referring to text books and notes and the model answer until you have completed your attempt.

Try to answer the question in the allotted time.

Review your attempt with the model answer and assess how much of the answer you achieved in the allocated exam time.

Fill in the self-assessment box below and decide on your best course of action.

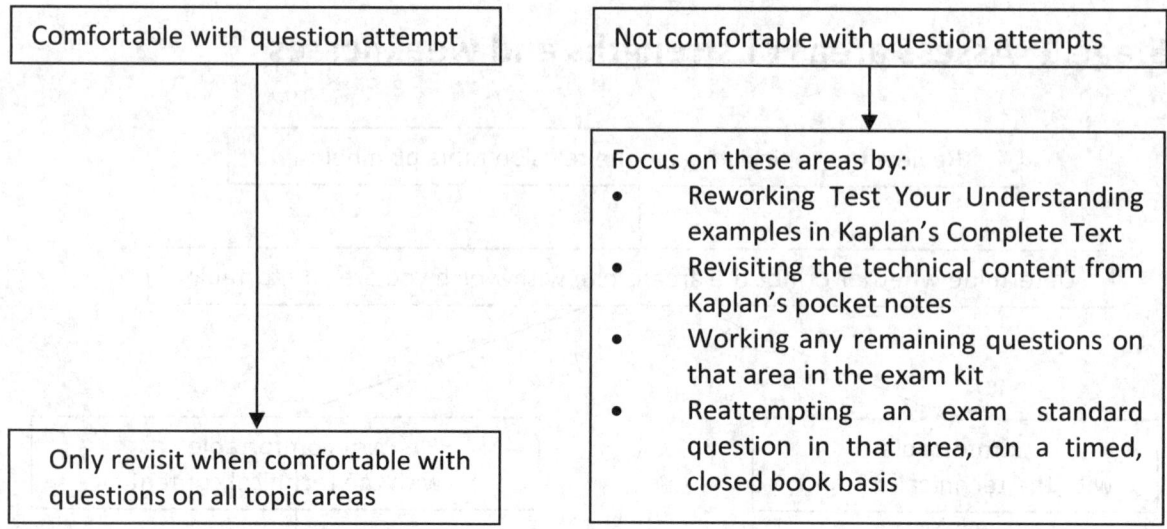

Note that:

 The 'footsteps questions' give guidance on exam techniques and how you should have approached the question.

 The 'clock questions' have an online debrief where a tutor talks you through the exam technique and approach to that question and works the question in full.

Stage 3: Final pre-exam revision

We recommend that you **attempt at least one three hour mock examination** containing a set of previously unseen exam standard questions.

It is important that you get a feel for the breadth of coverage of a real exam without advanced knowledge of the topic areas covered – just as you will expect to see on the real exam day.

Ideally this mock should be sat in timed, closed book, real exam conditions and could be:

- a mock examination offered by your tuition provider, and/or
- the pilot paper in the back of this exam kit, and/or
- the last real examination paper (available shortly afterwards on **My**Kaplan with 'enhanced walk through answers' and a full 'tutor debrief').

KAPLAN'S DETAILED REVISION PLAN

Very few of the recent P6 exam questions focus on just one area of tax.

This is especially true of the big, compulsory scenario questions, which often test several different areas.

This revision plan aims to lead you through a selection of the best questions, broadly grouped by the areas covered, and will ensure that you revise all of the key topics.

It is especially important that you practise the more recent questions, as the examining team has its own particular style.

Familiarisation with this style of questions will help to make sure that you are as well-prepared as possible for the real exam.

Topic	Complete Text Chapter	Pocket note Chapter	Questions to attempt	Tutor guidance	Date attempted	Self assessment
Corporation tax				Corporation tax is often an area that students struggle with, but in recent exams has regularly formed the basis of one of the compulsory scenario questions. For this reason, it would be a good idea to start by revising corporation tax to ensure that you have enough time to cover it thoroughly.		
Losses, anti-avoidance re trading losses c/f;	24	15	Q63 Daube Group,	The corporation tax scenario questions will often involve a group of companies; VAT is a regular feature too.		
Losses and gains groups;	27, 29	16	Q70 Opus Ltd Group	Use your Kaplan pocket notes to make sure that you are happy with all the different group definitions and implications before attempting these questions. You must also learn the reliefs available for the various types of losses, as it is easy to get these confused. Rollover relief is the only capital gains relief available to companies, making it a highly examinable area. VAT on land and buildings is a favourite area, and regularly features in questions. Don't worry if you find these questions hard – the scenario questions will get easier with practice. There are walkthrough answers to help you if you get stuck.		
Substantial shareholding exemption;	22	15				
Pre entry capital losses;	27	16				
Rollover relief;	9	8				
VAT: land and buildings and overseas aspects;	20	14				
Ethics	16	11				

PAPER P6: ADVANCED TAXATION (FA2015)

Topic	Complete Text Chapter	Pocket note Chapter	Questions to attempt	Tutor guidance	Date attempted	Self assessment
				Note that stamp duty and ethics often represent easy marks in this type of question.		
Gains groups; Degrouping charges; Rollover relief; Substantial shareholding exemption; Pre entry capital losses; Loan relationships; Ethics	27 27 9 22 27 22 16	16 16 8 15 16 15 11	Q73 Helm Ltd Group	Another excellent scenario question. Having attempted the previous two questions, you should start to find these easier as you become familiar with the style of question and the areas that are frequently tested. This question also includes loan relationship deficits, which often feature in questions.		
Gains groups; Sale of shares versus sale of assets; Admin VAT: groups and overseas; Patent box rules	27, 29 27 22 21, 27 22	16 15 16, 17 15	Q61 Particle Ltd Group	This big scenario question covers disposal of a subsidiary through sale of its shares or assets. Look at the mark allocations here to gauge how much you need to write. The corporation tax admin is pure F6 knowledge, highlighting how important it is that you retain this knowledge. This question covers VAT groups, which are regularly tested, and another popular area: overseas aspects. The question also tests the patent box rules. Use your Kaplan pocket notes to refresh your memory.		

KAPLAN'S DETAILED REVISION PLAN

Topic	Complete Text Chapter	Pocket note Chapter	Questions to attempt	Tutor guidance	Date attempted	Self assessment
Groups; Overseas aspects; Transfer pricing	27–29 28 23	16 17 16	Q64 Loriod plc Group	This was set as an optional question in the exam and covers some overseas aspects of corporation tax, including comparison of branch versus subsidiary, and the transfer pricing.		
Further issues: Research and development; Controlled foreign companies (CFCs); Degrouping charges; VAT: imports, capital goods scheme.	23 28 27 21	15 17 16 17	Q60 Palm plc, Q62 Cacao Ltd Group	Before attempting Q60, use your Kaplan pocket notes to make sure that you learn the rules governing the following: – enhanced relief available to companies for R&D expenditure, and – the conditions and possible exemptions for CFCs. There are also marks here again for degrouping charges and VAT for imports. Then attempt Q62, which is a big scenario question covering many of the same areas. The final section of Q62 covers VAT and the capital goods scheme. The examining team has said that the capital goods scheme is important, so make sure that you can explain how it works.		
Test question			Pilot Q1 Hutt plc	Now try attempting this question under exam conditions. You have 1.8 minutes per mark, so 70 minutes in total.		

PAPER P6: ADVANCED TAXATION (FA2015)

Topic	Complete Text Chapter	Pocket note Chapter	Questions to attempt	Tutor guidance	Date attempted	Self assessment
The Capital taxes	The key capital taxes are capital gains tax and inheritance tax. Inheritance tax often features as part of both a compulsory question and an optional question, often linked with capital gains tax.					
Inheritance tax basics; Income tax basics; Trusts	11–13 1 14	8 1 10	Q21 Alex; Q28 Surfe	Q21 is a good question to start with, covering the basic calculations and includes a straightforward income tax computation in part (a), and a written section on trusts. Trusts often feature as a small written section. Q28 also has a section on trusts and some basic inheritance tax computations, as well as some slightly trickier calculations. Related property and the transfer of a spouse's unused nil rate band are regularly tested, so make sure that you are happy with these.		
Inheritance tax: further computations; Business property relief (BPR); Admin	11–12 12 13	8 8 8	Q24 Kepler	This question includes popular complications: the diminution in value principle and BPR. BPR features in nearly every exam, so you must learn the conditions in detail. Also use your Kaplan pocket notes to make sure that you learn the payment dates for inheritance tax, particularly payment by instalment.		

KAPLAN'S DETAILED REVISION PLAN

Topic	Complete Text Chapter	Pocket note Chapter	Questions to attempt	Tutor guidance	Date attempted	Self assessment
Inheritance tax versus capital gains tax; Agricultural property relief; BPR; Gift relief, Principal private residence relief; Planning	13 12 12 9 9 13	8 8 8 6 6 12	Q20 Joan Ark, Q26 Fitzgerald and Morrison, Q25 Ernest and Georgina, Q2 Dokham (b)	One of the examining team's favourite tricks is to test both the inheritance tax and capital gains tax implications of lifetime gifts, and there are many questions on this area. Q20 is not in current exam style, but is a great question as it covers most of the calculations and reliefs available for both IHT and CGT. Before attempting this question, make sure that you revise the CGT reliefs thoroughly, and try not to get IHT and CGT confused! Note that part (ii) of this question, on the advantages of lifetime gifts, is very general. You will probably have to apply this knowledge in an exam question, and just pick out the points which are relevant. Have a go at Q26, a real past exam question from the optional section of the exam. This question covers gift relief for CGT in detail. Then try Q25 – but think carefully before you answer! The individuals are not married. Q2(b) also covers lifetime gifts, but with a slightly less obvious requirement.		
Test question			Q33 Pescara	Try answering this one under exam conditions.		

PAPER P6: ADVANCED TAXATION (FA2015)

Topic	Complete Text Chapter	Pocket note Chapter	Questions to attempt	Tutor guidance	Date attempted	Self assessment
Income tax				Income tax is not likely to be tested on its own at P6, but will often feature as part of a bigger question. For many of the questions set at this level, the examining team will not require you to do a whole income tax computation, but rather to start part way through. For example, you may have to calculate just the tax on some extra income, working in the margin. Be prepared to write about employment benefits as well as doing calculations.		
Property income; Employment benefits: share options, loans, use of assets; CGT: PPR relief; Ethics	3 2 9 16	1 2 6 11	Q1 Clifford and Amanda	A two part question, with part (a) on CGT and PPR relief, part (b) on income tax. Lease premiums are a tricky area, so you may want to revisit the test your understandings in the complete text before attempting this question. The examining team will often ask for explanations of how benefits are taxed. Think about how you would calculate the benefit, then write the process down in words, make sure your advice is clear and concise. Note the easy marks for ethics again.		
Termination payments; Share incentive plan; Marginal tax computations; CGT vs. IHT; Gift with reservation	2 2 2 13 12	2 2 2 8 8	Pilot Q5 Vikram Bridge	Parts (a) and (b) of this question cover CGT and IHT. Redundancy payments often feature as part of a bigger question. Share schemes are frequently tested, as they are not examined at F6. The last part of the question involves calculating extra tax on a dividend – by working in the margin		

KAPLAN'S DETAILED REVISION PLAN

Topic	Complete Text Chapter	Pocket note Chapter	Questions to attempt	Tutor guidance	Date attempted	Self assessment
Personal financial planning				You may be asked to advise on suitable investment products in the exam, particularly tax efficient forms of investment. Again, this is not likely to form the basis of a whole question, but will generally be combined with other areas.		
Enterprise investment scheme (EIS); VAT on land and buildings, capital goods scheme	3, 9, 15 20	6, 12 14	Q46 Gagarin	This is really two completely separate questions: one on EIS and the other on VAT. Use your Kaplan pocket notes to revise the conditions for EIS before attempting this question – you need a detailed knowledge of the rules to pass.		
Venture capital trusts (VCTs); Pensions;	3, 15 4	12 3	Q48 Tetra (c)	The rules for VCTs are very similar to the EIS rules, but you need to learn a few subtle differences. Pensions were covered at F6, but still appear in questions at P6.		
Test question			Q38 Poblano	Try attempting this question to exam time.		
Overseas aspects of personal tax				Overseas aspects for individuals are very popular in the exam, often appearing in optional questions but also sometimes in the compulsory scenario questions. Before attempting these questions, use your Kaplan pocket notes to revise the definitions of residence and domicile, and make sure that you can explain how a person's status affects the way they are taxed.		
Inheritance tax; Income tax	11 10	9	Q39 Sushi	A comprehensive test of your knowledge of the rules regarding domicile, deemed domicile and the implications for inheritance tax and income tax. The remittance basis for income tax is a popular exam topic, so make sure that you learn the rules.		
Income tax and capital gains tax	10	9	Q37 Boson	This is a great question to revise the temporary absence rules for CGT, with some income tax aspects too. It contains a both words and numbers and, as you must apply the rules to the scenario to score well.		

PAPER P6: ADVANCED TAXATION (FA2015)

Topic	Complete Text Chapter	Pocket note Chapter	Questions to attempt	Tutor guidance	Date attempted	Self assessment
Test question			Q43 Jodie	Try attempting this excellent scenario question, covering all aspects of overseas personal tax, to exam time.		
Business scenarios	There are lots of business scenarios for the examining team to test, and because of the many aspects of tax that apply, these often feature as big, compulsory questions. Much of the knowledge required is basic F6 knowledge, but you must make sure you keep this knowledge up to date.					
Commencement of trade with basic income tax; NICs; CGT: takeovers; VAT: land and buildings; IHT re lifetime gift	17 8 20 11	13 5 14 8	Q45 Adam Snook	This is a scenario involving an individual selling some assets to raise the money to start a business as a sole trader. There are many easy marks available for basic knowledge – the hard part is finding the relevant information and structuring your answer. There is a walkthrough answer for this question to give you further guidance, if needed.		
Change of accounting date and choice of year end	17	13	Q11 Piquet and Buraco (a)	This question requires careful thought about the impact of a change in year end on an individual's overlap profits.		
Cessation of trade; Partnerships; NICs; Corporation tax residence; VAT overseas aspects; Income tax residence	18 19 18 22 21 10	13 13 13 17 17 9	Q12 The Stiletto Partnership	Although this question actually deals with the incorporation of a partnership, it only covers the income tax and NIC implications – so is really just a question about cessation of trade with two alternative cessation dates. Make sure you are happy with the basics regarding the split of partnership profits, closing year assessments, and the NICs payable by self-employed individuals. Part (b) is a good written question on various overseas aspects of tax.		

KAPLAN'S DETAILED REVISION PLAN

Topic	Complete Text Chapter	Pocket note Chapter	Questions to attempt	Tutor guidance	Date attempted	Self assessment
Incorporation; CGT:	18	18	Q14 Vine (a) and (b);	Incorporation is a popular scenario as there are many different tax implications.		
Incorporation relief, Entrepreneurs' relief	9 9	6 6	Pilot Q3 Stanley Beech (a)	The previous question covered the income tax aspects of incorporation – these cover some of the other areas, particularly the CGT aspects with some planning points.		
Test question			Q18 Ziti	Try attempting this question to exam time.		
Employed versus self-employed; Lease versus buy; VAT: partial exemption	2 25 20	12 18 14	Pilot Q2 Pilar Mareno	Before attempting this question you may want to revisit the test your understandings covering VAT for a partially exempt business. Follow the instructions in the question – they guide you through the calculations in the correct order. An excellent question.		
Test question			Q36 Nucleus Resources	Try attempting this question to exam time.		
Family companies and planning scenarios	The following are also common scenarios that you need to be familiar with, although areas such as IR35, purchase of own shares and liquidations tend to only come up every few sittings in the exam.					
Business structure: unincorporated versus company; Loss reliefs; VAT registration Close companies; Ethics	26 24, 27 20 26 16	18 13, 15 14 18 11	Q13 Desiree Q51 Banda Ross	Before attempting these questions, you may want to use your Kaplan pocket notes to revise loss reliefs and the opening year assessment rules for individuals. Try not to confuse unincorporated businesses (individuals) and companies: the computations for individuals are all based around the tax year, whereas companies are taxed based on their chargeable accounting period. Q13 is very straightforward, so do that first.		

PAPER P6: ADVANCED TAXATION (FA2015)

Topic	Complete Text Chapter	Pocket note Chapter	Questions to attempt	Tutor guidance	Date attempted	Self assessment
Extraction of funds from a company	26	18	Pilot Q3 Stanley Beech (b)	Before attempting Q51 make sure you learn the rules for close companies: most small family companies are close. Again – note the easy marks for ethics! Extraction of funds from a company is an area you should be familiar with, but this question illustrates how the examining team likes to test common topics in a less obvious way.		
IR35	26	18	Q53 James (b)	You may want to revisit the test your understandings covering the calculation of deemed salary under IR35 before attempting this question.		
Purchase of own shares; Employee shareholder shares	26 2	18 2	Q52 Spica	Make sure you learn the conditions for purchase of own shares before you do this question. Part (b) tests the rules regarding employee shareholder shares.		
Liquidations; Disincorporation relief; Close companies	8, 26	5, 18	Q57 Banger Ltd and Candle Ltd	Liquidations are not tested regularly, but are fairly straightforward and mainly involve consideration of the difference in tax treatment between dividends and capital gains. This question also covers the more mainstream area of close companies, including close investment holding companies, and has been adapted to cover disincorporation relief		

Note that not all of the questions are referred to in the programme above.

We have recommended an approach to build up from the basic to exam standard questions where possible.

The remaining questions are available in the kit for extra practice for those who require more questions on some areas.

TAX RATES AND ALLOWANCES

Throughout this exam kit:

1   You should assume that the tax rates and allowances for the tax year 2015/16 and for the Financial year to 31 March 2016 will continue to apply for the foreseeable future unless you are instructed otherwise.

2   Calculations and workings need only to be made to the nearest £.

3   All apportionments should be made to the nearest month.

4   All workings should be shown.

INCOME TAX

		Normal rates %	Dividend rates %
Basic rate	£1 – £31,785	20	10
Higher rate	£31,786 – £150,000	40	32.5
Additional rate	£150,001 and above	45	37.5

A starting rate of 0% applies to savings income where it falls within the first £5,000 of taxable income.

Personal allowance

Personal allowance	£10,600
Transferable amount	£1,060
Income limit	£100,000

Residence status

Days in UK	Previously resident	Not previously resident
Less than 16	Automatically not resident	Automatically not resident
16 to 45	Resident if 4 UK ties (or more)	Automatically not resident
46 to 90	Resident if 3 UK ties (or more)	Resident if 4 UK ties
91 to 120	Resident if 2 UK ties (or more)	Resident if 3 UK ties (or more)
121 to 182	Resident if 1 UK tie (or more)	Resident if 2 UK ties (or more)
183 or more	Automatically resident	Automatically resident

Remittance basis charge

UK resident for:	Charge
7 out of the last 9 years	£30,000
12 out of the last 14 years	£60,000
17 out of the last 20 years	£90,000

Child benefit income tax charge

Where income is between £50,000 and £60,000, the charge is 1% of the amount of child benefit received for every £100 of income over £50,000.

Car benefit percentage

The relevant base level of CO_2 emissions is 95 grams per kilometre.

The percentage rates applying to petrol cars with CO_2 emissions up to this level are:

50 grams per kilometre or less	5%
51 grams to 75 grams per kilometre	9%
76 grams to 94 grams per kilometre	13%
95 grams per kilometre	14%

Car fuel benefit

The base level figure for calculating the car fuel benefit is £22,100.

Individual Savings Accounts (ISAs)

The overall investment limit is £15,240.

Pension scheme limits

Annual allowance	–	2014/15 and 2015/16	£40,000
	–	2012/13 and 2013/14	£50,000
Lifetime allowance			£1,250,000

The maximum contribution that can qualify for tax relief without any earnings is £3,600.

Authorised mileage allowances: cars

Up to 10,000 miles	45p
Over 10,000 miles	25p

TAX RATES AND ALLOWANCES

Capital allowances: rates of allowance

Plant and machinery
Main pool   18%
Special rate pool   8%

Motor cars
New cars with CO_2 emissions up to 75 grams per kilometre   100%
CO_2 emissions between 76 and 130 grams per kilometre   18%
CO_2 emissions above 130 grams per kilometre   8%

Annual investment allowance
Rate of allowance   100%
Expenditure limit   £500,000

Cap on income tax reliefs

Unless otherwise restricted, reliefs are capped at the higher of £50,000 or 25% of income.

CORPORATION TAX

Rate of tax   20%
Profit threshold   £1,500,000

Patent box

Net patent profit × ((main Rate − 10%)/main Rate)

VALUE ADDED TAX

Standard rate	20%
Registration limit	£82,000
Deregistration limit	£80,000

INHERITANCE TAX: Nil rate bands and tax rates

	£
6 April 2015 to 5 April 2016	325,000
6 April 2014 to 5 April 2015	325,000
6 April 2013 to 5 April 2014	325,000
6 April 2012 to 5 April 2013	325,000
6 April 2011 to 5 April 2012	325,000
6 April 2010 to 5 April 2011	325,000
6 April 2009 to 5 April 2010	325,000
6 April 2008 to 5 April 2009	312,000
6 April 2007 to 5 April 2008	300,000
6 April 2006 to 5 April 2007	285,000
6 April 2005 to 5 April 2006	275,000
6 April 2004 to 5 April 2005	263,000
6 April 2003 to 5 April 2004	255,000
6 April 2002 to 5 April 2003	250,000
6 April 2001 to 5 April 2002	242,000

Rate of tax on excess over nil rate band	– Lifetime rate	20%
	– Death rate	40%

Inheritance tax: Taper relief

Years before death	Percentage reduction
Over 3 but less than 4 years	20%
Over 4 but less than 5 years	40%
Over 5 but less than 6 years	60%
Over 6 but less than 7 years	80%

CAPITAL GAINS TAX

Rates of tax	– Lower rate	18%
	– Higher rate	28%
Annual exempt amount		£11,100
Entrepreneurs' relief	– Lifetime limit	£10,000,000
	– Rate of tax	10%

TAX RATES AND ALLOWANCES

NATIONAL INSURANCE CONTRIBUTIONS
(not contracted out rates)

Class 1	Employee	£1 – £8,060 per year	Nil
		£8,061 – £42,385 per year	12%
		£42,386 and above per year	2%
Class 1	Employer	£1 – £8,112 per year	Nil
		£8,113 and above per year	13.8%
		Employment allowance	£2,000
Class 1A			13.8%
Class 2		£2.80 per week	
		Small profits threshold	£5,965
Class 4		£1 – £8,060 per year	Nil
		£8,061 – £42,385 per year	9%
		£42,386 and above per year	2%

RATES OF INTEREST (assumed)

Official rate of interest	3%
Rate of interest on underpaid tax	3%
Rate of interest on overpaid tax	0.50%

STAMP DUTY LAND TAX

Non-residential properties

£150,000 or less	Nil
£150,001 – £250,000	1%
£250,001 – £500,000	3%
£500,001 and above	4%

Residential properties

£125,000 or less	0%
£125,001 – £250,000	2%
£250,001 – £925,000	5%
£925,001 – £1,500,000	10%
£1,500,001 and above	12%

STAMP DUTY

Shares	0.5%

TIME LIMITS AND ELECTION DATES

Income tax

Election/claim	Time limit	For 2015/16
Agree the amount of trading losses to carry forward	4 years from the end of the tax year in which the loss arose	5 April 2020
Current and prior year set-off of trading losses against total income (and chargeable gains)	12 months from 31 January following the end of the tax year in which the loss arose	31 January 2018
Three year carry back of trading losses in the opening years	12 months from 31 January following the end of the tax year in which the loss arose	31 January 2018
Three year carry back of terminal trading losses in the closing years	4 years from the end of the last tax year of trading	5 April 2020
Set-off of loss on the disposal of unquoted trading company shares against income	12 months from 31 January following the end of the tax year in which the loss arose	31 January 2018
Transfer of assets eligible for capital allowances between connected parties at TWDV	2 years from the date of sale	

National Insurance Contributions

Election/claim	Time limit	For 2015/16
Class 1 primary and secondary – pay days	17 days after the end of each tax month under PAYE system (14 days if not paid electronically)	22nd of each month
Class 1 A NIC – pay day	22 July following end of tax year (19 July if not paid electronically)	22 July 2016
Class 2 NICs – pay days	Paid under self-assessment with balancing payment	31 January 2017
Class 4 NICs – pay days	Paid under self-assessment with income tax	

Capital gains tax

Election/claim	Time limit	For 2015/16
Replacement of business asset relief for individuals (Rollover relief)	4 years from the end of the tax year: – in which the disposal occurred or – the replacement asset was acquired whichever is later	5 April 2020 for 2014/15 sale and 2015/16 acquisition
Holdover relief of gain on the gift of a business asset (Gift relief)	4 years from the end of the tax year in which the disposal occurred	5 April 2020
Disapplication of incorporation relief	2 years from the 31 January following the end of the tax year in which the business is transferred If sell all shares by 5 April following tax year of incorporation: Time limit 12 months earlier than normal claim date	31 January 2019 31 January 2018
EIS reinvestment relief	5 years from 31 January following the end of the tax year in which the disposal occurred	31 January 2022
Entrepreneurs' relief	12 months from 31 January following the end of the tax year in which the disposal occurred	31 January 2018
Determination of principal private residence	2 years from the acquisition of the second property	

Self-assessment – individuals

Election/claim	Time limit	For 2015/16
Pay days for income tax and class 4 NIC	1st instalment: 31 January in the tax year	31 January 2015
	2nd instalment: 31 July following the end of tax year	31 July 2015
	Balancing payment: 31 January following the end of tax year	31 January 2017
Pay day for CGT and class 2 NIC	31 January following the end of tax year	31 January 2017
Filing dates If return issued by 31 October in the tax year	Paper return: 31 October following end of tax year	31 October 2016
	Electronic return: 31 January following end of tax year	31 January 2017
If return issued after 31 October in the tax year	3 months from the date of issue of the return	
Retention of records Business records	5 years from 31 January following end of the tax year	31 January 2022
Personal records	12 months from 31 January following end of the tax year	31 January 2018
HMRC right of repair	9 months from date the return was filed	
Taxpayers right to amend a return	12 months from 31 January following end of the tax year	31 January 2018
Error or mistake claim	4 years from the end of the tax year	5 April 2020
HMRC can open an enquiry	12 months from submission of the return	
HMRC can raise a discovery assessment		
– No careless or deliberate behaviour	4 years from the end of the tax year	5 April 2020
– Tax lost due to careless behaviour	6 years from the end of the tax year	5 April 2022
– Tax lost due to deliberate behaviour	20 years from the end of the tax year	5 April 2036
Taxpayers right of appeal against an assessment	30 days from the assessment – appeal in writing	

Inheritance tax

Election/claim	Time limit	For 2015/16
Lifetime IHT on CLTs – pay day	Gift before 1 October in tax year: Following 30 April Gift on/after 1 October in tax year: 6 months after the end of the month of the gift	30 April 2015
Death IHT : on lifetime gifts within seven years of death (CLTs and PETs) and on the estate value	6 months after the end of the month of death	
Deed of variation	2 years from the date of death – in writing	
Transfer of unused Nil rate band to spouse or civil partner	2 years from the date of the second death	

Corporation tax

Election/claim	Time limit
Replacement of business asset relief for companies (Rollover relief)	4 years from the end of the chargeable accounting period: – in which the disposal occurred or – the replacement asset was acquired whichever is later
Agree the amount of trading losses to carry forward	4 years from the end of the chargeable accounting period in which the loss arose
Current year set-off of trading losses against total profits (income and gains), and 12 month carry back of trading losses against total profits (income and gains)	2 years from the end of the chargeable accounting period in which the loss arose
Surrender of current period trading losses to other group companies (Group relief)	2 years after the claimant company's chargeable accounting period
Election for transfer of capital gain or loss to another company within the gains group	2 years from the end of the chargeable accounting period in which the disposal occurred by the company actually making the disposal

TIME LIMITS AND ELECTION DATES

Self-assessment – companies

Election/claim	Time limit
Pay day for small and medium companies	9 months and one day after the end of the chargeable accounting period
Pay day for large companies	Instalments due on 14th day of: – Seventh, Tenth, Thirteenth, and Sixteenth month **after the start** of the chargeable accounting period
Filing dates	Later of: – 12 months from the end of the chargeable accounting period – 3 months form the issue of a notice to deliver a corporation tax return
Companies error or mistake claim	4 years from the end of the chargeable accounting period
HMRC can open an enquiry	12 months from the actual submission of the return
Retention of records	6 years from the end of the chargeable accounting period

Value added tax

Election/claim	Time limit
Compulsory registration Historic test: – Notify HMRC – Charge VAT Future test: – Notify HMRC – Charge VAT	 30 days from end of the month in which the threshold was exceeded Beginning of the month, one month after the month in which the threshold was exceeded 30 days from the date it is anticipated that the threshold will be exceeded the date it is anticipated that the threshold will be exceeded (i.e. the beginning of the 30 day period)
Compulsory deregistration	30 days from cessation
Filing of VAT return and payment of VAT	End of month following the return period

KAPLAN PUBLISHING

Section 1

PRACTICE QUESTIONS

TAXATION OF INDIVIDUALS

EMPLOYMENT

1   CLIFFORD AND AMANDA (ADAPTED)

You have received the following email from your manager, John Jones.

From	John Jones
Date	13 July 2016
To	Tax senior
Subject	Clifford and Amanda Johnson

I have just had a call from a prospective new client, Clifford Johnson. He and his wife are thinking of using us as tax advisers and during the course of the conversation, I have made some notes, which are attached to this e-mail.

Clifford is looking for some capital gains tax advice with regard to the disposal of a house. He has given me all of the relevant details we require at this stage.

Clifford has also informed me that his wife, Amanda, would like some income tax advice, as her remuneration package is due to change. On her behalf, he has supplied me with all the relevant details.

I have requested that I meet with both Clifford and Amanda next week to discuss their issues and I will be confirming the meeting with them by e-mail tomorrow.

Please can you review the attachment and prepare some notes for me to take to the meeting.

In your notes can you make sure you include the following:

(i)   A calculation of Clifford's capital gains tax liability for 2016/17 on the assumption that the Oxford house, together with its entire garden, is sold on 31 July 2016.

Please make some reference to the relevance of the size of the garden in your calculations.

(ii)   Some brief notes on the capital gains tax implications of the alternative of selling the Oxford house and garden by means of two separate disposals as proposed.

Do not bother to do any calculations on this option at this stage though.

(iii) A calculation of Amanda's income tax payable for the tax year 2015/16.

(iv) Some brief notes explaining the income tax implications for Amanda for the tax year 2016/17 of the additional benefits offered by her employer, Shearer plc.

Please can you also draft me a paragraph suitable for me to copy and paste into in my e-mail to Clifford tomorrow explaining our firm's policy when acting on behalf of both husband and wife.

We should also express any reservations we have in accepting and acting upon information supplied by Clifford in relation to Amanda's affairs.

Thanks

John Jones

The notes taken by your manager and attached to the e-mail are set out below:

To	The files
From	Tax manager
Date	13 July 2016
Subject	Clifford and Amanda Johnson – prospective new clients
Proposed meeting	w/c 17 July 2016
Clifford	Aged 54
Amanda	Aged 45
Date of marriage	1 February 2006

Oxford house

- Clifford moved into Amanda's house in London on the day they were married.
- Clifford's own house in Oxford, where he had lived since acquiring it for £129,400 on 1 August 2004, has been empty since the date of marriage, although he and Amanda have used it when visiting friends.
- Clifford has been offered £284,950 for the Oxford house and has decided that it is time to sell it.
- The house has a large garden such that Clifford is also considering an offer for the house and a part only of the garden.
- He would then sell the remainder of the garden at a later date as a building plot. His total sales proceeds will be higher if he sells the property in this way.
- Clifford is a higher rate taxpayer who has already realised taxable capital gains in 2016/17 in excess of his capital gains tax annual exempt amount.

Action required

Clifford would like to know:

- What his capital gains tax liability would be if he sold the house and its entire garden on 31 July 2016 for the offered price of £284,950, and
- The implications of his proposed two-part sale.

Amanda's current employment package

- Amanda began working for Shearer plc, a quoted company, on 1 June 2015 having had a two year break from her career.
- She earns an annual salary of £136,600 and was paid a bonus of £15,750 in August 2015 for agreeing to come and work for the company.
- As Amanda has made no pension provision to date Shearer plc agreed as part of her remuneration package to contribute £50,000 to a registered pension scheme on her behalf. This contribution was made on 1 September 2015.
- On 1 August 2015, Amanda was provided with a fully expensed company car, including the provision of private petrol, which had a list price when new of £23,400 and CO_2 emissions rate of 149 grams per kilometre.
- Amanda is required to pay Shearer plc £22 per month in respect of the private use of the car.
- In June and July 2015, Amanda used her own car whilst on company business. She drove 720 business miles during this two month period and was paid 34p per mile.
- Amanda had PAYE of £47,785 deducted from her gross salary in the tax year 2015/16.

Amanda's increased employment package

After working for Shearer plc for a full year, Amanda becomes entitled to the following additional benefits:

- The opportunity to purchase a large number of shares in Shearer plc on 1 July 2016 for £3.30 per share. It is anticipated that the share price on that day will be at least £7.50 per share. The company will make an interest-free loan to Amanda equal to the cost of the shares and will require the loan to be repaid within two years.
- Exclusive free use of the company sailing boat for one week in August 2016. The sailing boat was purchased by Shearer plc in January 2014 for use by senior employees and costs the company £1,400 a week in respect of its crew and other running expenses.

Amanda's other income

- Amanda received the following income from quoted investments in 2015/16:

	£
Dividends in respect of quoted trading company shares	1,395
Dividends paid by a Real Estate Investment Trust (out of tax exempt property income)	485

- On 1 June 2015 Amanda granted a nine year lease of a commercial investment property.
  She received a premium of £14,700 and receives rent of £2,100 per month.

Action required

According to Clifford, Amanda would like to know:

- Her income tax liability for 2015/16, and
- The income tax implications of additional employment benefits she will receive in 2016/17.

Required:

(a) Prepare the notes requested by your manager.

The notes should address all the issues and include the calculations you think are required.

The following marks are available for the four parts to be addressed:

(i) Clifford's capital gains tax liability if he accepts the offer price. **(5 marks)**

(ii) An explanation of the capital gains tax implications of two separate disposals. **(3 marks)**

(iii) Amanda's income tax payable for the tax year 2015/16. **(12 marks)**

(iv) Explanation of the income tax implications of the additional employment benefits. **(6 marks)**

Additional marks will be awarded for the presentation of the notes and the effectiveness with which the information is communicated. **(4 marks)**

You should assume that the rates and allowances for the tax year 2015/16 apply throughout this question.

(b) Draft the paragraph to insert in your manager's e-mail concerning the ethical issues of acting on behalf of both a husband and his wife. **(5 marks)**

(Total: 35 marks)

---

2 DOKHAM *Walk in the footsteps of a top tutor*

Dokham requires advice on his pension position at retirement, the rules relating to enterprise management incentive (EMI) schemes and the tax implications of his mother helping to pay his children's school fees.

The following information has been obtained from a telephone conversation with Dokham.

Dokham:

– Is 39 years old and married with two children.
– Is domiciled and resident in the UK.
– Has been offered a job by Criollo plc.
– His mother, Virginia, has offered to contribute towards Dokham's children's school fees.

The job offer from Criollo plc:

– Dokham's salary will be £70,000 per year.
– Criollo plc will make annual contributions of £8,000 into Dokham's personal pension scheme.
– Criollo plc will invite Dokham to join the company's EMI scheme.

Dokham's pension arrangements:

– Dokham has not made any pension contributions to date.
– Dokham intends to make gross annual contributions of £11,000 into a registered personal pension scheme.

PRACTICE QUESTIONS: SECTION 1

The EMI scheme:

- The scheme will have five members including Dokham.
- Criollo plc will grant Dokham an option to purchase 26,200 shares at a price of £9.00 per share. This will represent a holding of less than 1% of the company.
- The option can be exercised at any time until 31 December 2021.
- Criollo plc's current share price is £9.53.

Dokham has requested explanations of the following in respect of the job offer from Criollo plc:

- What would be the difference for me, from a tax point of view, if Criollo plc increased my salary by £8,000 instead of contributing into my personal pension scheme and I made additional gross annual pension contributions of £8,000?
- What benefits will I receive from the pension scheme, how will they be taxed and when can I receive them?
- Why might Criollo plc have told me that it is 'not possible' to increase the number of shares I can purchase within the EMI scheme?
- What are the tax implications for me when I exercise my EMI share option and when I sell the shares?

Virginia:

- Is 68 years old.
- Is domiciled and resident in the UK.
- Has taxable income of more than £125,000 per year.
- Owns a portfolio of quoted shares that is worth more than £500,000.
- Uses her capital gains tax and inheritance tax annual exemptions every year.
- Is considering three alternative ways of contributing towards Dokham's children's school fees.

The three alternative ways of contributing towards the children's school fees:

- Make a one-off gift to Dokham of £54,000 in cash.
- Make a one-off gift to Dokham of 9,800 shares (a holding of less than 1%) in Panatella plc, a quoted company, worth £54,000.
- Make a gift to Dokham of £8,000 in cash every year for the next seven years.

Required:

(a) Provide the information requested by Dokham in respect of the job offer from Criollo plc as set out above. **(9 marks)**

(b) Explain in detail the possible tax liabilities that could result from the three alternative ways proposed by Virginia to contribute towards the children's school fees. **(7 marks)**

(Total: 16 marks)

3 MORICE AND BABINE PLC *Walk in the footsteps of a top tutor*

Morice is the finance director of Babeen plc. Babeen plc is a non-close quoted trading company. Morice wants to provide information to the company's employees on a proposed Save As You Earn (SAYE) share option scheme, a medical care scheme and payments to employees for driving their own cars on business journeys.

The following information has been obtained from a telephone conversation with Morice.

Proposed SAYE scheme rules:

- Employees will invest in the scheme for five years.
- The scheme will permit monthly investments of between £5 and £750.
- The scheme will be open to all employees and directors who are at least 21 years old and have worked full-time for the company for at least three years.
- The share options granted under the scheme will enable employees to purchase shares for £2.48 each.

Detailed explanations, with supporting calculations, requested by Morice:

- Whether or not each of the proposed rules will be acceptable for a SAYE scheme.
- The tax and national insurance liabilities for the employee in the illustrative example below in respect of the grant and exercise of the share options, the receipt of the bonus and the sale of the shares on the assumption that the scheme referred to meets all of the HMRC conditions.

Illustrative example – SAYE scheme that meets HMRC conditions:

- The share options will be granted on 1 January 2017 to purchase shares at £2.48 each.
- The employee will invest £250 each month for five years.
- A bonus equal to 90% of a single monthly payment will be paid at the end of the five-year period.
- The amount invested, together with the bonus, will be used to exercise share options.
- The share options will be exercised on 31 December 2021 and the shares will be sold on the same day.
- The employee's interest in the employing company will be less than 1%.
- A share in the employing company will be worth: £3.00 on 1 January 2017
  £4.00 on 31 December 2021

Medical care scheme:

- Babeen plc is to offer free private health insurance to its employees.
- The health insurance will cost the company £470 annually per employee.
- The insurance would cost each employee £590 if they were to purchase it personally.
- Employees who decline the offer will be able to borrow up to £12,500 from Babeen plc to pay for medical treatment.
- The loans will be interest-free and repayable over four years.

Payments to employees for driving their own cars on business journeys:

- For each mile driven – 36 pence.
- For each mile driven whilst carrying a passenger – an additional 3 pence.

Required:

(a) Prepare the DETAILED explanations, with supporting calculations, as requested by Morice in respect of the proposed SAYE scheme. **(10 marks)**

(b) Explain the income tax and national insurance implications for the employees of Babeen plc of:

  (i) the medical care scheme **(3 marks)**

  (ii) the payments for driving their own cars on business journeys. **(4 marks)**

You should assume that the rates and allowances for the tax year 2015/16 apply throughout this question.

(Total: 17 marks)

4 PITA PLC *Walk in the footsteps of a top tutor*

Your firm has been asked to provide advice to Pita plc in respect of providing employees with financial assistance with childcare and encouraging them to work from home, the establishment of an enterprise management incentive scheme, and a redundancy package provided to an employee.

Pita plc:

– Is a UK resident company which trades in the UK and is quoted on the UK stock exchange.

– Has an issued share capital of 10,000,000 irredeemable £1 ordinary shares.

– Has gross assets of £24,000,000 and 180 employees.

Issues – Pita plc:

– Intends to provide assistance with childcare to employees and to encourage them to work from home.

– Intends to establish an enterprise management incentive (EMI) scheme for nine key employees.

– Has provided a redundancy package to Narn, an employee.

Financial assistance with childcare and encouraging working from home:

– Pita plc will provide employees with vouchers to purchase £42 of childcare per child per week.

– The vouchers will cost Pita plc 95 pence for each £1 of childcare purchased.

– Pita plc will pay employees an extra £3 per day when they work from home.

– The payments are intended to cover the additional household costs of working from home.

The EMI scheme:

– The scheme would reward seven full-time and two part-time key employees.

– Each key employee will be granted an option to acquire 10,000 shares at £1·75 per share.

– The options will be exercised in six years' time when the shares are expected to be worth £5 each.

– An ordinary share in Pita plc is expected to be worth £2 when the options are granted.

Redundancy package provided to Narn on 31 March 2016:

– Statutory redundancy of £8,100 paid on 31 March 2016.

– An additional payment of £26,000 made on 31 March 2016.

– Continued use of her company car until 30 September 2016.

– Pita plc paid £18,400 for Narn's diesel powered car; it had a list price of £19,500.

– The car has CO_2 emissions of 129 grams per kilometre.

Required:

(a) Explain whether or not the planned financial assistance with childcare and encouragement to work from home will give rise to taxable employment income for the employees. **(6 marks)**

(b) (i) Explain, with reference to the information provided, whether or not Pita plc is a qualifying company for the purpose of the enterprise management incentive (EMI) scheme and if it is able to make the scheme available to just the nine key employees. **(4 marks)**

   (ii) On the assumption that an EMI scheme is established, explain the income tax and capital gains tax implications for the employees in respect of the grant and exercise of the options and the sale of the shares, including the availability of entrepreneurs' relief. **(5 marks)**

(c) Explain, with supporting calculations, the taxable amounts arising in respect of the redundancy package provided to Narn. **(5 marks)**

(Total: 20 marks)

5 HYSSOP LTD *Walk in the footsteps of a top tutor*

Hyssop Ltd wishes to provide assistance with home to work travel costs for Corin, who is an employee, and also requires advice on the corporation tax implications of the purchase of a short lease and the value added tax (VAT) implications of the sale of a warehouse.

Hyssop Ltd:

– Is a UK resident trading company.

– Prepares accounts to 31 December each year.

– Is registered for VAT.

– Leased a factory on 1 February 2016.

Corin:

- Is resident and domiciled in the UK.
- Is an employee of Hyssop Ltd, who works only at the company's head office.
- Earns an annual salary of £55,000 from Hyssop Ltd and has no other source of income.

Hyssop Ltd – assistance with home to work travel costs:

- Hyssop Ltd is considering two alternatives to provide assistance with Corin's home to work travel costs.

Alternative 1 – provision of a motorcycle:

- Hyssop Ltd will provide Corin with a leased motorcycle for travelling from home to work.
- Provision of the leased motorcycle, including fuel, will cost Hyssop Ltd £3,160 per annum. This will give rise to an annual taxable benefit of £3,160 for Corin.
- Corin will incur no additional travel or parking costs in respect of his home to work travel.

Alternative 2 – payment towards the cost of driving and provision of parking place:

- Hyssop Ltd will reimburse Corin for the cost of driving his own car to work up to an amount of £2,240 each year.
- Corin estimates that his annual cost for driving from home to work is £2,820
- Additionally, Hyssop Ltd will pay AB Parking Ltd £920 per year for a car parking space for Corin near the head office.

Acquisition of a factory:

- Hyssop Ltd acquired a 40-year lease on a factory on 1 February 2016 for which it paid a premium of £260,000.
- The factory is used in Hyssop Ltd's trade.

Disposal of a warehouse:

- Hyssop Ltd has agreed to sell a warehouse on 31 December 2016 for £315,000, which will give rise to a chargeable gain of £16,520.
- Hyssop Ltd had purchased the warehouse when it was newly constructed on 1 January 2013 for £270,000 (excluding VAT).
- The warehouse was used by Hyssop Ltd in its trade until 31 December 2015, since when it has been rented to an unconnected party.
- Until 1 January 2016, Hyssop Ltd made only standard rated supplies for VAT purposes.
- Hyssop Ltd has not opted to tax the warehouse for VAT purposes.
- The capital goods scheme for VAT applies to the warehouse.

Required:

Note: You should ignore value added tax (VAT) for parts (a) and (b).

(a) Explain, with the aid of calculations, which of the two alternatives for providing financial assistance for home to work travel is most cost efficient for:

    (i)   Corin. **(5 marks)**

    (ii)   Hyssop Ltd. **(3 marks)**

(b) Explain, with the aid of calculations, the corporation tax implications for Hyssop Ltd of the acquisition of the leasehold premises on 1 February 2016, in relation to the company's tax adjusted trading profits for the year ended 31 December 2016 and its ability to roll over the gain on the sale of the warehouse. **(8 marks)**

(c) Explain, with the aid of calculations, the VAT implications of the disposal of the warehouse on 31 December 2016. **(4 marks)**

(Total: 20 marks)

UNINCORPORATED BUSINESSES

6   GLORIA SEAFORD (ADAPTED) *Online question assistance*

Gloria Seaford is UK resident but is not domiciled in the UK. She has owned and run a shop in the UK selling books, cards and small gifts as a sole trader since coming to the UK in June 2002.

Gloria was born on 4 January 1949 and on 1 November 2016 she started looking for a buyer for the business so that she could retire. She has received an offer of £335,000 for the shop premises from Ned Skillet who intends to convert the building into a restaurant.

The following information has been extracted from her client files and from a recent meeting with Gloria.

Gloria's business

- purchased current premises, which were built in 1996, in July 2015 for £267,000
- registered for value added tax
- plans to sell the shop premises to Ned on 28 February 2017 and cease to trade on that day
- estimates that on 28 February 2017 she will be able to sell the shelving and other shop fittings to local businesses for £1,400 (no item will be sold for more than cost)
- has agreed to sell all inventory on hand on 28 February 2017 to a competitor at cost plus 5%. This is expected to result in sales revenue of £8,300
- only other business asset is a van that is currently used 85% for business purposes. The van is expected to be worth £4,700 on 28 February 2017 and Gloria will keep it for her private use
- tax adjusted trading profit for the year ended 31 October 2016 was £39,245
- forecast tax adjusted trading profit for the period ending 28 February 2017, before taking account of the final sale of the business assets on that date and before deduction of capital allowances, is £11,500
- Gloria has overlap profits brought forward of £15,720.

PRACTICE QUESTIONS: SECTION 1

Capital allowances

- the tax written down value on the capital allowance general pool at 31 October 2016 was £4,050
- purchased equipment for £820 in November 2016
- the tax written down value of the van at 31 October 2016 was £4,130.

Other income in 2016/17

- taxable retirement pension of £5,312 received
- bank interest of £13,500 was credited to her bank account.

Capital assets and capital disposals

- on 1 November 2014 Gloria inherited the following assets from her aunt.

	Probate value £
Painting	15,200
17,500 shares in All Over plc	11,400

- sold the painting in May 2016 and realised a gain of £7,100
- at the end of April 2015 Gloria received notification that All Over plc, a quoted trading company, was in receivership and that there would be a maximum payment of 3 pence per share
- unused capital losses as at 6 April 2016 of £31,400.

Investment opportunities

- Eric Sloane, a business associate of Gloria, has provided her with the details of a number of investment opportunities including Bubble Inc, an investment company incorporated in the country of Oceania where its share register is maintained
- Gloria plans to buy a 2% share in Bubble Inc in May 2017, and expects to receive dividends of £12,000 per annum from 2017/18, which she will leave in an overseas bank account
- There is no foreign tax withheld on these dividends
- Gloria paid Eric £300 for his advice.

Required:

(a) State the value added tax implications of the sale by Gloria of her business assets and cessation of trade.

Calculations are not required for this part of the question. **(3 marks)**

(b) Compute Gloria's total income tax and national insurance liability for 2016/17.

(7 marks)

(c) (i) Compute Gloria's capital gains tax liability for 2016/17 ignoring any claims or elections available in respect of All Over plc. **(4 marks)**

(ii) Explain, with reasons, the relief available in respect of the fall in value of the shares in All Over plc, identify the years in which it can be claimed and state the time limit for submitting the claim. **(3 marks)**

(d) (i) Explain the options available to Gloria in respect of the UK tax on the dividends paid by Bubble Inc.

You should calculate the tax payable under each alternative for 2017/18, assuming that Gloria's other income remains the same as in 2016/17, and advise which basis should be chosen. **(8 marks)**

(ii) Explain the capital gains tax and inheritance tax implications of a future disposal of the shares.

Clearly state, giving reasons, whether or not the payment made to Eric is allowable for capital gains tax purposes. **(8 marks)**

You should assume that the rates and allowances for the tax year 2015/16 apply throughout this question.

(Total: 33 marks)

 Online question assistance

---

7 ELLROY (ADAPTED) *Walk in the footsteps of a top tutor*

Ellroy started an unincorporated business on 1 October 2016. He requires advice on his choice of accounting date, a possible change of accounting date and the use of the flat rate scheme for the purposes of VAT (value added tax).

The following information has been obtained from telephone conversations with Ellroy.

Ellroy:

- Is 47 years old.
- Is considering either a 31 March or a 30 September year end in 2017 and future years for his new business.
- Receives a share of profits from a partnership of more than £165,000 per year.

The budgeted trading profits of the business:

- It should be assumed that the profits set out below will accrue evenly in each trading period.
- The profits before deduction of capital allowances but after all other tax adjustments have been made are:

	£
Six months ending 31 March 2017	13,100
Year ending 31 March 2018	87,200
Year ending 31 March 2019	74,400

- Ellroy's only capital expenditure will be the purchase of two vans at a total cost of £22,000 in June 2017.

The VAT position of the business:

- The budgeted annual turnover and expenses of the fully established business are:

	£
Turnover (all standard rated)	100,000
Expenses: standard rated	21,000
zero rated	3,000
outside the scope of VAT	5,000

- All the figures exclude VAT.

Required:

(a) (i) Calculate the difference in the total income tax and national insurance that will be payable by Ellroy for the first three tax years of the business depending on whether he adopts a 31 March or 30 September year end.

(8 marks)

(ii) Explain the tax implications, including the effect on Ellroy's taxable profits for 2019/20 if, having initially adopted a 31 March year end, he were to change his accounting date and prepare accounts for the six months ending 30 September 2019.

You should consider the possibility of both rising and falling levels of profitability.

(7 marks)

(b) Explain, by reference to the budgeted annual turnover and expenses of the fully established business and with the aid of supporting calculations, the maximum flat rate percentage that can apply to Ellroy's business such that it would be financially beneficial for him to join the flat rate scheme.

(5 marks)

You should ignore the 1% discount for the first 12 months of registration.

(Total: 20 marks)

8 DANA *Walk in the footsteps of a top tutor*

Your manager has received a letter from Dana, a new client of your firm. Extracts from the letter and from an email from your manager are set out below.

Extract from the letter from Dana

> **Relief available in respect of a trading loss**
>
> I resigned from my job on 31 December 2013, having earned an annual salary of £40,000 for the previous three years. I spent the whole of 2014 planning my new business and began trading on 1 January 2015. The business was profitable initially but I made a loss in the year ended 30 September 2016.
>
> The results of the business have been:
>
> Period ended 30 September 2015 – a profit of £14,900.
> Year ended 30 September 2016 – a loss of £30,000.
>
> I own a number of rental properties that are let on long-term tenancies. On 1 February 2016, I sold one of these properties for £310,000. I paid £250,000 for this property on 1 December 2014.
>
> My taxable property business profits in recent tax years have been:
>
> | | £ |
> |---|---|
> | 2012/13 | 15,375 |
> | 2013/14 | 15,695 |
> | 2014/15 | 26,475 |
> | 2015/16 | 33,995 |
> | 2016/17 (estimated) | 44,595 |
>
> Please let me know how much tax I can save by relieving my trading loss for the year ended 30 September 2016.
>
> **Transfer of a rental property to a trust on 1 September 2016**
>
> On 1 September 2016, I transferred a rental property worth £270,000 to a trust for the benefit of my brother's children. I assume that there will be no tax liabilities for me or the trustees in respect of this gift. I also transferred a rental property to a trust in December 2011 and I am sure that no tax was paid in respect of that gift. I have never made any other gifts apart from gifts of cash to members of my family; none of these gifts exceeded £2,000.

Email from your manager

> Dana is unmarried and has no children. She is resident and domiciled in the UK.
>
> I have just spoken to Dana and she has provided me with the following additional information.
>
> – Dana received a bonus of £2,000 from her employer when she left her job in December 2013. The bonus was to thank her for all of the work she had done over the years.
>
> The results Dana has provided in respect of her unincorporated business have been adjusted for tax purposes but do not take account of expenditure she incurred during 2014. During that year, Dana spent £1,400 on petrol as she travelled around the UK visiting potential customers.

PRACTICE QUESTIONS: **SECTION 1**

> Dana had no income or capital gains in the tax years concerned other than those referred to in her letter and in the additional information set out above.
>
> **Work required:**
>
> Please prepare the following for me for my next meeting with Dana.
>
> (a) **Relief available in respect of the trading loss**
>
> A reasoned explanation, with supporting calculations, of the most tax efficient manner in which Dana's trading loss can be relieved, together with a calculation of the total tax relief obtained by following the most tax efficient strategy.
>
> I want you to consider all of the ways in which Dana could relieve the loss with the exception of carry forward for relief in the future. You should assume that gift relief will be claimed in respect of the transfer of the rental property to the trust on 1 September 2016 when carrying out this work.
>
> Your explanation should include:
>
> – a brief summary of the other reliefs available for relieving the loss, together with your reasons for rejecting them; and
> – the implications of the additional information provided by Dana.
>
> (b) **Transfer of the rental property to the trust on 1 September 2016**
>
> (i) **Capital gains tax**
>
> An explanation as to whether or not gift relief is available in respect of the transfer of the rental property on 1 September 2016 and, on the assumption that it is available, the action required in order to submit a valid claim.
>
> (ii) **Inheritance tax**
>
> In relation to Dana's gifts prior to 1 September 2016:
>
> – a list of the precise information we need to request from Dana in order to enable us to determine whether the gifts to her family members were exempt and to calculate the inheritance tax due on the transfer to the trust on 1 September 2016; and
> – an explanation of why the information is required.

Required:

Carry out the work required as requested in the email from your manager.

The following marks are available.

(a) Relief available in respect of the trading loss.

In respect of part (a) of this question you should:

(1) Ignore national insurance contributions.

(2) Assume that the tax rates and allowances for the tax year 2015/16 apply to all years. **(18 marks)**

(b) Transfer of the rental property to the trust on 1 September 2016.

(i) Capital gains tax **(2 marks)**

(ii) Inheritance tax. **(5 marks)**

(Total: 25 marks)

9   SPIKE *Walk in the footsteps of a top tutor*

Spike requires advice on the loss relief available following the cessation of his business and on the tax implications of share options and a relocation payment provided by his new employer.

Spike:

– Ceased to trade and sold his unincorporated business to an unrelated individual on 30 September 2015.
– Sold his house, 'Sea View', on 1 March 2016 for £125,000 more than he had paid for it.
– Began working for Set Ltd on 1 May 2016.
– Has no income or capital gains other than the amounts referred to in the information below.

Spike's unincorporated business:

– There are overlap profits from the commencement of the business of £8,300.
– The sale of the business resulted in net capital gains of £78,000.
– The tax adjusted profits/(loss) of the business have been:

		£
Year ended 31 December 2011	Profit	52,500
Year ended 31 December 2012	Profit	68,000
Year ended 31 December 2013	Profit	54,000
Year ended 31 December 2014	Profit	22,500
Nine months ending 30 September 2015	Loss	(13,500)

Remuneration from Set Ltd:

– Spike is being paid a salary of £65,000 per year.
– On 1 May 2016, Spike was granted an option to purchase ordinary shares in Set Ltd.
– On 1 July 2016, Set Ltd will pay Spike a relocation payment of £33,500.

The option to purchase ordinary shares in Set Ltd:

– Spike paid £3,500 for an option to purchase 7,000 ordinary shares, representing a 3.5% shareholding.
– The option is exercisable on 1 May 2020 at £4.00 per share.
– An ordinary share in Set Ltd was worth £5.00 on 1 May 2016 and is expected to be worth £8.00 on 1 May 2020.
– Set Ltd does not have any HM Revenue and Customs tax-advantaged (approved) share option schemes.

The relocation payment of £33,500:

– Spike sold 'Sea View', and purchased a new house, in order to live near the premises of Set Ltd.
– £22,000 of the payment is to compensate Spike for having to sell his house at short notice at a low price.
– £11,500 of the payment is in respect of the costs incurred by Spike in relation to moving house.

PRACTICE QUESTIONS: SECTION 1

Required:

(a) (i) Calculate the trading loss for the tax year 2015/16, and the terminal loss, on the cessation of Spike's unincorporated business. **(4 marks)**

(ii) Explain the reliefs available in respect of the losses calculated in part (i) and quantify the potential tax savings for each of them. **(10 marks)**

(b) (i) Explain all of the income tax and capital gains tax liabilities arising on Spike in respect of the grant and the exercise of the share options and the eventual sale of the shares in Set Ltd. **(4 marks)**

(ii) Explain the income tax implications for Spike of the relocation payment. **(2 marks)**

Notes:

(1) You should assume that the tax rates and allowances for the tax year 2015/16 apply to all tax years.

(2) Ignore national insurance contributions throughout this question.

(Total: 20 marks)

10 KANTAR *Walk in the footsteps of a top tutor*

Your manager has had a meeting with Kantar. Kantar recently appointed your firm to be his tax advisers. Extracts from the memorandum recording the matters discussed at the meeting and from an email from your manager are set out below.

Extract from the memorandum

> Kantar is resident and domiciled in the UK.
>
> Kantar has owned and operated his unincorporated business since 2002. In February 2016 Kantar disposed of some land. He used the proceeds to purchase equipment and vans on 1 May 2016 in order to expand his business.
>
> Kantar's only other income consists of UK property business income of £5,000 per year.
>
> **Capital transactions**
>
> | | |
> |---|---|
> | 1 November 2014 | Kantar inherited eight acres of land from his uncle. Kantar's uncle had purchased the land for £70,000 in 1997. At the time of the uncle's death, the land was worth £200,000. |
> | 5 November 2014 | Kantar gave £400 to each of his three nephews. |
> | 1 February 2016 | On this date, when the eight acres of land were worth £290,000, Kantar gave two acres, valued by an independent expert at £100,000, to his son. Capital gains tax gift relief was not available in respect of this gift. |
> | 2 February 2016 | Kantar sold the remaining six acres of land at auction for £170,000. |
>
> Kantar has not made any disposals for the purposes of capital gains tax other than those set out above.
>
> Kantar has not made any transfers of value for the purposes of inheritance tax other than those set out above.

Kantar's business

Kantar's business provides delivery services. The majority of its customers are members of the public. Kantar is not registered for the purposes of value added tax (VAT).

The recent actual and budgeted results of the business are set out below.

	Year ended 31 March		
	Actual 2015 £	Actual 2016 £	Budgeted 2017 £
Sales	48,000	65,000	96,000
Expenses	(6,000)	(8,000)	(13,000)
Profit per the accounts	42,000	57,000	83,000
Adjustments for tax purposes	2,000	1,000	4,000
Capital allowances	(1,000)	(1,000)	(155,000)
Tax adjusted profit/(loss)	43,000	57,000	(68,000)
Income tax liability for the tax year	8,827	14,203	Nil

In the year ending 31 March 2018, no capital allowances will be available to Kantar. With the exception of capital allowances, the results for the year ending 31 March 2018 are expected to be the same as those for the year ended 31 March 2017.

Extract from an email from your manager

Additional information

– The income tax liabilities in the memorandum take account of Kantar's UK property business income as well as his trading income and are correct.

– Kantar pays all of his tax liabilities on or before the due dates.

Please prepare notes for use in a meeting with Kantar.

The notes should address the following issues:

(a) **Capital transactions**

  (i) **Inheritance tax**

    – The availability of the small gifts exemption in respect of Kantar's gifts to his nephews.

    – A calculation of the potentially exempt transfer on 1 February 2016 after deduction of any available exemptions.

  (ii) A calculation of Kantar's chargeable gains and capital gains tax liability for the tax year 2015/16.

(b) **Budgeted trading loss for the year ending 31 March 2017**

(i) Calculations, with brief supporting explanations where necessary, of the tax which would be saved in respect of the offset of the trading loss for the tax year 2016/17 if:

(1) the loss is relieved as soon as possible

(2) the loss is carried forward for relief in the future.

A brief evaluation of your findings and the relevance to Kantar of the £50,000 restriction on the offset of trading losses.

(ii) On the assumptions that the trading loss is carried forward and that Kantar wishes to maximise his cash flow position, prepare a schedule of the dates and amounts of the payments on account and balancing payments Kantar would expect to make, post 1 January 2017, in respect of his tax liabilities for 2015/16, 2016/17 and 2017/18. Include brief explanations of the payments on account amounts.

(c) **Reporting of chargeable gains**

Kantar does not intend to report his chargeable gains on his income tax return as he believes that the tax authorities should be able to obtain this information from other sources. Explain the implications for Kantar, and our firm, of Kantar failing to report the chargeable gains to HM Revenue and Customs.

(d) **Value added tax (VAT)**

Explain, without performing any calculations, Kantar's obligation to compulsorily register for VAT; and state Kantar's ability, following registration, to recover the input tax incurred prior to registering.

Tax manager

Required:

Prepare the meeting notes requested in the email from your manager.

The following marks are available:

(a) **Capital transactions.**

(i) Inheritance tax. (4 marks)

(ii) Capital gains tax. (4 marks)

(b) **Budgeted trading loss for the year ending 31 March 2017.**

(i) Offset of the trading loss. (10 marks)

(ii) Further tax payments if the loss is carried forward.

Ignore National Insurance contributions and value added tax (VAT). (5 marks)

(c) Reporting of chargeable gains. (4 marks)

(d) Value added tax (VAT). (4 marks)

Professional marks will be awarded for the clarity of the calculations, analysis of the situation, the effectiveness with which the information is communicated, and the quality of the overall presentation. (4 marks)

(Total: 35 marks)

11 PIQUET AND BURACO *Walk in the footsteps of a top tutor*

Your firm has been asked to provide advice to two unrelated clients, Piquet and Buraco. Piquet, an unincorporated sole trader, requires advice on a proposed change to the date to which he prepares his accounts. Buraco requires advice on his residence status and the remittance basis.

(a) **Piquet:**

- Began trading as an unincorporated sole trader on 1 January 2009.
- Has always prepared accounts to 31 October.
- Has overlap profits of £15,000 for a five month overlap period.
- Is planning to change his accounting date to 28 February 2017.

Actual and budgeted tax adjusted trading profit of Piquet's business:

	Profit per month £	Profit for the period £
Year ended 31 October 2015	4,500	54,000
16 months ending 28 February 2017	5,875	94,000
Year ending 28 February 2018	7,333	88,000
Year ending 28 February 2019	9,000	108,000

Alternative choice of accounting date:

- Piquet is also considering a year end of 30 April.
- To achieve this, Piquet would prepare accounts for the 18 months ending 30 April 2017 and annually thereafter.

Required:

(i) On the assumption that Piquet changes his accounting date to 28 February, state the date by which he should notify HM Revenue and Customs of the change, and calculate the taxable trading profit for each of the tax years 2016/17 and 2017/18. **(3 marks)**

(ii) On the assumption that Piquet changes his accounting date to 30 April, state the basis periods for the tax years 2016/17 and 2017/18 and the effect of this change on Piquet's overlap profits. **(3 marks)**

(iii) Identify and explain TWO advantages for Piquet of using a year end of 30 April rather than 28 February. **(4 marks)**

(b) **Buraco's links with the country of Canasta:**

- Buraco is domiciled in Canasta.
- Buraco owns a home in the country of Canasta.
- Buraco's only income is in respect of investment properties in Canasta.
- Buraco frequently buys and sells properties in Canasta.

Buraco's links with the UK:

- Buraco's ex-wife and their 12 year-old daughter moved to the UK on 1 May 2015.

- Buraco first visited the UK in the tax year 2015/16 but was not UK resident in that year.

- Buraco did not own a house in the UK until he purchased one on 6 April 2016.

- Buraco expects to live in the UK house for between 100 and 150 days in the tax year 2016/17.

Required:

(i) Explain why Buraco will not satisfy any of the automatic overseas residence tests for the tax year 2016/17, and, on the assumption that he does not satisfy any of the automatic UK residence tests, explain how his residence status will be determined for that tax year. **(7 marks)**

(ii) On the assumption that Buraco is resident in the UK in the tax year 2016/17, state the tax implications for him of claiming the remittance basis for that year and explain whether or not there would be a remittance basis charge.
(3 marks)

(Total: 20 marks)

CHANGING BUSINESS SCENARIOS

12   THE STILETTO PARTNERSHIP (ADAPTED)

Assume today's date is 6 June 2016.

Clint, Ben and Amy are three partners in The Stiletto Partnership, who shared the profits of the business equally.

On 28 February 2016, the partners sold the business to Razor Ltd, in exchange for shares in Razor Ltd, with each former partner owning one third of the new company.

The following information has been extracted from client files and various telephone conversations with the partners.

The Stiletto Partnership

- Recent tax adjusted trading profits are as follows:

	£
Year ended 30 June 2015	107,124
1 July 2015 to 28 February 2016	96,795

- Estimated partnership's tax adjusted trading profits for the period from 1 March 2016 to 30 April 2016 would have been £20,760.

Clint Toon

- Born on 5 October 1948.
- Retired when the business was sold to Razor Ltd.
- Concerned that if the sale of the partnership, and his retirement, had been delayed until 30 April 2016, his total tax liability would have been reduced.
- His only other income is gross pension income of £8,100 per year, which he began receiving in the tax year 2014/15.
- Does not work for Razor Ltd and has not received any salary or dividends from the company.
- Overlap profits were £14,250 from when the partnership began trading.

Razor Ltd

- UK resident company that manufactures industrial cutting tools.
- On 1 July 2016, Razor Ltd will subscribe for the whole of the ordinary share capital of Cutlass Inc, a company newly incorporated in the country of Sharpenia.
- It is intended that Cutlass Inc will purchase partly finished tools from Razor Ltd and customise them in Sharpenia. The tools will then be sold back to Razor Ltd.
- It is anticipated that Cutlass Inc's annual taxable total profits will be approximately £120,000.
- Ben and Amy will be the directors of Cutlass Inc, although Ben will not be involved in the company's business on a day-to-day basis.

Amy Peters

- Currently resident and domiciled in the UK.
- Intends to spend one or two weeks each month in the country of Sharpenia looking after the company's affairs.
- The remainder of her time will be spent in the UK.
- She has employment contracts with both Razor Ltd and Cutlass Inc and her duties for Cutlass Inc will be carried out wholly in Sharpenia.
- Cutlass Inc will pay for Amy's flights to and from Sharpenia and for her husband and baby to visit her there twice a year.

The tax system in the country of Sharpenia

- The system of income tax and corporation tax in the country of Sharpenia is broadly similar to that in the UK although the rate of corporation tax is 38% regardless of the level of profits
- There is a double tax treaty between the UK and Sharpenia based on the OECD model treaty
- The clause in the treaty dealing with company residency states that a company resident in both countries under domestic law will be regarded under the treaty as being resident only in the country where it is effectively managed and controlled
- Sharpenia is not a member of the European Union.

Required:

(a) (i) Calculate Clint's taxable trading profits for the tax years 2015/16 and 2016/17 for both of the alternative retirement dates (28 February 2016 and 30 April 2016). **(3 marks)**

(ii) Analyse the effect of delaying the sale of the business of the Stiletto Partnership to Razor Ltd until 30 April 2016 on Clint's income tax and national insurance position.

You are not required to prepare detailed calculations of his income tax or national insurance liabilities. **(4 marks)**

(b) Draft a report as at today's date advising Cutlass Inc on its proposed activities.

The report should cover the following issues:

(i) The rate at which the profits of Cutlass Inc will be taxed.

This section of the report should explain:

– the company's residency position and what Ben and Amy would have to do in order for the company to be regarded as resident in the UK under the double tax treaty

– the meaning of the term 'permanent establishment' and the implications of Cutlass Inc having a permanent establishment in Sharpenia

– the rate at which the profits of Cutlass Inc will be taxed on the assumption that it is resident in the UK under the double tax treaty and either does or does not have a permanent establishment in Sharpenia. **(9 marks)**

(ii) The UK value added tax (VAT) implications for Razor Ltd of selling tools to and purchasing tools from Cutlass Inc. **(2 marks)**

(iii) The extent to which Amy will be subject to income tax in the UK on her earnings in respect of duties performed for Cutlass Inc and the travel costs paid for by that company. **(5 marks)**

Appropriateness of format and presentation of the report and the effectiveness with which its advice is communicated. **(2 marks)**

You should assume that the income tax rates and allowances for the tax year 2015/16 and the corporation tax rates and allowances for the Financial Year 2015 apply throughout this question.

(Total: 25 marks)

13 DESIREE (ADAPTED) *Walk in the footsteps of a top tutor*

Desiree requires advice on whether she should run her new business as an unincorporated sole trader or via a company together with the financial implications of registering voluntarily for value added tax (VAT).

The following information has been obtained from a meeting with Desiree.

Desiree:

- Resigned from her job with Chip plc on 31 May 2016.
- Had been employed by Chip plc on an annual salary of £60,000 since January 2013.
- Has no other income apart from bank interest received of less than £1,000 per year.
- Intends to start a new business, to be called Duchess, on 1 September 2016.

The Duchess business:

- The business will sell kitchen equipment and utensils.
- Market research consultants have estimated that 80% of its sales will be to commercial customers.
- The consultants were paid fees in November 2015 and March 2016.

Budgeted results of the Duchess business:

- The budgeted tax-adjusted trading profit/(loss) for the first three trading periods are:

	£
Ten months ending 30 June 2017	(46,000)
Year ending 30 June 2018	22,000
Year ending 30 June 2019	64,000

- The fees paid to the market research consultants have been deducted in arriving at the loss of the first period

Desiree's financial position:

- Desiree has not yet decided whether to run the business as an unincorporated sole trader or via a company.
- Her primary objective when deciding whether or not to operate the business via a company is the most beneficial use of the loss.

Registration for VAT:

- The turnover of the business is expected to exceed the VAT registration limit in January 2017.
- Desiree would consider registering for VAT earlier if it were financially advantageous to do so.
- Desiree will import some of her products from outside the EU, but is unsure of the VAT treatment.

PRACTICE QUESTIONS: SECTION 1

Required:

(a) (i) Calculate the taxable trading profit or allowable trading loss of the business for each of the first three taxable periods for the following alternative structures:

- the business is unincorporated
- the business is operated via a company. **(4 marks)**

(ii) Provide Desiree with a thorough and detailed explanation of the manner in which the budgeted trading loss could be used depending on whether she runs the business as an unincorporated sole trader or via a company and state which business structure would best satisfy her primary objective.

You are not required to prepare detailed calculations for part (ii) of this part of this question or to consider non-taxation issues. **(9 marks)**

(b) Explain in detail the financial advantages and disadvantages of Desiree registering voluntarily for VAT on 1 September 2016 and the VAT consequences of the imports from outside the EU, assuming she is VAT registered. **(7 marks)**

(Total: 20 marks)

14 VINE (ADAPTED) *Walk in the footsteps of a top tutor*

Vine requires advice on capital allowances, the incorporation of his business together with a subsequent sale of some of his shares, and the tax implications of measures intended to encourage his employees to become involved in a marketing strategy.

The following information has been obtained from a meeting with Vine.

Vine:

- Is 38 years old.
- Purchased a supermarket and began trading on 1 January 2016.
- Will make no capital disposals other than those referred to below.
- Has capital losses brought forward at 6 April 2016 of £6,400.

Vine's plans:

- Vine intends to incorporate the supermarket business, as detailed below, for commercial reasons.
- In June or July 2017 Vine intends to sell 20% of the new company to his store manager for £64,000.
- Vine is developing a marketing strategy called 'the active supermarket'.
- In October 2016 a false ceiling will be installed in the supermarket premises in order to conceal electrical wiring and water pipes.

The incorporation of Vine's business:

- All of the assets and liabilities of the business will be transferred to a new company, Passata Ltd, on 31 July 2016.
- Passata Ltd will be wholly owned by Vine.
- The consideration paid by Passata Ltd will be:
- the maximum amount of cash that can be paid without giving rise to a capital gains tax liability; and
- the issue of 1,200 £1 ordinary shares to Vine in respect of the remainder of the value of the business.
- The cash will be left on a loan account payable to Vine.

The assets and liabilities to be transferred to Passata Ltd:

	Cost £	Value £	Tax written down value on 31 July 2016 £
Premises	205,000	260,000	–
Equipment	55,000	35,000	22,000
Trading inventory		11,000	–
Liabilities		(10,000)	–
Goodwill	Nil	24,000	

- All of the equipment qualifies for capital allowances and no item is valued at more than cost.

The active supermarket:

- Passata Ltd will purchase six bicycles for a total of £2,400.
- The bicycles will be made available on loan to all employees for travelling to and from work and for making deliveries to customers.
- Employees will be paid 15 pence per mile if they use their own bicycles to make deliveries to customers.
- To provide help to enable those employees with children to start work earlier, Passata Ltd will provide childcare vouchers of £40 per week.
- On the first Monday of each month employees who cycle to work will receive a free breakfast.
- Each breakfast will cost Passata Ltd £8.

PRACTICE QUESTIONS: SECTION 1

Required:

(a) Explain:

   (i) the capital allowances implications for Vine of the transfer of the equipment to Passata Ltd; and

   (ii) whether or not the false ceiling to be installed in the supermarket premises will qualify as plant and machinery for the purposes of capital allowances.

   (4 marks)

(b) Calculate the chargeable gain arising on the proposed sale of the shares to the store manager and suggest a minor change in relation to the sale that would reduce the capital gains tax due. **(9 marks)**

(c) Outline the tax implications for Passata Ltd and its employees of the active supermarket marketing strategy. **(7 marks)**

You should ignore value added tax (VAT) when answering this question.

(Total: 20 marks)

15 FAURE *Walk in the footsteps of a top tutor*

Faure expects her new business to make a loss in its first trading period. She requires advice on the choice of year end and on the difference between employing her husband in the business and running the business as a partnership.

The following information has been obtained from discussions with Faure.

Faure:

- Is 44 years old and married to Ravel.
- Has not had an income tax liability since the tax year 2007/08.
- Intends to start a new business on 1 July 2016 under the trading name 'Bah-Tock'.
- 'Bah-Tock' will be Faure's only source of income.

The 'Bah-Tock' business:

- Is expected to make a loss throughout the first 12 months of trading.
- Is expected to be profitable from 1 July 2017 onwards.

Structure of the 'Bah-Tock' business:

- The business will be unincorporated.
- Faure and Ravel will both work full-time on the affairs of the business.
- Faure will either employ Ravel, and pay him a commercial salary, or the two of them will run the business as a partnership.

Ravel:

- Is 47 years old.
- Inherited a significant portfolio of quoted shares on the death of his mother in February 2008.
- Has annual taxable income, after deduction of the personal allowance, of £30,000.
- This income consists of bank interest and dividends only.

Required:

(a) Explain why a year end of 30 June, as opposed to 31 March, is likely to delay the first tax year in which the 'Bah-Tock' business makes a taxable profit rather than an allowable loss. **(4 marks)**

(b) On the assumption that the 'Bah-Tock' business will have a 30 June year end, analyse the issues that Faure and Ravel should be aware of from a tax viewpoint if:

(i) Faure employs Ravel

(ii) Faure and Ravel are partners in the business

and summarise your findings.

Notes in relation to part (b)

1   Your analysis should be based on the information provided and should be restricted to the situation where the business is loss-making.

2   You should address the effect of the choice of business structure on:

– the size of the loss made by the business

– the reliefs available to Faure and Ravel in respect of the initial losses

– the income tax and national insurance contributions liabilities of Faure and Ravel for the tax years 2016/17 and 2017/18. **(14 marks)**

(Total: 18 marks)

16   JEROME AND TRICYCLE LTD *Walk in the footsteps of a top tutor*

Jerome is an unincorporated sole trader who is about to sell his business to a company. He requires advice on the value added tax (VAT) implications of the sale of the business, whether a new lease in respect of a motor car for use by him should be entered into by him or by the company and the payment of travel expenses in respect of the family of an employee working overseas.

Jerome's business:

– Has annual taxable profits of £75,000 and is growing.

– Is registered for the purposes of VAT.

– Jerome leases a motor car in which he drives 20,000 miles per year of which 14,000 miles are on business. He anticipates that this level and pattern of mileage will continue in the future.

– The assets of the business include a building that was completed in 2014 and purchased by Jerome in April 2014 for £320,000.

The sale of Jerome's business to Tricycle Ltd:

– The business will be sold to Tricycle Ltd on 1 August 2016.

– Jerome will own the whole of the share capital of Tricycle Ltd.

– Tricycle Ltd will not change the nature of the business but will look to expand it by exporting its products to Italy.

PRACTICE QUESTIONS: SECTION 1

The lease of the motor car:

- The existing lease will end on 31 July 2016.
- A new lease will be entered into on 1 August 2016 by either Jerome or Tricycle Ltd.
- The annual leasing costs of the new car will be £4,400.

The motor car to be leased on 1 August 2016:

- Will be diesel powered and have a list price when new of £31,000.
- Will have CO2 emissions of 149 grams per kilometre.
- Will have annual running costs, including fuel, of £5,000 in addition to the leasing costs.

Remuneration to be paid by Tricycle Ltd to Jerome:

- A salary of £4,000 per month.
- If Tricycle Ltd leases the motor car, Jerome will use it for business and private purposes and will be provided with fuel for all of his motoring.
- If Jerome leases the motor car, he will be paid 50 pence per mile for driving it on business journeys.

Expansion into Europe:

- An employee of Tricycle Ltd will work for up to three months in Italy between April and July 2017.
- The employee will continue to be resident and domiciled in the UK.
- Tricycle Ltd will pay the travel costs of the employee's wife and three-year-old child when they visit him in June 2017.
- The travel costs will be taxable in the hands of the employee as employment income.

Required:

(a) Explain the value added tax (VAT) implications of the sale of Jerome's business to Tricycle Ltd. **(6 marks)**

(b) Prepare calculations for a 12-month period to show the total tax cost, for Tricycle Ltd and Jerome, of the car being leased by:

   (i) Tricycle Ltd

   (ii) Jerome.

   Ignore VAT for part (b) of this question. **(10 marks)**

(c) State the conditions that must be satisfied for a deduction for the travel costs paid by Tricycle Ltd to be given against the employee's total employment income.
(2 marks)

(Total: 18 marks)

17 FARINA AND LAUDA Walk in the footsteps of a top tutor

 Timed question with Online tutor debrief

Your manager has had a meeting with Farina and Lauda, potential new clients, who are partners in the FL Partnership.

The memorandum recording the matters discussed, together with an email from your manager, is set out below.

MEMORANDUM

To	The files
From	Tax manager
Date	5 December 2016
Subject	FL Partnership

Background

Farina and Lauda began trading as the FL Partnership on 1 May 2010. Accounts have always been prepared to 31 March each year. They are each entitled to 50% of the revenue profits and capital profits of the business.

On 1 March 2017, the whole of the FL Partnership business will be sold as a going concern to JH plc, a quoted trading company. The consideration for the sale will be a mixture of cash and shares. Capital gains tax relief on the transfer of a business to a company (incorporation relief) will be available in respect of the sale.

Farina and Lauda will both pay income tax at the additional rate in the tax year 2016/17 and anticipate continuing to do so in future years. They are very wealthy individuals, who use their capital gains tax annual exempt amounts every year. Both of them are resident and domiciled in the UK.

The sale of the business on 1 March 2017

The assets of the FL Partnership business have been valued as set out below. All of the equipment qualified for capital allowances.

	Value £	Cost £
Goodwill	1,300,000	Nil
Inventory and receivables	30,000	30,000
Equipment (no item to be sold for more than cost)	150,000	200,000
Total	1,480,000	

The total value of the consideration will be equal to the value of the assets sold. Farina and Lauda will each receive consideration of £740,000; £140,000 in cash and 200,000 shares in JH plc. Following the purchase of the FL Partnership, JH plc will have an issued share capital of 8,400,000 shares.

PRACTICE QUESTIONS: SECTION 1

Future transactions

Farina:

On 1 August 2017, Farina will make a gift of 15,000 of her shares in JH plc to the trustees of a discretionary (relevant property) trust for the benefit of her nieces and nephews. Farina will pay any inheritance tax liability in respect of this gift. The trustees will transfer the shares to the beneficiaries over the life of the trust.

Lauda:

On 1 June 2018, Lauda will give 40,000 of her shares in JH plc to her son.

For the purposes of giving our advice, the value of a share in JH plc can be assumed to be:

	£
On 1 March 2017	3
On 1 August 2017	4
On 1 June 2018	5

Email from your manager

I want you to prepare a memorandum for the client file in respect of the following:

(i) **Capital allowances**

A **detailed** explanation of the calculation of the capital allowances of the FL Partnership for its final trading period ending with the sale of its equipment to JH plc for £150,000 on 1 March 2017.

(ii) **Farina**

Brief explanations of:

(1) The manner in which any inheritance tax payable by Farina in her lifetime in respect of the gift of the shares to the trustees of the discretionary (relevant property) trust will be calculated and the date on which the tax would be payable.

(2) The availability of capital gains tax gift relief in respect of the transfer of the shares to the trustees of the discretionary (relevant property) trust and the subsequent transfers of shares from the trustees to the beneficiaries.

(iii) **Lauda**

A review of whether or not Lauda should disclaim incorporation relief.

The review should encompass the sale of the FL Partnership business, the gift of the shares to Lauda's son and the effect of incorporation relief on the base cost of the remaining shares owned by Lauda, as she intends to sell all of her shares in JH plc in the next few years.

It is important that you include a summary of your calculations and a statement of the key issues for me to discuss with Lauda. You should also include BRIEF explanations of the amount of incorporation relief available, the availability of any additional or alternative reliefs, and the date(s) on which any capital gains tax will be payable.

Tax manager

PAPER P6: ADVANCED TAXATION (FA2015)

Required:

(a) It is anticipated that Farina and Lauda will require some highly sophisticated and specialised tax planning work in the future.

Prepare a summary of the information which would be required, together with any action(s) which should be taken by the firm before it agrees to become the tax advisers to Farina and Lauda. **(5 marks)**

(b) Prepare the memorandum requested in the email from your manager. The following marks are available.

(i) Capital allowances. **(5 marks)**

(ii) Farina. **(7 marks)**

(iii) Lauda. **(14 marks)**

Ignore value added tax (VAT).

Professional marks will be awarded in part (b) for the overall presentation of the memorandum, the provision of relevant advice and the effectiveness with which the information is communicated. **(4 marks)**

(Total: 35 marks)

 Calculate your allowed time, allocate the time to the separate parts..................

18 ZITI *Walk in the footsteps of a top tutor*

Your manager has received a letter from Ziti. Ziti owns and runs an unincorporated business which was given to him by his father, Ravi. Extracts from the letter and from an email from your manager are set out below.

Extract from the letter from Ziti

I have decided that, due to my father's serious illness, I want to be able to look after him on a full-time basis. Accordingly, I am going to sell my business and use the proceeds to buy a house nearer to where he lives.

My father started the business in 2001 when he purchased the building referred to in the business assets below. He gave the business (consisting of the goodwill, the building and the equipment) to me on 1 July 2012 and we submitted a joint claim for gift relief, such that no capital gains tax was payable. I have no sources of income other than this business.

I have identified two possible methods of disposal.

(i) My preferred approach would be to close the business down. I would do this by selling the building and the equipment on 31 January 2017 at which point I would cease trading.

(ii) My father would like to see the business carry on after I sell it. For this to occur, I would have to continue trading until 30 April 2017 and then sell the business to someone who would continue to operate it.

In each case I would prepare accounts for the year ending 30 April 2016 and then to the date of cessation or disposal.

I attach an appendix setting out the information you requested in relation to the business.

Sadly, I have been told that my father is unlikely to live for more than three years. Please let me know whether his death could result in an inheritance tax liability for me in respect of the gift of the business.

My father's only lifetime gift, apart from the business given to me, was of quoted shares to a discretionary (relevant property) trust on 1 May 2008. The shares had a market value of £190,000 at the date of the gift and did not qualify for business property relief.

Appendix

Business assets (all figures exclude value added tax (VAT))

	Goodwill £	Building £	Equipment £
Original cost of the business assets	Nil	60,000	18,000
Market value at the time of my father's gift on 1 July 2012	40,000	300,000	9,000
Expected market value as at 31 January 2017 and 30 April 2017	40,000	330,000	10,000

Financial position of the business

The tax adjusted trading profits for the year ended 30 April 2015 were £55,000.

From 1 May 2015, it can be assumed that the business generates trading profits of £5,000 per month. The only tax adjustment required to this figure is in respect of capital allowances.

The tax written down value of the main pool as at 30 April 2015 was nil. I purchased business equipment for £6,000 on 1 August 2015. There have been no disposals of equipment since 30 April 2015.

Extract from an email from your manager

Additional background information

– Ziti and Ravi are both resident and domiciled in the UK.

– Ziti has overlap profits from when he took over the business of £9,000.

– All of the equipment is movable and no item has a cost or market value of more than £6,000.

– The business is registered for the purposes of VAT.

– No election has been made in respect of the building in relation to VAT.

> Please prepare notes, which we can use in a meeting with Ziti, which address the following issues:
>
> (a) **Sale of the business**
>
>   (i) Calculations to enable Ziti to compare the financial implications of the two possible methods of disposal. You will need to calculate:
>
>   – Ziti's taxable trading profits from 1 May 2015 onwards and the income tax thereon; and
>
>   – any capital gains tax (CGT) payable.
>
>   You should include:
>
>   – explanations of the availability of any CGT reliefs;
>
>   – a summary of the post-tax cash position; and
>
>   – any necessary assumptions.
>
>   (ii) Explanations of whether or not VAT would need to be charged on either or both of the alternative disposals.
>
> (b) **Inheritance tax**
>
> Calculations of the amount of inheritance tax which would be payable by Ziti for all possible dates of his father's death between 7 June 2016 and 30 June 2019. You should include an explanation of the availability of any inheritance tax reliefs.
>
> When calculating these potential inheritance tax liabilities you should assume that Ziti will sell the business on 30 April 2017.
>
> The best way for you to approach this is to identify the particular dates on which the inheritance tax liability will change.
>
> **Tax manager**

Required:

Prepare the meeting notes requested in the email from your manager.

The following marks are available.

(a) Sale of the business.

    (i) **Comparison of the financial implications of the alternative methods for disposing of the business.**

        Ignore National Insurance contributions. **(17 marks)**

    (ii) **Value added tax (VAT).** **(5 marks)**

(b) **Inheritance tax.** **(9 marks)**

Professional marks will be awarded for adopting a logical approach to problem solving, the clarity of the calculations, the effectiveness with which the information is communicated, and the overall presentation of the notes. **(4 marks)**

You should assume that today's date is 6 June 2016.

(Total: 35 marks)

PRACTICE QUESTIONS: SECTION 1

19 JONNY *Walk in the footsteps of a top tutor*

Your manager has had a meeting with Jonny who is establishing a new business. An extract from an email from your manager, a schedule and a computation are set out below.

You should assume that today's date is 10 September 2016.

Extract from the email from your manager

> Jonny's new business will begin trading on 1 November 2016. Jonny will use an inheritance he received following the death of his mother to finance this new venture.
>
> We have been asked to advise Jonny on his business and his inheritance. Some of the work has already been done; I want you to complete it.
>
> **Please prepare a memorandum for Jonny's client file addressing the following issues:**
>
> (a) **Unincorporated business**
>
> I attach a schedule which sets out Jonny's recent employment income and his plans for the new business. I think you will find it useful to read the schedule before you go through the rest of this email.
>
> You should assume that Jonny does not have any other sources of income or any taxable gains in any of the relevant tax years.
>
> (i) **Jonny's post-tax income**
>
> Jonny has asked for an approximation of his post-tax income position for the first two trading periods. I want you to prepare calculations in order to complete the following table, assuming that any available trading loss reliefs will be claimed in the most beneficial manner. You should include explanations of the options available to relieve the loss, clearly identifying the method which will maximise the tax saved (you do not need to consider carrying the loss forward).
>
> **Table to be completed**
>
> | | Strong demand £ | Weak demand £ |
> | --- | --- | --- |
> | Aggregate budgeted net profit of the first two trading periods | 39,200 | 2,800 |
> | Aggregate income tax (payable)/refundable in respect of the profit/loss for the first two tax years | ? | ? |
> | Budgeted post-tax income | ? | ? |
>
> Include a brief explanation as to why these calculations are only an approximation of Jonny's budgeted post-tax income.

KAPLAN PUBLISHING

(ii) **Salesmen**

Jonny intends to hire two salesmen to get the business started. Their proposed contractual arrangements are as set out in the attached schedule.

Explain which of the proposed contractual arrangements with the salesmen indicate that they would be self-employed and state any changes which should be made to the other arrangements in order to maximise the likelihood of the salesmen being treated as self-employed.

(iii) **New contracts for the business**

Jonny is hoping to obtain contracts with local educational establishments and has asked us to help. One of our clients is a college and an ex-client of ours provided services to a number of schools and colleges. Accordingly, we have knowledge and experience in this area.

Explain the extent to which it is acceptable for us to use the knowledge we have gained in respect of our existing client and ex-client to assist Jonny.

(b) **Jonny's inheritance from his mother**

Jonny's mother died on 31 July 2016. She left the whole of her estate, with the exception of a gift to charity, to Jonny. I attach a computation of the inheritance tax due; this was prepared by a junior member of staff and has not yet been reviewed. I can confirm, however, that all of the arithmetic, dates and valuations are correct. In addition, there were no other lifetime gifts, and none of the assets qualified for business property relief.

I want you to review the computation and identify any errors. You should explain each of the errors you find and calculate the value of the inheritance which Jonny will receive after inheritance tax has been paid.

Tax manager

Schedule – Employment income and plans for the new business

Jonny's income

Jonny worked full-time for many years until 30 June 2014 earning a salary of £6,000 per calendar month. From 1 July 2014, he worked part-time earning a salary of £2,000 per calendar month until he ceased employment on 31 March 2016.

Two budgets have been prepared for Jonny's business based on customer demand being either strong or weak. You should assume that no tax adjustments are required to Jonny's budgeted profit/loss figures for the first two trading periods.

For strong demand, the taxable trading profit for the first two tax years has been computed; these figures are correct and you do not need to check them. You will, however, need to calculate the equivalent figures for weak demand.

PRACTICE QUESTIONS: SECTION 1

	Strong demand £	Weak demand £
Budgeted net profit/(loss):		
Eight months ending 30 June 2017	9,200	(15,200)
Year ending 30 June 2018	30,000	18,000
Aggregate budgeted net profit of the first two trading periods	39,200	2,800
Taxable trading profit/(loss):		
2016/17	5,750	?
2017/18	19,200	?

Salesmen

Jonny is proposing to enter into the following contractual arrangements with two part-time salesmen:

– They will work on Tuesday and Wednesday mornings each week for a two-month period.

– They will be paid a fee of £300 for each new sales contract obtained. No other payments will be made.

– They will use their own cars.

– Jonny will lend each of them a laptop computer.

Computation – Inheritance tax payable on the death of Jonny's mother

Mother's lifetime gift	£
1 June 2012 – Gift of cash to Jonny	30,000

KAPLAN PUBLISHING

Mother's chargeable estate at death on 31 July 2016	£	£
Freehold property – Mother's home		530,000
UK quoted shares		400,000
Chattels – furniture, paintings and jewellery	40,000	
Less: Items individually worth less than £6,000	(25,000)	
		15,000
Cash		20,000
		965,000
Less: Gift to charity		(70,000)
Annual exemption		(3,000)
Chargeable estate		892,000
Less: Nil rate band	325,000	
Gift in the seven years prior to death (£30,000 – £6,000)	(24,000)	
		(301,000)
		591,000
Inheritance tax (£591,000 × 40%)		236,400

Required:

Prepare the memorandum as requested in the email from your manager. The following marks are available:

(a) Unincorporated business:

    (i) Jonny's post-tax income. **(15 marks)**

    (ii) Salesmen. **(4 marks)**

    (iii) New contracts for the business. **(5 marks)**

(b) Jonny's inheritance from his mother. **(7 marks)**

Professional marks will be awarded for following the manager's instructions, the clarity of the explanations and calculations, problem solving, and the overall presentation of the memorandum. **(4 marks)**

Notes

1. Assume that the tax rates and allowances for the tax year 2015/16 apply to all tax years.

2. Ignore national insurance contributions throughout this question.

(Total: 35 marks)

PRACTICE QUESTIONS: SECTION 1

CAPITAL TAXES

20 JOAN ARK

Joan Ark, aged 76, has asked for your advice regarding the following gifts that she has made during 2015/16.

(a) On 13 July 2015, Joan made a gift of 250,000 ordinary shares in Orleans plc, a quoted company into a discretionary trust for the benefit of her granddaughters.

On that day, the shares were quoted at 146p – 150p, with recorded bargains of 140p, 144p, 149p and 155p.

Joan originally purchased 200,000 shares in Orleans plc during 2000 at a cost of £149,000. Joan also bought 75,000 shares on 15 August 2013 for £69,375 and has subsequently bought 10,000 shares on 21 July 2014 for £14,800.

Orleans plc has an issued share capital of 10 million ordinary shares and Joan has never been a director or employee of the company.

(b) On 15 July 2015, Joan gave 20,000 of her 40,000 ordinary shares in Rouen Ltd, an unquoted trading company, to her son Michael. Rouen Ltd has an issued share capital of 100,000 ordinary shares. Joan's husband also owns 40,000 ordinary shares in the company.

On 15 July 2015, the relevant values of Rouen Ltd's shares were as follows:

Shareholding	Value per share £
100%	22.30
80%	17.10
60%	14.50
40%	9.20
20%	7.90

Joan purchased her 40,000 shares in Rouen Ltd during 2002 for £96,400. Her husband works for the company but Joan does not.

(c) On 4 November 2015, Joan gave her grandson an antique vase worth £18,500 as a wedding present. Joan purchased the vase during 2000 for £14,150.

(d) On 15 January 2016, Joan gave agricultural land with an agricultural value of £175,000 to her son Charles. Joan had purchased the land during 2004 for £92,000, and it has always been let out to tenant farmers.

The most recent tenancy agreement, which started in June 2006, will soon end, and Joan has obtained planning permission to build residential accommodation on the land. The value of the land with planning permission is £300,000.

Charles owns adjoining agricultural land, and the value of this land will increase from £210,000 to £250,000 as a result of the gift.

(e) On 31 March 2016, Joan made a gift of her main residence valued at £265,000 to her daughter Catherine. However, as a condition of the gift, Joan has continued to live in the house rent free.

The house was purchased on 1 July 1994 for £67,000, and Joan occupied it as her main residence until 31 December 1998. The house was unoccupied between 1 January 1999 and 31 December 2002, and it was rented out as furnished accommodation between 1 January 2003 and 30 June 2015.

Since 1 July 2015, Joan has again occupied the house as her main residence.

Joan has not previously made any lifetime transfers of assets. She is to pay any IHT and CGT liabilities arising from the above gifts.

Required:

(i) Advise Joan of the IHT and CGT implications arising from the gifts made during 2015/16.

Your answer should be supported by appropriate calculations, and should include an explanation of any reliefs that are available.

You should ignore the instalment option and the effect of the annual exemption for IHT purposes and the annual exempt amount for CGT purposes.

Marks for this part of the question will be allocated on the basis of:

5 marks to (a), 5 marks to (b), 3 marks to (c), 5 marks to (d), 7 marks to (e)

(25 marks)

(ii) Explain the main advantages of an individual making lifetime gifts for IHT purposes and the main factors to be considered in choosing which assets to gift. **(6 marks)**

Joan is a higher rate taxpayer for income tax purposes.

(Total: 31 marks)

21 ALEX (ADAPTED)

Assume today's date is 20 February 2016.

Alex, a widower, died on 5 February 2016. His will leaves £150,000 to charity and the remainder of his assets split in equal shares to his son, Brian and his daughter, Beatrice, who support his decision to benefit charitable causes.

The assets comprised in Alex's estate were as follows:

	Market value 5 February 2016 £
Residence	475,000
Building society account	15,000
NS&I investment account	55,000
NS&I savings certificates	180,000
Various chattels	40,000
Shares in Touriga Ltd	Note 1
Shares in Nacional plc	Note 2
Other quoted investments	115,000

Notes

(1) Touriga Ltd is an unquoted trading company. Alex bought his 2,450 ordinary shares (representing 35% of the issued shares) in September 2013 for £8.50 per share. The shares were worth £11.00 per share at the time of his death.

(2) Nacional plc is a quoted company in which Alex held 20,000 shares (representing less than 1% of the issued shares) at the time of his death. On 5 February 2016, the shares were listed ex div at 624p – 632p with marked bargains at 625p, 629p and 630p. A dividend of 18 pence per share was declared on 5 December 2015, and was received on 11 February 2016 by the executors.

Alex had made two lifetime gifts. The first was a villa in Spain. This was given to Brian in July 2010. The value at that time was £338,000. In addition, Alex settled an equal amount on a relevant property trust in March 2011. Alex agreed to pay any tax due on the gifts.

Prior to his death, Alex had the following income in 2015/16:

	£
Pension (gross – PAYE deducted at source £1,109)	13,285
Building society interest received	1,280
NS&I investment account interest received	870
Dividends received (other than from Nacional plc (Note 2 above))	8,100

Brian, Alex's son, is aged 58, is in poor health, and is not expected to live more than a few years. His wife died ten years ago, since when he has lived alone. He owns a house, currently worth £400,000 with an £80,000 mortgage outstanding and has other assets in the form of cash investments worth £80,000, and personal belongings worth £50,000.

Consequently, Brian has no need of his inheritance from Alex and so intends to gift his share of his father's estate to his two children, Colin and Charlotte, in equal shares.

Colin, who is 20, is in his second year at university, but Brian is worried that his son will spend all of the money at once. Charlotte, who is 17, is still at school but is likely to go to university in the near future.

Again, Brian worries about the money being spent unwisely, and therefore wishes to use some form of trust to control the capital sums gifted to both his children. Brian has made no lifetime gifts to date.

Required:

(a) Calculate the income tax (IT) payable/repayable for Alex for the income tax year 2015/16. (5 marks)

(b) Explain, with supporting calculations, the inheritance tax (IHT) implications (including any additional tax due on his lifetime gifts) arising on the death of Alex, and quantify the inheritance (after tax) due to Brian and Beatrice.

Assume that Alex's wife utilised all of her nil rate band when she died. (10 marks)

(c) (i) Explain how Brian could use a trust to maintain control of the capital he intends to gift to Colin and Charlotte following Alex's death and the inheritance tax (IHT) treatment of the trust. (4 marks)

(ii) State, giving reasons, what other inheritance tax (IHT) planning advice you would offer Brian with regard to setting up a trust for Colin and Charlotte with the assets he has inherited. (3 marks)

(Total: 22 marks)

22 MABEL PORTER *Online question assistance*

Assume today's date is 1 December 2016.

Mabel Porter is 76 years old and in poor health. Her husband, Luke, died on 1 June 2016 and she has no children.

Luke fully utilised his nil rate band for inheritance tax purposes during his lifetime.

In her will, Mabel has left the whole of her estate to Bruce and Padma, her brother's children. Bruce and Padma have always visited Mabel regularly although, since emigrating to South Africa in January 2013, Bruce now keeps in touch by telephone.

Mabel owns the following assets:

	Probate value 1 June 2016	Market value Today	Estimated at 30 June 2021
	£	£	£
House and furniture		325,000	450,000
Rolls Royce motor car		71,000	55,000
Diamond necklace		70,000	84,000
Cash and investments in quoted shares		120,000	150,000
Assets inherited from her husband, Luke:			
40,000 ordinary shares in BOZ plc	44,500	77,000	95,000
Land in the country of Utopia	99,000	75,000	75,000

Mabel has decided to give a substantial present to both Bruce and Padma on each of their birthdays on 1 February 2017 and 5 March 2017 respectively. She does not want to gift any asset that will give rise to a tax liability prior to her death and hopes that the gifts will reduce her eventual inheritance tax liability.

Bruce and Padma have agreed to sign any elections necessary to avoid tax arising on the gifts. It can be assumed that the market values of the assets will not change between now and when these gifts are made.

Mabel will give Bruce either the shares in BOZ plc or the land in the country of Utopia.

Luke purchased the shares in BOZ plc on 1 March 2013. BOZ plc is a quoted manufacturing company with an issued share capital of 75,000 ordinary shares. It owns investment properties that represent 8% of the value of its total assets. The land in Utopia consists of a small farm that has always been rented out to tenant farmers. It was purchased by Luke on 1 May 2012 and has an agricultural value at today's date of £58,000.

Mabel will give Padma either the Rolls Royce or the necklace.

Mabel purchased the Rolls Royce, new, in June 2011, for £197,000. She inherited the necklace from her grandmother in April 1991; its probate value at that time was £21,500.

Mabel's only lifetime gift was a gift of £210,000 to a discretionary trust on 1 May 2010 and she does not intend to make any further substantial gifts between now and her death. Mabel has capital losses of £15,100 as at 5 April 2016.

Required:

(a) Explain the immediate capital gains tax and inheritance tax implications of each of the four possible gifts.

Quantify the chargeable gain or loss and the potentially exempt transfer in each case and comment on the availability or otherwise of any reliefs. **(12 marks)**

(b) Mabel has two objectives when making the gifts to Bruce and Padma:

1 To pay no tax on any gift in her lifetime; and

2 To reduce the eventual liability to inheritance tax on her death.

Advise Mabel which item to gift to Bruce and to Padma in order to satisfy her objectives. Give reasons for your advice.

Your advice should include a computation of the inheritance tax saved as a result of the two gifts, on the assumption that Mabel dies on 30 June 2021. **(10 marks)**

(c) Without changing the advice you have given in (b), or varying the terms of Luke's will, explain how Mabel could further reduce her eventual inheritance tax liability and quantify the tax saving that could be made. **(3 marks)**

You should assume that the rates and allowances for the tax year 2015/16 will continue to apply for the foreseeable future.

(Total: 25 marks)

 Online question assistance

---

23 ALVARO PELORUS (ADAPTED)   *Walk in the footsteps of a top tutor*

Two years ago Alvaro Pelorus moved to the UK with his family to look after his father, Ray, who has recently died.

Alvaro requires some help in sorting out his father's tax affairs and is also concerned about his own liability to UK capital taxes. Alvaro and his family expect to return to their home in the country of Koruba in October 2016 once Ray's affairs have been settled.

The following information has been extracted from client files and from telephone conversations with Alvaro.

Alvaro Pelorus

– Aged 47 years old, married to Maria.
– The couple have two children, Vito and Sophie, aged 22 and 19 years respectively.
– Alvaro and Maria have lived in the country of Koruba since 1989 and are both domiciled in the country of Koruba.
– On 1 July 2014 the family moved to the UK to be near Alvaro's father, Ray, who was very ill.
– Alvaro and Maria are UK resident in the tax years 2014/15 and 2015/16.
– There is no double taxation agreement between the UK and Koruba.

Ray Pelorus

- Has been seriously ill and has not worked for the last three years.
- Died on 1 February 2016.
- UK domiciled, lived in the UK for the whole of his life.

Lifetime gifts by Ray

- 1 May 2012 gave Alvaro 95 acres of farm land situated in the UK
- market value of the land was £273,000, although its agricultural value was only £120,000
- Ray had acquired the land on 1 January 2004 and granted an agricultural tenancy on that date
- Alvaro continues to own the land as at today's date and it is still subject to the agricultural tenancy.
- 1 August 2015 gave Alvaro 6,000 shares in Pinger Ltd
- shares were valued at £195,000
- Pinger Ltd is a UK resident trading company
- gift relief was claimed in respect of this gift
- Ray had acquired 14,000 shares in Pinger Ltd on 1 April 2004 for £54,600, which represents a 4% interest in the company.

Assets owned by Ray on 1 February 2016

- UK assets, valued at £870,000 after deduction of all available reliefs, which includes cash ISA savings of £70,000.
- A house in the country of Pacifica valued at £94,000.
- The executors of Ray's estate have paid Pacifican inheritance tax of £1,800 and legal fees of £7,700 in respect of the sale of the Pacifican house.
- Ray left the whole of his estate to Alvaro.
- Ray left a note in his documents for his executors to remind them to claim relief for the transfer of his ISA savings to Alvaro.

Alvaro's capital assets and capital disposals

- Owns the family house in the UK, shares in UK and Koruban companies, and commercial rental property in the country of Koruba.
- In 2015/16 he made the following disposals of assets:

1 September 2015	sold the 6,000 shares in Pinger Ltd for £228,000
1 October 2015	sold 2,350 shares in Lapis Inc, a company resident in Koruba, for £8,270
	purchased 5,500 shares in the company on 1 September 2010 for £25,950
1 December 2015	transferred shares with a market value of £74,000 in Quad plc, a UK quoted company, to a UK resident discretionary trust for the benefit of Vito and Sophie
	had purchased the shares on 1 January 2015 for £59,500.

- Has not made any other transfers of value for the purposes of UK inheritance tax.

Maria's capital assets and capital disposals

- Only significant asset owned is the family home in the country of Koruba.
- Has not made any transfers of value for the purposes of UK inheritance tax.

Required:

(a) Calculate the inheritance tax (IHT) payable as a result of the death of Ray Pelorus.

Explain the availability or otherwise of agricultural property relief and business property relief on the two lifetime gifts made by Ray. **(8 marks)**

(b) (i) Explain how Alvaro may be assessed for capital gains tax purposes in 2015/16. **(7 marks)**

(ii) Calculate Alvaro Pelorus's capital gains tax liability for the tax year 2015/16 on the assumption that all available reliefs are claimed. You should assume that all of Alvaro's overseas income is remitted to the UK. **(8 marks)**

(c) (i) Explain the relief available on the transfer of ISA savings on death, and state whether or not Alvaro can make the claim for relief. **(3 marks)**

(ii) Explain the inheritance tax (IHT) implications and benefits of Alvaro Pelorus varying the terms of his father's will such that part of Ray Pelorus's estate is left to Vito and Sophie.

State the date by which a deed of variation would need to be made in order for it to be valid. **(3 marks)**

(iii) Identify any further planning opportunities available to Alvaro Pelorus in order to minimise the UK inheritance tax (IHT) due when he dies. He does not wish to make any lifetime gifts other than to his wife, Maria.

(6 marks)

You should assume that the rates and allowances for the tax year 2015/16 continue to apply for the foreseeable future. Alvaro is a higher rate taxpayer for income tax purposes.

(Total: 35 marks)

24 KEPLER (ADAPTED)

Kepler gave his nephew, Galileo, 600 shares (a 30% holding) in Messier Ltd on 1 June 2012. On 1 May 2016, Kepler died and left the remaining 1,400 shares in Messier Ltd to Galileo. Galileo intends to move to the UK from the country of Astronomeria to participate in the management of Messier Ltd.

The following information has been obtained from client files and meetings with the parties involved.

Kepler:

- Died on 1 May 2016.
- Was UK resident and domiciled.
- Has two nephews; Galileo and Herschel.
- In his will he left 1,400 shares in Messier Ltd valued at £546,000 to Galileo and the residue of his estate valued at £480,000 to Herschel.

Kepler – Lifetime gifts:

- 1 February 2011   Gave a house to Herschel valued at £311,000.
- 1 July 2011   Gave a watch costing £900 to each of his two nephews.
- 1 June 2012   Gave 600 shares in Messier Ltd to Galileo.

Messier Ltd:

- Unquoted company that transports building materials.
- Incorporated in the UK on 1 February 2003 when Kepler subscribed for 2,000 shares, the whole of its share capital.

Messier Ltd – Value of an ordinary share:

As at	1 June 2012	1 May 2016
	£	£
As part of a 100% holding	485	570
As part of a 70% holding	310	390
As part of a 30% holding	230	260

Messier Ltd – Asset values:

As at 1 June 2012	£
Premises	900,000
Surplus land rented to third party	480,000
Vehicles	100,000
Current assets	50,000

Galileo:

- Resident and domiciled in the country of Astronomeria where he has lived since birth.
- Lives in rented accommodation in Astronomeria.
- Intends to sell two paintings in order to provide funds to go towards the cost of relocating to the UK and purchasing a house here.
- Has a full time employment contract with Messier Ltd commencing on 1 September 2016.
- Intends to stay in the UK for at least five years.

The two paintings:

- Are situated in Astronomeria and are worth approximately £20,000 each.
- Have been owned by Galileo since 1 May 2001; their cost is negligible and can be ignored.

Employment contract with Messier Ltd:

- Galileo will be paid an annual salary of £52,000.
- Messier Ltd will assist Galileo with the cost of relocating to the UK.

PRACTICE QUESTIONS: SECTION 1

Required:

(a) (i) Calculate the inheritance tax payable (if any) by Galileo in respect of:

(1) the gift of shares in June 2012, and

(2) the inheritance of shares in May 2016 (8 marks)

(ii) Explain why Galileo is able to pay the inheritance tax due in instalments, state when the instalments are due and identify any further issues relevant to Galileo relating to the payments. (4 marks)

(b) Prepare a reasoned explanation of how any capital gains tax arising in the UK on the sale of the paintings can be minimised. (2 marks)

(c) (i) Explain how Messier Ltd can assist Galileo with the cost of relocating to the UK and/or provide him with interest-free loan finance for this purpose without increasing his UK income tax liability (3 marks)

(ii) State, with reasons, whether Messier Ltd can provide Galileo with accommodation in the UK without giving rise to a UK income tax liability.

(3 marks)

(Total: 20 marks)

25 ERNEST AND GEORGINA (ADAPTED) *Walk in the footsteps of a top tutor*

Ernest intends to sell a capital asset on 1 February 2017 and wishes to maximise his after tax sales proceeds. He is also seeking advice on his inheritance tax position and on his will.

The following information has been obtained from a telephone conversation with Ernest and from client files.

Ernest:

- Is 54 years old and unmarried.
- Lives with Georgina, who is 48 years old, and her adult daughter, Eileen.
- Earns a salary of £140,000 per year.
- Has as yet made no disposals of capital assets in the tax year 2016/17.
- Intends to sell either an oil painting or 7,700 shares in Neutron Ltd on 1 February 2017.

Oil painting:

- Ernest inherited the painting on the death of his uncle on 1 May 2012 when it was worth £23,800.
- Ernest's uncle purchased the painting on 1 July 1998 for £19,500.
- The painting is expected to be worth £47,000 on 1 February 2017.

Shares in Neutron Ltd:

- Qualified for income tax relief under the enterprise investment scheme (EIS) although Ernest did not claim any relief.
- 1 April 2009   Ernest subscribed for 18,600 shares at £8.90 per share.
- 1 March 2011   Ernest received a 1 for 4 bonus issue.
- 1 July 2014   Ernest purchased his full entitlement under a 1 for 10 rights issue at £4.20 per share.
- The shares are expected to be worth £5 each on 1 February 2017.

Neutron Ltd:

- Has an issued share capital of two million £1 ordinary shares.
- Is not quoted on any stock exchange.
- Manufactures and distributes radiation measuring equipment.

Inheritance tax planning and wills:

- Neither Ernest nor Georgina have made any lifetime gifts.
- In his will, Ernest has left the whole of his estate to Georgina.
- In her will, Georgina has left the whole of her estate to Eileen.
- Ernest and Georgina wish to minimise their total inheritance tax liability.
- They are willing to make lifetime gifts to each other but not to Eileen or any other person or organisation.

Current market values of assets owned:

	Ernest £	Georgina £
Family home	620,000	–
Antiques and works of art	400,000	60,000
Investment property	380,000	–
Shares in Neutron Ltd	127,875	–

Required:

(a) **Prepare calculations of the after tax sales proceeds that would be realised on the proposed sale of the painting and on the proposed sale of the shares on 1 February 2017.**

You should assume that Ernest will make any necessary beneficial claims or elections. **(7 marks)**

(b) **Prepare brief notes explaining the inheritance tax liabilities that will arise on the deaths of Ernest and Georgina if no action is taken to reduce such liabilities; identify any actions that could be taken in order to reduce these liabilities and explain the inheritance tax and capital gains tax implications of these actions.**

You are not required to prepare detailed calculations for part (b) of this question.

(13 marks)

You should assume that today's date is 1 December 2016 and that the rates and allowances for the tax year 2015/16 apply throughout the question.

(Total: 20 marks)

26 FITZGERALD AND MORRISON (ADAPTED) *Walk in the footsteps of a top tutor*

Fitzgerald and Morrison, two clients of your firm, require advice on the capital gains tax and inheritance tax implications of gifts they propose to make in the next few months. They are both higher rate taxpayers.

Fitzgerald

Gift of shares in Jay Ltd on 1 October 2016:

– To be made to Fitzgerald's nephew, Pat.
– Comprises the whole of Fitzgerald's 9% shareholding.
– Fitzgerald inherited the shares from his mother on 1 February 2016 when their market value was £32,000.
– The shares are expected to be worth £127,500 on 1 October 2016.

Jay Ltd

– An unquoted manufacturing company.
– Values of the company's assets as at 1 October 2016

	£
Premises	740,000
Plant and machinery (each item is worth more than £6,000)	160,000
Quoted company shares	250,000
Motor cars	30,000
Net current assets	80,000

Pat's plans:

– Pat is an employee of Jay Ltd and will continue to work for the company until he sells the shares.
– Pat intends to sell the shares in January 2018 and expects to receive £170,000.
– He will use the funds to finance a business venture.

Morrison

Gift of a painting on 1 September 2016:

– To be made to Morrison's daughter, Sula, on her wedding day.
– This will be Morrison's first gift since 1 May 2009.
– The painting is one of a set of three.
– Each of the individual paintings is expected to be worth £25,000 on 1 September 2016; a pair of paintings is expected to be worth £70,000 on that date.

The set of paintings:

– Morrison purchased the set of three paintings in April 2008.
– Each of the paintings has a base cost for capital gains tax purposes of £8,300.
– He gave one of the paintings to his wife on 1 May 2009.
– The complete set of three paintings is expected to be worth £120,000 on 1 September 2016.

Required:

(a) In respect of the gift of the shares by Fitzgerald and their subsequent sale by Pat:

    (i) Explain whether or not capital gains tax gift relief will be available on the gift, noting any additional information required. State the latest date for submission of a claim and identify who must sign it. **(4 marks)**

    (ii) Calculate the effect of submitting a valid claim for gift relief on the total capital gains tax liability of Fitzgerald and Pat on the assumption that the gift by Fitzgerald and the sale by Pat take place as planned. **(7 marks)**

    (iii) Explain whether or not business property relief will be available if Fitzgerald dies within seven years of making the gift. **(4 marks)**

(b) In respect of the gift of the painting by Morrison:

    (i) Calculate the value of the potentially exempt transfer, after deduction of all exemptions, for the purposes of inheritance tax **(3 marks)**

    (ii) Calculate the capital gain arising on the gift and comment on the availability of gift relief. **(2 marks)**

(Total: 20 marks)

27 CAPSTAN *Walk in the footsteps of a top tutor*

Capstan requires advice on the transfer of a property to a trust, the sale of shares in respect of which relief has been received under the enterprise investment scheme (EIS) and the sale of shares and qualifying corporate bonds following a takeover.

The following information was obtained from a meeting with Capstan.

Capstan:

- Expects to have taxable income in the tax year 2016/17 of £80,000.
- Transferred a UK property to a discretionary trust on 1 May 2016.
- Plans to sell ordinary shares in Agraffe Ltd and loan stock and ordinary shares in Pinblock plc.
- Will make all available claims to reduce the tax due in respect of his planned disposals.
- Entrepreneurs' relief is not available in respect of any of these disposals.

Transfer of a UK property to a discretionary trust:

- Capstan acquired the property in May 2008 for £285,000.
- The market value of the property on 1 May 2016 was £425,000.
- Capstan had used the property as a second home throughout his period of ownership.
- Capstan will pay any inheritance tax due on the gift of the property to the trust.

Sale of ordinary shares in Agraffe Ltd:

- Capstan subscribed for 18,000 shares in Agraffe Ltd for £32,000 on 1 February 2014.
- He obtained EIS relief of £9,600 against his income tax liability.
- Capstan intends to sell all of the shares for £20,000 on 1 July 2016.
- Capstan will relieve the loss arising on the shares in the most tax efficient manner.

Sale of loan stock and ordinary shares in Pinblock plc:

- Capstan will sell £8,000 7% Pinblock plc non-convertible loan stock for £10,600.
- Capstan will also sell 12,000 shares in Pinblock plc for £69,000.
- The sales will take place on 1 August 2016.

Capstan's acquisition of loan stock and ordinary shares in Pinblock plc:

- Capstan purchased 15,000 shares in Wippen plc for £26,000 on 1 May 2009.
- Pinblock plc acquired 100% of the ordinary share capital of Wippen plc on 1 October 2012.
- The takeover was for bona fide commercial reasons and was not for the avoidance of tax.
- Capstan received £8,000 Pinblock plc non-convertible loan stock (a qualifying corporate bond) and 20,000 ordinary shares in Pinblock plc in exchange for his shares in Wippen plc.
- The loan stock and the shares were worth £9,000 and £40,000 respectively as at 1 October 2012.

Required:

(a) Set out, together with supporting calculations, the inheritance tax and capital gains tax implications of the transfer of the UK property to the trust and the date(s) on which any tax due will be payable. **(6 marks)**

(b) Explain, with supporting calculations, in connection with the sale of shares in Agraffe Ltd
- the tax implications of selling them on 1 July 2016; and
- any advantages and disadvantages to Capstan of delaying the sale. **(7 marks)**

(c) Calculate Capstan's taxable capital gains for the tax year 2016/17. **(5 marks)**

In parts (a) and (b) you should clearly state any assumptions you have made together with any additional information that you would need to confirm with Capstan before finalising your calculations.

(Total: 18 marks)

28 SURFE *Walk in the footsteps of a top tutor*

Surfe has requested advice on the tax implications of the creation of a discretionary trust and a calculation of the estimated inheritance tax liability on her death. The following information was obtained at a meeting with Surfe.

Surfe:

- Is a 63-year-old widow who has two adult nephews.
- Intends to create a trust on 1 January 2017.

Death of Surfe's husband:

- Surfe's husband, Flud, died on 1 February 2009. He had made no gifts during his lifetime.
- In his will, Flud left £140,000 in cash to his sister and the remainder of his estate to Surfe.

The trust:

- The trust will be a discretionary (relevant property) trust for the benefit of Surfe's nephews.
- Surfe will give 200 of her ordinary shares in Leat Ltd and £100,000 in cash to the trustees of the trust on 1 January 2017.
- The inheritance tax due on the gift will be paid by Surfe.
- The trustees will invest the cash in quoted shares.

Leat Ltd:

- Leat Ltd has an issued share capital of 1,000 ordinary shares.
- Surfe owns 650 of the company's ordinary shares.
- The remaining 350 of its ordinary shares are owned by 'Kanal', a UK registered charity.
- Leat Ltd is a property investment company such that business property relief is not available.

Leat Ltd – Value of an ordinary share:

- As at

	1 January 2017 £	1 July 2019 £
As part of a holding of 75% or more	2,000	2,400
As part of a holding of more than 50% but less than 75%	1,000	1,200
As part of a holding of 50% or less	800	1,000

Surfe – Lifetime gifts:

- 1 February 2005   Surfe gave 350 ordinary shares in Leat Ltd to 'Kanal', a UK registered charity.
- 1 October 2016   Surfe gave £85,000 in cash to each of her two nephews.

Surfe's death:

- It should be assumed that Surfe will die on 1 July 2019.
- Her death estate will consist of the house in which she lives, worth £1,400,000, quoted shares worth £600,000 and her remaining shares in Leat Ltd.
- Her will divides her entire estate between her two nephews and their children.

Required:

(a) Outline BRIEFLY:

(i) The capital gains tax implications of:

(1) the proposed gift of shares to the trustees of the discretionary trust

(2) any future sale of the quoted shares by the trustees; and

(3) the future transfer of trust assets to Surfe's nephews. **(4 marks)**

(ii) The inheritance tax charges that may be payable in the future by the trustees of the discretionary trust.

You are not required to prepare calculations for part (a) of this question.

(2 marks)

(b) Calculate the inheritance tax liabilities arising as a result of Surfe's death on 1 July 2019. **(11 marks)**

(Total: 17 marks)

29 UNA (ADAPTED) *Walk in the footsteps of a top tutor*

Your manager has sent you an email, together with an attachment in respect of a new client called Una. The email and the attachment are set out below.

Email from your manager

> I have had a meeting with Una, a new client of the firm. Una is 74 years old and a widow. She has a son, Won, who is 49 years old.
>
> Una is resident and domiciled in the UK. Her annual taxable income is approximately £90,000. She makes sufficient capital gains every year to use her annual exempt amount.
>
> Una made a gift of cash of £40,000 to Won in May 2012. This is the only transfer she has made for the purposes of inheritance tax in the last seven years. Una has left the whole of her estate to Won in her will. Her estate is expected to be worth more than £3 million at the time of her death.
>
> For the purposes of this work I want you to assume that Una will die on 31 December 2021.
>
> **Gift to son**
>
> Una is considering making a gift to Won of either some farmland situated in the UK or a villa situated in the country of Soloria. Una has prepared a schedule setting out the details of the farmland and the villa. The schedule is attached to this email. Una will make the gift to Won on his birthday on 18 November 2016; she is not prepared to delay the gift, even if it would be advantageous to do so.

PAPER P6: ADVANCED TAXATION (FA2015)

The tax system in the country of Soloria

Capital gains tax   There is no capital gains tax in Soloria.

Inheritance tax   If Una still owns the villa at her death on 31 December 2021, the inheritance tax liability in Soloria would be £170,000.

If Una gifts the villa to Won on 18 November 2016 and dies on 31 December 2021, the inheritance tax liability in Soloria would be £34,000, all of which would be payable following Una's death.

The double taxation agreement between the UK and the country of Soloria includes an exemption clause whereby assets situated in one of the countries that is party to the agreement are subject to inheritance tax in that country only and not in the other country.

Gift to granddaughter

Una's granddaughter, Alona, will begin a three-year university course in September 2016. Una has agreed to pay Alona's rent of £450 per month while she is at university.

Undeclared income

Una purchased a luxury motor car for her own use in 2012, but found that many of her friends wanted to borrow it for weddings. In June 2013, she began charging £200 per day for the use of the car but is of the opinion that the income received cannot be subject to income tax as she only charges a fee 'to help cover the car's running costs'. However, I have considered the situation and concluded that the hiring out of the car has resulted in taxable profits.

Sale of painting in Railos

On 10 May 2015 Una took a valuable painting she owned from her home in the UK to the country of Railos. On 20 May 2015 she sold the painting for £62,000 more than she paid for it. Railos has no double taxation agreement with the UK and dos not exchange any financial information with UK authorities. Una has said that she does not intend to declare the capital gain as the painting was an overseas asset at the date of sale and she does not believe that she is liable to UK tax on this overseas asset.

I want you to prepare the following:

(a) **Gifts to son and granddaughter**

A memorandum for the client file that addresses the following issues.

(i)   In respect of the gift to Won

- Calculations of the potential reduction in the inheritance tax payable on Una's death as a result of each of the possible gifts to Won. The farmland will not qualify for business property relief, but you will need to consider the availability of agricultural property relief.
- Calculations of the capital gains tax liability in respect of each of the possible gifts.
- Explanations where the calculations are not self-explanatory, particularly in relation to the availability of reliefs, and a note of any assumptions made.
- A concise summary of your calculations in relation to these capital taxes in order to assist Una in making her decision as to which asset to give to Won.

- Any other tax and financial implications in respect of the gifts of which Una should be aware before she makes her decision.

    (ii) In respect of the payment of Alona's rent
    - The conditions that would need to be satisfied in order for the payments to be exempt for the purposes of inheritance tax.

(b) **Undeclared income and capital gain**

A **brief letter** to be sent from me to Una in relation to the luxury motor car and the gain on the painting sold in Railos.

The letter should explain the implications for Una and our firm of failing to declare the income from the car and the capital gain to HM Revenue and Customs and the implications for Una of not having declared the income sooner.

Tax manager

Attachment – Schedule from Una – Details of the farmland and villa

	Notes	Date acquired	Cost £	Estimated value 18 November 2016 £	Estimated value 31 December 2021 £
Farmland	1	September 2012	720,000	900,000	1,100,000
Villa	2	August 2002	510,000	745,000	920,000

Notes

(1) The agricultural value of the farmland is approximately 35% of its market value. The farmland has always been rented out to tenant farmers.

(2) I inherited the villa when my husband died on 14 January 2006. Its market value at that date was £600,000. The villa has never been my principal private residence. It is situated in the country of Soloria and rented out to long-term tenants. The income is subject to Solorian income tax at the rate of 50%. I do not own any other assets situated in Soloria.

(3) The whole of my husband's nil rate band was used at the time of his death.

Required:

(a) Prepare the memorandum requested in the email from your manager.

For guidance, the calculations in part (a) of this question are worth no more than half of the total marks available. **(21 marks)**

Professional marks will be awarded in part (a) for the overall presentation of the memorandum and the effectiveness with which the information is communicated.
(3 marks)

(b) Prepare the letter requested in the email from your manager. **(10 marks)**

A professional mark will be awarded in part (b) for the overall presentation of the letter. **(1 mark)**

Assume today's date is 15 June 2016.

(Total: 35 marks)

30 ASH *Walk in the footsteps of a top tutor*

Ash requires a calculation of his capital gains tax liability for the tax year 2015/16, together with advice in connection with entrepreneurs' relief, registration for the purposes of value added tax (VAT) and the payment of income tax.

Ash:

- Is resident in the UK.
- Had taxable income of £29,000 in the tax year 2015/16.
- Was the owner and managing director of Lava Ltd until 1 May 2015, when he resigned and sold the company.
- Is a partner in the Vulcan Partnership.

Ash – disposals of capital assets in the tax year 2015/16:

- The sale of the shares in Lava Ltd resulted in a capital gain of £235,000, which qualified for entrepreneurs' relief.
- Ash assigned a 37-year lease on a property for £110,000 on 1 May 2015.
- Ash sold two acres of land on 1 October 2015 for £30,000.
- Ash sold quoted shares and made a capital loss of £17,100 on 1 November 2015.

The lease:

- The lease was previously assigned to Ash for £31,800 when it had 46 years remaining.
- The property has always been used by Lava Ltd for trading purposes.
- Lava Ltd paid Ash rent, equivalent to 40% of the market rate, in respect of the use of the property.

The sale of the two acres of land:

- Ash purchased eight acres of land for £27,400 on 1 June 2008.
- Ash sold six acres of the land for £42,000 on 1 August 2011.
- The remaining two acres of land were worth £18,000 on 1 August 2011.

Vulcan Partnership (Vulcan):

- Has a 31 March year end
- Has monthly turnover of:

Standard-rated supplies	£400
Exempt supplies	£100
Zero-rated supplies	£5,600

- Its turnover is expected to increase slightly in 2017.
- None of its customers is registered for the purposes of VAT.
- Ash expects to receive less profit from Vulcan for the tax year 2016/17 than he did in 2015/16.

Required:

(a) (i) State the conditions that must be satisfied for Ash's assignment of the lease to be an associated disposal for the purposes of entrepreneurs' relief.

(3 marks)

(ii) Calculate Ash's capital gains tax liability for the tax year 2015/16 on the assumption that the assignment of the lease does qualify as an associated disposal and that entrepreneurs' relief will be claimed where possible.

The following lease percentages should be used, where necessary.

37 years   93.497

46 years   98.490

(7 marks)

(b) Discuss in detail whether the Vulcan Partnership may be required to register for value added tax (VAT) and the advantages and disadvantages for the business of registration. (7 marks)

(c) Set out the matters that Ash should consider when deciding whether or not to make a claim to reduce the payment on account of income tax due on 31 January 2017. (3 marks)

(Total: 20 marks)

31 CUTHBERT *Walk in the footsteps of a top tutor*

Cuthbert requires advice on the tax implications of the payment of capital gains tax by instalments and an error he has made in an income tax return. He has also requested calculations in respect of the inheritance tax payable on the death of his uncle, Pugh.

Cuthbert:

– Is resident and domiciled in the UK.

– Intends to give a building to his brother on 1 March 2017.

– Made an error in his income tax return for the tax year 2014/15.

Cuthbert – proposed gift of a building to his brother on 1 March 2017:

– The building is currently let to long-term tenants and has a market value of £460,000.

Cuthbert – error in his income tax return for the tax year 2014/15:

– HM Revenue and Customs have written to Cuthbert in respect of his income tax return.

– HM Revenue and Customs are claiming that Cuthbert has under-declared his UK property income.

Pugh – valuation of assets owned at death on 1 February 2016:

	£
Home in the UK	720,000
Vintage motor cars located in the country of Camberia	490,000
Quoted shares (holdings of less than 1%) registered in Camberia	330,000
Cash held in bank accounts in the UK	45,000

Pugh – UK inheritance tax liability:

– Was calculated on the basis that Pugh was domiciled in the country of Camberia and that he had made no lifetime gifts.
– Was paid on time.

Pugh – information discovered after the payment of the UK inheritance tax:

– Pugh had been domiciled in the UK since 1 January 2007.
– Pugh had made a gift of UK quoted shares (all holdings of less than 1%) to a trust on 10 June 2009.
– The quoted shares were worth £323,500 and Pugh paid any UK inheritance tax due.

The system of inheritance tax in the country of Camberia:

– There is no nil rate band and the rate of inheritance tax is 25%.
– Inheritance tax is only charged on the value of land and buildings and quoted shares owned at the time of death and located in Camberia.
– There is no double tax treaty between the UK and Camberia.

Required:

(a) Explain whether or not the capital gains tax due on the proposed gift of the building could be paid by instalments and the matters that Cuthbert would need to be aware of in respect of this method of payment. **(6 marks)**

(b) Explain how any penalty would be calculated if it is determined that Cuthbert made a careless error when completing his 2014/15 tax return. **(4 marks)**

(c) Calculate the UK inheritance tax liability in respect of Pugh's estate following the discovery of the additional information, together with the interest on overdue tax that will be payable if the inheritance tax is paid on 1 January 2017. **(10 marks)**

(Total: 20 marks)

32 BRAD (ADAPTED) *Walk in the footsteps of a top tutor*

Your manager has had a meeting with Brad, a client of your firm. Extracts from your manager's meeting notes together with an email from your manager are set out below.

Extracts from meeting notes

> **Personal details**
>
> Brad is 70 years old. He is married to Laura and they have a daughter, Dani, who is 38 years old.
>
> Brad had lived in the UK for the whole of his life until he moved with his wife to the country of Keirinia on 1 January 2013. He returned to live permanently in the UK on 30 April 2016. Whilst living in Keirinia, Brad was non-UK resident and he is now resident in the UK. He has always been domiciled in the UK.
>
> Brad has significant investment income and has been a higher rate taxpayer for many years.

PRACTICE QUESTIONS: SECTION 1

Capital gains

Whilst living in the country of Keirinia, Brad sold various assets as set out below. He has not made any other disposals since 5 April 2012.

Asset	Date of sale	Proceeds £	Date of purchase	Cost £
Quoted shares	1 December 2012	18,900	1 October 2011	14,000
Painting	1 June 2015	36,000	1 March 2011	15,000
Antique bed	1 March 2016	9,400	1 May 2013	7,300
Motor car	1 April 2016	11,000	1 February 2012	8,500

I explained that, although Brad was non-UK resident whilst living in Keirinia, these disposals may still be subject to UK capital gains tax because he will be regarded as only temporarily non-UK resident.

There is no capital gains tax in the country of Keirinia.

Inheritance tax planning

Brad's estate is worth approximately £5 million. He has not made any lifetime gifts and, in his will, he intends to leave half of his estate to his daughter, Dani, and the other half to his wife, Laura. I pointed out that it may be advantageous to make a lifetime gift to Dani. Brad agreed to consider giving Dani 1,500 of his shares in Omnium Ltd and has asked for a general summary of the inheritance tax advantages of making lifetime gifts to individuals.

Omnium Ltd is an unquoted manufacturing company which also owns a number of investment properties. Brad was given his shares in the company by his wife on 1 January 2012. The ownership of the share capital of Omnium Ltd is set out below.

	Shares
Laura (Brad's wife)	4,500
Brad	3,000
Vic (Laura's brother)	1,500
Christine (friend of Laura)	1,000
	10,000

The current estimated value of a share in Omnium Ltd is set out below.

Shareholding	Value per share £
Up to 25%	190
26% to 50%	205
51% to 60%	240
61% to 74%	255
75% to 80%	290
More than 80%	300

Email from your manager

In preparation for my next meeting with Brad, please prepare the following:

(a) **Capital gains tax**

An explanation, with supporting calculations, of the UK capital gains tax liability in respect of the disposals made by Brad whilst living in the country of Keirinia.

Your explanation should include the precise reasons for Brad being regarded as only temporarily non-UK resident and a statement of when the tax was/will be payable.

(b) **Inheritance tax**

(i) An explanation of the inheritance tax advantages of making lifetime gifts to individuals, in general.

(ii) In respect of the possible gift of 1,500 shares in Omnium Ltd to Dani:

– a calculation of the fall in value of Brad's estate which will result from the gift

– a detailed explanation of whether or not business property relief would be available in respect of the gift and, on the assumption that it would be available, the manner in which it would be calculated

– a brief statement of any other tax issues arising from the gift, which will need to be considered at a later date.

Tax manager

Required:

Carry out the work required as requested in the email from your manager.

The following marks are available.

(a) Capital gains tax. (8 marks)

(b) Inheritance tax.

(i) Explanation of the inheritance tax advantages of making lifetime gifts to individuals. (7 marks)

(ii) In respect of the possible gift of 1,500 shares in Omnium Ltd to Dani. (10 marks)

(Total: 25 marks)

33 PESCARA (ADAPTED) *Walk in the footsteps of a top tutor*

 Timed question with Online tutor debrief

Pescara requires advice on the inheritance tax payable on death and on the gift of a property, and on the capital gains tax due on a disposal of shares, together with the relief available in respect of the purchase of seed enterprise investment scheme shares.

Pescara and her parents:

- Pescara is a higher rate taxpayer who is resident and domiciled in the UK.
- Pescara's father, Galvez, died on 1 June 2007.
- Pescara's mother, Marina, died on 1 October 2016.
- Both Galvez and Marina were resident and domiciled in the UK.

Galvez – lifetime gifts and gifts on death:

- Galvez had not made any lifetime gifts.
- In his will, Galvez left cash of £80,000 to Pescara and a further £80,000 to Pescara's brother.
- Galvez left the remainder of his estate to his wife, Marina.

Marina – lifetime gifts and gifts on death:

- On 1 February 2011, Marina gave Pescara 375,000 shares in Sepang plc.
- Marina had made no other lifetime gifts.

Marina – gift of 375,000 shares in Sepang plc to Pescara:

- 1 January 2008   Marina purchased 375,000 shares for £420,000.
- 1 February 2011   Marina gave all of the shares to Pescara.

    The shares were quoted at £1.84 – £1.96

    The highest and lowest marked bargains were £1.80 and £1.92.

- The shares did not qualify for business property relief or capital gains tax gift relief.

Acquisition of Sepang plc by Zolder plc and subsequent bonus issue:

- 1 January 2013   Zolder plc acquired the whole of the ordinary share capital of Sepang plc.

    Pescara received 30 pence and two ordinary shares in Zolder plc, worth £1 each, for each share in Sepang plc.

    The takeover was for genuine commercial reasons and not for the avoidance of tax.

- 1 July 2014   Zolder plc declared a 2 for 1 bonus issue.

Pescara's actual and intended capital transactions in the tax year 2016/17:

			£
15 November 2016	Sale	1,000,000 shares in Zolder plc	445,000
1 April 2017	Purchase	Qualifying seed enterprise investment scheme (SEIS) shares	90,000

Pescara – gift of a UK property:

– Pescara intends to give a UK property to her son on 1 October 2017.

– Pescara intends to continue to use this property, rent-free, such that this gift will be a gift with reservation.

Required:

(a) Calculate the inheritance tax payable in respect of Marina's gift of the shares in Sepang plc, as a result of her death. **(7 marks)**

(b) (i) Calculate Pescara's capital gains tax liability for the tax year 2016/17 on the assumption that seed enterprise investment scheme (SEIS) relief is claimed in respect of the shares to be purchased on 1 April 2017 and that entrepreneurs' relief is not available. **(6 marks)**

(ii) State the capital gains tax implications of Pescara selling the SEIS shares at some point in the future. **(3 marks)**

(c) Explain how the proposed gift of the UK property will be treated for the purposes of calculating the inheritance tax due on Pescara's death. **(4 marks)**

(Total: 20 marks)

Calculate your allowed time, allocate the time to the separate parts...................

34 CADA *Walk in the footsteps of a top tutor*

Your firm has been asked to provide advice in connection with inheritance tax and capital gains tax following the death of Cada. The advice relates to the implications of making lifetime gifts, making gifts to charity, varying the terms of a will and other aspects of capital gains tax planning.

Cada and her family:

– Cada, who was UK domiciled, died on 20 November 2016.

– Cada is survived by two daughters: Raymer and Yang.

– Raymer has an adult son.

– Yang has no children.

Cada – Lifetime gifts and available nil rate band:

– Cada had not made any lifetime gifts since 30 November 2012.

– Cada's nil rate band available at the date of her death was £220,000.

Cada's death estate and the details of her will:

- Cada owned assets valued at £1,000,000 at the time of her death.
- Cada left her house, valued at £500,000, to Raymer.
- Cada left cash of £60,000 to a UK national charity.
- Cada left her remaining assets (including a portfolio of shares) valued at £440,000, to Yang.
- None of the remaining assets qualified for any inheritance tax reliefs.

Raymer:

- Is not an accountant, but has some knowledge of the UK tax system.
- Has made four observations regarding her mother's estate and her inheritance.

Raymer's four observations:

- 'My mother should have made additional gifts in her lifetime.'
- 'The tax rate on the chargeable estate should be less than 40% due to the gift to charity.'
- 'I do not intend to live in the house but will give it to my son on 1 July 2017.'
- 'My mother paid capital gains tax every year. However, when she died, some of her shareholdings had a value of less than cost.'

Cada's shareholdings at the time of her death:

- Quoted shares in JW plc valued at more than cost.
- Quoted shares in FR plc valued at less than cost.
- Unquoted shares in KZ Ltd valued at £nil.

Required:

(a) Explain the inheritance tax advantages, other than lifetime exemptions, which could have been obtained if Cada had made additional lifetime gifts of quoted shares between 1 December 2012 and her death. **(4 marks)**

(b) Calculate the increase in the legacy to the charity which would be necessary in order for the reduced rate of inheritance tax to apply and quantify the reduction in the inheritance tax liability which would result. **(5 marks)**

(c) Explain the capital gains tax and inheritance tax advantages which could be obtained by varying the terms of Cada's will and set out the procedures required in order to achieve a tax effective variation. **(6 marks)**

(d) In relation to capital gains tax, explain what beneficial actions Cada could have carried out in the tax year of her death in respect of her shareholdings. **(5 marks)**

(Total: 20 marks)

35 KING *Walk in the footsteps of a top tutor*

King, a wealthy client of your firm with a significant property portfolio, requires advice on the sale of some unquoted shares and on the capital gains tax and inheritance tax implications of transferring assets to a trust and to his two children.

King:

- Is resident and domiciled in the UK.
- Is an additional rate taxpayer.
- Has used his capital gains tax annual exempt amount for the tax year 2016/17.
- Has made one previous lifetime gift of £25,000 to his daughter, Florentyna, on 1 June 2015.
- It should be assumed that King will die on 1 May 2018.

King's family:

- King's daughter, Florentyna, is 34 years old and has two young children.
- Florentyna will have income from part time employment of £10,000 in the tax year 2016/17. This is her only source of taxable income.
- King's son, Axel, is 40 years old and has an 18 year old daughter, who is a university student.

King's plans:

- On 1 September 2016, King will sell some of his shares in Wye Ltd.
- On 1 October 2016, King will put a cottage he owns in Newtown and the after tax cash proceeds from the sale of the shares in Wye Ltd into an interest in possession trust for Florentyna and her children.
- On 1 March 2017, King will gift his share of a flat in Unicity to Axel.

Sale of shares in Wye Ltd:

- Wye Ltd is an unquoted investment company.
- King acquired 5,000 shares in Wye Ltd on 1 June 2002 at a cost of £5 each.
- These shares will be worth £45 each on 1 September 2016.
- King will sell sufficient shares to generate after tax proceeds of £30,000.

Cottage in Newtown:

- This property is wholly owned by King.
- It is expected to have a value of £315,000 on 1 October 2016.

Creation of the interest in possession trust:

- King will pay any inheritance tax arising as a result of the gifts made to the trust.
- Florentyna will be the life tenant and her two young children will be the remaindermen of the trust.
- Florentyna will live in the cottage in Newtown and the trustees will invest the cash in quoted shares which will generate annual dividends of £3,000.

Flat in Unicity:

- The flat in Unicity is jointly owned by King and his wife, Joy, in the proportions: King 75% and Joy 25%.

- King and Joy have recently signed a contract with Axel's daughter to rent the flat to her for three years starting on 1 September 2016.

- The rental agreement is on a commercial basis.

- King has obtained the following expected valuations for the flat as at 1 March 2017:

	With vacant possession	Without vacant possession
	£	£
Value of a 25% share	60,000	40,000
Value of a 75% share	220,000	160,000
Value of the whole property	340,000	250,000

Required:

(a) Calculate the minimum number of shares in Wye Ltd which King must sell to generate after-tax proceeds of £30,000. **(3 marks)**

(b) (i) Advise King, with the aid of supporting calculations, of the capital gains tax and immediate inheritance tax implications of the proposed gift of assets into the interest in possession trust on 1 October 2016. **(6 marks)**

(ii) Explain how Florentyna will be taxed on the income arising in the trust and calculate the additional income tax, if any, payable by her in respect of this income for the tax year 2016/17. **(4 marks)**

(c) Explain, with the aid of supporting calculations, why the disposal of the flat in Unicity may be caught by the associated operations rules and the increase in the inheritance tax liability which would arise on King's death on 1 May 2018 if these rules were to apply. **(7 marks)**

(Total: 20 marks)

MULTI TAX PERSONAL INCLUDING OVERSEAS

36 NUCLEUS RESOURCES (ADAPTED) *Online question assistance*

 Walk in the footsteps of a top tutor

You have received the following memorandum from your manager.

To	Tax senior
From	Tax manager
Date	28 November 2016
Subject	Maria Copenhagen and Nucleus Resources

I spoke to Maria Copenhagen this morning. We arranged to meet on Thursday 4 December to discuss the following matters.

Nucleus Resources

Maria is planning a major expansion of her business, Nucleus Resources. I attach a schedule, prepared by Maria, showing the budgeted income and expenditure of the business for a full year. Maria wants to know how much additional after tax income the expansion of the business will create depending on whether she employs the two additional employees or uses a sub-contractor, Quantum Ltd.

Quoted shares

In October 2014 Niels, Maria's husband, received a gift of shares with a value of £170,000 from his uncle. The shares are quoted on the Heisenbergia Stock Exchange. The uncle died in November 2016 and Maria wants to know whether there will be any UK inheritance tax in respect of the gift. The uncle had been living in the country of Heisenbergia since moving there from the UK in 1995 and had made substantial gifts to other close relatives in 2013 and 2014. Inheritance tax of £30,600 has been charged in Heisenbergia in respect of the gift to Niels.

According to Maria, Niels is considering transferring the shares to a trust for the benefit of their two sons.

Please prepare the following:

(a) In respect of Nucleus Resources:

Calculations of the additional annual after tax income that would be generated by the expansion of the business under the two alternatives i.e. the recruitment of the additional employees and the use of the sub-contractor. You should check to see if Maria is currently an additional rate taxpayer. If she is, you can simply deduct tax and national insurance at the marginal rates from the additional profits.

Don't worry about the precise timing of the capital allowances in respect of the car, just spread the total allowances available for the car equally over the period of ownership. Also, watch out for the VAT implications of the expansion; there is bound to be an effect on the recoverability of input tax due to the business being partially exempt.

PRACTICE QUESTIONS: SECTION 1

(b) In respect of the quoted shares:

  (i) A list of the issues to be considered in order to determine whether or not the gift from the uncle is within the scope of UK inheritance tax and the treatment of any inheritance tax suffered in the country of Heisenbergia.

  (ii) A brief outline of the tax implications of transferring the shares to the trust and the taxation of the trust income paid to the beneficiaries. The shares are currently worth £210,000.

  (iii) Notes on the extent to which it is professionally acceptable for me to discuss issues relating to the shares with Maria.

I want to be able to use the calculations and notes in my meeting with Maria (or in a subsequent meeting with Niels) and I may not have much time to study them beforehand so please make sure that they are clear, concise and that I can find my way around them easily.

Thank you

Tax manager

The schedule prepared by Maria is set out below.

Nucleus Resources – Estimated income and expenditure for a full year

Notes

1   The figures in the 'expansion' column relate to the expansion only and will be in addition to the existing business.

2   Nucleus Resources is registered for VAT.

3   All amounts are stated exclusive of VAT.

4   Materials and overheads are subject to VAT at 20%. The expenditure cannot be attributed to particular supplies.

		Existing business £	*Expansion* £
Turnover:	Standard rated	40,000	190,000
	Exempt	90,000	–
Expenditure:			
Materials and overheads		37,000	See
Wages		35,000	below

Costs relating to the expansion

In order to expand the business I will either recruit two additional employees or sub-contract the work to Quantum Ltd, an unconnected company. Details of the expenditure relating to these two possibilities are set out below.

Employees

Employee 1 would be paid a salary of £55,000. He would also be provided with a petrol driven car with a list price when new of £12,800 (including VAT) and a CO_2 emission rate of 109 grams per kilometre. It can be assumed that the car will be sold in five years' time for £2,000. Employee 2 would be paid a salary of £40,000 and would not be provided with a car.

There would also be additional materials and overheads, net of VAT at 20%, of £20,000.

Quantum Ltd

Quantum Ltd would charge an annual fee of £140,000 plus VAT.

There would be no additional materials or overheads.

Niels and Maria Copenhagen are both clients of your firm. The following information has been obtained from their files.

Niels Copenhagen

- Resident and domiciled in the UK.
- Niels has not made any previous transfers for the purposes of inheritance tax.
- Married to Maria. They have two children; Hans (11 years old) and Erik (8 years old).

Maria Copenhagen

- Resident and domiciled in the UK.
- Trades as 'Nucleus Resources', an unincorporated business.
- Receives annual gross rental income from an interest in possession trust of £110,000.

Required:

Prepare the meeting notes requested by your manager. The following marks are available.

(a) Calculations of the annual additional after tax income generated by the expansion of Maria's business under each of the two alternatives. **(14 marks)**

(b) (i) The issues to be considered in order to determine whether or not the gift from the uncle is within the scope of UK inheritance tax and the treatment of any inheritance tax suffered in the country of Heisenbergia. **(6 marks)**

 (ii) The tax implications of transferring the shares to the trust and the taxation of any trust income paid to the beneficiaries, Hans and Erik. **(7 marks)**

 (iii) The extent to which it is professionally acceptable to discuss issues relating to the shares with Maria. **(4 marks)**

Appropriateness of the format and presentation of the notes and the effectiveness with which the information is communicated. **(4 marks)**

You should assume that today's date is 1 December 2016 and that the rates and allowances for the tax year 2015/16 apply throughout the question.

(Total: 35 marks)

 Online question assistance

37 BOSON (ADAPTED) *Walk in the footsteps of a top tutor*

Boson has been working overseas and is about to return to the UK. He requires advice on his capital gains tax position and on whether to retain an overseas investment property or to sell it and invest the funds in the UK.

The following information has been obtained from telephone conversations with Boson.

Boson's current position:

– He is UK domiciled.
– He had lived in the UK all of his life until he moved to the country of Higgsia on 10 January 2012 to take up a full time employment contract overseas.
– He sold shares in Meson plc whilst living in Higgsia.
– He purchased a house in Higgsia but retained his principal private residence in the UK.

Boson's future:

– Boson plans to cease his employment overseas and return permanently to his home in the UK on 20 December 2016.
– He has signed an employment contract with Graviton Ltd, which commences on 20 January 2017.
– He is considering selling the house in Higgsia and investing the after tax proceeds in a portfolio of quoted shares in UK companies or, alternatively, retaining the house and renting it out.

Sales of shares in Meson plc:

– Meson plc is a UK resident quoted company.
– Boson inherited 19,500 shares on 1 August 2005 when they were worth £2 each.
– Boson sold 10,000 shares on 1 May 2012 for £11 each.
– Boson sold the remaining shares on 1 November 2016 for £15 each.

House in the country of Higgsia:

– Purchased by Boson on 1 May 2012 for £105,000.
– Could be rented out for £11,000 per year after deduction of allowable expenses.
– Is currently worth and could be sold for £200,000.

The tax system in the country of Higgsia:

– Non-residents of Higgsia are charged income tax at 30% on income arising in the country of Higgsia.
– No capital gains tax.
– No double tax treaty with the UK.

Employment contract with Graviton Ltd:

– Boson will be paid an annual salary of £35,500.

Portfolio of quoted shares:

– The portfolio would be expected to generate annual dividends at the rate of approximately 4.3% of the capital invested.

Required:

(a) Advise Boson, by reference to his residence position, as to whether or not the sales of the shares in Meson plc on 1 May 2012 and 1 November 2016 and the possible sale of the house in the country of Higgsia will be subject to capital gains tax.

State what he should do in order to ensure that any gains arising are not subject to capital gains tax.

You are not required to prepare calculations for part (a) of this question.

(10 marks)

(b) (i) Calculate Boson's annual rental income after deduction of all taxes in respect of the house in Higgsia. **(4 marks)**

(ii) On the assumption that the house in Higgsia is sold for £200,000, with no capital gains tax payable, calculate the annual after tax income generated if the whole amount is invested in the portfolio of quoted shares. **(3 marks)**

(iii) Calculate the maximum by which the rate of return on the portfolio of quoted shares could fall before the after tax income generated would cease to exceed the return from renting out the house in Higgsia. **(3 marks)**

You should assume that today's date is 1 December 2016 and that the rates and allowances for the tax year 2015/16 and the FA2015 rules apply throughout the question.

(Total: 20 marks)

38 POBLANO (ADAPTED) *Walk in the footsteps of a top tutor*

Your manager has had a meeting with Poblano. Poblano is the Finance Director of Capsicum Ltd, a subsidiary of Scoville plc. He is a higher rate taxpayer earning £60,000 per year and currently has no other income. Scoville plc together with its subsidiaries and its directors have been clients of your firm for many years.

The memorandum recording the matters discussed at the meeting and an extract from an email from your manager detailing the tasks for you to perform are set out below.

Memorandum recording matters discussed at meeting with Poblano

To The files

From Tax manager

Date 4 June 2016

Subject Poblano

I had a meeting with Poblano on 3 June 2016.

(i) **Working in Manchester**

Poblano currently lives and works in Birmingham. However, Capsicum Ltd has recently acquired the Manchester operations of the group from a fellow subsidiary of Scoville plc. As a result of this, Poblano is going to be based in Manchester from 1 August 2016 for a period of at least five years. He will be paid an additional £15,000 per year during this period.

Poblano does not want to relocate his family to Manchester for personal reasons. He has been offered the use of a furnished flat in Manchester belonging to Capsicum Ltd to live in during the week. He will drive home each weekend.

Details of the company's flat are set out below.

	£
Current market value	490,000
Purchase price (1 June 2013)	443,000
Annual value	8,500
Monthly contribution required from Poblano	200

Alternatively, if he does not live in the flat, Capsicum Ltd will pay him a mileage allowance of 50 pence per mile to cover the cost of travelling to Manchester every Monday and returning home every Friday. During the week, whilst he is in Manchester, Poblano will stay with his aunt, paying her rent of £325 per month.

Poblano estimates that he will drive 9,200 miles per year travelling to Manchester each week and that he will spend £1,400 per year on petrol. There would also be additional depreciation in respect of his car of approximately £1,500 per year. Capsicum Ltd has a policy of not providing its employees with company cars.

Poblano expects to be better off due to the increase in his salary. He wants to know how much better off he will be depending on whether he lives in the company flat or receives the mileage allowance and stays with his aunt.

(ii) **Senior accounting officer rules**

Poblano is aware that there are some special rules affecting senior accounting officers. He asked me for a brief summary of the rules and whether or not they could apply to him.

(iii) **Father's property in the country of Chilaca**

Paprikash (Poblano's father) owns a property in the country of Chilaca that he uses for holidays. It has always been intended that the property would be left to Poblano in his father's will. However, Paprikash has recently agreed to give the property to Poblano now, if to do so would make sense from a tax point of view. Paprikash may still wish to use the property occasionally in the future.

The property is currently worth £600,000. However, due to the economic situation in the country of Chilaca, it is possible that this figure could either rise or fall over the next few years.

Paprikash is domiciled in the UK. He is in poor health and is not expected to live for more than a further five years. His total assets, including the property in the country of Chilaca, are worth £2 million.

Paprikash makes gifts on 1 May each year in order to use his annual exemption. His only other gift in the last seven years was to a trust on 1 June 2015. The gift consisted of a number of minority holdings of quoted shares valued at £290,000 in total. The trust is for the benefit of Poblano's daughter, Piri. It can be assumed that Paprikash will not make any further lifetime gifts.

There is no capital gains tax or inheritance tax in the country of Chilaca.

(iv) **Trust created for the benefit of Poblano's daughter**

The trust was created on 1 June 2015 as noted above. Poblano's daughter, Piri, received income from the trust for the first time in March 2016. Poblano did not have any further information on the trust and agreed to bring the relevant documentation to our next meeting. Piri's only other income is an annual salary of approximately £35,000.

PAPER P6: ADVANCED TAXATION (FA2015)

Tax manager

E-mail from your manager

I want you to prepare notes for a meeting that we will both attend with Poblano. You will be leading the meeting.

Set out the information so that it is easy for you to find what you need as we go through the various issues. Include the briefest possible notes where the numbers are not self-explanatory.

The meeting notes need to include:

(i) **Working in Manchester**

– Calculations showing how much better (or worse) off Poblano will be under each of the alternatives as compared to his current position. If he is worse off under either of the alternatives, include a calculation of the amount of salary he would have to be paid, in addition to the £15,000, so that he is not out of pocket.

– An explanation of the tax treatment for the recipients of the mileage allowance to be paid to Poblano and the rent to be paid to his aunt.

– Any further information required and the effect it could have on the calculations you have prepared.

(ii) **Senior accounting officer rules**

The information requested by Poblano.

(iii) **Father's property in the country of Chilaca**

– Calculations of the inheritance tax liability that will become due in respect of the property in the country of Chilaca depending on whether the property is gifted to Poblano on 1 August 2016 or via his father's will.

You should assume the following:

– His father, Paprikash, will die on either 31 December 2018 or 31 December 2020.

– The property will be worth £600,000 on 1 August 2016.

– Three possible values of the property at the date of Paprikash's death: £450,000, £600,000 and £900,000.

You should calculate the inheritance tax for each of the 12 possible situations on the property only, assuming that Paprikash does not use the property after the date of the gift.

You should start by calculating the tax on a lifetime gift with Paprikash's death on 31 December 2018. If you then think about the relationships between the different situations you should find that the calculations do not take too long.

In order for the calculations to be comparable, when calculating the tax on the gift via Paprikash's will, you should assume that any available nil band is deductible from the property.

– Conclusions drawn from the calculations.

– Any other issues that we should draw to Poblano's attention.

(iv) **Trust created for the benefit of Poblano's daughter**

– A summary of the tax treatment of the income received by Poblano's daughter Piri, as beneficiary, depending on the nature of the trust.

I understand from Poblano that the only income of the trust is dividend income.

Required:

Prepare the meeting notes requested in the email from your manager.

The following marks are available.

(i)	Working in Manchester	(10 marks)
(ii)	Senior accounting officer rules	(3 marks)
(iii)	Father's property in the country of Chilaca	(12 marks)
(iv)	Trust created for the benefit of Poblano's daughter.	(6 marks)

Professional marks will be awarded for the appropriateness of the format and presentation of the notes and the effectiveness with which the information is communicated. **(4 marks)**

(Total: 35 marks)

39 SUSHI (ADAPTED) *Walk in the footsteps of a top tutor*

An extract from an e-mail from your manager regarding a meeting with a client, Sushi, together with an e-mail from Sushi are set out below.

E-mail from your manager

> I have just had a meeting with Sushi who has been a client of the firm since she moved to the UK from the country of Zakuskia in May 2002.
>
> Sushi is 57 years old and was born in the country of Zakuskia. Her father died in 2009 and, as you will see from her e-mail, her mother died in October 2016. Her father and mother were both domiciled and resident in the country of Zakuskia throughout their lives.
>
> Zakuskian inheritance tax is charged at the rate of 24% on all land and buildings situated within the country that are owned by an individual at the time of death. There is no capital gains tax in the country of Zakuskia. There is no double tax treaty between the UK and the country of Zakuskia.
>
> Until the death of her mother, Sushi's only assets consisted of her house in the UK, a number of investment properties also situated in the UK, and cash in UK bank accounts. Her total UK assets are worth approximately £3 million. Sushi is an additional rate taxpayer and realises taxable capital gains of more than £20,000 each year. She has made significant cash gifts to her son in the past and, therefore, does not require an explanation of the taxation of potentially exempt transfers or the accumulation principle. Sushi is resident in the UK.
>
> I want you to write notes addressing the points below:

(i) **UK inheritance tax and the statue**

An explanation of:

– The UK inheritance tax implications of the death of Sushi's mother.

– Which of Sushi's assets will be subject to UK inheritance tax when she dies. This will require some careful and detailed consideration of her domicile position both now and in the future.

– The manner in which UK inheritance tax would be calculated, if due, on any land and buildings situated in the country of Zakuskia that are owned by Sushi when she dies.

– Why the gift of the statue to her son, as referred to in her e-mail, will be a potentially exempt transfer, and how this treatment could be avoided.

The statue has not increased in value since the death of Sushi's mother. Accordingly, the proposed gift of the statue to Sushi's son will not give rise to a capital gain.

(ii) **The Zakuskian income**

The Zakuskian income will be subject to tax in the UK because Sushi is UK resident. Accordingly, we need to think about whether or not Sushi should claim the remittance basis. In order to do this I want you to prepare calculations of the increase in her UK tax liability due to the Zakuskian income on the assumption that the remittance basis **is not** available and then on the assumption that it **is** available. You should assume that Sushi remits £100,000 (gross) to the UK each year in accordance with her plans. In relation to the taxation of the Zakuskian income, your notes should include explanations of the meaning of the terms 'remittance basis' and 'remittance', and whether or not the remittance basis is available to Sushi, together with your conclusions based on your calculations but no other narrative. You should include brief footnotes to your calculations where necessary to aid understanding of the figures.

There is no need to consider the implication of capital gains on overseas assets as Sushi does not intend to dispose of any of her Zakuskian assets, apart from the statue, for the time being.

Thank you

Tax manager

E-mail from Sushi

My mother died on 1 October 2016 and left me the whole of her estate. I inherited the following assets.

The family home in the country of Zakuskia
Investment properties in the country of Zakuskia
Cash in Zakuskian bank accounts
Paintings and other works of art in the country of Zakuskia

The works of art include a statue that has been owned by my family for many years. I intend to bring the statue to the UK in December 2016 and give it to my son on his birthday on 1 July 2017. The statue was valued recently at £390,000.

The assets inherited from my mother will generate gross annual income of approximately £200,000 before tax, all of which is subject to 10% Zakuskian income tax. I intend to bring half of this income into the UK each year. The balance will remain in a bank account in Zakuskia.

I would like to meet with you to discuss these matters.

Thank you for your help.

Sushi

Required:

Prepare the notes requested in the e-mail from your manager. The following marks are available.

(i) UK inheritance tax and the statue (12 marks)

(ii) The Zakuskian income. (13 marks)

You should assume that today's date is 6 December 2016 and that the rates and allowances for 2015/16 continue for the foreseeable future.

(Total: 25 marks)

40 MIRTOON (ADAPTED)

  Online question assistance and Walk in the footsteps of a top tutor

Your manager has sent you an email, together with an attachment, in respect of a client called Mirtoon. The email and the attachment are set out below.

Email from your manager

Mirtoon intends to leave the UK in January 2017 in order to live in the country of Koro. He has entered into a full-time contract of employment for a fixed term of four years but he may stay in Koro for as long as ten years. He will buy a house in Koro and will not make any return trips to the UK whilst he is living in Koro.

Mirtoon plans to sell his house in the UK and cease his business prior to his departure. Details of these proposals, together with information regarding agricultural land owned by Mirtoon, are set out in the attached extract from his email.

Background information

Mirtoon is 52 years old and divorced. He has always been resident and domiciled in the UK. He will continue to be UK domiciled whilst living in the country of Koro.

He does not own any buildings other than his home. He receives bank interest in respect of UK bank deposits of £22,600 per year. He will continue to hold these bank deposits whilst living in the country of Koro.

Mirtoon has not made any disposals for the purposes of capital gains tax in the tax year 2016/17. He has capital losses brought forward as at 5 April 2016 of £3,100.

Mirtoon is self-employed. He has overlap profits brought forward in respect of his business of £7,600. He is registered for value added tax (VAT) and makes standard rated supplies only. He has never made any claims in respect of entrepreneurs' relief.

I want you to prepare the following:

(a) **Mirtoon's financial position**

Mirtoon wants to know how his plans to dispose of assets and his departure from the UK will affect his financial position. The details of his plans are in the following attachment. He has asked us to prepare a calculation of **the total** of the following amounts:

- The after tax proceeds from the sale of his home and business assets.
- The tax saving in respect of the offset of his trading losses.

 The trading losses should be offset against the total income of the tax year 2015/16; there is no need to consider any other loss reliefs.

 In order to accurately determine the tax effect of the relief available, you should prepare calculations of Mirtoon's income tax liability for 2015/16 both before and after the offset of the losses.

- Any other tax liabilities arising as a result of Mirtoon's plans to leave the UK.

You should include explanatory notes where this is necessary to assist Mirtoon's understanding of the calculations. This may be particularly useful in relation to the availability of any reliefs and allowances and the tax relief available in respect of the offset of the trading losses.

(b) **A letter to be sent from me to Mirtoon that addresses the following matters**

 (i) VAT: The VAT implications of the cessation of the business and the sale of the business assets.

 (ii) Income tax and capital gains tax: Whether or not Mirtoon will be liable to UK income tax and capital gains tax whilst he is living in the country of Koro by reference to his residence and domicile status.

 You should include specific reference to the capital gains tax implications of the proposed sale of the agricultural land in June 2018. Also comment on the implications of Mirtoon selling his UK home whilst he is in Koro rather than prior to his departure.

 There is no double tax treaty between the UK and the country of Koro.

 (iii) Inheritance tax: Mirtoon has asked me to discuss some ideas he has had in relation to reducing the potential inheritance tax liability on his death. To help me with this, please include a summary of the rules relating to associated operations.

Tax manager

Attachment – Extract from an email from Mirtoon

Sale of house

I plan to sell my house on 31 December 2016 for £850,000. I purchased the house for £540,000 on 1 July 2006 and I have lived there ever since that date. Two rooms, representing 20% of the property, have always been used exclusively for the purposes of my business.

Sale of business assets

My business made a tax adjusted profit in the year ended 30 June 2015 of £95,000. However, in the year ended 30 June 2016 it made a tax adjusted loss of £20,000. I have not been able to find a buyer for the business and will therefore cease trading on 31 December 2016. I will then sell any remaining business assets.

I expect to be able to sell the business assets, consisting of machinery and inventory, for £14,000, with no asset being sold for more than cost. The business will make a tax adjusted loss of £17,000 in the six months ending 31 December 2016 after taking account of the sale of the business assets.

Agricultural land

In May 2012 my father gave me 230 acres of agricultural land situated in the UK. A capital gain of £72,000 arose in respect of this gift and my father and I submitted a joint claim for gift relief. I expect the value of the land to increase considerably in 2017 and I intend to sell it in 2018.

Required:

(a) The calculations showing how Mirtoon's disposal of assets and subsequent departure from the UK will affect his financial position as requested in the email from your manager, assuming that the house is sold on 31 December 2016.

Ignore national insurance contributions. **(16 marks)**

(b) Prepare the letter to Mirtoon requested in the email from your manager. The following marks are available.

(i) Value added tax (VAT) **(3 marks)**

(ii) Income tax and capital gains tax **(10 marks)**

(iii) Inheritance tax. **(2 marks)**

Professional marks will be awarded for the extent to which the calculations are approached in a logical manner in part (a) and the effectiveness with which the information is communicated in part (b). **(4 marks)**

You should assume that today's date is 9 December 2016. **(Total: 35 marks)**

 Online question assistance

41 SHUTTELLE (ADAPTED) *Walk in the footsteps of a top tutor*

Your firm has been asked to provide advice to Shuttelle in connection with personal pension contributions and to three non-UK domiciled individuals in connection with the remittance basis of taxation for overseas income and gains.

(a) **Personal pension contributions:**

- Shuttelle has been the production director of Din Ltd since 1 February 2003.
- Shuttelle joined a registered personal pension scheme on 6 April 2013.

Shuttelle's tax position for the tax year 2015/16:

- Shuttelle's only source of income is her remuneration from Din Ltd.
- Shuttelle's annual salary is £204,000.
- Shuttelle lived in a house owned by Din Ltd for a period of time during the tax year 2015/16.

The house provided by Din Ltd for Shuttelle's use:

- Was purchased by Din Ltd on 1 January 2003 for £500,000 and has an annual value of £7,000.
- Shuttelle lived in the house from 1 February 2003 until 30 June 2015.
- The house had a market value of £870,000 on 6 April 2015.

Contributions to Shuttelle's personal pension scheme:

- Shuttelle has made the following gross contributions:
  6 April 2013 – £19,000
  6 April 2014 – £38,000
  6 April 2015 – £120,000
- Din Ltd contributes £4,000 to the scheme in each tax year.

Required:

(i) Calculate Shuttelle's income tax liability for the tax year 2015/16. **(8 marks)**

(ii) Calculate the amount of tax relief obtained by Shuttelle as a consequence of the gross personal pension contributions of £120,000 she made on 6 April 2015. **(3 marks)**

(b) **The remittance basis of taxation:**

– Advice is to be provided to three non-UK domiciled individuals.
– Each of the three individuals is more than 18 years old.

Details of the three individuals:

Name	Lin	Nan	Yu
Tax year in which the individual became UK resident	2005/06	2000/01	2005/06
Tax year in which the individual ceased to be UK resident	Still resident	2014/15	Still resident
Overseas income and gains for the tax year 2015/16	£39,200	£68,300	£130,700
Overseas income and gains remitted to the UK for the tax year 2015/16	£38,500	Nil	£1,400

Required:

(i) In respect of each of the three individuals for the tax year 2015/16:

(1) explain whether or not the remittance basis is available

(2) on the assumption that the remittance basis is available to ALL three individuals, state, with reasons, the remittance basis charge (if any) that they would have to pay in order for their overseas income and gains to be taxed on the remittance basis.

The following mark allocation is provided as guidance for this requirement:

(1) 3 marks

(2) 4 marks

(7 marks)

(ii) Give TWO examples of actions that would be regarded as remittances other than simply bringing cash into the UK. (2 marks)

(Total: 20 marks)

42 KESME AND SOBA *Walk in the footsteps of a top tutor*

Kesme and Soba, a married couple, require advice on Kesme's taxable income and rent-a-room relief, the capital gain on a future sale of the family home, and the assets which will be received by Soba under Kesme's will.

Kesme:

– Is UK resident and UK domiciled.
– Is married to Soba.
– Has not made any lifetime gifts for the purposes of inheritance tax.

Soba:

– Is UK resident but non-UK domiciled.
– Has elected to be treated as UK domiciled for the purposes of inheritance tax.

Kesme's income for the tax year 2015/16:

- State retirement pension of £7,900 (gross).
- A pension from a former employer of £24,100 (gross).
- Rental income in respect of furnished rooms in the family home.
- Interest in respect of 8% loan stock in Ramen plc.

Rental income in respect of furnished rooms in the family home:

- Kesme and Soba purchased the family home on 1 July 1991 and have lived there since that date.
- Three furnished rooms have been rented out to an individual tenant since 6 April 2015.
- The tenant does not share Kesme and Soba's living accommodation or take meals with them.
- The three rooms represent 30% of the property.
- The annual rent is £14,400 and there are allowable expenses of £1,600 per year.

8% loan stock in Ramen plc:

- Kesme purchased £18,000 of 8% loan stock on 1 May 2008.
- Interest is payable on 31 May and 30 November annually.
- Kesme sold the 8% loan stock on 30 September 2015 cum interest.

Kesme's estate and his will:

- Kesme's share of the family home, a plot of land and chattels are worth £1,280,000 in total.
- The plot of land is worth £370,000 and is situated in the UK.
- Kesme has left the plot of land to his daughter.
- Kesme has left the residue of his estate to his wife, Soba.

Required:

(a) Explain the availability and operation of rent-a-room relief in relation to Kesme and calculate his taxable income for the tax year 2015/16 on the assumption that the relief is claimed. **(8 marks)**

(b) Explain the effect of renting out the furnished rooms on the amount of the taxable capital gain on a future sale of the family home. **(6 marks)**

(c) Explain the implications of the election made by Soba to be treated as UK domiciled for the purposes of inheritance tax, and calculate the value of the residue of the estate which she would receive under Kesme's will if he were to die on 6 June 2015. **(6 marks)**

(Total: 20 marks)

43 JODIE *Walk in the footsteps of a top tutor*

Your manager has received a letter from Jodie in connection with her proposed emigration from the UK. Extracts from the letter and from an email from your manager are set out below.

Extract from the letter from Jodie

I was born in 1975 and I have always lived in the UK. I plan to leave the UK and move to the country of Riviera on 5 April 2017. My intention is to move to Riviera permanently and acquire a new home there. However, if my children are not happy there after four years, we will return to the UK.

My husband died three years ago. My brother lives in Riviera and is the only close family I have apart from my children. I will not have any sources of income in the UK after 5 April 2017.

I intend to work part time in Riviera so that I can look after my children. In the tax year 2017/18, I will return to the UK for a holiday and stay with friends for 60 days; for the rest of the tax year I will live in my new home in Riviera.

My unincorporated business

I prepared accounts to 31 December every year until 31 December 2015. I then ceased trading on 31 May 2016. I made a tax adjusted trading loss in my final period of trading of £18,000.

I was unable to sell my business as a going concern due to the decline in its profitability. Accordingly, on 31 May 2016 I sold my business premises for £190,000. I paid £135,000 for these premises on 1 June 2002. I also sold various items of computer equipment, which I had used in my business, for a total of £2,000. This equipment cost me a total of £5,000. I retained the remaining inventory, valued at £3,500, for my own personal use.

My taxable income for the last five tax years is set out below. There is no property income in the 2016/17 tax year because I sold my rental property in May 2015.

	2012/13	2013/14	2014/15	2015/16	2016/17
	£	£	£	£	£
Trading income	64,000	67,000	2,000	3,000	Nil
Property income	15,000	13,000	14,000	2,500	Nil
Bank interest	2,000	2,000	3,000	3,500	8,000 (est.)

PAPER P6: ADVANCED TAXATION (FA2015)

Other matters

On 30 April 2016 I sold my house, which is built on a one hectare plot, for £400,000. I purchased the house for £140,000 in March 1994 and lived in it throughout my period of ownership. I have been living in a rented house in the UK since 1 May 2016. My tenancy of this rented house will end on 5 April 2017.

When we spoke, you mentioned that you wanted details of any gifts I have received. The only item of significance is 2,000 ordinary shares in Butterfly Ltd which my mother gave to me on 14 May 2014 when the shares were worth £60,000. Butterfly Ltd is a UK resident trading company.

My mother and I submitted a joint claim for capital gains tax holdover relief on the gift of these Butterfly Ltd shares, such that no capital gains tax was payable. I recently received an offer of £68,000 for these shares, but I decided not to sell them. My mother had inherited the shares from her brother on 18 December 2001 when they were worth £37,000. Neither I nor my mother have ever worked for Butterfly Ltd.

Extract from an email from your manager

Additional information

- Jodie's business has always been registered for the purposes of value added tax (VAT). The sales proceeds in respect of the business assets are stated net of VAT.

- Jodie has overlap profits from the commencement of her business of £6,500.

Please prepare paragraphs for inclusion in a letter from me to Jodie addressing the following issues.

(a) UK tax residence status and liability to UK income tax

- Assuming Jodie leaves the UK in accordance with her plans, explain how her residence status for the tax year 2017/18 will be determined and conclude on her likely residence status for that year. To help, I have already concluded that Jodie will not be regarded as non-UK resident using the automatic overseas tests so there is no need to consider these tests.

- State how becoming non-UK resident will affect Jodie's liability to UK income tax.

(b) Relief available in respect of the trading loss

- Calculate the income tax relief which Jodie would obtain if she were to claim terminal loss relief in respect of her trading loss. You should not consider any other ways in which the loss could be relieved.

- There is no need to calculate Jodie's tax liabilities for each of the years concerned; just calculate the tax which will be saved due to the offset of the loss and explain how you have determined this figure.

(c) **Capital gains tax**

Assuming that Jodie becomes non-UK resident from 6 April 2017 and does not return to the UK for at least four tax years:

– explain how this will affect her liability to UK capital gains tax in the tax year 2017/18 and future years, and in 2016/17 (the tax year prior to departure); and

– calculate her capital gains tax liability for the tax year 2016/17. You should include explanations of the chargeable gains which have arisen or may arise in that year and the tax rate(s) which will be charged.

(d) **Other matters**

– Explain how leaving the UK will affect the UK inheritance tax liability on any gifts Jodie may make in the future.

– Explain the matters which Jodie should be aware of in relation to VAT in respect of the cessation of her business. I have already checked that Jodie charged the correct amount of VAT when she sold the business premises and the computer equipment.

Tax manager

Required:

Prepare the paragraphs for inclusion in a letter from your manager to Jodie as requested in the email from your manager.

The following marks are available:

(a)	UK tax residence status and liability to UK income tax.	(7 marks)
(b)	Relief available in respect of the trading loss.	(8 marks)
(c)	Capital gains tax.	(11 marks)
(d)	Other matters.	(5 marks)

Professional marks will be awarded for following the manager's instructions, the clarity of the explanations and calculations, the effectiveness with which the information is communicated, and the overall presentation. (4 marks)

Notes

1. You should assume that the tax rates and allowances for the tax year 2015/16 apply to all tax years.

2. Ignore national insurance contributions throughout this question.

(Total: 35 marks)

44 CATE AND RAVI *Walk in the footsteps of a top tutor*

Cate requires advice on the after tax cost of taking on a part time employee and the tax implications of starting to sell items via the internet. Cate's husband, Ravi, requires advice in relation to capital gains tax on the disposal of an overseas asset.

Cate:

– Is resident and domiciled in the UK. She is aged 48.

– Is married to Ravi.

– Runs a successful unincorporated business, D-Designs.

– Receives dividends of £27,000 each year.

– Wants to sell some second-hand books online.

D-Designs business:

– Was set up by Cate in 2008.

– Is now making a taxable profit of £90,000 per annum.

– Operates a number of dress shops and already employs six full time staff.

– Requires an additional part-time employee.

Part time employee – proposed remuneration package:

Salary of £12,000 per annum.

– Qualifying childcare vouchers of £25 per week for 52 weeks a year.

– Mileage allowance of 50 pence per mile for the 62 mile round trip required each week to redistribute stock between the shops. This will be for 48 weeks in the year.

– This employment will be the employee's only source of taxable income.

Sale of second-hand books:

– Cate inherited a collection of books from her mother in December 2014.

– Cate intends to sell these books via the internet.

– Some of the books are in a damaged state and Cate will get them rebound before selling them.

Ravi:

– Is domiciled in the country of Goland.

– Has been resident in the UK since his marriage to Cate in February 2008.

– Has UK taxable income of £125,000 in the tax year 2015/16.

– Realises chargeable gains each year from disposals of UK assets equal to the capital gains tax annual exempt amount.

– Sold an investment property in Goland in February 2016 for £130,000, realising a chargeable gain of £70,000. None of the proceeds from the sale of this property have been remitted to the UK.

Required:

(a) Calculate the annual cost for Cate, after income tax and national insurance contributions, of D-Designs employing the part time employee. **(9 marks)**

(b) Discuss whether the profit from Cate's proposed sale of books via the internet will be liable to either income tax or capital gains tax. **(5 marks)**

(c) Advise Ravi on the options available to him for calculating his UK capital gains tax liability for the tax year 2015/16. Provide supporting calculations of the tax payable by him in each case. **(6 marks)**

(Total: 20 marks)

PERSONAL FINANCE, BUSINESS FINANCE AND INVESTMENTS

45   ADAM SNOOK (ADAPTED)   *Walk in the footsteps of a top tutor*

Your manager has had a meeting with Adam Snook and has sent you a copy of the following memorandum.

To	The files
From	Tax manager
Date	1 December 2016
Subject	Adam Snook

Adam Snook (AS) has been entertaining children at parties as a hobby for the last two years. On 1 June 2016, his aunt gave him shares in Brill plc, a quoted company, worth £88,040. As a result, AS intends to give up his job on 31 December 2016 (he is a regional sales manager with Rheims Ltd) and purchase a small theatre from which he will carry on a business of providing entertainment for children's parties.

The business

AS will begin advertising and charging for attending children's parties on 1 January 2017. He estimates that his net profit for the first five months (until the theatre opens) will only be £400 per month. Accordingly, he has agreed to work part-time for his existing employer from 1 January 2017 until 31 May 2017 for a salary of £1,050 per month.

AS will purchase the theatre on 1 April 2017. He estimates that it will take six weeks or so to renovate the theatre such that it should be ready for business by 1 June 2017 at the latest. AS will seek to rent out the theatre for the days when it is not required for his business.

We agreed that the business should prepare accounts to 31 March each year. AS does not wish to form a limited company.

The supply of entertainment at the theatre will be standard rated for the purposes of value added tax (VAT) and AS will register for VAT on 1 June 2017.

The finance required

The costs of establishing the business, exclusive of recoverable VAT, are set out below.

	£
Purchase price of the theatre	215,000
Renovation of the theatre	45,000
Equipment and other costs	50,000
Finance required	310,000

AS sold 42,600 shares in Snapper plc for £104,370 on 1 December 2016 and intends to sell £25,000 6% Snapper plc non-convertible loan stock next week for £29,900. He will use the net proceeds of these sales to finance the business and obtain the balance of the funds required via a bank overdraft at an annual interest rate of 10%. The shares and loan stock in Snapper plc were acquired as follows:

- AS was given 14,200 shares in Brill plc by his aunt on 1 June 2016. At that time, the shares were worth £88,040.
- On 1 November 2016, Brill plc was acquired by Snapper plc. Both Brill plc and Snapper plc are UK resident trading companies.
- AS received 42,600 shares in Snapper plc together with £25,000 6% Snapper plc non-convertible loan stock (a qualifying corporate bond) in exchange for his shares in Brill plc.
- The shares and the loan stock were worth £97,980 and £28,400 respectively as at 1 November 2016.

Other background information

AS is 35 years old. His full time salary with Rheims Ltd is £25,200 per annum. He is provided with a diesel company car that had a list price when new of £13,950 and a CO_2 emission rate of 142 grams per kilometre. He is not provided with free fuel. He will return the car to the company on 31 December 2016.

AS's aunt is 71 years old and is domiciled in the UK. This is the first substantial gift that she has made to AS although he suspects that she has made similar gifts to other relatives in the past.

AS is also drafting his will and wants to understand how any amounts left to charity would affect the inheritance position on his death.

Tax manager

An extract from an email from your manager is set out below.

Please prepare a memorandum for me, incorporating the following:

(a) (i) Calculations to support the amount of external finance required by Adam including a note of any assumptions made.

Don't forget to take his capital gains tax liability into account but ignore any possible inheritance tax liability.

PRACTICE QUESTIONS: SECTION 1

> (ii) A proposal which will increase the after tax proceeds from the sale of the Snapper plc loan stock, together with the amount of the increase.
>
> A reasoned recommendation of a more appropriate form of external finance for the business.
>
> (b) Explanations of the following matters:
>
> (i) Adam's liability to class 2 and class 4 national insurance contributions in 2016/17.
>
> (ii) The income tax relief available in respect of both the cost of purchasing and renovating the theatre.
>
> (iii) For value added tax (VAT) purposes: the effect of renting out the theatre on Adam's ability to recover input tax, the implications of opting to tax the theatre and the factors affecting the decision to opt to tax.
>
> (c) An explanation of the inheritance tax payable by Adam in respect of the gift from his aunt depending on when his aunt dies and an explanation of the consequences of charitable bequests.
>
> We will be under significant fee pressure on this job so please don't do any unnecessary work – I'm sure that time spent thinking about what needs to be done before you start will save you time in the long run.
>
> **Tax manager**

Required:

Prepare the memorandum requested by your manager.

You should assume that today's date is 3 December 2016.

Marks are available for the components of the memorandum as follows:

(a) (i) Calculations to support the amount of external finance required.

You should state any assumptions you have made in preparing the calculations. **(10 marks)**

(ii) A proposal which will increase the after tax proceeds from the sale of the Snapper plc loan stock and a reasoned recommendation of a more appropriate form of external finance. **(3 marks)**

(b) Explanations of the various matters. **(11 marks)**

(c) The inheritance tax payable by Adam in respect of the gift from his aunt and an explanation of the consequences of charitable bequests. **(7 marks)**

Additional marks will be awarded for the appropriateness of the format and presentation of the memorandum and the effectiveness with which the information is communicated.

(4 marks)

You should assume that the tax rates and allowances for the tax year 2015/16 will continue to apply for the foreseeable future.

(Total: 35 marks)

46 GAGARIN (ADAPTED)

Gagarin wishes to persuade a number of wealthy individuals who are business contacts to invest in his company, Vostok Ltd. He also requires advice on the recoverability of input tax relating to the purchase of new business premises.

The following information has been obtained from a meeting with Gagarin.

Vostok Ltd:

- An unquoted UK resident company, set up in 2010.
- Gagarin owns 100% of the company's ordinary share capital.
- Has 18 employees.
- Provides computer based services to commercial companies.
- Requires additional funds to finance its expansion.

Funds required by Vostok Ltd:

- Vostok Ltd needs to raise £420,000.
- Vostok Ltd will issue 20,000 shares at £21 per share on 31 August 2016.
- The new shareholder(s) will own 40% of the company.
- Part of the money raised will contribute towards the purchase of new premises for use by Vostok Ltd.

Gagarin's initial thoughts:

- The minimum investment will be 5,000 shares and payment will be made in full on subscription.
- Gagarin has a number of wealthy business contacts who may be interested in investing.
- Gagarin has heard that it may be possible to obtain tax relief for up to 58% of the investment via the enterprise investment scheme.

Wealthy business contacts:

- Are all UK resident higher rate and additional rate taxpayers.
- May wish to borrow funds to invest in Vostok Ltd if there is a tax incentive to do so.

New premises:

- Will cost £456,000 including value added tax (VAT).
- Will be used in connection with all aspects of Vostok Ltd's business.
- Will be sold for £600,000 plus VAT in six years' time.
- Vostok Ltd will waive the VAT exemption on the sale of the building.

The VAT position of Vostok Ltd:

- In the year ending 31 March 2017, 28% of Vostok Ltd's supplies will be exempt for the purposes of VAT.
- This percentage is expected to reduce over the next few years.
- Irrecoverable input tax due to the company's partially exempt status exceeds the de minimis limits.

PRACTICE QUESTIONS: SECTION 1

Required:

(a) Prepare notes for Gagarin to use when speaking to potential investors.

The notes should include:

(i) The tax incentives immediately available in respect of the amount invested in shares issued in accordance with the enterprise investment scheme.

(5 marks)

(ii) The answers to any questions that the potential investors may raise in connection with the maximum possible investment, borrowing to finance the subscription and the implications of selling the shares. (9 marks)

You should assume that Vostok Ltd and its trade qualify for the purposes of the enterprise investment scheme and you are not required to list the conditions that need to be satisfied by the company, its shares or its business activities.

(b) Calculate the amount of input tax that will be recovered by Vostok Ltd in respect of the new premises in the year ending 31 March 2017 and explain, using illustrative calculations, how any additional recoverable input tax will be calculated in future years.

(6 marks)

(Total: 20 marks)

47 CALISIA *Walk in the footsteps of a top tutor*

Your manager has sent you an email with two attachments in respect of a new client called Calisia. The first attachment is an extract from a letter from Calisia, in which she has asked the firm to consider how she can increase the income of her daughter, Farfisa, and to review her own inheritance tax position.

The second attachment is a schedule setting out what your manager wants you to do in order to prepare for a meeting with Calisia.

Attachment 1 – Extract from letter from Calisia

(a) **Farfisa – Additional income**

My daughter, Farfisa, will leave home and start her first job on 1 October 2016 in London. She will be working for Jelmini Ltd and will be paid a salary of £28,000 (gross) per year. Jelmini Ltd will also provide Farfisa with an interest free loan of £2,700 in order for her to purchase suitable business clothing. The loan is to be repaid on 30 September 2018.

We have estimated that Farfisa's expenses will be £2,500 per month (of which £550 will be rent) so her salary after tax will be insufficient. At present Farfisa has no other income so I have identified three possible transfers of capital that I could make to her in order to generate the income she requires.

KAPLAN PUBLISHING

(i) **Gift of shares quoted on the UK stock exchange**

I would give Farfisa sufficient quoted shares to generate the additional income she requires. On average the quoted shares would generate dividends equal to 4% of their current market value. It can be assumed that, on average, the capital gain arising on the quoted shares will equal a quarter of their market value. I do not hold more than 1% of the share capital of any quoted company.

(ii) **Sale of investment property followed by gift of proceeds**

I own a two-bedroom investment property situated in London. I bought it in 2006 for £90,000 and it is now worth £260,000. I have always rented it out to tourists such that it qualifies as commercially let furnished holiday accommodation.

I would give Farfisa the net proceeds of the sale after paying any tax and other costs. Farfisa would place the cash on bank deposit; I estimate that the deposit would earn interest at 3% (gross). Farfisa would only spend the interest, not the capital, so I would then give Farfisa quoted shares to generate the remainder of the additional income she requires as in (i) above.

(iii) **Gift of investment property**

Under this option, instead of selling the property, I would give it to Farfisa who would then receive the annual rental income, after all allowable expenses, of £5,100. Again, I would then give Farfisa quoted shares to generate the remainder of the additional income she requires as in (i) above.

(b) **Calisia – Inheritance tax**

I would like to discuss my inheritance tax position with you so that I can understand the amount of tax that would be payable if I were to die now. I set out below the assets I own together with their current market values. I have not included my home as I assume that it is not subject to inheritance tax. I have never made any lifetime gifts and neither did my husband before he died. I intend to leave £150,000 to the Fairness for All political party when I die and the rest of my estate to Farfisa.

	£
Investment property in London	260,000
Investment property in the country of Sakura	380,000
Share (25%) in the 'Therson Partnership'	700,000
Building used by the 'Therson Partnership'	440,000
Shares quoted on the UK stock exchange	1,300,000
Art and antiques	200,000
Motor cars	100,000
Cash and other possessions	320,000

PRACTICE QUESTIONS: SECTION 1

Attachment 2 – Schedule from your manager

Preparation for the meeting with Calisia

(a) **Farfisa – Additional income**

During the meeting I only want to focus on any immediate tax liabilities as opposed to liabilities that may or may not arise in the future.

Prepare notes, with supporting calculations, showing Calisia's capital gains tax liability in respect of:

- each of the three possibilities identified by her; and
- a fourth possibility (which I expect to be more tax efficient) whereby Calisia gifts the property to Farfisa who then lives in it. Any shortfall in income could then be satisfied by renting out the second bedroom. You should include a calculation of the minimum monthly rent that would need to be charged in order to provide sufficient income for Farfisa.

Start by calculating the excess of Farfisa's budgeted expenditure over her salary after all taxes for a 12-month period. This will enable you to determine the value of shares she will need to be given under each of the possibilities in order to provide her with the income she needs. Remember to take into account any income tax due on the income received by Farfisa when calculating the income she will retain in respect of the assets transferred.

Conclude with a summary, showing the capital gains tax payable in respect of each of the four alternatives.

Please include a note of the stamp duty or stamp duty land tax implications of each proposal.

You should assume the following:

- a sale or gift of the investment property will result in legal fees of £6,000
- there will be no disposal costs in relation to any gift of shares
- all claims and elections necessary to reduce immediate tax liabilities will be made.

Further information

Calisia and Farfisa are resident and domiciled in the UK.

Calisia is a higher rate taxpayer who makes sufficient capital gains every year to utilise her annual exempt amount.

Calisia has not made a claim for entrepreneurs' relief in the past.

(b) **Calisia – Inheritance tax**

Calisia is domiciled in the UK and has not made any lifetime gifts. I want you to prepare a comprehensive explanation of how Calisia's inheritance tax liability would be calculated if she were to die today. Please try to identify all of the issues that are relevant to Calisia's situation together with any matters that need to be confirmed with her in order for reliefs and/or exemptions to be available. I do not want you to perform any calculations as we do not have sufficient information at present.

Further information

Calisia's husband died in 2007. He had not made any lifetime gifts and he left the whole of his estate, consisting principally of quoted shares and UK property, to Calisia.

Required:

(a) Farfisa – Additional income

Prepare the notes and supporting calculations as set out in the schedule from your manager. **(21 marks)**

(b) Calisia – Inheritance tax

Prepare the explanation as set out in the schedule from your manager. **(10 marks)**

Professional marks will be awarded for the effectiveness with which the information is communicated and the extent to which the calculations are approached in a logical manner. **(4 marks)**

Assume today's date is 6 June 2016. **(Total: 35 marks)**

48 TETRA *Walk in the footsteps of a top tutor*

Tetra has recently been made redundant and joined a trading partnership. He requires advice on the redundancy payments he has received, a potential investment in a venture capital trust and on making pension contributions. He has also asked for a calculation of his class 4 national insurance contributions in respect of his income from the partnership.

Tetra:

- Is 44 years old.
- Was made redundant by Ivy Ltd on 31 March 2016.
- Became a partner in the Winston partnership on 1 June 2016.
- Is considering two alternative investments.

Redundancy payments made by Ivy Ltd to Tetra:

- Statutory redundancy of £4,200.
- A non-contractual payment of £46,000 as compensation for loss of office.
- £7,000 in consideration of Tetra agreeing not to work for any competitor of Ivy Ltd for 12 months.

The Winston Partnership:

- Prior to 1 June 2016, there were two partners in the partnership: Zia and Fore.
- Budgeted tax adjusted trading profits of the partnership
- Year ending 31 December 2016 – £300,000
- Year ending 31 December 2017 – £380,000
  Profit sharing arrangements

		Zia	Fore	Tetra
Up to 31 May 2016 –	Profit share	60%	40%	N/A
From 1 June 2016 –	Annual salary	–	£24,000	£18,000
	– Profit share	40%	30%	30%

Two alternative investments:

In the tax year 2016/17 Tetra will either:

- subscribe £32,000 for shares in a venture capital trust; or
- make a payment of £32,000 to a registered personal pension fund.

PRACTICE QUESTIONS: SECTION 1

Required:

(a) Explain briefly whether or not the redundancy payments made by Ivy Ltd to Tetra are subject to income tax. **(3 marks)**

(b) Calculate the class 4 national insurance contributions payable by Tetra for the tax year 2016/17. **(7 marks)**

(c) Compare the effect of the two alternative investments on Tetra's income tax liability for the tax year 2016/17 and identify any non-tax matters relevant to the investment decision of which he should be aware.

For part (c) of this question it should be assumed that Tetra's net income in the tax year 2016/17 (before deduction of the personal allowance) will be £130,000, none of which is savings income or dividend income. **(8 marks)**

(Total: 18 marks)

49 MONISHA AND HORNER *Walk in the footsteps of a top tutor*

 Timed question with Online tutor debrief

Your firm has been asked to advise two unrelated clients, Monisha and Horner. The advice relates to furnished holiday accommodation, tax planning for a married couple, and the personal service company (IR35) rules.

(a) **Monisha:**

- Is married to Asmat.
- Earns a salary of £80,000 per year and realises chargeable gains of £6,000 per year.
- Owns a UK investment property, which is let to short-term tenants.

Asmat:

- Looks after the couple's children and has no income or chargeable gains.
- Expects to return to work on 6 April 2022 on an annual salary of £18,000.

The UK investment property owned by Monisha:

- The property cost £270,000 and is currently worth £300,000.
- The letting does not qualify as a commercial letting of furnished holiday accommodation.
- Annual income and expenditure

	£
Rental income	20,000
Repairs and maintenance	1,600
Council tax	1,200
Agent's fees	2,000

- Monisha claims the wear and tear allowance in respect of this property.
- The property will be sold on 5 April 2023 and is expected to create a chargeable gain of £100,000.

Proposals to reduce the couple's total tax liability:

– Monisha will give a 20% interest in the investment property to Asmat on 1 April 2017.
– The couple will ensure that, from 6 April 2017, the letting of the investment property will qualify as a commercial letting of furnished holiday accommodation.
– From the tax year 2017/18 onwards, Monisha will claim annual capital allowances equal to the current annual wear and tear allowance.

Required:

(i) State the conditions which must be satisfied in order for the letting of a UK furnished property to qualify as a commercial letting of furnished holiday accommodation. **(3 marks)**

(ii) Calculate the total tax saving in the six tax years 2017/18 to 2022/23 if ALL of the proposals to reduce the couple's tax liabilities are carried out.

In respect of the second proposal, you should assume that the letting will qualify as a commercial letting of furnished holiday accommodation for the whole of the period of joint ownership and that all beneficial reliefs are claimed.

You should ignore inheritance tax. **(10 marks)**

(b) **Horner:**

– Horner owns all of the shares of Otmar Ltd.
– All of the income of Otmar Ltd is subject to the personal service company (IR35) rules.
– Budgeted figures for Otmar Ltd for the year ending 5 April 2017 are set out below.

Where applicable, these amounts are stated exclusive of value added tax (VAT).

	£
Income in respect of relevant engagements carried out by Horner	85,000
Costs of administering the company	3,900
Horner's annual salary	50,000
Dividend paid to Horner	15,000
Contributions paid into an occupational pension scheme in respect of Horner	2,000

Required:

(i) Outline the circumstances in which the personal service company (IR35) rules apply. **(3 marks)**

(ii) Calculate the deemed employment income of Horner for the year ending 5 April 2017. **(4 marks)**

(Total: 20 marks)

 Calculate your allowed time, allocate the time to the separate parts.....................

50 STELLA AND MARIS (ADAPTED) *Walk in the footsteps of a top tutor*

Your firm has been asked to provide advice to two unrelated clients, Stella and Maris. Stella requires advice on the tax implications of making an increased contribution to her personal pension scheme. Maris requires advice regarding the lump sum payment she has received from her pension scheme and the inheritance tax exemptions available on her proposed lifetime gifts.

(a) **Stella:**

– Is resident and domiciled in the UK.

– Receives a gross salary of £80,000 each year.

– Has income from a portfolio of unfurnished properties, totalling £92,000 in the tax year 2016/17.

– Has no other source of taxable income.

– Wishes to make an increased contribution to her personal pension scheme in the tax year 2016/17.

Personal pension scheme contributions:

– Stella has contributed £40,000 (gross) to her personal pension scheme in each of the four tax years 2012/13, 2013/14, 2014/15 and 2015/16.

– Stella wishes to make an increased contribution of £90,000 (gross) in the tax year 2016/17.

Required:

Calculate Stella's income after tax and pension contributions for the tax year 2016/17 if she does pay £90,000 (gross) into her personal pension scheme.

(Total: 10 marks)

(b) **Maris:**

– Is resident and domiciled in the UK and is widowed.

– Has three married children and five grandchildren under the age of 12.

– Attained the age of 68 on 30 January 2016 and decided to vest some of her pension benefits on that date.

– Wishes to make regular gifts to her family in order to reduce inheritance tax on her death.

Personal pension fund:

– Maris had a money purchase pension scheme which was valued at £1,550,000 on 30 January 2016.

– Maris would like some advice on the tax implications of drawing a lump sum from this pension.

Assets and income:

- In addition to pension income and savings income totalling around £60,000, Maris receives dividends from shareholdings in quoted companies of around £45,000 each year.

- The shareholdings in quoted companies are currently valued at £980,000.

- Maris wishes to gift some of the shares or the dividend income to her children and grandchildren on their birthdays each year.

- Maris already makes gifts each year to use her annual exemption for inheritance tax purposes.

Required:

(i) Explain how an amount withdrawn by Maris as a lump sum from her pension may be taxed. **(4 marks)**

(ii) Advise Maris of TWO relevant exemptions from inheritance tax which she will be able to use when making the birthday gifts, together with any conditions she will need to comply with in order to obtain them. **(6 marks)**

(Total: 20 marks)

TAXATION OF CORPORATE BUSINESSES

FAMILY COMPANY ISSUES

51 BANDA ROSS (ADAPTED) *Walk in the footsteps of a top tutor*

You have received the following email from your manager, Kara Weddell.

From	Kara Weddell
Date	3 December 2016
To	Tax senior
Subject	Banda Ross

I've put a copy of a letter from a potential new client, Banda Ross, on your desk. I've arranged a meeting with Banda for Friday this week to discuss the most appropriate structure for her new business, 'Aral'.

I spoke to Banda yesterday and obtained the following additional information.

- Banda has owned the whole of the ordinary share capital of Flores Ltd since 1 January 2013.

- Flores Ltd pays Banda a salary of £15,635 per annum and pays dividends to her of £20,250 on 31 July each year.

- Banda does not intend to take any income from Aral until the tax year 2019/20 at the earliest.

- Flores Ltd is Banda's only source of income.

Banda also mentioned that Flores Ltd made some sort of 'informal loan' to her in 2013 of £21,000 to pay for improvements to her house. I decided not to press her about this over the phone but I need to discuss with her what she meant by 'informal' and whether or not the loan has been disclosed to HM Revenue and Customs.

Please prepare the following schedules for me to use as a basis for our discussions. I will give Banda copies of schedules (a) and (b) but not schedule (c), as some of its contents may be sensitive.

(a) Calculations of the anticipated tax adjusted trading profit/loss of Aral for its first three trading periods.

(b) Explanations, together with relevant supporting calculations, of the tax relief available in respect of the anticipated trading losses depending on whether the business is run as a sole trader or a limited company. When considering the use of a limited company, don't forget that it could be owned by Banda or by Flores Ltd.

Please include a recommendation based on your figures but do not address any other issues regarding the differences between trading as a sole trader and as a company; I just want to focus on the losses for the moment.

(c) Explanatory notes of the tax implications of there being a loan from Flores Ltd to Banda and whether or not such a loan might affect our willingness to provide her with tax advice.

Take some time to think about your approach to this before you start; I want you to avoid preparing any unnecessary calculations and to keep the schedules brief.

Thank you

Kara

The letter referred to in Kara's email is set out below.

Dear Kara

Aral business

I am the managing director of Flores Ltd, a company that manufactures waterskiing equipment. I am looking for a tax adviser to help me with my next business venture.

When I began the Flores business in 2011 it was expected to make losses for the first year or so. I was advised not to form a company but to trade as a sole trader and to offset the losses against my income of earlier years. I followed that advice and transferred the business to Flores Ltd on 1 January 2013, once it had become profitable. Flores Ltd has made taxable trading profits of approximately £120,000 each year since it was formed. It prepares accounts to 30 June each year.

For the past few months, I have been researching the windsurfing market. I must have spent at least £6,000 travelling around the UK visiting retailers and windsurfing clubs (half of which was spent on buying people lunch!). However, it was all worthwhile as on 1 January 2017 I intend to start a new business, 'Aral', manufacturing windsurfing equipment.

PAPER P6: ADVANCED TAXATION (FA2015)

> The budgeted results for the first three trading periods of the Aral business are set out below:
>
> | | | £ |
> |---|---|---|
> | 6 months ending 30 June 2017 | Trading loss | (25,000) |
> | Year ending 30 June 2018 | Trading loss | (13,000) |
> | Year ending 30 June 2019 | Trading profit | 77,000 |
>
> The figures above have been adjusted for tax purposes but take no account of the tax relief available in respect of the equipment and car to be acquired on 2 January 2017. The business will rent its premises but will purchase equipment (machinery, computers, shelving etc.) at a cost of £12,500. The equipment should last approximately three years so there will be no further acquisitions of equipment until the year ending 30 June 2020. The business will also buy a second hand car with CO_2 emissions of 125 g/km for £10,875. The car will be available for general staff use on business trips and will be left at the work premises every night.
>
> The next decision I need to make is whether the new business should trade as a company or as an unincorporated entity. It would make more sense commercially to form a company immediately but I would be willing to use the same approach as I used when establishing the Flores business if this maximises the relief obtained in respect of the trading losses. I want to obtain relief for the losses now; I do not want the losses carried forward for relief in the future unless there are no other options available.
>
> Yours sincerely
>
> Banda

Required:

Prepare the schedules requested by Kara.

Marks are available for the three schedules as follows:

(a) Tax adjusted trading profit/loss of the new business (Aral) for its first three trading periods. **(5 marks)**

(b) The tax relief available in respect of the anticipated trading losses, together with supporting calculations and a recommended structure for the business. **(18 marks)**

(c) Explanatory notes, together with relevant supporting calculations, in connection with the loan. **(8 marks)**

Additional marks will be awarded for the appropriateness of the format and presentation of the schedules, the effectiveness with which the information is communicated and the extent to which the schedules are structured in a logical manner. **(4 marks)**

You should assume that the tax rates and allowances for the tax year 2015/16 and for the financial year to 31 March 2016 apply throughout the question.

You should ignore value added tax (VAT). **(Total: 35 marks)**

52 SPICA (ADAPTED)

Spica, one of the director shareholders of Acrux Ltd, has been in dispute with the other shareholders over plans to expand the company's activities overseas. In order to resolve the position it has been agreed that Spica will sell her shares back to the company.

Another director, Mimosa, would like some information about the consequences of becoming an employee shareholder.

The following information has been obtained from client files and meetings with the parties involved.

Acrux Ltd:

– An unquoted UK resident trading company.

– Share capital consists of 50,000 ordinary shares issued at £1.25 per share in July 2007.

– None of the other shareholders has any connection with Spica.

The purchase of own shares:

– The company will purchase all of Spica's shares for £8 per share.

– The transaction will take place by the end of 2016.

Spica:

– Purchased 8,000 shares in Acrux Ltd for £3.95 per share on 30 September 2011.

– Has no income in the tax year 2016/17.

– Has chargeable capital gains in the tax year 2016/17 of £2,800, but does not anticipate making any capital gains in the foreseeable future.

– Has houses in the UK and the country of Solaris and divides her time between them.

Mimosa

– Has been offered £25,000 worth (approximately 7%) of shares in Acrux Ltd as consideration for entering an employee shareholder agreement.

– Currently has no shares.

– Has an annual salary of £70,000 but no other income.

Required:

(a) (i) Prepare detailed calculations to determine the most beneficial tax treatment of the payment Spica will receive for her shares. **(7 marks)**

(ii) Identify the points that must be confirmed and any action necessary in order for capital treatment to apply to the transaction. **(4 marks)**

(b) (i) Explain, with supporting calculations, the immediate tax implications for Mimosa of accepting the employee shareholder shares in Acrux Ltd.
(4 marks)

(ii) Explain the capital gains tax implications of a future disposal of the shares.
(3 marks)

(iii) State briefly any other factors that Mimosa should consider before entering the employee shareholder agreement. **(2 marks)**

(Total: 20 marks)

53 JAMES (ADAPTED) *Walk in the footsteps of a top tutor*

James is about to be made redundant by Quark Ltd. He is seeking advice on the taxation of his redundancy payment and on the sale of shares acquired via an approved share incentive plan. He intends to form Proton Ltd, which is expected to be treated as a personal service company, and wants to know how much better or worse off he will be as compared to the job he is about to lose.

The following information has been obtained from a meeting with James.

James – Income, national insurance and capital gains tax position:

- James is paid a salary of £70,000 per year by Quark Ltd.
  He has no income other than that from Quark Ltd and Proton Ltd in the tax year 2016/17.
- He withdrew shares from the Quark Ltd approved share incentive plan on 1 September 2016.
- His disposal of the shares in Quark Ltd is his only disposal for the purposes of capital gains tax in the tax year 2016/17.

Withdrawal and sale of shares from the Quark Ltd approved share incentive plan:

- James has been awarded free shares on 1 June every year since 2012.
- James withdrew all of the shares in the plan on 1 September 2016 and immediately sold them.

Redundancy and future plans:

- Quark Ltd will make James redundant on 31 January 2017.
- The company will make a redundancy payment to James of £38,500.
- In accordance with its usual policy, the company will also pay James £17,500 in lieu of notice.
- James will form a new company, Proton Ltd.

Proton Ltd – Activities:

- Proton Ltd will provide services to Quark Ltd and to other companies.
- The services will be carried out by James personally.
- All of Proton Ltd's income will be in respect of relevant engagements and therefore subject to the personal service company (IR35) legislation.

Proton Ltd – Estimated income and outgoings for a full year:

	£
Gross fee income	80,000
Salary paid to James	48,000
Administrative expenses	3,000
Travel expenses reimbursed to James	1,500
Dividends paid to James	18,000

Notes:

1 Where applicable, the above amounts are stated excluding value added tax (VAT).

2 The travel expenses are those which will be necessarily incurred by James in performing the work for Quark Ltd and the other customers of Proton Ltd. These expenses were not incurred by James as an employee of Quark Ltd.

Required:

(a) Identify the income tax, national insurance contribution and capital gains tax implications, if any, of the withdrawal and subsequent sale of the shares in Quark Ltd, the redundancy payment and the payment in lieu of notice. (7 marks)

(b) (i) Prepare calculations to determine the effect on James's annual income, after deduction of all taxes, of working for Proton Ltd rather than Quark Ltd.
(8 marks)

(ii) Calculate the effect on James's annual income, after deduction of all taxes, if the income of Proton Ltd were not regarded as being in respect of relevant engagements. (2 marks)

(c) Give three examples of specific contractual arrangements that would assist in arguing that the relationships between Proton Ltd and its customers do not amount to relevant engagements such that they would no longer be covered by the personal service company (IR35) legislation. (3 marks)

You should assume that today's date is 1 December 2016 and that the rates and allowances for the tax year 2015/16 apply throughout the question.

(Total: 20 marks)

54 FEDORA AND SMOKE LTD (ADAPTED) *Walk in the footsteps of a top tutor*

Fedora wants to improve the overall financial position of his family and his company, Smoke Ltd. He is considering three possibilities: repaying a loan to the company, employing his wife, Wanda, in the business, and selling a piece of land owned by the company.

The following information has been obtained from a telephone conversation with Fedora and from client files.

Fedora:

– Fedora's only income is his annual salary of £80,000 from Smoke Ltd together with annual taxable benefits of £6,600.

Smoke Ltd:

– Is wholly owned by Fedora.
– Manufactures precision engineering tools.
– Already has several employees.
– Has a year end of 31 March.

Fedora's plans:

– Repay an interest-free loan of £18,400 made to him by Smoke Ltd in February 2011.
– Smoke Ltd to employ Wanda.
– Smoke Ltd to sell part of the land surrounding its factory.

Smoke Ltd to employ Wanda:

– Wanda would carry out duties currently performed by Fedora and would be paid an annual salary of £20,000.
– Wanda's salary would represent an arm's length price for the work that she would perform.
– Fedora's salary would be reduced by £20,000 to reflect the reduction in the level of his duties.
– Wanda's only income is bank interest of £470 per year. She has notified the bank that she is a non-taxpayer.

Smoke Ltd to sell land:

– The land is currently used by Smoke Ltd for parking vehicles.
– The land was purchased together with the factory on 1 April 1998 for £174,000.
– The land would be sold on 1 February 2017 for £22,000.
– The value of the factory together with the remaining unsold land on 1 February 2017 will be £491,000.
– Smoke Ltd will use £19,000 of the sales proceeds to acquire engineering machinery in March 2017.

Required:

(a) Explain, with the aid of supporting calculations, the tax implications for both Fedora and Smoke Ltd of the proposed repayment by Fedora of the loan from Smoke Ltd. **(5 marks)**

(b) Calculate the annual net effect on the total of the tax liabilities of Fedora, Wanda and Smoke Ltd of Smoke Ltd employing Wanda under the arrangements set out above. **(7 marks)**

(c) Calculate the taxable gain arising on the sale of the land in the year ending 31 March 2017 on the assumption that any beneficial claim available is made.

Explain in detail the beneficial claim available, state the amount of the gain relieved and the manner in which any deferred part of the gain will be charged in the future. **(8 marks)**

Note: The following figures from the Retail Prices Index should be used.

April 1998   162.6
February 2017   279.5 (assumed)

(Total: 20 marks)

55 TRIFLES LTD, VICTORIA AND MELBA (ADAPTED)   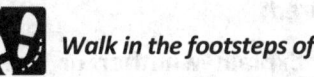 *Walk in the footsteps of a top tutor*

Trifles Ltd intends to carry out a purchase of its own shares. The shareholders from whom the shares are to be purchased require advice on their tax position. Trifles Ltd also intends to loan a motorcycle to one of the shareholders.

The following information has been obtained from the shareholders in Trifles Ltd.

Trifles Ltd:

- Is an unquoted company specialising in the delivery of small, high value items.
- Was incorporated and began trading on 1 February 2009.
- Has an issued share capital of 10,000 ordinary shares subscribed for at £2 per share.
- Has four unrelated shareholders: Torte, Baklava, Victoria and Melba.
- Intends to purchase some of its own shares from Victoria and Melba.
- Victoria and Melba have been directors of the company since they acquired their shares but will resign immediately after the purchase of their shares.

The purchase by Trifles Ltd of its own shares:

- Will take place on 28 February 2017 for Victoria's shares, and on 31 March 2017 for Melba's shares at an agreed price of £30 per share.
- Will consist of the purchase of all of Victoria's shares and 450 shares from Melba.

Victoria:

- Is resident in the UK.
- Is a higher rate taxpayer with taxable income of £50,000 who will make no other capital disposals in the tax year 2016/17.
- Has a capital loss carried forward as at 5 April 2016 of £4,100.
- Will have no link with Trifles Ltd following the purchase of her shares.
- Inherited her holding of 1,500 ordinary shares on the death of her husband, Brownie, on 1 February 2015.
- Brownie paid £16,500 for the shares on 1 February 2013.
- The probate value of the 1,500 ordinary shares was £16,000 on 1 February 2015.

Melba:

- Is resident in the UK.
- Is a higher rate taxpayer.
- Acquired her holding of 1,700 ordinary shares when Trifles Ltd was incorporated.
- Following the purchase of her shares Melba's only link with Trifles Ltd will be her remaining ordinary shareholding and the use of a motorcycle belonging to the company.

The motorcycle:

- Will be purchased by Trifles Ltd for £9,000 on 1 April 2017.
- Will be made available on loan to Melba for the whole of the tax year 2017/18.
- Melba will pay Trifles Ltd £30 per month for the use of the motorcycle.

Required:

(a) Explain whether or not Victoria and/or Melba satisfy the conditions relating to period of ownership and reduction in level of shareholding such that the amount received from Trifles Ltd on the purchase of own shares may be treated as a capital event. **(7 marks)**

(b) Calculate Victoria's after tax proceeds from the purchase of her shares:
- if the amount received is treated as capital; and
- if the amount received is treated as income. **(7 marks)**

(c) Explain, with supporting calculations where necessary, the tax implications of the purchase and loan of the motorcycle for both Melba and Trifles Ltd. **(6 marks)**

Ignore value added tax (VAT).

(Total: 20 marks)

56 SANK LTD AND KURT LTD (ADAPTED) *Walk in the footsteps of a top tutor*

Sank Ltd and Kurt Ltd are two unrelated clients of your firm. Sank Ltd requires advice in connection with the payment of its corporation tax liability and the validity of a compliance check enquiry it has received from HM Revenue and Customs. Kurt Ltd requires advice in connection with the purchase of machinery and expenditure on research and development.

(a) Sank Ltd:
- Has had augmented profits above the threshold for corporation tax for many years.
- Has a large number of related 51% group companies.
- Will prepare its next accounts for the 11 months ending 30 September 2016.
- Has received a compliance check enquiry from HM Revenue and Customs.

Taxable total profits for the 11 months ending 30 September 2016:
- Figures prepared on 31 March 2016 indicated taxable total profits for this 11-month period of £640,000.
- As at 1 June 2016, taxable total profits for this 11-month period are expected to be £750,000.

The compliance check enquiry from HM Revenue and Customs:
- HM Revenue and Customs raised the enquiry on 31 May 2016.
- It relates to Sank Ltd's corporation tax return for the year ended 31 October 2013.
- No amendments have been made to the corporation tax return since it was submitted.

Required:

In relation to Sank Ltd:

(i) Explain the definition of a related 51% group company and the significance of Sank Ltd having a large number of related 51% group companies. (3 marks)

(ii) Explain, with supporting calculations, the payment(s) required in respect of the company's corporation tax liability for the 11 months ended 30 September 2016 and the implications of the increase in the expected taxable total profits. (6 marks)

(iii) In relation to the date on which the compliance check enquiry into the corporation tax computation for the year ended 31 October 2013 was raised, explain the circumstances necessary for it to be regarded as valid.

You should assume that Sank Ltd has not been fraudulent or negligent.

(3 marks)

(b) **Kurt Ltd:**
- Was incorporated and began to trade on 1 August 2015.
- Is owned by Mr Quinn, who also owns three other trading companies.
- Has made a tax adjusted trading loss in the eight months ending 31 March 2016.
- Has no other income or chargeable gains in the eight months ending 31 March 2016.
- Is expected to be profitable in future years.
- Is a small enterprise for the purposes of research and development.

Expenditure in the period ending 31 March 2016:
- Machinery for use in its manufacturing activities – £340,000.
- The cost of staff carrying out qualifying scientific research in connection with its business – £28,000.

Required:

In relation to Kurt Ltd, explain the tax deductions and/or credits available in the period ending 31 March 2016 in respect of the expenditure on machinery and scientific research and comment on any choices available to the company.

(8 marks)

(Total: 20 marks)

57 BANGER LTD AND CANDLE LTD (ADAPTED) Walk in the footsteps of a top tutor

Banger Ltd and Candle Ltd are two unrelated companies.

The management of Banger Ltd requires advice on the implications for one of the company's shareholders of the use of a motor car owned by the company and the proposed liquidation of the company.

The management of Candle Ltd has asked for a calculation of the company's corporation tax liability. Candle Ltd is a close investment-holding company.

(a) **Banger Ltd:**

- Banger Ltd is a UK resident trading company.
- 65% of the company's share capital is owned by its managing director, Katherine.
- The remaining shares are owned by a number of individuals who do not work for the company.

Motor car provided to minority shareholder throughout year ended 31 March 2016:

- Banger Ltd paid £17,400 for the motor car, which had a list price when new of £22,900.
- The car has a petrol engine and has CO_2 emissions of 117 grams per kilometre.

Liquidation of Banger Ltd:

- It is intended that a liquidator will be appointed on 31 January 2017 to wind up the company.

Distributions of company assets to shareholders being considered by Banger Ltd:

- A total distribution of £280,000 in cash to the minority shareholders prior to 31 January 2017.
- The distribution of a building with a market value of £720,000 to Katherine after 31 January 2017.

Required:

(i) Explain, with supporting calculations, the amount of the minority shareholder's taxable income in respect of the use of the motor car.

(3 marks)

(ii) Explain the tax implications for the minority shareholders and Katherine of the distributions that the company is considering. (4 marks)

(iii) State the corporation tax implications for Banger Ltd of the distribution of the building to Katherine and explain briefly, with reasons, whether or not disincorporation relief could be claimed. (3 marks)

PRACTICE QUESTIONS: SECTION 1

(b) **Candle Ltd:**
   – Is a UK resident close investment-holding company.

The results of Candle Ltd for the year ended 31 March 2016:

	£
Interest receivable	41,100
Chargeable gains realised in the country of Sisaria (net of 18% Sisarian tax)	15,580
Chargeable gains realised in the UK (excluding the sale of shares in Rockette plc)	83,700
Fees charged by a financial institution re an issue of loanstock	14,000
Interest payable on debentures	52,900
General expenses of management	38,300

Sale of shares in Rockette plc on 1 January 2016:

– Candle Ltd purchased a 2.2% holding of the shares in Rockette plc for £31,400 in 2002.

– Piro plc acquired 100% of the ordinary share capital of Rockette plc on 1 January 2016.

– Candle Ltd received shares in Piro plc worth £147,100 and cash of £7,200 in exchange for its shares in Rockette plc.

– Piro plc's acquisition of Rockette plc was a commercial transaction and was not part of a scheme to avoid tax.

– The relevant indexation factor is 0.510.

Required:

Calculate the corporation tax liability of Candle Ltd for the year ended 31 March 2016, giving an explanation of your treatment of the disposal of the shares in Rockette plc.

You should assume that Candle Ltd will claim all reliefs available to reduce its tax liability and you should state any further assumptions you consider necessary.

(10 marks)

(Total: 20 marks)

58 BAMBURG LTD *Walk in the footsteps of a top tutor*

Charlotte is the owner of Bamburg Ltd. She requires advice on the value added tax (VAT) flat rate scheme, the sale of a substantial item of machinery, and the alternative methods by which she can extract additional funds from the company.

Charlotte:

– Is UK resident and UK domiciled.

– Owns 100% of the ordinary share capital of Bamburg Ltd.

– Earns an annual salary from Bamburg Ltd of £46,000 and has no other income.

– Has two ideas to generate additional cash in Bamburg Ltd.

– Wants to receive an additional £14,000 (after the payment of all personal taxes) from Bamburg Ltd on 30 June 2016.

KAPLAN PUBLISHING

Bamburg Ltd:

- Is a UK resident trading company.
- Is registered for VAT.
- Has budgeted sales revenue for the year ending 31 March 2017 of £120,000 excluding VAT.
- Makes wholly standard rated supplies apart from £6,000 of exempt supplies.
- Has a nil tax written down value on its main pool as at 31 March 2016.
- Will not purchase any plant and machinery in the year ending 31 March 2017.

Charlotte's ideas to generate additional cash in Bamburg Ltd:

- 'Bamburg Ltd should join the VAT flat rate scheme in order to save money.'
- 'Bamburg Ltd should sell the 'Cara' machine and offset the resulting loss against its profits.'

The 'Cara' machine:

- Was purchased on 1 January 2013 for £94,000.
- Rollover relief was claimed in respect of this purchase to defer a chargeable gain of £13,000.
- The 'Cara' machine is currently worth £80,000.
- Following the sale of the 'Cara' machine, Bamburg Ltd will rent a replacement machine.

Alternative methods of extracting an additional £14,000 from Bamburg Ltd:

- Bamburg Ltd to pay Charlotte a bonus.
- Bamburg Ltd to pay Charlotte a dividend.
- Bamburg Ltd to make an interest free loan of £14,000 to Charlotte.

Required:

(a) Explain, with reference to the information provided, whether or not Bamburg Ltd would be permitted to join the value added tax (VAT) flat rate scheme and set out the matters which would need to be considered in order to determine whether or not it would be financially beneficial for the company to do so. **(5 marks)**

(b) Explain the tax and financial implications of Bamburg Ltd selling the 'Cara' machine during the year ending 31 March 2017. **(5 marks)**

(c) (i) Prepare calculations to determine whether it would be cheaper for Bamburg Ltd to pay Charlotte a bonus or a dividend, such that she would receive £14,000 after the payment of all personal taxes. **(5 marks)**

(ii) Explain the immediate tax implications for Bamburg Ltd and Charlotte of Bamburg Ltd making an interest free loan of £14,000 to Charlotte. **(5 marks)**

(Total: 20 marks)

59 NOCTURNE LTD *Walk in the footsteps of a top tutor*

Nocturne Ltd, a partially exempt company for the purposes of value added tax (VAT), requires advice on the corporation tax implications of providing an asset to one of its shareholders; the income tax implications for another shareholder of making a loan to the company; and simplifying the way in which it accounts for VAT.

Nocturne Ltd:

– Is a UK resident trading company.

– Prepares accounts to 31 March annually.

– Has four shareholders, each of whom owns 25% of the company's ordinary share capital.

– Owns a laptop computer, which it purchased in October 2012 for £1,200, and which has a current market value of £150.

– Has purchased no other plant and machinery for several years and the tax written down value of its main pool at 31 March 2016 was £Nil.

Provision of a laptop computer to one of Nocturne Ltd's shareholders:

– Nocturne Ltd is considering two alternative ways of providing a laptop computer in the year ending 31 March 2017 for the personal use of one of its shareholders, Jed.

– Jed is neither a director nor an employee of Nocturne Ltd.

– Option 1: Nocturne Ltd will buy a new laptop computer for £1,800 and give it immediately to Jed.

– Option 2: Nocturne Ltd will gift its existing laptop to Jed and will purchase a replacement for use in the company for £1,800.

Loan from Siglio:

– Siglio will loan £60,000 to Nocturne Ltd on 1 October 2016 to facilitate the purchase of new equipment.

– Siglio is both a shareholder of Nocturne Ltd and the company's managing director.

– Nocturne Ltd will pay interest at a commercial rate on the loan from Siglio.

– Siglio will borrow the full amount of the loan from his bank on normal commercial terms.

VAT – partial exemption:

– Nocturne Ltd is partially exempt for the purposes of VAT.

– Nocturne Ltd's turnover for the year ended 31 March 2016 was £240,000 (VAT exclusive).

– Nocturne Ltd's turnover for the year as a whole for VAT purposes comprised 86% taxable supplies and 14% exempt supplies.

- The input VAT suffered by Nocturne Ltd on expenditure during the year ended 31 March 2016 was:

	£
Wholly attributable to taxable supplies	7,920
Wholly attributable to exempt supplies	1,062
Unattributable	4,150

- Nocturne Ltd expects its turnover and expenditure figures to increase by approximately 25% next year.

- Siglio has heard about an annual test for computing the amount of recoverable input VAT during an accounting period and would like more information about this.

Required:

(a) Explain, with the aid of supporting calculations, which of the two proposed methods of providing the laptop computer to Jed would result in the lower after-tax cost for Nocturne Ltd.

You should ignore value added tax (VAT) for part (a) of this question. **(7 marks)**

(b) Explain the income tax implications for Siglio of providing the loan to Nocturne Ltd.

(4 marks)

(c) (i) Determine, by reference to the de minimis tests 1 and 2, Nocturne Ltd's recoverable input VAT for the year ended 31 March 2016. **(4 marks)**

(ii) Advise Siglio of Nocturne Ltd's eligibility for the annual test for computing the amount of recoverable input VAT for the year ending 31 March 2017 and the potential benefits to be gained from its use. **(5 marks)**

(Total: 20 marks)

GROUPS, CONSORTIA AND OVERSEAS COMPANY ASPECTS

60 PALM PLC (ADAPTED)

Palm plc recently acquired 100% of the ordinary share capital of Nikau Ltd from Facet Ltd. Palm plc intends to use Nikau Ltd to develop a new product range, under the name 'Project Sabal'. Nikau Ltd owns shares in a non-UK resident company, Date Inc.

The following information has been extracted from client files and from a meeting with the Finance Director of Palm plc.

Palm plc:

- Has more than 40 wholly owned subsidiaries.
- All group companies prepare accounts to 31 March.
- Acquired Nikau Ltd on 1 November 2016 from Facet Ltd, an unrelated company.

PRACTICE QUESTIONS: SECTION 1

Nikau Ltd:

- UK resident company that manufactures domestic electronic appliances for sale in the European Union (EU).
- Large enterprise for the purposes of the additional relief available for research and development expenditure.
- Trading losses brought forward as at 1 April 2016 of £195,700.
- Budgeted taxable trading profit of £360,000 for the year ending 31 March 2017 before taking account of 'Project Sabal'.
- Nikau owns 35% of the shares in Date Inc and received dividend income of £382,000 in the year ending 31 March 2017 in respect of these shares.

'Project Sabal':

- Development of a range of electronic appliances, for sale in North America and to VAT registered customers in the European Union.
- Project Sabal will represent a significant advance in the technology of domestic appliances.
- Nikau Ltd will spend £70,000 on staffing costs and consumables researching and developing the necessary technology between now and 31 March 2017. Further costs will be incurred in the following year.
- Sales to North America will commence in 2018 and are expected to generate significant profits from that year.

Shares in Olive Ltd:

- In order to finance the purchase of Nikau Ltd, Palm plc sold its shares in another 100% subsidiary Olive Ltd.
- The shares in Olive Ltd were purchased on 1 June 2002 for £338,000, and sold on 1 November 2016 for £1,400,000
- Olive Ltd is a property investment company.
- On 2 May 2012 Spring Ltd, another 100% subsidiary of Palm plc, transferred a property to Olive Ltd for its then market value £900,000. The building had cost Spring Ltd £380,000 in October 2002.

Date Inc:

- A controlled foreign company resident in the country of Palladia.
- Annual chargeable profits, which are caught by the controlled foreign company legislation, are approximately £1,200,000, of which approximately £1,137,000 is distributed to its shareholders each year.

The tax system in Palladia:

- No taxes on income or capital profits.
- 4% withholding tax on dividends paid to shareholders resident outside Palladia.

Required:

(a) Prepare detailed explanatory notes, including relevant supporting calculations, on the effect of the following issues on the amount of corporation tax payable by Nikau Ltd and Palm plc for the year ending 31 March 2017.

    (i) The costs of developing 'Project Sabal' and the significant commercial changes to the company's activities arising out of its implementation.

(10 marks)

    (ii) The shares held in Date Inc and the dividend income received from that company. **(2 marks)**

    (iii) The sale of shares in Olive Ltd. **(3 marks)**

(b) Explain why making sales of Sabals in North America will have no effect on Nikau Ltd's ability to recover its input tax. **(5 marks)**

You should assume that the corporation tax rates and allowances for the financial year to 31 March 2016 will continue to apply for the foreseeable future.

You should ignore indexation allowance. **(Total: 20 marks)**

61 PARTICLE LTD GROUP (ADAPTED) *Walk in the footsteps of a top tutor*

An extract from an e-mail from your manager is set out below.

> I attach a schedule I received this morning from Max Constant, the new managing director of the Particle Ltd group of companies. With Max in charge this client has recently become a lot more lively!
>
> This e-mail will make more sense when you have read Max's schedule so I suggest you read that first.
>
> **Report**
>
> Please prepare a report to the management of Particle Ltd addressing the four areas of advice requested by Max. The report should also cover the following additional points.
>
> Sale of Kaon Ltd – the value added tax (VAT) implications of selling the trade and assets of the business.
>
> Muon Inc – any tax problems in connection with the loan.
>
> Payment of corporation tax – the advantage of group payment arrangements.
>
> **Further information**
>
> The information in Max's schedule is pretty clear but you will see that there are two question marks in connection with the assets of Kaon Ltd. I've spoken to him about this and to check on a couple of other things and I set out below some additional information that you will need.
>
> – All of the companies are UK resident with the exception of Muon Inc, which is resident in the country of Newtonia. Newtonia is not in the European Union (EU) and there is no double tax treaty between Newtonia and the UK.
>
> – Shortly after its acquisition, Muon Inc approached a number of financial institutions for a loan. However, the interest rates demanded were so high that Particle Ltd has made the loan to Muon Inc instead. Particle Ltd is charging 4% interest on the loan. By the way, Muon Inc is not a controlled foreign company.

PRACTICE QUESTIONS: SECTION 1

- The goodwill of Kaon Ltd has been created within the company since its formation on 1 May 2007.
- Kaon Ltd purchased its premises (Atom House) from Baryon Ltd on 1 March 2009 for its market value at that time of £490,000. Baryon Ltd purchased Atom House on 1 July 2005 for £272,000. Three months later, on 1 October 2005, Baryon Ltd sold another building (Bohr Square) for £309,400 making a capital gain of £89,000 and claimed rollover relief in respect of the purchase of Atom House. No option to tax for VAT purposes has been made in respect of Atom House.

Max has a reasonable knowledge of the UK tax system so keep the narrative in the report brief. As always, assume that all beneficial claims will be made and include a reference to them in the report.

Tax manager

The schedule from Max Constant is set out below.

Particle Ltd Group – Situation as at 1 December 2016

Background information

- Particle Ltd owns 100% of its five subsidiaries. All six companies are trading companies preparing accounts to 31 March.
- Their approximate annual taxable profits are included in the group structure below.
- None of the companies receive any franked investment income and there are no unused trading losses within the group.
- Baryon Ltd has a capital loss of £37,100 brought forward in respect of a disposal on 1 May 2010.
- Particle Ltd, Baryon Ltd and Kaon Ltd have a group VAT registration.

Group structure

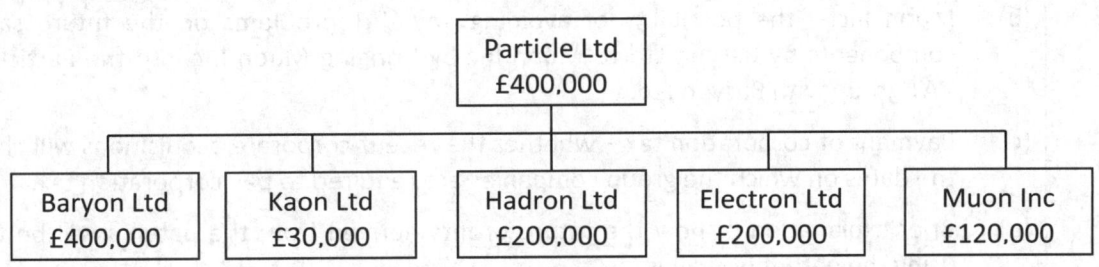

Notes

1. Baryon Ltd has been a subsidiary since 2001.
2. Kaon Ltd was incorporated by Particle Ltd on 1 May 2007. This company is to be sold – see below.
3. Hadron Ltd, Electron Ltd and Muon Inc were all purchased on 1 August 2015 from three unrelated individual vendors.

The sale of Kaon Ltd

The sale will take place on 31 January 2017. We have received offers from two separate purchasers.

Offer 1 – Sale of shares

We have been offered £650,000 for the whole of the company's share capital.

Offer 2 – Sale of trade and assets of the business

We have been offered £770,000 for the company's trade and assets as follows:

	Offer	Cost	Tax written down value
	£	£	£
Office premises (Atom House)	604,000	490,000?	N/A
Machinery and equipment	46,000	80,000	65,000
Goodwill	120,000	Nil	?
	770,000		

This will leave Kaon Ltd with net current liabilities of £25,000, which it will pay out of the sale proceeds of the business.

Particle Ltd is in the process of developing a new manufacturing technique and will patent the technique. I have read that there are some special tax rules for the taxation of any profits derived from a patent, but have found the rules difficult to understand.

Advice required

(a) Sale of Kaon Ltd – the after tax proceeds in respect of each of the two offers.

(b) Muon Inc – the possibility of avoiding any VAT problems on the future sale of components by Baryon Ltd to Muon Inc by bringing Muon Inc into the Particle Ltd VAT group with Baryon Ltd.

(c) Payment of corporation tax – whether the recent corporate acquisitions will change the dates on which the group companies are required to pay corporation tax.

(d) Brief explanation of how the future profits derived from the patents will be taxed using the patent box rules.

Required:

Prepare the report requested by your manager.

The report should include explanations together with supporting calculations.

The following marks are available for the four areas of the report.

(i) The sale of Kaon Ltd – after tax proceeds and VAT.

Marks for (i) are allocated as follows:

Sale of the share capital – 2 marks,

Sale of the trade and assets of the business – 12 marks. (14 marks)

(ii) Muon Inc – VAT and issues in connection with the loan. (5 marks)

(iii) Payment of corporation tax – payment dates and group payment arrangements. (7 marks)

(iv) The taxation of profits derived from patents. (5 marks)

Appropriateness of the format and presentation of the report and the effectiveness with which the information is communicated. (4 marks)

The following indexation factors should be used.

July 2005 to March 2009	0.099
July 2005 to January 2017	0.389
May 2007 to January 2017	0.294
March 2009 to January 2017	0.263

The relevant patent box percentage is 80%.

You should assume that today's date is 1 December 2016 and that the rates and allowances for the financial year to 31 March 2016 apply throughout the question.

(Total: 35 marks)

62 CACAO LTD GROUP (ADAPTED) *Walk in the footsteps of a top tutor*

Extracts from e-mails from your manager and a client, Maya, together with information obtained from client files are set out below.

Email from your manager

> I have forwarded an e-mail to you from Maya who owns The Cacao Ltd group of companies. Maya is a scientist and relies on us for all of her tax advice.
>
> Please write a memorandum addressing the matters raised by Maya whilst taking into account the following instructions and additional information.
>
> (i) **The corporation tax liability for the year ending 30 September 2017**
>
> Last week, Maya and I prepared a budget for the group for the year ending 30 September 2017 and arrived at the figures set out below for the three subsidiaries.
>
> | | Ganache Ltd £ | Truffle Ltd £ | Fondant Ltd £ |
> |---|---|---|---|
> | Taxable trading profit | 45,000 | 168,000 | 55,000 |
> | Chargeable gain (does not qualify for rollover relief) | Nil | 42,000 | Nil |
>
> These figures do not take into account the additional expenditure identified by Maya as set out in her e-mail below or the capital allowances available in respect of any capital expenditure in the year.

When calculating the total corporation tax liability of the three subsidiaries as requested by Maya I want you to:

- calculate the corporation tax liabilities based on the above figures on the assumption that the purchase of Praline Inc, as described in Maya's e-mail, will take place as planned

- explain, with supporting calculations, the potential effects of the additional expenditure identified by Maya on the total of the liabilities you have calculated.

When preparing these calculations you should take advantage of any opportunities available to reduce the total corporation tax liability of the companies.

We do not have sufficient information regarding the financial position of Cacao Ltd at present so you should generally ignore any effect of that company's results on the tax position of the subsidiaries.

However, you should assume that Cacao Ltd will be using £400,000 of the group's annual investment allowance for plant and machinery for the year ending 30 September 2017.

(ii) **Praline Inc**

It is possible that Praline Inc will be a controlled foreign company.

Accordingly, in addition to addressing Maya's point about the interest, the memorandum should include the following:

- a detailed analysis of the information we have and any further information we require in order to determine whether or not Praline Inc will be a controlled foreign company when it is purchased by Cacao Ltd or could become one at some time in the future

- the implications of Praline Inc being a controlled foreign company

- a summary of your findings so that Maya will understand the likely ways in which Praline Inc's profits will be taxed.

You should assume that Praline Inc will retain its profits in the country of Noka and will not pay any dividends to Cacao Ltd.

(iii) **Fondant Ltd**

You will need to include a brief outline of the capital goods scheme in order to address Maya's query. I would also like you to draw her attention to the partial exemption percentage used by Fondant Ltd when preparing its VAT returns. It may be advantageous for the company to use the partial exemption percentage for the previous year rather than calculating it for each particular quarter as it appears to be doing at the moment.

Tax manager

E-mail from Maya

The corporation tax liability for the year ending 30 September 2017

Following on from our discussion of the subsidiaries' budgeted profits for the year ending 30 September 2017, I have now identified some additional expenditure. Ganache Ltd will spend £11,000 on hiring temporary staff to carry out scientific research in connection with its business activities.

In addition, I have finalised the capital expenditure budget. Truffle Ltd and Ganache Ltd will purchase manufacturing equipment at a cost of £86,000 and £29,000 respectively.

Most of this additional expenditure will need to be borrowed. Please let me know the budgeted total corporation tax liability for the three subsidiaries, after taking account of the proposed expenditure, so that I can estimate the group's total borrowing requirements.

Praline Inc

I am hopeful that Cacao Ltd will be able to purchase the whole of the share capital of Praline Inc, probably towards the end of 2016. Praline Inc is incorporated in the country of Noka. The company's main source of income is investment income. The great thing is that the rate of corporation tax in the country of Noka is only 12%.

At the moment Praline Inc's annual profit is in the region of £36,000 but I intend to transfer additional investment properties to it in the future in order to take advantage of the low rate of tax.

I have not agreed a price for Praline Inc yet. However, I am conscious that the necessary funds will be borrowed by Cacao Ltd resulting in costs in that company in respect of arrangement fees and interest. Bearing in mind that Cacao Ltd's taxable profits are very small, does that mean that these costs will not give rise to a tax deduction?

Fondant Ltd

As you know, Fondant Ltd rents the premises from which it runs all of its activities. It has recently been offered the chance to buy the building (for a price likely to be in the region of £450,000) rather than renewing the lease.

In the quarter ended 31 March 2016 the company was only able to recover 62% of the VAT charged on the rent and I expect this percentage to fall over the next year or two. I wondered if the irrecoverable VAT problem could be solved if Fondant Ltd were to purchase the building.

Regards Maya

Extracts from the client files for the Cacao Ltd group of companies.

	Cacao Ltd	Ganache Ltd	Truffle Ltd	Fondant Ltd
Shareholders	Maya (100%)	Cacao Ltd (100%)	Cacao Ltd (100%)	Cacao Ltd (100%)
Residency	UK	UK	UK	UK
Trading company?	Yes	Yes	Yes	Yes
As at 1 October 2015:				
Trading loss brought forward	–	–	–	–
Capital loss brought forward	–	–	–	£23,000
VAT partially exempt?	No	No	No	Yes

Notes

1   The subsidiaries have always been owned by Cacao Ltd.

2   The group is small for the purposes of research and development expenditure.

Required:

Prepare the memorandum requested in the email from your manager.

The following marks are available.

(i) The corporation tax liability for the year ending 30 September 2017 (8 marks)

(ii) Praline Inc (13 marks)

(iii) Fondant Ltd. (6 marks)

Professional marks will be awarded for the appropriateness of the format and presentation of the memorandum and the effectiveness with which the information is communicated. (4 marks)

You should assume that today's date is 7 June 2016 and that the rates and allowances for the financial year to 31 March 2016 continue to apply for the foreseeable future.

(Total: 31 marks)

63 DAUBE GROUP (ADAPTED) *Walk in the footsteps of a top tutor*

Your manager has had a meeting with Mr Daube, a potential new client. The memorandum recording the matters discussed at the meeting and an extract from an e-mail from your manager detailing the tasks for you to perform are set out below.

Memorandum recording matters discussed at meeting with Mr Daube

To:	The files
From:	Tax manager
Date:	3 December 2016
Subject:	Mr Daube – Corporate matters

I had a meeting with Mr Daube on 2 December 2016. He wants us to advise him on the sale of Shank Ltd, one of his companies, and on the sale of a number of buildings.

Mr Daube owns the Hock Ltd group of companies and Knuckle Ltd as set out below. The dates in brackets are the dates on which the companies were purchased. Neither Mr Daube nor his companies have any interests in any other companies.

All five companies are UK resident trading companies with a 31 March year end. All of the companies, with the exception of Shank Ltd, are profitable.

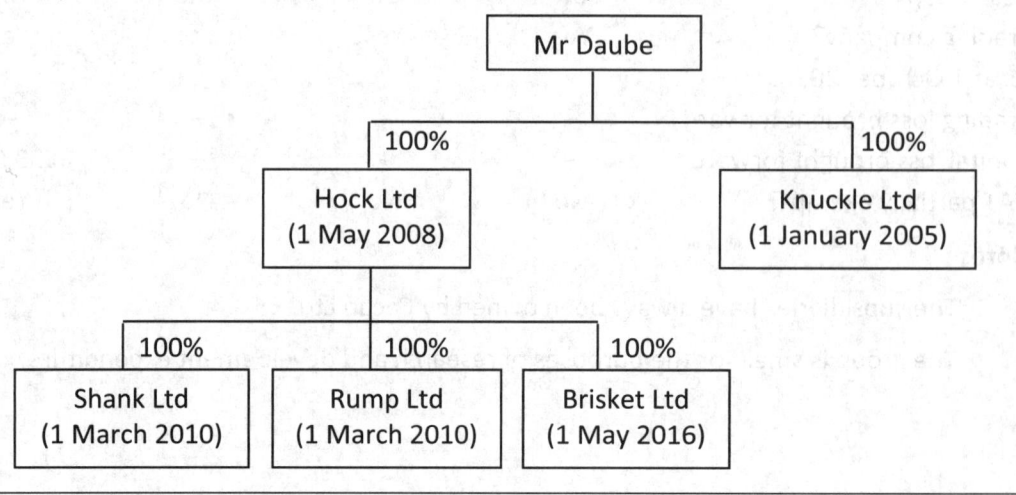

(i) **Sale of Shank Ltd**

Shank Ltd has made trading losses for a number of years and, despite surrendering the maximum possible losses to group companies, it has trading losses to carry forward as at 31 March 2016 of £35,000. Shank Ltd is expected to make a further trading loss of £54,000 in the year ending 31 March 2017 and has no other sources of income.

Mr Daube is of the opinion that the company will only become profitable following significant financial investment, which the group cannot afford, together with fundamental changes to its commercial operations.

Accordingly, Hock Ltd entered into a contract on 1 November 2016 to sell the whole of the ordinary share capital of Shank Ltd to Raymond Ltd (an independent third party) on 1 February 2017 for £270,000; an amount that is considerably less than the group paid for it.

(ii) **Sales of buildings**

The following buildings are to be sold during the year ending 31 March 2017, with the exception of the Monk building which was sold on 1 March 2016. Rollover relief will not be claimed in respect of any of the gains arising

	Gar building	*Cray building*	*Monk building*	*Sword building*
Owned by:	Shank Ltd	Rump Ltd	Brisket Ltd	Knuckle Ltd
Cost:	£210,000	£240,000	£380,000	See below
Estimated indexation allowance factors:	0.350	0.250	0.070	0.480
Date of sale:	1 January 2017	1 February 2017	1 March 2016	1 February 2017
Purchaser:	Hock Ltd	Quail plc	Hare plc	Pheasant plc
Estimated proceeds:	£370,000	£420,000	£290,000	£460,000

On 30 June 2006 Knuckle Ltd sold its original premises, the Pilot building, for £270,000 resulting in a chargeable gain of £60,000. On 1 January 2007 it purchased the Sword building for £255,000 and claimed rollover relief in respect of the gain on the Pilot building.

Tax manager

Email from your manager

I have just had a further conversation with Mr Daube. He informed me that:

– Brisket Ltd acquired the Monk building on 1 January 2013.
– Quail plc, Hare plc and Pheasant plc are all unrelated to Mr Daube and his companies.
– None of the companies will make any other chargeable gains or allowable losses in the year ending 31 March 2017.
– Knuckle Ltd has identified a number of potential overseas customers and expects to begin selling its products to them in 2017. At the moment, all of Knuckle Ltd's supplies are standard rated for the purposes of value added tax (VAT).

I want you to draft a report for Mr Daube dealing with the matters set out below.

> (i) **Sale of Shank Ltd**
>
> – The alternative ways in which the company's trading losses can be relieved. I want some precise detail here so please try to consider all of the possibilities and any anti-avoidance legislation that may restrict the use of the losses.
>
> – The tax treatment of the loss arising on the sale of Shank Ltd.
>
> – An explanation of the threshold applicable for all of the companies for the payment of corporation tax by instalment for the year ending 31 March 2017.
>
> (ii) **Sales of buildings**
>
> On the assumption that the three future building sales go ahead as planned:
>
> – Calculations of the chargeable gain/allowable loss arising on the sale of each of the four buildings.
>
> – The alternative ways in which any capital losses arising can be relieved. I need a detailed explanation of the options available together with any restrictions that will apply. Watch out for the Monk building because the loss was incurred prior to the purchase of Brisket Ltd.
>
> – The need to charge VAT on the sales of the buildings.
>
> – The stamp duty land tax implications of the sales of the buildings.
>
> (iii) **Potential sales by Knuckle Ltd to overseas customers**
>
> – The VAT implications.
>
> **Tax manager**

Required:

(a) Prepare the report as set out in the e-mail from your manager.

The following marks are available.

(i)	Sale of Shank Ltd	(12 marks)
(ii)	Sales of buildings	(10 marks)
(iii)	Potential sales by Knuckle Ltd to overseas customers.	(4 marks)

Professional marks will be awarded in part (a) of question 1 for the appropriateness of the format of the report and the effectiveness with which the information is communicated. **(4 marks)**

(b) Prepare a summary of the information required and any action that should be taken before the firm agrees to become tax advisers to Mr Daube and his companies. **(5 marks)**

(Total: 35 marks)

64 LORIOD PLC GROUP *Walk in the footsteps of a top tutor*

The Loriod plc group intends to acquire an overseas business. It requires advice on the relief available in respect of any initial losses made by the business, the use of foreign tax credits and transfer pricing.

The following information has been obtained from the management of the Loriod plc group.

Loriod plc group:

- Loriod plc is a UK resident trading company.
- Loriod plc has a large number of wholly-owned UK resident trading subsidiary companies.
- It should be assumed that all group companies pay corporation tax at the main rate of 20%.
- Elivar Ltd, one of the Loriod plc group subsidiaries, is to acquire the 'Frager' business.
- The purchase of the 'Frager' business will follow either Strategy A or Strategy B.

Elivar Ltd:

- Makes qualifying charitable donations of £2,000 each year.
- Has taxable total profits of approximately £90,000 per year.

The 'Frager' business:

- Is carried on in the country of Kuwata and is owned by Syme Inc, a company resident in Kuwata.
- Manufactures components used by Elivar Ltd and other Loriod plc group companies.
- Carries on the same trade as Elivar Ltd.
- Is expected to make a loss in the year following its acquisition by Elivar Ltd.
- Is expected to have taxable profits of £130,000 per year following the year of acquisition.

Strategy A:

- Elivar Ltd will purchase the trade and all of the assets of Syme Inc such that Elivar Ltd will be carrying on the 'Frager' business through a permanent establishment in Kuwata.
- The permanent establishment will be controlled from the UK.

Strategy B:

- Elivar Ltd will purchase the whole of the share capital of Syme Inc such that Syme Inc will be a subsidiary of Elivar Ltd resident in Kuwata.
- It has been determined that Syme Inc would not be a controlled foreign company.

The tax system in the country of Kuwata:

- Is broadly the same as that in the UK with a corporation tax rate of 14%.
- Trading losses may only be utilised by companies resident in Kuwata.
- Kuwata is not a member of the European Union and there is no double tax treaty between the UK and Kuwata.

Required:

(a) Provide a detailed explanation of the relief available in respect of the expected loss to be made by the 'Frager' business depending on whether the purchase follows Strategy A or Strategy B. (7 marks)

(b) For this part of the question it should be assumed that the purchase has followed Strategy A and that the 'Frager' business is now profitable.

Explain, with supporting calculations, how to determine the maximum loss that can be surrendered to Elivar Ltd by the Loriod plc group companies if relief in respect of the tax suffered in Kuwata is not to be wasted. (5 marks)

(c) For this part of the question it should be assumed that the purchase has followed Strategy B.

Explain the effect of the prices charged by the subsidiary in Kuwata to other companies in the Loriod plc group on the total tax paid by the group and the implications of the transfer pricing legislation. (6 marks)

(Total: 18 marks)

65 DRENCH, HAIL LTD AND RAIN LTD (ADAPTED) *Online question assistance*

 Walk in the footsteps of a top tutor

Your manager has sent you a schedule of information received from a client, named Drench, who is the managing director of Hail Ltd. Hail Ltd is a UK resident trading company with a year end of 30 June and Drench owns the whole of the company's ordinary share capital. The schedule is set out below together with an email from your manager.

Schedule of information from Drench

Acquisition of Rain Ltd

I intend to buy 100% of the ordinary share capital of Rain Ltd, a UK resident trading company, on 1 January 2017. I will either purchase the shares personally or Hail Ltd will acquire Rain Ltd as a 100% subsidiary.

Rain Ltd is one of two companies currently wholly-owned by Flake Ltd. All three of the companies in the Flake Ltd group are trading companies. Following its acquisition Rain Ltd will change its year end from 30 September to 30 June such that it will prepare accounts for the nine months ending 30 June 2017.

Budgeted results of Rain Ltd

The budgeted financial results of Rain Ltd for the nine months ending 30 June 2017 are set out below. The results depend on whether or not the company acquires new contracts in 2017. All of the company's sales are standard rated for the purposes of value added tax (VAT). The chargeable gain is in respect of the disposal of a 0.3% shareholding in a quoted company.

	Nine months ending 30 June 2017	
	Without the new contracts	With the new contracts
	£	£
Sales revenue (exclusive of VAT)	380,000	1,425,000
Tax adjusted (loss)/profit	(110,000)	285,000
Chargeable gain	50,750	50,750

Other relevant information

In the year ended 30 September 2016 Rain Ltd realised a tax adjusted trading loss of £27,000 and had no other income or chargeable gains. The trading loss was surrendered as group relief to companies within the Flake Ltd group.

Rain Ltd's main asset is a building which is currently worth £340,000. The building was purchased from Mist Ltd, the other 100% subsidiary of Flake Ltd, on 1 July 2013 for its book value of £248,000. The market value of the building at that time was £260,000. Mist Ltd had purchased the building on 1 January 2004 for £170,000.

Hail Ltd is budgeted to realise taxable total profits in the year ending 30 June 2017 of £100,000.

Email from your manager

I want you to prepare the following:

(a) A memorandum for the client file that explains the following matters, providing supporting calculations where relevant:

(i) **Acquisition of Rain Ltd**

A comparison of the tax implications of:

— Drench acquiring Rain Ltd personally; and

— Hail Ltd acquiring Rain Ltd.

Drench is aware of the general implications of forming a group. Accordingly, your comparison should focus on the following specific issues.

On the assumption that Rain Ltd DOES NOT obtain the new contracts

— The manner in which the loss for the nine months ending 30 June 2017 should be relieved in order to maximise the tax relief obtained; the tax relief should be quantified where possible.

Drench wants the loss to be used as soon as possible and only to be carried forward as a last resort.

— The tax implications of Hail Ltd making a payment to Rain Ltd in respect of any group relief losses surrendered.

On the assumption that Rain Ltd DOES obtain the new contracts

— The corporation tax liability of Rain Ltd for the nine months ending 30 June 2017.

— The date by when Rain Ltd will need to pay its corporation tax liability for the period in order to avoid interest charges.

> The tax treatment of Rain Ltd's building, including
>
> - any potential tax liabilities that may arise on the acquisition of Rain Ltd, and
> - the base cost of the building for the purposes of calculating the chargeable gain or loss arising on the future disposal by Rain Ltd.
>
> (ii) **Loan from Hail Ltd to Drench and VAT cash accounting scheme**
>
> - The tax implications for Hail Ltd of Drench borrowing £18,000 from the company on 1 February 2017. The loan will be interest-free and will be repaid by Drench on 1 February 2023.
> - The advantages of the VAT cash accounting scheme and whether it will be possible for Rain Ltd to operate the scheme.
>
> (b) **A briefing note to me**
>
> Our firm will be assisting Rain Ltd to obtain the new contracts. We have experience in this area as we used to have a client that successfully applied for government building contracts. The client moved to a rival firm at the end of 2014.
>
> To what extent is it acceptable for us to use the knowledge we gained in respect of our ex-client to assist Rain Ltd?
>
> **Tax manager**

Required:

(a) Prepare the memorandum including supporting calculations requested in the email from your manager. The following marks are available.

    (i)   Acquisition of Rain Ltd   **(15 marks)**

    (ii)   Loan from Hail Ltd to Drench and VAT cash accounting scheme.   **(8 marks)**

Professional marks will be awarded in part (a) for the extent to which the calculations are approached in a logical manner and the effectiveness with which the information is communicated.   **(2 marks)**

The following figures from the Retail Prices Index should be used where necessary.

January 2004	183.1
July 2013	249.7
January 2017	266.9 (assumed)

(b) Prepare the briefing note requested in the email from your manager.   **(5 marks)**

You should assume that today's date is 9 December 2016.   **(Total: 30 marks)**

 Online question assistance

PRACTICE QUESTIONS: SECTION 1

66 JANUS PLC GROUP (ADAPTED) *Walk in the footsteps of a top tutor*

Your manager has had a meeting with Mrs Pairz, the Group Finance Director of the Janus plc group of companies. The memorandum recording the matters discussed at the meeting is set out below.

Memorandum recording matters discussed at the meeting with Mrs Pairz

To   The files
From   Tax manager
Date   15 June 2016
Subject   Janus plc group

Mrs Pairz has recently been appointed the Group Finance Director of the Janus plc group. She has asked for advice on the use of the trading loss of Janus plc for the year ended 31 March 2016 and on a number of other matters.

The Janus plc group of companies

The group structure indicating the trading loss of Janus plc and the taxable total profits of each of the other group companies for the year ended 31 March 2016 is set out below. All of the companies are UK resident trading companies.

Janus plc purchased Seb Ltd, together with its subsidiary, Viola Ltd, on 1 December 2015 from Mr Twinn. Mr Twinn has never owned any other companies. There have not been any other changes to the group structure in recent years.

The minority holdings in Castor Ltd and Pollux Ltd are owned by UK resident individuals. The minority holding in Duet Ltd is owned by Bi plc, a UK resident company, such that Duet Ltd is a consortium company.

The group policy is for an amount equal to the corporation tax saved to be paid for any losses transferred between group companies.

Each of the companies is separately registered for the purposes of value added tax (VAT).

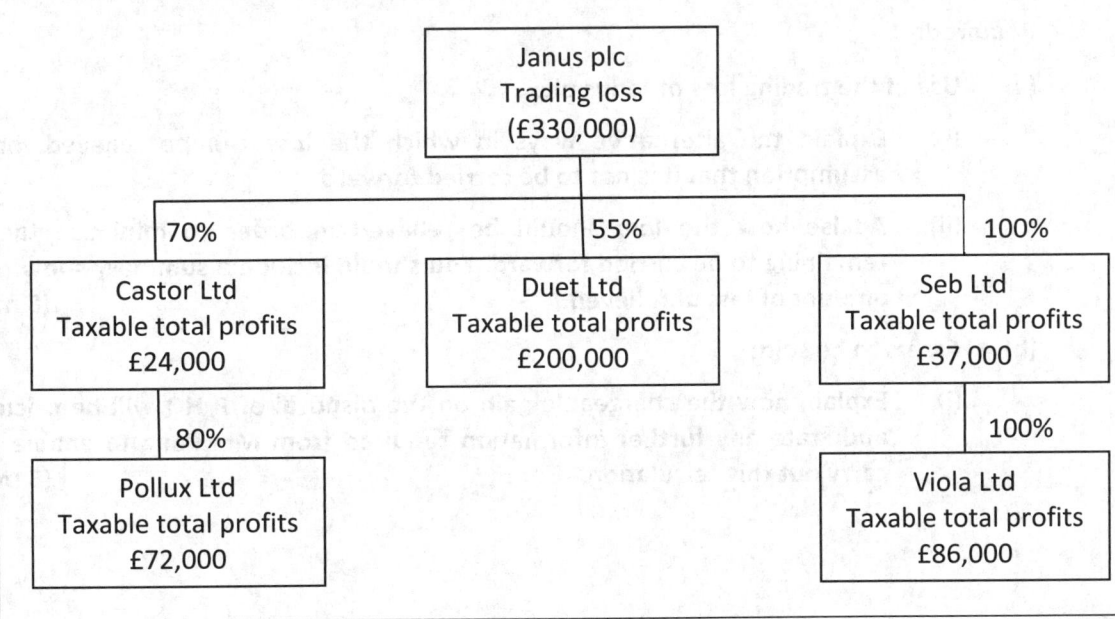

Additional information in respect of Janus plc

- Janus plc made a chargeable gain of £44,500 in the year ended 31 March 2016.
- Janus plc had taxable total profits in the year ended 31 March 2015 of £95,000 and did not make any charitable donations in the year.

Assets to be sold

(i) Pollux Ltd is to sell its administrative premises, 'P HQ', to Janus plc on 1 July 2016 for their market value of £285,000. Pollux Ltd acquired these premises from Castor Ltd on 1 March 2013 for their market value of £240,000.

(ii) Viola Ltd is to sell a warehouse to an unrelated company on 1 August 2016 for £350,000 plus VAT of £70,000. Viola Ltd acquired this warehouse on 1 February 2015 for £320,000 plus VAT of £64,000.

Mrs Pairz understands that the input tax relating to the warehouse should be recovered in accordance with the capital goods scheme because Viola Ltd is a partially exempt company, but suspects that the calculations may not have been done correctly.

The relevant VAT recovery percentages for Viola Ltd are:

Year ended 31 March 2015	70%
Year ended 31 March 2016	55%
Period from 1 April 2016 to 1 August 2016	50%

(iii) Castor Ltd is to sell patent rights to an unrelated company on 1 September 2016 for £41,000. Castor Ltd acquired these patent rights for use in its trade on 1 September 2012 for £45,000. The patent rights are being written off in Castor Ltd's accounts on a straight-line basis over a ten-year period. Castor Ltd has not and will not be making the election to apply the patent box rules.

Investment in Kupple Inc

Janus plc intends to purchase 15% of the ordinary share capital of Kupple Inc on 1 October 2016. Kupple Inc is a profitable trading company, resident in the country of Halven. Kupple Inc will provide consultancy services to Janus plc. This is intended to be a short-term commercial investment; Janus plc will sell the shares at some point in the next two years.

Required:

(a) Use of the trading loss of Janus plc:

    (i) Explain the alternative ways in which the loss can be relieved, on the assumption that it is not to be carried forward.

    (ii) Advise how the loss should be relieved in order to minimise the loss remaining to be carried forward. You should include a summary showing the amount of loss unrelieved.

    (8 marks)

(b) Assets to be sold:

    (i) Explain how the chargeable gain on the disposal of P HQ will be calculated and state any further information required from Mrs Pairz to enable us to carry out this calculation.

    (5 marks)

(ii) Calculate the input tax recoverable from/repayable to HM Revenue and Customs in respect of the warehouse for each of the three years ending 31 March 2017, on the assumption that the sale of the warehouse goes ahead as planned. **(4 marks)**

(iii) Explain, with supporting calculations, the corporation tax implications of the sale of the patent rights. **(3 marks)**

(c) Investment in Kupple Inc:

(i) Explain the VAT implications for Janus plc of purchasing consultancy services from Kupple Inc. **(2 marks)**

(ii) Explain the corporation tax treatment of any profit or loss arising on the eventual sale of the shares in Kupple Inc. **(4 marks)**

(d) Janus plc group senior accounting officer:

Explain, briefly, whether or not Mrs Pairz will be the senior accounting officer of the Janus plc group, the circumstances in which the rules relating to the group's tax accounting systems will apply to the Janus plc group, and the statutory responsibilities of a senior accounting officer when the rules apply. **(4 marks)**

(Total: 30 marks)

67 FLAME PLC GROUP *Walk in the footsteps of a top tutor*

Your manager has had a meeting with Gordon, the Group Finance Director of the Flame plc group of companies.

Flame plc is quoted on the UK stock exchange. An extract from the memorandum prepared by your manager after the meeting, together with an email from him detailing the tasks for you to perform, is set out below.

Extract from the memorandum prepared by your manager

> **Background**
>
> Flame plc is a UK resident company, which has annual taxable profits of more than £200,000. It owns the whole of the ordinary share capital of Inferno Ltd, Bon Ltd and six other companies. All of the companies in the Flame plc group are UK resident companies with a 31 March year end.
>
> **Flame plc – sale of Inferno Ltd**
>
> Flame plc purchased the whole of the ordinary share capital of Inferno Ltd on 1 March 2012 for £600,000. The value of Inferno Ltd has increased and Gordon has decided to sell the company. For the purposes of our work, we are to assume that the sale will take place on 1 January 2017. The budgeted taxable profits of Inferno Ltd for the nine months ending 31 December 2016 are £160,000.

The sale will be carried out in one of two ways:

(i) a sale by Flame plc of the whole of the ordinary share capital of Inferno Ltd for £1 million; or

(ii) a sale by Inferno Ltd of its trade and assets for their market value.

Gordon needs to know the tax cost for the Flame plc group of each of these options to help him in his negotiations.

Inferno Ltd owns the following assets.

	Note	Cost £	Current market value £
Equipment	1, 3	100,000	60,000
Milling machine	2, 3	95,000	80,000
Goodwill	4	Nil	530,000
Building – business premises	5	300,000	490,000

Notes

(1) No item of equipment will be sold for more than cost.

(2) The milling machine is an item of fixed plant and machinery that was purchased on 1 June 2013. Inferno Ltd claimed rollover relief in respect of the purchase of this machine to defer a chargeable gain of £8,500 made on 1 May 2012.

(3) Capital allowances have been claimed in respect of the equipment and the milling machine. The tax written down value of the main pool of Inferno Ltd as at 1 April 2016 was zero. There have been no additions or disposals since that date.

(4) The goodwill has been generated internally by Inferno Ltd since it began trading on 1 May 2007.

(5) Inferno Ltd purchased the building from Flame plc on 15 March 2012 for its market value at that time of £300,000. Flame plc had purchased the building on 1 January 2008 for £240,000.

Flame plc – employee share scheme

Gordon is planning to introduce a share option scheme in order to reward the senior managers of Flame plc.

Bon Ltd – the grant of a lease

Part of the trading premises of Bon Ltd, a subsidiary of Flame plc, is surplus to requirements. Bon Ltd intends to grant a lease to an independent third-party company in respect of that part of its premises.

Bon Ltd – refund of corporation tax

Bon Ltd received a refund of corporation tax from HM Revenue and Customs on 1 June 2016. The company has not been able to identify any reason for this refund.

PRACTICE QUESTIONS: SECTION 1

Email from your manager

(a) I want you to draft a report to the Group Finance Director that addresses the following:

  (i) **Flame plc – sale of Inferno Ltd**

  The tax cost of each of the two possible ways of carrying out the sale. Please note that I have already considered the availability of the substantial shareholding exemption and concluded that it will not be available in respect of the sale of Inferno Ltd because the Flame plc group is not a trading group.

  The report should include concise explanations of matters where the calculations are not self-explanatory.

  (ii) **Flame plc – employee share scheme**

  – The tax advantages for the employees of introducing an approved company share option plan (CSOP) as opposed to an unapproved share option scheme.

  – Why a CSOP would be a suitable approved scheme for Gordon to choose.

  – The restrictions within the CSOP rules in respect of the following:

   – The number of share options that can be granted to each employee.

   – The price at which the shares can be sold to the employees.

  (iii) **Bon Ltd – the grant of a lease**

  The value added tax (VAT) implications for the lessee if Bon Ltd were to opt to tax the building prior to granting the lease.

(b) **Bon Ltd – refund of corporation tax**

Prepare a summary of the actions that we should take and any matters of which Bon Ltd should be aware in respect of the refund of corporation tax.

Tax manager

Required:

(a) Draft the report to the Group Finance Director requested in the email from your manager. The following marks are available.

  (i) Flame plc – sale of Inferno Ltd

  Notes for part (a)(i):

  (1) For guidance, approximately equal marks are available for calculations and explanations.

  (2) The following indexation factors should be used, where necessary.

   January 2008 to March 2012   0.148
   January 2008 to January 2017   0.272 (assumed)
   March 2012 to January 2017   0.108 (assumed)   (15 marks)

(ii)   Flame plc – employee share scheme   (8 marks)

(iii) Bon Ltd – the grant of a lease.   (3 marks)

Professional marks will be awarded in part (a) for the overall presentation of the report, the provision of relevant advice and the effectiveness with which the information is communicated.   (4 marks)

(b)   Prepare the summary requested in the email from your manager. (5 marks)

You should assume that today's date is 7 December 2016.

(Total: 35 marks)

68 LIZA   *Walk in the footsteps of a top tutor*

Liza requires detailed advice on rollover relief, capital allowances and group registration for the purposes of value added tax (VAT).

Liza's business interests:

– Liza's business interests, which have not changed for many years, are set out below.

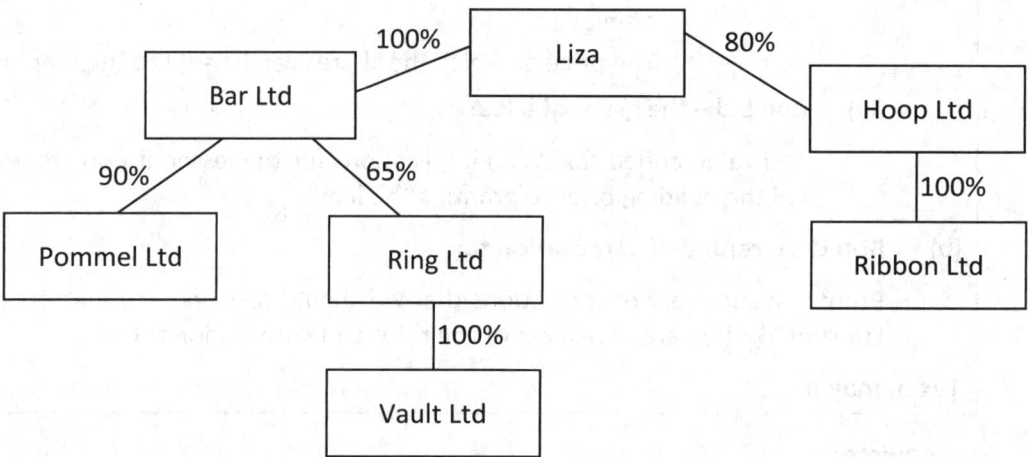

– All six companies are UK resident trading companies with a 31 March year end.
– All of the minority holdings are owned by individuals, none of whom is connected with Liza or with each other.

A building ('Building I') sold by Bar Ltd:

– Bar Ltd sold Building I on 31 May 2016 for £860,000.
– Bar Ltd had purchased the building on 1 June 2010 for £315,000 plus legal fees of £9,000.
– On 5 June 2010, Bar Ltd had carried out work on the building's roof at a cost of £38,000 in order to make the building fit for use.
– On 1 July 2015, Bar Ltd spent £14,000 repainting the building.
– Bar Ltd used Building I for trading purposes apart from the period from 1 January 2012 to 30 June 2013.
– It is intended that the chargeable gain on the sale will be rolled over to the extent that this is possible.

PRACTICE QUESTIONS: SECTION 1

A replacement building ('Building II') purchased by Bar Ltd:

- Bar Ltd purchased Building II, new and unused, for £720,000 on 1 May 2016.
- Bar Ltd uses two thirds of this building for trading purposes; the remaining one-third is rented out.

The trading activities of the Bar Ltd and Hoop Ltd groups of companies:

- The number of transactions between the Bar Ltd group and the Hoop Ltd group is increasing.
- Vault Ltd makes zero rated supplies; all of the other five companies make standard rated supplies.

Required:

(a) (i) Calculate the chargeable gain on the sale of Building I, ignoring any potential claim for rollover relief. **(3 marks)**

   (ii) In relation to claiming rollover relief in respect of the disposal of Building I, explain which of the companies in the Bar Ltd and Hoop Ltd groups are, and are not, able to purchase qualifying replacement assets, and state the period within which such assets must be acquired; **(4 marks)**

   (iii) Explain, with the aid of supporting calculations, the additional amount that would need to be spent on qualifying assets in order for the maximum amount of the gain on Building I to be relieved by rollover relief. **(4 marks)**

Notes:

(1) You should ignore Value Added Tax (VAT) when answering part (a) of this question.

(2) The following figures from the Retail Prices Index should be used, where necessary.

   June 2010   224.1
   July 2015   258.7 (assumed)
   May 2016   262.7 (assumed)

(b) Explain the capital allowances that are available in respect of the electrical, water and heating systems that were acquired as part of Building II. **(2 marks)**

(c) Explain which of the companies in the Bar Ltd and Hoop Ltd groups would be able to register as a single group for the purposes of value added tax (VAT) and discuss the potential advantages and disadvantages of registering them as a single VAT group. **(7 marks)**

(Total: 20 marks)

69 SPETZ LTD GROUP Walk in the footsteps of a top tutor

 Timed question with Online tutor debrief

The management of the Spetz Ltd group requires advice on the value added tax (VAT) annual adjustment for a partially exempt company, the tax position of a company incorporated and trading overseas, and the income tax treatment of the costs relating to an employee working abroad.

The Spetz Ltd group of companies:

- Spetz Ltd has a large number of subsidiaries.
- Novak Ltd and Kraus Co are two of the 100% subsidiaries of Spetz Ltd.
- Novak Ltd has a VAT year end of 30 September.
- Spetz Ltd acquired Kraus Co on 1 October 2015.
- Meyer, an employee of Spetz Ltd, has been seconded to work for Kraus Co.

Novak Ltd – Figures for the year ended 30 September 2016:

	£
Taxable supplies (excluding VAT)	1,190,000
Exempt supplies	430,000
Input tax:	
– attributed to taxable supplies	12,200
– attributed to exempt supplies	4,900
– unattributed	16,100
– recovered on the four quarterly returns prior to the annual adjustment	23,200

Kraus Co:

- Is incorporated in, and trades through, a permanent establishment in the country of Mersano.
- Has no taxable income or chargeable gains apart from trading profits.
- Has taxable trading profits for the year ended 30 September 2015 of £520,000, all of which arose in Mersano.
- Is not a controlled foreign company.
- Has not made an election to exempt its overseas trading profits from UK tax.

The tax system in the country of Mersano:

- It can be assumed that the tax system in the country of Mersano is the same as that in the UK.
- However, the rate of corporation tax is 18%.
- There is no double tax treaty between the UK and Mersano.

Meyer:

- Will work for Kraus Co in the country of Mersano from 15 December 2016 to 31 March 2017.
- Will continue to be employed by Spetz Ltd.
- Will continue to be resident and domiciled in the UK.

The costs relating to Meyer's secondment to Kraus Co:

- Meyer will be reimbursed for the cost of the flights at the start and end of the contract.
- Meyer will return to the UK for a holiday in February 2017, and will pay his own transport costs.
- Meyer will be reimbursed for the cost of laundry and telephone calls home.
- Spetz Ltd does not have a Form P11D dispensation (PAYE dispensation) in place with HM Revenue and Customs.

Required:

(a) Calculate the value added tax (VAT) partial exemption annual adjustment for Novak Ltd for the year ended 30 September 2016 and state when it must be reported to HM Revenue and Customs. You should state, with reasons, whether or not each of the three de minimis tests is satisfied. **(7 marks)**

(b) (i) Explain how to determine whether or not Kraus Co is resident in the UK.
(3 marks)

(ii) Explain, with supporting calculations, the UK corporation tax liability of Kraus Co for the year ended 30 September 2016 on the assumption that it is resident in the UK, and discuss the advantages and disadvantages of making an election to exempt its overseas profits from UK tax. **(5 marks)**

(c) Explain the UK income tax implications for Meyer of the costs relating to his secondment to Kraus Co. **(5 marks)**

(Total: 20 marks)

 Calculate your allowed time, allocate the time to the separate parts.....................

70 OPUS LTD GROUP   *Walk in the footsteps of a top tutor*

> *Timed question with Online tutor debrief*

Your manager is due to attend a meeting with the finance director of Opus Ltd. A schedule of information obtained from the client files and an email from your manager in connection with the Opus Ltd group are set out below.

Schedule of information

Opus Ltd – holdings in other companies as at 31 March 2016

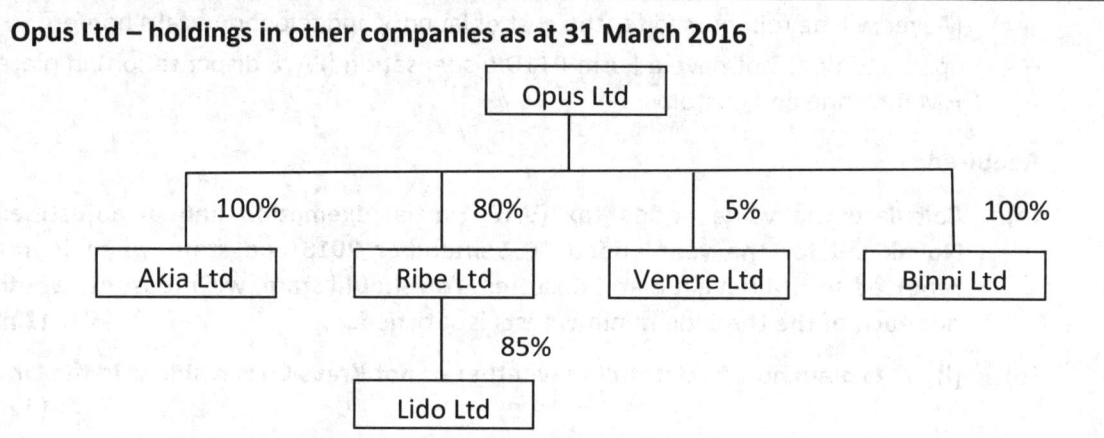

Results for the period ended 31 March 2016

	Opus Ltd £	Akia Ltd £	Ribe Ltd £	Lido Ltd £	Venere Ltd £	Binni Ltd £
Trading profit/(loss)	10,000	(93,000)	41,000	75,000	160,000	78,000
Property income	8,000	–	–	–	–	–
Chargeable gain	Note 3	6,000	–	21,000	–	–

Notes

Holdings in other companies

1. All of the companies are UK resident trading companies.

2. All of the companies, including Binni Ltd, have always been large due to a large number of overseas related 51% group companies.

3. Opus Ltd – acquisition of the holdings in other companies

    – Opus Ltd acquired Akia Ltd and the shareholding in Ribe Ltd (together with its subsidiary Lido Ltd) on 1 January 2000.

    – Venere Ltd has an issued share capital of 1,000,000 ordinary shares. Opus Ltd acquired 170,000 ordinary shares in Venere Ltd on 1 July 2005 for £65,000. It sold 120,000 of these shares on 1 October 2015 for £150,000. The indexation factor from July 2005 to October 2015 is 0·352.

    – Opus Ltd acquired Binni Ltd on 1 December 2015.

PRACTICE QUESTIONS: SECTION 1

4. The minority interests in Ribe Ltd and Lido Ltd are owned by individuals.

5. Venere Ltd is a 75% subsidiary of Jarrah Ltd, a company with no connections to the Opus Ltd group.

Results for the period ended 31 March 2016

6. All of the companies, with the exception of Binni Ltd, have prepared accounts for the year ended 31 March 2016. Binni Ltd has prepared accounts for the ten months ended 31 March 2016.

7. Where necessary, the results shown above have been adjusted for tax purposes.

8. Akia Ltd's trading loss includes writing down allowances in the main pool of £35,000.

9. Akia Ltd is not expected to return to profitability for a number of years.

10. Ribe Ltd has trading losses brought forward of £68,000 as at 1 April 2015.

Email from your manager

Please carry out the following work in preparation for the Opus Ltd meeting.

(a) **Relieving the trading losses of Akia Ltd and Ribe Ltd**

The objective of the group is to relieve all losses as soon as possible.

Prepare calculations, together with supporting explanations, to show how the group's objective can best be achieved, clearly identifying any losses to be carried forward as at 31 March 2016 and any further information which may need to be obtained.

There may be some interesting planning possibilities here; you should think carefully about the tax position of each company.

(b) **Sale of the shares in Venere Ltd**

Opus Ltd has received an offer of £80,000 for its remaining 50,000 ordinary shares in Venere Ltd. If the sale were to go ahead, it would take place on 30 June 2016. However, the management of Opus Ltd are of the opinion that the results of Venere Ltd for the year ending 31 March 2017 will be such that the shares could be worth as much as £100,000 if the sale were to be delayed until 30 April 2017.

Set out the matters which the management of Opus Ltd should consider in order to decide on which of the two dates it would be more financially advantageous to sell the shares in Venere Ltd. When calculating the indexation allowance, use an approximate indexation factor of 0·455 for the period from 1 July 2005 until the date of sale.

KAPLAN PUBLISHING

(c) **Error in the corporation tax return of Binni Ltd**

A detailed review of the results of Binni Ltd for the year ended 31 May 2015 has revealed that no adjustment was made in respect of an amount of disallowable expenditure. As a result of this, the company's corporation tax liability for the year was understated by £8,660. I have told the company that there may be interest and penalties in respect of this error.

Explain how the interest on the underpaid tax will be calculated and state the matters which would need to be considered if the company were unwilling to disclose the error to HM Revenue and Customs.

Tax manager

Required:

Carry out the work required as requested in the email from your manager.

The following marks are available.

(a) Relieving the trading losses of Akia Ltd and Ribe Ltd. (14 marks)

(b) Sale of the shares in Venere Ltd. (5 marks)

(c) Error in the corporation tax return of Binni Ltd.

You are not required to calculate the amount of interest payable or to consider any penalty which may be charged. (6 marks)

(Total: 25 marks)

 Calculate your allowed time, allocate the time to the separate parts....................

71 BOND LTD *Walk in the footsteps of a top tutor*

You have received an email with an attachment from your manager relating to a new client of your firm.

The attachment is a memorandum prepared by the client, Mr Stone, who owns the whole of the ordinary share capital of Bond Ltd. The email from your manager contains further information in relation to the Bond Ltd group of companies and sets out the work you are to perform. The attachment and the email are set out below.

PRACTICE QUESTIONS: SECTION 1

Attachment – Memorandum from Mr Stone

Bond Ltd group of companies

Formation of the group

The Bond Ltd group consists of Bond Ltd, Ungar Ltd and Madison Ltd.

1 April 2014	I purchased the whole of the ordinary share capital of Bond Ltd.
1 December 2014	Bond Ltd purchased the whole of the ordinary share capital of Ungar Ltd.
1 October 2016	Madison Ltd was incorporated on 1 October 2016. Bond Ltd acquired 65% of the ordinary share capital of Madison Ltd on that date.

Bond Ltd – Results for the six months ended 30 September 2016

	£	Notes
Trading losses brought forward	(20,000)	1
Tax adjusted trading income for the period	470,000	2, 3
Chargeable gain	180,000	4

Notes

1. On 31 March 2014, Bond Ltd had trading losses to carry forward of £170,000. The company's total taxable trading income for the two years ended 31 March 2016 was only £150,000, such that on 31 March 2016 it had trading losses to carry forward of £20,000.

2. Bond Ltd's trade consists of baking and selling bread and other baked products. Up to 31 March 2016, its main product had always been low cost bread which was sold to schools, hospitals and prisons. In April 2016, Bond Ltd introduced a new range of high quality breads and cakes. This new range is sold to supermarkets and independent retailers and, for the six months ended 30 September 2016 represents 65% of the company's turnover and 90% of its profits.

3. In order to produce the new product range, Bond Ltd invested £285,000 in plant and machinery in April 2016. The tax adjusted trading income is after deducting capital allowances of £285,000 (i.e. 100% of the cost of the plant and machinery).

    The tax written down value brought forward on the company's main pool as at 1 April 2016 was zero and there were no other additions or disposals of plant and machinery in the period.

4. The chargeable gain arose on the sale of a plot of land on 1 May 2016 for proceeds of £350,000. The land had always been used in the company's business but was no longer required.

Ungar Ltd

The trade of Ungar Ltd consists of baking high quality cakes. Ungar Ltd trades from premises purchased on 1 July 2015 for £310,000.

Ungar Ltd also develops new baking processes and techniques which it has patented. It uses these processes and techniques itself and licenses the patents to other manufacturers.

Madison Ltd

Madison Ltd purchased a building for £400,000 (plus 20% value added tax (VAT)) and machinery for £300,000 (plus 20% VAT) and began to trade on 1 October 2016.

Madison Ltd is partially exempt for the purposes of VAT. In the year ending 30 September 2017, its VAT recovery percentage is expected to be 80%. However, I expect this percentage to fall slightly in future years.

Email from your manager

Additional information

- Bond Ltd, Ungar Ltd and Madison Ltd are all resident in the UK.

- Bond Ltd and Ungar Ltd had always prepared accounts to 31 March. However, in 2016 it was decided to change the group's year end to 30 September and accounts have been prepared for the six months ended 30 September 2016.

- The original cost of the land sold by Bond Ltd on 1 May 2016 was £150,000. The chargeable gain of £180,000 is after the deduction of indexation allowance and is correct.

Please carry out the following work:

(a) **Corporation tax liability of Bond Ltd**

Calculate the corporation tax liability of Bond Ltd for the six months ended 30 September 2016 based on the information provided by Mr Stone. You should review Mr Stone's capital allowances figure of £285,000 and assume the company will claim the maximum possible rollover relief.

Include notes on the following matters.

(i) The capital allowances available.

(ii) The use of Bond Ltd's trading losses brought forward bearing in mind that Mr Stone only recently acquired the company.

(iii) The availability of rollover relief in respect of the chargeable gain on the land.

You should **ignore VAT** when carrying out this work.

We will need to do further work in order to finalise this computation. In the meantime, make a note of any assumptions you have made in order to complete the computation as far as possible for now.

(b) **Ungar Ltd – Patent box regime**

State, giving reasons, whether or not the patent box regime is available to Ungar Ltd and briefly describe the operation of the regime.

(c) **Madison Ltd – Recovery of input tax**

Explain how much of the input tax in respect of the purchase of the building and machinery can be recovered by Madison Ltd in the year ending 30 September 2017 and how this may be adjusted in future years. Include an example of a possible adjustment in the year ending 30 September 2018.

Tax manager

PRACTICE QUESTIONS: SECTION 1

Required:

Carry out the work required as requested in the email from your manager.

The following marks are available:

(a) Corporation tax liability of Bond Ltd.

For guidance, approximately two-thirds of the available marks relate to the written notes. **(17 marks)**

(b) Ungar Ltd – Patent box regime. **(4 marks)**

(c) Madison Ltd – Recovery of input tax. **(4 marks)**

(Total: 25 marks)

72 KLUBB PLC *Walk in the footsteps of a top tutor*

Klubb plc, a client of your firm, requires advice on the penalty in respect of the late filing of a corporation tax return, the establishment of an approved tax efficient share scheme, and its shareholding in an overseas resident company.

Klubb plc:

– Is a UK resident trading company.

– Has been charged a penalty in respect of the late filing of corporation tax returns.

– Intends to establish an approved tax efficient share plan.

– Purchased 30% of the ordinary share capital of Hartz Co from Mr Deck on 1 April 2016.

Late filing of corporation tax returns:

– Klubb plc prepared accounts for the 16 month period ended 31 March 2015.

– The corporation tax returns for this period were filed on 31 May 2016.

Approved tax efficient share plan:

– The plan will be either an approved share incentive plan (SIP) or an approved company share option plan (CSOP).

– If a SIP, the shares would be held within the plan for five years.

– If a SIP, members will not be permitted to reinvest dividends in order to purchase further shares.

– If a CSOP, the options would be exercised within five years of being granted.

– In both cases it can be assumed that the plan members would sell the shares immediately after acquiring them.

Klubb plc wants the share plan to be flexible in terms of:

– The employees who can be included in the plan.

– The number or value of shares which can be acquired by each plan member.

Hartz Co:

- Is resident in the country of Suta.
- Mr Deck continues to own 25% of the company's ordinary share capital.
- Kort Co, a company resident in the country of Suta, owns the remaining 45%.

Budgeted results of Hartz Co for the year ending 31 March 2017:

- Trading profits of £330,000.
- Chargeable gains of £70,000.
- All of Hartz Co's profits have been artificially diverted from the UK.
- Hartz Co will pay corporation tax at the rate of 11% in the country of Suta.
- Hartz Co will not pay a dividend for the year ending 31 March 2017.

Required:

(a) State the corporation tax returns required from Klubb plc in respect of the 16 month period ended 31 March 2015 and the due dates for filing them.

Explain the penalties which may be charged in respect of the late filing of these returns. **(4 marks)**

(b) Compare and contrast an approved share incentive plan with an approved company share option plan in relation to:

- the flexibility desired by Klubb plc regarding the employees included in the plan and the number or value of shares which can be acquired by each plan member; and
- the income tax and capital gains tax implications of acquiring and selling the shares under each plan. **(9 marks)**

(c) (i) Explain whether or not Hartz Co will be regarded as a controlled foreign company (CFC) for the year ending 31 March 2017 and the availability or otherwise of the low profits exemption. **(4 marks)**

(ii) On the assumption that Hartz Co is a CFC, and that no CFC exemptions are available, calculate the budgeted CFC charge for Klubb plc based on the budgeted results of Hartz Co for the year ending 31 March 2017. **(3 marks)**

(Total: 20 marks)

73 HELM LTD GROUP   *Walk in the footsteps of a top tutor*

Your manager has had a number of telephone conversations with Gomez, a potential new client. Gomez owns the whole of the ordinary share capital of Helm Ltd. Extracts from the memorandum prepared by your manager setting out the matters discussed and an email from your manager in connection with the Helm Ltd group are set out below.

Extracts from the memorandum

Helm Ltd

The past and present members of the Helm Ltd group are set out below.

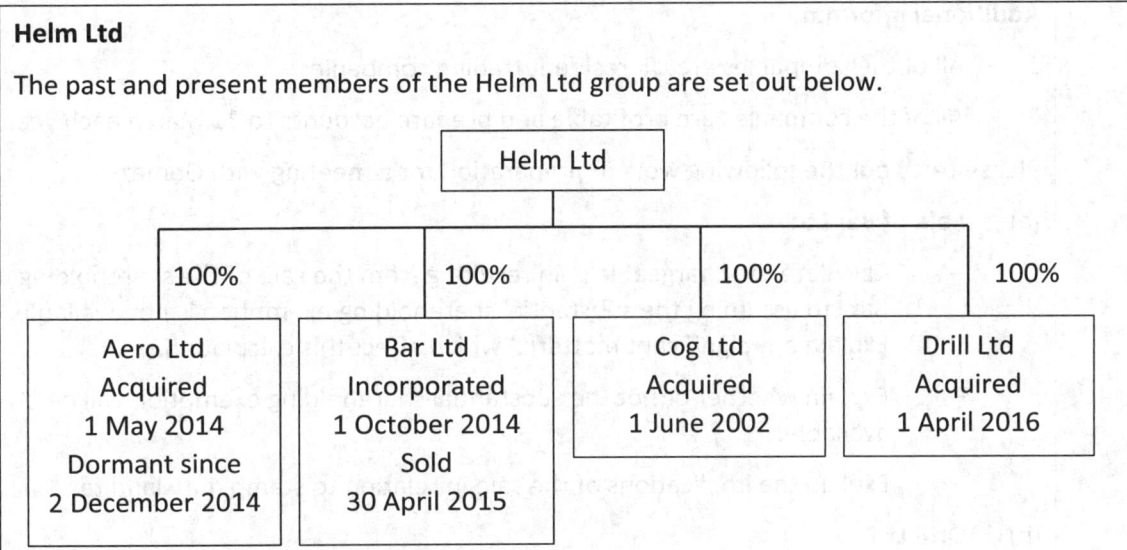

Year ended 31 March 2016

Sale of Bar Ltd

The whole of the ordinary share capital of Bar Ltd was sold to an unconnected party on 30 April 2015 for £1,200,000. Bar Ltd was incorporated on 1 October 2014, when Helm Ltd subscribed £1,000,000 for 200,000 ordinary shares.

Bar Ltd was formed to purchase the entire trade and assets of Aero Ltd for £1,000,000. This purchase occurred on 1 December 2014. The assets consisted of a building valued at £830,000, inventory and receivables. The building had cost Aero Ltd £425,000 on 1 July 1994 and was valued at £880,000 on 30 April 2015 when it was still owned by Bar Ltd.

Year ending 31 March 2017

Purchase of Drill Ltd

Helm Ltd purchased the whole of the ordinary share capital of Drill Ltd on 1 April 2016. Drill Ltd has capital losses to carry forward as at 31 March 2016 of £74,000.

The business of Drill Ltd is to be expanded in the year ending 31 March 2017.

- Drill Ltd intends to borrow £1,350,000 in order to finance the purchase of a building and to provide additional working capital. Drill Ltd will be required to pay an arrangement fee of £35,000 in order to obtain this loan.

- The building will cost Drill Ltd £1,200,000. To begin with, this building will be larger than Drill Ltd requires. One quarter of the building will be rented out to a third party until Drill Ltd needs the additional space.

Cog Ltd

On 1 May 2016, Cog Ltd sold a warehouse for £470,000. Cog Ltd had owned the warehouse for almost two years and had rented it to a tenant throughout this period. Cog Ltd had always intended to bring the warehouse into use in its trade at some point in the future, but before this could happen, it sold the warehouse and realised a chargeable gain of £82,000.

Email from your manager

Additional information

1   All of the companies are UK resident trading companies.

2   All of the companies are profitable and prepare accounts to 31 March each year.

Please carry out the following work in preparation for a meeting with Gomez.

(a) **Sale of Bar Ltd**

– Calculate the chargeable gain resulting from the sale of the shareholding in Bar Ltd assuming the substantial shareholding exemption is not available. Explain any significant matter(s) which affect this calculation.

– Explain whether or not the substantial shareholding exemption will be available.

– Explain the implications of the sale in relation to stamp duty land tax.

(b) **Drill Ltd**

Explain how tax relief may be obtained in respect of the arrangement fee and the interest payable on the loan of £1,350,000 (you should be aware that Drill Ltd receives less than £50 of interest income each year).

(c) **Cog Ltd – chargeable gain on the sale of the warehouse**

Explain:

– whether or not the chargeable gain on the sale of the warehouse can be relieved by rollover relief; and

– how Drill Ltd's capital losses can be relieved; in particular, whether or not they can be offset against the chargeable gain made on the sale of the warehouse by Cog Ltd.

(d) **Becoming tax advisers to Gomez and the Helm Ltd group of companies**

Prepare a summary of the information we require, and any actions which we should take before we agree to become tax advisers to Gomez and the Helm Ltd group of companies.

Tax manager

PRACTICE QUESTIONS: SECTION 1

Required:

Carry out the work required as requested in the email from your manager. The following marks are available:

(a) Sale of Bar Ltd. (11 marks)

The following figures from the Retail Prices Index should be used, where necessary.

July 1994	144.0
October 2014	251.9
December 2014	253.4
April 2015	255.7

(b) Drill Ltd. (5 marks)

(c) Cog Ltd – chargeable gain on the sale of the warehouse. (4 marks)

(d) Becoming tax advisers to Gomez and the Helm Ltd group of companies. (5 marks)

(Total: 25 marks)

74 SPRINT LTD AND IRON LTD (ADAPTED) *Walk in the footsteps of a top tutor*

Your manager has received a letter from Christina. Christina is the managing director of Sprint Ltd and owns the whole of that company's ordinary share capital. Sprint Ltd is a client of your firm. Extracts from the letter from Christina and an email from your manager are set out below.

Extract from the letter from Christina

> I intend to purchase the whole of the ordinary share capital of Iron Ltd on 1 November 2016. My company, Sprint Ltd, purchases components from Iron Ltd, so the two companies will fit together well. I hope to increase the value of Iron Ltd over the next three to five years and then to sell it at a profit.
>
> I need your advice on the following matters:
>
> **Corporation tax payable**
>
> Iron Ltd has not been managed particularly well. It has had significant bad debts and, as a result, is in need of more cash. To help determine its financial requirements, I need to know how much corporation tax Iron Ltd will have to pay in respect of its results for the 16-month period ending 30 June 2017. Iron Ltd's tax adjusted trading income for this period is budgeted to be only £30,000. In fact, if we discover further problems, it is quite possible that Iron Ltd will make a trading loss for this period; but please base your calculations on the budgeted profit figure of £30,000.
>
> Iron Ltd has no income other than trading income. Following the acquisition, Iron Ltd will sell a small industrial building for £160,000 and an item of fixed machinery for £14,000 on 1 December 2016. The industrial building and the item of fixed machinery were both purchased on 1 June 2013 for £100,000 and £13,500 respectively. At that time, rollover relief of £31,800 was claimed against the acquisition of the industrial building and £3,200 against the acquisition of the item of fixed machinery.

PAPER P6: ADVANCED TAXATION (FA2015)

Ownership of Iron Ltd

I need to decide whether I should purchase the shares in Iron Ltd personally or whether the shares should be purchased by Sprint Ltd. I will be the managing director of Iron Ltd regardless of who purchases the shares.

My preference would be to own Iron Ltd personally. However, I would be interested to learn of any advantages to the company being owned by Sprint Ltd. When Iron Ltd is eventually sold, I intend to use the proceeds to purchase a holiday home in Italy.

Value added tax (VAT)

Iron Ltd is not registered for the purposes of VAT. The current management of the company has told me that the level of bad debts is keeping the company's cash receipts in a 12-month period below the registration limit of £82,000. However, I suspect that when I have the opportunity to look at the figures in more detail, it will become apparent that the company should be registered.

Extract from the email from your manager

Additional information

1 Sprint Ltd owns the whole of the ordinary share capital of Olympic Ltd. Both these companies are profitable and prepare accounts to 30 June each year. Both companies are registered for the purposes of VAT.

2 Sprint Ltd, Olympic Ltd and Iron Ltd are all UK resident trading companies.

3 Sprint Ltd will sell a warehouse on 1 February 2017. This will result in a capital loss of £38,000.

4 Iron Ltd currently makes up its accounts to 28 February each year. Following its acquisition, however, its next set of accounts will be for the 16 months ending 30 June 2017.

4 Iron Ltd currently has no related 51% group companies.

Please carry out the work set out below.

There will be quite a few points to draw to Christina's attention, so keep each one fairly brief.

(a) **Iron Ltd – Corporation tax payable**

Assuming the entire ordinary share capital of Iron Ltd is purchased by Christina personally on 1 November 2016, calculate the corporation tax payable by Iron Ltd in respect of the 16-month period ending 30 June 2017, and state when this tax will be due for payment.

(b) **Ownership of Iron Ltd**

Explain the tax matters which Christina needs to be aware of in order to decide whether the ordinary share capital of Iron Ltd should be purchased by herself, personally, or by Sprint Ltd. You should assume that Iron Ltd will be required to register for VAT. You should consider the tax implications of both:

– the ownership of Iron Ltd, and

– the eventual sale of Iron Ltd (by either Christina or Sprint Ltd).

PRACTICE QUESTIONS: SECTION 1

> You should recognise that, regardless of who purchases and subsequently sells Iron Ltd, Christina intends to use the proceeds for personal purposes and that she is a higher rate taxpayer.
>
> **(c)   VAT registration**
>
> Set out the matters which Christina should be aware of in relation to the need for Iron Ltd to register for VAT and the implications for that company of registering late.
>
> **Tax manager**

Required:

Carry out the work required as requested in the email from your manager. The following marks are available:

(a)   Iron Ltd – Corporation tax payable.

Note: The following figures from the Retail Prices Index should be used, where necessary.

June 2013	249.7
December 2016	265.7

(9 marks)

(b)   Ownership of Iron Ltd.   (13 marks)

(c)   Value added tax (VAT) registration.   (3 marks)

(Total: 25 marks)

75   CINNABAR LTD   *Walk in the footsteps of a top tutor*

Cinnabar Ltd requires advice on the corporation tax treatment of expenditure on research and development, the sale of an intangible asset, and a proposed sale of shares. Cinnabar Ltd has also requested advice on the potential to claim relief for losses incurred in a new joint venture.

Cinnabar Ltd:

–   Is a UK resident trading company.

–   Has one wholly-owned UK subsidiary, Lapis Ltd.

–   Is a small enterprise for the purposes of research and development expenditure.

–   Prepares accounts to 31 March each year.

–   Intends to enter into a joint venture with another UK company, Amber Ltd. This joint venture will be undertaken by a newly incorporated company, Beryl Ltd.

Research and development expenditure – year ended 31 March 2016:

– The expenditure on research and development activities was made up as follows:

	£
Computer hardware	44,000
Software and consumables	18,000
Staff costs	136,000
Rent	30,000
	228,000

– The staff costs include a fee of £10,000 paid to an external contractor, who was provided by an unconnected company.

– The remainder of the staff costs relates to Cinnabar Ltd's employees, who are wholly engaged in research and development activities.

– The rent is an appropriate allocation of the rent payable for Cinnabar Ltd's premises for the year.

Sale of an intangible asset to Lapis Ltd:

– The intangible asset was acquired by Cinnabar Ltd in May 2011 for £82,000.

– The asset was sold to Lapis Ltd on 1 November 2015 for its market value on that date of £72,000, when its tax written down value was £65,600.

Sale of shares in Garnet Ltd:

– Cinnabar Ltd acquired a 12% shareholding in Garnet Ltd, a UK resident trading company, in July 2010 for £120,000.

– Cinnabar Ltd sold one third of this shareholding on 20 October 2015.

– Cinnabar Ltd intends to sell the remaining two thirds of this shareholding on 30 November 2016 for £148,000.

– It would be possible to bring forward this sale to October 2016 if it is beneficial to do so.

Beryl Ltd:

– Will be incorporated in the UK and will commence trading on 1 January 2017.

– Is anticipated to generate a trading loss of £80,000 in its first accounting period ending 31 December 2017.

– Will have no sources of income other than trading income.

Alternative capital structures for Beryl Ltd:

– Two alternative structures have been proposed for the shareholdings in Beryl Ltd:

– **Structure 1:** 76% of the shares in Beryl Ltd will be held by Amber Ltd, with the remaining 24% held by Cinnabar Ltd;

– **Structure 2:** 70% of the shares will be held by Amber Ltd, 24% by Cinnabar Ltd and the remaining 6% held personally by Mr Varis, the managing director of Amber Ltd.

Required:

(a) (i) Explain, with supporting calculations, the treatment for corporation tax purposes of the items included in Cinnabar Ltd's research and development expenditure for the year ended 31 March 2016. **(5 marks)**

(ii) Explain the corporation tax implications for Cinnabar Ltd of the sale of the intangible asset to Lapis Ltd. **(2 marks)**

(b) Calculate the after-tax proceeds which would be received on the proposed sale of the Garnet Ltd shares on 30 November 2016 and explain the potential advantage of bringing forward this sale to October 2016.

Note: The following indexation factor should be used where necessary:

July 2010 to November 2016 – 0.1903 **(5 marks)**

(c) Explain, with supporting calculations, the extent to which Cinnabar Ltd can claim relief for Beryl Ltd's trading loss under each of the proposed alternative capital structures. **(8 marks)**

(Total: 20 marks)

Section 2

ANSWERS TO PRACTICE QUESTIONS

TAXATION OF INDIVIDUALS

EMPLOYMENT

1 CLIFFORD AND AMANDA (ADAPTED)

>
>
> **Key answer tips**
>
> This is a very long question to read through. It is important to be clear as to the requirements of the question as you read through it. Break the information in the question down into the different parts of the requirements. The requirements are all separate so that the answer to one part does not affect the answer to another. Once you have identified which bit of the question relates to which bit of the requirement, you should be able to set down your answer.
>
> Part (b) is a short section dealing with a potential conflict of interest. You must be prepared to write about ethical and professional issues.

(a) **Notes to Manager**

To: Tax manager
Date: 13 July 2016
From: Tax senior
Subject: Notes for meeting with Clifford and Amanda Johnson

(i) **Clifford**

Capital gains tax liability on sale of house – 2016/17

	£
Proceeds	284,950
Less: Cost	(129,400)
Capital gain	155,550
Less: PPR exemption (£155,550 × 36/144) (W)	(38,888)
Chargeable gain	116,662
Capital gains tax (£116,662 × 28%)	32,665

Size of the garden

It has been assumed that the garden is no more than half a hectare or, if larger, is required for the reasonable enjoyment of the house.

If this is not the case, there will be no principal private residence relief in respect of the gain on the excess land.

Working: PPR relief

		Months
Period of ownership	(1 August 2004 – 31 July 2016)	144
Actual occupation	(1 August 2004 – 31 January 2006)	18
Deemed occupation	(last 18 months of ownership)	18
		36

Tutorial note

The last 18 months of ownership of any property that has been the taxpayer's principal private residence at some time, is exempt.

(ii) **The implications of selling the Oxford house and garden in two separate disposals**

- The additional sales proceeds would result in an increase in Clifford's capital gains and consequently his tax liability.
- When computing the gain on the sale of the house together with a small part of the garden, the allowable cost would be a proportion of the original cost as the part disposal rules would need to be used.
- That proportion would be A/A + B where
  A is the value of the house and garden that has been sold, and
  B is the value of the part of the garden that has been retained.
- Principal private residence relief would be available in the same way as in (i) above.
- When computing the gain on the sale of the remainder of the garden, the cost would be the remainder of the cost (i.e. the original cost of the property less the amount used in computing the gain on the earlier part disposal).
- Principal private residence relief would not be available as the land sold is not a dwelling house or part of one.

Tutorial note

*Principal private residence relief should be available if the parcel of land was sold **before** the house and the rest of the garden rather than afterwards.*

(iii) **Amanda**

Income tax payable – 2015/16

	£
Salary (£136,600 × 10/12)	113,833
Bonus on joining the company	15,750
Car benefit (W1)	3,568
Fuel benefit (W1)	3,536
Claim in respect of business mileage (720 × (45p – 34p))	(79)
Employment income	136,608
Excess pension contribution (£50,000 – £40,000)	10,000
Property income (W2)	33,348
Dividends – REIT (£485 × 100/80)	606
Dividends – Quoted shares (£1,395 × 100/90)	1,550
Total income	182,112
Less: PA (reduced to £Nil as ANI > £121,200)	
(£100,000 + (2 × £10,600))	(Nil)
Taxable income	182,112

Analysis of income (see tutorial note)

Excess pension £10,000   Dividends £1,550   Other income £170,562

Income tax payable

£		£
31,785	× 20% (Other income)	6,357
118,215	× 40% (Other income)	47,286
150,000		
20,562	× 45% (Other income)	9,253
170,562		
1,550	× 37.5% (Dividends)	581
10,000	× 45% (Pension annual allowance charge)	4,500
182,112		
Income tax liability		67,977
Less	Tax credits	
	On dividends (£1,550 × 10%)	(155)
	On REIT (£606 × 20%)	(121)
	PAYE	(47,785)
Income tax payable		19,916

Tutorial note

Dividends from REITs are treated as 'other property income' (not as dividends) and are taxed at 20%/40%/45% (not 10%/32.5%/37.5%).

The annual allowance (AA) for pension contributions is £40,000. Where the total employer and employee gross contributions exceed the AA, the individual becomes taxable on the excess. In this case only the employer contributes into the scheme, however they contribute £50,000. Accordingly, £10,000 is taxable.

Amanda has no unused relief from earlier years as she was not a member of a registered scheme in the preceding 3 years.

Workings

(W1) **Car and fuel benefits**

CO_2 emissions 149 g/km, car and fuel available for 8 months in 2015/16

	%
Petrol	14
Plus: (145 – 95) × 1/5	10
Appropriate percentage	24

	£
Car benefit (£23,400 × 24% × 8/12)	3,744
Less: Contributions for private use (£22 × 8)	(176)
	3,568
Fuel benefit (£22,100 × 24% × 8/12)	3,536

(W2) **Property income**

	£
Rent receivable (£2,100 × 10)	21,000
Assessment – granting of a 9 year lease (W3)	12,348
Property income	33,348

(W3) **Assessment on granting of 9 year sub-lease**

	£
Premium received on granting 9 year sub-lease	14,700
Assessable as property income £14,700 × (51 – 9)/50	12,348

ANSWERS TO PRACTICE QUESTIONS: SECTION 2

(iv) **Income tax implications of the additional benefits**

- Amanda is an employee earning more than £8,500. Accordingly, the purchase of shares at a discount, the provision of a low interest loan and the free use of a company asset may give rise to taxable benefits.

- Amanda will pay income tax at 40% on the taxable amount in respect of each of the benefits, increasing to 45% (37.5% for dividends) if her income exceeds £150,000.

Shares

- Amanda does not appear to be acquiring the shares under an approved share incentive scheme. Therefore, a taxable benefit will arise, equal to the excess of the market value of the shares over the price paid by Amanda.

- No taxable benefit will arise if the loan does not exceed £10,000 (i.e. if she purchases 3,030 shares or less for £3.30 each).

- Where the loan is for more than £10,000, the taxable benefit is the value of the loan multiplied by the official rate of interest of 3% multiplied by the proportion of the year for which it is outstanding (i.e. 9/12 for 2016/17).

- Any interest paid by Amanda in respect of the loan will reduce the taxable benefit.

Use of the sailing boat

- Where an asset is made available for the use of an employee earning more than £8,500 per annum or a director, the annual taxable benefit is 20% of the value of the asset when it is first made available for any employee.

- The annual benefit is apportioned where, as here, the asset is not available for the whole year.

- There will also be a taxable benefit of £1,400 in respect of the weekly running expenses.

(b) **Paragraph to insert in e-mail to Clifford**

Acting for Amanda

Thank you for supplying the information about Amanda's affairs and for informing us that she would like us to act on her behalf as well as on behalf of yourself.

We will however need to talk with Amanda directly to verify the information supplied and she will need to instruct us herself as to her requirements of the firm.

However, at this stage we are bound to inform you that acting on behalf of both parties of a husband and wife relationship may, at times, present us with a potential conflict of interest.

We therefore will need agreement from both of you that you understand and agree to us acting for both of you. It may be advisable for you to seek independent advice as to whether this is appropriate.

We can however assure you that different personnel within the firm will deal with your separate affairs, but they will work together where there are mutually beneficial reasons for doing so. However, if there is ever any cause for concern that there is a potential conflict of interest, all facts will be disclosed to both parties.

2 DOKHAM *Walk in the footsteps of a top tutor*

Key answer tips

This question is really two separate questions, which could be answered in any order.

Part (a) covers pensions and EMI schemes – neither of which are generally liked by students.

Part (b) covers the frequently tested area of IHT vs CGT for lifetime gifts, but this was perhaps not obvious from the requirement.

The highlighted words in the written sections are key phrases that markers are looking for.

(a) **The information requested by Dokham**

Tutor's top tips

This part of the question is tricky, and you need to think carefully before you answer.

There are several specific questions to address, and you need to make sure that you leave enough time to cover all of them to increase your chance of passing.

Additional salary instead of pension contributions

Tutor's top tips

Think about what you are comparing here:

1 *Dokham receives an employer's pension contribution, which is a tax free benefit, or*

2 *Dokham receives extra salary, which is subject to income tax and NICs, and pays his own personal pension contribution, which saves income tax.*

There is no need to prepare full tax computations. Dokham has a salary of £70,000, so is clearly a higher rate tax payer and is above the NIC limit. Any extra income tax will therefore be at 40%, and extra NICs at 2%.

Employer pension contributions:

There are no tax implications for you when Criollo plc makes contributions into your personal pension scheme.

If you received additional salary instead:

- Your taxable income would increase by £8,000 resulting in additional income tax of £3,200 (£8,000 × 40%).

- However, you would pay the additional pension contributions net of 20% income tax (saving you £1,600) and, as a result of the pension contributions, £8,000 of your taxable income would be taxed at 20% rather than 40% (saving you a further £1,600).
- Accordingly, the effective income tax implications of the two alternatives are the same.
- However, you would have to pay additional national insurance contributions of £160 (£8,000 × 2%) if Criollo plc paid you additional salary of £8,000.

Benefits from the pension scheme

Tutor's top tips

Even if you do not know the detailed rules here, you should be aware that pension income is taxable, and that part of the pension fund can be taken as a tax free lump sum.

You cannot receive any benefits from the pension scheme until you are 55 (unless you are incapacitated by ill health).

Once you are 55, you can receive up to a quarter of the lower of the value of the fund or the lifetime allowance as a tax free one-off payment.

The lifetime allowance is currently £1,250,000. Accordingly, if the fund exceeds this amount, the maximum tax free lump sum payment is £312,500.

The balance of the fund (up to the amount of the lifetime allowance) can be withdrawn at any time as pension income which is taxed as 'other income' at 20/40/45%.

Any withdrawals are subject to income tax at the appropriate rate as and when received.

The number of shares within the Enterprise Management Incentive (EMI) scheme

Tutor's top tips

To score well on this section you needed a good knowledge of the conditions and operation of the EMI scheme.

The value of shares over which you can be granted options within the EMI scheme rules is restricted to £250,000.

This rule results in a maximum number of shares of 26,232 (£250,000/£9.53) at the current share price of £9.53.

Accordingly, it appears that Criollo plc is intending to grant you an option in respect of the maximum possible number of shares whilst allowing for a small increase in the company's share price between now and when the option is granted to you.

It is therefore not possible to increase the number of shares you are allowed to purchase.

Exercise of option and sale of shares

When you exercise the option and purchase shares in Criollo plc:

- You will be liable to income tax and national insurance on the amount by which the value of the shares at the time the option is granted exceeds the price you pay for the shares, i.e. £13,886 (26,200 × (£9.53 – £9)).

When you sell the shares:

- The excess of the sale proceeds over the amount paid for them plus the amount charged to income tax, i.e. £249,686 ((26,200 × £9) + £13,886) less your capital gains tax annual exempt amount (currently £11,100) if available, will be subject to capital gains tax.

    As you are a higher rate taxpayer the rate of tax will be 28%. However, if you sell your shares at least 12 months after the date the share options are granted, the capital gains tax rate will only be 10% as entrepreneurs' relief will be available.

Tutorial note

*Usually, there are no income tax implications on the exercise of options under an approved EMI scheme. However, if the exercise price is less than the value at **grant**, then the shortfall will be subject to income tax and NICs when the option is **exercised**.*

For EMI shares the ownership period for entrepreneurs' relief begins when the options are granted and there is no need to own at least 5% of the company ordinary share capital.

(b) **The tax implications of Virginia contributing towards the children's school fees**

Tutor's top tips

This section is similar to those seen in previous exams, but the wording of the question which refers to 'contributions towards school fees' may have confused some students.

It is really just a question about three lifetime gifts, and the 'possible tax liabilities' here are CGT and IHT.

One-off gift to Dokham of cash of £54,000

Inheritance tax

- The gift will be a potentially exempt transfer for the purposes of inheritance tax.
- There will be no inheritance tax liability if Virginia survives the gift for seven years.

- If Virginia were to die within seven years of the gift:
  - Inheritance tax would be charged at 40% on the excess of the gift over the available nil rate band.

    The available nil rate band is the nil rate band (currently £325,000) as reduced by chargeable transfers in the seven years prior to the gift.

    Chargeable transfers include, broadly, transfers into trust in the seven years prior to the gift and transfers to individuals prior to the gift that take place within the seven years prior to death.
  - Any inheritance tax due in respect of the gift will be reduced by 20% if Virginia survives the gift for three years and by a further 20% for each additional year she survives.
- Any tax due will be payable by Dokham within six months of the end of the month of death.

Capital gains tax

- There is no liability to capital gains tax on a gift of cash.

One-off gift to Dokham of quoted shares worth £54,000

Inheritance tax

- The inheritance tax implications are the same as for the one-off cash gift of £54,000.

Capital gains tax

- Virginia will be subject to capital gains tax at 28% on the excess of the value of the shares over the price she paid for them.

Tutorial note

Gift relief would not be available on the gift of the shares as Panatella plc is a quoted company and Virginia owns less than 5% of the company.

Gift to Dokham of cash of £8,000 every year for the next seven years

Inheritance tax

- Virginia should argue that this series of gifts represents normal expenditure out of her income such that each gift is an exempt transfer for the purposes of inheritance tax.

  For this exemption to be available, Virginia would have to show that:
  - Each gift is part of her normal expenditure.
  - The gifts are made out of income rather than capital.
  - Having made the gifts, she still has sufficient income to maintain her usual standard of living.

  Virginia's taxable income of more than £120,000 per year would help to support this argument.

- If the exemption in respect of normal expenditure out of income is not available, each gift of £8,000 would be a potentially exempt transfer and the inheritance tax implications of each gift would be the same as for the one-off cash gift of £54,000.

Capital gains tax

- Again, there will be no liability to capital gains tax on these cash gifts.

> **Examiner's comments**
>
> The pension scheme element of part (a) was not done particularly well. Candidates struggled in an attempt to produce detailed calculations when a few well-chosen sentences would have been much more efficient. Many candidates failed to consider national insurance contributions and there was particular confusion in relation to the employer's contributions to the pension scheme with many candidates deducting the contributions from the employee's salary.
>
> The main problem here was an inability to set down a clear explanation of the rules. Before starting to write an answer, candidates should be willing to stop and think in order to plan what they want to say. Also, as, part of their preparation for the exam, candidates should practise explaining the tax implications of transactions in writing in order to improve their ability to get to the point in a clear and precise manner.
>
> A small minority of candidates failed to address the three additional questions raised by the client in respect of pension scheme benefits. This was a shame as there were some relatively straightforward marks available here.
>
> The enterprise management incentive scheme element of part (a) again required candidates to address particular points as opposed to writing generally. Although many candidates were aware that there was a maximum value to the options granted under such a scheme, not all of them applied the rule to the facts of the question in terms of the restriction on the number of share options granted by the company. A significant number of candidates confused the enterprise management incentive scheme with the enterprise investment scheme.
>
> Part (b) concerned a grandmother who wished to help finance the school fees of her grandchildren. It was done well by many candidates. Those who did not do so well were often too superficial in their explanations; the question required candidates to 'explain in detail'. Also, weaker candidates failed to consider the capital gains tax implications of the gifts and/or the possibility of the exemption in respect of normal expenditure out of income being available in relation to inheritance tax. Of those who did address capital gains tax, many thought, incorrectly, that gift relief would be available in respect of the proposed gift of quoted shares.

ANSWERS TO PRACTICE QUESTIONS: SECTION 2

ACCA marking scheme		
		Marks
(a)	Additional pension contributions	
	Income tax	2.5
	National insurance contributions	1.0
	Benefits from the pension scheme	3.0
	Enterprise management incentive scheme	
	Maximum number of shares	1.5
	Exercise of option	1.5
	Sale of shares	1.5
		11.0
	Maximum	9.0
(b)	One-off gift of cash	
	Potentially exempt transfer	1.0
	Death within seven years	2.0
	Taper relief	1.0
	Payment of tax	1.0
	Capital gains tax	0.5
	One-off gift of shares	
	Inheritance tax	0.5
	Capital gains tax	1.0
	Series of gifts	
	Exemption for normal expenditure out of income	1.0
	Able to maintain standard of living	1.0
	If exemption not available	0.5
		9.5
	Maximum	7.0
Total		**16.0**

3 MORICE AND BABEEN PLC *Walk in the footsteps of a top tutor*

Key answer tips

This question covers provision of benefits to employees. It is not likely to have been a popular question in the exam, as there are 10 marks purely on the SAYE scheme – an area that had not been tested before in the P6 exam. However, part (b) covers some much more mainstream benefits.

Part (a) requires in-depth knowledge of the SAYE scheme conditions, which may have put off many students. However, there are 7 marks available for applying the tax treatment of an approved share scheme to figures given in the question, so a solid pass could still have been obtained without precise knowledge of the SAYE conditions.

Part (b) on the income tax and national insurance implications of private medical insurance, beneficial loans and the use of an employee's own car for business journeys should have been a gift. These are all F6 areas.

The highlighted words in the written sections are key phrases that markers are looking for.

(a) **SAYE scheme**

Tutor's top tips

This part of the question is slightly unusual for an optional question as the requirement at the end of the question does not actually tell you what you need to do.

If you look back at the information in the question you will see that there are really two requirements here:

1 Explain whether or not each of the proposed rules will be acceptable for a SAYE scheme.

2 Explain, with calculations, the tax and national insurance liabilities for the employee in the illustrative example.

Whether or not the proposed rules will be acceptable for a SAYE scheme

Tutor's top tips

You need to have a good knowledge of the SAYE scheme conditions to be able to answer this part of the question, then you need to apply these conditions to the scenario to ensure that you score a good mark.

The investment period of five years is acceptable. SAYE schemes can run for three or five years.

The minimum monthly investment of £5 is acceptable, but the maximum of £750 is not acceptable. The maximum monthly investment for an approved scheme is £500.

The scheme must be open to all employees:

- It is not acceptable to have a minimum age limit of 21.
- It is also not acceptable to exclude part time employees.
- However, it is acceptable to exclude employees who have worked for the company for less than three years.

Tutorial note

It is acceptable to exclude employees who have worked for the company for less than a qualifying period, as long as the period chosen does not exceed five years.

The share options can be granted at a discount, as long as the exercise price is no less than 80% of the market value at the date of grant. The price of £2.48 will, therefore, be acceptable, as long as the market value at 1 January 2017 is not more than £3.10 (£2.48/80%) per share.

ANSWERS TO PRACTICE QUESTIONS: SECTION 2

Tutor's top tips

You are asked to explain, with calculations, the tax and national insurance liabilities for the employee in respect of:

- grant of the share options
- exercise of the share options
- receipt of the bonus, and
- sale of the shares.

Even if you did not know the conditions for the SAYE scheme, you should still be able to answer most of this part of the requirement if you knew the general tax treatment for approved share option schemes.

Note that there are four different aspects to deal with here, so make sure that you cover all of these and clearly label your answer.

Grant of share options

There is no tax liability on the grant of the share options.

Exercise of share options

There is no tax liability on the exercise of the share options.

Receipt of the bonus

There is no tax liability on the receipt of the bonus.

Sale of shares

There will be a chargeable gain on the sale of the shares, which will be subject to capital gains tax.

The cost of the shares will be:

	£
Amount saved (£250 × 12 months × 5 years)	15,000
Add: Bonus (90% × £250)	225
Total cost	15,225

The number of shares purchased at exercise will therefore be £15,225/£2.48 per share	6,139

The gain on disposal of 6,139 shares will be as follows:

	£
Proceeds (6,139 × £4.00)	24,556
Less: Cost (6,139 × £2.48)	(15,225)
Chargeable gain	9,331

KAPLAN PUBLISHING

161

Tutor's top tips

Don't stop here. You need to explain how the gain will be taxed, but there is no information about the tax position of the illustrative employee.

Have they used their annual exempt amount?

Are they a basic rate or a higher rate taxpayer?

You need to consider all possibilities.

This gain may be covered by the annual exempt amount of £11,100, if the employee has no other chargeable disposals in 2021/22 (the tax year of sale), in which case no tax will be payable.

If the annual exempt amount is not available, the rate of capital gains tax will depend on the level of the employee's taxable income:

- If the employee has taxable income of more than £31,785, then the gain will be taxed at 28%.
- If the employee has taxable income of less than £31,785, gains falling into the basic rate band will be taxed at 18% with the excess being taxed at 28%.

Entrepreneurs' relief will not be available as the employee will not own 5% of the company's ordinary share capital.

National insurance

There are no national insurance implications in respect of a SAYE scheme.

(b) **Income tax and national insurance implications for the employees of Babeen plc**

Tutor's top tips

*The benefits set out here were tested at F6. F6 level knowledge is often tested at P6, and **explaining** the tax treatment of benefits, rather than just calculating them, is a popular requirement.*

Note that you are only asked to talk about the tax implications for the employees in this question, not the employer.

(i) **Medical care scheme**

Private health insurance

Private health insurance is a taxable benefit for P11D employees (those earning at least £8,500).

The benefits will be the cost to the employer of £470.

Interest-free loans

As long as the amount borrowed does not exceed £10,000 at any point in the tax year, there will be no taxable benefit.

If the employee borrows more than £10,000 there will be a taxable benefit.

The benefit is calculated by multiplying the official rate of interest of 3% by the amount outstanding during the tax year, giving a maximum annual benefit of:

(£12,500 × 3%) = £375

If the amount borrowed changes during the year, there are two alternative methods of calculating the benefit:

- The average method, based on the average amount outstanding

  = (balance b/f + balance c/f) ÷ 2

- The strict method, based on the actual amounts outstanding during the year.

Either the taxpayer or HMRC can elect for the strict method.

These taxable benefits will be subject to income tax at 20% if they fall within the basic rate band or 40% if the employee is a higher rate taxpayer.

Employees do not pay national insurance contributions on private health insurance or beneficial loans.

(ii) **Payments for driving their own cars**

Tutor's top tips

Don't forget to refer to the tax tables given in the exam. The authorised mileage allowances are provided.

However, you do need to learn the authorised allowance for passengers, as this is not given.

Mileage allowance

Employees are allowed to receive a tax free mileage allowance of 45p per mile for the first 10,000 business miles per tax year, and 25p per mile thereafter.

- If they receive less than these approved amounts, the shortfall can be deducted from taxable employment income. This means that employees of Babeen plc will be able to deduct a shortfall of 9p per mile (45p − 36p) for the first 10,000 business miles.
- If they receive more than the approved amounts, the excess will be subject to income tax.

Passenger allowance

There is a tax free allowance of 5p per mile for carrying a passenger, so the 3p per mile paid will be tax free. However, the shortfall of 2p per mile (5p − 3p) is not tax deductible.

National insurance

As the mileage allowance is no more than 45p per mile, there will be no national insurance contributions payable. There will also be no national insurance contributions payable on the additional 3p per mile.

Tutorial note

Even if the employee drove more than 10,000 miles and had a taxable benefit in respect of the mileage allowance, there would still be no national insurance contributions payable.

However, if the employer paid more than 45p per mile, the excess would be subject to national insurance.

Examiner's comments

In order to score well in part (a) it was important for candidates to address each of the detailed rules in the question as opposed to writing generally about share option schemes. Many candidates who attempted this question were knowledgeable about Save As You Earn schemes but only a minority took a sufficiently disciplined approach to score well.

The explanation of the tax liabilities in respect of the shares acquired under the scheme was not done particularly well. Many candidates lacked precise knowledge of this area such that they did not know that no tax would be charged until the shares were sold. In addition, it needed to be recognised that the position of each employee would vary depending on whether or not they had made any other capital gains and on the level of their taxable income; very few candidates considered these matters.

The medical care scheme in part (b) was not handled particularly well in that many candidates incorrectly stated that the provision of health insurance would be an exempt benefit for the employees. However, this was not too important as it was only a minor part of the answer. The provision of an interest free loan was also not dealt with as well as might have been expected. The question stated that the loan would be 'up to £12,500' so it was necessary to point out that loans of no more than £10,000 would be exempt.

The explanation of the implications of the payments to employees for driving their own cars was handled well. The only common error was the failure to recognise that there would be no national insurance implications.

The question asked for the tax implications 'for the employees' as opposed to the tax implications generally. Accordingly, it was necessary to consider the national insurance issues for the employees (but not the employer) and there was no need to address the ability of the employer to obtain tax relief for the costs incurred.

ANSWERS TO PRACTICE QUESTIONS: SECTION 2

ACCA marking scheme			
			Marks
(a)	Scheme rules		
	Investment period and investment limits		1.5
	Eligible employees		1.5
	Share price		1.5
	Illustrative example		
	Grant and exercise of option, receipt of bonus		1.5
	Gain		1.5
	Capital gains tax		3.0
	National insurance contributions		1.0
			11.5
		Maximum	10.0
(b) (i)	Health insurance		0.5
	Interest-free loan		2.5
	National insurance contributions		0.5
(ii)	Driving on company business		
	Income tax		2.0
	National insurance contributions		1.0
	Carrying passengers		1.5
			8.0
		Maximum	7.0
Total			17.0

4 PITA PLC *Walk in the footsteps of a top tutor*

Key answer tips

This question is split into 3 parts and focuses on employment issues. This question was the most popular of the optional questions when it was set.

Part (a) covers the income tax implications of childcare vouchers and payments to employees who work from home.

Part (b) requires application of the conditions which should be satisfied for companies issuing options under the enterprise management incentive (EMI) scheme. This part of the question requires some detailed knowledge.

In addition the examining team asks if the shares are eligible for entrepreneurs' relief.

Part (c) covers the income tax implications of redundancy packages and the car benefit.

There are a lot of easy marks available here and the question is broken down into different parts which makes it easy to understand. Well prepared students should have been able to score high marks in this question as it is knowledge based.

The highlighted words in the written sections are key phrases that markers are looking for.

KAPLAN PUBLISHING

Tutor's top tips

You could attempt the question in any order and could do the easy parts first.

(a) **Financial assistance with childcare and encouraging working from home**

Tutor's top tips

There are 6 marks available for this section, so try to make sure that you have at least 6 separately identifiable points in your answer.

Tutorial note

For the childcare vouchers the exempt amount is based on the employee's marginal tax rate.

Employees working from home can receive £4 per week as exempt income towards household expenses incurred.

Vouchers to purchase childcare

The cost of providing the vouchers (as opposed to the value of the services which they can be used to purchase) will be taxable employment income as reduced by the following exemption.

The exemption will only be available where the vouchers are available to all employees and the care is provided by an approved child carer. The amount of the exemption varies depending on the marginal rate of income tax paid by each employee. This marginal rate of tax is determined by reference to the employee's employment income only.

The exemption is:

£55 per week for a basic rate taxpayer

£28 for a higher rate taxpayer

£25 for an additional rate taxpayer.

Payments for working from home

These payments will not result in taxable employment income where an employee receives no more than £4 per week (or £18 per month).

Payments in excess of these limits will be taxable in full unless the employee is able to provide evidence of the additional household costs incurred.

ANSWERS TO PRACTICE QUESTIONS: SECTION 2

Tutor's top tips

Credit was available for identifying the exemption limits in respect of the vouchers and payments but it was possible to score full marks without this knowledge.

(b) (i) **Ability to establish an enterprise management incentive (EMI) scheme**

Tutor's top tips

The EMI scheme allows unquoted trading companies to reward key employees by allowing them to benefit from an increase in share price. Only relatively small companies (similar to companies eligible for the enterprise investment scheme) are eligible for the EMI.

Pita plc is a qualifying company for the purposes of the EMI scheme because:

- it has gross assets of no more than £30 million; and
- it has fewer than 250 full-time employees; and
- it has a permanent establishment in the UK.

Under the EMI scheme rules, Pita plc is allowed to make the scheme available to just its nine key employees. However, the two part-time key employees cannot join the scheme unless they work for Pita plc for at least 25 hours per week or, if lower, 75% of their working time.

Tutorial notes

1 The following conditions would also be relevant but the information necessary to address them was not provided in the question.

- An employee owning 30% or more of the company's ordinary shares would not be permitted to join the scheme.

- Pita plc must carry on a qualifying trade and must not be controlled by another company.

2 The answer does not include the need for the shares to be fully paid up irredeemable ordinary shares as the requirement refers to the conditions relating to the company and the employees, and not to the shares.

KAPLAN PUBLISHING

(ii) **Income tax and capital gains tax implications for the employees**

Tutor's top tips

You must deal with both the income tax and capital gains tax aspects of the share options.

There is no income tax charge if the option price corresponds to the market value of the shares at the date of grant of the option, otherwise any shortfall is subject to income tax.

The difference between the sale proceeds and the market value when the options are granted is subject to capital gains tax.

EMI shares are eligible for entrepreneurs' relief even if the shareholder owns less than 5% of the ordinary share capital, and the period of ownership begins at the date the options are granted, not the date of the exercise.

There will be no income tax on the grant of the share options.

The options are to be exercised within ten years of the date on which they were granted. Accordingly, income tax will only be charged on the excess of the market value of the shares at the time the options were granted over the option price, i.e. 25 pence per share (£2·00 — £1·75).

When the shares are sold, there will be a capital gain per share equal to the excess of the sales proceeds over the market value at the time the options were granted, i.e. £3 per share (£5 – £2).

On a disposal of EMI shares in Pita plc, entrepreneurs' relief will be available where:

- Pita plc was a trading company throughout the year prior to the disposal.
- The shareholder was employed by the company throughout the year prior to disposal.
- The options were granted at least one year prior to the date of the disposal of the shares.

There is no requirement for the individual to own at least 5% of the shares in the company where the shares are EMI shares.

(c) **Redundancy package for Narn**

Tutor's top tips

There are a number of items in the redundancy package and each must be considered in turn.

Redundancy of £30,000 is exempt as long it is ex-gratia (non-contractual) and does not coincide with retirement.

Statutory redundancy is exempt but reduces the £30,000 limit.

If the payment is a reward for services – past, present or future then it will be treated as contractual employment income and the exemption is not available.

The question does not state the circumstances in which the additional payment is made so you should explain why it may be taxable.

When calculating the car benefit, remember that the car is diesel (add 3% to the %) and only available for part of the year, so the benefit must be time apportioned.

The statutory redundancy payment is covered by the £30,000 exemption which is available in respect of termination payments which are not in respect of services provided by the employee.

The additional amount of £26,000 will be taxable in full if:

- Narn was contractually entitled to receive it, or
- it was in respect of work done by Narn, or
- it was in respect of a restriction placed on Narn's future working activities.

If the payment is not taxable in full, £21,900 (£30,000 – £8,100) will be exempt and the balance of £4,100 will be taxable.

The continued use of the company car will result in a taxable benefit in the tax year 2015/16 after Narn has left the company.

The benefit will be £2,242 (W).

Working: Car benefit

List price £19,500, CO_2 emissions of 129 g/km, rounded down to 125, diesel engine.

Relevant % = (14% + (125 – 95) ÷ 5) + 3% diesel) = 23%

Benefit = (£19,500 × 23% × 6/12) = £2,242

Examiner's report

In part (a) the taxation of vouchers to be used for the purchase of childcare was tackled well by the majority of candidates. The majority of candidates were aware that an exemption was available in respect of the provision of such vouchers, with many knowing that the amounts of the exemption depend on the employee's marginal rate of tax. The rules regarding the ability of an employer to make tax-free payments to employees who work from home were not as well known, such that very few candidates scored well on this aspect of the question.

Part (b) tested various aspects of the Enterprise Management Incentive (EMI) scheme and was split into two sub-requirements.

The first part of part (b) was done reasonably well. The majority of candidates knew that there were conditions relating to the number of employees and the gross assets of the company, although not all knew the precise detail of the conditions. Most candidates were also aware that it is acceptable for an EMI scheme to be provided to key employees (rather than to all of a company's employees) but many did not realise that part-time employees are not permitted to be members of such a scheme.

The second part was arguably a more difficult requirement and was not done particularly well.

As always, those candidates who adopted a methodical approach and dealt with the grant, exercise and sale as three separate issues did better than those who tried to address everything at once.

Candidates will almost always benefit from starting a new paragraph for each new issue that needs to be addressed.

In the final part of the question concerning a redundancy package, all three matters were handled well by many candidates with most candidates demonstrating awareness of the £30,000 exemption.

The one area where almost all candidates could have improved their performance was the additional payment. The question was deliberately silent as to the reason for and the nature of the payment. It was up to candidates to raise the matter as to whether or not the payment was for work carried out or a restriction to be placed on the employee's future working activities, such that it would be taxable in full.

ANSWERS TO PRACTICE QUESTIONS: SECTION 2

ACCA marking scheme		
		Marks
(a) Vouchers to purchase childcare		
Taxable employment income		1.0
Availability of exemption		1.0
Amount of exemption		2.0
Payments for working from home		2.5
		6.5
	Maximum	6.0
(b) (i) Qualifying company		3.0
Qualifying employees		2.0
		5.0
	Maximum	4.0
(ii) Grant of options		1.0
Exercise of options		1.5
Sale of shares		3.0
		5.5
	Maximum	5.0
(c) Statutory redundancy		1.0
Additional payment		3.0
Continued use of car		2.0
		6.0
	Maximum	5.0
Total		20.0

5   HYSSOP LTD   *Walk in the footsteps of a top tutor*

Key answer tips

This question is really three separate questions covering: employment benefits, payment of a lease premium by a company and the VAT capital goods scheme.

It is a good question, covering areas that you should be familiar with.

As usual, there are a few twists, such as partial business use for rollover relief and the fact that the lease premium is a depreciating asset, but there are still enough basic marks here for you to score a pass if you missed these trickier points.

The highlighted words in the written sections are key phrases that markers are looking for.

KAPLAN PUBLISHING

(a) **Assistance with home to work travel costs for Corin**

Tutor's top tips

This part requires explanation and calculation of the cost of two alternative benefits from the point of view of the employee and the company. This type of requirement regularly appears in the P6 exam.

The key is to think about cash flows and to remember to include tax payable and tax savings.

Don't forget to consider national insurance contributions; these are payable by the employer on all benefits, but the employee only pays them on cash benefits.

You are specifically asked which is the most cost efficient for both Corin and Hyssop Ltd, so there will be marks for following through your figures and stating this.

(i) **Cost to Corin**

Alternative 1 – Provision of a motorcycle

Corin is a higher rate taxpayer, so will pay income tax at 40% on the annual taxable benefit.

Corin will have no national insurance liability in respect of this benefit.

The total cost of this option will be:

Income tax on benefit (£3,160 × 40%) = total cost   £1,264

Alternative 2 – Payment towards the cost of driving and provision of parking place

Provision of a parking place at or near an employee's normal place of work is an exempt benefit for income tax.

Corin will pay income tax at 40% on the cash received as reimbursement of his driving costs, together with class 1 national insurance contributions at 2%.

The total cost of this option will be:

	£
Cost of driving	2,820
Less: Amount reimbursed	(2,240)
Additional cost of driving	580
Income tax and NICs on cash received (£2,240 × 42%)	941
Total cost	1,521

The most cost efficient option for Corin is therefore provision of the motorcycle.

Tutorial note

The statutory mileage rates are not relevant in this case as the driving costs are not related to journeys made in the course of Corin carrying out his duties of employment.

(ii) **Cost to Hyssop Ltd**

Alternative 1 – Provision of a motorcycle

Hyssop Ltd will have to pay class 1A national insurance contributions of 13.8% in respect of the provision of the motorcycle.

The total cost to Hyssop Ltd is therefore:

	£
Lease cost	3,160
Employer's class 1A NICs (£3,160 × 13.8%)	436
Total cost	3,596

Alternative 2 – Payment towards the cost of driving and provision of parking place

As the provision of the parking place is an exempt benefit for income tax, there will be no class 1A liability for Hyssop Ltd.

Hyssop Ltd will have a class 1 national insurance liability at 13.8% in respect of the reimbursement of driving costs.

The total cost to Hyssop Ltd is therefore:

	£
Cost of driving reimbursed	2,240
Parking cost	920
Employer's class 1 NICs (£2,240 × 13.8%)	309
Total cost	3,469

The most cost efficient option for Hyssop Ltd is therefore the payment towards the cost of driving and provision of the parking place.

Hyssop Ltd will be able to deduct all the costs for corporation tax purposes under both options.

Tutorial note

As the amounts are deductible for corporation tax purposes under both options, there is no need to calculate the after-tax cost to Hyssop Ltd.

(b) **Corporation tax implications of the acquisition of the 40-year lease**

Tutor's top tips

This part tests F6 knowledge of the allowable deduction for a premium paid on a short lease. You may have forgotten the formula, but could still gain marks for knowing that there is a deduction from trading profits over the life of the lease and that it should be time apportioned in the year of payment.

There are also marks here for discussing rollover relief – a very popular topic in the P6 exam, so make sure that you are able to explain and apply the rules.

Allowable deduction

As Hyssop Ltd has paid a premium on the grant of a short lease on a property which is going to be used in its trade, a deduction is available for each year of the lease in calculating Hyssop Ltd's taxable trading income.

The annual deduction is calculated as:

$$\frac{\text{Amount of premium taxed as income on the landlord}}{\text{Number of years of the lease}}$$

The amount of the premium which is taxed as income on the landlord is £57,200 (£260,000 – (£260,000 × (40 – 1) × 2%)).

The annual deduction available to Hyssop Ltd is £1,430 (£57,200/40).

As the lease was only acquired on 1 February 2016, the deduction available in the year ended 31 December 2016 is restricted to £1,311 (£1,430 × 11/12).

Tutorial note

Alternatively, the amount of premium taxed as income on the landlord could be calculated as (£260,000 × (51 – 40)/50)) = £57,200.

Rollover relief: gain on warehouse

The factory is used in Hyssop Ltd's trade, so the lease is a qualifying business asset, and it was acquired within the 12 months before the disposal of the warehouse. Therefore the full business use element of the gain arising may be deferred to the extent that the proceeds relating to the business use of the warehouse have been reinvested in the lease.

The warehouse will have been owned by Hyssop Ltd for four years (1 January 2013 to 31 December 2016).

The warehouse has been used by Hyssop Ltd in its trade for three years (1 January 2013 to 31 December 2015).

The proceeds relating to the business use element of the gain are £236,250 (75% × £315,000). This is less than the £260,000 premium reinvested in the acquisition of the lease, therefore the full 75% of the chargeable gain relating to the business use of the warehouse can be deferred against the acquisition of the lease. Accordingly, £12,390 (£16,520 × 75%) may be deferred.

The lease is for less than 60 years and so is a wasting asset for capital gains purposes. Accordingly, the gain will be deferred until the earliest of:

– The date of disposal of the lease

– The date the leased factory ceases to be used in Hyssop Ltd's business

– 1 February 2026 (ten years after the acquisition of the lease).

The remaining gain of £4,130 (£16,520 × 25%), relating to the non-business use, will be included in Hyssop Ltd's corporation tax computation for the year ending 31 December 2016.

(c) **Value added tax (VAT) implications of the disposal of the warehouse**

Tutor's top tips

VAT for land and buildings and the capital goods scheme are popular topics in the P6 exam, so you should be prepared to answer a question on this area.

At the date of sale, the warehouse is more than three years old. Accordingly, because Hyssop Ltd has not opted to tax it, the disposal will be exempt from VAT.

As the warehouse was newly constructed when it was purchased, VAT of £54,000 (£270,000 × 20%) would have been charged and, as the warehouse was used in its standard-rated business, this would have been wholly reclaimed by Hyssop Ltd in the year ended 31 December 2013.

As the disposal is exempt from VAT, VAT will have to be repaid to HM Revenue and Customs (HMRC) as the warehouse is deemed to have 0% taxable use for the remainder of the ten-year adjustment period under the capital goods scheme. The amount of £32,400 (£54,000 × 6/10 × (100% – 0%)) will be repayable to HMRC as a result of the disposal.

Tutorial note

A further £5,400 (£54,000 × 1/10 × (100% – 0%)) will also be repayable to HMRC in respect of the year ending 31 December 2016 as the warehouse has been rented out throughout this year, with no option to tax.

> **Examiner's comments**
>
> The first part required candidates to consider two possible ways in which an employer could provide financial assistance to an employee in respect of home to work travel and to advise on the most cost efficient method.
>
> Although this was, arguably, very straightforward, it was not easy to get right. As always, those candidates who thought before writing did considerably better than those who simply wrote. In particular, they recognised the importance of national insurance contributions.
>
> Most candidates identified the income tax and corporation tax implications of the two alternatives. The one point that many missed out on was the fact that the provision of a parking space is an exempt benefit.
>
> The problems related to the national insurance position. Some candidates missed this out completely. Others were simply not orderly enough, such that they did not earn as many marks as they could have done.
>
> Candidates needed to recognise that the provision of a motorcycle to an employee would result in a liability to class 1A national insurance contributions for the employer but no liability to national insurance contributions for the employee. Whereas, making a payment towards an employee's driving costs would result in a liability to class 1 national insurance contributions for both the employer and the employee.
>
> Many candidates wrote about the statutory mileage rates, but these are only relevant where payments are in respect of journeys made when carrying out employment duties, which was not the case here.
>
> The second part of the question concerned a premium paid in respect of a lease and the availability of rollover relief. This part was not done particularly well.
>
> There were two distinct aspects to this part of the question.
>
> The first concerned the tax deduction available in respect of the premium paid. Most candidates were able to make a start on this but very few made it to the end. The first task was to determine the amount of the premium that would be taxed on the landlord as income. This amount was then divided by the number of years of the lease in order to determine the annual deduction. The deduction in the current period was then 11/12 of the annual deduction because the lease was entered into when there were eleven months of the accounting period remaining.
>
> The second part of the question concerned the availability of rollover relief. Most candidates knew the basics of rollover relief. However, they did not score as well as they could have done for two reasons:
>
> - The asset sold had not been used for the purposes of the trade for the whole of the period of ownership. As a result, although rollover relief was available, only the business-use proportion of the gain could be relieved and only that proportion of the proceeds needed to be reinvested in qualifying business assets.
>
> - They failed to realise that the lease was a depreciating asset for the purposes of rollover relief, such that the gain would be deferred until the earliest of the date of disposal of the lease, the date the leased building ceased to be used in the business and ten years after the acquisition of the lease.

ANSWERS TO PRACTICE QUESTIONS: SECTION 2

> The final part of the question concerned the capital goods scheme for VAT and was not done particularly well. The capital goods scheme is not easy to explain and many candidates were unable to organise their thoughts and provide a coherent explanation of the implications of the disposal of a building.
>
> Candidates would help themselves if they told the story from the beginning.
>
> - The first point to make was that the input tax on the purchase of the building would have been recovered in full.
>
> - It was then necessary to recognise that the sale of the building would be an exempt supply.
>
> - As a result of the exempt supply, there will be deemed to be 0% taxable use of the building for the remainder of the 10-year adjustment period resulting in a repayment of VAT to HMRC.

ACCA marking scheme

			Marks
(a)	(i)	Cost of motorcycle option	1.5
		Cost of driving costs reimbursement option	3.0
		Conclusion	0.5
			5.0
	(ii)	Cost of provision of motorcycle	1.5
		Cost of driving costs reimbursement	1.0
		All costs deductible for corporation tax	0.5
		Conclusion	0.5
			3.5
		Maximum	3.0
(b)		Deduction:	
		Available against taxable trading income	1.0
		Amount	3.0
		Deferral relief available	3.0
		Date gain crystallises	2.0
			9.0
		Maximum	8.0
(c)		Disposal exempt	1.5
		Initial reclaim	1.0
		Repayment of VAT reclaimed previously y/e 31 December 2016	2.0
			4.5
		Maximum	4.0
Total			**20.0**

KAPLAN PUBLISHING

UNINCORPORATED BUSINESSES

6   GLORIA SEAFORD (ADAPTED) *Online question assistance*

Key answer tips

Parts (a) to (c) of this question are reasonably straightforward sections dealing with the income tax, VAT and capital gain implications of a trader who is giving up business.

Whenever a question refers to an individual's residence and domicile status, you should be on the lookout for income and assets whose tax treatment may be affected. In this question it was part (d) where this information was relevant.

(a)   **Value added tax (VAT) implications of the sale by Gloria of the business assets**

- The sale of the premises is an exempt supply for VAT purposes because they are more than three years old. Accordingly, Gloria cannot recover any VAT incurred on any costs relating to the sale.

- Gloria must charge VAT on the shelving, shop fittings and the inventory of cards and small gifts.

- The sale of the inventory of books will be zero-rated.

- Gloria is making a taxable supply to herself of the van. However, there is no need to account for VAT as the amount due of £940 (£4,700 × 20%) is less than £1,000.

- Gloria must inform HMRC by 30 March 2017 that she has ceased to trade. Her VAT registration will be cancelled with effect from 28 February 2017.

Tutorial note

This is not a transfer of a going concern: the assets are being sold to different purchasers and the building is to be used for a different purpose.

(b)   **Income tax and national insurance liability – 2016/17**

Tutorial note

An individual's tax status is only important for income tax in determining their liability to UK tax on overseas income and the availability of the personal allowance.

The question says that Gloria is resident in the UK, but not UK domiciled.

As she is UK resident in 2016/17, Gloria is liable to tax on all of her UK income and is entitled to a full personal allowance.

Her domicile is not important in this part as she has no source of overseas income.

Income tax liability

	£
Trading income (W1)	32,434
Retirement pension	5,312
Bank interest (£13,500 × 100/80)	16,875
Total income	54,621
Less: Personal allowance	(10,600)
Taxable income	44,021

Analysis of income:
Savings income £16,875, Other income £27,146

£	£
27,146 × 20% (other income)	5,429
4,639 × 20% (savings income)	928
31,785	
12,236 × 40% (savings income)	4,894
44,021	
Income tax liability	11,251

National insurance liability

Gloria has no class 2 or class 4 national insurance contributions liability as she was over the state pensionable age on 6 April 2016.

Workings

(W1) Trading income

Closing year rules apply:

Year of cessation	2016/17
Penultimate year	2015/16

Accounts assessed in penultimate year (CYB) = y/e 31 October 2015

The year of cessation will assess all profits not yet assessed less overlap relief.

	£	£
Year ended 31 October 2016		39,245
Period ending 28 February 2017	11,500	
Profit on closing inventory (£8,300 × 5/105)	395	
Capital allowances (W2)	(2,986)	
		8,909
		48,154
Less: Overlap profits		(15,720)
Trading income		32,434

(W2) **Capital allowances**

	Pool £	Van £	B.U. %	Allowances £
TWDV b/f	4,050	4,130		
Addition	820	–		
Less: Proceeds	(1,400)	(4,700)		
	3,470	570		
Balancing allowance	(3,470)	–		3,470
Balancing charge	–	(570)	× 85%	(484)
	Nil	Nil		
Total allowances				2,986

(c) (i) **Capital gains tax liability – 2016/17**

Tutorial note

The question says that Gloria is resident in the UK, but not UK domiciled.

Her non-UK domicile status is however not important in this part as she has not disposed of any overseas assets.

Accordingly, in 2016/17, Gloria is liable to capital gains tax on the net taxable gains arising on all of her UK asset disposals with a full annual exempt amount.

Calculation ignoring the negligible value claim

	£	£
Gains not qualifying for entrepreneurs' relief		
Gain on painting	7,100	
Gains qualifying for entrepreneurs' relief		
Gain on shop (£335,000 – £267,000)		68,000
Less: Capital losses b/f (Note)	(7,100)	(24,300)
Less: Annual exempt amount	(Nil)	(11,100)
	Nil	32,600
Capital gains tax:		
Qualifying gains (£32,600 × 10%)		3,260

Tutorial note

Entrepreneurs' relief is available on the disposal of the shop as although Gloria is not disposing of the whole or part of the business as a going concern, the relief is available on the disposal of assets of an individual's trading business that has now ceased.

Furthermore, the assets have been held at least 12 months prior to the disposal and the disposal of assets is to take place within three years of the cessation of trade.

Capital losses and the AEA are set against non-qualifying gains first, as these would otherwise be taxed at 28% (as Gloria is a higher rate taxpayer).

The rate of CGT on a gain qualifying for entrepreneurs' relief is 10%.

(ii) **Relief in respect of the fall in value of the shares in All Over plc**

The shares in All Over plc are worth three pence each and are of negligible value. Gloria can make a negligible value claim in order to realise the loss on the shares without selling them.

	£
Value (17,500 × 3p)	525
Cost (probate value)	(11,400)
Capital loss on making the claim	(10,875)

Gloria can claim the loss in any year in which the shares are of negligible value provided she notifies HMRC within two years of the end of that year.

Accordingly, she can claim to realise the loss in 2015/16 or even in 2014/15 if she can show that the shares were of negligible value in that year.

Alternatively, she can claim the loss in 2016/17 or a later year if that would give rise to a greater tax saving.

(d) (i) **Options for UK tax in respect of dividends paid by Bubble Inc**

If Gloria invests in Bubble Inc shares, she will own an overseas asset and will be in receipt of overseas income. Her tax status is therefore important in determining how she will be assessed to UK taxes.

The important factors in determining Gloria's liability to tax are as follows:

- She is resident in the UK, but not UK domiciled
- Her unremitted dividends from Bubble Inc will be > £2,000.

Accordingly, she will be taxed as follows:

Income tax

- She will be assessed on the dividends on an arising basis with full personal allowance available **unless** a claim for the remittance basis is made

- If a claim for the remittance basis is made:
  - The dividends arising in that year will only be assessed in the UK if they are remitted into the UK
  - As Gloria plans to leave the dividends in her overseas bank account, they will not be taxed in the UK
  - Note that they will be taxed even if remitted in a later year when the remittance basis is not claimed
  - No personal allowance available in the year the remittance basis is claimed
  - In addition, Gloria will be liable to a £60,000 remittance basis tax charge as she has been UK resident for more than 12 out of the previous 14 tax years.

Income tax liability

	Arising basis £	Remittance basis £
Retirement pension	5,312	5,312
Bank interest (£13,500 × 100/80)	16,875	16,875
Dividends from Bubble Inc (£12,000 × 100/90)	13,333	Nil
Total income	35,520	22,187
Less: Personal allowance	(10,600)	(Nil)
Taxable income	24,920	22,187

Analysis of income:
Arising basis: Dividend income £13,333, Savings income £11,587
Remittance basis: Savings income £16,875, Other income £5,312

£	£	£	£
5,000 × 0% (savings)	5,312 × 20% (other)	Nil	1,062
6,587 × 20% (savings)	16,875 × 20% (savings)	1,317	3,375
11,587	22,187		
13,333 × 10% (dividends)		1,333	
24,920	22,187		
		2,650	4,437
Plus: Remittance basis charge		Nil	60,000
Income tax liability		2,650	64,437
Less: Tax deducted at source			
Dividends (£13,333 × 10%)		(1,333)	(Nil)
Bank interest (£16,875 × 20%)		(3,375)	(3,375)
Income tax payable/(repayable)		(2,058)	61,062

ANSWERS TO PRACTICE QUESTIONS: SECTION 2

Tutorial note

The overseas dividends are treated like UK dividends in that they are grossed up at 100/90 and have a deemed tax credit of 10%. This tax credit is not repayable, and should be deducted before the tax credit on the bank interest, which can be repaid.

If the dividends had foreign tax withheld, they would be grossed up for the foreign tax first, and then for the 10% notional credit. Double tax relief would then be available for the foreign tax in the normal way.

- Gloria should clearly not claim the remittance basis in 2017/18
- Note that the remittance basis claim is made on a year by year basis

Tutorial note

Note that even if Gloria had not been UK resident for 7 out of the last 9 years, it would not be beneficial for her to claim the remittance basis.

(ii) **Implications of future disposal of shares**

Capital gains tax

- **Individuals are subject to capital gains tax on worldwide assets if they are resident in the UK.**

- However, because Gloria is non-UK domiciled and the shares are situated abroad, the treatment of gains and losses on the disposal of overseas assets depends on whether Gloria's unremitted overseas income and gains in the tax year that the shares are sold exceed £2,000 as follows:

If unremitted overseas income and gains ≤ £2,000

– Only assessed on gains if proceeds are remitted to the UK
– Overseas losses will be allowable
– The annual exempt amount is available

If unremitted overseas income and gains ≤ £2,000

– Assessed on gains on all overseas disposals on an arising basis **unless** an election is made for the remittance basis to apply
– If the election is not made (i.e. arising basis applies)
  – all gains assessed
  – annual exempt amount available
  – overseas losses are allowable

- If the election is made (i.e. remittance basis applies)
  - only assessed to gains if proceeds are remitted into the UK
  - annual exempt amount is not available
  - overseas losses are not allowable unless a further election is made
  - the election will apply to both income and gains
  - Gloria cannot elect for it to apply to just one or the other

Tutorial note

The remittance basis election applies to both income and gains.

*As Gloria has been resident in the UK for 12 out of the last 14 tax years she will have to pay the remittance basis charge of £60,000 in any tax year where her unremitted income and gains exceed £2,000 **and** she claims the remittance basis.*

- Any tax suffered in Oceania in respect of the gain is available for offset against the UK capital gains tax liability arising on the shares.

Investment advice costs

In computing a capital gain or allowable loss, a deduction is available for the incidental costs of acquisition. However, to be allowable, such costs must be incurred wholly and exclusively for the purposes of acquiring the asset.

The fee paid to Eric related to general investment advice and not to the acquisition of the shares and therefore, would not be deductible in computing the gain.

Inheritance tax

For IHT, Gloria's domicile status is important in deciding how she will be taxed.

Assets situated abroad owned by non-UK domiciled individuals are excluded property for the purposes of inheritance tax.

However, Gloria will be deemed to be UK domiciled (for the purposes of inheritance tax only) if she has been resident in the UK for 17 out of the 20 tax years ending with the year in which the disposal occurs.

Gloria has been living in the UK since June 2002 and would therefore, appear to have been resident for 15 tax years (2002/03 to 2016/17 inclusive).

If Gloria is deemed to be UK domiciled such that the shares in Bubble Inc are not excluded property, business property relief will not be available because Bubble Inc is an investment company.

ANSWERS TO PRACTICE QUESTIONS: **SECTION 2**

7 ELLROY (ADAPTED) *Walk in the footsteps of a top tutor*

Key answer tips

This optional question is based on F6 level knowledge of opening year rules for sole traders, change of accounting date and the flat rate scheme for VAT.

You should know the opening year rules for assessment of trading profits, as these are still regularly tested in the P6 exam.

However, the flat rate scheme for VAT is a less mainstream area, and if you had forgotten the rules for this you would be advised not to choose this question in the exam!

The question also features change of accounting date calculations – which is a new topic for paper P6.

The highlighted words in the written sections are key phrases that markers are looking for.

(a) (i) **Difference in Ellroy's total tax liability depending on his choice of year end**

Tutor's top tips

You could potentially spend a very long time on this part of the question if you calculated the total income tax and NIC for three different tax years with two different year ends!

As Ellroy already has partnership profits of more than £165,000, you know that he must already be an additional rate taxpayer, and is above the upper limit for class 4 NICs.

This means that you just need to calculate the taxable profits for the new business for each tax year, then multiply the difference by 47% to calculate the extra tax/tax saving.

Remember that the basis of assessment rules are applied to the adjusted accounting profits.

The order to approach the calculation of taxable profits is as follows:

1 *Calculate trading profits for each accounting period (already given in the question for the March year end).*

2 *Deduct capital allowances for each accounting period (just the annual investment allowance for the accounting period in which the vans are purchased).*

3 *Apply the opening year rules to match the profits to the tax years.*

This answer shows the examiner's model answer, although there are alternative ways of presenting the answer – see the end of the answer for an alternative.

KAPLAN PUBLISHING

	2016/17 £	2017/18 £	2018/19 £
March year end:			
Six months ending 31 March 2017	13,100		
Year ending 31 March 2018 (£87,200 – £22,000)		65,200	
Year ending 31 March 2019			74,400
September year end:			
1 October 2016 to 5 April 2017 (£34,700 (W1) × 6/12)	17,350		
Year ending 30 September 2017 (W1)		34,700	
Year ending 30 September 2018 (W1)			80,800
Increase/(fall) in profit due to adopting a September year end	4,250	(30,500)	6,400
Income tax and class 4 national insurance contributions at 47%	1,997	(14,335)	3,008
Reduction in total tax liability over the three years			9,330

Tutorial note

The income tax and class 4 national insurance contributions on the change in the level of profits will be at 45% and 2% respectively due to the level of Ellroy's partnership income.

Working: Tax adjusted profits – 30 September year end

	£
Year ending 30 September 2017	
Adjusted trading profit:	
Six months ending 31 March 2017	13,100
Six months ending 30 September 2017 (£87,200 × 6/12)	43,600
Less: Capital allowances (AIA)	(22,000)
	34,700

	£
Year ending 30 September 2018	
Adjusted trading profit:	
Six months ending 31 March 2018 (£87,200 × 6/12)	43,600
Six months ending 30 September 2018 (£74,400 × 6/12)	37,200
	80,800

ANSWERS TO PRACTICE QUESTIONS: SECTION 2

Alternative calculation of reduction in total tax liability

	March year end £	Sept year end £
2016/17	13,100	17,350
2017/18	65,200	34,700
2018/19	74,400	80,800
	152,700	132,850

Reduction in assessable profits if Sept year end
(£152,700 – £132,850)   £19,850

Income tax and NIC saving @ 47%   £9,330

(ii) **The effect on Ellroy's total taxable profits of changing his year end**

Tutor's top tips

Even if you could not remember the rules on change of accounting date, you could have made a few sensible points to score some marks here.

Remember that overlap profits are dependent on the date chosen as the year end. If the year end is changed, we either create more, or use up existing, overlap profits.

*Under the current year basis we always try to tax the 12 month accounting period ended in the tax year. If we have a short accounting period ended in the tax year, as will happen here, we need to make this up to 12 months by taxing the **12 months** to the new accounting date.*

Remember to address the specific requirement and consider what will happen if profitability increases and is profitability decreases.

With a 31 March year end, Ellroy's basis period for the tax year 2019/20 will be the year ending 31 March 2020.

If Ellroy were to change his year end to 30 September and prepare accounts for the six months ending 30 September 2019, he would have a six-month trading period ending in the tax year 2019/20.

His basis period for 2019/20 would be the 12 months ending 30 September 2019, such that the profits for the six months ending 31 March 2019 would be taxed again in 2019/20 having already been taxed in 2018/19.

The profits taxed twice would be classified as overlap profits and would be relieved when the trade ceases or, potentially, on a future change of accounting date.

Accordingly, by changing his year end, in the tax year 2019/20 Ellroy would be taxed on the profits arising in the six months ending 31 March 2019 rather than those arising in the six months ending 31 March 2020.

If Ellroy's profits are rising, the change in accounting date will reduce his taxable profits for 2019/20.

If Ellroy's profits are falling, the change in accounting date will cause his taxable profits for 2019/20 to increase.

Ellroy would need to notify HM Revenue and Customs of the change in accounting date by 31 January 2021 in order for the change to be valid in 2019/20.

(b) **Maximum flat rate percentage**

Tutor's top tips

This is a tricky little section requiring application of your knowledge of the VAT flat rate scheme.

The key here is to work out the VAT currently paid by Ellroy, and then calculate this as a % of VAT inclusive turnover.

If the flat rate % is less than this, it would be beneficial for Ellroy to join the flat rate scheme. If it is more than this, then the scheme is not worthwhile.

The annual VAT payable by the business when calculated in the normal way is set out below.

	£
Output tax (£100,000 × 20%)	20,000
Input tax (£21,000 × 20%)	(4,200)
Payable to HMRC	15,800

Under the flat rate scheme a business continues to charge its customers output tax in the normal way but pays a fixed percentage of its VAT inclusive turnover to HMRC rather than calculating output tax minus input tax.

The VAT due under the flat rate scheme in respect of Ellroy's business would be £120,000 (£100,000 × 1.20) multiplied by the flat rate percentage.

The percentage necessary to result in VAT payable of £15,800 is 13.167% (£15,800/ £120,000).

Accordingly, the scheme will be financially beneficial if the flat rate percentage for Ellroy's business is no more than 13%.

Tutorial note

Flat rate scheme percentages increase in increments of either a half or a whole percentage point. Accordingly, the scheme would be financially beneficial if the relevant percentage is 13% but not if it is 13.5%.

ANSWERS TO PRACTICE QUESTIONS: SECTION 2

> **Examiner's comments**
>
> Part (a) concerned the various aspects of the trader's year end and was in two parts.
>
> Part (i) required calculations of the difference in the trader's tax liability depending on the year end adopted. This was not hard but it was not done particularly well. Many candidates failed to give the annual investment allowance on the vans and were also unable to apply the opening year rules to the facts of the question. In addition, many candidates would have benefited by thinking before they started calculating. The trader was an additional rate taxpayer so it was not necessary to prepare any income tax computations; it was merely necessary to calculate the difference in the taxable profits by reference to each of the two year ends and then to multiply by 47%.
>
> Part (ii) required explanations of the tax implications of a change of accounting date. This was the more difficult part of the question and was not done well. In particular, candidates needed to think rather than write in order to come up with sensible points to say but most were unable to explain the implications well.
>
> Part (b) concerned VAT and the flat rate scheme and was done reasonably well. Again, however, it required some thought in order to solve the problem and many candidates chose to write down everything they knew about the scheme, most of which did not earn marks, rather than trying to answer the question set.

ACCA marking scheme

				Marks
(a)	(i)	Taxable profits with a 31 March year end		2.0
		30 September year end		
		Tax adjusted profits for the trading periods		2.5
		Assessable profits		2.0
		Effect on total tax and national insurance liability		2.0
				8.5
			Maximum	8.0
	(ii)	Basis periods		1.5
		Profits taxed twice		2.0
		Effect on taxable profits		2.5
		Requirement to notify HMRC		1.0
				7.0
(b)		VAT payable in the normal way		1.5
		Basis of flat rate scheme		2.0
		Calculation of maximum percentage		2.0
		Conclusion		0.5
				6.0
			Maximum	5.0
Total				**20.0**

8 DANA Walk in the footsteps of a top tutor

Key answer tips

This question covers two unrelated issues: trading loss relief for a sole trader, and the capital tax implications of transferring an asset into a trust.

Most of the marks in the question are for explanations of the different ways in which a trading loss can be relieved. As Dana has only been in business for a few years it is necessary to first apply the opening year rules before considering the loss relief. The examiner does not want discussion of losses carried forward so this restricts the choices available. This part of the question tests F6 knowledge, showing how important it is to retain knowledge from the previous stage. As the loss available to be relieved is below £50,000, there is no need to consider the maximum cap on the amount of loss that can be offset in this question.

In part (b)(i) the capital gains implication of the gift of a property to a trust is not a problem provided you remember that gift relief is available for gifts of any type of asset (not just business assets) where there is an immediate charge to inheritance tax. As there is a chargeable lifetime transfer when putting an asset into a trust, gift relief is available for any asset put into a trust.

There are no inheritance tax calculations required in (b)(ii) but it is tricky to write enough to pick up all the marks.

The highlighted words in the written sections are key phrases that markers are looking for.

Tutor's top tips

The actual requirements at the end of the question only tell you how many marks are available for each section. The real requirements can be found in the information provided within the stem of the question.

(a) **Relief available in respect of trading loss**

Tutor's top tips

The examiner requires explanations supported by calculations. You need to plan carefully how to structure and present your answer.

Offsetting a loss in the most tax efficient manner means that you get the highest tax saving. Since the examiner has removed the option of carrying the loss forward you have two remaining loss options to consider.

1   *Offset against total income in the tax year of loss and/or the previous tax year. Once the loss has been offset against income it can then be extended to cover gains.*

ANSWERS TO PRACTICE QUESTIONS: SECTION 2

> 2   As the business has only recently started, opening year loss relief is available whereby a loss incurred in any of the first 4 tax years of trading can be carried back against total income of the preceding 3 years, on a FIFO basis.
>
> If there is sufficient loss it may be possible to use both options.
>
> Before you can consider relief for the trading loss you need to establish the:
>
> (a)   amount of the loss and which tax year(s) it falls into, and
>
> (b)   level of taxable income and gains for all the possible years of claim.
>
> Fortunately the examiner tells you to ignore national insurance contributions which removes one complication.
>
> Note also that as the loss is below £50,000, there is no cap on the loss relief.

A trading loss for tax purposes of £22,500 (W2) has arisen in the tax year 2016/17.

It can be relieved against Dana's total income of 2016/17, the year of the loss, and/or 2015/16.

Alternatively, because the loss has arisen in one of the first four tax years of trading, it can be relieved against Dana's total income of the three years prior to the year of the loss starting with the earliest year (i.e. 2013/14).

The income taxable at the higher rate in each of the tax years is set out below.

	2013/14 £	2014/15 £	2015/16 £	2016/17 £
Employment income (W1)	32,000	–	–	–
Trading income (W2)	–	4,500	6,000	–
Rental income	15,695	26,475	33,995	44,595
Less: Personal allowance	(10,600)	(10,600)	(10,600)	(10,600)
	37,095	20,375	29,395	33,995
Less: Basic rate band	(31,785)	(31,785)	(31,785)	(31,785)
Income taxable at the higher rate	5,310	Nil	Nil	2,210
Basic rate band remaining			(2,390)	
Taxable gains ((£310,000 – £250,000) – £11,100)			48,900	
Gains taxable at the higher rate			46,510	

> **Tutor's top tips**
>
> It is important that you work in the margins to calculate tax saving. You do not have time to set out numerous personal tax computations.
>
> The table above shows one method of quickly identifying income and gains taxed in the higher rate band and enables you to see where the loss will save most tax.

The claims against total income are all or nothing claims such that the trading loss will be offset in full in one of 2013/14 or 2015/16 or 2016/17, depending on which relief is claimed.

Because an opening year's claim would relieve the loss in full in 2013/14, it is not possible to relieve the loss in 2014/15.

The year with the most income taxable at the higher rate is 2013/14.

Relieving the loss of £22,500 in that year would save income tax as follows:

£		£
5,310	× 40%	2,124
17,190	× 20%	3,438
22,500		5,562

Relieving the loss in 2016/17 would clearly save less tax, as there is less income taxable at the higher rate in that year than there is in 2013/14.

There is no income taxable at the higher rate in 2015/16 but there are capital gains.

Relieving the loss against the total income in the basic rate band would allow an equivalent amount of capital gains to be taxed in the basic rate band rather than the higher rate band.

Accordingly, relieving the loss in 2015/16 would save tax as follows:

	£
Income tax (£22,500 × 20%)	4,500
Capital gains tax (£22,500 × (28% – 18%))	2,250
	6,750

The most beneficial claim is to relieve the loss in 2015/16 in order to save tax of £6,750.

Tutor's top tips

Your answer should include all the other possible reliefs with reasons for rejecting them.

Note that the question says that gift relief will be claimed in respect of the transfer of the property into the trust on 1 September 2016, therefore there is no chargeable gain in 2016/17 to consider.

The sale of the rental property however will give rise to a gain in 2015/16 and there are no capital gains tax reliefs available to defer this gain as the property is an investment asset.

Implications of the additional information provided by Dana:

- The bonus is in respect of work carried out by Dana for her employer. Accordingly, it is taxable in full in the year of receipt.
- The cost of travelling around the UK in 2014 would have been allowable had it been incurred after Dana began to trade. Accordingly, because it was incurred in the seven years prior to commencing to trade, it is treated as if it had been incurred on the first day of trading.

Tutor's top tips

The examiner wants you to include the implications of the additional information provided by Dana. Do not miss out on these two easy marks.

Tutorial note

Note that pre-trading expenditure incurred in the seven years prior to commencing trade is tax allowable provided it would be allowed if it were incurred whilst trading.

Do not confuse this rule with the recoverability of input VAT on pre-registration expenditure which only applies to services incurred in the six months prior to registration.

Workings

(W1) Employment income – 2013/14

	£
Salary for nine months (£40,000 × 9/12)	30,000
Bonus – taxable	2,000
	32,000

(W2) Trading income – opening year rules

	£
2014/15 (1 January 2015 to 5 April 2015) £13,500 (W3) × 3/9	4,500
2015/16 (1 January 2015 to 31 December 2015) £13,500 – £7,500 (£30,000 × 3/12)	6,000
2016/17 (year ended 30 September 2016) Loss (£30,000 – £7,500)	(22,500)

The trading loss of £7,500 deducted in arriving at the taxable profit for the tax year 2015/16 is excluded from the loss available for relief in respect of the tax year 2016/17.

Tutorial note

Remember that loss relief cannot be double counted. Where a loss is utilised in calculating a trading income assessment in an earlier year, that part of the loss must be excluded in the calculation of the trading income assessment in the following year.

(W3) Trading profit – nine months ended 30 September 2015

	£
Original figure per question	14,900
Less: Pre-trading expenditure	(1,400)
	13,500

(b) Transfer of the rental property to the trust – 1 September 2016

(i) Capital gains tax

Dana can claim gift relief in respect of the transfer of the property to the trustees because a lifetime transfer to any trust is a chargeable lifetime transfer subject to inheritance tax.

The gift relief election must be signed by Dana and submitted by 5 April 2021 (i.e. four years after the end of the tax year in which the gift was made).

Tutor's top tips

There are two marks available for capital gains tax. The points highlighted above are likely to be worth a half mark each.

Note that normally gift relief claims need to be signed by both the donor and donee. However, where an asset is put into a trust, only the donor needs to sign the claim.

(ii) Inheritance tax

Information required from Dana:

In respect of the transfer to the trust in December 2011

- The value of the property at the time of the gift.

  The gift in December 2011 is within the seven-year period prior to the gift on 1 September 2016, such that it will affect the nil rate band available in respect of the latter gift.

In respect of the gifts to family members

- Date, value, recipient and occasion of each gift.

  This information is required in order to determine whether the gifts to family members are exempt or not. This will affect the annual exemptions available in respect of each of the gifts to the trusts.

In addition to the annual exemption, the following lifetime gifts are exempt:

- Gifts of less than £250 in total to any individual in a tax year.
- Gifts of no more than £1,000, made on the occasion of a marriage or civil partnership.
- Regular gifts made out of income that do not affect Dana's standard of living.

ANSWERS TO PRACTICE QUESTIONS: SECTION 2

Tutorial note

Dana is unmarried and has no children. Accordingly, the exemption available for any gifts she makes on the occasion of marriage is a maximum of £1,000.

Examiner's comments

In part (a), the treatment of pre-trading expenditure was done well by only a minority of candidates. Other candidates either missed it out altogether or deducted it from the taxable profit for the tax year 2013/14 rather than the profit of the first trading period. The opening year rules and the treatment of the loss within those rules were done well by the majority of candidates. This was a significant improvement over the performance in recent exams.

Once the profits and losses had been determined, candidates needed to consider the reliefs available in respect of the loss. There were two aspects to this.

First, candidates needed to know all of the available reliefs for the losses. This was done very well by the vast majority of candidates.

Secondly, candidates needed to compare the different reliefs and then calculate the total tax relief obtained by the most efficient strategy. Performance of this second task was mixed with some candidates calmly and efficiently calculating the tax due before and after claiming relief in order to determine the tax saving, whilst others wrote about how to do it in general terms without actually doing it. This is perhaps a confidence issue; candidates should ensure that they have practised as many questions as possible prior to sitting the exam and, once in the exam, should have the self-belief to address the figures and come up with specific advice.

Part (b)(i) concerned the availability of gift relief on the transfer of a rental property to a trust and was not done particularly well.

The issue here was that gift relief would be available because the transfer was immediately subject to inheritance tax. This is true regardless of the nature of the asset, such that those candidates who focussed on whether or not the property was a business asset had missed the point. This was not too great a problem as there were only two marks available. However, a minority of candidates made things worse by ignoring the fact that this question part needed to be answered in approximately 3.5 minutes and wrote about gift relief at length, thus wasting time.

Part (b)(ii) concerned Dana's inheritance tax position. Those candidates who made a genuine attempt to answer the question here did well. The technical issues in this question were:

- the transfer of the rental property in December 2011 was a chargeable lifetime transfer, such that we needed a value for the property in order to determine the nil band available for the transfer in September 2016.

- the gifts of cash to family members were potentially exempt transfers, such that they would not affect the nil band whilst Dana is alive.

- the cash gifts may be exempt depending on the amount given, the date of the gift and the reason for the gift. Exempt gifts would not use Dana's annual exemptions, such that they may be available for relief against the transfer to the trust.

KAPLAN PUBLISHING

This question was different from past inheritance tax questions and required some thought before it could be answered. It was not technically difficult but required candidates to address the specific question; the minority of candidates who wrote about inheritance tax in general terms and ignored the specifics of the question did poorly, as did those who tried to calculate inheritance tax liabilities. Some candidates let themselves down by writing that they needed 'the details of the gifts' without specifying what those details were and why they needed them.

ACCA marking scheme

				Marks
(a)		Identification of years in which relief available		4.0
		Employment income		1.0
		Trading income		4.0
		Income taxable at the higher rate		4.0
		Capital gains taxable at the higher rate		1.5
		Tax savings		5.0
		Notes in respect of additional information		2.0
				21.5
			Maximum	18.0
				Marks
(b)	(i)	Capital gains tax		2.0
	(ii)	Inheritance tax		
		Gift in December 2011		1.5
		Gifts to family members		
		Information required		1.5
		Relevance of information		3.0
				6.0
			Maximum	5.0
Total				25.0

9 SPIKE *Walk in the footsteps of a top tutor*

Key answer tips

The question is divided into 3 unrelated parts.

Part (a)(i) requires a calculation of the trading loss using closing year rules as well as a calculation of the terminal loss.

In part (a)(ii), using the calculations from part (a)(i), you are required to explain the reliefs available for the losses **and** quantify the tax saving for each option.

Part (b)(i) requires an explanation of the income tax and capital gains tax implications of unapproved share options.

Part (b)(ii) is an easy part of the question involving a relocation payment to an employee.

The highlighted words in the written sections are key phrases that markers are looking for.

(a) (i) **Loss relief available on the cessation of the trade**

Tutor's top tips

There are two parts to this loss calculation. The first is calculating a loss on cessation using closing year rules and including overlap profits.

The second part is a calculation of the terminal loss. Don't forget that if part of the answer is a profit, the figure to include for the terminal loss is £Nil.

Trading loss – 2015/16

	£
Loss for the period from 1 January 2015 to 30 September 2015	13,500
Add: Overlap profits	8,300
Trading loss for the last tax year of assessment	21,800

Tutorial note

The basis period for the tax year 2015/16 runs from 1 January 2015 (the end of the basis period for the previous 'penultimate' year) until 30 September 2015 (the cessation of trade).

Terminal loss

	£	£
6 April 2015 to 30 September 2015:		
Loss (£13,500 × 6/9)		9,000
Add: Overlap profits		8,300
		17,300
1 October 2014 to 5 April 2015:		
1 October 2014 to 31 December 2014 profit (£22,500 × 3/12)	5,625	
1 January 2015 to 5 April 2015 loss (£13,500 × 3/9)	(4,500)	
Net profit ignored for the purposes of the terminal loss	1,125	Nil
Terminal loss		17,300

(ii) **The reliefs available in respect of the trading loss and the terminal loss**

Tutor's top tips

Make sure you consider the reliefs separately. Deal with the 'normal' loss calculated on cessation first. The loss can be offset against total income and gains of the current tax year and/or the previous tax year.

The key here was that Spike had some capital gains. The gains on the sale of the business are taxed at 10% as entrepreneurs' relief is available. The gain on the sale of the house may be exempt as it was Spike's principal private residence. However we are not told if he occupied throughout the entire period of ownership so some of the gain may be taxable at 28%.

Clearly it is more beneficial to offset any loss against the gains subject to 28% in priority to gains taxed at 10%.

Don't forget that if trading losses are to be offset against gains, they must be offset against total income first.

The terminal loss can be carried back against trading profits only of the previous three years on a LIFO basis.

Don't forget to discuss all options and quantify the saving. You will then be able to decide which option is the best one.

Note that carry forward is not an option as the trade has ceased!

Relief of the loss for the tax year 2015/16

The loss for the tax year 2015/16 can be offset against Spike's total income of 2015/16 and/or 2014/15.

Once the loss has been offset against the total income of a particular tax year, it can also be offset against the capital gains of that same year.

Spike has no income in the tax year 2015/16. But, a claim can be made for the whole of the loss to be relieved against his 2015/16 capital gains (a partial claim cannot be made).

Relieving the loss against the gains on the sale of the business assets would save capital gains tax at the rate of 10% due to the availability of entrepreneurs' relief. The tax saved would be £2,180 (£21,800 × 10%).

Spike's sale of his house will be an exempt disposal of his principal private residence if he has always occupied it, or is deemed to have always occupied it. If part of the gain on the house is taxable, capital gains tax will be payable at 28% because the gains on the business assets will have used the basic rate band. Accordingly, if this is the case, the loss should be offset against any gain on the house in priority to the gain on the business assets.

In the tax year 2014/15, the loss would be offset against the total income of £22,500. The claim cannot be restricted in order to obtain relief for the personal allowance (PA) of that year. Therefore the whole loss would be utilised, part of the PA would be wasted and the tax saved would be £2,380 ((£22,500 − £10,600) × 20%).

ANSWERS TO PRACTICE QUESTIONS: SECTION 2

Relief of the terminal loss

The terminal loss of £17,300 can be offset against the trading profit of the business for 2015/16 and the three preceding tax years, starting with the latest year.

The trading profit in the tax year 2015/16 is £Nil, such that all of the terminal loss will be relieved in the tax year 2014/15. This would utilise all of the terminal loss, part of the PA would be wasted and would save tax of £2,380 ((£22,500 − £10,600) × 20%).

The excess of the trading loss of 2015/16 over the terminal loss is £4,500 (£21,800 − £17,300). This amount is treated as a separate loss and can be offset against total income and capital gains in 2015/16 and 2014/15 as set out above.

However, there is no income in 2015/16 and once the terminal loss has been relieved in the tax year 2014/15, Spike's remaining total income of £5,200 (£22,500 − £17,300) is less than the personal allowance. Thus there is no taxable income and, therefore, no further tax saving to be achieved in either of the two relevant years.

Accordingly, the remaining £4,500 loss should be relieved against the capital gains of 2015/16. This would save tax of £450 (£4,500 × 10%) if the loss is relieved against the gains on the sale of the business, or £1,260 (£4,500 × 28%) if it is relieved against a non-exempt gain arising on the sale of the house.

Tutorial note

*It is important to remember that losses in the **last year** are carried back on a **LIFO** basis, and losses in the **first years** on a **FIFO** basis.*

If you incorrectly set the terminal loss against general income in 2012/13 on a FIFO basis, the tax saving would have been at 40% and you would have recommended the wrong option.

(b) (i) **The option to purchase ordinary shares in Set Ltd**

Tutor's top tips

This was a straightforward part of the question testing income tax and capital gains implications of a share option scheme that is not tax-advantaged. The examiner states in the question that the company does not have any tax-advantaged (approved) schemes.

There will be no tax liability in respect of the grant of the option.

When Spike exercises the option and acquires the shares, he will be subject to income tax on the excess of the market value of the shares at that time over the price paid for the option and the shares, i.e. £3.50 (£8.00 − £0.50 − £4.00) per share.

Accordingly, there will be an income tax liability of £9,800 (7,000 × £3.50 × 40%) when the option is exercised on the assumption that Spike continues to be a higher rate taxpayer.

On the sale of the shares, the excess of the sales proceeds per share over £8.00 (the market value of the shares when the option was exercised) will be taxed as a capital gain.

The capital gain, less the annual exempt amount, will be subject to capital gains tax at 28% on the assumption that Spike continues to be a higher rate taxpayer. Entrepreneurs' relief will not be available unless Spike has acquired more shares, such that he owns at least 5% of the company's share capital.

(ii) **The relocation payment**

Tutor's top tips

You may not have identified that the compensation payment was fully taxable but you should remember that up to £8,000 of relocation payments are a tax free benefit.

The compensation in respect of the sale of the house at short notice at a low price will be regarded as having been derived from employment, such that it will be taxable in full.

£8,000 of the payment in respect of the costs of moving house will be exempt; the remaining £3,500 (£11,500 – £8,000) of the payment will be taxable.

Examiner's comments

Part (a)(i) was short and direct; it was intended to ensure that all candidates attempting this question addressed the two possibilities that needed to be considered when they went on to part (ii) and had to explain the reliefs available in respect of the loss.

Very few candidates made a reasonable job of part (a)(i); the majority of candidates simply did not know the rules. Accordingly, many candidates simply did not appreciate the difference between the loss of the tax year and the terminal loss. Of those candidates who were aware that the terminal loss is calculated in its own particular way, very few knew how to do it. In addition, many candidates deducted the overlap profits from the loss rather than using them to increase the loss.

In part (ii) things did not really improve. Although many candidates were aware that there was the possibility of carrying back a loss on cessation to the three years prior to the loss, there was a lack of precision as regards the rules and a confused approach to the figures.

When dealing with losses, there are only really two things that need to be known: the years in which the losses can be offset and the type of income or gains that the losses can be offset against. Marks were available in part (ii) for knowing these fundamental rules but they were not awarded as frequently as one might have expected.

ANSWERS TO PRACTICE QUESTIONS: **SECTION 2**

> The approach of most candidates to part (ii) was not as measured or considered as was necessary. Candidates would have benefited from clearly defining the possibilities in their minds and then writing brief, precise points that addressed each of the possibilities. Instead, most candidates wrote too much that was confused and often contradictory. In addition, because they did not give themselves sufficient time to consider the possibilities, many candidates did not consider the possibility of relieving the capital gains. Those that did often did so in general terms as opposed to addressing the particular gains in the question.
>
> Part (b) was done reasonably well. There were many satisfactory answers to part (b)(i) but also many unsatisfactory ones. The candidates who did well tended to be those who were better organised and were methodical in their approach. In particular, the requirement listed the three matters to address: the grant, exercise and sale of the shares. Some candidates did not address all three of these matters, making it much more difficult to pass this part of the question.
>
> Part (ii) concerned the £8,000 exemption available in respect of relocation costs and was answered well.

ACCA marking scheme				
				Marks
(a)	(i)	Loss for the tax year 2015/16		1.0
		Terminal loss		3.0
				4.0
	(ii)	Relief of the loss for the tax year 2015/16		
		The reliefs available		2.0
		Tax savings – 2015/16		
		Business assets		1.5
		House		2.0
		Tax savings – 2014/15		1.0
		Relief of the terminal loss		
		The reliefs available		3.0
		Tax savings – terminal loss		1.0
		Tax savings – excess of trading loss over terminal loss		1.5
				12.0
			Maximum	10.0
(b)	(i)	Grant		1.0
		Exercise		2.0
		Sale of shares		2.0
				5.0
			Maximum	4.0
	(ii)	Relocation payment		2.0
Total				20.0

KAPLAN PUBLISHING

10 KANTAR *Walk in the footsteps of a top tutor*

Key answer tips

This multi-tax question covers IHT and CGT for lifetime disposals, sole trader loss reliefs, self-assessment payment dates, ethics and VAT registration. Much of this is F6 level material. It is very important to maintain your F6 level knowledge, as P6 questions often test brought forward knowledge.

Part (a) is a reasonably straightforward section on IHT and CGT for lifetime gifts. These two taxes are often tested together in the P6 exam, so it is important to learn the differences between them.

The use of trading losses, tested in part (b)(i) is a popular area that is often examined. Look out for the offset of losses against gains (from (a)(ii)). Even if you missed this, you should still have been able to score a pass by following through and summarising the tax savings that could be achieved.

Part (b)(ii) requires a payment schedule for payments on account and balancing payments. Despite being an F6 level topic, this is tricky, and requires some thought about the payments that would actually be due following the use of losses. You also had to recognise that POAs could be reduced.

Part (c) offers easy marks for a discussion of tax evasion, an area that has been tested several times before. This is a standalone section, and could be attempted before the other parts of the question.

Part (d) also offers easy marks for those who remember the rules seen at F6 for compulsory VAT registration, and also pre-registration input VAT.

The highlighted words in the written sections are key phrases that markers are looking for.

Tutor's top tips

The requirements at the end of the question serve only to highlight the number of marks available for each section. The real requirements are in the email from your manager.

Highlight the requirements as you come across them, and don't forget to keep looking back at them to make sure your answer is focused.

The requirement asks for 'notes for a meeting', with some brief explanations required. This means that you must keep narrative to a minimum and should write in very short sentences. Bullet points are ideal.

(a) (i) **NOTES FOR MEETING**

Tutor's top tips

The biggest challenge in part (a) is recognising which values apply for IHT and which for CGT. The value for IHT is based on the diminution in value of the donor's estate, whereas CGT treats a gift as a disposal at market value.

For CGT only, the cost is also required.

Inheritance tax

Small gifts exemption

The small gifts exemption is available where the total gifts to an individual in a tax year are no more than £250.

Accordingly, the exemption was not available in respect of the gifts to Kantar's nephews.

Potentially exempt transfer – 1 February 2016

	£
Value of the land prior to the gift	290,000
Value of the land after the gift	(170,000)
Diminution in value	120,000
Less: Annual exemption – 2015/16	(3,000)
– 2014/15 (£3,000 – (3 × £400))	(1,800)
Value of PET	115,200

(ii) **Capital gains tax liability – 2015/16**

Tutor's top tips

This part of the question deals with a part disposal followed by the sale of the remainder of the asset. Part disposals are an F6 level topic, but also appear in the P6 exam.

Remember that if part of an asset is sold, then only part of the cost can be deducted:

Cost × A/(A + B)

Where:

A is the value of the part sold (the proceeds), and
B is the value of the remainder.

When the remainder of the asset is sold, the remainder of the cost can be deducted.

	£	£
Gift on 1 February 2016 (part disposal)		
Proceeds at market value	100,000	
Less: Cost		
£200,000 × (£100,000/(£100,000 + £170,000))	(74,074)	
		25,926
Sale on 2 February 2016 (sale of remainder)		
Proceeds	170,000	
Less: Cost (£200,000 – £74,074)	(125,926)	
		44,074
Chargeable gains		70,000
Less: Annual exempt amount		(11,100)
Taxable gains		58,900
Capital gains tax (£58,900 × 28%)		16,492

Tutorial note

1 As both the part disposal and the sale of the remainder take place during 2015/16, you could take a shortcut and calculate the total chargeable gains as follows:

	£
Total proceeds (£100,000 + £170,000)	270,000
Less: Total cost	(200,000)
Total chargeable gains	70,000

You would still score full marks if you adopted this approach, as long as you explained your answer.

2 Rollover relief will not be available in respect of the chargeable gain on the sale of the land, as it is not a business asset.

(b) (i) **Budgeted trading loss – year ending 31 March 2017**

Tutor's top tips

Trading losses for sole traders are often tested in the exam, and you must learn the rules.

The question first asks for tax savings if the loss is relieved 'as soon as possible'. Think about all of the possible reliefs here: the loss can be set against total income for the current year and/or the previous year, but can also be set against gains for those years. You have just calculated some gains in part (a), so you need to consider setting the loss against these gains as well. Even if your figures are wrong, you will be given marks for following through.

If you missed the relief against gains, you would still score some marks if you carried the excess loss forward and set it against future trading profits.

ANSWERS TO PRACTICE QUESTIONS: SECTION 2

> *The income tax liabilities for each tax year are given in the question, so there is no point in recalculating these!*
>
> *Watch for the property income: the total income each year is the trading profit plus the property income. This will impact on the amount of loss used.*
>
> *Brief explanations are required, so your answer should have words as well as numbers.*

(1) **Loss relieved as soon as possible**

The loss would be offset against Kantar's general income of the tax year 2015/16. This would reduce his taxable income, and therefore his income tax liability, to nil. The tax saving would therefore be the whole of his liability for 2015/16 of £14,203.

The £50,000 restriction on the offset of trading losses only applies where losses are offset against income other than profits from the same trade. Accordingly, as only £5,000 of the loss is being offset against the property business income, the restriction would not apply to Kantar in the tax year 2015/16.

The loss remaining after the offset against general income could then be offset against Kantar's chargeable gains of 2015/16. Following the offset of the loss against his income, the whole of Kantar's basic rate band would be available when calculating the tax due on the unrelieved taxable gains. The capital gains tax saved would be £4,859 (below).

The total of income tax and capital gains tax saved would be £19,062 (£14,203 + £4,859).

	£
Chargeable gains (from (a)(ii))	70,000
Less: Loss relief (£68,000 − (£57,000 + £5,000))	(6,000)
	64,000
Less: Annual exempt amount	(11,100)
Taxable gains	52,900

Capital gains tax liability

£		
31,785	× 18%	5,721
21,115	× 28%	5,912
52,900		
		11,633
Capital gains tax with no loss relief (from (a)(ii))		16,492
Reduction in capital gains tax liability		4,859

KAPLAN PUBLISHING

Tutorial note

Alternative calculation at the margin:

	£
BRB available against gains – tax saving (£31,785 x (28% – 18%))	3,179
Loss relief against gains – tax saving (£6,000 x 28%)	1,680
	4,859

(2) **Loss carried forward for relief in the future**

Tutor's top tips

Remember that trading losses carried forward can only be offset against future trading profits from the same trade and not against any other income.

The loss would be offset against Kantar's trading income for 2017/18.

	Without loss relief £	With loss relief £
Expected trading profit y/e 31.3.18 (£83,000 + £4,000)	87,000	87,000
Less: Trading loss brought forward	–	(68,000)
	87,000	19,000
UK property business income	5,000	5,000
	92,000	24,000
Less: Personal allowance	(10,600)	(10,600)
Taxable income	81,400	13,400

Income tax

£	£			
31,785	13,400	× 20%	6,357	2,680
49,615	–	× 40%	19,846	
81,400	13,400		26,203	2,680

Tax saved in respect of the trading loss
(£26,203 – £2,680)   23,523

Carrying the loss forward would increase the amount of tax relief obtained. However, Kantar cannot be certain of the level of his future trading profits and carrying the loss forward would also delay the relief obtained.

(ii) **Future tax payments assuming the trading loss is carried forward**

Tutor's top tips

This section revises your F6 knowledge of payments on account (POAs) and balancing payments under self-assessment.

Remember that payments should be made as follows (ignoring NICs as stated in the requirement):

31 January during the tax year – first POA	50% x previous year's IT
31 July after the tax year – second POA	50% x previous year's IT
31 January after the tax year – balancing payment	balance of current year's IT + CGT

Your answer should make it clear which tax year the payments relate to, and the dates on which any payments are due. You are only asked to set out payments due after 1 January 2017.

As always, you will be given credit for following through with your figures.

	Notes	£
2015/16		
Balancing payment 31 January 2017		
Income tax (£14,203 – £8,827)	1	5,376
Capital gains tax (from (a)(ii))		16,492
		———
		21,868
		———
2016/17		
Payments on account:		
31 January 2017	2	Nil
31 July 2017		Nil
Balancing payment 31 January 2018		Nil
2017/18		
Payments on account:		
31 January 2018	3	Nil
31 July 2018		Nil
Balancing payment 31 January 2019 (from (b)(i)(2))		2,680

Notes:

1. Kantar will have made payments on account equal to his tax liability for 2014/15 (the previous tax year).

2. Kantar should apply to reduce his payments on account to nil as he does not expect to have a tax liability for the tax year 2016/17.

3. Kantar will not have to make any payments on account for the tax year 2017/18 as he will not have a tax liability for the tax year 2016/17.

(c) **Reporting of chargeable gains**

Tutor's top tips

Ethical issues appear in every P6 exam for roughly 4 – 5 marks. These can be very easy marks to obtain, and you could attempt this section before attempting parts (a) and (b).

However, there are only 4 marks available here, so you should not need to write more than four or five sentences to obtain full marks.

Any late payment of capital gains tax could result in interest and/or penalties being payable by Kantar.

Failure to disclose the chargeable gains could amount to the criminal offence of tax evasion. It may also be necessary to submit a report under the money laundering rules.

We cannot be associated with a client who has engaged in deliberate tax evasion, as this poses a threat to the fundamental principles of integrity and professional behaviour.

We should not continue to act for Kantar unless he agrees to disclose the chargeable gains to HM Revenue and Customs. If we ceased to act for Kantar, we would notify the tax authorities, although we would not provide them with any reason for our action.

(d) **Value added tax (VAT)**

Tutor's top tips

This section revises your F6 knowledge of VAT registration and pre-registration input VAT. Again, this section could be attempted before attempting parts (a) and (b) and offers easy marks to those who remember the rules.

Kantar must monitor his sales each month in order to identify when his taxable supplies for a 12-month period exceed £82,000 (the registration threshold). He must notify HM Revenue and Customs within 30 days of the end of the relevant 12 month period and will become registered from the end of the month following the 12 month period.

Once Kantar has registered, he will be able to recover input tax incurred:

– in the four years prior to registration in respect of goods he still owns; and

– in respect of services acquired by him in the six months prior to registering.

ANSWERS TO PRACTICE QUESTIONS: SECTION 2

Tutorial note

The recovery of input tax will reduce the expenses incurred by the business. It will also reduce the cost of the equipment purchased in the year ending 31 March 2017 for the purposes of capital allowances.

Examiner's comments

In part (a) both parts were answered reasonably well but it felt as though many candidates spent too much time on them. This may have been because it was the first question and thus time may not have appeared to be such a pressing issue. However, of course, any overruns on this part would still have caused candidates to run out of time later on in the exam.

Part (a) was only worth 8 marks in total and so should have been completed in less than 15 minutes, but some candidates found the time to explain the meaning of potentially exempt transfers, the manner in which they are taxed and the other exemptions that may be available rather than simply addressing the requirements of this particular question part.

Candidates will always benefit from answering the specific requirements of the question and from not digressing into other, irrelevant, areas.

In part (a)(i) candidates' knowledge was satisfactory. The only common error was the failure to identify the fall in value of the donor's estate as a result of the gift.

In part (a)(ii) the key issue here was the A/A+B calculation of the cost in respect of the first disposal. The majority of candidates knew that such a calculation was necessary but many did not know exactly how to perform it. In addition, a minority of candidates failed to recognise that the base cost of the whole of the land was its value at the time of the uncle's death.

Part (b)(i) was not tackled particularly well. Many candidates did not know the rules for the offset of trading losses well enough and were unable to determine an approach to answer the question efficiently. As always, it was necessary to think first and decide how to approach the question in order to prepare the required answer.

With trading losses there are two main things that candidates need to know; 1) what the losses can be offset against and 2) when. Many candidates did not possess this precise knowledge and others treated the individual taxpayer as a company or made other fundamental errors.

Many candidates also failed to make use of the information in the question. In particular, the tax liability for the tax year 2015/16 was given in the question but many candidates calculated it themselves, thus wasting time.

A final problem was that some candidates were unwilling to commit themselves to an answer, such that they described some of the issues but did not prepare calculations. This made it difficult for them to score particularly well.

In part (b)(ii) many candidates had an awareness of the rules but their knowledge was somewhat vague and confused, such that they were unable to apply it to the facts.

Some candidates tried to describe the system but this did not satisfy the requirement. Other candidates presented their answers in confusing ways without explaining which tax year and/or which payments they were referring to.

For a candidate who knew the rules, this part of the question was not particularly challenging, although it did require thought and care. Unfortunately, very few candidates had sufficient precise knowledge to produce an acceptable answer.

Part (c) was answered well by the majority of candidates. However, the problem here was that many candidates wrote far too much. There were only four marks available, so four decent sentences were sufficient, yet many candidates wrote the best part of a page. Candidates should think before they write and decide on the points they intend to make. They should then make each point concisely, and they should make it only once.

Answers to part (d) of the question were generally satisfactory. Candidates' knowledge of the rules regarding VAT registration was generally sound, although some candidates displayed a tendency to write generally rather than to address the specifics of the question. In addition, candidates need to take care to be precise in their use of language and terminology. The historic test relates to supplies in the 'previous 12 months', and not the sales of 'the trading period', and HMRC must be notified 'within 30 days' as opposed to 'within a month'. Candidates' knowledge of the rules regarding the recovery of pre-registration input tax was not as strong as that relating to registration but was still generally of an acceptable standard.

ACCA marking scheme				
				Marks
(a)	(i)	Small gifts exemption		1.5
		Potentially exempt transfer		2.5
				4.0
	(ii)	Chargeable gain in respect of the gift on 1 February 2016		2.0
		Chargeable gain in respect of the sale on 2 February 2016		1.0
		Capital gains tax liability		1.0
				4.0
(b)	(i)	Loss relieved as soon as possible		
		Income tax		1.0
		Capital gains tax		3.0
		Loss carried forward		
		Taxable incomes		2.5
		Tax liabilities and saving		2.0
		£50,000 restriction		1.0
		Evaluation		1.0
		Explanatory notes		1.5
				12.0
			Maximum	10.0
	(ii)	Payments required if loss carried forward		
		2015/16		2.5
		2016/17		1.5
		2017/18		2.0
				6.0
			Maximum	5.0

ANSWERS TO PRACTICE QUESTIONS: SECTION 2

		Marks
(c)	Implications for Kantar	2.0
	Fundamental principles	1.0
	Cease to act	2.5
		5.5
	Maximum	4.0
(d)	When registration required	2.0
	VAT incurred prior to registration	2.0
		4.0
	Format and presentation	1.0
	Analysis	1.0
	Quality of explanations	1.0
	Quality of calculations	1.0
		4.0
Total		**35.0**

11 PIQUET AND BURACO

Key answer tips

This question covers two areas of the syllabus: change of accounting date and residence, including the remittance basis. If you had not studied these two areas in detail you would struggle to gain a pass here, and would be advised not to choose this question.

Part (a) requires calculations of assessable profits following a change of accounting date, with explanations of the implications of choosing another date. These assessments are tricky, and require very good knowledge of the rules. There are easy marks for stating the date for notifying HMRC, and also the advantages of having a 30 April year end.

Part (b)(i) requires application of the new statutory residence tests. Although this is a technically challenging area, lots of help could be gained by looking at the tax rates and allowances at the front of the exam paper and applying to the scenario.

Part (b)(ii) offers 3 marks for the remittance basis rules, which have been tested several times before. The main pitfall here would be spending too long explaining all the rules, rather than just answering the question set.

The highlighted words in the written sections are key phrases that markers are looking for.

Tutor's top tips

This is really two separate, standalone questions. You could attempt parts (a) and (b) in whichever order you like, as long as you clearly label your answer.

(a) (i) **Accounting date changed to 28 February**

Tutor's top tips

The basis of assessment rules for sole traders are very important and are often tested in the P6 exam. You need to be confident in dealing with:

- *Opening years*
- *Change of accounting date*
- *Closing years*

Piquet must notify HM Revenue and Customs of the change by 31 January 2018 (31 January following the tax year in which the change is made).

Taxable trading profit

	£
2016/17	
16 months ending 28 February 2017	94,000
Less: Relief for overlap profits (£15,000 × 4/5)	(12,000)
	82,000
2017/18	
Year ended 28 February 2018	88,000

(ii) **30 April year end – Basis periods and overlap profits**

The basis period for the tax year 2016/17 will be the 12 months ended on the new accounting date in the tax year (i.e. the 12 months ended 30 April 2016).

This will create additional overlap profits, as the profits for the six months ended 31 October 2015 have already been subject to tax in the tax year 2015/16. The additional overlap profits will be £27,000 (6/12 × £54,000).

The basis period for the tax year 2017/18 will be the 12 months ending 30 April 2017.

Tutorial note

The level of overlap profit depends on the sole trader's accounting year end date, and will change if the accounting year end is changed.

The number of months' worth of overlap profit can be found by counting the number of months from the accounting year end to the end of the tax year (5 April).

Applying this to the dates in the question:

Year end:	No. of months of overlap
31 October	5
28 February	1
30 April	11

This means that if the year end is changed from 31 October to 28 February, the overlap profit must fall from 5 months' worth to 1 month worth (i.e. 4 months' worth will be used).

If the year end is changed from 31 October to 30 April, the overlap profit must increase from 5 months' worth to 11 months' worth (i.e. 6 months' worth of extra overlap will be created).

(iii) The advantages of a 30 April year end

Tutor's top tips

You are asked to identify and explain TWO advantages of using a 30 April year end, so try to make sure you do this.

Choice of year end for a sole trader is a popular planning area that you should be prepared to discuss.

Financial benefit

It would be financially advantageous for Piquet to have an accounting date earlier in the tax year (30 April) rather than later in the tax year (28 February) because the profits of his business are increasing.

The earlier year end date will result in an earlier period of profits, and therefore a lower amount of profits, being subject to tax.

For example, in the tax year 2017/18, the profit for the 12 months ending 30 April 2017 will be less than the profit for the 12 months ending 28 February 2018.

Time for tax planning

The nearer an accounting date is to the start of the tax year, the sooner the taxable profit for that tax year will be known. This means that there will be more time for plans to be made and carried out in relation to, for example, payments on account and pension contributions.

Cash flow benefit

The interval between earning profits and paying the tax on those profits is greater where the year end is earlier rather than later in the tax year.

For example, the payments of tax for the year ended 30 April 2018 are due on 31 January 2019 and 31 July 2019, whereas the payments for the year ended 28 February 2018 would be due a year earlier.

Tutorial note

Note that only two advantages were required.

Credit was also available to candidates who explained the effect of a trader's year end on the basis period in the tax year of cessation.

(b) (i) **Residence status – 2016/17**

Tutor's top tips

The requirement for this part of the question is very specific, and you will not be given credit for providing information that is not requested.

There are only two aspects of residency to discuss:

1   The automatic overseas residence tests (i.e. automatic non-UK residence tests)
2   The sufficient ties tests.

No credit was given for considering the automatic UK residence tests in detail as the question clearly states that these are not satisfied.

You must apply your knowledge to the scenario, and you will not score marks for writing about residency in general terms.

When considering the sufficient ties tests, you should discuss all possibilities. Buraco could either fall into the '91 – 120 days in the UK' bracket, or the '121 – 182 days in the UK' bracket.

Automatic overseas residence tests

Buraco will not satisfy any of the automatic overseas residence tests for the tax year 2016/17 because he will have been in the UK for 46 days or more in that tax year.

Tutorial note

The 90-day test does not apply to Buraco because he does not work full time overseas.

Residence status – 2016/17

Buraco was not UK resident for any of the three previous tax years, accordingly:

–   if he is in the UK for between 100 and 120 days, he will be resident if he has three or more of the four relevant UK ties; or

–   if he is in the UK for between 121 and 150 days, he will be resident if he has two or more UK ties.

Buraco does not satisfy the tie relating to work, as he does not work in the UK.

Buraco satisfies the close family tie and the accommodation tie, as he has a minor child in the UK and a house which he has stayed in during the year.

Accordingly, as he satisfies two of the ties, he will be UK resident if he is in the UK for more than 120 days.

If he is in the UK for less than 120 days, he will only be resident if he satisfies the final tie relating to time spent in the UK during either of the two previous tax years. This tie will be satisfied if Buraco spent more than 90 days in the UK during the tax year 2015/16.

(ii) **Tax implications of claiming the remittance basis**

Tutor's top tips

Make sure that you apply your knowledge to the scenario and set out the implications for Buraco. He has only been in the UK since 2015, so there will be no remittance basis charge.

There are just three marks available, so you should try to have three separate points in your answer.

If Buraco claims the remittance basis in 2016/17, he will only be subject to UK tax on his overseas income and overseas chargeable gains remitted to the UK.

However, Buraco would not be entitled to the income tax personal allowance or the capital gains tax annual exempt amount.

There would not be a remittance basis charge because Buraco was not resident in the UK for seven of the nine tax years prior to 2016/17.

Examiner's comments

The calculations in parts (a)(i) and (ii) would have been straight forward for those candidates who knew the rules and had practised applying them. Unfortunately, most candidates who attempted this question did not know the rules, such that very few scored well on these parts of the question.

In part (a)(iii) many candidates were able to identify one advantage but few were able to come up with two. This was disappointing as the choice of year end is a basic aspect of tax planning for the unincorporated trader and one that candidates should be confident of.

Candidates should recognise that change of accounting date is not part of the Paper F6 (UK) syllabus and must therefore be regarded as an area that will be examined regularly in future Paper P6 (UK) exams.

In part (b)(i) candidates' appeared to be well-prepared for a question on this area of the syllabus with good levels of knowledge.

However, it was important for candidates to realise that this was a question that required their knowledge to be applied to the specific facts and that it was not enough to simply set down everything they knew on the topic. For example, candidates should have realised that, depending on the number of days spent in the UK (which was left imprecise in the question) the relevant number of ties was either two or three. Then, it was not sufficient to list the ties, it was necessary to state whether or not they were met by the individual concerned. It was then good exam technique to draw the various aspects of the explanation together into a form of summary or conclusion.

The other common mistake made by candidates when answering this question was to include irrelevant information in their answers. A significant number of candidates explained the automatic UK residency tests despite the wording of the requirement. Such explanations would not have scored any marks as they were irrelevant to the requirement and thus such candidates put themselves under unnecessary time pressure as a result.

PAPER P6: ADVANCED TAXATION (FA2015)

> Part (b)(ii), the final part of the question, concerned the remittance basis. This was answered well by many candidates. There were only two matters to note here. Firstly, some candidates' knowledge of the rules governing the remittance basis charge was somewhat imprecise. Secondly, a minority of candidates set out the rules but did not apply them to the individual concerned.

		ACCA marking scheme		Marks
(a)	(i)	Date		1.0
		Calculations		2.0
				3.0
	(ii)	Basis periods		1.5
		Overlap profits		1.5
				3.0
	(iii)	Identification of issue – one mark each		2.0
		Explanation of issue – one mark each		2.0
				4.0
(b)	(i)	Automatic overseas residence tests		1.0
		Days and ties		2.5
		Work, family and accommodation ties		3.0
		90 days tie		1.5
		Conclusion		1.0
				9.0
			Maximum	7.0
	(ii)	UK tax on overseas income and gains		1.0
		Personal allowance and annual exempt amount		1.0
		No remittance basis charge		2.0
				4.0
			Maximum	3.0
Total				**20.0**

CHANGING BUSINESS SCENARIOS

12 THE STILETTO PARTNERSHIP (ADAPTED)

>
>
> **Key answer tips**
>
> This question is really two separate questions.
>
> The first part is about incorporation of a partnership, but this time deals with the income tax and national insurance implications instead of the more common CGT implications.
>
> This section is really just asking you to look at the effect of delaying cessation of trade until the following tax year, and tests your basic F6 knowledge of closing year assessments. There is a slight twist in that Clint was born in 1948 – you need to think about how this will impact on his NICs.
>
> The second part is a written section on various overseas aspects of tax for companies and individuals. Overseas aspects of tax are very popular in P6, so you must make sure you learn the rules.
>
> There were 2 easy marks available here for structuring your answer as a report.

(a) (i) **Clint's assessable trading income**

Selling the business on 30 April 2016 rather than 28 February 2016 would mean that the final year of trading would be 2016/17 rather than 2015/16.

Clint's taxable trading income under each of the alternative cessation dates is as follows:

	2015/16 £	2016/17 £
Sale of business on 28 February (W)	53,723	–
Sale of business on 30 April (W)	35,708	24,935

(ii) **The implications of delaying the sale of the business**

The implications of delaying the sale of the business until 30 April would have been as follows:

- Clint would have received an additional two months of profits amounting to £6,920 (£20,760 × 1/3)

- Clint's trading income in 2015/16 would have been reduced by £18,015 (£53,723 – £35,708), all of which would have been subject to income tax at 40%. His additional trading income in 2016/17 of £24,935 would all have been taxed at 20%.

- Clint's class 4 national insurance contributions would be unaffected. Clint is not liable to class 4 national insurance contribuions in 2015/16 or 2016/17 as he is over 65 at the start of the tax year.

- Changing the date on which the business was sold would have had no effect on Clint's class 2 liability as he has not been required to make class 2 contributions since reaching the age of 65.

Working: Trading income assessments

Cessation on 28 February 2016

Business ceases in 2015/16.

Penultimate year is 2014/15 and would have assessed y/e 30 June 2014 profits.

Final assessment in 2015/16 therefore assesses profits from 1 July 2014 to the date of cessation, less overlap profits.

2015/16	Total £		Clint's share £
Year ended 30 June 2015	107,124		
1 July 2015 to 28 February 2016	96,795		
	203,919	× 1/3	67,973
Less: Overlap profits			(14,250)
Trading income assessment			53,723

Cessation on 30 April 2016

Business ceases in 2016/17

Penultimate year is 2015/16 and would assess y/e 30 June 2015 profits.

Final assessment in 2016/17 will assess profits from 1 July 2015 to the date of cessation, less overlap profits.

2015/16	Total £		Clint's share £
Year ended 30 June 2015	107,124	× 1/3	35,708
2016/17			
1 July 2015 to 28 February 2016	96,795		
1 March to 30 April 2016	20,760		
	117,555	× 1/3	39,185
Less: Overlap profits			(14,250)
Trading income assessment			24,935

(b) **Report to the management of Razor Ltd**

To The management of Razor Ltd
From Tax advisers
Date 6 June 2016
Subject The proposed activities of Cutlass Inc

(i) **Rate of tax on profits of Cutlass Inc**

When considering the manner in which the profits of Cutlass Inc will be taxed it must be recognised that the system of corporation tax in Sharpenia is the same as that in the UK.

The profits of Cutlass Inc will be subject to corporation tax in the country in which it is resident or where it has a permanent establishment. It is desirable for the profits of Cutlass Inc to be taxed in the UK rather than in Sharpenia as the rate of corporation tax in the UK on annual profits of £120,000 will be 20% whereas in Sharpenia the rate of tax would be 38%.

Residency of Cutlass Inc

Cutlass Inc will be resident in Sharpenia, because it is incorporated there. However, it will also be resident in the UK if it is centrally managed and controlled from the UK. For this to be the case, Amy and Ben should hold the company's board meetings in the UK.

Under the double tax treaty between the UK and Sharpenia, a company resident in both countries is treated as being resident in the country where it is effectively managed and controlled. For Cutlass Inc to be treated as UK resident under the treaty, Amy and Ben would need to ensure that all key management and commercial decisions are made in the UK and not in Sharpenia.

Permanent establishment

A permanent establishment is a fixed place of business, including an office, factory or workshop, through which the business of an enterprise is carried on. A permanent establishment will also exist in a country if contracts in the company's name are habitually concluded there.

The trading profits of Cutlass Inc will normally be taxable in Sharpenia if they are derived from a permanent establishment in Sharpenia even if it can be established that Cutlass Inc is UK resident under the double tax treaty.

Double taxation

If Cutlass Inc is UK resident but has a permanent establishment in Sharpenia, its trading profits will be subject to corporation tax in both the UK and Sharpenia with double tax relief available in the UK. The double tax relief will be the lower of the UK tax and the Sharpenian tax on the trading profits. Accordingly, as the rate of tax is higher in Sharpenia than it is in the UK, there will be no UK tax to pay on the company's trading profits and the rate of tax on the profits would be the rate in Sharpenia (i.e. 38%).

Alternatively, Cutlass Inc could make an election for the profits from the overseas permanent establishment to be exempt in the UK. However, this would not affect the tax position as the double tax relief means that there is no tax to pay in the UK in any case (as explained above). Again, the rate of tax on the profits would be the rate in Sharpenia (i.e. 38%).

If Cutlass Inc is UK resident and does **not** have a permanent establishment in Sharpenia, its profits will be taxable in the UK at the rate of 20% and not in Sharpenia.

(ii) **Value added tax (VAT)**

Goods exported to Sharpenia are zero rated. Razor Ltd must retain appropriate documentary evidence that the export has taken place.

Razor Ltd must account for VAT on the value of the goods purchased from Cutlass Inc at the time the goods are brought into the UK. The VAT payable should be included as deductible input tax on the company's VAT return.

(iii) **Amy's UK income tax position**

Amy will remain UK resident as she will still spend at least 183 days in the UK each tax year.

Accordingly, she will continue to be subject to UK tax on her worldwide income including her earnings in respect of the duties she performs for Cutlass Inc. The earnings from these duties will also be taxable in Sharpenia as the income arises in that country.

The double tax treaty between the UK and Sharpenia will either exempt the employment income in one of the two countries or give double tax relief for the tax paid in Sharpenia. The double tax relief will be the lower of the UK tax and the Sharpenian tax on the income from Cutlass Inc.

Amy will not be subject to UK income tax on the expenses borne by Cutlass Inc in respect of her flights to and from Sharpenia provided her journeys are wholly and exclusively for the purposes of performing her duties in Sharpenia.

The amounts paid by Cutlass Inc in respect of Amy's family travelling to Sharpenia will be subject to UK income tax as Amy will not be absent from the UK for a continuous period of at least 60 days.

Key answer tips

You should use headings in your report, particularly in part (i), to make it easier for the marker to follow. You must also make sure that you apply your knowledge to the scenario, which you can show by using the names of the people and companies involved in your answer. If you just write out the rules you will not score many marks.

ANSWERS TO PRACTICE QUESTIONS: SECTION 2

13 DESIREE (ADAPTED) *Walk in the footsteps of a top tutor*

Key answer tips

This question covers the familiar scenario of sole trader versus company, with some easy marks on voluntary VAT registration.

Part (a) requires calculation of taxable profits or losses for the first three periods, and was almost identical to a requirement set in one of the compulsory questions in a previous exam.

Part (a)(ii) requires discussion of the use of losses for a sole trader compared to a company. This is a typical textbook scenario with no tricks, and you should score well here as long as you have learnt the rules.

Part (b) requires discussion of voluntary VAT registration – an F6 topic, but one which most students are likely to be happy with. There are also marks for discussing imports – a popular P6 topic. The danger here is not applying the discussion to the specific scenario.

The highlighted words in the written sections are key phrases that markers are looking for.

(a) (i) **Taxable profit/allowable loss for each of the first three taxable periods**

Tutor's top tips

Think carefully before attempting this section.

If the business is unincorporated, the losses must be matched to tax years before reliefs can be claimed.

However, if the business is set up as a company, the loss reliefs will be for chargeable accounting periods, so no further adjustments will be needed.

Make sure that your answer is clearly labelled!

KAPLAN PUBLISHING

Business is unincorporated

	Loss £	Assessable profit £
2016/17 – Actual basis (1 September 2016 to 5 April 2017) (£46,000 × 7/10)	(32,200)	Nil
2017/18 – First 12 months (1 September 2016 to 31 August 2017)		
1 September 2016 to 30 June 2017 – Loss	(46,000)	
Loss allocated to 2016/17	32,200	
1 July 2017 to 31 August 2017 – Profit (£22,000 × 2/12)	3,667	
	(10,133)	Nil
2018/19 – Current year basis (Year ending 30 June 2018)		22,000

Tutorial note

Remember that when you apply the opening year rules to losses there is no overlap!

Losses can only be relieved once, and if they are matched with two tax years in the assessments, they must be removed from the later year.

Business is operated via a company

	Loss £	Assessable profit £
Ten months ending 30 June 2017	(46,000)	Nil
Year ending 30 June 2018		22,000
Year ending 30 June 2019		64,000

(ii) **Advice on whether or not the business should be incorporated**

Tutor's top tips

You must learn the loss reliefs available to individuals and companies, as these often feature in exam questions.

Don't write about all the loss reliefs available; just pick the ones that are relevant. For example, in this question, there is no point in talking about reliefs on cessation of trade.

When writing about loss reliefs, make sure that you use very specific language. For example, don't just say 'losses can be carried forward'; say that 'losses can be carried forward against the first available future trading profits from the same trade'.

You must also apply the reliefs to the scenario.

The two key considerations for both the unincorporated business and the company are:

- *Amount of tax saved, and*
- *Timing of the relief.*

There is no point in preparing full computations of the tax saved, as the question states that detailed calculations are not required.

Business is operated via a company

If the business is operated via a company, the loss of the ten month period ending 30 June 2017 will be carried forward for offset against future trading profits of the same trade.

The earliest that any of the company's losses will be relieved is the year ending 30 June 2018 thus reducing the corporation tax payable on 1 April 2019.

However, the tax savings will only arise if the budgeted profits are achieved. If the business does not achieve profitability the losses will be wasted.

Business is unincorporated

If the business is unincorporated, the loss in each of the two tax years can be offset against:

- The total income of the year of loss and/or the previous year
- The total income of the three years prior to the year of loss starting with the earliest of the three years.

This enables Desiree to obtain immediate relief for the losses.

Desiree has employment income in 2016/17 of only £10,000 (£60,000 × 2/12) together with bank interest of less than £1,000. Most of this income will be covered by her personal allowance.

Her total income in earlier years is her salary of £60,000 and the bank interest. Accordingly, she should offset the losses against the income of 2015/16 and earlier years rather than the income of 2016/17.

The loss of 2016/17 could be offset against the total income of 2015/16 (the previous year) or 2013/14 (the first of the three years prior to 2016/17).

The loss of 2017/18 could be offset against the total income of 2014/15 (the first of the three years prior to 2017/18).

This will obtain full relief for the losses at a mixture of basic and higher rates of tax.

Conclusion

Desiree's primary objective is the most beneficial use of the loss.

She should therefore run the business as an unincorporated sole trader in order to obtain relief for the losses as soon as possible.

Tutor's top tips

Make sure that you state your conclusion. As long as it is consistent with your analysis, you will be given credit.

There is no loss relief cap for the relief as the trading loss is less than £50,000.

(b) **Financial advantages and disadvantages of Desiree registering voluntarily for VAT**

Tutor's top tips

This section of the question is mainly based on F6 knowledge and is very straightforward.

You could attempt this part of the question first, just in case you run out of time on part (a).

Advantages

- Registering for VAT will enable the business to recover input tax, where possible, on expenses and capital expenditure.

  This will reduce the costs incurred by the business thus reducing its losses and its capital allowances.

- The VAT incurred on the fees paid to the market research consultants in March 2016 can be recovered as pre-registration input tax.

  The payment in November 2015 is more than six months prior to registration and therefore the input tax in relation to it cannot be recovered.

Disadvantages

- The business will have to charge its customers VAT at 20%.

  This will represent an increase in the prices charged to those customers who are unable to recover VAT (i.e. domestic customers and non-registered business customers).

  Desiree may need to consider reducing prices in order to reduce the impact of the additional VAT on these customers.

Treatment of non-EU imports

- VAT will be payable by Desiree at the place of importation.
- If the goods are kept in a bonded warehouse or free zone, then the payment of VAT is delayed until they are removed from the warehouse/zone.
- Desiree can then reclaim the VAT as input tax on the VAT return for the period during which the goods were imported.

> **Examiner's comments**
>
> Part (a)(i) required candidates to calculate the taxable trading profit or allowable trading loss depending on whether the business vehicle was a company or an unincorporated business. The majority of candidates scored high marks here although some had difficulty calculating the figure for the second tax year of an unincorporated business based on the first 12 months of trading. Those who did not do so well simply did not know the basic mechanical rules and either missed out this part of the question or tried to make it up. The opening and closing years rules for unincorporated traders are examined regularly and candidates preparing for future sittings are likely to benefit from being able to handle them.
>
> Part (a)(ii) required candidates to provide a 'thorough and detailed explanation' of the manner in which the losses could be used depending on the choice of business vehicle. This part of the question was done well by almost all of the candidates who attempted it. In order to maximise marks here it was necessary to be precise in terms of language used. For example, it was not sufficient to state that losses can be carried forward against future profits. Instead, candidates needed to state that losses could be carried forward for offset against future profits of *the same trade*.
>
> There was also a requirement to state which business structure would best satisfy the client's objectives. The mark available for this was missed by those candidates who had stopped thinking and were simply writing down everything they knew about loss relief.
>
> The other difficulty which candidates had with this part of the question was a failure to recognise that not all possible loss reliefs were available due to the particular facts of the question. Candidates should ensure that they do not write at length about matters which are irrelevant.
>
> The final part of the question concerned the 'financial' advantages and disadvantages of registering voluntarily for VAT. Many candidates let themselves down by not reading the question carefully such that they simply listed all the advantages and disadvantages they could think of without focusing on the word financial or the particular facts surrounding the client. This meant that they missed the possibility of recovering pre-registration VAT, which was often the difference between an OK mark and a good mark.

ACCA marking scheme			
			Marks
(a)	(i)	Business is unincorporated	
		Application of opening year rules	2.5
		Losses counted once only	1.0
		Business is operated via a company	1.0
			4.5
		Maximum	4.0
	(ii)	Business is operated via a company	2.5
		Business is unincorporated	
		Reliefs available	2.5
		Application to Desiree's position	3.0
		Conclusion	1.0
			9.0
(b)		Advantages	
		Recovery of input tax	1.5
		Pre-registration input tax	1.5
		Disadvantages	1.5
		VAT treatment of non-EU imports	3.0
			7.5
		Maximum	7.0
Total			**20.0**

14 VINE (ADAPTED) *Walk in the footsteps of a top tutor*

Key answer tips

This question mainly covers incorporation, a popular exam scenario.

Part (a) covers capital allowances, and is very straightforward.

Part (b) deals with the disposal of shares after incorporation, and requires calculation of the gain at incorporation first. This section is very similar to the first part of question 3 of the pilot paper.

Part (c) covers the tax implications of company bicycles, child care vouchers and free breakfasts. These are not areas that are tested regularly, but are only worth four marks.

The highlighted words in the written sections are key phrases that markers are looking for.

(a) **Capital allowances**

The transfer of the equipment to Passata Ltd

The market value of the equipment exceeds its tax written down value such that a sale would normally result in additional taxable income for Vine in the form of a balancing charge.

However, because Vine and Passata Ltd will be connected persons (Vine will control Passata Ltd), an election is available to transfer the equipment at the opening tax written down value, rather than market value, such that no balancing charge will arise.

Tutorial note

To be eligible to transfer assets at TWDV (tax written down value), the owner of the business must be 'connected' to the new company, which means that they must control the shares in the new company.

A claim must be made for this treatment within two years of the incorporation.

The false ceiling to be installed in the supermarket premises

For the purposes of capital allowances, the meaning of the term machinery is taken to be its ordinary, everyday meaning. The meaning of the term plant has been considered in many cases and certain items are dealt with by statute.

Case law tends to draw a distinction between items that perform a function in the operation of the business, and may therefore be plant, and those which comprise the setting in which the business is carried on, which are not plant.

It has been held that a false ceiling does not perform a function but is merely part of the setting in which the business is carried on. Accordingly, the false ceiling will not qualify as plant and machinery.

Tutorial note

You are not expected to know details of specific tax cases in the exam, but you are expected to be aware of some of the key decisions made.

Even if you had not come across false ceilings before, you could have scored the marks here by applying basic tax principles.

(b) **The proposed sale of the shares to the store manager**

Tutor's top tips

Before calculating the chargeable gain on the sale of the shares, you need to work out the base cost of the shares.

The base cost of the shares will be the market value of the assets exchanged for shares, less any gains deferred on incorporation.

The gains deferred on incorporation will be the total net chargeable gains arising multiplied by the value of shares acquired, then divided by the total value of the consideration received.

You need to approach the calculations in the following order:

1   *Calculate the net chargeable gains on the incorporation of the business.*

2   *Calculate the gains deferred (i.e. the incorporation relief).*

    This is tricky – the question states that the consideration will be a mixture of shares and cash/loans, such that there is no capital gains tax liability.

    A gain equal to the capital losses plus the annual exempt amount should therefore remain chargeable, and the rest will be deferred.

3   *Once the deferred gain has been calculated, the value of the shares can be calculated from the following formula:*

    Incorporation relief = Net chargeable gains × (Value of shares ÷ total value)

4   *The final step is to deduct the incorporation relief from the value of the shares, to give the CGT base cost of the shares.*

Chargeable gain on the disposal of shares

	£
Proceeds	64,000
Less: Cost (20% × £187,614 (W1))	(37,523)
Chargeable gain	26,477

Tutor's top tips

Even if you did not manage to correctly calculate the base cost of the shares, you will score marks for consistency here!

Entrepreneurs' relief

Entrepreneurs' relief would reduce the tax rate on the gain to 10%.

However, it is only available if the shares have been owned for at least a year.

Accordingly, Vine should delay the sale until August in order to qualify for the relief.

Tutor's top tips

There is a clue in the question that entrepreneurs' relief is not currently available: the examiner asks you to suggest a minor change that would reduce the chargeable gain.

The timing of a sale is often relevant for CGT, and may affect the availability of reliefs, annual exemption, and also the payment date.

Workings

(W1) Base cost of the shares

	£
Value of the business transferred	320,000
Amount left on loan account (W2)	(70,886)
Market value of the shares received	249,114
Less: Incorporation relief (W3)	(61,500)
Base cost of shares	187,614

(W2) Loan account

	£
Value of the business transferred	320,000
Market value of shares received (W3)	(249,114)
Loan account required	70,886

(W3) Incorporation relief

	£
Gains on assets transferred:	
Premises (£260,000 – £205,000)	55,000
Goodwill	24,000
Total net chargeable gains	79,000
Less: Capital loss available	(6,400)
Annual exempt amount	(11,100)
Incorporation relief	61,500

Therefore to calculate the market value of the shares to be received to achieve incorporation relief of £61,500:

Incorporation relief

= Total net chargeable gains × (MV of shares ÷ MV of business)

£61,500 = £79,000 × (MV of shares ÷ £320,000)

MV of shares = £249,114

Tutorial note

Entrepreneurs' relief is not relevant on the incorporation of the business as Vine will not have owned the business for at least one year.

(c) **The tax implications of the active supermarket marketing strategy**

>
>
> *Tutor's top tips*
>
> Some of the benefits covered here are rather obscure, and have not been tested in the past.
>
> However, even if you did not know the rules, you could still score some marks by applying basic principles:
>
> - bicycles are plant and machinery, so would qualify for capital allowances
> - staff costs are generally allowable deductions for the employer
> - there is a tax free mileage allowance for bicycles just like there is for cars.

Passata Ltd

The cost of the bicycles will qualify for capital allowances.

The mileage allowance paid to employees, the cost of the child care vouchers and the cost of the breakfasts will be tax allowable expenses.

Employees

Bicycles

The loan of the bicycles will not give rise to a taxable benefit provided they are used mainly for travel to and from work and for business purposes.

Mileage allowance

A tax-free mileage allowance of up to 20 pence per mile can be paid to employees who use their own bicycles for business purposes.

The employees of Passata Ltd will be entitled to a tax deduction from their employment income if the company pays them less than this amount.

Accordingly, with the mileage rate set at 15 pence per mile, they will be entitled to a tax deduction of 5 pence per business mile cycled.

Child care vouchers

The child care vouchers are less than £55 per week, so will be tax free for any employees who are basic rate taxpayers.

However, higher rate taxpayers are only entitled to £28 per week tax free and thus would be taxed on a benefit of £12 (£40 – £28) per week.

The tax free allowance for additional rate taxpayers is lower still at £25 per week, so any employees in this category would have a taxable benefit of £15 (£40 – £25) per week.

Breakfasts

The provision of free breakfasts gives rise to a taxable benefit equal to the cost of the breakfast.

ANSWERS TO PRACTICE QUESTIONS: SECTION 2

Examiner's comments

Part (a) concerned the capital allowances implications of incorporating the business and the allowances available in respect of a false ceiling to be installed in a supermarket. It was not done particularly well. Many candidates thought that on incorporation the assets would be transferred to the company at tax written down value whereas the correct position is that a balancing charge would arise unless a succession election were entered into. A number of candidates wrote that a balancing charge or a balancing allowance would arise when it was clear from the facts that it would be a balancing charge.

Part (b) required candidates to prepare calculations in order to determine the base cost of the shares received on incorporation and the subsequent gain on the sale of some of the shares. Common errors here included calculating a capital loss on the equipment (not available due to the availability of capital allowances) and giving entrepreneurs' relief on the incorporation (not available as the business had not been owned for a year). The quality of the answers to this part of the question depended on the clarity of the candidates' knowledge. There were many candidates who knew how to perform the necessary calculations and whose only common error was the failure to deduct the gain relieved on incorporation from the base cost of the shares. There was then another group of candidates who had no clear knowledge of the rules and consequently did not score well.

Candidates were asked to suggest a minor change in relation to the sale of shares that would reduce the chargeable gain. Suggestions needed to be sensible and commercial and not, as put forward by a number of candidates, 'reduce the selling price of the shares'.

The final part of the question concerned the provision of bicycles and other related benefits to employees.

Candidates were asked to outline the tax implications for the company and its employees of the various benefits. There were four benefits, so all answers should have consisted of eight brief elements. Unfortunately, most answers were not that well organised with candidates addressing the issues in what was often a haphazard manner such that they did not score as well as they could have done.

KAPLAN PUBLISHING

ACCA marking scheme		
		Marks
(a)	Transfer of the equipment	2.5
	False ceiling	2.0
		4.5
	Maximum	4.0
(b)	Incorporation:	
	Gains arising	2.0
	Calculation of the loan account	3.0
	Gain on the sale of the shares	2.0
	Entrepreneurs' relief	2.0
		9.0
(c)	Passata Ltd	2.0
	Employees	
	Use of bicycles	1.0
	Mileage allowance	1.5
	Child care vouchers	2.0
	Free breakfasts	1.0
		7.5
	Maximum	7.0
Total		20.0

15 FAURE *Walk in the footsteps of a top tutor*

Key answer tips

This question covers two different areas: choice of year end for a sole trader business, and employee versus partner.

Part (a) requires explanation of how choice of year end will affect taxable profits. This is tricky unless you have a good knowledge of the opening year rules for sole traders.

Part (b) requires discussion of taking on a spouse either as an employee or as a partner. This is a scenario you should be familiar with, and is likely to have been a popular question in the exam.

The highlighted words in the written sections are key phrases that markers are looking for.

(a) **The advantage of a 30 June year end**

Tutor's top tips

To answer this part of the question you might find it easiest to set out the opening year assessments for the two alternative year ends, and then summarise these in words.

If the business has a 30 June year end the opening year assessments will be as follows:

		£
2016/17	1 July 2016 – 5 April 2017	Loss
2017/18	Year ended 30 June 2017	Loss
2018/19	Year ended 30 June 2018	Profit

A profit will not be assessed until 2018/19.

If the business adopts a year end of 31 March the opening year assessments will be as follows:

		£
2016/17	1 July 2016 – 5 April 2017	Loss
2017/18	Year ended 31 March 2018:	
	1 April 2017 – 30 June 2017 (3 months)	Loss
	1 July 2017 – 31 March 2018 (9 months)	Profit
2018/19	Year ended 31 March 2019	Profit

It can be seen that with the March year end, 9 months' worth of profit will be assessed in 2017/18. This will be offset against the loss for the three months to 30 June 2017, but may produce an overall net taxable profit.

Choosing 30 June as the year end is, therefore, likely to delay the first tax year in which the Bah-Tock business makes a taxable profit.

Tutorial note

The opening year rules for sole traders are tricky, but they do often get tested in the P6 exam. It is important that you retain your F6 knowledge of these rules.

(b) (i) **Tax issues if Faure employs Ravel**

Tutor's top tips

Try not to just write everything you know about taking on a spouse as an employee.

There are some specific points that the examiner wishes you to address, so you should use these to structure your answer.

To score well here you must apply your knowledge to the specific scenario given in the question. Remember that the business will be loss-making for 2016/17 and 2017/18 if a 30 June year end is chosen, as set out in part (a).

Size of the loss

Faure will pay Ravel a salary, and will also pay employer's class 1 national insurance contributions at 13.8% on any salary above £8,112, subject to a £2,000 'employment allowance'.

Both the salary and the employer's national insurance contributions are tax deductible, and will increase the loss made by the business.

Reliefs available for initial losses

Faure

As Faure has had no income tax liability since 2007/08, there is no possibility of carrying back the losses made in 2016/17 or 2017/18.

The only option will be to carry forward the loss against future trading profits of the same trade. Relief will not be obtained until 2018/19 at the earliest.

Ravel

Ravel will have no losses under this option.

Income tax and national insurance liabilities for 2016/17 and 2017/18

Faure

As Faure will have a trading loss for 2016/17 and 2017/18, she will have no income tax, class 2 or class 4 national Insurance liability in respect of the business for those two years.

Faure will not utilise her personal allowance (PA) in either year, and has not for many years.

As her husband (Ravel) is a basic rate taxpayer, with effect from 6 April 2015, she can elect to transfer £1,060 of her unused PA (10% x £10,600) to him.

Tutorial note

Remember that class 2 and class 4 contributions are only payable if a sole trader is making profits in excess of limits, and are not payable where the business is loss-making.

For class 2 the taxable trading profit limit is £5,965 and for class 4 the taxable trading profit limit is £8,060.

Ravel

Ravel will pay income tax on his salary at 20% up to the basic rate limit of £31,785.

If the election to transfer £1,060 of PA is made by Faure, Ravel will benefit from a tax reducer of £212 (£1,060 x 20%).

As a result of the extra income if Faure employs Ravel:

- Ravel's bank interest and dividends may be pushed into the higher rate band, and be taxed at 40% and 32.5% respectively, with tax credits of 20% and 10% of the gross figures.

- Previously, the tax on the savings and dividends would have been covered by the tax credits. However, if these move into the higher rate band there will be extra tax to pay.

- Note that if Ravel becomes a higher rate taxpayer, it will no longer be possible for Faure to elect to transfer £1,060 unused PA to Ravel.

- Ravel will also be subject to employees' class 1 national Insurance contributions at 12% of any salary in excess of £8,060, and possibly 2% if in excess of £42,385.

(ii) **Tax issues if Faure and Ravel are partners in the business**

Tutorial note

Remember that partners in a partnership are taxed on their share of the profit/loss as if they were sole traders.

Size of the loss

The loss will be split between Faure and Ravel in accordance with their agreed profit sharing ratio. This could be an equal split, but does not have to be.

Reliefs available for initial losses

Faure

Again, the only option for Faure will be to carry forward the loss against future trading profits of the same trade. Relief will not be obtained until 2018/19 at the earliest.

Ravel

Ravel has the option of offsetting his share of the loss against his total income:

- for the tax year of the loss and/or the previous tax year; or
- for the three tax years preceding the year of the loss on a first in-first out basis.

Where the loss is relieved against interest income Ravel will be able to recover the tax he has paid in respect of that income. For interest falling into the basic rate band this will be 20%.

There is a cap on the amount of losses that can be offset against other income, being the higher of £50,000 or 25% of adjusted total income

Where the loss is relieved against dividend income falling into the basic rate band there will be no repayment as the 10% tax credit on dividends is not repayable.

Alternatively, Ravel could choose to carry forward the loss against future profits of the same trade. This is likely to save tax at a higher rate, as Ravel will probably be a higher rate taxpayer once the business is profitable. However, this is not guaranteed and there would be a cash flow disadvantage, as relief would be delayed.

Income tax and national insurance liabilities for 2016/17 and 2017/18

Both Faure and Ravel will have trading losses for 2016/17 and 2017/18, and will have no income tax, class 2 or class 4 national insurance liabilities in respect of the business for those two years.

Ravel may be assessed on his bank interest and dividend income if losses are carried back. If this is the case, Faure can transfer £1,060 of her PA to Ravel to obtain the benefit of a tax reducer of £212.

Summary

Tutor's top tips

The examiner asks you to summarise your findings, so there will be marks available for doing this.

As long as your summary is consistent you should be given credit!

It would appear to be better for Faure and Ravel to run the business in partnership.

There would be no immediate tax liabilities, and Ravel would be able to obtain relief for losses immediately, or at a higher rate than Faure in the future.

If Faure employs Ravel, there will be tax to pay in 2016/17 and 2017/18 even though the business will be making losses, and the benefit of transferring unused PA will be lost.

Examiner's comments

Part (a) concerned the choice of year end for the new business; it was answered poorly by a majority of candidates but very well by the remainder.

The question was slightly unusual in that it required candidates to explain why something was true; namely that one year end rather than another would be likely to delay the first tax year in which the business makes a taxable profit. This required candidates to apply their technical knowledge to the facts of the question.

In order to answer this question, candidates needed to know the opening year rules for an unincorporated business. However, they also had to reach the conclusion set out in the question. The problem here was that many candidates did not pause and think about what they had been asked to do. Instead, they simply wrote about opening years in relation to overlap profits, utilisation of losses or tax payment dates.

Candidates who did well either thought before they began writing, such that they submitted very concise answers that neatly summarised the position, or explored the opening year rules for each of the year ends and reached the required conclusion.

Part (b) required a comparison of employing someone with going into partnership with them. There were lots of marks available, many of which were straightforward and, on the whole, this part was answered reasonably well. However, many candidates could have done considerably better if they had recognised all of the help that was provided to them in the question and had taken the time to consider whether or not they had addressed all of the relevant points.

Candidates' first impression on reading this question may have been favourable in that the technical area was one they were likely to be comfortable with (although the lack of numbers may have worried some). However, in order to maximise their marks candidates needed to follow the instructions given in the notes to the question.

Note 1 required candidates' answers to be restricted to losses; this was ignored by many candidates. Note 2 provided a structure to what was otherwise an awkward open ended question; unfortunately, this suggested structure was also ignored by many candidates.

ANSWERS TO PRACTICE QUESTIONS: SECTION 2

> Those candidates who ignored the notes lost marks for two reasons; they wasted time writing about matters that did not score (principally the taxation of profits) and they failed to address all of the relevant issues (as listed in note 2).
>
> For example, candidates wrote about how class 4 national insurance contributions would be calculated when they should have written that no such contributions would be due until the business was profitable.

ACCA marking scheme			
			Marks
(a)		30 June year end	2.0
		31 March year end	2.0
		Comparison	0.5
			4.5
		Maximum	4.0
(b)	(i)	Faure employs Ravel	
		Effect on results of business	1.0
		Class 1 national insurance contributions	1.5
		Faure – income tax	2.0
		Ravel – income tax	2.5
	(ii)	Faure and Ravel are partners in the business	
		Allocation of loss and no taxable income	1.5
		Faure – use of loss	0.5
		Ravel – use of loss	
		Alternatives available	2.5
		Tax relief and timing	2.5
		Class 2 national insurance contributions	1.0
		Conclusion	1.0
			16.0
		Maximum	14.0
Total			**18.0**

16 JEROME AND TRICYCLE LTD *Walk in the footsteps of a top tutor*

Key answer tips

The question covers three different areas: the VAT implications of a sale of a business; the different tax implications if the car is leased by the employee or employer and the tax treatment of overseas travel expenses for an employee.

Part (a) on VAT is very easy and is a popular area in the P6 exam provided you have learnt the conditions.

Part (b) is trickier and you need to be careful with your computations to avoid getting lost.

Part (c) is not a mainstream area but easy marks were available if you knew the rules for employee expenses while working abroad.

The highlighted words in the written sections are key phrases that markers are looking for.

(a) **Value added tax (VAT) – Sale of the business**

Tutor's top tips

The transfer of a business as a going concern is often tested in the P6 exam, so you must learn the conditions. There are easy marks here purely for stating these conditions.

However, you may not have spotted that there is an issue with the building, as it is less than three years old and therefore a 'new' building for VAT purposes.

HM Revenue and Customs should be notified of the sale of the business within 30 days. Jerome's VAT registration will need to be cancelled unless it is to be taken over by Tricycle Ltd.

VAT must be charged on the sale of the business assets unless it qualifies as a transfer of a going concern. For the sale of the business to be regarded as a transfer of a going concern, the following conditions must be satisfied:

- The business must be a going concern.
- Tricycle Ltd must use the assets to carry on the same kind of business as that carried on by Jerome.
- Tricycle Ltd must be VAT registered or be required to be VAT registered as a result of the purchase (based on the turnover of the purchased business in the previous 12 months).
- There should be no significant break in trading before or after the purchase of the business.

Tutorial note

Usually when a business deregisters for VAT, there is a final VAT charge payable based on the market value of inventory and non-current assets on which input VAT was claimed earlier. This final VAT charge is not payable if it is less than £1,000.

When a business is sold as a going concern, the final VAT charge is not payable as long as the above conditions are satisfied.

Even if the transfer satisfies the above conditions, Jerome will need to charge VAT on the sale of the building as it is a commercial building that is less than three years old. The only exception to this is if Tricycle Ltd makes an election to tax the building at the time of purchase.

(b) **Tax costs incurred in respect of the motor car**

Tutorial note

*It is important to fully understand each option before performing the computations. You must consider the effect on both Jerome and Tricycle Ltd for **both** options.*

*If the **car is leased by Tricycle Ltd** then:*

- *Jerome will have to pay income tax on the car and fuel benefits at 40%.*
- *Tricycle Ltd will have to pay class 1A NICs on the benefits at 13.8%.*
- *The lease payments relate to a high emission car, therefore 15% will be disallowed in computing the company's taxable profits.*
- *85% of the lease payments, running costs and class 1A NICs are allowable expenses for calculating taxable profits and will result in a corporation tax saving at 20% because the company is a small company.*

*If the **car is leased by Jerome** then:*

- *Jerome will have to pay income tax on the mileage allowance received in excess of the AMAP rates (First 10,000 miles at 45p, above 10,000 miles at 25p). These rates are given in the exam.*
- *Jerome also has to pay class 1 NICs on the difference between 50p and 45p, but only at 2% as his salary is above the NIC upper limit.*
- *Tricycle will only have to pay class 1A NICs on the difference between 50p and 45p at 13.8%.*
- *The mileage allowance paid and the NICs are allowable expenses for calculating taxable profits and will save corporation tax at 20%.*

(i) **Motor car is leased by Tricycle Ltd**

Jerome

	£
Taxable benefit in respect of private use of the motor car (£31,000 × 27%) (W)	8,370
Taxable benefit in respect of private fuel (£22,100 × 27%)	5,967
	14,337
Income tax at 40% – payable by Jerome (Note 1)	5,735

Tricycle Ltd

	Allowable expenses £	Tax £
Lease payments (£4,400 × 85%) (Note 2)	3,740	
Running costs	5,000	
Class 1A NICs (£14,337 × 13.8%)	1,979	1,979
	10,719	
Reduction in corporation tax liability (£10,719 × 20%)		(2,144)
Net taxes saved by Tricycle Ltd		(165)
Total tax cost for Jerome and Tricycle Ltd (£5,735 – £165)		5,570

Tutorial notes

1   Jerome's salary of £48,000 per year exceeds the personal allowance plus the basic rate band, such that he will be a higher rate taxpayer.

2   High emission car leasing payments are not all allowable; 15% are disallowable and added back in the adjustment of profits computation. Therefore only 85% of the cost is allowable.

Working: Appropriate percentage

	%
Diesel	17
Plus: ((145 – 95) ÷ 5)	10
	27

ANSWERS TO PRACTICE QUESTIONS: SECTION 2

(ii) Motor car is leased by Jerome

Jerome

	£
AMAPs	
10,000 × 45p	4,500
4,000 × 25p	1,000
	5,500
Amount received (14,000 × 50p)	7,000
Taxable benefit	1,500
Income tax at 40% – payable by Jerome	600
Class 1 NICs payable by Jerome (Note 2):	
14,000 miles × (50p – 45p) × 2%	14
Total tax payable by Jerome	614

Tricycle Ltd

	Allowable expenses £	Tax £
Mileage allowance paid (14,000 × 50p)	7,000	
Class 1 NICs payable by Tricycle Ltd:		
14,000 × (50p – 45p) × 13.8%	97	97
	7,097	
Reduction in corporation tax liability (£7,097 × 20%)		(1,419)
Net taxes saved by Tricycle Ltd		(1,322)
Net taxes saved by Jerome and Tricycle Ltd (£1,322 – £614)		708

Tutorial notes

1   The calculations reflect the tax implications of the two alternatives. Jerome controls the company such that the non-tax costs incurred (lease payments, running costs and mileage allowances) are going to be incurred regardless of who leases the car and are therefore only relevant to the extent that they increase or reduce a tax liability.

However, Jerome may need to extract funds from the company in order to pay the costs relating to the motor car. This would give rise to further tax liabilities that would need to be considered.

2   Class 1 NICs are payable by Jerome and Tricycle Ltd in respect of mileage allowances paid in excess of the AMAP rate of 45p (i.e. the rate for the first 10,000 miles).

NICs are payable on the excess over 45p on all business mileage, even if the mileage exceeds 10,000.

Jerome's salary of £48,000 exceeds the NIC upper limit of £42,385 such that the rate of Jerome's NICs will be 2%.

(c)   Conditions for travel costs to be deductible

Tutor's top tips

The rules tested here do not often feature in the P6 exam, but gave two easy marks if you had learnt them.

- The employee must be absent from the UK for a continuous period of at least 60 days for the purposes of performing the duties of his employment.
- The journey must be from the UK to the place where the employee is carrying out the duties of his employment.
- A deduction is only available for two outward and two return journeys by the same person(s) in the same tax year.

Tutorial note

Note that these rules only apply to travel costs of the employee's spouse / civil partner and children under 18.

Other expenses which can be deducted include travel costs for the employee to travel to and from the overseas employment and accommodation paid by the employer.

ANSWERS TO PRACTICE QUESTIONS: SECTION 2

Examiner's comments

In part (a) candidates first needed to recognise that the sale was a transfer of a business as a going concern such that VAT should not be charged. This was done well with the majority of candidates listing the conditions that needed to be satisfied.

Candidates were then expected to realise that the building being sold was a commercial building that was less than three years old. Accordingly, VAT would need to be charged in respect of the building unless the purchaser made an election to tax the building at the time of purchase. Very few candidates identified this point.

Part (b) required calculations of the total tax cost for Tricycle Ltd and Jerome in relation to the lease of car. The car would be leased by Jerome, an employee of the company, or by Tricycle Ltd. This was a practical problem that was not particularly technically difficult but required care and thought in order to score well. It was not done as well as it should have been.

The point here was that Jerome owned Tricycle Ltd such that he was interested in the total tax cost to himself and the company in respect of each of the two options.

Candidates needed to recognise that there were tax implications for both the employer, Tricycle Ltd, and the employee, Jerome, in each situation. For example, if Jerome leased the car, the payment of 50 pence per business mile was tax deductible for the company but resulted in taxable income for Jerome. There was also the need to consider national insurance contributions as well as income tax and corporation tax.

The main problem for candidates was a lack of exam technique. In particular, weaker candidates did not spend sufficient time thinking about the different tax implications for both parties in each situation but focussed on Jerome when he leased the car and on Tricycle Ltd when it leased the car.

There was also considerable confusion as to what represented a 'tax cost'. A tax cost (or saving) was either income/expenditure at an appropriate tax rate or a direct tax cost due to the arrangement, for example class 1A national insurance contributions. Many candidates did not multiply income/expenditure by tax rates or simply got lost in the distinction between what is taxable and what is allowable for tax purposes. This led to various errors including, indicating that the benefit in respect of the car was an allowable expense for the company or that the leasing costs paid by Jerome were deductible from taxable income.

The final part of the question concerned the payment of travel expenses in respect of a family of an employee working overseas. This was a minor part of the question for two marks. It rewarded those (few) candidates who had acquired a knowledge of the less frequently examined areas of the syllabus.

PAPER P6: ADVANCED TAXATION (FA2015)

ACCA marking scheme			
			Marks
(a)	Administration – one mark for relevant point		1.0
	Charge VAT unless transfer of a going concern		1.0
	Conditions (one mark each, maximum three marks)		3.0
	Land and buildings		2.5
			7.5
		Maximum	6.0
(b) (i)	Motor car leased by Tricycle Ltd		
	Income tax payable by Jerome		2.5
	Net taxes saved by Tricycle Ltd		3.0
	Net tax cost		0.5
(ii)	Motor car leased by Jerome		
	Total tax payable by Jerome		3.0
	Net taxes saved by Tricycle Ltd		1.5
	Net tax saved		0.5
			11.0
		Maximum	10.0
(c)	Conditions – one mark each		2.0
Total			**18.0**

17 FARINA AND LAUDA *Walk in the footsteps of a top tutor*

Key answer tips

This question is in two main parts: two partners in a partnership planning to sell their business to a company in exchange for cash and shares, and then planning to make disposals of the shares acquired on incorporation.

Part (a) was the guaranteed 5 marks on ethics which tests the information required and action to be taken before becoming tax advisers to two partners. This part is usually at the end of the question, but as it is an independent part it can be attempted at any point. The topic is straightforward and should provide easy marks, however you need to make sure that you make reference in your answer to the partnership scenario given.

Part (b) firstly requires the capital allowances on the sale of the business to the company and should also provide 5 easy marks for F6 knowledge. However, detailed explanations (not computations) are required, but only in relation to the final trading period.

Secondly, the IHT and CGT implications of the transfer of shares into a discretionary (relevant property) trust are covered for 7 marks. The majority of the marks in this part are for providing an explanation of the calculation of an IHT liability although the consideration of CGT implications and gift relief are also required.

The last part of this question was the trickiest part as it requires a review of whether or not one of the partners should disclaim incorporation relief for 14 marks. A methodical approach and good use of headings and sub-headings to break your answer down is needed. It is important to deal with each step in turn – the sale of the business followed by a gift of shares, and then subsequent sale of shares in the future.

The question states that incorporation relief is available on the sale of the business, but you need to calculate the tax that would be charged in respect of these transactions both with and without incorporation relief and then make some sensible comments regarding your findings.

The highlighted words in the written sections are key phrases that markers are looking for.

Tutor's top tips

As is the norm for Section A questions in recent sittings, the requirements for part (b) that appear at the end of the question only tell you how many marks are available for each section of the memorandum. The real requirements can be found in the information provided in the stem of the question.

As you read through highlight any requirements and instructions that you find. The requirements in this question are all in the email from the manager.

In part (b) the examiner has asked for a memorandum which addresses certain issues and you may find it useful to number these requirements so that you can tick them off as you attempt them.

Make sure you set out your answer in the required format. For a memorandum you need a suitable heading which will identify to whom it is addressed. Numbered headings which agree to the numbered points in the manager's email will make your answer easier to mark Question 1 will always have 4 professional marks to cover presentation, relevant advice and quality of communication.

(a) **Becoming tax advisers to Farina and Lauda**

Tutor's top tips

Be careful to answer the specific question here and address the facts of the scenario.

*The question does not ask for lists of information needed in order to be able to give advice once they are clients – it wants information required **before** becoming advisers.*

Also note that the partners will want the provision of specialised tax advice.

Information required in respect of Farina and Lauda:
- evidence of their identities; and
- their addresses.

Action to be taken by the firm:
- The firm should contact their existing tax advisers. This is to ensure that there has been no action by either Farina or Lauda which would, on ethical grounds, preclude the acceptance of the appointment.
- The firm should consider whether becoming tax advisers to Farina and Lauda would create any threats to compliance with the fundamental principles of professional ethics. Where such threats exist, the appointment should not be accepted unless the threats can be reduced to an acceptable level via the implementation of safeguards.
- With this in mind, the firm must ensure that it has sufficient competence to carry out the sophisticated tax planning required by Farina and Lauda.
- In addition, it is possible that providing advice to Farina and Lauda on the sale of their business could give rise to a conflict of interest, as a course of action (for example, the timing of the sale) which is beneficial for one of them may not be beneficial for the other. The firm should obtain permission from both Farina and Lauda to act for both of them and should consider making a different member of the firm responsible for each of them.

(b)
MEMORANDUM

To	The files
From	Tax senior
Date	6 December 2016
Subject	The FL Partnership

The purpose of this memorandum is to advise Farina and Lauda, the partners in the FL Partnership, on the sale of the business to JH plc and on the proposed disposals of shares in JH plc in the future.

(i) **Capital allowances of the FL Partnership for its final trading period**

Tutor's top tips

Detailed explanations are required, not numbers.

Remember that only 5 marks are available and only the final period of trading needs to be considered.

There will be no annual investment allowance, first year allowances or writing down allowances in the period in which the business ceases.

Instead, there will be a balancing adjustment; either a balancing allowance or a balancing charge.

The balancing adjustment will be calculated as follows:

		£
TWDV b/f at the start of the period		X
Add: Additions in the period		X
Less: Disposals during the period		
Lower of cost and sales proceeds		(X)
		X
Less: Proceeds on the sale of the equipment (1 March 2017)		(150,000)
Balancing allowance/(balancing charge)		X/(X)

It will not be possible to elect to transfer the equipment to JH plc at its tax written down value (rather than market value) because Farina and Lauda will not be connected with JH plc. This is because they will not control the company.

Tutorial note

On incorporation, if the previous owners of the business control the company incorporating the business, a succession election can be made to transfer the assets at TWDV instead of market value. As a result, balancing adjustments can be avoided on incorporation, but this will affect the base cost of the assets taken over by the company.

(ii) **Farina**

(1) **Inheritance tax**

Tutor's top tips

An explanation of how to calculate the IHT is required. Be careful to explain, in detail, each step of the thought process in a logical / chronological order.

Try to be succinct and precise in your explanation, and don't forget the easy mark for stating the due date of payment which is easily gained, but easily lost if you do not remember to write it down.

The gift of the JH plc shares to the trustees will be a chargeable lifetime transfer, such that inheritance tax may be due at the time of the gift. Business property relief will not be available as JH plc is a quoted company and Farina will not be a controlling shareholder.

The shares will be valued at £4 per share, such that the value of the gift will be £60,000 (15,000 × £4).

This will be reduced by the annual exemptions for the tax year 2017/18 and also for the tax year 2016/17 if they have not been used against any other gifts. The annual exemption is £3,000.

The excess of this value over the available nil rate band will be subject to inheritance tax at 25% because the tax will be paid by Farina.

The available nil rate band will be £325,000 as reduced by any chargeable transfers made by Farina in the previous seven years.

Any inheritance tax due will be payable on 30 April 2018.

Tutorial note

The gift is on 1 August 2017 which is in the first half of the tax year 2017/18.

The lifetime IHT is therefore due on the following 30 April (i.e. 30 April 2018).

If the gift had fallen into the second half of the tax year the IHT would be due 6 months after the end of month in which the gift took place.

(2) **Capital gains tax gift relief**

Tutor's top tips

Although it is not clear from the requirement, there are only 1.5 marks for this part. Therefore it is important to be brief and to the point.

Gift relief will be available in respect of the transfer of the shares to the trustees because, as noted above, the transfer is immediately subject to inheritance tax.

For the same reason, gift relief will also be available in respect of any subsequent transfers of shares from the trustees to the beneficiaries.

Tutorial note

Gift relief is available where there is an immediate charge to IHT.

When the shares are put into the trust it is a CLT for IHT purposes, and therefore there is an immediate charge to IHT.

When the shares are distributed out of the trust there will also be an immediate charge to IHT (known as an exit charge).

Accordingly, as there is an immediate charge to IHT, gift relief is available both when the shares are put into the trust and when they are distributed.

(iii) **Lauda**

Tutor's top tips

With many things to consider it is important to break down the answer and to think through each stage carefully:

- The sale of the business – with and without incorporation relief.
- The gift of the shares.
- The subsequent sale of shares.

Make sure you address all of the requirements, including a statement of key issues to discuss, brief explanations, availability of alternative reliefs and the due date of payment.

The sale of the business will result in a chargeable gain in respect of the goodwill.

The gain, equal to the market value of the goodwill of £1,300,000, will be split equally between Farina and Lauda, such that Lauda's chargeable gain will be £650,000.

As all of the equipment qualified for capital allowances, no capital losses will arise on its sale.

Tutorial note

The only chargeable asset is goodwill and therefore there is only one gain to consider.

Inventory and receivables are not chargeable as they are working capital, not capital assets.

Note that if the equipment was sold at a profit then there would a chargeable gain arising, unless the examiner specifically states that they were all small items with cost and market values that did not exceed £6,000.

Tutor's top tips

Incorporation relief defers the gain on incorporation until the later disposal of shares. It is therefore necessary to consider all the series of events both with, and without, claiming incorporation relief.

If the relevant conditions are satisfied then incorporation relief is automatically applied to the gain.

For incorporation relief to be disapplied the taxpayer must make an election within 2 years from the 31 January following the end of the tax year in which the transfer took place.

With incorporation relief

The sale of the business – 1 March 2017

	£
Capital gain on the sale of the goodwill	650,000
Less: Incorporation relief	
£650,000 × (£600,000/£740,000) (Note 1)	(527,027)
Taxable gain	122,973
Capital gains tax at 10% (Note 2)	12,297

The tax will be payable on 31 January 2018.

Lauda's base cost in the shares in JH plc

	£
Market value of the shares received (200,000 × £3)	600,000
Less: Incorporation relief	(527,027)
Base cost	72,973

The gift of 40,000 shares on 1 June 2018 (Note 3)

	£
Proceeds at market value (40,000 × £5)	200,000
Less: Cost (£72,973 × (40,000/200,000))	(14,595)
Taxable gain	185,405
Capital gains tax at 28% (Note 4)	51,913

The tax will be payable on 31 January 2020.

Explanatory notes

1. Incorporation relief is restricted by reference to the value of the shares divided by the value of the total consideration received. Lauda will receive a total of £740,000, consisting of cash of £140,000 and shares worth £600,000 (200,000 × £3).

2. Capital gains tax will be charged at 10% because entrepreneurs' relief will be available. This relief is available because the business is a trading business, it is to be sold as a going concern and has been owned for at least a year. It is assumed that Lauda has not exceeded the lifetime limit of £10,000,000 and will claim this relief.

3. Gift relief will not be available in respect of this gift because the shares are quoted and Lauda will hold less than 5% of the company (200,000/8,400,000 = 2.38%).

4. Capital gains tax will be charged at 28% because Lauda pays income tax at the additional rate. Entrepreneurs' relief will not be available because Lauda will hold less than 5% of JH plc.

ANSWERS TO PRACTICE QUESTIONS: SECTION 2

Tutorial note

In order for entrepreneurs' relief to be available in respect of the gift of the shares, Lauda would also need to be an employee of JH plc and work for the company on a part time or full time basis.

Without incorporation relief

Tutor's top tips

Consideration is needed of the same three events without incorporation relief, followed by a summary of findings and comments arising from the comparison.

The sale of the business on 1 March 2017

	£
Capital gain on the sale of the goodwill	650,000
Capital gains tax at 10% (Note 1 below)	65,000

The tax will be payable on 31 January 2018.

Lauda's base cost in the shares in JH plc

	£
Market value of the shares received (200,000 × £3)	600,000

The gift of 40,000 shares on 1 June 2018 (Note 2 below)

	£
Proceeds at market value (40,000 × £5)	200,000
Less: Cost (£600,000 × 40,000/200,000)	(120,000)
Taxable gain	80,000
Capital gains tax at 28% (Note 2 below)	22,400

The tax will be payable on 31 January 2020.

Explanatory notes

1. Entrepreneur's relief (ER) will still be available if incorporation relief is disapplied in this scenario.

    FA2015 has introduced legislation to deny ER on chargeable gains relating to goodwill where the goodwill is acquired by a close company and the individual becomes a shareholder in the company.

    However, in this scenario the acquiring company is a plc and therefore very unlikely to be a close company (i.e. unlikely to be controlled by its directors or by five or fewer participators).

KAPLAN PUBLISHING

2 Capital gains tax will be charged at 28% because Lauda pays income tax at the additional rate. Entrepreneurs' relief will not be available because Lauda will hold less than 5% of JH plc.

Summary

	With incorporation relief £	Without incorporation relief £
CGT on:		
Sale of the business	12,297	65,000
Gift of the shares on 1 June 2018	51,913	22,400
	64,210	87,400

The effect of incorporation relief on the base cost of the shares

	£	£
Reduction in base cost due to incorporation relief		527,027
Base cost re: gift of the shares on 1 June 2018		
Without incorporation relief	120,000	
With incorporation relief	(14,595)	
Increase in the base cost of the gift		(105,405)
Overall reduction in base cost		421,622
Additional tax at 28%		118,054

Tutorial note

The examiner's model answer above could be simplified as shown below.

The base cost of the remaining 160,000 shares would be as follows:

If incorporation relief is claimed: £72,973 × (160,000/200,000) = £58,378

If incorporation relief is not claimed: £600,000 × (160,000/200,000) = £480,000

Reduction in base cost = (£480,000 – £58,378) = £421,622 as above

Key issues

Tutor's top tips

As a result of your calculation, consider what issues you need to bring to Lauda's attention.

If Lauda were to disclaim incorporation relief, she would have higher initial capital gains tax liabilities.

However, disclaiming incorporation relief will result in a higher base cost in the shares, such that on a sale of the shares in the future, there will be tax savings which will exceed the increased initial liability.

Tutorial note

1   *Incorporation relief reduces the capital gains tax payable on the sale of the business and the gift of the shares by £23,190 (£87,400 – £64,210). When this amount is deducted from the additional tax due because of the reduced base cost, we arrive at an overall increase in the capital gains tax liability of £94,864 (£118,054 – £23,190).*

    This overall increase in the capital gains tax liability is simply the tax on the deferred gain of £527,027 at 28% in the future rather than at 10%, due to the availability of entrepreneurs relief, now:

    £527,027 × (28% – 10%) = £94,865 (and a rounding difference of £1).

2   *Capital gains tax holdover relief in respect of gifts of business assets will not be available on the sale of the business to JH plc, because Farina and Lauda are not going to gift the business to the company; they are going to sell the business at market value, which will be received in the form of cash and shares.*

Examiner's comments

Part (a) should have been straightforward but, on the whole, it was not done particularly well. The main problem was a lack of thought before answering the question.

The question asked for the information required before becoming advisers to the partners but a significant number of candidates listed the information they would need in order to be able to give advice to them once they had become clients (including personal details, information in respect of prior years and so on). Candidates will always benefit from reading the requirement carefully and thinking before they begin to write their answers. It is important to think about the specifics of the situation, for example, the fact that the partners required sophisticated and specialised tax planning work, such that the firm needed to be sure that it had staff with sufficient knowledge and competence.

Again, part (b)(i) was reasonably straightforward and again, on the whole, it was not done well. The question asked for a detailed explanation of the calculation of the capital allowances for the final trading period of the business. Accordingly, the answer should have explained how the balancing adjustment would be calculated and explained why the assets could not be transferred at tax written down value.

However, many answers included detailed calculations of capital allowances over many years (despite the fact that the question did not include the information necessary to prepare such calculations) or tried to explain everything about capital allowances, very little of which was relevant to this particular question. A short thoughtful answer was able to score three marks whereas many answers covering more than a page only scored a single mark.

Part (b)(ii) was done very well by most candidates. However, performance in respect of the availability of capital gains tax gift relief was not quite as strong; candidates must learn when the various capital gains tax reliefs are available. Gift relief is available where a transfer is immediately subject to inheritance tax regardless of the nature of the assets disposed of.

Part (b)(iii) was the more demanding part of this question. It required a review of whether or not one of the partners should disclaim incorporation relief for 14 marks. There was guidance in the question as to what the review should encompass. This part of the question was not done well.

The first thing to note is that many candidates did not have a thorough attempt at this part of the question. Many answers were very short, despite the number of marks available, and some candidates omitted it altogether.

Other candidates avoided producing calculations and simply wrote about the issues in general terms which was never going to be particularly successful.

In addition, most candidates who attempted the question did not give it sufficient thought before starting their answers. As a result, many answers were confused and did not cover sufficient ground to score well.

In particular, it was often not obvious which aspect of the question was being addressed and the summary of calculations and statement of key issues required by the question were often missing. Finally, many candidates addressed inheritance tax in this part of the question, which was not required and, therefore, could not score any marks.

In addition to the general problems regarding the approach to the question, there were two specific technical problems.

Firstly, the majority of candidates tried to calculate the gain on the disposal of the business by reference to the total value of the assets sold as opposed to calculating the gain on each individual chargeable asset. There was only one chargeable asset in the question, goodwill, so all that was needed was the gain on the goodwill.

Secondly, many candidates then struggled with the calculation of incorporation relief and its effect on the base cost of the shares.

The general impression was that many candidates had not practised sufficient past exam questions, such that they were unable to plan their approach to a question of this type and then to carry that plan out.

Marks were available for professional skills in question 1. In order to earn these marks candidates had to provide a suitable amount of appropriate narrative, calculations that were clear and logical and sensible analysis in relation to the position of Lauda in an appropriately formatted memorandum. On the whole, the performance of candidates in this area was good with the majority of candidates producing a memorandum in a style that was easy to follow.

ANSWERS TO PRACTICE QUESTIONS: SECTION 2

ACCA marking scheme			
			Marks
(a)	Information required		1.0
	Contact existing tax adviser		1.0
	Fundamental principles		1.0
	Competence		1.0
	Conflict of interest		2.0
			–––
			6.0
		Maximum	5.0
			–––
(b)	(i) Allowances available		1.5
	Calculation of balancing adjustment		2.0
	Consideration of transfer at tax written down value		1.5
			–––
			5.0
			–––
	(ii) Inheritance tax		
	Tax may be payable at time of gift		1.0
	Business property relief		1.5
	Valuation and exemptions		1.5
	Inheritance tax and due date		3.0
	Gift relief		1.5
			–––
			8.5
		Maximum	7.0
			–––
	(iii) Capital gain on sale of business		1.5
	With incorporation relief		
	Incorporation relief		1.5
	Capital gains tax and due date		1.0
	Capital gain on gift of shares		2.0
	Capital gains tax and due date		1.0
	Without incorporation relief		
	Capital gains tax on sale of business		1.0
	Capital gains tax on gift of shares		1.5
	Explanations		4.0
	Summary and key issues		4.0
			–––
			17.5
		Maximum	14.0
			–––
	Format and presentation		1.0
	Analysis		1.0
	Quality of explanations and calculations		2.0
			–––
			4.0
			–––
Total			**35.0**
			–––

KAPLAN PUBLISHING

18 ZITI *Walk in the footsteps of a top tutor*

Key answer tips

This question has two distinct parts:

Part (a) relates to the disposal of an unincorporated business on two alternative disposal dates (31 January 2017 and 30 April 2017). The examining team expects you to compare the after tax sale proceeds after payment of both income tax and capital gains tax.

This is the most demanding part of the question and a methodical approach is necessary together with a sound understanding of the current year basis closing year rules and capital allowances.

With regard to capital gains tax, Ravi (Ziti's father) gave the business to Ravi back in July 2012 and claimed full gift relief, so you need to consider the impact of this on Ravi's disposal and also think about whether entrepreneurs' relief is available.

There are 5 easy marks on VAT, for a comparison of the disposal of assets following a cessation of trade and the disposal of a business as a going concern.

Part (b) relates to the inheritance tax payable by Ziti if Ravi was to die any time between 7 June 2016 and 30 June 2019. This is challenging as you need to consider when the inheritance tax liability would change. As long as you realise that that the two main factors affecting the IHT liability are business property relief and taper relief, you should be able to earn sufficient marks to pass this part of the question.

The highlighted words in the written sections are key phrases that markers are looking for.

Tutor's top tips

As is the norm for section A questions, the requirements that appear at the end of the question only tell you how many marks are available for each section of the answer. The real requirements can be found in the information provided in the stem of the question.

As you read through the question, highlight any requirements and instructions that you find. The requirements in this particular question are all in the email from the manager.

The question has asked for meeting notes which address certain issues and you may find it useful to tick the issues off as you attempt them.

Make sure that you set out your answer in the required format. For meeting notes you need a suitable heading which will identify the subject. Use of sub-headings for each part which agree to the points in the manager's email will make your answer easier to mark.

Question 1 will always have 4 professional marks to cover presentation, relevant advice and quality of communication.

NOTES FOR MEETING

Prepared by   Tax senior
Date   6 June 2016
Subject   Ziti – sale of business and inheritance tax

(a) **Sale of the business**

    (i) **Post-tax income and sales proceeds**

    Income tax position

Tutor's top tips

As long as you methodically deal with each alternative disposal date, it should be easy to pass this part of the question, which is all based on F6 knowledge.

Step 1:   Find Ziti's profits assessed based on the closing year rules.

Step 2:   Find the income tax payable based on the profits assessed.

The key to success is recognising that the two alternative cessation dates fall into two different tax years.

If Ziti ceases to trade on 31 January 2017 then the final tax year is 2016/17, whereas if he ceases just three months later on 30 April 2017, the final tax year will be 2017/18.

This has an impact on the closing year assessments.

Cessation on 31 January 2017 would require two sets of accounts, for:
- the year ended 30 April 2016
- the 9 months ended 31 January 2017.

However, both of these will be assessed in 2016/17.

Cessation on 30 April 2017 would also require two sets of accounts, for:
- the year ended 30 April 2016
- the year ended 30 April 2017.

The year ended 30 April 2016 will be assessed in 2016/17, and the year ended 30 April 2017 will be assessed in 2017/18, requiring two income tax computations.

In both cases the profits for the year ending 30 April 2015 would be assessed under the current year basis in 2015/16, but you were only required to consider the trading profits from 1 May 2015 onwards in this question.

It was also important to appreciate the effect that the capital allowances would have on the assessment of profits on cessation, based on the timing of capital additions and disposals.

Remember to get the easy mark for deducting overlap profits (profits taxed twice on commencement) from the final year's assessment!

Business cessation on 31 January 2017 in the tax year 2016/17

Adjusted profits for accounting periods	y/e 30.4.2016 £	9 m/e 31.1.2017 £
Trading income		
(12 × £5,000) / (9 × £5,000)	60,000	45,000
Less: Capital allowances (£6,000 × 100% AIA)	(6,000)	
Add: Balancing charge (TWDV £Nil – £10,000 MV)		10,000
Adjusted trading profit	54,000	55,000

Assessment of profit

2016/17	£
Year ended 30 April 2016	54,000
Period ended 31 January 2017	55,000
Less: Overlap profits	(9,000)
Taxable trading profit	100,000

Tutor's top tips

Strictly, the capital allowances should be calculated for each accounting period before then matching the profits to the tax year using the closing year rules, as set out above.

The alternative presentation below shows you how the answer could be calculated more quickly by taking some shortcuts.

Either presentation would be acceptable in the exam.

Alternative presentation:
Assessment of profits

2016/17	£
Trading income (1 May 2015 to 31 January 2017)	
(21 × £5,000)	105,000
Add: Net balancing charge (£6,000 – £10,000) (Note)	4,000
Less: Overlap profits	(9,000)
Taxable trading profit	100,000

Tutorial note

There would be an AIA of £6,000 on the purchase of the equipment during the year ended 30 April 2016, leaving a tax written down value of zero, then a balancing charge of £10,000 in the final accounting period on the sale of all the equipment in the general pool.

With cessation on 31 January 2017, both the AIA and the balancing charge will be assessed 2016/17, but with cessation on 30 April 2017 the allowance and charge will fall into two different tax years.

Tutor's top tips

The examining team wants you to quantify the post-tax proceeds so you have to find the income tax payable based on profits of £100,000 in 2016/17. Remember the personal allowance of £10,600 is only restricted once income exceeds £100,000, so the full PA is available.

Don't worry if you have the wrong figure for taxable trading profit. As long as you calculate the income tax based on your figure, you could still score full marks here.

Income tax payable

	2016/17 £
Taxable trading profit (above)	100,000
Less: Personal allowance	(10,600)
Taxable income	89,400

£	
31,785 × 20%	6,357
57,615 × 40%	23,046
89,400	
Income tax payable	29,403

KAPLAN PUBLISHING

Business disposal on 30 April 2017 in the tax year 2017/18

Adjusted profits for accounting periods	y/e 30.4.2016 £	y/e 30.4.2017 £
Trading income (12 × £5,000) / (12 × £5,000)	60,000	60,000
Less: Capital allowances (£6,000 × 100% AIA)	(6,000)	
Add: Balancing charge (TWDV £Nil – £10,000 MV)		10,000
Adjusted trading profit	54,000	70,000

Assessment of profits

2016/17 £
Year ended 30 April 2016 54,000

2017/18
Year ended 30 April 2017 70,000
Less: Overlap profits (9,000)

Taxable trading profit 61,000

Income tax payable

	2016/17 £	2017/18 £
Taxable trading profit (above)	54,000	61,000
Less: Personal allowance	(10,600)	(10,600)
Taxable income	43,400	50,400

£ £		
31,785 / 31,785 × 20%	6,357	6,357
11,615 / 18,615 × 40%	4,646	7,446
43,400 / 50,400		
Income tax payable	11,003	13,803

Capital gains tax (CGT) position

Tutor's top tips

When computing the capital gain on the disposal of the business, it is necessary to deal with each asset separately. Gains will only arise on chargeable assets.

With cessation on 31 January 2017, Ziti is closing down the business so a disposal only arises on the building and the equipment, not the goodwill.

Alternatively, with the disposal on the 30 April 2017, the business is being sold as a going concern so it is necessary to consider the gain on the goodwill as well.

The question asks for explanations of the availability of any CGT reliefs as well as any necessary assumptions, so there will be marks available for these.

Sale of assets on 31 January 2017

	£
Capital gains:	
Building (£330,000 – £60,000 (W))	270,000
Equipment	Nil
	270,000
Less: Annual exempt amount	(11,100)
Taxable gains	258,900
CGT at 10%	25,890

No capital gains or losses will arise in respect of the equipment, as movable items (chattels) with a cost and market value of not more than £6,000 are exempt from CGT.

Working: Deemed cost of building

	£
Market value at date of gift	300,000
Less: Gain on gift held over (£300,000 – £60,000)	(240,000)
Deemed cost for Ziti	60,000

Tutorial note

The assets were originally given to Ziti by Ravi, and a gift relief claim was made, which means that when Ziti now disposes of the business, his base cost will be the same as the original cost (Ravi's cost).

Sale of business on 30 April 2017

Tutor's top tips

There will now be a gain on the goodwill in addition to the gain on the building.

The CGT liability computed earlier on the building will simply increase by the tax on this goodwill gain which is £4,000 (£40,000 x 10%).

You do not have to do the entire computation again.

	£
CGT due in respect of the sale of the building on 31 January 2017 (as above)	25,890
CGT due in respect of the sale of goodwill (£40,000 × 10%)	4,000
	29,890

Availability of entrepreneurs' relief:

Entrepreneurs' relief is available where a business which has been owned for at least a year:

- is sold; or
- ceases to be carried on and its assets are sold within three years of cessation.

Accordingly, the relief will be available in both situations.

Summary of post-tax cash

Tutor's top tips

When computing the after-tax proceeds consider only the cash inflows and cash outflows. This is a very popular area and one that features regularly in the exam.

Cash inflows will consist of the trading income and sale proceeds received from the sale of the assets.

Cash outflows will consist of the capital cost of the equipment and the income tax and capital gains tax liabilities payable.

ANSWERS TO PRACTICE QUESTIONS: SECTION 2

	Sale on 31 January 2017 £	Sale on 30 April 2017 £
Trading income (£5,000 × 21/24)	105,000	120,000
Equipment purchased 1 August 2015	(6,000)	(6,000)
Sale proceeds:		
Goodwill	–	40,000
Building	330,000	330,000
Equipment	10,000	10,000
Less: Income tax	(29,403)	
(£11,003 + £13,803)		(24,806)
CGT	(25,890)	(29,890)
Post-tax cash	383,707	439,304

Delaying the sale until 30 April 2017 would:

- be financially beneficial; and
- delay the payment of both the income tax for the profits taxed in the tax year 2017/18 and the CGT.

Assumption:

Ziti has not used his annual exempt amount.

(ii) **Value added tax (VAT)**

Tutor's top tips

The VAT implications arising on a cessation of trade is an area that is regularly examined and represents a very easy 5 marks.

In both cases, Ziti is ceasing to trade and would have to deregister for VAT.

The difference between the two options is that the disposal on 31 January 2017 is not a transfer of a going concern (so output VAT would be payable) whereas the transfer on 30 April 2017 is a TOGC (so no output VAT is payable as long as certain conditions are satisfied).

Watch out for the building: remember that there are special rules for buildings. The question has confirmed that no option to tax has been made and the building is more than 3 years old.

Sale on 31 January 2017

VAT will need to be charged at 20% on the sale of the equipment.

The sale of the building will be an exempt supply, as it is a commercial building, more than three years old and no election has been made for it to be a taxable building.

KAPLAN PUBLISHING

Sale on 30 April 2017

VAT will need to be charged at 20% on the equipment and the goodwill unless the sale qualifies as a transfer of a going concern.

For the sale of the business to be regarded as a transfer of a going concern, the following conditions must be satisfied:

- The business must be a going concern.
- The purchaser must use the assets to carry on the same kind of business as that carried on by Ziti.
- The purchaser must be VAT registered or be required to be VAT registered as a result of the purchase (based on the supplies made by the purchased business in the previous 12 months).
- There should be no significant break in trading before or after the purchase of the business.

(b) **Inheritance tax**

Tutor's top tips

The question asked you to compute the IHT liability payable by Ziti for all possible dates based on Ravi dying between 7 June 2016 and 30 June 2019. The question did also give a hint and indicated that the best way to approach this is to identify the dates on which the IHT liability would change.

The first aspect to consider is the availability of 100% business property relief. If Ravi died while Ziti still owned the business then 100% BPR would be available. However, if Ravi died after Ziti had sold the business then no BPR would be available.

After computing the inheritance tax liability, you then need to consider how the liability would change if Ravi was fortunate enough to survive for a longer period. For every consecutive year thereafter, the IHT liability would be reduced by 20% as a greater amount of taper relief would be available.

In common with previous P6 case study questions, it is imperative to spend a few minutes planning your approach prior to starting the question.

You should have identified 4 different periods.

(1) 7.6.2016 – 30.4.2017

during this period Ziti still owns the business so 100% BPR is available and no IHT liability would arise.

(2) 1.5.2017 – 30.6.2017

during this period no BPR is available as Ziti will have sold the business.

The IHT liability would be reduced by 40% taper relief as the period between the gift to Ziti and the date of Ravi's death is between 4 – 5 years.

(3) 1.7.2017 – 30.6.2018

taper relief of 60% is available as the period between the gift to Ziti and the date of Ravi's death is between 5 – 6 years.

ANSWERS TO PRACTICE QUESTIONS: SECTION 2

(4) 1.7.2018 – 30.6.2019

taper relief of 80% is available as the period between the gift to Ziti and the date of Ravi's death is between 6 – 7 years.

The easiest way to approach the question is to compute the IHT liability based on the second period above and then reduce this liability by the increased taper relief.

Summary

Date of death	Note	Liability £
7 June 2016 to 30 April 2017	1	Nil
1 May 2017 to 30 June 2017	2	48,480
1 July 2017 to 30 June 2018	3(i)	32,320
1 July 2018 to 30 June 2019	3(ii)	16,160

Notes

1 If Ravi were to die whilst Ziti still owns the business, there would be no inheritance tax liability due to the availability of 100% business property relief on the transfer of an unincorporated business which has been owned by the transferor (Ravi) for at least two years.

2 Business property relief will not be available if Ziti does not own the business when Ravi dies, because he does not intend to reinvest all of the proceeds into replacement business property.

Taper relief will be available once Ravi has survived the gift by at least three years.

	£	£	£
Value transferred (£40,000 + £300,000 + £9,000)			349,000
Less: Annual exemptions (2012/13 and 2011/12 b/f)			(6,000)
			343,000
Nil rate band		325,000	
GCTs in 7 years before the gift (1.7.2005 – 1.7.2012):			
Chargeable transfer		190,000	
Less: Annual exemptions (2008/09 and 2007/08)	(6,000)		
			(184,000)
NRB available			(141,000)
Taxable amount			202,000

KAPLAN PUBLISHING

		£
	Inheritance tax at 40%	80,800
	Less: Taper relief (4 – 5 years) (40% × £80,800)	(32,320)
	Inheritance tax payable	48,480

3 Additional taper relief

		£
(i)	Taper relief of 60% (5 – 6 years)	32,320
(ii)	Taper relief of 80% (6 – 7 years)	16,160

Examiner's report

The first part of part (a) concerned the tax implications of the disposal of the business and was split into two sub-requirements. It was quite substantial and was worth 17 marks. Stronger candidates structured their answers in such a way that it was very clear which of the possible methods of disposal they were addressing and then dealt with the two methods one at a time. Weaker candidates did not spend sufficient time thinking about the facts of the question and simply dealt with a disposal without making it clear which of the possibilities they were considering.

The income tax aspects of the disposal revolved around the closing year rules for the unincorporated trader. There were two possible dates for the disposal: 31 January 2017 (in the tax year 2016/17) and 30 April 2017 (in the tax year 2017/18). It was important to be able to identify the tax years of the proposed disposal and the basis of assessment for each of the relevant years.

Many candidates did not have a clear understanding of these basic rules, such that they were not able to identify the relevant tax years or to accurately calculate the taxable profits for each of the relevant tax years. The unincorporated trader is an important element of the syllabus and is examined at almost every sitting; candidates must ensure that they are competent at applying the opening years rules, closing years rules and relief for losses.

The trader had purchased equipment, which was then to be sold on the cessation of the business. This required knowledge of the fundamentals of capital allowances including the annual investment allowance (AIA) and the balancing charge on disposal. Most candidates identified the AIA but many then omitted to follow the story through to the disposal, such that the balancing charge was left out. In addition, weaker candidates prepared comprehensive (and time-consuming) calculations of capital allowances in order to arrive at an AIA of £6,000, when all that was required was a statement in the calculation of the trading profit that the AIA was £6,000.

The treatment of overlap profits, the personal allowance and the calculation of income tax was done well by the vast majority of candidates.

The capital gains tax implications of the sale of the business were straightforward and were handled reasonably well. However, one common error was to treat the sale of the business as if it were a sale of a single asset as opposed to a sale of the individual assets of the business. It is important to calculate a chargeable gain on the disposal of each individual asset and not to group assets together as a single disposal.

Many candidates concluded that the capital gains tax implications were the same regardless of which of the methods of disposal took place. However, this was not the case because there was a disposal of goodwill only where the business was sold as a going concern. This affected both the disposal proceeds of the assets and the capital gains tax arising.

Finally, candidates were required to prepare a summary.

From the point of view of the client there are many detailed issues and calculations to consider here so it is important to be able to bring matters together in a manner which is useful and informative.

The summary was worth a maximum of three marks and simply required figures from earlier calculations to be brought together in one place. In order to score the maximum marks available, candidates had to include the trading income and the proceeds from the sale of the assets together with both the income tax and the capital gains tax. It was also important to exclude any non-cash items. Very few candidates managed to score all three marks; and many candidates failed to produce any sort of summary.

The second part of part (a) was handled well by the majority of candidates with many candidates demonstrating a good knowledge of the various conditions necessary for a sale to be regarded as a transfer of a going concern.

The second part of the question concerned the basic mechanics of inheritance tax; it was done well by many candidates. The question concerned the gift of a business and the subsequent death of the donor.

Almost all candidates identified the gift of the business as a potentially exempt transfer that would become chargeable following the death of the donor within seven years. They were also competent at dealing with the annual exemptions, the nil rate band (with one exception – see below), the tax rate and taper relief.

The one area where a lot of candidates did not perform as well was when it came to business property relief (BPR). To begin with, many candidates omitted BPR altogether. BPR is a significant relief that all candidates should be aware of. It is important to slow down in the exam and make sure that you work through the tax implications of the particular situation in a logical way. So, with inheritance tax, assets need to be valued, then reliefs (including BPR) need to be considered, then exemptions, followed by the nil band, tax rate and taper relief.

Those candidates who did include BPR in their answers often failed to realise that if the business was sold by Ziti (the donee) before the death of his father (the donor), BPR would not be available because the rules require the donee to own the assets gifted at the date of the donor's death.

The point referred to above regarding the nil rate band relates to the relevance of the chargeable lifetime transfer (CLT) made by the donor of the business on 1 May 2008. It was thought by some candidates that this gift would have no effect on the nil rate band available as it was more than seven years prior to the death of the donor. However, because the CLT was made within seven years of the gift of the business on 1 July 2012, the nil rate band available when calculating the tax due in respect of the gift of the business has to be reduced by the amount of the CLT.

ACCA marking scheme

			Marks
(a)	(i)	Income tax position	
		Basis periods	2.0
		Trading income	1.5
		Capital allowances	3.0
		Overlap profits	1.0
		Cessation on 31 January 2017	
		Income tax payable	1.0
		Cessation on 30 April 2017	
		Income tax payable	1.0
		Capital gains tax position	
		Capital gains	2.5
		Capital gains tax	1.5
		Availability of entrepreneurs' relief	2.0
		Summary	3.0
		Assumption	1.0
			19.5
		Maximum	**17.0**
	(ii)	Sale on 31 January 2017	1.5
		Sale on 30 April 2017	
		Charge VAT unless it is a transfer of a going concern	1.0
		Conditions (one mark each, maximum three marks)	3.0
			5.5
		Maximum	**5.0**
(b)		Death prior to disposal of business	2.0
		Death post disposal of business	
		Value of gift	1.5
		Annual exemptions	1.0
		Business property relief	1.5
		Taper relief	1.0
		Nil rate band	1.5
		Inheritance tax liabilities	2.0
			10.5
		Maximum	**9.0**
		Approach to problem solving	1.0
		Clarity of calculations	1.0
		Effectiveness of communication	1.0
		Overall presentation	1.0
		Maximum	**4.0**
Total			**35.0**

ANSWERS TO PRACTICE QUESTIONS: SECTION 2

19 JONNY *Walk in the footsteps of a top tutor*

Key answer tips

This question is in four separate parts, which could be answered in any order.

All of the areas covered are mainstream areas, and much of the technical knowledge tested is brought forward knowledge from F6: unincorporated businesses and trading losses, employed vs. self-employed factors and basic inheritance tax.

It is very important to retain your F6 knowledge, as it is often tested in the P6 exam.

Remember that there will always be roughly 5 marks available in section A of the exam for discussing ethical issues. These are often some of the easiest marks to obtain, as there are a limited number of different scenarios that could be examined.

The highlighted words in the written sections are key phrases that markers are looking for in your letter.

Tutor's top tips

As is usual for section A questions, the requirement at the end of the questions just tells you how many marks are available for each part of the question. The real requirements are in the email from the manager.

As you read through, you may find it useful to highlight any requirements and instructions that you find. Refer back to these and tick them off as you answer the question, to ensure that you do not leave anything out.

Note that the requirement asks for a memorandum, so there will be marks available for using the correct format.

KAPLAN PUBLISHING

Memorandum

To   The files
Prepared by Tax senior
Date   10 September 2016
Subject   Jonny – new business, inheritance tax and other matters

(a) **Unincorporated business**

  (i) **Jonny's post-tax income**

Tutor's top tips

Although unincorporated businesses and trading losses are F6 topics, the P6 examining team has said that unincorporated businesses will be tested in every paper, so you must ensure that you can remember and apply the rules.

In order to answer this question, there are a number of steps to be undertaken:

(1) Apply the opening year assessment rules and calculate the taxable trading profit/loss for the first two tax years based on the weak demand figures.

(2) Explain the options available for relieving the loss and select the most tax efficient option.

(3) Calculate the tax payable/saved for each of the first two tax years for both strong and weak demand.

(4) Calculate the post-tax income.

Do not waste time in calculating the taxable trading profits for strong demand as these figures are provided in the question.

Weak demand – taxable trading profit/(loss) for the first two tax years

	£	£
2016/17 (1 November 2016 to 5 April 2017)		
Loss (£15,200 × 5/8)		(9,500)
2017/18 (1 November 2016 to 31 October 2017)		
1 November 2016 to 30 June 2017		
Loss	(15,200)	
Less: Recognised in 2016/17	9,500	
		(5,700)
1 July 2017 to 31 October 2017		
Profit (£18,000 × 4/12)		6,000
Profit		300

Options for loss relief with weak demand

The loss of £9,500 for 2016/17 can be offset against:

(i) Total income of 2016/17 and/or 2015/16.

In 2016/17, Jonny will have no taxable income.

In 2015/16, Jonny had employment income of £24,000 (12 × £2,000), such that he was a basic rate taxpayer.

Or

(ii) Total income of 2013/14, 2014/15 and 2015/16 in that order.

In 2013/14, Jonny had employment income of £72,000 (12 × £6,000), such that he had more than £9,500 of income taxable at the higher rate.

The loss should therefore be offset in 2013/14, resulting in a tax refund of £3,800 (£9,500 × 40%).

Income tax payable/refundable

	Strong demand		Weak demand	
	2016/17	2017/18	2016/17	2017/18
	£	£	£	£
Taxable trading profit	5,750	19,200	Nil	300
Less: Personal allowance	(5,750)	(10,600)	Nil	(300)
Taxable income	Nil	8,600	Nil	Nil
Income tax payable at 20%	Nil	1,720	Nil	Nil
Income tax refundable (above)			(3,800)	

Tutor's top tips

The question provides a table to be completed, so make sure that you do this. There are easy marks available for following through and calculating the post-tax income figures, regardless of whether your figures for the tax payable and tax savings are correct.

Post-tax income position

	Strong	Weak
	£	£
Aggregate budgeted net profit of the first two trading periods (per email)	39,200	2,800
Aggregate income tax (payable)/refundable for the first two tax years	(1,720)	3,800
Budgeted post-tax income	37,480	6,600

These post-tax income figures are an approximation because the total income arises in a period of 20 months (1 November 2016 to 30 June 2018), whereas the total income tax payable is in respect of only 17 months (five months in 2016/17 and the whole of 2017/18).

Tutorial note

You could also have stated that the figures are an approximation as they are based on estimates, which may change.

(ii) **Salesmen**

Tutor's top tips

This part requires straightforward application of employed vs. self-employed factors. The key to scoring well here is to apply the factors to the scenario, not just list them all out. The requirement asks specifically for indicators of self-employment, so there is no need to discuss anything else.

Proposed contractual arrangements indicating self-employed status

– The salesmen will be paid a fee by reference to the work they do. This will enable them to earn more by working more efficiently and effectively.

– The salesmen will not be paid sick pay or holiday pay; such payments would be indicative of employed status.

– The salesmen will be required to use their own cars.

Suggested changes in order to maximise the likelihood of the salesmen being treated as self-employed

– It would be helpful if the salesmen were able to work on the days they choose rather than being required to work on specific days.

– The salesmen should be required to provide their own laptop computer rather than borrowing one from Jonny.

Tutorial note

The period for which the salesmen will work is not a relevant factor in determining their status. However, the longer they are appointed for, the more likely it is that the factors indicating employment (for example, the degree of control over the worker) will be present.

(ii) **New contracts for the business**

Tutor's top tips

There are 5 marks available here, so try to make sure that you make 5 separately identifiable points in your answer.

- ACCA's Code of Ethics and Conduct includes confidentiality as one of the fundamental principles of ethics on which we should base our professional behaviour.

- Where we have acquired confidential information as a result of our professional and business relationships, we are obliged to refrain from using it to our own advantage or to the advantage of third parties.

- This principle of confidentiality applies to both ex-clients and continuing clients.

- As a result of this, we should not use any confidential information relating to our existing clients or ex-clients to assist Jonny.

- We are permitted to use the experience and expertise we have gained from advising our clients.

(b) **Jonny's inheritance from his mother**

Tutor's top tips

This part of the question involves correcting errors in an inheritance tax computation, which requires good basic knowledge of inheritance tax.

Take note of the information in the email from the manager: you are told that the arithmetic, dates and valuations are correct, and also that there were no other lifetime gifts and no business property relief.

The exclusion of chattels less than £6,000 and application of the annual exemption to the death estate are common errors, so should have been easy to spot.

Even if you did not spot all of the errors, you would still score marks for following through and calculating the value of the inheritance receivable by Jonny.

Errors identified

1 Chattels (for example, furniture, paintings and jewellery) with a value of less than £6,000 are not exempt for the purposes of inheritance tax (although they are exempt for the purposes of capital gains tax).

2 The annual exemption is not available in respect of transfers on death.

3   The reduced rate of inheritance tax of 36% will apply. This is because:

   – the chargeable estate, before deduction of the charitable donation but after deduction of the nil rate band, is £689,000 (£619,000 (£591,000 + £25,000 + £3,000) + £70,000); and

   – the gift to the charity of £70,000 is more than 10% of this amount.

Value of inheritance receivable by Jonny

	£
Chargeable estate per draft computation	892,000
No exemption for chattels valued at less than £6,000	25,000
No annual exemption	3,000
	920,000
Less: Nil rate band	(301,000)
Inheritance tax at 36%	619,000
	222,840
Assets inherited by Jonny (£530,000 + £400,000 + £40,000 + £20,000 – £70,000)	920,000
Less: Inheritance tax payable	(222,840)
Inheritance receivable by Jonny	697,160

Examiner's comments

Part (a), which was in three parts, related to a sole trader business. Part (a)(i) required candidates to calculate an individual's post-tax income for the first two tax years of trading, after considering the optimum relief for a trading loss in the first accounting period. A small number of candidates achieved full, or nearly full marks for this part but a significant minority made no or very little attempt to address this part of this question, suggesting a lack of preparation for this type of question. Unincorporated business are tested in every paper, and questions frequently demand consideration of basis periods and/or relief for trading losses, so question practice on these areas should always form an important part of all candidates' preparation for this exam.

Relief for trading losses is a technically demanding area, which requires accurate knowledge of what reliefs are available in which situations, and the precise rules or conditions in each case. Many candidates confined themselves to discussing just one method of loss relief, whereas careful reading of the question indicated that there were different options available and a decision was to be made regarding the optimum method of relief, thereby suggesting that more than one method of relief was available.

It appeared that many candidates would have benefited from pausing and thinking more before they started to write. It is important in a question dealing with relief for losses that a well-considered and logical approach is taken. Weaker candidates prepared detailed income tax computations for several tax years in the apparent hope that this would eventually lead to being able to determine the rate of tax paid in each year, and an ability to calculate the tax refund suggested by the question. The problem with this approach was that it was very time consuming and tended to produce redundant information as tax years were included for which it was not possible to offset the loss. Candidates should be advised to consider first of all the tax years in which they believe loss relief is available, before launching into a series of detailed computations for which there are no marks available.

Part (a)(ii) concerned the employment status of two part-time salesmen and was done extremely well. The majority of candidates were able to identify which of the specific contractual arrangements given in the question concerning the work to be done by the salesmen indicated self-employment and any changes required to the other arrangements in order to maximise the likelihood of the salesmen being treated as self-employed. Many candidates gave the impression of being very confident with this topic, and happy to write at length about the different arrangements, giving the impression that they may well have exceeded the four marks worth of time which should have been allocated to this part. Candidates should always take note of the number of marks available for each question part and resist the temptation to elaborate unnecessarily on areas with which they are very comfortable.

Part (a)(iii) covered the ethical issue of confidentiality in relation to using knowledge and experience gained from dealing with both current and ex-clients to assist a new client. This part was done very well by the vast majority of candidates, with many scoring full marks. It was pleasing to see that most candidates related well to the specific client and the facts given in the scenario.

Part (b) of this question required candidates to identify errors in an inheritance tax computation on a death estate, and to calculate the amount to be received by the sole beneficiary of the estate, after the correct inheritance tax had been paid.

Performance on this part of the question was mixed, with a disappointing number of candidates believing that the capital gains tax exemption for chattels with a value below £6,000 also applies to inheritance tax, and that inheritance tax annual exemptions are available against assets in the death estate. These are fundamental errors which candidates at P6 should not be making. Candidates should ensure that they are able to identify and apply correctly the different exemptions available for capital gains tax and inheritance tax as these are tested on a very regular basis.

In order to calculate the correct amount of inheritance tax to be paid after correcting the errors found, the majority of candidates rewrote the entire death estate. This succeeded in gaining the relevant marks, but was probably fairly time-consuming, and candidates are encouraged to try and adopt a more efficient approach, focusing on the effect of correcting the error on the value of the chargeable estate as this would save time.

Questions at P6 frequently ask for a calculation of after-tax proceeds – here, the amount receivable by the sole beneficiary of the estate. Candidates need to think more carefully about the starting point for this type of calculation. Here, it wasn't the value of the chargeable estate, as this includes a deduction for the nil rate band.

Candidates needed to identify the actual value which would be received prior to making this deduction. Failure to identify the correct starting point is a common error.

PAPER P6: ADVANCED TAXATION (FA2015)

ACCA marking scheme			
			Marks
(a)	(i)	Taxable trading profit/(loss) for weak demand	3.0
		Income tax payable or refundable	
		Strong demand	2.0
		Weak demand	2.0
		Advice on use of loss	
		Options available	3.0
		Recommendation	3.0
		Summary	1.0
		Calculation only an approximation	2.0
			———
			16.0
		Maximum	15.0
			———
	(ii)	One mark for each relevant point Maximum	4.0
	(iii)	One mark for each relevant point Maximum	5.0
(b)		Identification of errors	4.5
		Calculations	
		Inheritance tax liability	2.0
		Inheritance receivable by Jonny	1.5
			———
			8.0
		Maximum	7.0
			———
		Followed instructions	1.0
		Clarity of explanation and calculations	1.0
		Problem solving	1.0
		Overall presentation	1.0
			———
		Maximum	4.0
			———
Total			**35.0**

ANSWERS TO PRACTICE QUESTIONS: SECTION 2

CAPITAL TAXES

20 JOAN ARK

Key answer tips

This is a good practice question covering the IHT and CGT implications of lifetime gifts in part (a), with a written requirement on general IHT planning points in part (b).

The style of question is more like the Section B optional questions, although it is much longer than the Section B questions you will see under the current exam format.

When attempting part (a), the best approach is to run through each disposal twice: once to deal with the IHT implications, then again to deal with the CGT implications.

If you try to cover both taxes at once, it is very easy to get them confused! You must also make sure that your answer is clearly labelled so that the marker knows exactly which tax and which gift you are discussing.

(i) **IHT and CGT implications of gifts made in 2015/16**

(a) **Ordinary shares in Orleans plc**

IHT implications

For IHT purposes, a discretionary trust is a 'relevant property trust' and lifetime gifts into trusts are chargeable lifetime transfers.

BPR is not available as the shares are quoted and Joan does not have a controlling interest.

There would be two annual exemptions available against this gift; however, the question says to ignore the effect of the annual exemption.

The shares are valued at the lower of:

- Quarter up method = 147p (146p + ¼ × (150p −146p)) per share, or
- Average of the marked bargains = 147.5p ((140p + 155p) ÷ 2).

As Joan is to pay any IHT, the gift is a net gift and will be taxed at 25%.

	£
Transfer of value (250,000 × 147p)	367,500
Less: BPR	(Nil)
Exemptions	(Nil)
Net chargeable transfer	367,500
Less: NRB	(325,000)
Taxable amount	42,500
IHT payable (£42,500 × 25%)	10,625

KAPLAN PUBLISHING

The tax payable by Joan is due by 30 April 2016.

Gross gift to c/f = (£367,500 + £10,625) = £378,125

If Joan dies within seven years, before 13 July 2022, a further IHT liability may arise.

CGT implications

For CGT purposes, the shares are deemed to have been sold for their market value.

This is calculated as the mid-price = 148p ((146p + 150p) ÷ 2)

There are no acquisitions on the same day or in the next 30 days; therefore, the disposal of shares is from the share pool as follows:

	Number	Cost £
2000 – Purchase	200,000	149,000
August 2013 – Purchase	75,000	69,375
July 2014 – Purchase	10,000	14,800
	285,000	233,175
July 2015 – Gift	(250,000)	(204,539)
	35,000	28,636

The chargeable gain is calculated as follows:

	£
Market value (250,000 × 148p)	370,000
Less: Cost	(204,539)
Chargeable gain	165,461

Joan does not have a 5% interest in the company and therefore the shares are not qualifying business assets for gift relief purposes.

However, Joan can elect to defer all of the gain with a gift relief claim as there is an immediate charge to IHT.

Therefore there is no capital gains tax payable.

Tutorial note

If gift relief is claimed, the full gain is deferred, therefore entrepreneurs' relief is not a consideration.

However, even if gift relief were not claimed, entrepreneurs' relief would not be available as Joan is not an employee and does not own a 5% interest. The gain would therefore be taxed at 28% (as Joan is a higher rate taxpayer), not 10%.

(b) **Ordinary shares in Rouen Ltd**

IHT implications

Joan's gift of shares in Rouen Ltd in July 2015 to her son will be a PET, calculated as follows:

	£
Value of shares held before the transfer (see Tutorial note)	
40,000 × £17.10 (part of a 80% holding)	684,000
Value of shares held after the transfer	
20,000 × £14.50 (part of a 60% holding)	(290,000)
Value transferred	394,000
Less: BPR (100%) (see Tutorial note)	(394,000)
Chargeable amount	Nil

As a PET there is no lifetime IHT payable.

If Michael still owns the shares at the date of Joan's death, 100% BPR is still available and there will be nil taxable amount.

An IHT liability will arise if Joan dies before 15 July 2022 and Michael has disposed of the shares before that date.

Tutorial note

When valuing the shares for IHT purposes, the related property provisions must be taken into account. Joan is therefore disposing of 20,000 shares out of a combined 80% holding of shares held by her husband.

Business property relief at the rate of 100% will be available as the shares are unquoted trading company shares held for more than two years.

CGT implications

A capital gain will arise as follows:

	£
MV of 20% holding (20,000 × £7.90)	158,000
Less: Cost £96,400 × (20,000/40,000)	(48,200)
Chargeable gain	109,800

Provided Joan and her son jointly elect, the gain can be held over as a gift of business assets, since Rouen Ltd is an unquoted trading company.

Therefore there is no capital gains tax payable.

Tutorial note

If gift relief is claimed, the full gain is deferred, therefore entrepreneurs' relief is not a consideration.

However, even if gift relief were not available, entrepreneurs' relief would not be available as Joan does not work for Rouen Ltd. The gain would therefore be taxed at 28%.

Key answer tips

For IHT purposes, the diminution in the value of Joan's estate is the starting point.

For CGT purposes, the deemed proceeds is the market value of the asset gifted (i.e. a 20% holding).

Note that the diminution in value concept does not apply to CGT and the related property provisions do not apply to CGT.

(c) **Antique vase**

IHT implications

The gift of the vase is in consideration of marriage, and will therefore qualify for an exemption of £2,500 as it is a gift from a grandparent to grandchild.

The balance of the gift of £16,000 (£18,500 – £2,500) will be a PET made on 4 November 2015, with no tax unless Joan dies within seven years.

CGT implications

The gift of the vase is a disposal of a non-wasting chattel. The gain is calculated as £4,350 (£18,500 – £14,150).

Gift relief is not available as a vase is not a qualifying business asset and there is no immediate charge to IHT.

The CGT liability due on 31 January 2017 is therefore £1,218 (£4,350 × 28%) (ignoring the annual exempt amount).

(d) **Agricultural land**

IHT implications

The gift of the agricultural land will be a PET for £300,000 on 15 January 2016 and will not become chargeable unless Joan dies within seven years.

The increase in the value of her son Charles' property is irrelevant in valuing the PET. Only the diminution in the value of Joan's estate as a result of the gift is relevant.

If the PET becomes chargeable as a result of Joan dying before 15 January 2023, agricultural property relief at the rate of 100% based on the agricultural value of £175,000 will be available. This is because the land is let out for the purposes of agriculture and has been owned for at least seven years.

However, relief will only be available if, at the date of Joan's death, Charles still owns the land and it still qualifies as agricultural property.

CGT implications

The gift of agricultural land to Charles will be valued at its open market value on the date of the gift of £300,000.

Since the land qualifies for agricultural property relief it is also eligible for gift relief for CGT purposes. Joan and Charles can therefore jointly elect that the gain of £208,000 (£300,000 – £92,000) is held over as a gift of business assets.

Therefore there is no capital gains tax payable.

Tutorial note

Entrepreneurs' relief is not a consideration as the full gain is deferred with a gift relief claim.

However, even if gift relief were not available, entrepreneurs' relief would not be available for the disposal of investment assets. The gain would therefore be taxed at 28%.

(e) **Main residence**

IHT implications

The gift of the main residence is a gift with reservation because although Joan has gifted the freehold interest, she retains an interest in the property as she has continued to live rent free in the property.

The gift will be treated as a PET for £265,000 as normal on 31 March 2016, but Joan will still be treated as beneficially entitled to the property.

If Joan continues to live in the property rent free until her death, it will be included in her estate when she dies at its market value at that date, although relief will be given should there be a double charge to IHT.

Joan could avoid these provisions by paying full consideration for the use of the property. The gift of the main residence will simply be a PET on 31 March 2016 with no gift with reservation implications.

CGT implications

The gift of the main residence is a chargeable disposal for CGT purposes and the time of the disposal is when the ownership of the asset passes to the donee.

The reservation of benefit is therefore not relevant for CGT, and a normal CGT computation is required on 31 March 2016.

	£
Deemed consideration	265,000
Less: Cost	(67,000)
	198,000
Less: PPR exemption (W1)	(81,931)
Letting relief (W2)	(40,000)
Chargeable gain	76,069
Capital gains tax (£76,069 × 28%)	21,299
Due date	31 January 2017

Workings

(W1) **Principal private residence exemption**

		Notes	Months	Exempt	Chargeable
1.07.94 – 31.12.98	Owner occupied		54	54	
1.01.99 – 31.12.02	Unoccupied	1	48	36	12
1.01.03 – 30.06.15	Rented out	2	150	9	141
1.07.15 – 31.03.16	Owner occupied		9	9	
			261	108	153

PPR exemption = (108/261) × £198,000 = £81,931

Notes

1. Three years allowed for no reason provided the property is owner occupied at some time before and sometime after the period of absence.

2. The last 18 months are always exempt. They fall partly into the final period of owner occupation but partly in the period when the property was rented out.

(W2) **Letting relief**

Lower of:		£
(a)	PPR exemption	81,931
(b)	Maximum	40,000
(c)	Period not exempted by PPR but the property is let (141/261) × £198,000	106,966

(ii) **Main advantages in lifetime giving for IHT purposes**

Possible advantages of lifetime giving include:

- Making use of lifetime IHT exemptions such as the annual exemption, small gifts exemption, marriage exemptions in reducing a taxpayer's chargeable estate at death.

- Gifts between individuals will not become liable to IHT unless the donor dies within seven years of making the gift.

- If the donor does die prematurely there may still be an IHT advantage in lifetime giving because usually:
  - The value of the asset for calculating any additional IHT arising upon death is fixed at the time the gift is made, unless the asset falls in value, in which case fall in value relief may be available.
  - The availability of tapering relief (providing the donor survives at least three years) may help reduce the effective IHT rate.

Main factors to consider in choosing assets to gift

The main factors to consider include:

(i) Whether or not a significant CGT liability will arise upon making the gift.

Lifetime gifting may give rise to CGT. This therefore needs to be balanced against the fact that no CGT liability will arise upon death (i.e. if the assets are left in the estate and gifted in a will). Death results in the 'tax free' uplift of the chargeable assets included in the deceased's estate to market value.

The availability of CGT reliefs (primarily gift relief for business assets or if there is an immediate charge to IHT) and CGT exemptions (e.g. annual exempt amount) to ensure there is no CGT liability on the lifetime gift is therefore relevant in selecting assets.

Some assets are completely exempt from CGT, such as cash. Giving cash during lifetime would not give rise to a CGT liability.

(ii) Whether an asset is appreciating in value.

Because any additional IHT arising as a result of death will be based on the (lower) value of the asset at the date of gift it may be advantageous to select assets that are likely to significantly appreciate in value.

Even if the value of the asset decreases, fall in value relief may be available so that lifetime giving does not result in more tax than leaving the asset in the death estate.

(iii) Whether the donor can afford to make the gift.

Whilst lifetime gifting can result in significant IHT savings this should not be at the expense of the taxpayer's ability to live comfortably, particularly in old age.

(iv) The availability of significant IHT reliefs, particularly BPR.

There may be little point in selecting an asset that already qualifies for 100% relief.

21 ALEX (ADAPTED)

Key answer tips

This question includes some nice easy marks for basic income tax and inheritance tax computations, with a written section on the use of trusts.

There are a few tricky points in part (b) – make sure that you calculate the lifetime tax before trying to calculate the death tax on lifetime transfers, as the PET uses the nil band on death but does not affect the nil band when calculating the lifetime tax on the CLT.

Where shares are quoted 'ex div' you must add the dividend to the estate too. Don't forget to include the income tax from part (a) – this will be a mark for consistency, even if your figure is wrong.

Trusts are only likely to feature as part of a question in the exam, as in part (c).

(a) **Income tax payable/repayable – 2015/16**

	Total	Other income	Savings income	Dividends
	£	£	£	£
Pension	13,285	13,285		
B.Soc interest (£1,280 × 100/80)	1,600		1,600	
NS&I interest (received gross)	870		870	
Dividends – other (£8,100 × 100/90)	9,000	–		9,000
– Nacional plc (Note 1)	4,000			4,000
Total income	28,755	13,285	2,470	13,000
Less: PA	(10,600)	(10,600)		
Taxable income	18,155	2,685	2,470	13,000

Income tax

£			£
2,685	× 20% (Other income)		537
2,315	× 0% (Savings income) (Note 2)		–
5,000			
155	× 20% (Savings income) (Note 2)		31
13,000	× 10% (Dividends)		1,300
18,155			

		£
Income tax liability		1,868
Less: Tax at source		
On dividends (£13,000 × 10%)		(1,300)
On savings (£1,600 × 20%)		(320)
PAYE		(1,109)
Income tax repayable		(861)

Tutorial note

1   Alex will be taxed on his income due and payable up to the date of death. He will have a full (non-apportioned) personal allowance for 2015/16, the tax year of death.

Re-the Nacional plc dividends:

- The dividends are declared before Alex's death and are therefore included in Alex's last income tax computation even though they are received post death.

- Gross dividends to include = (20,000 × 18p × 100/90) = £4,000

The ACCA have confirmed that this is the treatment they expect for dividends declared pre-death, received post death.

2   Note that to the extent that savings income falls in the first £5,000 of taxable income, that part is taxed at 0%. The remainder of the savings income is taxed at the basic rate for savings of 20%.

(b) **Inheritance tax liability on Alex's death**

Lifetime inheritance tax

July 2010 – PET

- The gift in July 2010 was a potentially exempt transfer (PET).
- No IHT is payable at the time of the gift.
- IHT only becomes payable when Alex dies within seven years.

March 2011 – CLT

- The transfer into the discretionary trust in March 2011 was a chargeable lifetime transfer (CLT).
- Lifetime IHT is due when the gift is made and additional tax is due as Alex dies within seven years of the gift.
- The value of the CLT was £338,000.
- No annual exemptions were available, as these are allocated in date order against the PET in July 2010.
- The lifetime tax on the CLT was as follows:
  (£338,000 – £325,000 nil rate band) × 25% = £3,250
- The gross chargeable transfer was therefore £341,250 (£338,000 + £3,250).

Tutorial note

1   The question tells you that when Alex's wife died, she had utilised all of her nil rate band. As a result, only Alex's nil rate band is available.

Had his wife not utilised her nil rate band, the proportion of unused nil rate band could be transferred to Alex on his death.

> 2 Where the donor suffers the lifetime tax due, the tax rate used to calculate lifetime tax is 25% (i.e. 20/80).
>
> All of the nil rate band is available against this lifetime gift; the PET is ignored as it is not chargeable during Alex's lifetime, although it does use the annual exemptions.

Additional inheritance tax due at death

IHT on PET in July 2010

The PET becomes chargeable on death, as Alex died within seven years of making the gift. As there are no lifetime transfers in the previous seven years, all of the nil rate band is available.

		£
Value transferred		338,000
Less: Annual exemptions: 2010/11		(3,000)
2009/10		(3,000)
PET		332,000
IHT due (£332,000 – £325,000) × 40%		2,800
Less: Taper relief (5 – 6 years) (60%)		(1,680)
IHT due on death		1,120

This additional tax is paid by Brian (see Tutorial note).

IHT on CLT in March 2011

The PET has used up the nil rate band, so the CLT in March 2011 is fully taxable as follows:

	£
IHT due on gross gift (£341,250 × 40%)	136,500
Less: Taper relief (4 – 5 years) (40%)	(54,600)
	81,900
Less: IHT paid during lifetime	(3,250)
IHT due on death	78,650

This additional tax is paid by the trustees of the discretionary trust (see tutorial note).

Tutorial note

The additional tax on PETs and CLTs as a result of death is always paid by the donee.

Estate at death

	£	£
Residence		475,000
Touriga shares (W1)	26,950	
Less: Business property relief	(26,950)	
		Nil
Nacional shares (W2)		128,800
Building society account		15,000
NS&I investment account		55,000
NS&I savings certificates		180,000
Chattels		40,000
Other quoted investments		115,000
Income tax repayment (part (a))		861
		1,009,661
Less: Exempt charitable legacy		(150,000)
Gross chargeable estate = taxable estate		859,661

The nil rate band has already been used against gifts made in the seven years prior to death.

IHT on estate (£859,661 × 36%) (W3)   309,478

The inheritance due to each of Brian and Beatrice is £288,566 (W4).

Workings

(W1) **Touriga Ltd**

The total value of Touriga Ltd shares at death = (£11.00 × 2,450) = £26,950.

As these shares are unquoted trading company shares and have been held for more than two years, 100% business property relief applies.

(W2) **Nacional plc**

The Nacional plc shares are valued at the lower of:

(i) Quarter up method

= (624p + (632p − 624p) × 1/4) = 626p

(ii) Average of highest and lowest marked bargains

= (625p + 630p) × ½ = 627.5p

Value of 20,000 shares = (626p × 20,000) = £125,200

As the shares are quoted ex-div at the date of death, the value of the shares in the death estate, needs to include the value of the next net dividend (18p × 20,000 = £3,600).

The total value of the shares is therefore £128,800 (£3,600 + £125,200).

(W3) **Rate of tax**

	£
Taxable estate	859,661
Add: Exempt legacy to charity	150,000
Baseline amount	1,009,661
Apply 10% test	
£1,009,661 × 10%	100,966

As the exempt charitable legacy exceeds £100,966, the estate is taxed at 36% instead of 40%.

(W4) **Share of inheritance**

	£
Value of estate	859,661
Value of Touriga shares	26,950
	886,611
IHT payable from estate	(309,478)
Estate value to share	577,133

Half share to each of Brian and Beatrice (£577,133 ÷ 2) = £288,566.

(c) (i) **Use of a trust**

Relevant property trusts

Brian has the choice of setting up an interest in possession trust or a discretionary trust.

However, regardless of the type of trust set up, if the trust is set up by Brian during his lifetime it will be a 'relevant property trust' for IHT purposes.

A relevant property trust is taxed as follows:

- Gifts into a relevant property trust are chargeable lifetime transfers (CLTs). They attract IHT at half the death rate to the extent that the cumulative lifetime transfers in the last seven years of the settlor (Brian) exceed the nil rate band (£325,000).
- The tax can be paid by the trustees out of the settled assets (i.e. borne by the trust).
- Once the assets are settled in a relevant property trust, the trust will suffer a 10 year charge (the 'principal charge').
- The charge is 6%.
- If capital assets are removed from the trust (i.e. distributed to the beneficiaries), an exit charge is also levied.

Type of trust

Given Brian's desire to retain control over the assets, it would appear that a discretionary trust would be advisable, rather than an interest in possession trust.

This is because:

- The trustees of a discretionary trust have the discretion (hence the name) over how the funds will be used.
- They can thus control the assets comprising the inheritance, while allowing Colin or Charlotte access to some or all of the income.
- It is likely that Brian himself would wish to be a trustee and he could therefore control how his children accessed the money, both the income and capital.
- In contrast, if an interest in possession trust is set up, the beneficiaries Colin and Charlotte would be legally entitled to the income generated by the trust each year and it must be paid to them.
- In the trust deed the capital must be directed to pass at a set future date or as a consequence of a future event.

(ii) **Inheritance tax planning**

If Brian creates a discretionary trust by making a lifetime gift of the inherited assets, this will be a CLT and will give rise to a charge to IHT with a further liability arising if Brian dies within seven years.

Therefore, Brian should be advised to pass his inheritance directly to his children by using a deed of variation to alter the disposition of Alex's estate.

Provided the deed includes a statement that the deed is effective for inheritance tax purposes, the transfer into the trust will be treated as a legacy under the will.

There will be no alteration in the tax payable on Alex's estate but Brian will not have a CLT, there will be no lifetime tax on setting up the trust and Brian will have preserved his own nil rate band for use against future lifetime gifts or the value of his own estate on death.

Tutorial note

If Brian had chosen to set up an interest in possession trust, if set up on death (under a deed of variation of Alex's will), it will be an Immediate Post Death Interest trust (IPDI) and not a 'relevant property trust'. As a result, different rules apply to the taxation of trust.

22 MABEL PORTER *Online question assistance*

Key answer tips

This question covers the popular area of CGT versus IHT for lifetime gifts, with IHT calculations on death and further IHT planning.

You must make sure that your answer is well structured and well labelled in part (a) – you are looking at four gifts in total, and need to consider CGT and IHT. The best way to approach this is to deal with one tax at a time. Think about all the CGT implications, remembering to state which reliefs are not available, as well as those that are; then deal with the IHT implications in the same way.

As long as your advice and calculation of the tax saving in (b) is consistent with your analysis in part (a), you could still score full marks here.

(a) **Tax implications of the four possible gifts**

All four possible gifts would be potentially exempt transfers (PETs) such that no inheritance tax would be due at the time of the gift.

The chargeable gain or allowable loss arising on each gift will be computed by reference to the market value of the asset as at the date of the gift.

Gift to Bruce of shares in BOZ plc

Capital gains tax

The gift will result in a chargeable gain of £32,500 (£77,000 – £44,500).

BOZ plc is Mabel's personal trading company as she is able to exercise at least 5% of the voting rights. Accordingly, the shares qualify for gift relief.

However, gift relief would only be available if Bruce (the recipient of the gift) were UK resident. This is unlikely to be the case as he emigrated to South Africa in January 2013; therefore gift relief is not available.

Entrepreneurs' relief is not available as although BOZ plc is Mabel's personal trading company and she has owned the shares for more than a year, she does not work for BOZ plc.

Key answer tips

Where an individual owns shares in a plc, you should generally assume that they hold less than a 5% interest and that they don't work for the company, unless clearly told otherwise.

Inheritance tax

The value transferred will be reduced by business property relief at the rate of 50% because Mabel owns a controlling shareholding in the company.

Luke's period of ownership can be taken into account in order to satisfy the two-year period of ownership requirement.

The relief is restricted because the company owns excepted assets.

	£
Value transferred	77,000
Less: BPR (£77,000 × 92% × 50%)	(35,420)
Annual exemptions – 2016/17 and 2015/16 (£3,000 × 2)	(6,000)
PET	35,580

Gift to Bruce of the land in Utopia

Capital gains tax

The gift will result in a capital loss of £24,000 (£99,000 – £75,000).

This loss is available for relief against chargeable gains made by Mabel in 2016/17 or future years.

Mabel and Bruce (aunt and nephew) are not connected persons for the purposes of capital gains tax and therefore, there is no restriction on Mabel's use of the losses.

Inheritance tax

Agricultural property relief is not available because the land is not situated in the UK or the EEA.

Business property relief is also not available because the farm is an investment asset, not a business asset.

The value of the PET will therefore be:

	£
Value transferred	75,000
Less: Annual exemptions – 2016/17 and 2015/16 (£3,000 × 2)	(6,000)
PET	69,000

Tutorial note

BPR is available on worldwide business property, whereas APR is only available on farm land and buildings situated in the UK or the EEA.

The minimum period of ownership rules also have to be satisfied. Even if the farm had been in the UK or EEA, APR would not be available as a tenanted farm must be owned by the donor and occupied and farmed by the tenant for at least 7 years prior to the transfer.

Gift to Padma of the Rolls Royce motor car

Capital gains tax

No gain or loss will arise as cars are exempt assets for the purposes of capital gains tax.

Inheritance tax

The PET will equal the market value of the car of £71,000.

There are no annual exemptions available as they have already been used against the gift to Bruce.

Gift to Padma of the necklace

Capital gains tax

The gift will result in the following chargeable gain.

	£
Deemed proceeds (market value)	70,000
Less: Cost (probate value when inherited)	(21,500)
Chargeable gain	48,500

Gift relief is not available as the necklace is not a business asset.

Inheritance tax

The value of the PET will equal the market value of the necklace of £70,000.

There are no annual exemptions available as they have already been used against the gift to Bruce.

Key answer tips

Watch out for the dates here – the gift to Padma will be made after the gift to Bruce.

(b) **Recommendation of gifts to make**

Mabel's criteria in deciding which assets to give are:

- The gifts must not give rise to any tax liabilities prior to her death.

    The gifts will not give rise to inheritance tax prior to Mabel's death because they are potentially exempt transfers. Accordingly, in satisfying this criterion, it is only necessary to consider capital gains tax.

- If possible, the gifts should reduce the inheritance tax due on her death.

Bruce

A gift of the shares in BOZ plc would result in a chargeable gain of £32,500.

This exceeds Mabel's capital losses brought forward of £15,100 and the annual exempt amount of £11,100, such that a capital gains tax liability would arise.

Accordingly, she should give Bruce the land in Utopia. This will result in a capital loss of £24,000.

Padma

There would be no capital gains tax on either of the proposed gifts to Padma.

The car is an exempt asset and the chargeable gain arising on the necklace would be relieved by Mabel's capital losses and the annual exempt amount as follows:

		£
Chargeable gain		48,500
Less:	Capital loss on the gift to Bruce of the land	(24,000)
	Capital losses brought forward (restricted)	(13,400)
		11,100
Less:	Annual exempt amount	(11,100)
Taxable gain		Nil

Accordingly, the gift to be made to Padma should be chosen by reference to the amount of inheritance tax saved.

Mabel should give Padma the necklace as its value is expected to increase.

Key answer tips

Don't worry if you made some mistakes in part (a) – as long as you have provided clear, consistent advice with reasons, you should still score full marks here.

IHT payable if the lifetime gifts to Bruce and Padma are not made

IHT payable on Mabel's lifetime gift – during her lifetime

1 May 2010 – Gift into discretionary trust

		£
Transfer of value		210,000
Less: Annual exemptions	– 2010/11	(3,000)
	– 2009/10 b/f	(3,000)
Net chargeable amount		204,000

The gift is covered by the NRB and therefore no IHT was paid.

Gross chargeable amount	204,000

IHT payable on Mabel's lifetime gift – due to her death

If Mabel dies on 30 June 2021, this gift is more than 7 years before death and therefore no IHT payable.

As there are no other lifetime gifts, the full NRB is available against the death estate.

Death estate

	£	£
House and furniture		450,000
Rolls Royce car		55,000
Diamond necklace		84,000
Cash and investments		150,000
Shares in BOZ plc	95,000	
Less: BPR (50% × £95,000 × 92%)	(43,700)	
		51,300
Land in Utopia		75,000
Chargeable estate		**865,300**
IHT payable (£865,300 − £325,000) × 40%		216,120

Tutorial note

Luke has fully utilised his nil rate band, so there is no unused proportion to transfer to Mabel.

IHT payable if Mabel makes the lifetime gifts to Bruce and Padma

IHT payable on Mabel's lifetime gifts – during her lifetime

1 May 2010 – Gift into discretionary trust

As before, the IHT payable will be £Nil as the gift of £204,000 is covered by the NRB.

1 February 2017 – Gift to Bruce – Land in Utopia

	£
Transfer of value	75,000
Less: Annual exemption – 2016/17	(3,000)
– 2015/16 b/f	(3,000)
PET – chargeable amount	**69,000**

No IHT payable during lifetime as the gift is a PET.

5 March 2017 – Gift to Padma – Diamond necklace

	£
Transfer of value	70,000
Less: Annual exemptions (already used)	(Nil)
PET – chargeable amount	70,000

No IHT payable during lifetime as the gift is a PET.

IHT payable on Mabel's lifetime gifts – due to her death

1 May 2010 – Gift into discretionary trust

As before, if Mabel dies on 30 June 2021, this gift is more than 7 years before death and therefore no IHT payable

1 February 2017 – Gift to Bruce – Land in Utopia

	£	£
Chargeable amount		69,000
NRB at death	325,000	
Less: Gross transfers in last 7 years (1.2.10 – 1.2.17)	(204,000)	
		(121,000)
Taxable amount		Nil

No IHT payable as the gift is covered by the NRB.

5 March 2017 – Gift to Padma – Diamond necklace

	£	£
Chargeable amount		70,000
NRB at death	325,000	
Less: Gross transfers in last 7 years (5.3.10 – 5.3.17) (£204,000 + £69,000)	(273,000)	
		(52,000)
Taxable amount		18,000
IHT payable (£18,000 × 40%)		7,200
Less: Taper relief (5.03.17 to 30.06.21) (4 – 5 years) (40%)		(2,880)
		4,320
Less: IHT paid in lifetime (PET)		(Nil)
IHT due on death		4,320

Death estate

	£	£
House and furniture		450,000
Rolls Royce car		55,000
Cash and investments		150,000
BOZ plc shares (as before)		51,300
Chargeable estate		706,300
NRB at death	325,000	
Less: Gross transfers in last 7 years (30.6.14 – 30.6.21) (£69,000 + £70,000)	(139,000)	
		(186,000)
Taxable estate		520,300
IHT payable (£520,300 × 40%)		208,120

Quantifying the IHT saving as a result of making the lifetime gifts

	£
Total IHT payable if the gifts are not made	216,120
Total IHT payable if the gifts are made (£4,320 + 208,120)	(212,440)
Total IHT saved	3,680

Key answer tips

Even if you recommended different gifts, you could still score full marks for calculating the tax saving by comparing the tax payable without the gifts and the tax payable with the gifts (remembering that the assets given would no longer be in the death estate!).

(c) **Further advice**

Mabel should consider delaying one of the gifts until after 1 May 2017 such that it is made more than seven years after the gift to the discretionary trust.

Both PETs would then be covered by the nil rate band resulting in a saving of inheritance tax of £4,320 (from (b)).

Mabel should ensure that she uses her inheritance tax annual exemption of £3,000 every year by, say, making gifts of £1,500 each year to both Bruce and Padma. The effect of this will be to save inheritance tax of £1,200 (£3,000 × 40%) every year.

She could also make use of the normal expenditure out of income exemption.

23 ALVARO PELORUS (ADAPTED) *Walk in the footsteps of a top tutor*

Key answer tips

This question is all about the capital taxes (IHT and CGT), with the added complication that Alvaro and his wife are not UK domiciled.

This question has been altered to reflect the extensive changes to the rules governing the taxation of non-domiciled individuals which were introduced in the Finance Act 2008.

The highlighted words in the written sections are key phrases that markers are looking for.

Tutor's top tips

Make sure you read the question carefully and identify the relationship between the individuals involved. Part (a) is all about the IHT payable on Ray's death; parts (b) and (c) relate to his son, Alvaro, who is disposing of assets whilst still alive.

The best way to approach the calculations in part (a) is to deal with each transfer separately, starting with the earliest gift. Note that the requirement specifically asks you to explain the availability or otherwise of APR and BPR, so make sure that you do this. The words 'or otherwise' are a hint that perhaps these reliefs may not both be available!

As Ray is UK domiciled, he will be subject to IHT on his UK and overseas assets, with double tax relief available for any overseas tax suffered

(a) **Inheritance tax (IHT) payable as a result of the death of Ray Pelorus**

Lifetime gifts

IHT is payable in respect of the potentially exempt transfers (PETs) made in the seven years prior to Ray's death and on the death estate.

PET on 1 May 2012 – Gift of farm land

	£
Value transferred	273,000
Less: Agricultural property relief (100% of agricultural value)	(120,000)
Annual exemptions – 2012/13 and 2011/12 (£3,000 × 2)	(6,000)
PET – gross chargeable amount	147,000

No IHT is due during lifetime. There is no IHT on death as the PET is less than the available nil rate band of £325,000.

KAPLAN PUBLISHING

Availability of agricultural property and business property relief

Agricultural property relief is available on the agricultural value of the land on Ray's death because:

- Ray owned the tenanted land for at least seven years prior to the gift to Alvaro, and
- Alvaro still owned the land when Ray died.

Business property relief (BPR) is not available on the excess of the market value over the agricultural value because the land was held by Ray as an investment and not a business asset.

Tutorial note

Another condition for the availability of APR is that the farm must be occupied and farmed by the tenant throughout Ray's ownership and must still qualify as agricultural property on Ray's death. This condition was not however included in the examiner's model answer, but would have been a mark earning point.

PET on 1 August 2015 – Gift of shares in Pinger Ltd

	£
Transfer of value	195,000
Less: BPR (100%)	(195,000)
PET – gross chargeable amount	Nil

No IHT payable during lifetime as the gift is a PET and has £Nil chargeable value.

IHT payable on death:

	£	£
Chargeable amount (as above)		Nil
Add: BPR (see below)		195,000
Less: Annual exemptions (see tutorial note)		
– 2015/16 and 2014/15 (£3,000 × 2)		(6,000)
PET – chargeable amount on death		189,000
NRB at death	325,000	
Gross transfers in the previous 7 years (1.8.08 – 1.8.15)	(147,000)	
NRB available		(178,000)
Taxable amount		11,000
IHT on death (£11,000 × 40%)		4,400
Less: Taper relief (less than 3 years)		(Nil)
Less: Lifetime IHT paid		(Nil)
IHT payable		4,400

Availability of business property relief

Although the shares qualified for BPR at the time the PET was made, BPR is not available when the PET becomes chargeable because Alvaro did not own the shares at the date of Ray's death (tutorial note).

Tutorial note

The gift of shares was on 1 August 2015, Alvaro sold the shares on 1 September 2015, and Ray died on 1 February 2016. Therefore Alvaro did not own the shares at the date of Ray's death.

BPR is clawed back if the asset is not owned by the donee at the date of the donor's death, unless the sale proceeds have been reinvested in qualifying replacement assets.

There is nothing in the question to suggest that Alvaro invested the proceeds from the sale of the shares in replacement business property, therefore BPR is not available in the death calculation.

To calculate the chargeable amount on death, the BPR must be added back. However, provided they have not been used against a CLT during his lifetime, the annual exemptions are still available against this PET when calculating the chargeable amount.

Death estate

	£	£
UK assets		870,000
House in Pacifica (W)		89,300
Chargeable estate		959,300
NRB at death (Note 1)	325,000	
Gross transfers in the previous 7 years		
(1.2.09 – 1.2.16) (£147,000 + £189,000)	(336,000)	
NRB available		(Nil)
Taxable estate		959,300
IHT (£959,300 × 40%)		383,720
Less: Double tax relief – the lower of:		
Overseas tax suffered	1,800	(1,800)
UK IHT on the house (£89,300 × 40%) (Note 2)	35,720	
IHT payable		381,920

Working: House in Pacifica

	£	£
Value as at 1 February 2016		94,000
Less: Legal fees – the lower of:		
The fees incurred	7,700	
Maximum (5% × £94,000)	4,700	(4,700)
Value to include in the estate		89,300

Tutor's top tips

1 There is no mention of Ray's wife, whether she is still alive or predeceased him. Without further information in the question you should assume there is no unutilised spouse nil rate band available.

2 As there is no nil band available to set against the death estate, the rate of UK tax suffered is simply 40%.

Remember that if there is some nil band remaining, the average estate rate will be less than 40%, and is calculated by dividing the tax by the chargeable estate.

The UK rate of tax on foreign property can then be calculated and compared with the overseas tax suffered.

(b) (i) **Alvaro Pelorus**

Assessment to capital gains tax – 2015/16

Tutor's top tips

This section requires you to know about the complex rules for non-UK domiciled individuals. You must make sure that you learn these rules, as overseas aspects of tax are very popular in the exam.

In 2015/16 Alvaro is resident, but not UK domiciled.

Accordingly, he is assessed to UK CGT in the normal way on all of his disposals of UK assets.

However, the treatment of his capital gains and losses on his disposals of overseas assets depends on whether the amount of his unremitted overseas income and gains exceeds £2,000.

He has no unremitted income (per the question), and only disposes of one overseas asset in 2015/16, which gives rise to a capital loss. His total unremitted gains and income is therefore less than £2,000, so:

- His overseas loss is allowable.
- He will automatically be assessed on all of his UK gains with a full annual exempt amount available, and
- There is no need to make an election.

ANSWERS TO PRACTICE QUESTIONS: SECTION 2

(ii) **Alvaro Pelorus**

Capital gains tax (CGT) liability – 2015/16

Tutor's top tips

As Alvaro is UK resident, he must pay tax on his UK gains. You must then apply the non-domicile rules to decide on the tax treatment of any overseas gains or losses, and the availability of the annual exempt amount.

	£
Shares in Pinger Ltd (W1)	200,200
Shares in Lapis Inc (W4)	(2,818)
Shares in Quad plc (W5)	Nil
Net chargeable gains	197,382
Less: Annual exempt amount	(11,100)
Taxable gains	186,282
Capital gains tax (£186,282 × 28%)	52,159

Workings

(W1) Shares in Pinger Ltd – UK asset

	£
Proceeds (September 2015)	228,000
Less: Base cost (W2)	(23,400)
IHT payable by Alvaro on the PET (Note 1)	(4,400)
Chargeable gain (Note 2)	200,200

Tutorial note

1   Relief is available in respect of any inheritance tax payable on the gift of the shares on 1 August 2015.

    Although IHT will not have been paid at the time of this gift (as it was a PET for IHT purposes), following the death of Ray Pelorus, the PET becomes chargeable and IHT is paid in respect of this gift.

    As a result, the capital gains tax due in respect of the disposal of the shares in Pinger Ltd will be re-computed in order to take account of the IHT relief. However, the P6 examiner does not expect you to know this point.

2   Alvaro is not entitled to entrepreneurs' relief as the shares are not shares in his personal trading company (he owns < 5% interest) and he does not appear to work for the company. The gain will therefore be taxed at 28%, not 10%.

KAPLAN PUBLISHING

(W2) **Base cost of shares in Pinger Ltd**

	£
Market value (1 August 2015)	195,000
Less: Gift relief on gift by Ray (W3)	(171,600)
Alvaro's base cost in the shares	23,400

(W3) **Gift relief on gift by Ray to Alvaro**

	£
Market value as at 1 August 2015	195,000
Less: Cost (£54,600 × 6,000/14,000)	(23,400)
Gift relief claimed	171,600

(W4) **Shares in Lapis Inc – Overseas asset**

	£
Proceeds	8,270
Less: Cost (£25,950 × 2,350/5,500)	(11,088)
Capital loss	(2,818)

The overseas capital loss is available for relief because although Alvaro is domiciled outside the UK, he has unremitted overseas gains of ≤ £2,000 (see part (b)(i)).

(W5) **Shares in Quad plc**

	£
Deemed proceeds	74,000
Less: Cost	(59,500)
	14,500
Less: Gift relief (see tutorial note)	(14,500)
Chargeable gain	Nil

Tutorial note

Gift relief is available on the transfer of any asset to a discretionary trust because the transfer is subject to an immediate charge to inheritance tax.

Gift relief is optional and is given before considering entrepreneurs' relief.

Therefore Alvaro should consider whether or not he wants to make the gift relief claim or leave the gains to be chargeable and claim entrepreneurs' relief instead, if the conditions are satisfied.

However, the Quad plc shares do not qualify as the company is a plc and unless the question clearly states otherwise, it is assumed that:

- *he will have a less than 5% interest*
- *he does not work for the company, and*
- *he has held the shares for less than a year.*

He will therefore claim gift relief to defer the gain. The question states that you should assume that all available reliefs are claimed.

(c) (i) **Transfer of Ray's ISA savings on death**

Tutor's top tips

Note that this part of the question has two parts:

- *explain the relief available on the transfer of ISA savings on death, which is a straightforward explanation of the rules, and then*
- *consider the possibility of Alvaro (the son) claiming the relief – which is not possible.*

If on death ISA savings are left to the spouse / civil partner:

- the gift is an exempt legacy, and
- in addition, an ISA allowance equal to the deceased individual's ISA savings can be claimed by the surviving spouse / civil partner.

As a result, the deceased individual's ISA savings will retain their beneficial tax treatment (i.e. exemption from income tax and capital gains tax) in the future, in the hands of the surviving spouse / civil partner.

However, Ray has left his entire estate to his son, Alvaro, and therefore this relief is not available.

Tutorial note

It is unclear as to whether Ray has a spouse (or civil partner) and, if so, whether they are still alive, still married or divorced or have predeceased Ray. Assuming that a spouse (or civil partner) is no longer alive, a claim for this relief is not possible.

If however a wife (or civil partner) is alive and they were still married on the date of Ray's death, they would be entitled to the allowance even if the ISA assets were left to someone else (e.g. Alvaro).

If this is the case, there will be no exempt legacy in the death estate computation, but the surviving spouse (or civil partner) would be able to invest an additional amount of their own funds into an ISA to benefit from the ISA exemptions in the future.

(ii) **Variation of Ray's will**

Tutor's top tips

Don't forget that it is possible to change a person's will after they have died, as long as all beneficiaries agree. This can be a useful tax planning tool.

Note however that the question just asks you to consider varying the will in favour of the grandchildren Vito and Sophie – so do not waste time talking about the possibility of Ray having a surviving spouse (or civil partner) and possible tax savings that could arise in that scenario.

The variation by Alvaro of Ray's will, such that assets are left to Vito and Sophie, will not be regarded as a gift by Alvaro. Instead, provided the deed states that it is intended to be effective for IHT purposes, it will be as if Ray had left the assets to the children in his will.

This strategy, known as skipping a generation, will have no effect on the IHT due on Ray's death but will reduce the assets owned by Alvaro and thus his potential UK IHT liability.

A deed of variation is more tax efficient than Alvaro making gifts to the children as such gifts would be PETs and IHT may be due if Alvaro were to die within seven years.

The deed of variation must be entered into by 31 January 2018 (i.e. within two years of the date of Ray's death).

(iii) **IHT planning opportunities**

Tutor's top tips

Read the question carefully – it says that Alvaro does not wish to make any lifetime gifts other than to his wife. This means that there will be no marks available for discussion of lifetime gifts to people other than Maria!

The key point here is that Alvaro is not UK domiciled, and therefore will be taxed on his UK assets, but not overseas assets. If he can divest himself of UK assets, he will reduce the IHT due when he dies.

Alvaro will be subject to UK IHT on his UK assets only (e.g. land and chattels situated in the UK, shares registered in the UK and cash held in UK branches of banks) as he is domiciled in Koruba.

UK IHT will be charged on the excess of the value of these assets over Alvaro's available nil rate band.

Until 30 November 2022, Alvaro's available nil rate band is £257,000 (£325,000 – (£74,000 – £6,000)) due to the gift to the discretionary trust.

In order to minimise his UK IHT liability Alvaro should reduce the value of his UK assets by making gifts to Maria or selling the UK assets to third parties and acquiring foreign assets.

Maria can own UK assets equal to her available nil rate band of £325,000 without incurring a UK IHT liability on death.

There will be no CGT on the gifts even if Alvaro is UK resident, because transfers between spouses take place at no gain, no loss.

For the purposes of IHT, the gifts will be covered by the spouse exemption. The £325,000 limit on transfers to a non-UK domiciled spouse does not apply where the donor spouse is also non-UK domiciled.

Accordingly, Alvaro can gift assets to Maria with no UK tax consequences.

Alternatively, Alvaro can leave all of his UK assets to Maria on his death. There will be no IHT payable on Alvaro's death due to the spouse exemption. On Maria's death, Alvaro's unused nil rate band can be claimed against her estate, along with her nil rate band.

Alvaro should not sell any UK assets to third parties until he is non-UK resident otherwise he will be subject to UK CGT. Once he is non-UK resident the disposals will not have any UK tax consequences.

Tutorial note

The £325,000 limit on inter-spouse transfers only applies where the donor spouse is UK domiciled and the recipient spouse is non-UK domiciled.

The nil rate band unused on the death of a spouse (or civil partner) can be used to reduce the inheritance tax payable on the death of the surviving spouse (or civil partner).

24 KEPLER (ADAPTED)

Key answer tips

This is a reasonable capital taxes question but with some complications. The calculation of inheritance tax on the lifetime gift of shares is something a well prepared student should have no problems with. You might have been puzzled when asked to calculate Galileo's inheritance tax payable on the shares he inherited on Kepler's death when there is none. The examiner did give a clue by saying tax payable (if any).

Payment by instalments is important in practice and the rules should be learnt.

You must also make sure that you are happy with the overseas aspects of personal tax, as these are very popular in the exam.

There are some easy marks in the last sections asking for advice about employment benefits.

(a) (i) **Galileo – Inheritance tax payable**

Gift of shares in June 2012

The gift of shares to Galileo was a potentially exempt transfer. It has become chargeable due to Kepler's death within seven years of the gift.

Any tax arising on a PET which becomes chargeable on death is payable by the donee (i.e. Galileo).

	£	£
Value of Kepler's holding prior to the gift to Galileo (2,000 × £485)		970,000
Less: Value of Kepler's holding after the gift (1,400 × £310)		(434,000)
Transfer of value		536,000
Less: Business property relief (W1)		(367,843)
Less: Annual exemption – 2012/13		(3,000)
– 2011/12 b/f (W2)		(1,200)
Chargeable amount		163,957
Nil rate band at death	325,000	
Gross chargeable transfers in last 7 years (W2)	(305,000)	
Nil rate band available		(20,000)
Taxable amount		143,957

	£
Inheritance tax (£143,957 × 40%)	57,583
Less: Taper relief (3 – 4 years) (£57,583 × 20%)	(11,517)
Inheritance tax payable by Galileo	46,066

Inheritance of shares in May 2016

The inheritance tax payable in respect of the shares in the death estate will be paid by the executors and borne by Herschel, the residuary legatee.

None of the tax will be payable by Galileo.

Tutorial note

As Galileo is inheriting a specific gift, he will not suffer any tax. The tax will be taken from the balance of the estate.

Workings

(W1) Business property relief

BPR at 100% is available on unquoted trading company shares held for at least two years. However, BPR is restricted if the company has excepted assets.

Excepted assets and total assets

	Total assets	Excluding excepted assets
	£	£
Premises	900,000	900,000
Surplus land	480,000	–
Vehicles	100,000	100,000
Current assets	50,000	50,000
	1,530,000	1,050,000
BPR (£536,000 × 100% × (£1,050,000/£1,530,000))		367,843

Tutorial note

Excepted assets are those which have not been used wholly or mainly for business in the last two years and are not likely to be required for future use in the business.

(W2) **Lifetime gifts in the 7 years before 1 June 2012**

	1 Feb 2011	1 July 2011
	£	£
Transfer of value	311,000	1,800
(2 × £900)		
Less Annual exemptions		
– 2010/11	(3,000)	
– 2009/10 b/f	(3,000)	
– 2011/12		(1,800)
	305,000	Nil

- No tax is due at the time of the gifts as they are PETs.
- Both gifts fall within 7 years of Kepler's death and therefore become chargeable on death.
- Therefore, the GCTs in the 7 years before the gift in June 2012 are £305,000.

(ii) **Payment by instalments**

The inheritance tax can be paid by instalments because Messier Ltd is an unquoted company controlled by Kepler at the time of the gift and is still unquoted at the time of his death.

The tax is due in ten equal annual instalments starting on 30 November 2016.

Interest will be charged on any instalments paid late; otherwise the instalments will be interest free because Messier is a trading company that does not deal in property or financial assets.

All of the outstanding inheritance tax will become payable if Galileo sells the shares in Messier Ltd.

Tutorial note

Candidates were also given credit for stating that payment by instalments is available because the shares represent at least 10% of the company's share capital and are valued at £20,000 or more.

(b) Minimising capital gains tax on the sale of the paintings

Galileo will only become resident from the date he arrives in the UK as he will be starting to work full time in the UK for a period of one year or more and he did not have sufficient ties in the UK in order to be UK resident prior to coming to the UK. Further, the split year basis applies to him as he was not UK resident in the previous year, is UK resident in the current year and arrived in the UK part way through the current year to begin work in the UK.

Prior to that date he will not be resident such that he will not be subject to UK capital gains tax.

Galileo should sell the paintings before he leaves Astronomeria; this will avoid UK capital gains tax completely.

Tutorial note

If Galileo sells the paintings after arriving in the UK and becoming UK resident, then as a non-domiciled individual, the taxation of his gains depends on how much of them he remits to the UK.

If his unremitted gains exceed £2,000 then Galileo must choose whether to be taxed on all his gains (arising basis) but keep his entitlement to the capital gains annual exempt amount, or to be taxed only on the gains remitted to the UK (remittance basis) and lose the annual exempt amount.

If he chooses the remittance basis then he will not have to pay the £30,000 annual charge as he has not been resident in the UK for at least 7 out of the last 9 tax years.

If his unremitted gains are less than £2,000, then the remittance basis of taxation applies automatically and he will be entitled to a capital gains annual exempt amount.

However, since he wants to use the proceeds of selling his paintings to help buy a house, it is likely he will bring in all the money raised from the sale and consequently will automatically be taxed on the whole of his gains under the remittance basis, with the capital gains annual exempt amount being available.

(c) (i) Relocation costs

Direct assistance

Messier Ltd can bear the cost of certain qualifying relocation costs of Galileo up to a maximum of £8,000 without increasing his UK income tax liability.

Qualifying costs include the legal, professional and other fees in relation to the purchase of a house, the costs of travelling to the UK and the cost of transporting his belongings. The costs must be incurred before the end of the tax year following the year of the relocation (i.e. by 5 April 2018).

Assistance in the form of a loan

Messier Ltd can provide Galileo with an interest-free loan of up to £10,000 without giving rise to any UK income tax.

(ii) **Tax-free accommodation**

It is not possible for Messier Ltd to provide Galileo with tax-free accommodation.

The provision of accommodation by an employer to an employee will give rise to a taxable benefit unless it is:

- necessary for the proper performance of the employee's duties (e.g. a caretaker); or
- for the better performance of the employee's duties and customary (e.g. a hotel manager); or
- part of arrangements arising out of threats to the employee's security (e.g. a government minister).

As a manager of Messier Ltd, Galileo is unable to satisfy any of the above conditions.

Examiner's comments

This question was the most popular of the optional questions. It concerned inheritance tax, capital gains tax and income tax together with certain implications of moving to the UK from overseas. There were five separate parts to this question, all of which had to be addressed in the time. A number of candidates failed to tailor their answers to the number of marks available and wasted time producing inappropriately long answers.

Part (a) required candidates to calculate the inheritance tax payable by the donee of a potentially exempt transfer following the death of the donor. This was done well by many candidates although a minority did not consider business property relief, which was an important element of the question. Those who did consider business property relief often failed to recognise the existence of excepted assets in the company.

Candidates were also asked to explain why the tax could be paid in instalments and to state when the instalments were due. This was not handled particularly well; many candidates did not know the circumstances in which payment by instalments is available and the payment dates given often lacked precision.

Part (b) concerned the liability to capital gains tax of an individual coming to the UK. It was only for two marks but it illustrated continued confusion on the part of many as to the treatment of someone who is not resident. Such a person is not subject to UK capital gains tax on personal investment assets and the remittance or otherwise of the proceeds is irrelevant. Candidates preparing for future exams should ensure that they fully understand the rules.

Part (c) involved the desire to assist an employee's relocation to the UK without giving rise to an income tax liability. This was done rather well with many candidates identifying the possibility of a tax free loan and relocation assistance.

ANSWERS TO PRACTICE QUESTIONS: SECTION 2

		ACCA marking scheme	
			Marks
(a)	(i)	Diminution in value	1.0
		Business property relief	1.5
		Annual exemptions	1.5
		Available nil band	1.5
		Inheritance tax at 40%	0.5
		Taper relief	1.0
		Tax due in respect of shares in death estate	1.0
			8.0
	(ii)	Valid reason for payment by instalments being available	1.0
		When due	1.0
		Interest on instalments	1.5
		Implication of Galileo selling the shares	1.0
			4.5
		Maximum	4.0
(b)		Residence position	1.0
		Advice	1.0
			2.0
(c)	(i)	Relocation costs	
		Tax free with maximum	1.0
		Examples of qualifying costs (0.5 each, maximum 1)	1.0
		Deadline	0.5
		Interest-free loan	
		Maximum tax-free amount	1.0
			3.5
		Maximum	3.0
	(ii)	Provision of accommodation will be taxed	1.0
		Reasons why not exempt	2.0
			3.0
Total			**20.0**

KAPLAN PUBLISHING

25 ERNEST AND GEORGINA (ADAPTED) *Walk in the footsteps of a top tutor*

> **Key answer tips**
>
> This question is in two separate parts. Part (a) is purely computational, and involves some fairly straightforward CGT computations.
>
> Part (b) is purely written, and requires you to give advice about IHT and CGT.
>
> The highlighted words in the written sections are key phrases that markers are looking for.

(a) **Ernest – Maximisation of after tax sales proceeds**

> *Tutor's top tips*
>
> *Make sure that you answer the specific question here. If you just calculate the gains and capital gains tax, you will not score full marks. You must also calculate the after tax proceeds (i.e. the cash proceeds less the tax), not the (gains less the tax).*
>
> *If the examiner just asks you to 'calculate', there is no point in providing a detailed narrative to your answer, although you must label your calculations sufficiently so that the marker can see what you are calculating.*

Sale of painting

	£	£
Proceeds	47,000	47,000
Less: Cost (probate value)	(23,800)	
	———	
Capital gain	23,200	
Less: Annual exempt amount	(11,100)	
	———	
Taxable gain	12,100	
	———	
Less: Capital gains tax (£12,100 × 28%)		(3,388)
		———
After tax sales proceeds		43,612
		———

Sale of shares

	£	£
Proceeds (£7,700 × £5)	38,500	38,500
Less: Cost (W1)	(52,780)	
	———	
Allowable loss	(14,280)	
	———	
Less: Capital gains tax		(Nil)
Plus: Income tax refund (see tutorial note) (£14,280 × 40%)		5,712
		———
After tax sales proceeds		44,212
		———

ANSWERS TO PRACTICE QUESTIONS: SECTION 2

Tutorial note

If the disposal of qualifying EIS shares gives rise to a gain, it is exempt provided the shares have been held for at least three years.

However, if the disposal gives rise to a capital loss, the loss is an allowable loss.

Furthermore, if a claim is made, the capital loss on the sale of the shares in Neutron Ltd can be offset against Ernest's income in the year of disposal and/or the previous year and thereby obtain relief at 40% (rather than setting against capital gains in the future which would save tax at 18% or possibly 28%).

This is because Ernest subscribed for the shares and, as they qualified for relief under the enterprise investment scheme (EIS), Neutron Ltd satisfies the conditions necessary to qualify as a trading company for the purposes of offsetting any capital loss on disposal against income.

As the examiner just asks you to 'prepare calculations', you do not need to provide explanations of the elections claimed.

Working: Neutron Ltd – Cost of shares sold

		Number		£
1 April 2009	Purchase	18,600	@ £8.90	165,540
1 March 2011	Bonus issue – 1 for 4	4,650	@ Nil	Nil
		23,250		
1 July 2014	Rights issue – 1 for 10	2,325	@ £4.20	9,765
		25,575		175,305
1 February 2017	Proposed sale			
	(7,700/25,575 × £175,305)	(7,700)		(52,780)
Balance c/f		17,875		122,525

(b) **Planning for inheritance tax**

Tutor's top tips

Read the information carefully!

It is easy to miss the fact that Ernest and Georgina are not married, and will not therefore benefit from the inter-spouse exemption for IHT purposes and will not benefit from the no gain, no loss transfers rule for CGT purposes.

The examiner has stated that credit was available for pointing this out, or for identifying the advantage of the couple getting married.

Do not confuse two people living together with a civil partnership. A civil partnership is where two people of the same sex officially register their partnership, and thereafter the couple are treated exactly the same as a married couple.

KAPLAN PUBLISHING

> *Note also that the examiner does not state who will die first, so you need to consider both alternatives: Ernest dying first and Georgina dying first.*
>
> *There is no point in talking about making lifetime gifts to Eileen, as the information says that Ernest and George are only willing to make gifts to each other.*
>
> *Note also that the examiner does not require you to prepare calculations.*

Current position

- The shares in Neutron Ltd will be fully relieved via business property relief and therefore will not give rise to any inheritance tax either on Ernest's death or in the case of their subsequent disposal (on death or by lifetime gift) by whoever inherits them.

Tutorial note

The minimum two years ownership period does not apply to inherited assets that qualified for business property relief at the time of the previous death.

If Ernest dies before Georgina

- Ernest's estate, as reduced by the nil band of £325,000, will be taxed at 40%.
- When Georgina dies, her estate (including those assets inherited from Ernest), as reduced by the nil band of £325,000, will be taxed at 40%.
- Problem:

  Some of Ernest's assets will be taxed twice, once on his death and again on the death of Georgina.

  Quick succession relief will mitigate the double taxation if the deaths occur within five years of each other but only to a limited extent.

If Georgina dies before Ernest

- Georgina's estate of £60,000 will be covered by the nil rate band such that there will be no inheritance tax liability.
- When Ernest dies, his estate, as reduced by the nil band of £325,000, will be taxed at 40% (as above).
- Problem:

  Georgina is wasting most of her nil rate band due to an insufficiency of assets.

Advice to Ernest

1   Ernest should give assets worth £265,000 to Georgina.

    This gift will be a potentially exempt transfer but will become a chargeable transfer if Ernest dies within seven years.

    Even so, the gift must improve Ernest's inheritance tax position. This is because:

    - the value of the assets given will be frozen at the time of the gift
    - the gift will be reduced by the annual exemption, and
    - taper relief will be available if Ernest survives the gift by at least three years.

On Georgina's death, £325,000 of her estate (i.e. £265,000 more than before), will not give rise to any inheritance tax as it will be covered by her nil rate band.

Accordingly, there will be no inheritance tax liability in respect of the value of the gift if Ernest survives the gift by seven years. This will save inheritance tax of £106,000 (£265,000 at 40%).

The gift will be a disposal at market value for the purposes of capital gains tax. However, if any of the antiques or works of art have a cost and current market value of less than £6,000, these will be exempt from capital gains tax. The family home will also be exempted by principal private residence relief provided Ernest has not been absent from the home for substantial periods. Ernest should take advantage of his CGT annual exempt amount each year in making gifts.

The gift should not be made out of the Neutron Ltd shares because of the availability of the 100% business property relief.

2   Ernest should change his will and leave some assets directly to Eileen. These assets will then be subject to inheritance tax once only rather than potentially twice saving inheritance tax up to a maximum of 40%.

Tutor's top tips

Don't panic if you missed the fact that Ernest and Georgina are not married.

You could still score a pass mark here for demonstrating knowledge of business property relief, the nil band, rates of tax, the effect of lifetime giving on IHT and CGT and general planning points.

Examiner's comments

This question concerned capital gains tax and inheritance tax and was the most popular of the Section B questions.

Part (a) required calculations of the after tax sales proceeds on the sale of a painting and some shares. Almost all candidates scored high marks for this part.

However, a significant minority merely calculated tax liabilities and not the after tax proceeds. This was important as the sale of the shares resulted in a loss such that, before taking account of the relief available in respect of the loss, the after tax sales proceeds was simply the proceeds and not zero as many candidates wrote.

There was also a common technical error in the answers to this question in that many candidates incorrectly treated the rights issue shares as a separate identifiable acquisition rather than as part of the original purchase.

The ability to offset the loss on the shares against income was a tricky point that was missed by the majority of candidates.

Part (b) required candidates to consider the inheritance tax position of an unmarried couple with unequal estates.

This part of the question was done well by the majority of those who attempted it and there was clearly a good knowledge of the subject. However, many candidates would have scored more marks if they had slowed down, written less and thought more. For example, it was relatively common for candidates to omit any reference to business property relief even though they were probably well aware of the existence of the relief.

The candidates who did best worked their way through the question logically and addressed specifics. They considered what would happen on the death of Ernest followed by the death of Georgina and then what would happen if the deaths occurred the other way around. They then explained, in a clear and succinct manner, the need to transfer assets to Georgina.

	ACCA marking scheme	
		Marks
(a)	Sale of painting	
	Capital gain	1.0
	Annual exempt amount	0.5
	Capital gains tax payable	0.5
	After tax sales proceeds	0.5
	Sale of shares	
	Cost of shares sold	2.0
	Capital loss	0.5
	Tax saving in respect of losses	1.5
	After tax sales proceeds	0.5
		7.0
(b)	Current position	
	Business property relief on the shares in Neutron Ltd	1.5
	Ernest dies before Georgina	
	Tax on Ernest's death estate	1.0
	Tax on Georgina's death estate	1.0
	Identification of problem	1.0
	Quick succession relief	1.0
	Georgina dies before Ernest	
	Tax on Georgina's death estate	0.5
	Tax on Ernest's death estate	0.5
	Identification of problem	1.0
	Advice	
	Gift assets to Georgina	1.0
	Inheritance tax implications	1.5
	Potential inheritance tax saving	1.0
	Capital gains tax implications	2.0
	Should not gift shares in Neutron Ltd	0.5
	Change will and leave assets to Eileen	1.0
	Potential inheritance tax saving	0.5
		15.0
	Maximum	13.0
Total		20.0

ANSWERS TO PRACTICE QUESTIONS: SECTION 2

26 FITZGERALD AND MORRISON (ADAPTED) *Walk in the footsteps of a top tutor*

Key answer tips

This is a classic question on IHT and CGT on lifetime gifts, covering gift relief, entrepreneurs' relief, business property relief and related property.

It is a typical exam question and the interaction of IHT and CGT on lifetime gifts is an important part of the syllabus. It would be a good choice of question in the exam as there are easy marks to be had, and there are no obscure areas of the syllabus.

The highlighted words in the written sections are key phrases that markers are looking for.

(a) **Fitzgerald – gift of shares**

  (i) **Availability of gift relief**

Tutor's top tips

Being able to list the conditions for reliefs such as gift relief, rollover relief, entrepreneurs' relief, incorporation relief, etc., is a valuable skill for the exam.

You may need to provide a written answer, as here, rather than simply applying the rules to the numbers in the question.

The shares qualify for gift relief because Jay Ltd is an unquoted trading company.

For gift relief to be available, Pat must be resident in the UK.

A claim for gift relief would have to be submitted by 5 April 2021.

The claim must be signed by Fitzgerald and Pat.

  (ii) **Capital gains tax saved**

Tutor's top tips

Here gift relief is applied to shares, and it is therefore important to consider, as this is the donor's personal company, whether the company holds any chargeable assets which are not business asset (i.e. investments such as quoted company shares).

When comparing the chargeable business assets with the chargeable assets, remember that current assets, cars and non-wasting chattels with cost and proceeds of less than £6,000 are not chargeable.

KAPLAN PUBLISHING

Fitzgerald's chargeable gain

Gain not qualifying for entrepreneurs' relief

	£
Deemed proceeds – market value	127,500
Less: Cost (probate value)	(32,000)
	95,500
Less: Gift relief (£95,500 × £900,000/£1,150,000 (W))	(74,739)
Chargeable gain	20,761

If a gift relief claim is not made, Fitzgerald's gain would increase by the amount of the gift relief and his capital gains tax liability would increase by £20,927 (£74,739 × 28%).

Working

	Chargeable assets £	Chargeable business assets £
Premises	740,000	740,000
Plant and machinery	160,000	160,000
Quoted company shares	250,000	–
Motor cars	–	–
Net current assets	–	–
	1,150,000	900,000

Tutorial note

Entrepreneurs' relief will not be available as Fitzgerald has not owned the shares for 12 months. It is therefore not necessary to consider any wastage of entrepreneurs' relief by making a gift relief claim.

Pat's chargeable gain

Gain qualifying for entrepreneurs' relief

	£
Proceeds	170,000
Less: Cost (£127,500 – £74,739)	(52,761)
Chargeable gain	117,239

If a gift relief claim is not made, Pat's gain would fall by the amount of the gift relief and his capital gains tax liability would reduce by £7,474 (£74,739 × 10%) due to the availability of entrepreneurs' relief.

The tax saved as a result of the claim is £13,453 (£20,927 – £7,474).

Tutorial note

Proof of the tax saving

	Claim £	No claim £
Fitzgerald's gain	20,761	95,500
Less: Annual exempt amount	(11,100)	(11,100)
Taxable gain	9,661	84,400
Capital gains tax at 28%	2,705	23,632

	£	£
Pat's gain – gift relief claimed	117,239	
Pat's gain – no gift relief claimed ((£170,000 – £127,500))		42,500
Less: Annual exempt amount	(11,100)	(11,100)
Taxable gain	106,139	31,400
Capital gains tax at 10%	10,614	3,140
Total capital gains tax	13,319	26,772

The capital gains tax saved as a result of making the claim is £13,453 (£26,772 – £13,319).

Candidates who recognised that the tax saving could be calculated by reference to the gift relief as £74,739 × (28% – 10%) = £13,453 received full marks.

(iii) **Availability of business property relief**

Tutor's top tips

Like the capital gains tax reliefs mentioned above, it is important to be able to list the conditions for inheritance tax reliefs such as business property relief and agricultural property relief etc.

The shares qualify for business property relief because Jay Ltd is an unquoted company.

There is no need for Fitzgerald to have owned the shares for two years prior to the gift to Pat provided the shares were eligible for business property relief when he inherited them from his mother.

However, for business property relief to be available, Pat must either still own the shares when Fitzgerald dies or must have reinvested all of the sales proceeds in qualifying business property within three years of any sale.

(b) (i) **Potentially exempt transfer**

 Tutor's top tips

You need to be clear on the different valuation rules between capital gains tax and inheritance tax.

For CGT purposes, assets are transferred at market value, but for IHT the valuation is based on the diminution in value of the donor's estate, taking into account related property rules.

When looking at a question which involves both taxes, don't fall into the trap of automatically using the same values for both calculations (although in many instances the values will be the same).

The potentially exempt transfer is calculated by reference to the fall in value of Morrison's estate.

	£
Value before the gift	
– two paintings (£70,000/(£70,000 + £25,000) × £120,000)	88,421
Value after the gift	
– one painting (£25,000/(£25,000 + £25,000) × £70,000)	(35,000)
Transfer of value	53,421
Less: Marriage exemption	(5,000)
Annual exemption (current and brought forward)	(6,000)
Potentially exempt transfer	42,421

Tutorial note

The painting owned by Morrison's wife is related property. Accordingly, for the purposes of inheritance tax, Morrison's painting(s) must be valued as a proportion of the value of the whole of the related property when determining the fall in value of his estate as a result of the gift.

The related property formula needs to be learnt to deal with this kind of calculation.

It is as follows:

$$\frac{\text{Value of donor's property}}{\text{Value of donor's property} + \text{value of related property}} \times \text{Value of combined property}$$

Before the gift Morrison owned two paintings (worth £70,000) and his wife owned one (worth £25,000). The combined value of their related property was £120,000.

Following the gift Morrison owned only one painting (worth £25,000) and his wife still owned one painting (worth £25,000). The combined value of their related property was £70,000.

It is the fall in the related property value of Morrison's property which is used for inheritance tax purposes.

(ii) **Capital gain and gift relief**

Tutor's top tips

It is easy to gain two marks here, as the capital gain calculation is simply the market value less the cost (although it is a non-wasting chattel it was bought and 'sold' for more than £6,000).

Gift relief is not available on non-business assets, therefore there is no need to discuss it any further.

The gain, computed by reference to the market value of the painting, will be £16,700 (£25,000 – £8,300).

A painting is not a qualifying asset for the purposes of gift relief.

Examiner's comments

This question concerned inheritance tax and capital gains tax in respect of two proposed gifts. The question was in two parts.

The first part concerned the availability of gift relief and business property relief and required calculations of the effect of submitting a valid claim for gift relief. The calculations were done reasonably well with many candidates identifying the need to restrict the gift relief due to the existence of chargeable assets that were not business assets. The explanations of the availability of the reliefs were not done so well. The majority of candidates knew that an election for gift relief needed to be signed by both the donor and the donee but there was a general lack of precise knowledge as to which assets qualify for which reliefs. In relation to business property relief, many candidates thought the ownership requirements related to the donee rather than the donor.

The second part required calculations of a potentially exempt transfer and the capital gain arising in respect of a gift of a painting. The inheritance tax aspects of this part were difficult and were not done particularly well with the exception of the available exemptions. The capital gains tax aspects were more straightforward and were done well with the exception of weaker candidates who did not know which assets qualify for gift relief.

This question highlighted confusion between capital gains tax and inheritance tax and between gift relief and business property relief; candidates must learn these rules if they are to be successful in this exam.

			ACCA marking scheme	
				Marks
(a)	(i)		Unquoted trading company	1.0
			Need to determine status of donee	1.0
			Date	1.0
			Signatories	1.0
				4.0
	(ii)		Tax saved by Fitzgerald	
			Gain before gift relief	0.5
			Gift relief	1.5
			No entrepreneurs' relief	0.5
			Capital gains tax saved	1.0
			Additional tax payable by Pat	
			Capital gain	1.0
			Entrepreneurs' relief	1.0
			Additional tax	1.5
			Total tax saved	0.5
				7.5
			Maximum	7.0
	(iii)		Unquoted company	0.5
			Ownership period	2.0
			Pat still owns the shares	2.0
				4.5
			Maximum	4.0
(b)	(i)		Fall in value	2.0
			Exemptions	1.0
				3.0
	(ii)		Capital gain	1.0
			Availability of gift relief	1.0
				2.0
Total				**20.0**

27 CAPSTAN *Walk in the footsteps of a top tutor*

Key answer tips

This question is in three parts and covers IHT and CGT on the transfer of a property to a trust; withdrawal of EIS relief and sale of shares and qualifying corporate bonds following a takeover. These parts could be answered in any order.

Part (a) is likely to have been popular in the exam, as IHT versus CGT for lifetime gifts is an area that is very regularly tested.

Part (b) covers the sale of EIS shares. Most students are likely to be aware of the withdrawal of EIS relief, but may not be familiar with the restriction of the capital loss on sale. However, there are still some easy marks to be had here.

The last part of the question requires calculation of CGT for shares and qualifying corporate bonds acquired following a takeover. Takeovers are an important area in the exam and have appeared in many P6 exams.

The highlighted words in the written sections are key phrases that markers are looking for.

(a) **Transfer of a UK property to a discretionary trust**

Inheritance tax

Tutor's top tips

There are no tricks in this part of the question. What is required is a straightforward calculation of IHT for a chargeable lifetime transfer. You should be able to score full marks.

Note that you are required to state any assumptions you have made and additional information you require. As long as your assumptions are sensible, you should be given credit.

The transfer is a chargeable lifetime transfer.

The lifetime inheritance tax is calculated as follows:

	£
Transfer value	425,000
Less: Annual exemptions – 2016/17	(3,000)
– 2015/16 b/f	(3,000)
Chargeable amount	419,000
Less: Nil rate band available	(325,000)
Taxable amount	94,000
Inheritance tax at 25% (Capstan is paying the tax)	23,500

The inheritance tax is due on 30 April 2017.

Tutorial note

Lifetime tax on a CLT is due on the later of:

- *6 months from the end of the month of transfer, or*
- *30 April following the tax year of transfer.*

Assumptions

- Capstan has made no other previous transfers in 2015/16 or in 2016/17, so there are two annual exemptions available.
- Capstan has made no chargeable lifetime transfers in the seven years prior to 1 May 2016, so the whole of the nil rate band is available.

Capital gains tax

	£
Proceeds (market value)	425,000
Less: Cost	(285,000)
Chargeable gain	140,000
Less: Gift relief	(140,000)
Taxable gain	Nil

Gift relief is available on the transfer because the gift is immediately chargeable to inheritance tax.

The full gain will be deferred against the cost of the property for the trustees, and there will be no immediate tax payable.

Tutor's top tips

The examiner did not expect you to show the calculation of the gain in this question, as the full gain can be deferred using gift relief.

(b) **Sale of shares in Agraffe Ltd**

Tutor's top tips

In this part of the question, you are asked to **explain** with supporting calculations.

The written part of the answer is therefore likely to score as many marks as the numbers, if not more marks.

Even if you do not know the detailed rules for calculating the EIS relief withdrawn, you can still score marks for explaining what will happen.

Withdrawal of income tax relief

If the shares in Agraffe Ltd are sold on 1 July 2016, they will have been owned for less than three years.

The EIS income tax relief obtained when the shares were purchased will be withdrawn. As the shares are sold at a loss, the relief withdrawn will be based on 30% of the proceeds received.

This will result in a liability of £6,000 (£20,000 × 30%).

Tutorial note

When the EIS shares were acquired, a tax credit of 30% of the amount subscribed would have been claimed, i.e. £9,600 (£32,000 × 30%).

If the EIS shares are sold within less than three years at a profit, then all of this tax credit will be reclaimed. However, if the shares are sold at a loss then only an amount equal to 30% of the proceeds will be reclaimed.

Note that you could still score a good pass mark on this part of the question even if you did not know this rule.

Capital loss

There will also be a capital loss on the sale of the shares. However, when calculating the loss, the cost of the shares will be reduced by the EIS relief *not* withdrawn:

	£
Original EIS relief claimed (£32,000 × 30%)	9,600
Less: EIS relief withdrawn (above)	(6,000)
EIS relief not withdrawn	3,600

The capital loss is as follows:

	£
Proceeds	20,000
Less: Cost (£32,000 – £3,600) (Note 1)	(28,400)
Allowable loss	(8,400)

As the allowable loss arises on unquoted shares that Capstan subscribed for, Capstan could offset the loss against his total income for 2016/17 and/or 2015/16. There is no cap on the use of the loss as it is less than £50,000.

This would save income tax at 40% as Capstan is a higher rate taxpayer, which would be better than saving capital gains tax at 28%.

Tutorial note

1   To avoid double counting of relief, the capital loss on the disposal of the EIS shares must take account of the income tax relief already given on the cost of the shares. The income tax relief given is deducted from the cost in the gain computation.

2   An election is available to convert a capital loss into a trading loss if the capital loss arises on the disposal of unquoted trading company shares that were originally subscribed for.

Impact of delaying sale

Advantage

If Capstan delayed the sale of the shares until after 1 February 2017 there would be no withdrawal of EIS relief as he would then have held them for three years.

However, the capital loss on sale of the shares would be reduced by £9,600, not £3,600. This would give £6,000 less loss to set against other income.

The net effect of this would be:

	£
EIS repayment saved	6,000
Less: Income tax repayment lost through reduced capital loss (£6,000 × 40%)	(2,400)
Net saving	3,600

Disadvantage

If the sale is delayed, the sale price could fall still further and lead to a larger financial loss for Capstan.

There would also be a cash flow disadvantage if the sale was delayed.

(c) **Capstan's taxable capital gains for the tax year 2016/17**

Tutor's top tips

Read the question carefully: the examiner asks you to calculate taxable gains, so there is no point in going any further than this and calculating the tax due.

	£
Pinblock plc loan stock (W2)	4,224
Shares in Pinblock plc (W3)	56,266
Total chargeable gains	60,490
Less: Annual exempt amount	(11,100)
Taxable gains	49,390

Tutor's top tips

The examiner has stated that candidates who assumed in their answer to part (b) above that the loss arising on the sale of the shares in Agraffe Ltd would be set off against Capstan's capital gains were given full credit in this part of the question.

Workings

Tutor's top tips

In order to calculate the gains, you first need to allocate the original cost of the Wippen plc shares between the Pinblock plc shares and the loan stock in Pinblock plc, based on the market values at the time of the takeover.

(W1) **Allocation of cost at time of takeover**

	Market value £	Apportioned cost £
Consideration received:		
20,000 Ordinary shares in Pinblock plc	40,000	
(£40,000/£49,000) × £26,000		21,224
Loan stock in Pinblock plc	9,000	
(£9,000/£49,000) × £26,000		4,776
	49,000	26,000

Tutorial note

The Pinblock plc shares 'step in the shoes' of the Wippen plc shares (i.e. they take over part of the cost of the Wippen plc shares).

The loan stock is treated as if it is cash, and is used as 'proceeds' for a part disposal of the Wippen plc shares. This gain is calculated at the time of the takeover, frozen and is deferred until the loan stock is sold.

(W2) **Gain on sale of loan stock**

The loan stock has increased in value from £9,000 to £10,600. However, as the loanstock is a qualifying corporate bond, any gain arising is exempt from capital gains tax.

However, the gain that arose at the time of the takeover when the shares in Wippen plc were exchanged for the loan stock in Pinblock plc will become chargeable on the sale of the loan stock.

	£
Proceeds (market value on 1 October 2012)	9,000
Less: Cost (W1)	(4,776)
Chargeable gain	4,224

(W3) **Gain on sale of 12,000 shares in Pinblock plc**

	£
Proceeds	69,000
Less: Cost ((12,000/20,000) × £21,224)(W1)	(12,734)
Chargeable gain	56,266

Examiner's comments

Part (a) required candidates to consider both the capital gains tax and inheritance tax implications of the transfer of a property to a discretionary trust. The inheritance tax implications were addressed very well by all but a tiny minority of candidates. The only common error was a failure to set out any assumptions made as required by the note to the question.

The capital gains tax element of this part was not answered well. The problem here was that most candidates did not think; instead they simply deducted the cost from the proceeds and addressed rates of tax. Some candidates then realised that gift relief was available and that, per the question, all available claims would be made. As a result, although they had wasted some time, they were still able to score full marks. Other candidates, however, did not address the gift relief point and consequently did not score any marks for the capital gains tax element of the question.

Part (b) concerned the sale of shares in respect of which EIS relief had been claimed. Almost all candidates identified the claw back of the relief if the shares were sold within three years of the acquisition. However, many stated that the whole of the relief obtained would be withdrawn as opposed to a proportion of it.

The implications of delaying the sale were not identified particularly well. Many candidates simply stated the opposite of what they had already written, i.e. that the relief obtained would not be withdrawn if the shares were held for three years. More thoughtful candidates considered other matters and recognised that delaying the sale delayed the receipt of the sales proceeds and that the value of the shares might change (for the better or the worse).

The final part of the question concerned the sale of shares and qualifying corporate bonds that had been acquired following a paper for paper exchange. This part was done well by those candidates who knew how to handle this type of transaction.

The first task was to recognise that the cost of the original shares needed to be apportioned between the new shares and the corporate bonds. Many candidates knew what they were doing here and were on the way to doing well in this part of the question.

However, there was often confusion as to the treatment of the sale of the corporate bonds. Many candidates who knew that corporate bonds are exempt from capital gains tax went on to calculate a gain on the sale and include it in the taxable capital gains for the year. Also, many candidates were not able to identify the gain on the original shares that was frozen at the time of the paper for paper exchange and then charged when the corporate bonds were sold.

ACCA marking scheme

			Marks
(a)	Inheritance tax:		
	Explanations and assumptions		3.5
	Calculations		2.0
	Capital gains tax		1.5
			7.0
		Maximum	6.0
(b)	Withdrawal of EIS relief		2.0
	Loss on sale		1.5
	Offset of loss		1.0
	Advantage of delay		2.0
	Disadvantage of delay		1.0
			7.5
		Maximum	7.0
(c)	Sale of loan stock		3.5
	Gain on sale of shares		1.0
	Annual exempt amount		0.5
		Maximum	5.0
Total			18.0

28 SURFE Walk in the footsteps of a top tutor

Key answer tips

This is a question in two parts, covering CGT and IHT aspects of discretionary trusts, and textbook IHT computations for lifetime gifts and a simple death estate. This is likely to have been a popular choice in the exam as IHT is always tested, and so should be very familiar to students.

Part (a) on trusts should offer some easy marks, as the level of knowledge expected of students is very basic. You may have been tempted to give chapter and verse on all aspects of trusts rather than just focusing on the specific areas requested and thus may have run out of time to complete the question.

Part (b) covers straightforward IHT computations. There are a couple of tricky points, such as the valuation of shares with related property and diminution in value, and also the calculation of the proportion of the husband's unused nil rate band. However, there should be enough marks available for basic computations for you to score a good mark.

The highlighted words in the written sections are key phrases that markers are looking for.

(a) (i) **Capital gains tax implications**

Tutor's top tips

The examiner asks you to outline **briefly** the capital gains tax implications of:

1   transfer of shares **into** a trust
2   sale of shares by the trustees, **within** the trust
3   transfer of shares **out of** the trust.

There are only four marks available here, and there is usually a half to one mark available per point, so that should give you an idea of how much the examiner expects you to write.

Gift of shares to trustees of the discretionary trust

The gift of shares will be treated as a disposal at market value for capital gains tax purposes, and a chargeable gain will arise.

However, as the transfer will be a chargeable lifetime transfer for the purposes of inheritance tax, the gain may be deferred by making a gift relief claim.

Surfe must elect to claim gift relief by 5 April 2021 (i.e. within four years of the end of the tax year of the gift).

ANSWERS TO PRACTICE QUESTIONS: SECTION 2

Tutorial note

Usually, a gift relief claim requires a joint election to be signed by the donor and the donee.

However, where the claim relates to a transfer into a trust, only the donor has to sign the election.

Sale of quoted shares by the trustees

The gain on sale of shares will be taxable on the trustees, and the capital gains tax payable will be paid from the trust assets.

Tutorial note

You could also have stated that there will be an annual exempt amount available of £5,550 (half of the full annual exempt amount of £11,100), and that tax on any excess will be payable at 28%.

However, you are only expected to have a very basic knowledge of the capital gains tax treatment of trusts, so the examiner did not expect you to make these points.

Transfer of trust assets to Surfe's nephews

Transfer of assets from the trust will again be treated as a disposal at market value and a chargeable gain will arise.

As there will also be an inheritance tax charge, the gain may be deferred against the cost for the nephews by making a gift relief claim.

Both the trustees and the nephew must sign the gift relief election, which should be submitted within four years of the end of the tax year in which the transfer occurs.

(ii) **Inheritance tax**

The trustees will be subject to extra tax on the chargeable lifetime transfer from Surfe to the trust, if Surfe dies within seven years of the transfer.

There will be a principal charge of 6% of the value of trust assets payable by the trustees every ten years.

When assets are transferred out of the trust, there will be an exit charge of up to 6% of the value of the assets transferred.

These tax charges will be paid from the trust assets.

Tutorial note

The rules governing the inheritance tax treatment of discretionary trusts are complex. However, you are only expected to have a very basic knowledge of the tax charges that may arise within the trust.

(b) **Inheritance tax payable on Surfe's death on 1 January 2019**

Tutor's top tips

There will be three different elements to the tax payable on Surfe's death:

1. Tax on potentially exempt transfers (PETs) within seven years prior to death.
2. Further tax on chargeable lifetime transfers (CLTs) within seven years prior to death.
3. Tax on the death estate.

Before you can calculate the death tax, you need to establish the tax that was paid during lifetime, as this will be deducted from the death tax.

It is very important that you clearly label your answer so that the marker can see whether you are calculating lifetime tax or death tax.

Lifetime tax

Tutor's top tips

Always work chronologically, starting with the earliest gift.

1 February 2005 – Gift to charity

Gifts to charity are exempt from IHT.

1 October 2016 – Gifts to nephews

These gifts are potentially exempt transfers.

	£
Transfer of value (£85,000 × 2)	170,000
Less: Annual exemption	
Current year (2016/17)	(3,000)
Previous year (2015/16)	(3,000)
Gross transfer	164,000

No lifetime tax is payable.

Tutorial note

Remember that PETs are not chargeable during lifetime, and do not affect the nil rate band, although they do still use up the annual exemptions.

ANSWERS TO PRACTICE QUESTIONS: SECTION 2

1 January 2017 – transfer of shares and cash to trust

This transfer is a chargeable lifetime transfer.

	£	£
Value of shares (W1)		400,000
Cash		100,000
Transfer of value		500,000
Less: Annual exemption		
Current year (2016/17)		(used)
Previous year (2015/16)		(used)
Net chargeable amount		500,000
Nil rate band (NRB) at date of gift (2016/17)	325,000	
Less: Gross chargeable transfers in 7 years pre gift	(Nil)	
NRB available		(325,000)
Taxable amount		175,000
Inheritance tax at 25% (Surfe is paying the tax)		43,750
Gross chargeable transfer c/f (£500,000 + £43,750)		543,750

Tutorial note

The question states that Surfe (the donor) will pay the lifetime tax, so the rate of tax is 25% and you must add the tax to the gift to calculate the gross transfer for use in future calculations.

If the trustees (the donee) agreed to pay the tax, the tax would be at 20% and the gross amount would be £500,000.

Death tax: 1 July 2019

1 October 2016 – Gifts to nephews

This PET is within seven years prior to death and is now chargeable

	£
Gross chargeable amount	164,000
NRB at death (W2) (all available)	(504,167)
Taxable amount	Nil

There is no tax payable as this gift is covered by the NRB.

1 January 2017 – transfer of shares and cash to trust

		£
Gross chargeable transfer		543,750
NRB at death (W2)	504,167	
Less: Gross chargeable transfers in 7 years pre gift	(164,000)	
NRB available		(340,167)
Taxable amount		203,583
Inheritance tax at 40%		81,433
Less: Taper relief		
(1.1.17 to 1.7.19) less than 3 years		(Nil)
		81,433
Less: Lifetime tax paid		(43,750)
Inheritance tax payable on death		37,683

Tutor's top tips

You should only be penalised once for any mistake that you make.

If you have the wrong gross chargeable transfer brought forward, or the wrong NRB, you can still score marks for calculating the IHT at 40%, stating that taper relief is not available and deducting your figure for lifetime tax paid.

1 July 2019 – death estate

		£
House		1,400,000
Quoted shares		600,000
Shares in Leat Ltd (based on 80% holding) (W1)		
(450 × £2,400)		1,080,000
		3,080,000
NRB at death (W2)	504,167	
Less: Gross chargeable transfers in 7 years pre death		
(£164,000 + £543,750)	(707,750)	
NRB available		(Nil)
Taxable amount		3,080,000
Inheritance tax at 40%		1,232,000

ANSWERS TO PRACTICE QUESTIONS: SECTION 2

Tutorial note

The value of the Leat Ltd shares included in the death estate is based on the value of the combined holding, including the related property held by the charity, at the date of death.

Workings

(W1) Gift of shares to the trust on 1 January 2017

	No. of shares before gift	No. of shares After gift
Surfe	650	450
Kanal (related property)	350	350
	1,000	800
Combined holding as a % of total shares	100%	80%
Value per share at date of gift	£2,000	£2,000

Transfer of value:	£
Value of Surfe's holding prior to the gift (650 × £2,000)	1,300,000
Less: Value of Surfe's holding after the gift (450 × £2,000)	(900,000)
Transfer of value	400,000

Tutorial note

The value of the Leat Ltd shares is based on the value of the combined holding, including the related property held by the charity, at the date of the gift.

The most common example of related property is property held jointly by spouses, but property that has been transferred by the donor (or their spouse) to a charity or political party is also deemed to be related property for as long as the charity still owns the property (and for five years after they dispose of it).

Remember also that the value for IHT is calculated as the diminution in value of the donor's estate, and is found by calculating the value of Surfe's shares before the gift and deducting the value after the gift.

(W2) Nil rate band on death

	£
Surfe's NRB as at the date of death	325,000
Unused nil rate band of Flud ((£312,000 − £140,000)/£312,000) × £325,000)	179,167
	504,167

KAPLAN PUBLISHING

Tutorial note

As Surfe's husband did not use all of his NRB, the excess can be transferred to Surfe to be used on her death.

The amount transferred is based on the proportion that was unused when Surfe's husband died, but this proportion is then applied to the NRB in force at the date of Surfe's death.

Note that the fact that the date of the husband's death is more than seven years before Surfe's is irrelevant. The unused proportion of the deceased spouse's NRB can always be transferred regardless of the date of the first death.

Examiner's comments

Part (a) required an outline of the capital gains tax implications of various transactions relating to the trust and the inheritance tax charges that may be payable in the future by the trustees. It was important for candidates to be methodical in their approach to this question. There were three transactions to be addressed in relation to capital gains tax whereas the inheritance aspects of the question were more open ended.

The majority of candidates knew some of the capital gains tax implications of the transactions but very few knew all of them. In particular, there was a lack of understanding that capital gains would arise when the trustees transfer trust assets to the beneficiaries of the trust. As always, when dealing with capital gains tax, it is vital to consider the availability of reliefs; gift relief is available when assets are transferred to a discretionary trust and again when they are transferred to the beneficiaries.

The inheritance aspects of part (a) were not handled as well as the capital gains tax aspects. The majority of candidates failed to mention the ten-yearly charges and exit charges payable out of the trust's assets.

Part (b) required a calculation of the inheritance tax liability arising on the death of an individual who had made a number of lifetime gifts. This was a fairly straightforward question, albeit with a couple of tricky points within it, but it was not handled particularly well.

There was a lack of appropriate structure to candidates' answers that indicated that, perhaps, there had been insufficient practice of this area. Inheritance tax computations should all look the same, starting with the tax on any chargeable lifetime transfers, followed by the consideration of gifts within seven years of death and ending with the death estate. However, many candidates began with the death estate and worked their way backwards towards the lifetime gifts; a method that was never going to be successful.

There was confusion as to which gift benefited from the annual exemptions and in respect of the utilisation of the nil rate band. There was also a general lack of knowledge of the impact of related property on the valuation of a gift. Other technical errors, made by a minority of candidates, included the treatment of cash as an exempt asset and business property relief being given in respect of the shares owned by the taxpayer.

On the positive side, the majority of candidates identified the availability of the husband's nil rate band and the death estate was handled well.

ANSWERS TO PRACTICE QUESTIONS: **SECTION 2**

ACCA marking scheme				Marks
(a)	(i)	Gift of shares		1.5
		Future sale of quoted shares		0.5
		Transfer of trust assets to beneficiaries		1.5
		Election details		1.0
	(ii)	Inheritance tax		2.5
				7.0
			Maximum	6.0
(b)	Inheritance tax in respect of lifetime gifts			
	Gift to charity			0.5
	Gifts to nephews			1.5
	Gift to trust			
		Shares – fall in value		2.0
		Cash and nil rate band		1.0
		Lifetime tax		1.0
		Gross chargeable transfer		0.5
		Nil rate band		2.5
		Inheritance tax payable on death		1.5
	Inheritance tax in respect of death estate			1.5
				12.0
			Maximum	11.0
Total				**17.0**

29 UNA (ADAPTED) *Walk in the footsteps of a top tutor*

Key answer tips

Part (a) is a classic question which involves the gift of two alternative assets: farmland in the UK or a villa in Soloria. The examiner is looking for an understanding of both inheritance tax and CGT.

Part (b) examines the non-disclosure of income and gains to HMRC and an explanation of the implications of tax evasion. Remember that there will always be up to 5 marks in each exam on ethics. A good knowledge of income tax penalties was also required here.

The highlighted words in the written sections are key phrases that markers are looking for.

Tutor's top tips

As is usual for Section A questions, the actual requirements at the end of the question only indicate how many marks are available for each section. The real requirements can be found in the information provided within the question.

As you read through, highlight any requirements and instructions that you find and make sure that you address them all in your answer. The requirements in this question are all in the email from the manger.

The examiner has asked for a memorandum which addresses certain issues and you may find it useful to number these requirements so that you can tick them off as you attempt each one.

Make sure you set out your answer in the required format (memorandum in part (a) and letter in part (b)) as there are 4 relatively easy presentation and style marks available.

In part (a) the examiner has made it clear that the calculations are worth a maximum of half the marks available and is hinting to you that he is also looking for explanations and analysis.

(a) **MEMORANDUM**

To   The files

From   Tax senior

Date   15 June 2016

Subject Una – Gifts to son and granddaughter

The purpose of this memorandum is to provide advice to Una on the tax implications of a gift to be made to her son, Won, and the payment of rent on behalf of her granddaughter, Alona. For the purposes of this memorandum, it has been assumed that the gift to Won will be made on 18 November 2016 and that Una's death will occur on 31 December 2021.

(i) **Gift to Won**

Tutor's top tips

The key to success in this part is dealing with each tax separately and then understanding the cumulative effect.

Make sure that your answer is clearly labelled so that the examiner can see clearly which gift and which tax you are dealing with.

Don't forget to provide written explanations regarding the availability of reliefs, and also state any assumptions you have made. You do not, however, need to explain any other aspects of IHT or CGT.

Inheritance tax

Tutor's top tips

You are calculating the **reduction** in inheritance tax as a result of each of the gifts.

This means that you need to compare the IHT assuming the asset is gifted with the IHT assuming the asset is left in the death estate.

Note that the gift of cash to Won in May 2012 is an exempt / tax free PET as it takes place more than 7 years before the date of death (31.12.21), so it will have no effect on the calculations.

Farmland situated in the UK

Tutor's top tips

The key to success here was knowledge of the seven year ownership rule for agricultural property relief, where the property is rented out.

If the property is given on 18 November 2016 it will not be eligible for APR because it has been owned and let out for less than seven years.

However, if the farmland is retained until Una's death on 31 December 2021 it will form part of her death estate and will now be eligible for APR because it has been let out for at least 7 years.

If you missed this point, there were still marks available for basic points such as using the annual exemptions during lifetime, taking into account the nil rate band, taper relief, and using the correct rate of IHT.

If Una owns the farmland at her death

– it will be included in her death estate

	£
Market value in death estate	1,100,000
Less: Agricultural property relief (£1,100,000 × 35%) (100% of agricultural value)	(385,000)
Included in death estate (tutorial note)	715,000
IHT payable on death at 40%	286,000

If Una gifts the farmland to Won

– it will be a PET (Note 1) which becomes chargeable on death

	£	£
Market value (Note 2)		900,000
Less: Annual exemptions		
– 2016/17 and 2015/16		(6,000)
PET		894,000
NRB available on death	325,000	
Less: GCTs in previous 7 years (Tutorial note)	(Nil)	
NRB available		(325,000)
Taxable amount		569,000
IHT at 40%		227,600
Less: Taper relief		
(death within five to six years of the gift) (60%)		(136,560)
		91,040
Less: Lifetime IHT (£Nil as gift is a PET)		(Nil)
IHT payable on PET on death		91,040
Plus: Additional tax on death estate due to use of NRB against the PET and therefore not available against the death estate (tutorial note) (£325,000 × 40%)		130,000
IHT payable on death		221,040
Potential saving if gifted during lifetime (£286,000 – £221,040)		64,960

Notes

1 There will be no UK inheritance tax when the gift is made as it will be a potentially exempt transfer.

2 Agricultural property relief will not be available in respect of a gift on 18 November 2016 as Una will not have owned the farm for the requisite seven years.

This is on the assumption that the farmland did not replace other agricultural property which, together with this farmland, had been owned for seven out of the previous ten years (tutorial note).

Tutorial note

If the farmland is retained until death, it is assumed the nil rate band will have already been allocated to the remainder of the death estate and therefore the additional tax due because of the inclusion of the farmland in the estate at death will be calculated at 40%.

For the lifetime gift, all of the NRB will be available on death to match against this gift, as the previous lifetime gift in May 2012 was a PET which became completely exempt and therefore there is £Nil amount to be cumulated.

You must also take into account the extra tax payable on the death estate if the farmland is gifted during the lifetime, due to the use of the nil rate band against the PET.

The requirement also asks you to state any assumptions made. In the model answer the examiner gave credit for mentioning that it is assumed that the replacement property provisions for APR do not apply (Note 2 above).

Villa situated in Soloria

Tutor's top tips

An important point to appreciate here is that the double tax agreement contains an exemption clause which exempts the villa in Soloria from UK IHT.

It is therefore not necessary to give double tax relief in the usual way (i.e. the lower of UK and overseas tax); you only need to consider Soloria IHT and compare the Soloria IHT liabilities given in the question (£170,000 and £34,000).

The villa in Soloria is, however, subject to UK CGT.

There will be no UK inheritance tax on either a lifetime gift of the villa or including it in the estate due to the exemption clause in the UK–Soloria double taxation agreement.

There will be no inheritance tax in Soloria until Una's death.

The gift will save inheritance tax in Soloria as set out below:

	£
Liability if Una owns the villa at her death on 31 December 2021	170,000
Liability if Una gifts the villa to Won on 18 November 2016	(34,000)
Inheritance tax saved	136,000

Capital gains tax

Tutor's top tips

Remember that CGT is only payable on gifts during lifetime, not on death.

Farmland situated in the UK

A gift of the farmland would result in a liability to capital gains tax as set out below. No business asset reliefs would be available as the farmland is an investment asset (as opposed to a business asset), does not qualify for agricultural property relief and the gift does not give rise to an immediate charge to inheritance tax.

	£
Proceeds (market value)	900,000
Less: Cost	(720,000)
Capital gain	180,000
Capital gains tax at 28% (Una is a higher rate taxpayer)	50,400

Tutorial note

If the farmland had qualified for APR, then gift relief would be available.

The gain will be taxed at 28% as Una is a higher rate taxpayer who has already used up her annual exempt amount.

Villa situated in Soloria

A gift of the villa would result in a liability to UK capital gains tax as set out below. The villa is an investment and not a business asset, such that no capital gains tax business reliefs would be available.

There is no capital gains tax in Soloria.

	£
Proceeds (market value)	745,000
Less: Deemed cost (probate value)	(600,000)
Capital gain	145,000
Capital gains tax at 28% (Una is a higher rate taxpayer)	40,600

Tutorial note

Una is resident and domiciled in the UK and accordingly is subject to CGT on her worldwide assets.

The villa is an investment asset, so no CGT business reliefs are available, such as gift relief or entrepreneurs' relief.

Summary of position re capital taxes

Tutor's top tips

There are two marks available for providing a concise summary of your calculations. Even if your calculations are wrong, you will still score these marks if you summarise them as requested.

	Farmland	Villa
	£	£
Inheritance tax – potential saving	64,960	136,000
Capital gains tax – liability	(50,400)	(40,600)
Net tax saving	14,560	95,400

Other tax implications in respect of the gift to Won

Tutor's top tips

Here the examiner was looking for an appreciation of the timing of the tax payments and an explanation of the other tax implications, particularly stamp duty land tax and income tax.

Remember that there is no SDLT on gifts.

Note also that where an income-generating asset is given, the income will then accrue to the donee.

You should still be given credit if you have mentioned any of these points elsewhere in your answer.

Inheritance tax

If Una were to die after 18 November 2022, there would be an additional 20% taper relief in the UK. If she were to survive the gift by seven years, there would be no UK inheritance tax in respect of the asset gifted and the inheritance tax nil rate band would be available against the death estate.

Stamp duty land tax

There is no stamp duty land tax in the UK on a gift of land. The situation in Soloria would need to be investigated if a gift of the villa is proposed.

Financial implications in respect of the gift to Won

The potential gifts are income generating assets. Accordingly, Una should be aware that the gift will reduce her available income. The income in respect of the villa is subject to income tax in Soloria at the rate of 50%, such that no UK income tax is payable due to double tax relief. The income in respect of the farmland is subject to UK income tax at the rate of 40%.

The capital gains tax would be payable on 31 January 2018 (31 January following the end of the tax year in which the gift is made). This is at least four years prior to the eventual inheritance tax saving. Because gift relief is not available, it would be possible to pay the capital gains tax in ten equal annual instalments (provided Won continues to own the asset gifted), but interest would be charged on the balance outstanding.

Tutorial note

CGT can be paid in ten equal annual instalments for gifts of land that do not qualify for gift relief.

(ii) **Payment of Alona's rent**

Tutor's top tips

There are easy marks here for discussing the exemption for normal expenditure out of income.

However, to score well you must apply your knowledge to the facts in the question.

The payments of Alona's rent will be exempt if they represent normal expenditure out of income.

For this exemption to be available, Una would have to prove that:

- each gift is part of her normal expenditure
- the gifts are made out of income rather than capital
- having made the gifts, she still has sufficient income to maintain her usual standard of living.

Una will have annual income of £90,000 as reduced by income tax and the post tax income in respect of whichever asset she gifts to Won. She must be able to demonstrate that her annual income exceeds her normal expenditure by the annual rental cost of £5,400 (£450 × 12).

(b) **LETTER TO UNA**

Tutor's top tips

There are two aspects to address here:

- the impact for the taxpayer of not declaring income and gains, particularly the penalties that could be levied
- the professional issues relating to the firm of accountants.

It is important that you address both of these in order to score well.

You may have been tempted to discuss the badges of trade. However, these were not required here, as the manager has already concluded that the hiring of the car 'has resulted in taxable profits'.

Firm's address

Una's address

15 June 2016

Dear Una

Tutor's top tips

You are writing to Una, so you should address her as 'you', otherwise you may not score the professional mark for this part of the question.

Income received in respect of the luxury motor car

I set out below our advice in relation to the income received in respect of the luxury motor car.

Amount of taxable profit

I have considered the circumstances surrounding the rental income in respect of the car and concluded that the profits from the hiring of the car are liable to income tax. In determining the taxable profit, the income you have received can be reduced by the expenses relating to the running and maintenance of the car. We can assist you in determining the taxable profit.

Effect of non-disclosure

The taxable profit must be reported to HM Revenue and Customs (HMRC); failure to disclose the profit would amount to tax evasion, a criminal offence.

HMRC will charge interest on any tax liabilities that are overdue.

A penalty may also be charged in respect of the non-declaration of the income. The maximum penalty for a deliberate non-disclosure of income is 70% of the tax liability.

This penalty may be reduced if the income is disclosed to the authorities at a time when there is no reason to believe that the non-disclosure is about to be discovered and full assistance is provided to the authorities to enable them to quantify the error (i.e. unprompted disclosure). The minimum penalty in these circumstances is 20% of the tax liability.

>
>
> *Tutorial note*
>
> The penalty applied here would be the 'standard penalty' that now applies for incorrect returns and failure to notify liability to tax.
>
> The level of penalty depends on the taxpayer's behaviour, and the maximum penalties are as follows:
>
> - Genuine mistake – no penalty
> - Failure to take reasonable care – 30%
> - Deliberate understatement but no concealment – 70%
> - Deliberate understatement with concealment – 100%
>
> In all cases the penalties are based on the 'potential lost revenue' (i.e. the unpaid tax).
>
> Penalties can be reduced if the taxpayer discloses the error to HMRC, and the reduction in the penalty is greater for unprompted disclosure than for prompted disclosure.

Capital gain on the sale of the painting in Railos

As a UK resident, you are liable to UK capital gains tax on your worldwide assets. The location of the asset at the date of sale does not matter; it will be a chargeable disposal. The fact that the painting was situated in the UK, you then took it to Railos and then sold it does not reduce your liability to UK capital gains tax.

Effect of non-disclosure

The capital gain must therefore be reported to HMRC; failure to disclose the gain would amount to tax evasion, a criminal offence.

A penalty of 100% of the unpaid tax is likely to be charged in respect of the non-declaration of the gain as it could be classified as deliberate with concealment.

Furthermore, the penalties for offshore non-compliance rules will apply.

Where HMRC discover that a taxpayer has deliberately moved an asset overseas to a country that does not exchange financial information with the UK, in order to prevent (or delay) HMRC knowing about it, and then conceal taxable income and/or gains arising, they have the power to charge higher tax-geared penalties.

Impact for our firm

In addition, you will appreciate that we would not wish to be associated with a client who has engaged in deliberate tax evasion, as this poses a threat to the fundamental principles of integrity and professional behaviour.

Accordingly, we cannot continue to act for you unless you are willing to disclose the hiring activity and the offshore capital gain to HM Revenue and Customs and to pay any ensuing tax liabilities.

We are required to notify the tax authorities if we cease to act for you, although we would not provide them with any reason for our action.

ANSWERS TO PRACTICE QUESTIONS: SECTION 2

>
>
> **Tutor's top tips**
>
> Ethics and tax evasion are popular areas in the exam.
>
> The tax advisor must recommend that the client discloses the relevant information to HMRC.
>
> If the client does not disclose the information then the tax advisor must resign and recommend that the client seeks legal advice. HMRC must be notified of the resignation without giving the reason why, in order to protect client confidentiality.

Yours sincerely

Tax manager

> **Examiner's comments**
>
> Part (a) was answered reasonably well. In particular, only a minority of candidates confused the rules of inheritance tax and capital gains tax. Also, many candidates demonstrated strong technical knowledge of the mechanics of inheritance tax and agricultural property relief. Now that inheritance tax has been part of Paper F6 for a while, candidates sitting Paper P6 can expect to see more questions in this style (i.e. questions which work at the margin rather than requiring complete tax computations).
>
> The one common error in relation to inheritance tax was a failure to realise that the earlier cash gift had no effect on the nil band in respect of the later gift as it was made more than seven years prior to death. Other, less common, errors included deducting taper relief from the value transferred rather than from the inheritance tax liability and deducting the annual exemptions from the death estate.
>
> The capital gains tax elements of the question were not handled as well as inheritance tax. Many candidates did not know the conditions relating to the availability of capital gains tax reliefs and simply assumed, incorrectly, that gift relief would be available. A substantial minority also forgot the fundamental point that there is no capital gains tax on death and calculated liabilities in respect of both lifetime gifts and gifts via Una's will.
>
> However, the main problems experienced by candidates related to exam technique. There were three particular problems; failing to read the question sufficiently carefully, failing to address all of the requirements and running over time.
>
> When reading the question, many candidates failed to identify the relevance of the exemption clause in the double taxation agreement. The effect of the clause was to exempt the overseas villa from UK inheritance tax.
>
> This meant that, when dealing with the villa, candidates needed only to consider the tax suffered overseas. Those candidates who failed to appreciate this did not lose many marks but wasted time calculating UK inheritance tax on the villa.
>
> The question required calculations of the 'possible reduction in the inheritance tax payable as a result of Una's death' in respect of each of the possible lifetime gifts. This required candidates to compare the tax arising on a lifetime gift with that arising if the asset passed via Una's will for both of the assets.

KAPLAN PUBLISHING

There was then the need to consider the capital gains tax on the lifetime gift whilst remembering that there would be no capital gains tax if the assets were retained until death. Finally, candidates were asked to provide a concise summary of their calculations 'in order to assist Una in making her decision'.

The problem was that many candidates were not sufficiently methodical such that they did not carry out all of the necessary tasks and missed out on easy marks. In particular, many candidates did not provide the final summary.

The final problem in relation to exam technique related to time management: it was evident that some candidates did not have a sufficient sense of urgency when answering this question. This resulted in lengthy explanations of how inheritance tax, and, to a lesser extent, capital gains tax, is calculated together with details of Una's plans.

The question asked for 'explanations where the calculations are not self-explanatory, particularly in relation to the availability of reliefs'. Candidates need to think carefully before providing narrative as writing is very time consuming. They should identify, in advance, the points they are planning to make and should then make each point in as concise a manner as possible. There is likely to be a mark for each relevant point so each one should take no more than two short sentences.

Part (b) required a letter in relation to the non-declaration of income and was done reasonably well. There were two elements to a good answer: the penalties that could be levied on the taxpayer and the professional issues relating to the firm of accountants. The two elements were indicated clearly in the question which stated that 'the letter should explain the implications for Una and our firm'. Those candidates who failed to address both elements struggled to do well.

The part involving the sale of the painting and the new offshore non-compliance penalties has been added to the original question.

	ACCA marking scheme	
		Marks
(a)	Calculations	
	Farmland – inheritance tax	
	Owned at death	2.0
	Lifetime gift	4.0
	Farmland – capital gains tax	1.0
	Villa – inheritance tax (Soloria)	1.0
	Villa – capital gains tax (UK)	1.5
	Notes on availability of relevant reliefs – one mark each	3.0
	Other relevant tax and financial implications – one mark each	5.0
	Relevant assumption	1.0
	Summary of position re capital taxes	2.0
	Payment of rent	3.0
		23.5
	Maximum	21.0
	Professional marks for the overall presentation of the memorandum and the effectiveness with which the information is communicated	3.0

ANSWERS TO PRACTICE QUESTIONS: SECTION 2

		Marks
(b)	Determination of taxable profit	1.0
	Liability to CGT on sale of painting	1.0
	The need to disclose	4.0
	Interest and penalties	3.0
	Offshore penalties for non-compliance	3.0
		12.0
	Maximum	10.0
	Professional mark for the overall presentation of the letter	1.0
Total		**35.0**

30 ASH *Walk in the footsteps of a top tutor*

Key answer tips

This is a question with three independent parts which could have been attempted in any order.

The first part deals with capital gains and is a mix of very easy marks (land part disposal) and trickier marks (lease assignment).

The second part deals with VAT registration for a business dealing with both taxable and exempt supplies but does not require any calculations.

The third part covers a tax administration issue about whether to reduce a payment on account which tests knowledge brought forward from F6.

The highlighted words in the written sections are key phrases that markers are looking for.

(a) (i) **Availability of entrepreneurs' relief – assignment of the lease**

Tutor's top tips

This should be straightforward provided you have learned the rules! Remember you must apply the rules to the facts of the question to earn the marks. There are three marks available and three conditions, so one mark for each.

The following conditions must be satisfied in order for the assignment of the lease to qualify as an associated disposal such that entrepreneurs' relief will be available:

- Ash's disposal of the shares in Lava Ltd must qualify for entrepreneurs' relief.
- The lease must have been owned by Ash and used for the purposes of the trade of Lava Ltd for at least a year.
- Ash must have sold the shares in Lava Ltd and the lease as part of a process of withdrawing from participating in the business of Lava Ltd.

KAPLAN PUBLISHING

Tutorial note

Entrepreneurs' relief is not available on an associated disposal if full commercial rent is charged for the use of the asset.

In this question, rent is charged, but not the full market rate. Therefore entrepreneurs' relief is available on part of the gain, but not all of the gain.

(ii) **Capital gains tax liability – 2015/16**

Tutor's top tips

You have already been told that the sale of shares in Lava Ltd qualified for entrepreneurs' relief, and you can see that the land sale does not qualify as there is no mention of any business.

The best way to present the calculation of gains tax when there are gains both qualifying and non-qualifying for entrepreneurs' relief is in two columns. The annual exempt amount and the capital loss on the sale of the quoted shares should be deducted from the non-qualifying gains first.

Even if you calculated the gain on the lease incorrectly you would still get the marks available for including it in your summary and taxing it.

	Entrepreneurs' relief available £	Entrepreneurs' relief not available £
Gain on sale of shares	235,000	
Gain on assignment of lease (£79,812 (W1) × 60%/40%) (Note 1)	47,887	31,925
Gain on sale of land (W2)		21,780
Loss on sale of quoted shares		(17,100)
	282,887	36,605
Less: Annual exempt amount		(11,100)
	282,887	25,505
Capital gains tax (Note 2)		
Gains qualifying for entrepreneurs' relief (£282,887 × 10%)		28,289
Gains not qualifying for entrepreneurs' relief (£25,505 × 28%)		7,141
CGT liability		35,430

ANSWERS TO PRACTICE QUESTIONS: SECTION 2

Tutorial notes

1   Entrepreneurs' relief in respect of the lease will be restricted to 60% of the gain, due to the rent charged by Ash to Lava Ltd which is equivalent to 40% of the market rate.

2   Ash's taxable income is less than his basic rate band. However, the gains qualifying for entrepreneurs' relief use up the remainder of the basic rate band first, such that all of the non-qualifying gains are taxed at 28%.

Workings

(W1)   **Gain on the assignment of the lease**

	£
Proceeds (for a 37 year lease)	110,000
Less: Deemed cost (£31,800 × (93.497 ÷ 98.490))	(30,188)
Chargeable gain	79,812

Tutorial note

A lease is a wasting asset whose cost depreciates in accordance with a curved line table.

	£
Proceeds	X
Less: Cost × (% for life left at disposal ÷ % for life left at acquisition)	(X)
Capital gain	X

(W2)   **Gain on the sale of the remainder land**

	£	£
Proceeds		30,000
Less: Deemed cost of the remainder		
Original cost	27,400	
Part disposal cost		
£27,400 × (£42,000 ÷ (£42,000 + £18,000))	(19,180)	
		(8,220)
Chargeable gain		21,780

(b) **Vulcan Partnership (Vulcan) – Value added tax (VAT) registration**

Tutor's top tips

You are asked to discuss in detail whether the Vulcan Partnership may be required to register and the advantages and disadvantages of registration. This gives you three headings to structure your answer.

You must apply your knowledge to the facts of the question. You will not earn marks for listing everything you know about VAT registration.

You are not required to perform any calculations, although you may find it useful to establish the current level of annual taxable supplies.

Whether or not Vulcan may be required to register

Subject to the exceptions noted below, Vulcan will be required to register for VAT once its cumulative taxable supplies (those that are standard rated and zero rated) in a 12-month period exceed £82,000.

However, Vulcan will not be required to register if HM Revenue and Customs are satisfied that its total supplies for the following 12 months will be less than £80,000.

Vulcan could request to be exempt from registration because only a small proportion of its supplies are standard rated. This exemption will be available provided it would be in a repayment position if registered.

Advantages of registration

Vulcan will be able to recover all of its input tax if the amount relating to exempt supplies is de minimis. Where Vulcan's exempt supplies is not de minimis, it will still be able to recover the majority of its input tax.

Registration will prevent third parties from knowing the size of Vulcan's business.

Disadvantages of registration

Registration will add to the amount of work required to administer the business. In addition, Vulcan may be subject to financial penalties if it fails to comply with the obligations imposed by the VAT regime.

The partnership's customers would be unable to recover any output tax charged by the partnership as they are not registered for VAT. Accordingly, the prices charged to the small proportion of customers purchasing standard rated items would increase unless Vulcan decides to reduce its profit in respect of these sales.

(c) **Payment on account on 31 January 2017**

Tutor's top tips

This should be straightforward provided you could remember the rules.

ANSWERS TO PRACTICE QUESTIONS: SECTION 2

The payment on account due on 31 January 2017 is the first payment in respect of Ash's income tax payable (income tax liability as reduced by tax deducted at source) for 2016/17. The payment due is half of the income tax payable for 2015/16 unless Ash makes a claim to reduce the payment.

Ash can make a claim to reduce the payment if he expects the amount payable for 2016/17 to be less than that for 2015/16. The income tax payable for 2016/17 is likely to be less than that for 2015/16 due, principally, to Ash receiving less profit from Vulcan.

Ash will need to estimate his income tax payable for 2016/17 in order to decide whether or not to reduce the payment on account. Ash will be charged interest if the payment on account is reduced to an amount that is less than half of the final agreed amount payable for 2016/17. In addition, a penalty may be charged if Ash is fraudulent or negligent when he makes the claim to reduce the payment.

Examiner's comments

Part (a)(i) required a statement of the conditions necessary for the disposal of an asset to be an associated disposal for the purposes of entrepreneurs' relief and was not done well. This is not an area of the syllabus that one would expect to see examined regularly and many candidates will have known immediately on reading the requirement that they did not know the answer. However, the sensible approach would then have been to write a very brief answer with some sensible comments on entrepreneurs' relief. It was pretty likely that this would then score one of the three marks available.

In general part (a)(ii) was done well by many candidates. There was no problem in deciding what needed to be done, so those candidates who did poorly simply did not have sufficient knowledge of the rules.

The majority of part (b) was done very well including, in particular, the advantages and disadvantages of registering for VAT. However, some candidates' answers lacked precision when it came to the circumstances where compulsory registration is required in that taxable supplies were not clearly defined and/or the 12-month period was not clearly stated. Other candidates wasted time by writing far too much on the recovery of input tax. The one area where performance was not good was the exceptions to the need to register, which were only referred to by a very small number of candidates.

Part (c) concerned an area that candidates would have been familiar with but it approached it from a slightly unusual angle: it was not done well. Candidates needed to use their common sense as much as anything else here and to recognise that the claim would need to be made before the end of the tax year. This in turn meant that the tax liability would need to be estimated and that interest would be payable if the final liability turned out to be more than the estimated liability. Making these two points would have scored two of the three marks available for this part of the question.

PAPER P6: ADVANCED TAXATION (FA2015)

ACCA marking scheme			
			Marks
(a)	(i)	Conditions – 1 mark each	3.0
	(ii)	Taxable capital gains	
		Assignment of lease	2.5
		Sale of land	2.0
		Other matters	1.5
		Capital gains tax	1.5
			7.5
		Maximum	7.0
(b)		Requirement to register	1.5
		Exceptions	2.0
		Advantages	2.0
		Disadvantages	2.0
			7.5
		Maximum	7.0
(c)		Context	1.5
		Circumstance in which a claim can be made	1.0
		Interest and penalties	1.5
			4.0
		Maximum	3.0
Total			**20.0**

31 CUTHBERT *Walk in the footsteps of a top tutor*

Key answer tips

This question has three unrelated parts. Half the marks are for administration issues and half for inheritance tax.

Part (a) covers the payment of capital gains tax by instalments. Although the rules are straightforward this area is a relatively peripheral topic in a huge syllabus, such that many students would know little about this topic.

Part (b) deals with the penalty for careless errors and tests brought forward F6 knowledge.

Part (c) tests inheritance tax and the effect of domicile and unusually requires calculations rather than explanations.

The highlighted words in the written sections are key phrases that markers are looking for.

(a) **Payment of capital gains tax (CGT) by instalments**

Tutor's top tips

If you know nothing about paying CGT by instalments then do not waste time here but move on to the rest of the question. This section is straightforward but only if you know the rules.

Remember to apply your knowledge to the facts of the question instead of writing generally.

Availability

Payment of CGT by instalments is available in respect of gifts of certain assets, including land and buildings, where gift relief is not available.

Gift relief will not be available in respect of the gift of the building as the building is not used in a business and is let to a long-term tenant such that it cannot be a furnished holiday letting.

Tutorial note

Payment of CGT by instalments is available for gifts of:

(i)   *land or an interest in land*

(ii)   *shares from a controlling interest*

(iii)   *shares out of a minority interest in an unquoted company*

provided the donor is not entitled to gift relief.

The instalment option is also available if the consideration for the disposal is received over a period exceeding eighteen months. In this case the instalments of tax will be spread over the period in which the consideration is received, or eight years if shorter.

Matters that Cuthbert would need to be aware of

It is necessary to make an election to pay by instalments before the date that the CGT is normally due (i.e. 31 January 2018).

There will be ten annual instalments beginning on 31 January 2018.

Interest will be charged on the outstanding balance of the tax liability.

Cuthbert will be required to pay all of the remaining instalments immediately if the property is sold because Cuthbert and his brother are connected persons for the purposes of CGT.

(b) **The penalty due in respect of a careless error in Cuthbert's tax return**

The maximum penalty for a careless error is 30% of the potential lost revenue. The potential lost revenue is the additional tax due following the correction of the error.

The penalty may be reduced depending on the level of disclosure Cuthbert provides to HM Revenue and Customs (HMRC) in terms of telling them about the error, providing them with assistance in quantifying it and allowing them access to his records.

Any disclosure provided by Cuthbert will be regarded as prompted, rather than unprompted, because Cuthbert is aware that HMRC suspect that an error has been made.

Tutorial note

Error penalties increase with the severity of the offence.

	Maximum penalty (% of revenue lost)
Genuine mistake	No penalty
Careless/failure to take reasonable care	30%
Deliberate but no concealment	70%
Deliberate with concealment	100%

(c) **Pugh – UK inheritance tax (IHT) liability**

Tutor's top tips

Most of the marks for this part of the question are for a straightforward calculation of inheritance tax with double tax relief.

The examiner tells you in the requirements how to calculate the overseas tax (i.e. charge 25% on the value of the land (none) and shares (£330,000) situated in Camberia).

There are also vintage cars in Camberia but these are not liable to Camberian tax.

Inheritance tax on death

Gift in the seven years prior to death

There would be no tax due in respect of the gift on 10 June 2009 as the gross transfer of £317,500 (W1) is covered by the nil rate band of £325,000.

Death estate

Pugh was UK domiciled and will therefore be subject to IHT on his Camberian assets as well as his UK assets.

	£	£
Home in the UK		720,000
Cash held in bank accounts in the UK		45,000
Vintage motor cars located in Camberia		490,000
Quoted shares registered in Camberia		330,000
Gross chargeable estate		1,585,000
Nil rate band at death	325,000	
Less: GCTs in the previous seven years (W1)	(317,500)	
Nil rate band available		(7,500)
Taxable amount		1,577,500

		£
IHT at 40%		631,000
Less: Double tax relief		
Lower of:		
(i) UK tax on estate (£330,000 × 39.811% (W2)) = £131,376		
(ii) Overseas tax on estate (£330,000 × 25%) = £82,500		(82,500)
IHT payable on estate		548,500

Tutorial note

Business property relief is available on worldwide relevant business property, but is not available in respect of quoted shares unless the donor controls the company. Accordingly, there is no BPR available on the Camberia quoted shares.

Interest due

	£
Original IHT already paid on estate (W3)	176,000
Additional IHT due (£548,500 – £176,000)	372,500

Interest of £3,725 (£372,500 × 3% × 4/12) will be charged in respect of the four month period from the due date of 31 August 2016 (i.e. six months after the end of the month of death) until the tax is paid on 1 January 2017.

Tutor's top tips

Even if you cannot calculate the interest you should set out the period for which any interest is charged.

Workings

(W1) CLT in the seven years prior to death – 10 June 2009

	£	£
Value transferred		323,500
Less: AEs (2009/10 and 2008/09)		(6,000)
Net chargeable amount		317,500
Less: Nil rate band for 2009/10	325,000	
GCTs in 7 years before gift (10.6.02 – 10.6.09)	(Nil)	
Nil rate band available		(325,000)
Taxable amount		Nil

	£
Lifetime IHT	Nil
Gross chargeable transfer c/f (£317,500 net + £Nil tax)	317,500

(W2) **Average estate rate**

Average estate rate (AER) = (£631,000 ÷ £1,585,000) × 100 = 39.811%

(W3) **Original estate – calculation of IHT liability**

> *Tutor's top tips*
>
> To calculate the interest on overdue tax it is necessary to calculate the inheritance tax originally paid when it was thought that Pugh was not domiciled and had not made any previous transfers.
>
> In that case, inheritance tax would only be charged on death on UK assets, his home and his bank account.

The original calculation would have excluded the assets located in Camberia and ignored the lifetime gift to the trust.

	£	£
Home in the UK		720,000
Cash held in bank accounts in the UK		45,000
Original estate total		765,000
Less: Nil rate band at death	325,000	
GCTs in 7 years pre death (lifetime gifts ignored in original computation)	(Nil)	
Nil rate band available		(325,000)
Taxable estate		440,000
IHT at 40%		176,000

> **Examiner's comments**
>
> Part (a) required detailed knowledge of the payment of capital gains tax by instalments. It was the most difficult part of the question and was not done well. The fundamental problem here was that candidates simply did not know the rules, such that they had very little to say. The smart candidates kept their answers brief and moved on to the easier marks in part (b) and, particularly, part (c).
>
> Part (b) concerned the penalty for making a careless error in a tax return. The question stated that the error was careless but many candidates described the full range of penalties available for all error types thus wasting time.

ANSWERS TO PRACTICE QUESTIONS: SECTION 2

> Having said that, candidates' performance in this part of the question was good with the exception of the meaning of potentially lost revenue (PLR), the figure on which the penalty would be based. PLR is the additional tax due following the correction of the error and not the amount of the undeclared income.
>
> Part (c) required calculations of inheritance tax and was done well. Almost all candidates understood the relevance of the taxpayer being UK domiciled rather than non-UK domiciled and most candidates handled the chargeable lifetime transfer correctly.
>
> There were two common areas where marks were lost. First, many candidates omitted to calculate the original inheritance tax liability that would have been paid before the additional information was discovered. This calculation was necessary in order to calculate the tax underpaid. Secondly, many candidates were not sure of the due date for inheritance tax or, if they knew the six-month rule, they did not know how to apply the rule to the facts.
>
> A minority of candidates did not know the mechanics of inheritance tax particularly well. As a result, they did not deal with the nil rate band correctly or they included the chargeable lifetime transfer in the death estate. Other errors involved applying capital gains tax exemptions to inheritance tax and failing to calculate an estate rate in order to justify the double tax relief available.

	ACCA marking scheme	
		Marks
(a)	Payment of capital gains tax by instalments	
	Availability of payment by instalments	1.5
	Availability of gift relief	1.5
	Matters that Cuthbert would need to be aware of	
	Need for election	1.5
	Payment and interest	2.0
	Subsequent sale of asset	1.0
		7.5
	Maximum	6.0
(b)	Maximum penalty	1.5
	Disclosure	1.5
	Minimum penalty	1.5
		4.5
	Maximum	4.0
(c)	Gift in the seven years prior to death	1.5
	Death estate – if UK domiciled	
	Assets in UK	1.0
	Assets in Camberia	1.5
	Nil rate band	1.0
	Inheritance tax and double tax relief	2.5
	Death estate – if non-UK domiciled	1.0
	Interest on underpayment	1.5
		10.0
Total		**20.0**

32 BRAD (ADAPTED)   *Walk in the footsteps of a top tutor*

> **Key answer tips**
>
> The question covers two unrelated issues.
>
> Part (a) requires an explanation of why an individual is only temporarily non UK resident and calculations of the UK capital gains tax.
>
> The payment date is also required which is an easy mark to gain, but easily forgotten and lost if you are not careful.
>
> Part (b) relates to IHT and is divided into two parts. The first part asks for a general explanation of the IHT advantages of making lifetime gifts. The second part concerned a particular gift of shares and required knowledge of the valuation rules and business property relief in order to calculate a transfer of value and provide a detailed explanation of BPR. Finally, any other tax issues arising from the gift was another requirement.
>
> The highlighted words in the written sections are key phrases that markers are looking for.

(a) **Capital gains tax**

> *Tutor's top tips*
>
> *The examiner frequently tests the capital gains tax of an individual who leaves the UK, returns within 5 years, and whilst overseas disposes of assets. These are known as the temporary non-UK resident rules or temporary absence abroad rules. You are asked for an explanation of the rules as well as the calculations, so make sure you provide the explanations.*
>
> *Note that the rules only apply to assets owned before the individual loses their UK resident status and as such the antique bed does fall within the rules as it is purchased whilst Brad is abroad. Also note that the disposal of the motor car is exempt, regardless of these rules.*

Brad will be regarded as only temporarily non-UK resident whilst living in Keirinia because:

- he was absent from the UK for less than five years; and
- having always lived in the UK prior to moving to Keirinia, he was UK resident for at least four of the seven tax years immediately prior to the year of departure.

As a temporary non-UK resident, Brad will be subject to UK capital gains tax on the assets sold whilst he was temporarily overseas, which he owned at the date of his departure from the UK.

Accordingly, the antique bed is excluded from these rules as it was both bought and sold during the period of absence.

The profit on the sale of the motor car is ignored as motor cars are exempt assets for the purposes of capital gains tax.

The shares were sold in 2012/13, before Brad left the UK, so the gain on these shares was subject to tax in that year. However, there will have been no tax to pay as the capital gain of £4,900 (£18,900 − £14,000) was covered by the annual exempt amount for 2012/13.

The capital gains tax due on the sale of the painting is calculated as follows.

	£
Capital gain (£36,000 − £15,000)	21,000
Less: Annual exempt amount	(11,100)
Taxable gain	9,900
Capital gains tax at 28%	2,772

The gain on the sale of the painting is subject to tax in 2016/17, the tax year in which Brad returned to the UK, and not in the year of sale.

Accordingly, the tax is due on 31 January 2018.

(b) **Inheritance tax**

(i) **The inheritance tax advantages of making lifetime gifts to individuals**

Tutor's top tips

The question asks for the IHT advantages of lifetime gifts. Make sure you discuss all the issues as this part is worth 7 marks.

Note that only the advantages are required, so there is no need to mention disadvantages.

A lifetime gift to an individual is a potentially exempt transfer. It will be exempt from inheritance tax if the donor survives the gift by seven years.

If the donor dies within seven years of making the gift, such that the gift is chargeable to inheritance tax, the value used will be the value at the time of the gift and not the value at the time of death. Any increase in the value of the asset will be ignored, although relief will be available if the asset falls in value following the gift.

Certain exemptions are only available in respect of lifetime gifts (i.e. they cannot be deducted from the death estate).

These exemptions are:

- the annual exemption of £3,000 each year
- gifts in consideration of marriage/civil partnership up to certain limits
- regular gifts out of income that do not affect the donor's standard of living
- the small gifts exemption of £250 per donee per tax year.

Any inheritance tax due on the donor's death will be reduced by taper relief if the donor survives the gift by more than three years.

The tax due will be reduced by 20% if the donor survives the gift by more than three but less than four years. The percentage reduction will increase by 20% for each additional year that the donor survives the gift.

(ii) **In respect of the possible gift of 1,500 shares in Omnium Ltd to Dani**

Tutor's top tips

There are three elements to this part of the question so make sure you attempt all parts.

*The first part is a calculation of the transfer of value. For IHT, this is based on the **fall in value** or **diminution in value** of Brad's estate.*

However, the shares in Omnium Ltd are also owned by Brad's wife, so there is a related property calculation as part of the transfer of value.

*Remember that if we are dealing with related property and shares we apportion the value of the combined ownership based on the **number** of shares.*

The formula is:

A/(A+B) × combined ownership

where A is donor's number of shares and B is the related property's number of shares.

In this answer the examiner has used the short cut calculation possible for valuing shares. In the question you are given the value per share, so all you need to do is to value Brad's shares using the price per share based on the combined percentage ownership.

Fall in value of Brad's estate

Before the gift, Brad owned a 30% interest and his wife a 45% interest; therefore the couple have a combined ownership interest of 75%.

After the gift, Brad's ownership would be 15% and therefore the combined ownership of the couple will drop to 60%.

The fall in value of Brad's estate on a gift of 1,500 shares in Omnium Ltd using the related property rules will be (Tutorial note):

	£
Value of shares held prior to the gift (3,000 × £290)	870,000
Value of shares held after the gift (1,500 × £240)	(360,000)
	510,000

ANSWERS TO PRACTICE QUESTIONS: SECTION 2

Tutorial note

Using the A /(A + B) rules:

	£
Value of shares held prior to the gift:	
(7,500 × £290) × (3,000 ÷ (3,000 + 4,500))	870,000
Value of shares held after the gift:	
(6,000 × £240) × (1,500 ÷ (1,500 + 4,500))	(360,000)
	510,000

Ignoring the related property rules:

	£
Value of shares held prior to the gift (3,000 × £205)	615,000
Value of shares held after the gift (1,500 × £190)	(285,000)
	330,000

The higher fall in value of £510,000, produced by reference to related property, will be used.

Tutor's top tips

The examiner's solution shows the transfer of value with and without using related property. Don't worry if you didn't get this point. Technically, both calculations are necessary and the higher transfer of value is the answer. However, this is almost always going to be the value using the related property.

Business property relief

Tutor's top tips

The requirement asks for a detailed explanation of whether or not BPR is available. The examiner has offered clues in the question as Omnium Ltd owns a number of investment properties. Business property relief will not be available if the business of Omnium Ltd consists wholly or mainly of dealing in securities, stocks or shares or land and buildings or the making or holding of investments.

If BPR is available then the investment properties are excepted assets such that BPR will only be available on:

The transfer of value × (Non-excepted assets ÷ Total assets)

Business property relief will not be available if the business of Omnium Ltd consists wholly or mainly of dealing in securities, stocks or shares or land and

KAPLAN PUBLISHING 363

buildings or the making or holding of investments. Accordingly, it will be necessary to determine the significance of the investment properties to the activities of Omnium Ltd as a whole.

Brad must have owned the shares for at least two years at the time of the gift. This condition is satisfied.

Business property relief will not be available unless Dani still owns the shares at the time of Brad's death (or had died whilst owning the shares) and the shares continue to qualify for the relief.

If all of the conditions set out above are satisfied, business property relief will be available at the rate of 100%, because Omnium Ltd is an unquoted company.

However, where the company has excepted assets, business property relief will be restricted to:

100% × (Value of non-excepted assets ÷ Value of total assets) × the fall in value

Excepted assets are assets that have not been used for the purposes of the company's business in the two years prior to the transfer and are not required for such use in the future. Some or all of Omnium Ltd's investment properties may be classified as excepted assets.

Tutorial note

Business property relief will only be relevant if Brad were to die within seven years of making the gift, such that the potentially exempt transfer became a chargeable transfer.

Business property relief would also be available if Dani disposed of the shares prior to Brad's death and acquired qualifying replacement property within three years of the disposal.

Other tax issues

The gift of shares will be a disposal at market value for the purposes of capital gains tax. Gift relief will be available but will be restricted because of the investment properties owned by Omnium Ltd.

Gifts of shares are not subject to stamp duty.

Tutorial note

The question asked for a brief statement only of the other tax issues.

The capital gains gift relief restriction is calculated as:

Capital gain × (Chargeable business assets ÷ Chargeable assets).

Don't forget stamp duty – this is an easy mark!

ANSWERS TO PRACTICE QUESTIONS: SECTION 2

> **Examiner's comments**
>
> In part (a) the majority of candidates had some knowledge of the temporary non-UK resident rules and quite a reasonable knowledge of capital gains tax generally, such that they scored reasonably well. Most candidates knew the five-year rule although a much smaller number stated the four years out of seven rule.
>
> A minority of candidates stated a rule correctly in general terms but failed to apply it to the facts of the question. For example, some candidates stated that assets bought and sold during the period of absence were not subject to UK capital gains tax but then went on to calculate a gain in respect of the antique bed.
>
> Other candidates failed to apply the basics. For example, a minority of candidates omitted the annual exempt amount whilst others either provided an incorrect payment date or failed to provide one at all.
>
> When providing a payment date it is important to make it clear which tax year is being addressed. There were several possible relevant tax years in this question so stating a date without a year could not score unless the candidate explained in general terms how the date is determined (i.e. 31 January after the end of the tax year).
>
> In the first part of part (b) many candidates did very well but the performance of the majority was unsatisfactory.
>
> The advantages of lifetime giving are scattered throughout the inheritance tax system with certain exemptions only being available in respect of lifetime gifts, potentially exempt transfers being exempt once the donor has lived for seven years, taper relief once the donor has lived for at least three years, and the value of a gift being frozen at the time of the gift together with the availability of relief for any fall in value of the assets gifted.
>
> Most candidates would have known all of these rules but many did not include them all in their answers. Instead they wrote at length about some of them whilst omitting others. In particular, many candidates did not address the exemptions available in respect of lifetime giving. This is likely to be because candidates simply started writing and kept writing until they felt they had written enough. These candidates would have benefited from thinking their way through the inheritance tax system and noting each of the advantages of lifetime giving before they started writing.
>
> The valuation, which involved fall in value together with related property, in the second part of (b) was done well with many candidates scoring full marks. A minority of candidates were not aware that it is only the spouse's property that is related whilst others failed to appreciate that it is only the donor's property that is valued (the related property is only relevant when determining the valuation).
>
> The business property relief was done well with the majority of candidates identifying the two year rule and the relevance of the investments. Fewer candidates stated the need for the donee to continue owning the shares until the death of the donor.
>
> Candidates did not do so well when it came to identifying other tax issues. Most candidates simply repeated the basics of the inheritance tax rules in relation to potentially exempt transfers when what was required here was consideration of capital gains tax and stamp duty.

PAPER P6: ADVANCED TAXATION (FA2015)

ACCA marking scheme				Marks
(a)		Conditions		2.0
		Antique bed and motor car		1.5
		Quoted shares		2.0
		Painting		3.5
				9.0
			Maximum	8.0
(b)	(i)	Seven year rule		1.0
		Valuation		2.0
		Exemptions		3.0
		Taper relief		2.0
				8.0
			Maximum	7.0
	(ii)	Fall in value		3.5
		Availability of business property relief		
		Business of Omnium Ltd		1.5
		Brad's ownership of the shares		1.0
		Circumstances on Brad's death		1.0
		Calculation of business property relief		
		Rate of relief		1.0
		Excepted assets		2.0
		Other tax matters		2.5
				12.5
			Maximum	10.0
Total				25.0

33 PESCARA (ADAPTED) *Walk in the footsteps of a top tutor*

Key answer tips

Part (a) requires the calculation of death tax on a potentially exempt transfer. It is slightly complicated in that the donor is a widow and her husband did not utilise all of his nil rate band on death, but otherwise it is straightforward.

Part (b) requires the calculation of tax due on the sale of shares which were originally acquired via a gift and had subsequently been the subject of a takeover and a bonus issue. An explanation of the treatment on the subsequent disposal of an investment in SEIS shares is also required.

Part (c) requires a straightforward explanation of the IHT payable on death in respect of a gift with reservation. However, detail knowledge needs to be displayed, including an explanation of double charges relief to score highly on this part.

The highlighted words in the written sections are key phrases that markers are looking for.

ANSWERS TO PRACTICE QUESTIONS: SECTION 2

Tutor's top tips

The calculation of death tax due on a PET which becomes chargeable on death, with careful consideration of the nil rate band available, is a classic requirement. All of this part draws on F6 knowledge and should provide some relatively easy marks.

(a) **Marina**

Inheritance tax payable in respect of the gift of the shares in Sepang plc

		£	£
Transfer of value (375,000 × £1.86) (W1)			697,500
Less: Annual exemption – 2010/11			(3,000)
– 2009/10 b/f			(3,000)
Potentially exempt transfer now chargeable			691,500
Less: Marina's NRB at death		325,000	
NRB transferred from Galvez (W2)		151,667	
NRB available			(476,667)
Taxable amount			214,833
IHT at 40%			85,933
Less: Taper relief (1.2.11 – 1.10.16) (5 – 6 years) (60%)			(51,560)
			34,373
Less: IHT paid in lifetime			(Nil)
IHT payable			34,373

Workings

(W1) **Value of shares in Sepang plc as at 1 February 2011**

Lower of:

(i)	Quarter up = (£1.84 + ((£1.96 – £1.84) × 1/4))		£1.87
(ii)	Mid-market = ((£1.80 + £1.92) × 1/2)		£1.86
	Therefore, value of shares used		£1.86

KAPLAN PUBLISHING

(W2) **Nil rate band transferred from Galvez**

	£
Nil rate band available in 2007/08	300,000
Legacies to Pescara and her brother (2 × £80,000)	(160,000)
Unused NRB	140,000
Unused % of current year NRB available to transfer to Marina (£325,000 × (£140,000 ÷ £300,000))	151,667

Tutorial note

Galvez had no lifetime gifts and therefore the calculation of the unused NRB just considers legacies in his will.

If there had been any CLTs or PETs in the seven years pre death, they would have to be taken into consideration as they would also utilise some of Galvez's NRB available on death.

An alternative method of calculating Marina's NRB which is acceptable is:

- Galvez had an unused NRB = (£140,000 ÷ £300,000) = 46.667%
- Marina can claim 146.667% of the current NRB = (£325,000 × 146.667%) = £476,667.

Remember that an individual can never claim more than 200% of the current NRB.

(b) (i) **Pescara**

Capital gains tax liability – 2016/17

Tutor's top tips

The base cost of the original Sepang plc shares following the gift to Pescara must be established first. Then the takeover consideration received from Zolder plc, in return for the original shares in Sepang plc, must be quantified in order to allocate the base cost of the original shares to the two elements of the takeover consideration received.

The bonus issue must then be brought into the share pool of the new Zolder plc shares acquired before the gain is calculated on the disposal of some of the shares from the share pool.

ANSWERS TO PRACTICE QUESTIONS: SECTION 2

	£
Proceeds: sale of 1,000,000 shares	445,000
Less: Cost (W1)	(269,565)
Chargeable gain	175,435
Less: SEIS reinvestment relief (50% × £90,000)	(45,000)
Annual exempt amount	(11,100)
Taxable gain	119,335
Capital gains tax at 28%	33,414

Tutorial note

SEIS reinvestment relief allows the exemption of gains on any asset.

The maximum amount of relief that can be claimed is the lowest of:

1 50% of the chargeable gain = (50% × £175,435) = £87,718, or

2 50% of amount invested in qualifying SEIS shares (maximum 50% × £100,000)
   = (50% × £90,000) = £45,000, or

3 Any amount up to the lower of (1) or (2).

Therefore, any amount up to £45,000 could be claimed.

Remember that this CGT reinvestment relief is in addition to the income tax relief available which allows the deduction of 50% of the cost of the investment in SEIS shares to be deducted from the income tax liability in the tax year of investment.

Working

(W1) Base cost of 1,000,000 shares in Zolder plc

	Number	£
Original shares in Sepang plc		
Market value of gift (part (a))	375,000	697,500
Exchanged for shares in Zolder plc		
Cost of new shares (W2)	750,000	606,522
Bonus issue (2:1)	1,500,000	Nil
	2,250,000	606,522
Cost of shares to be sold		
(1,000,000/2,250,000) × £606,522	(1,000,000)	(269,565)
Balance c/f	1,250,000	336,957

KAPLAN PUBLISHING

Tutorial note

1 The base cost of shares in Sepang plc to Pescara will be the market value at the time of the gift (i.e. £697,500).

   The question says that gift relief is not available on these shares and therefore there will be no gain deferred against this base cost.

2 Bonus shares are free shares to existing shareholders. The number of shares received are therefore brought into the share pool at nil cost.

(W2) **Takeover of Sepang plc**

	MV of consideration received £	Allocation of original base cost £
Cash (375,000 × 30p)	112,500	
(£112,500/£862,500) × £697,500		90,978
Shares (375,000 × 2 × £1)	750,000	
(£750,000/£862,500) × £697,500		606,522
	862,500	697,500

(ii) **Pescara – Capital gains tax implications of selling the SEIS shares**

Tutor's top tips

There are only three marks available here, so a short but succinct summary of the position is required.

This part could have been answered independently at the beginning to bank some easy marks first.

The treatment of the gain or loss arising on the SEIS shares depends on when they are sold.

- If they are sold within three years of their purchase, any gain arising will be chargeable and any loss will be allowable.

- If they are sold more than three years after their purchase, any gain arising will be exempt.

  If the sale results in a loss, the loss will be allowable but will be reduced by the SEIS income tax relief obtained in respect of the shares.

In addition, if the SEIS shares are sold within three years, all or part of the capital gains tax reinvestment relief will be withdrawn, depending on the amount of shares sold and whether or not the sale is at arm's length.

(c) **Pescara – Gift of a UK property**

Tutor's top tips

This is a straightforward independent part on gifts with reservation which should produce some easy marks and could have been answered at the beginning if preferred.

The gift of a property will be a potentially exempt transfer (PET). The value of this PET will be the market value of the property at the time of the gift.

The amount which will be subject to inheritance tax in respect of this gift with reservation depends on whether or not the reservation of benefit is lifted (i.e. Pescara stops using the property rent-free, before she dies).

(i) If the reservation of benefit is lifted prior to Pescara's death, there will be a further PET equal to the value of the property at that time. This will only be chargeable if Pescara dies within the subsequent seven years.

(ii) If the reservation of benefit is still in place when Pescara dies, the value of the property at the time of her death will be included in her death estate.

Where Pescara dies within seven years of the original PET, such that it is chargeable to inheritance tax, and either (i) or (ii) applies, the original PET or (i)/(ii) will be taxed, whichever results in the higher tax liability.

Tutorial note

1 Where Pescara dies within seven years of the original PET, double charges relief is available.

 If the reservation has been lifted, the original PET and the deemed PET both become chargeable.

 If the reservation is still in place, the original PET becomes chargeable but HMRC require the house to be included in the estate computation at death.

 Double charges relief ensures that, in either case, the higher of these two liabilities will actually be chargeable.

2 Pescara would be advised to stop using the property (or to start paying a market rent) if she wishes the gift to be advantageous from the point of view of inheritance tax.

3 Note that if Pescara was just to make incidental use of the property (such as living in the property while visiting her son) so that the benefit derived is minimal, then the GWR rules would not apply

> **Examiner's comments**
>
> The majority of candidates performed well in part (a) and scored high marks. Less well-prepared candidates were unable to value the shares in Sepang plc and/or the amount of the nil rate band to be transferred from the donor's deceased husband. This was because they either did not know the rules or were unable to apply them to the facts in the question. Some candidates failed to identify that the husband's nil rate band was available for transfer.
>
> Part (b) concerned capital gains tax and was in two parts; neither part was done particularly well. In part (i) the calculation of the base cost of the shares required a certain amount of work.
>
> It was first necessary to realise that, due to the fact that gift relief was not claimed on the original gift (the question stated that gift relief was not available), the base cost of the original shares was their market value at the time of the gift. Following the takeover, this original cost had to be split between the new shares and cash received by reference to the market value of the consideration. Finally, the bonus issue increased the number of shares but had no effect on the total base cost.
>
> A significant number of candidates lost marks here because they side-stepped the first two stages of this calculation by attributing a cost to the new shares equal to their market value at the time of the takeover. The majority of candidates had no problem with the bonus issue.
>
> When calculating the amount subject to capital gains tax it was necessary to deduct EIS deferral relief equal to the whole of the £50,000 invested in EIS shares. Many candidates confused this relief with the relief available in respect of income tax when EIS shares are acquired. *Note: This is the examiner's comment on the original question, which has since been adapted to test SEIS reinvestment relief instead of EIS relief.*
>
> The first problem that some candidates had in part (b)(ii) was that they answered the question by reference to income tax rather than capital gains tax. Many of those who did address capital gains tax did not score as many marks as they might have done because they were not methodical in their approach. It was important to (briefly) consider four possible situations (i.e. sale of the shares at a profit or a loss both within and after the three-year period).
>
> Part (c) was not done particularly well as those candidates who clearly had some knowledge did not pay sufficient attention to the requirement.
>
> The question asked how the gift would be treated for the purposes of calculating the inheritance tax due on death. This required consideration of the value to be used, whether or not the reservation was lifted prior to death and the relief available in order to avoid double taxation.
>
> Many candidates wrote more broadly about gifts with reservation, explaining the rationale behind the rules and the actions necessary in order for the reservation to be lifted. These generalisations did not score any marks.

ANSWERS TO PRACTICE QUESTIONS: SECTION 2

ACCA marking scheme			
			Marks
(a)		Value of shares	2.0
		Annual exemptions	1.0
		Nil rate band	2.5
		Inheritance tax liability	1.5
			7.0
(b)	(i)	Proceeds less cost	4.0
		SEIS reinvestment relief, annual exempt amount and liability	2.0
			6.0
	(ii)	Sale of SEIS shares	3.5
		Withdrawal of SEIS reinvestment relief	1.0
			4.5
		Maximum	3.0
(c)		The initial gift	1.0
		Reservation lifted within seven years	1.5
		Reservation in place at death	1.0
		Avoidance of double taxation	1.5
			5.0
		Maximum	4.0
Total			**20.0**

34 CADA *Walk in the footsteps of a top tutor*

Key answer tips

This question covers the very regularly tested area of CGT versus IHT, with planning points re: lifetime gifts, the reduced rate of IHT for substantial legacies to charity, deed of variation and CGT planning. It is likely to have been a very popular question, although parts of it are actually quite challenging.

Part (a) requires you to think about IHT advantages of lifetime gifts, but not the use of lifetime exemptions. The only other advantages were the freezing in value of appreciating assets, and taper relief.

Part (b) covers the reduced rate of IHT for substantial legacies to charity. This is a relatively new area that has not been tested before this sitting. You must keep up to date with changes in the tax rules, as the examining team likes to test new areas.

There are some easy marks in part (c) for stating the procedures for a deed of variation to be tax effective.

KAPLAN PUBLISHING

Part (d) is less obvious, and requires you to spot the issue that capital losses are not available at death, but can be crystallised during lifetime to save CGT, either by selling shares that have gone down in value or by making a negligible value claim for shares that are worthless.

The highlighted words in the written sections are key phrases that markers are looking for.

(a) **The inheritance tax advantages of additional lifetime gifts**

Tutor's top tips

Think carefully before answering this part of the question. Cada would not have survived more than 7 years after these lifetime gifts, so they would not become exempt. You are specifically told not to discuss lifetime exemptions, so there will be no marks if you do.

The question also states that 'none of the remaining assets qualified for any inheritance reliefs', so there is no point in discussing business property relief either.

Also, there are no marks here for discussing CGT, as the requirement only asks for IHT advantages.

It is therefore important to cover the points regarding appreciating assets and taper relief thoroughly in order to get the four marks available.

Any additional lifetime gifts of quoted shares would have become chargeable on Cada's death on 20 November 2016.

However, the value charged to tax would have been the value of the shares at the time of the gift and not their value at the time of death.

Any increase in the value of the shares would therefore have been ignored, although relief would have been available if the shares had fallen in value following the gift.

Taper relief would have been available in respect of any gifts made in the period 1 December 2012 to 20 November 2013 (i.e. those gifts made more than three years prior to death).

This would only be relevant in respect of that amount of the gifts made which exceeded the nil rate band available of £220,000. In these circumstances, because the gift would have been made between three and four years prior to death, taper relief would have reduced the tax charged on the gift by 20%.

(b) **Additional gift to charity**

Tutor's top tips

It is a good idea to set out your computations before and after the additional gift to charity side by side, so that you only have to write out the headings once.

The breakdown of the estate is shown here for completeness, but you could obtain full credit by taking the total estate value of £1,000,000 straight from the question.

ANSWERS TO PRACTICE QUESTIONS: SECTION 2

> *This section is only worth five marks, so will be quite time pressured.*
>
> *Make sure that you fully answer the question by identifying both the increase in the legacy required and the IHT saving. Even if your increased legacy is wrong, you will still score marks for calculating the tax saving based on your figures.*

	Before additional gift to charity £	After additional gift to charity £
House	500,000	500,000
Cash	60,000	60,000
Other assets including share portfolio	440,000	440,000
	1,000,000	1,000,000
Less: Gift to charity (W)	(60,000)	(78,000)
Gross chargeable estate	940,000	922,000
Less: Nil rate band	(220,000)	(220,000)
Taxable estate	720,000	702,000
Inheritance tax at 40%/36%	288,000	252,720

Reduction in the inheritance tax liability
(£288,000 – £252,720)   35,280

Additional gift to charity (£78,000 – £60,000)   18,000

Tutorial note

The reduced rate of 36% applies where the gift to charity is at least 10% of the individual's baseline amount.

The baseline amount consists of the assets owned at death reduced by liabilities, exemptions, reliefs, and the nil rate band but before the deduction of the charitable gift.

An alternative method of calculating the baseline amount
= (Taxable estate plus charitable donation)

Working: Additional charitable donation required

	£
Taxable estate	720,000
Add back: Charitable donation	60,000
Baseline amount	780,000
Charitable donation required for 36% rate to apply: 10% × baseline amount	78,000

KAPLAN PUBLISHING

(c) **Variation of Cada's will**

Tutor's top tips

Although you may have learnt some of the tax advantages of a deed of variation, such as skipping a generation, you will not score marks in this section unless you apply your knowledge to the scenario.

Potential tax advantages

(i) **Gift to charity**

An additional £18,000 gift to charity could be carried out via a variation of Cada's will. This would result in the tax saving set out in (b) above.

(ii) **The house**

There are two reasons to vary the terms of Cada's will, such that the house is left directly to Raymer's son.

Capital gains tax

Without the variation, the proposed gift of the house by Raymer to her son will result in a chargeable gain equal to the excess of the value of the house on 1 July 2017 (the date of the proposed gift) over its probate value of £500,000.

The principal private residence exemption would not be available, as Raymer does not intend to live in the house.

Gift relief would not be available as a house is not a qualifying asset for this relief.

Inheritance tax

Without the variation, the gift of the house by Raymer to her son would be a potentially exempt transfer for the purposes of inheritance tax and would become a chargeable transfer if Raymer were to die within seven years of the gift.

Procedures

–   The variation of the will must be made in writing within two years of death by the person(s) who would benefit under the will (i.e. Raymer and Yang).

–   It must be stated that the variation is intended to replace the terms of the will for the purposes of inheritance tax and capital gains tax.

Tutorial note

The additional gift to charity would have to come out of the legacy to Yang, since Raymer only inherited the house.

It would be beneficial for Yang to sign the deed of variation, since it will cost £18,000 in additional charitable legacies, however, it will save tax of £35,280. All the inheritance tax due on the death estate will come out of Yang's inheritance, since she is the residual legatee. By signing the deed of variation to give an additional £18,000 to charity, Yang will actually inherit an additional £17,280 (£35,280 – £18,000).

(d) **Capital gains tax – Beneficial actions in respect of shareholdings**

Tutor's top tips

The key to success in this section was spotting that Cada owned shares that had fallen in value. As there is no capital gains tax on death, relief can only be obtained for these capital losses during lifetime.

There are no marks for discussing the annual exempt amount, as the question states that Cada pays capital gains tax every year, so must already be using her AEA.

Following her death, the capital gains tax base costs of Cada's shareholdings are equal to their market value as at the date of death. Accordingly, any losses which accrued up to the date of death are no longer available for relief.

Cada could have sold the shares in FR plc (valued at less than cost) prior to her death in order to realise the accrued capital losses. The capital losses could have been offset against any chargeable gains in 2016/17.

A negligible value claim could have been submitted in respect of the shares in KZ Ltd. The shares would have been treated as having been sold and reacquired at their market value, resulting in an allowable capital loss. This loss would have been available for relief against Cada's chargeable gains in 2016/17 (the year in which the claim would have been made) or in either of the two preceding tax years, provided the shares were of negligible value in those years.

Any capital losses in excess of chargeable gains in 2016/17 could have been carried back and offset against gains in the three tax years prior to death, relieving later years before earlier years.

Tutorial note

Candidates were not required to consider the possibility of a loss arising in respect of the unquoted shares being offset against the taxpayer's income.

Examiner's comments

The first thing to note in part (a) was that this part of the question concerned inheritance tax and not capital gains tax. The question also stated that candidates should not consider lifetime exemptions, for example the annual exemption. Many candidates did not identify these important points and thus wrote about both of these areas rather than focussing on the question requirements.

In addition, many candidates wrote at length about business property relief. This was not relevant because business property relief is available in respect of both lifetime gifts and the death estate and thus additional lifetime gifts by the deceased would not have resulted in additional relief. Other candidates were of the opinion that lifetime gifts will reduce the value of the death estate (true) and therefore reduce the inheritance tax due on death (not necessarily true). These candidates had failed to recognise the inheritance tax due in respect of potentially exempt transfers in the seven years prior to death (which these transfers inevitably would be due to the facts of the question).

Most candidates would have benefited from reading the question more carefully (and, for example, ignoring the annual exemption) and thinking more (thus recognising that business property relief was not relevant) and then writing a shorter answer that may very well have scored more marks.

Having said that, the majority of candidates correctly identified taper relief as an advantage of lifetime gifts and many explained the concept of value freezing. However, very few candidates were able to explain fall in value relief correctly.

Part (b) required candidates to calculate the increase in the legacy to charity that would be necessary for the reduced rate of inheritance tax to apply. Candidates appeared to be well-prepared for a question on this area of the syllabus and this part was answered particularly well with the exception of a very small minority who were simply not aware of the rules regarding the 36% rate of tax.

In part (c) the tax advantages are not obscure, but they do require some thought and they are not particularly easy to explain. Candidates would have benefited from slowing down and thinking about how best to express what they wanted to say rather than writing in the hope that the necessary words would eventually appear on the page.

As always, candidates had to apply their knowledge to the facts in the question. As far as capital gains tax was concerned, many candidates knew that there was no capital gains tax on death but failed to think about the potentially undesirable implication of the proposed gift of the house and how that implication could be avoided. In respect of inheritance tax, many candidates saw that this was linked to generation skipping but mentioning the term 'generation skipping' was not in itself sufficient.

Candidates had to explain that the variation would avoid the need for Raymer to make a potentially exempt transfer and therefore removed the possibility of such a transfer being chargeable to inheritance tax in the event that Raymer died within seven years of making the gift.

The majority of candidates were able to explain the procedures necessary in order to achieve a valid variation of the terms of the will.

ANSWERS TO PRACTICE QUESTIONS: SECTION 2

> Many candidates were unsure of the answer to part (d) despite having sufficient knowledge to deal with it. Unfortunately, instead of calmly thinking about it, they wrote about various aspects of capital gains tax, and inheritance tax, until they ran out of time. In particular, many candidates wrote about using any unused annual exempt amount despite being told in the question that the individual paid capital gains tax every year.
>
> The key issue here was that, because there is no capital gains tax on death, any unrealised losses in respect of shares worth less than cost are lost. Candidates simply had to point out, for example, that the quoted shares that were valued at less than cost at the time of death should have been sold prior to death in order to realise a loss that could then have been offset against chargeable gains.

ACCA marking scheme		
		Marks
(a)	Value frozen	
	Identify issue	1.0
	Relief for fall in value	1.0
	Taper relief for gifts more than three years prior to death	
	Identify issue	1.0
	Explain effect	1.5
		4.5
	Maximum	4.0
(b)	Original liability	2.5
	Additional gift to charity	2.5
	Net saving	1.0
		6.0
	Maximum	5.0
(c)	Potential tax advantages	
	Additional gift to charity	1.0
	House	3.5
	Procedures	2.0
		6.5
	Maximum	6.0
(d)	No relief for accrued losses	1.0
	Quoted shares where cost exceeds market value	1.0
	Unquoted shares	2.0
	Use of losses	2.0
		6.0
	Maximum	5.0
Total		**20.0**

35 KING *Walk in the footsteps of a top tutor*

Key answer tips

This question covers capital gains tax, inheritance tax, and the taxation of trust income.

You might find it easiest to start with the inheritance tax, as the gift of the cottage into an IIP trust has implications for inheritance tax and capital gains tax on the same disposal.

The highlighted words in the written sections are key phrases that markers are looking for.

(a) **Minimum number of shares in Wye Ltd to be sold**

Tutor's top tips

It would be easy to spend a long time on part (a), but it is only worth a small number of marks, so ensure you do not overrun.

Each share sold will generate sale proceeds of £45 and result in a chargeable gain of £40 (£45 – £5).

King's annual exempt amount for the tax year 2016/17 has already been used.

King is an additional rate taxpayer so will pay capital gains tax at 28% on his taxable gains.

The capital gains tax in respect of a single share is £11.20 (£40 × 28%).

The after-tax proceeds from the sale of a single share is therefore:

= (£45.00 – £11.20) = £33.80

Therefore the number of shares to be sold to generate £30,000 in after-tax proceeds is 888 (£30,000 ÷ £33.80).

Tutorial note

Alternative calculation, if X is the number of shares to be sold:

$45y - (40y \times 28\%) = 30,000$

$45y - 11.2y = 30,000$

$33.8y = 30,000$

$y = 888$

Proof of calculation:		
	£	£
Sale proceeds (888 x £45)	39,960	39,960
Less: Cost (888 x £5)	(4,440)	
Chargeable gain	35,520	
CGT @ 28%	9,946	(9,946)
After tax proceeds		30,014

(b) (i) **Gifts into the interest in possession trust**

Capital gains tax

Tutor's top tips

Take care; the proposed gifts are the cash proceeds from the sale of the shares (not the shares themselves) and the cottage. It appears that the cottage has never been King's PPR (he owns a significant property portfolio and no periods of occupation are described) so no PPR relief will be available to reduce his capital gains tax.

£30,000 cash

This is an exempt asset for capital gains tax purposes.

Cottage in Newtown

A chargeable gain will arise on the gift of the property by reference to its market value at the date of the gift.

Gift relief will be available on the transfer as it is a chargeable lifetime transfer for inheritance tax purposes.

King does not need the trustees' consent for this; he alone can elect for the full gain arising to be deferred such that no capital gains tax will be payable now.

The election must be submitted by 5 April 2021 (i.e. within four years after the end of the tax year in which the transfer is made).

Inheritance tax

Tutor's top tips

There is no need to separate the two gifts in order to calculate the inheritance tax as they are both being given to the same donee on the same day.

The transfer into an interest in possession trust is a chargeable lifetime transfer and accordingly an immediate lifetime charge arises.

	£	£
Transfer of value (£30,000 + £315,000)		345,000
Less: Annual exemption		
Current year (2016/17)		(3,000)
Previous year (2015/16) (used)		(Nil)
Net chargeable amount		342,000
Nil rate band (NRB) at date of gift (2016/17)	325,000	
Less: Gross chargeable transfers in 7 years pre gift	(Nil)	
NRB available		(325,000)
Taxable amount		17,000
Inheritance tax at 25% (King is paying the tax)		4,250

Tutorial note

Potentially exempt transfers use the annual exemptions but have no effect on the nil rate band while the donor is still alive.

(ii) **Income tax payable on the trust income by Florentyna**

Tutor's top tips

The taxation of trusts is often tested in questions with inheritance tax so make sure you do not neglect it in your studies.

As the trust is an interest in possession trust, all of the income must be paid out to the life tenant of the trust, Florentyna.

The only income will comprise dividends from the quoted shares so it will be received by Florentyna net of a notional 10% tax credit and taxed as dividend income in her hands.

Florentyna's 2016/17 personal allowance will have been used against her employment income. Therefore, as Florentyna is a basic rate taxpayer, she will be liable to income tax at the rate of 10% on the grossed up dividend income. However, there will be no additional tax to pay as the liability will be covered by the accompanying tax credit from the trust.

(c) **Gift of the flat in Unicity**

Tutor's top tips

Part (c) is an unusual requirement but there are easy marks available for noting that King's AE for 2016/17 has already been used by the CLT and that his NRB on death will have been used by the PET and CLT. The application of the related property rules will also gain credit.

Associated operations

For the purposes of inheritance tax associated operations may be defined as:

(a) two or more operations which affect the same property; or

(b) any two or more operations, where one is effected with reference to the other(s).

Where the rules apply, the series of transactions will be regarded as a single gift at the time of the final transaction in the series such that the total value transferred will be subject to tax.

The flat will be gifted to Axel, subject to a pre-existing tenancy agreement between King and Joy, as original owners of the property, and Axel's daughter as tenant.

Because of this agreement, the property will not have a right to vacant possession, such that its value will be reduced.

The creation of the tenancy agreement and subsequent gift of the property may therefore be considered to constitute 'associated operations' for inheritance tax purposes by HM Revenue and Customs (HMRC).

If this is the case, HMRC may treat the letting agreement with Axel's daughter and the transfer of the property to Axel as a single transaction, such that the transfer of the flat will be valued on a vacant possession basis for inheritance tax purposes.

Increase in inheritance tax liability

King's share of the property is valued on a related property basis.

King's annual exemption for 2016/17 has already been used by the CLT on 1 October 2016.

If King dies on 1 May 2018, his nil rate band will be fully used against his two previous lifetime gifts (to Florentyna and the trust).

When the potentially exempt transfer becomes chargeable, the value of the gross chargeable transfer will be increased by £67,143 (W) to £267,143 and there will be an additional inheritance liability due to the application of the 'associated operations' rules of £26,857 (£67,143 × 40%).

Working: Increase in value of the gift of property

Without vacant possession

	£
Value of the gift: £250,000 × $\dfrac{£160,000}{£160,000 + £40,000}$	200,000

With vacant possession

Value of the gift: £340,000 × $\dfrac{£220,000}{£220,000 + £60,000}$	267,143
Difference in gross chargeable amount (£267,143 − £200,000)	67,143

Examiner's comments

Part (a) required candidates to calculate the number of shares that needed to be sold in order to realise post-tax proceeds of £30,000. This was done relatively well by the majority of candidates, although only a minority of candidates managed to arrive at the correct answer.

A minority of candidates did not know how to solve this problem and simply calculated a tax liability based on an assumed number of shares sold. For those candidates who could see what needed to be done, the main mistake that was made in arriving at post-tax proceeds was to deduct the tax liability from the gain as opposed to from the sale proceeds.

Part (b) concerned the transfer of assets to a trust and was in two parts.

Part (i) required candidates to advise on the capital gains tax and inheritance tax implications of the transfer of the assets. This was a straightforward requirement where candidates simply needed to know the basic rules and to be organised and methodical. For example, it was important to deal with the two taxes separately and not at the same time.

The capital gains tax implications were done well with most candidates recognising that gift relief was available because the gift was immediately chargeable to inheritance tax. The only common mistake was a failure to point out that cash is an exempt asset for the purposes of capital gains tax.

The inheritance tax implications were also handled reasonably well although some candidates were unable to follow through the position in relation to the availability of the annual exemptions. Also, many candidates reduced the available nil rate band due to the gift to the daughter on 1 June 2014.

This was incorrect because the gift to the daughter was a potentially exempt transfer that will only become subject to inheritance tax if the donor dies within seven years. Therefore it has no effect on the nil rate band whilst the donor is alive.

Part (ii) concerned the income tax position of the life tenant of the trust. This was done well by those candidates who knew the rules. The only difficulty here was to ensure that the answer given was comprehensive and referred to the need to gross up the income, the rate of tax and the availability of the tax credit.

The final part of the question concerned inheritance tax and, in particular, related property and associated operations. This was a challenging part of the question but there were plenty of accessible marks for those candidates who were willing to be brave and to simply apply their knowledge to the facts. It was therefore important that candidates did not simply decide that they had not learnt the rules relating to associated operations, such that they were unable to answer the question. Basic knowledge of inheritance tax, including the need to take account of related property, went a long way towards obtaining reasonable marks here.

ACCA marking scheme

			Marks
(a)	Calculation of number of shares		3.0
(b)	(i)	Capital gains	4.0
		Inheritance tax	3.0
			7.0
		Maximum	6.0
	(ii)	Life tenant entitled to full income	1.0
		10% notional tax credit	1.0
		No additional tax payable, with reasons	2.5
			4.5
		Maximum	4.0
(c)	Explanation of associated operations		1.0
	Application to gift of flat		1.5
	Implication – value with vacant possession		1.0
	Increase in inheritance tax liability		4.5
			8.0
		Maximum	7.0
Total			**20.0**

PAPER P6: ADVANCED TAXATION (FA2015)

MULTI TAX PERSONAL INCLUDING OVERSEAS

36 NUCLEUS RESOURCES (ADAPTED) *Online question assistance*

 Walk in the footsteps of a top tutor

Key answer tips

This question is really two unconnected questions.

The first part is all about a sole trader expanding her business, either by taking on some employees or paying a company to do some work for her. You need to work out which option will leave her financially better off.

The second part covers mainly IHT and CGT. There are a couple of issues here: you need to think about the impact of domicile on IHT, and the tax implications of a lifetime transfer into a trust. In addition, there is a small section on ethical issues.

The highlighted words in the written sections are key phrases that markers are looking for.

Tutor's top tips

Read the memorandum in the question carefully. The examiner gives you some helpful tips on how to approach this part of the question.

You need to check whether Maria is already an additional rate taxpayer, to avoid the need to prepare full income tax computations.

You also need to think about VAT as this is a partially exempt business. The examiner indicates that the recoverability of input VAT is bound to be affected.

If the amount of VAT recoverable changes as a result of the expansion, this will affect the amount of after tax income for Maria.

Remember also that you are considering the options from Maria's point of view, so you do not need to consider the tax position of the employees or company doing the work for Maria, just the extra income after tax generated for Maria herself.

Make sure that you show your workings clearly, so that if you do make some mistakes you can still gain marks for consistency.

Notes for meeting with Maria Copenhagen

(a) **After tax income generated by the expansion of Nucleus Resources**

Maria is an additional rate taxpayer, as the current net income from the business and IIP trust of £168,000 (£40,000 + £90,000 – £37,000 – £35,000 + £110,000) exceeds £150,000.

Maria's personal allowance would already be reduced to £Nil as her net income exceeds £121,200.

Accordingly, the profit generated by the expansion will be subject to tax at a total of 47% (income tax at 45% and class 4 national insurance at 2%).

Tutorial note

In the real exam answer the examiner worked out the net after tax income at £168,000 (i.e. ignoring the VAT impact).

However, the net after tax income before considering the options is in fact £162,894 (£168,000 less irrecoverable VAT £5,106 (W1)).

Either way, with £168,000 or £162,894, the purpose of this first paragraph is just to establish that she is an additional rate taxpayer and therefore the impact of each option can be calculated at the marginal rates.

Employ additional employees :

	£
Additional turnover	190,000
Existing irrecoverable VAT will be recoverable (W1, W2)	5,106
	195,106
Salaries (£55,000 + £40,000)	95,000
Class 1 NIC ((£95,000 – (£8,112 × 2)) × 13.8%) (Note (1))	10,871
Cost in respect of car (W4)	2,443
Additional overheads	20,000
	128,314
Net additional income (£195,106 – £128,314)	66,792
Additional income after tax (£66,792 × 53% (Note (2)))	35,400

Tutorial note

1   The £2,000 employment allowance will already have been claimed against the class 1 secondary NICs relating to the existing employees. Accordingly there is no £2,000 deduction against the additional class 1 secondary NICs in relation to the additional employees.

2   If the total tax rate at the margin is 47%, the after tax income generated by the expansion will be 53% (100% – 47%).

Use Quantum Ltd:

	£
Additional turnover	190,000
Additional irrecoverable VAT (£9,912 (W3) – £5,106 (W1))	4,806
Quantum Ltd annual fee	140,000
	144,806
Net additional income (£190,000 – £144,806)	45,194
Additional income after tax (£45,194 × 53%)	23,953

Tutor's top tips

Don't worry if you didn't get this completely right. If you have calculated after tax income correctly based on your figures, you will still score marks here. There were some very easy marks for just putting in the extra income and expenses.

Workings

(W1) Existing business – Irrecoverable VAT due to partial exemption

Partial exemption percentage (£40,000 ÷ £130,000) (Note)	31%
	£
Total input tax (£37,000 × 20%)	7,400
Attributable to taxable supplies (£7,400 × 31%)	(2,294)
Attributable to exempt supplies	5,106

De minimis tests:

(1) Total monthly input tax is £617 (£7,400 ÷ 12) on average, which is less than £625. However, as the value of exempt supplies is more than 50% of the total supplies, test 1 is not satisfied.

(2) Total input tax less input tax directly attributable to taxable supplies is £7,400 (£7,400 – £Nil), which gives a monthly average of £617, as above, but again the value of exempt supplies is more than 50% of the total supplies, so test 2 is not satisfied.

(3) Monthly input tax relating to exempt supplies is £425 (£5,106 ÷ 12) on average, which is less than £625. However, as the input VAT relating to exempt supplies is more than 50% of the total input VAT, test 3 is not satisfied either.

Therefore the VAT attributable to exempt supplies cannot be recovered.

Tutorial note

Remember that when a business makes a mixture of both taxable and exempt supplies, input VAT can usually only be reclaimed on purchases attributable to taxable supplies.

Any mixed input VAT needs to be apportioned using the formula:

Taxable supplies ÷ total supplies = % recoverable.

This % is always rounded up to the next whole %.

However, if the input VAT relating to exempt supplies is very small (i.e. below the de minimis limits), then the whole amount can be reclaimed.

(W2) **Expanded business with employees**

Irrecoverable VAT due to partial exemption

Partial exemption percentage

((£40,000 + £190,000) ÷ (£130,000 + £190,000))	72%
	£
Total input tax ((£37,000 + £20,000) × 20%)	11,400
Attributable to taxable supplies (£11,400 × 72%)	(8,208)
Attributable to exempt supplies	3,192

This is below the annual de minimis limit of £7,500 (£625 × 12) and is less than half of the total input tax. Accordingly, all of the input tax can be recovered.

Tutorial note

As this de minimis test is satisfied, there is no need to consider the two further tests.

Therefore, as a result of expanding the business and taking on employees, £5,106 (W1) of irrecoverable VAT becomes recoverable.

Tutorial note

The approach in this answer is that used by the examiner in his model answer and was therefore the way in which he expected you to deal with the situation, given his hint that the recoverability of input VAT is 'bound to be affected'.

> *However, you may have assumed that the examiner's comment in Note 4 that 'the expenditure cannot be attributed to particular supplies' only related to the existing business and that all of the input VAT on the additional overheads of £20,000 is fully recoverable as they directly relate to a wholly taxable supply (i.e. the new project).*
>
> *If so, this is a very valid assumption. If you stated this assumption and prepared you answer on this basis, you should still have gained full marks.*

(W3) **Expanded business using Quantum Ltd**

Irrecoverable VAT due to partial exemption

Partial exemption percentage (W2)	72%
	£
Total input tax ((£37,000 + £140,000) × 20%)	35,400
Attributable to taxable supplies (£35,400 × 72%)	(25,488)
Attributable to exempt supplies	9,912

De minimis tests:

(1) Total monthly input tax is £2,950 (£35,400 ÷ 12) on average. As this exceeds £625, test 1 is not satisfied.

(2) Total input tax less input tax directly attributable to taxable supplies is £35,400 (£35,400 − £Nil), which gives a monthly average of £2,950, as above. As this exceeds £625 test 2 is not satisfied.

(3) Monthly input tax relating to exempt supplies is £826 (£9,912 ÷ 12) on average. As this exceeds £625, test 3 is not satisfied either.

Therefore the VAT attributable to exempt supplies cannot be recovered.

Tutorial note

As in (W2), you may have assumed that the examiner's comment in Note 4 that 'the expenditure cannot be attributed to particular supplies' only related to the existing business and that all of the input VAT on the annual charge of £140,000 is fully recoverable as it directly relates to a wholly taxable supply (i.e. the new project).

If so, this is a very valid assumption. The examiner has said that if you stated this assumption and prepared you answer on this basis, you should still have gained full marks.

(W4) **Cost in respect of car**

	£
Annual cost ((£12,800 − £2,000) ÷ 5) (Note)	2,160
Class 1A NIC (£2,048 (W5) × 13.8%)	283
	2,443

Tutorial note

*The examiner specifically tells you to spread the effect of the capital allowances evenly. All you need to remember is that the **total** capital allowances available will be equal to the net cost of the car to the business (i.e. the proceeds less the original cost). This effect will actually be spread over a longer period than 5 years, as the car will be added to the general pool and no balancing allowance will be given on disposal, and instead WDAs will continue to be claimed on a reducing balance basis. However you have been told in the question to spread the allowances over the period of ownership of the car.*

Don't forget that as an employer, Maria will have to pay class 1A NICs as she will be providing a benefit to an employee.

(W5) **Car benefit**

CO_2 emissions 109 g/km, available all tax year

	%
Basic petrol percentage	14
Plus: (105 – 95) × 1/5	2
Appropriate percentage	16

Car benefit (£12,800 × 16%) £2,048

(b) (i) **Inheritance tax on the quoted shares**

Tutor's top tips

Make sure that you answer the specific question here. In the first part, the examiner asks you for the 'issues to be considered' in order to determine whether the gift will be subject to UK IHT.

What he is really asking you to consider is two things:

'is Neil's uncle UK domiciled', and

'are the shares UK or overseas assets'?

Consideration of the availability of double taxation relief is then required.

*There are six marks available, so try to make sure that you have at least six separately identifiable points in your answer, and show that you have **applied** your knowledge by using facts provided in the information in the question.*

The inheritance tax position depends on the domicile of the uncle and the location of the quoted shares.

KAPLAN PUBLISHING

- If the uncle was domiciled in the UK when he made the gift in October 2014, the value of the shares at the time of the gift will be subject to inheritance tax.
- If the uncle was domiciled in Heisenbergia, the gift will only be subject to UK inheritance tax if the shares are UK assets.

Uncle's domicile

- If the uncle was not UK domiciled in 1995 it seems very unlikely from what we know that he would have acquired a UK domicile whilst living in Heisenbergia.
- If the uncle was UK domiciled at the time he left the UK in 1995, he will continue to be UK domiciled unless he acquired a domicile of choice in Heisenbergia.
- In order to have acquired a domicile of choice in Heisenbergia, the uncle would have had to have severed his ties with the UK and exhibited a clear intention of making Heisenbergia his permanent home.

Location of the quoted shares

- The shares are UK assets if the company is incorporated in the UK or the shares are registered in the UK.

Tutorial note

The location of the shares may also be affected by any double tax treaty between the UK and Heisenbergia.

Inheritance tax suffered in Heisenbergia

- Any UK inheritance tax due in respect of the gift can be reduced by double tax relief in respect of the inheritance tax charged in Heisenbergia.

(ii) **Creation of the trust**

Tutor's top tips

The first part of the requirement simply asks for the 'tax implications' of transferring the shares to the trust. So, you need to consider all of the capital tax implications of the gift here: IHT, CGT and also stamp duty.

The second part requires an outline of the taxation of trust income received by a beneficiary.

Inheritance tax

- The lifetime transfer of shares to the trust would be a chargeable lifetime transfer.
- The value transferred would be reduced by the annual exemptions for the year of the gift and the previous year.

- As the company is quoted, business property relief (at 50%) will only be available in respect of the shares if Niels controls the company, which is unlikely to be the case.
- As Niels has not made any previous chargeable transfers, the transfer would be covered by his £325,000 nil rate band; there would be no inheritance tax due.

Capital gains tax

- The transfer of the shares to the trust represents a chargeable disposal at market value.
- Gifts holdover relief would be available (because the gift is immediately chargeable to inheritance tax) such that any gain arising could be deducted from the trustees' base cost of the shares rather than being charged.

Stamp duty

- There is no stamp duty on a gift.

Income tax

- Niels will be subject to income tax on any amounts received from the trust by his sons, subject to a *de minimis* limit of £100 per annum. This is because the boys are both minors and the trust was created with capital provided by their parent, Niels.
- A tax credit will be given in respect of the income tax paid by the trustees.

(iii) **Discussion of issues with Maria**

Tutor's top tips

The examiner always includes ethical issues in his exams, up to a maximum of 5 marks. These sections are usually very straightforward, as long as you have not run out of time!

- Maria and Niels are separate clients and must be treated as such from the point of view of confidentiality.
- We must not disclose information relating to Niels to anyone, including Maria, unless we have permission from Niels (or such disclosure as is required by law or professional duty). Accordingly, we should check to see if we have written permission from Niels to discuss his affairs with his wife.
- Unless we have permission from Niels, we should not discuss the situation relating to the proposed transfer of shares to the trust. This is because we cannot explain the situation to Maria without referring to Neils' tax position, i.e. the lack of previous chargeable transfers.
- Maria's question concerning inheritance tax on the gift from the uncle is different because it can be answered without making any reference to the tax affairs of Niels. It is, arguably, a general question on the workings of inheritance tax. There would be no breach of confidentiality if we discussed this matter with Maria.

- However, we know that it is not a general question and we should still consider the potential problems that could arise in discussing matters with Maria that relate to the personal affairs of Niels without first obtaining permission from Niels.

Examiner's comments

Part (a) required calculations of the annual additional after tax income generated by two alternative business expansion proposals. These calculations were made more complicated by the fact that the client's business was partially exempt for the purposes of VAT (value added tax).

This required an approach similar to that tested in question 2 of the Pilot paper but was only attempted by a minority of candidates. However, with the exception of the VAT aspects, the majority of candidates made a good attempt at this part of the question and produced clear, logical calculations which identified most of the relevant issues.

One surprising but common error was to treat the car benefit as a cost incurred by the business. In addition, a minority of candidates wasted time by providing lengthy explanations which were not asked for.

Part (b) tested three technical areas relating to the client. The general approach in this question was good, with well structured documents addressing the majority of the issues being prepared by many candidates.

Part (i) concerned the inheritance tax implications of a gift from an individual who may or may not have been domiciled in the UK. Somewhat surprisingly, many candidates struggled with this.

The most common error was to focus on the domicile status of the recipient of the gift rather than the donor. There was also some discussion of the remittance basis which had no relevance here.

Stronger candidates began by stating the general rule as regards domicile and location of assets in relation to inheritance tax and then applied the rules to the specific facts in the question.

The majority of candidates made sensible comments about the availability of double tax relief.

Part (ii) concerned the transfer of shares to a trust. The inheritance tax aspects were handled well and the stronger candidates also addressed the capital gains tax and income tax aspects. As always, it was important to identify all of the issues first and then ensure that they were all addressed in the time available. Otherwise, the only issue covered was inheritance tax and too few marks were earned.

Part (iii) concerned the extent to which it is acceptable to discuss a client's affairs with that client's spouse. The majority of candidates were quite clear on the inappropriateness of such behaviour and scored well. However, a significant minority did not attempt this part demonstrating either a lack of time management or poor knowledge of this area of the syllabus.

		ACCA marking scheme	
			Marks
(a)		VAT position	
		Existing business	3.0
		Expand with employees	2.0
		Expand using Quantum Ltd	2.0
		Employ additional staff	
		Turnover	0.5
		Irrecoverable VAT	1.0
		Salaries and class 1 NIC	1.5
		Car	
		Cost	1.0
		Class 1A NIC	1.5
		Additional overheads	0.5
		Income after tax	1.0
		Use Quantum Ltd	
		Turnover	0.5
		Irrecoverable VAT	1.0
		Annual fee	0.5
		Income after tax	0.5
			16.5
		Maximum	14.0
(b)	(i)	Relevance of domicile	1.0
		Relevance of location of shares	1.0
		Uncle's domicile in 1995	2.0
		Acquisition of domicile of choice in Heisenbergia	1.0
		Location of shares	1.0
		Double tax relief	1.0
			7.0
		Maximum	6.0
	(ii)	Inheritance tax	
		Chargeable lifetime transfer	1.0
		Annual exemptions	0.5
		Business property relief	0.5
		Covered by nil rate band	1.0
		Capital gains tax	
		Gain by reference to market value	1.0
		Gift relief available	1.0
		Income tax	
		Payable by Niels, with reasons	2.0
		Tax credit for tax paid by trustees	0.5
		Stamp duty	1.0
			8.5
		Maximum	7.0

				Marks
(b)	(iii)	Two separate clients		1.0
		Statement of general rule		1.0
		Transfer of shares to trust		1.5
		Inheritance tax on gift from uncle		2.0
				5.5
			Maximum	4.0
		Appropriate style and presentation		2.0
		Effectiveness of communication		1.0
		Logical structure		1.0
				4.0
Total				35.0

37 BOSON (ADAPTED) *Walk in the footsteps of a top tutor*

Key answer tips

This question is mainly about overseas aspects of income tax and CGT. Overseas aspects of tax are tested regularly in P6, so you must make sure that you learn the rules. You cannot assume that they will always be tested in the optional section of the exam and can therefore be avoided!

The highlighted words in the written sections are key phrases that markers are looking for.

(a) **Boson – Capital gains tax**

Tutor's top tips

The danger here is that you simply write down the definition of residence, which will score very few marks.

You must apply your knowledge to the specific scenario and give advice per the detailed requirement.

Note that the new FA2015 rules which cover the disposal of UK property by a non-UK resident individual are not applicable in this question as it is concerned with a non-UK resident individual considering the disposal of an overseas property.

Boson's capital gains tax position

Boson will have been non-resident whilst living in Higgsia. As he left the UK to work full time overseas, he would have lost his UK residence on 10 January 2012.

Accordingly, he will not be subject to capital gains tax on disposals made during the period in Higgsia unless he is classed as a temporary non-resident.

Boson will be treated as a temporary non-resident if he returns to the UK on or before 9 January 2017.

This is because:

- he was UK resident for four of the seven years prior to leaving the UK, and
- he will have been absent for less than five years.

As a temporary non-resident:

- Any capital gains made whilst overseas on assets owned at the time Boson left the UK will be subject to capital gains tax in the year of return (i.e. if he returns as planned on 20 December 2016 in 2016/17).
- Gains on assets purchased after he left the UK do not come within the temporary non-resident rules.

Boson will become UK resident from the date he returns to the UK as he is ceasing full time work abroad and returning permanently. He will then be subject to capital gains tax on his worldwide assets.

Tax planning advice

Sale of the shares in Meson plc on 1 May 2012 and 1 November 2016

Boson owned the shares at the time he left the UK and has already made the disposals whilst abroad.

Accordingly, it would be advisable if Boson delayed his return to the UK until after 9 January 2017 in order to avoid the gains being charged to capital gains tax.

Sale of the house in Higgsia

Boson purchased the house after leaving the UK and is considering selling it in the future.

As he purchased it after leaving the UK, the disposal will not fall within the temporary non-resident rules. Therefore, the disposal will not be subject to capital gains tax if Boson sells the house in a tax year prior to his return.

However, if he sells the house after his return, or during the tax year of his return (if he returns within five years), he will be liable to CGT on the disposal.

So, again, it would be advisable if Boson deferred his return to the UK until after 9 January 2017 and sold the house prior to this date.

Tutorial note

If the property in Higgsia was chargeable to CGT in the UK, it would not qualify for principal private residence relief, as an individual can only have one principal private residence at a time. The information in the question clearly states that Boson retained his principal private residence in the UK.

(b) (i) **Rental income after deduction of all taxes**

	£
Rental income	11,000
Higgsian income tax suffered (£11,000 × 30%)	3,300

UK income tax:

£	
6,885 × 20% (W1)	1,377
4,115 × 40%	1,646
11,000	

	£
Income tax liability	3,023
Less: Double tax relief (lower of UK and foreign tax)	(3,023)
	Nil
Total tax on overseas rental income	3,300
Income after deduction of all taxes (£11,000 – £3,300)	7,700

Tutorial note

Watch out here. The rental income will have suffered £3,300 overseas tax at source. The question to ask yourself is whether or not any more UK tax is also due.

*The total tax suffered is the overseas tax, plus any **extra** tax due in the UK. As the UK tax is completely covered by DTR, it will not reduce Boson's net income.*

Working: Remainder of basic rate band

	£
Salary	35,500
Less: Personal allowance	(10,600)
Taxable income in the UK	24,900
Basic rate band	31,785
Remainder of basic rate band	6,885

ANSWERS TO PRACTICE QUESTIONS: SECTION 2

(ii) **Dividend income after deduction of all taxes**

	£
Dividend income (£200,000 × 4.3%)	8,600
Taxable dividend income (£8,600 × 100/90)	9,556

UK income tax:

£	
6,885 × 10% (remaining BR band as before)	688
2,671 × 32.5%	868
9,556	

	£
Income tax liability	1,556
Less: Tax credit (£9,556 × 10%)	(956)
Income tax payable	600
Income after deduction of all taxes (£8,600 – £600)	8,000

Tutorial note

Remember that UK dividends received are deemed to be net of 10% tax, so must be grossed up to calculate the tax, but the cash received will be the £8,600 cash dividend less the income tax payable.

Beware in your calculation of the income tax payable!

Because the dividend falls partly in the basic rate band and partly in the higher rate band, you cannot calculate the income tax payable on the dividends by applying the effective rate of 25% to the net dividend here.

(iii) **Maximum fall in rate of return on portfolio of quoted shares**

Tutor's top tips

This section of the question is somewhat unusual, and not something that has ever been tested before. The best advice is to have a go, but don't get bogged down – it's only worth 3 marks!

		£
Maximum fall in after tax income (£8,000 – £7,700)		300

		£
Maximum fall in dividend income (£300/0.75) (see tutorial note)		400
Minimum dividend income (£8,600 – £400)		8,200

		%
Minimum rate of return (£8,200/£200,000)		4.1
Rate of return can fall by (4.3% – 4.1%)		0.2

Tutorial note

The effective rate of tax on dividend income that falls within the higher rate band is 25% ((32.5% – 10%) × 100/90). A reduction in net dividend income of £300 would all fall within the higher rate band

Examiner's comments

Part (a) required candidates to advise Boson on his liability to capital gains tax by reference to his residence position. Candidates needed to be methodical here and begin by pointing out that someone who is not resident is not subject to capital gains tax on investments. It was then necessary to relate this rule to Boson and to consider the applicability of the temporary non-resident rules. It was important that candidates clearly addressed the specific assets in the question (the shares and the house) rather than making general comments that could apply to anyone.

This part of the question was done reasonably well despite being quite tricky. The majority of candidates were aware of the temporary non-resident rules and some good attempts were made to apply them. One significant error, which was relatively common, was to think that the remittance basis was also relevant to Boson.

Candidates sitting the exam in the future should read my article on the international aspects of personal taxation and ensure that they are confident of the detail of the rules and the situations in which the remittance basis applies.

Part (b) concerned the taxation of investment income and was in three parts.

The first part required a calculation of rental income in respect of a house situated overseas after deduction of all taxes. This was a straightforward calculation of income less income tax liability, incorporating double tax relief, and was done well. Candidates who identified the remainder of the basic rate band after taking account of the salary and the personal allowance were more likely to calculate the tax on the rental income (as opposed to the tax on all of the individual's income) and were thus in a better position to satisfy the requirement correctly.

ANSWERS TO PRACTICE QUESTIONS: SECTION 2

Part (ii) required a calculation of dividend income after deduction of all taxes. Again, this was a straightforward task, but many candidates let themselves down by failing to address the basics of the UK tax system. In particular, the dividend was often not grossed up and the tax credit was often omitted. Many candidates seem to find it difficult to apply their basic knowledge when dealing with a single element of income as opposed to a full income tax computation. When reviewing the model answer you should note that those candidates who calculated the remainder of the basic rate tax band in part (i) were in a position to use that information to calculate the tax on the dividends in this part.

Part (iii) required candidates to use the 25% effective rate of tax on dividends (for a higher rate taxpayer) in order to calculate the amount by which the rate of return on a portfolio of shares could fall before the after tax income generated would cease to exceed the return from renting out the overseas house. This was a commercial, practical problem but was quite tricky and was not done well.

ACCA marking scheme

				Marks
(a)		Position whilst living in Higgsia		
		Not subject to UK capital gains tax with reason		2.0
		Circumstances giving rise to temporary non-resident status		2.0
		Implications of temporary non-resident status		2.0
		Position on returning to the UK		
		Subject to capital gains tax with reason		1.5
		Sales of shares		1.5
		Potential sale of house		2.0
				11.0
			Maximum	10.0
(b)	(i)	Higgsian income tax		0.5
		UK income tax		
		Remainder of basic rate band		
		Salary		0.5
		Personal allowance		0.5
		Excess over basic rate band		0.5
		Tax at appropriate rates		0.5
		Double tax relief		1.0
		Income after deduction of all taxes		0.5
				4.0
	(ii)	Taxable dividend income		1.0
		Tax at appropriate rates		1.0
		Tax credit		0.5
		Income after deduction of all taxes		0.5
				3.0
	(iii)	Maximum fall in dividend income		1.5
		Minimum rate of return required		1.0
		Maximum fall in rate of return		0.5
				3.0
	Total			20.0

38 POBLANO (ADAPTED) *Walk in the footsteps of a top tutor*

Key answer tips

This is a lengthy question, and the biggest problem is sorting out the information and the requirements whilst also leaving enough time to answer the question. There are really four separate questions here, which could be attempted in any order, as there is no follow through of information.

Part (i) covers a comparison of net income for two different employment packages. This type of question is very popular at P6, and once you have seen one they are all very similar. The accommodation benefit is pure F6 knowledge, and illustrates how important it is to retain this knowledge. However, even without this you should still be able to score a good pass here.

Part (ii) deals with the rules for senior accounting officers, and there are easy marks here if you have learnt these rules.

Part (iii) covers the popular topic of inheritance tax, but in a rather unusual way. The '12 possible situations' may put you off attempting this section, but the examiner does provide guidance on how to approach it – so if you heed his words and do not panic you should be able to score some marks.

The final part of the question, part (iv), covers the income tax treatment of trusts. Trusts are generally not a popular area with students, although this section is actually very straightforward if you have learnt the rules.

The highlighted words in the written sections are key phrases that markers are looking for.

Tutor's top tips

Again, the requirements at the end of the question serve only to highlight the number of marks available for each section. The real requirements are mainly in the email from the manager and in the memorandum given at the start of the question.

Highlight the requirements as you come across them, and don't forget to keep looking back at them to make sure your answer is focused.

The first requirement asks for 'notes for a meeting', with the 'briefest possible notes' where the numbers are not self-explanatory. This means that you must keep narrative to a minimum and should write in very short sentences. Bullet points are ideal.

ANSWERS TO PRACTICE QUESTIONS: SECTION 2

MEETING NOTES

Date   7 June 2016

Subject   Poblano

(i)   **Working in Manchester – Poblano's financial position**

Tutor's top tips

Poblano wants to know how much better or worse off he will be compared to his current position. This means that you need to think about the additional net cash (or deficit) after taking into account any tax charges and expenses.

The first paragraph of the question states that Poblano earns £60,000 per year, so it is clear that any extra taxable employment income will be subject to 40% income tax and 2% NICs.

Living in the company flat

The calculations set out below are based on the information currently available.

		£
Additional salary		15,000
Less:	Income tax (£15,000 × 40%)	(6,000)
	Class 1 primary NICs (£15,000 × 2%)	(300)
	Petrol and depreciation (£1,400 + £1,500) (Note 1)	(2,900)
Additional salary after income tax, NICs and motoring expenses		5,800
Less:	Income tax on benefit in respect of the use of the flat (£17,140 (W) × 40%)	(6,856)
	Contribution towards the flat to be made by Poblano (£200 × 12)	(2,400)
Poblano would be worse off by		(3,456)
Additional salary required for Poblano not to be out of pocket (£3,456 ÷ 58%)		5,959

Tutor's top tips

Remember to state the additional salary needed, and remember that this will also be received net of 40% income tax and 2% NICs, so needs to be grossed up by 100/58 (or divided by 58%).

If Poblano's additional salary and benefits increased his adjusted net income to more than £100,000 he would start to lose his personal allowance but that is not the case here.

KAPLAN PUBLISHING

Not living in the company flat

	£
Additional salary after income tax, NICs and motor expenses (as above)	5,800
Plus: Mileage allowance (9,200 × 50p)	4,600
Less: Income tax and NICs on mileage allowance (£4,600 × 42%) (Note 2)	(1,932)
Rent (£325 × 12) (Note 3)	(3,900)
Poblano would be better off by	4,568

Notes

1 The depreciation is not an immediate cost but will increase the funds needed by Poblano to purchase his next car.

Poblano will not be able to claim a tax deduction for these costs as they relate to travelling to and from work and not to the performance of his duties.

2 The mileage allowance would be subject to tax and national insurance contributions as Poblano would be travelling to and from work and not in the performance of his duties.

Manchester will not be a temporary workplace for Poblano because he expects to work there for more than two years.

Tutorial note

The mileage allowance is not exempt and the authorised mileage allowance of 45p per mile is irrelevant here, as the travel from home to work is private mileage, not a business trip.

If Poblano had been sent to Manchester for less than two years, then the travel would represent travel from home to a temporary workplace, and would qualify as a business trip.

In this case, only the excess allowance of 5p per mile (50p – 45p) would be taxable, rather than all of it.

3 Poblano's aunt will not be subject to income tax on the rent.

This is because it will be in respect of a (presumably) furnished room in her house and the rent does not exceed £4,250 per year.

Tutor's top tips

The question specifically asks for an explanation of the tax treatment of the mileage allowance and the rent paid to Poblano's aunt, so make sure that you provide this.

Further information required

- The cost of the furniture provided in the flat – there will be an annual taxable benefit equal to 20% of the cost.
- Any running costs (utilities and maintenance etc.) in respect of the flat borne by Capsicum Ltd – there will be a taxable benefit equal to the costs incurred.
- Any capital improvements made to the property before the start of the tax year for which the benefit is being calculated.

Working: Taxable benefit in respect of the use of the flat

	£
Annual value	8,500
Additional benefit (£443,000 – £75,000) × 3% (Note)	11,040
	19,540
Contribution to be made by Poblano (£200 × 12)	(2,400)
Accommodation benefit	17,140

Note: The cost of £443,000 will be increased by any capital improvements made to the property before the start of the tax year for which the benefit is being calculated.

Tutorial note

The current value of the property (when Poblano moves in) is not relevant in this case, as the property has been owned by the employer for less than six years.

(ii) **Responsibilities of a senior accounting officer**

The rules require the senior accounting officer of a qualifying company or group of companies to:

- Ensure that a company's accounting systems are adequate for the purposes of calculating the company's tax liabilities.
- Certify to HM Revenue and Customs that such accounting systems exist for each financial year.
- Notify HM Revenue and Customs of any inadequacies in the accounting systems.

The rules apply to a company, or a group of companies, with turnover of more than £200 million and/or a statement of financial position total of more than £2 billion.

Penalties apply for non-compliance with the rules.

The senior accounting officer of Capsicum Ltd is the director or officer with overall responsibility for the company's financial accounting arrangements. This could be Poblano or another director within the group.

(iii) **Property in Chilaca**

Inheritance tax liabilities

Tutor's top tips

This section of the question may have appeared daunting, as there are 12 possible situations to deal with. However, there are actually very few calculations needed, as a number of the situations result in the same amount of tax.

The examiner does hint at this in the question, and often does give advice concerning the approach he wants you to take with parts of his questions.

Make sure that you follow his advice!

Key answer tips

Watch out for the following:

- There is no annual exemption, as Paprikash already makes gifts each year that use this.

- There is no lifetime tax, as a gift to an individual is a PET. The issue therefore revolves around charges arising as a result of death.

  In all cases, the nil band will be reduced by the gift in 2015, as this is less than seven years before the date of the gift/death.

- Death tax on a lifetime gift is usually based on the value of the gift at the date of gift, not at the date of death (*unless* the property falls in value), so any increases in value since the date of the gift are irrelevant for calculating death tax on a lifetime gift.

- Taper relief will be available for lifetime gifts, but only if the donor survives for at least three years.

Lifetime on 1 August 2016 – PET

Assumed Value at death (Note 1)	Death on 31 December 2018: IHT arising: (Note 2)		Death on 31 December 2020: IHT arising (Note 3)	
£		£		£
450,000	(£450,000 – £35,000) × 40% =	166,000	(£166,000 × 60%) =	99,600
600,000	(£600,000 – £35,000) × 40% =	226,000	(£226,000 × 60%) =	135,600
900,000	(£600,000 – £35,000) × 40% =	226,000	(£226,000 × 60%) =	135,600

Gift via will on 31 December 2018 or 31 December 2020 (Note 4)

Assumed Value at death (Note 1)	Death on 31 December 2018 or 2020: IHT arising: (Note 2)	
£		£
450,000	(£450,000 – £35,000) × 40% =	166,000
600,000	(£600,000 – £35,000) × 40% =	226,000
900,000	(£900,000 – £35,000) × 40% =	346,000

Notes

1   When Paprikash makes the gift it will be a potentially exempt transfer, thus, if the value of the property at the time of death is less than it was at the time of the gift, the inheritance tax payable will reflect the fall in value.

    If the value at the time of death is higher than at the time of the gift, the 'frozen' value at the time of the gift is charged to tax at the death rates.

2   The nil band remaining following the gift into trust on 1 June 2015 will be:

    (£325,000 – £290,000 CLT in June 2015) = £35,000.

Tutorial note

The value of the CLT on 1 June 2015 is £290,000 as:

- the gift is a gift of a minority shareholding in quoted shares, which does not qualify for business property relief (BPR), and
- the annual exemptions have already been utilised.

3   31 December 2020 would be between four and five years after the gift such that 40% taper relief would be available. Accordingly, the liability will be 60% of the liability calculated in respect of death occurring on 31 December 2018.

4   The date of death will not affect the amount of inheritance tax due.

Tutorial note

Note 4 is true, but only because it is assumed in the answer that the nil rate band does not change in the future.

In practice, the nil rate band can change in each tax year and therefore the amount of tax payable could be affected by the date of death.

Inheritance tax liabilities – conclusions

If the property is gifted on 1 August 2016, the inheritance tax due on death will never be more than the amount due if the property is transferred via Paprikash's will, even if the value of the property falls prior to the date of death.

Making a lifetime gift would turn out to be particularly beneficial if:

- The value of the property increases, as the tax would be based on the value as at 1 August 2016 rather than the value at the time of death.
- Paprikash survives the gift by more than three years such that taper relief would be available.

Tutor's top tips

Even if your calculations are not correct, you will still be able to score marks for drawing sensible conclusions.

Other issues

Tutor's top tips

The examiner asks for any 'other issues' that should be drawn to Poblano's attention. The most obvious issue is the continuing use of the property by Paprikash, which is mentioned a couple of times in the question.

There is also the issue of capital gains tax potentially arising on lifetime gifts.

Gift with reservation

Once the property has been given to Poblano, the occasional use of it by Paprikash may result in the gift being treated as a gift with reservation.

In these circumstances, the gift would be ignored for inheritance tax purposes and the property would then be included in Paprikash's death estate at its value at the time of death.

In order to ensure that the gift is effective for inheritance tax purposes Paprikash should have only minimal use of the property unless he pays Poblano a market rent.

Tutorial note

There is HMRC guidance that suggests that visits of up to two weeks a year without the son, and up to a month with the son, would be acceptable as 'minimal' use for these purposes. Knowledge of this guidance is not expected in the exam, but is of interest!

If the father pays a full commercial rent for the use of the property gifted, the gift with reservation rules will not apply. The gift will only be treated as a PET.

Capital gains tax

Lifetime gift

If Paprikash is resident in the UK in the year in which he gives the property to Poblano, it will be necessary to calculate a capital gain on the gift of the property.

The gain would be the market value of the property less its cost. The gain, less any available annual exempt amount, would be taxed at 18% or 28% depending on Paprikash's taxable income.

Tutorial note

If Paprikash is not resident in the UK in the year in which he gives the property to Poblano, the gain will be exempt from capital gains tax (subject to the temporary residence overseas rule).

Gift on death in the will

There would be no capital gains tax if the property were given to Poblano on death, via Paprikash's will.

(iv) **Tax treatment of trust income received by Poblano's daughter**

Tutor's top tips

Be careful that you don't waste time here. The examiner only wants you to talk about the tax treatment of the **income** received from the trust by Poblano's daughter.

There are six marks available, so your answer needs to reflect this. Note that the examiner does not tell you what type of trust it is, so you need to discuss the different types of trust and the tax treatment of income received from each.

The question clearly states that the income is dividend income, so don't bother discussing any other types of income.

The trust will be either an interest in possession trust or a discretionary trust:

- It will be an interest in possession trust if Piri has an absolute right to the income generated by the trust assets.
- It will be a discretionary trust if the trustees have the right to accumulate the income and pay it to Piri when they choose.

It is understood that the only income received by the trustees of the trust is dividend income.

Interest in possession trust

- The income to which Piri is entitled must be grossed up at 100/90.
- Where the income falls into Piri's basic rate band (after calculating the tax on her salary) it will be taxed at 10%.
- The balance of the income will be taxed at 32.5%.
- There will be a 10% tax credit.

Discretionary trust

- The income received must be grossed up at 100/55.
- Where the income falls into Piri's basic rate band it will be taxed at 20%.
- The balance of the income will be taxed at 40%.
- There will be a 45% tax credit.

Tutorial note

The 10% tax credit in respect of the dividend from the interest in possession trust is not refundable, whereas the 45% tax credit relating to the income from the discretionary trust is refundable.

Given the level of Piri's salary, this is not likely to be an issue, as her tax liability is not likely to be reduced below zero.

Examiner's report

This was a substantial question in four parts. Although some of the question parts could be seen as easier or harder than others, all of the parts had some easily accessible marks and candidates benefited from attempting all parts rather than only attempting those that appeared to be straightforward.

Part (i) concerned the implications of a change to an employee's location of work. On the whole this part of the question was done reasonably well. However, in order to score a high mark for this part it was necessary to focus on the client's financial position and calculate how much better or worse off he was going to be as a result of the change. This required candidates to think in terms of income and costs (with tax as a cost) and to recognise that costs that are not tax deductible are still costs and are therefore still relevant. This aspect of the question was not handled particularly well.

The calculation of the benefit in respect of the flat provided by the company was done well. However, the majority of candidates failed to recognise that the mileage allowance related to travel to and from work and was therefore taxable in full.

It was pleasing to note that fewer candidates than in the past provided lengthy explanations of what they were going to do before getting on and doing it. However, the question asked for an explanation of the tax treatment of two particular points; the receipt of the mileage allowance and the receipt of the rent. Many candidates failed to provide these explanations. As noted above, in respect of question 1, candidates must identify and carry out all of the tasks in the question in order to maximise their marks.

Part (ii) concerned the rules introduced in the Finance Act 2009 in relation to senior accounting officers. These rules were a significant development in the personal responsibility of individuals for the behaviour of their employing companies and were covered in great detail in the financial press at the time. However, the majority of candidates were not aware of them and, consequently, found it difficult to score well on this part of the question.

Part (iii) of the question concerned inheritance tax and the advantages of lifetime giving. At first sight it was a daunting question requiring the consideration of three possible property values, two dates of death and a lifetime gift or gift via will; a total of 12 possible situations. However, there was guidance from the 'manager' as to where to start together with the reassurance that 'you should find that the calculations do not take too long'.

It was very pleasing to find that the majority of candidates had no problem with this part of the question and that their knowledge of the basic mechanics of inheritance tax was sound. Candidates benefited from thinking rather than writing such that they were then able to realise that, for example, with a lifetime gift, the only difference between the two possible dates of death was the availability of taper relief. The best answers were admirably short and to the point.

The one area where candidates could have done better was in identifying the possible gift with reservation. The failure by many candidates to do this indicates, yet again, that some candidates do not take enough care in identifying all that has been asked of them.

The final part of the question concerned the tax treatment of income received from a trust. This was a test of knowledge, as opposed to application of knowledge, and candidates should have scored well.

However, the marks for this part were not as high as expected because candidates were not sufficiently careful in their approach. As always, the advice here is to stop and think. The question made it clear that the nature of the trust was not known and therefore candidates were expected to consider the income tax position of receipts from both an interest in possession trust and a discretionary trust. There was also the need to be specific and precise, as regards grossing up fractions and tax rates, rather than superficial and general in order to maximise the marks obtained.

PAPER P6: ADVANCED TAXATION (FA2015)

ACCA marking scheme		
		Marks
(i)	Salary less tax, national insurance contributions and motoring expenses	2.0
	Living in the company flat	
	Tax on the benefit	2.0
	Contribution	0.5
	Additional salary required	1.0
	Further information required	2.0
	Staying with aunt in Manchester	
	Calculations	1.5
	Mileage allowance	1.5
	Rent paid to aunt	1.5
		12.0
	Maximum	10.0
(ii)	Senior accounting officer	3.5
		3.5
	Maximum	3.0
(iii)	Inheritance tax liabilities	
	Nil band	1.0
	Lifetime gift	
	Value at time of gift and tax rate	1.0
	Fall in value post gift	1.0
	Taper relief	1.0
	Gift via will	1.5
	Full set of outcomes	0.5
	Conclusions (1 mark each, maximum 2 marks)	2.0
	Explanatory notes (½ mark each)	2.0
	Gift with reservation	2.5
	Capital gains tax	1.5
		14.0
	Maximum	12.0
(iv)	Nature of the trust	2.0
	Tax treatment (2 × 2 marks)	4.0
		6.0
	Appropriate style and presentation	2.0
	Effectiveness of communication	2.0
		4.0
Total		**35.0**

ANSWERS TO PRACTICE QUESTIONS: SECTION 2

39 SUSHI (ADAPTED) *Walk in the footsteps of a top tutor*

Key answer tips

This question is in two separate parts.

Part (i) deals with inheritance tax, in particular the impact of domicile on an individual's inheritance tax liability. Domicile has been a very popular area in recent exams, so you must learn the rules in detail.

Part (ii) covers the remittance basis. This is another popular area in the exam. The rules are complex, and again must be learnt.

The highlighted words in the written sections are key phrases that markers are looking for.

Tutor's top tips

The requirement at the end of the question just tells you how many marks are available for each section. The detailed requirements are all within the email from the manager.

You may find it useful to number these requirements so that you can tick them off as you attempt them.

Think about how you will structure your answer before you start; address only the questions set and do not deviate, otherwise you are likely to run out of time!

(i) **UK inheritance tax and the statue**

On the death of Sushi's mother

Sushi's mother was not UK domiciled, and would therefore only be subject to UK inheritance tax on UK assets.

As Sushi's mother had no UK assets, there will be no UK inheritance tax due on her death.

Tutorial note

It is the domicile of the **donor** that is important in determining whether or not inheritance tax is due on overseas assets, not the domicile of the recipient.

KAPLAN PUBLISHING

On Sushi's death

>
>
> *Tutor's top tips*
>
> Sushi has both UK and overseas assets, both of which should be considered.
>
> You do not know whether or not Sushi has acquired UK domicile, and you do not know when she will die, so you need to discuss all possibilities.
>
> Make sure that you **apply** the domicile rules to Sushi and give clear advice.

UK assets

Sushi's UK assets will be subject to UK inheritance tax, regardless of her domicile status.

Overseas assets

However, her overseas assets will only be subject to tax if she is UK domiciled or deemed to be UK domiciled.

Domicile

A person's domicile is the country in which they have their permanent home.

At birth, a person's domicile of origin is inherited from their father. Sushi would therefore have inherited the domicile of Zakuskia.

Even though she has been living in the UK for a number of years, she will remain domiciled in Zakuskia unless she acquires a domicile of choice in the UK.

To do this, she must acquire a permanent home in the UK and sever all ties with Zakuskia.

However, even if Sushi has not chosen to be UK domiciled, she will be deemed to be domiciled in the UK, for inheritance purposes only, once she has been resident in the UK for 17 out of the last 20 tax years (ending with the tax year in which any assets are transferred).

As Sushi has been resident in the UK since May 2002, she will be deemed domiciled in the UK from 2018/19 onwards.

This means that from 2018/19 onwards, both her UK assets and her overseas assets will be subject to UK inheritance tax.

Should Sushi die before 2018/19, her overseas assets will only be subject to UK inheritance tax if she has acquired a domicile of choice in the UK.

Land and buildings in Zakuskia

Tutor's top tips

You are asked to explain **how** the inheritance will be calculated, should the overseas land and buildings be taxable in the UK.

Think about the steps you would take if you were preparing an inheritance tax computation, and try to put these into words.

Valuation

The land and buildings will be valued at the date of Sushi's death. This value will be converted to sterling using the exchange rate on that day that gives the lowest sterling figure.

Any additional administration expenses incurred in Zakuskia will be deducted, subject to a maximum of 5% of the property value.

Calculation of inheritance tax

The nil rate band will be deducted from Sushi's death estate, including the land and buildings, and the excess will be subject to tax at 40%.

Double tax relief will be available for the lower of the overseas tax suffered, or the UK tax on the land and buildings.

The UK tax on the land and buildings will be calculated at the average estate rate.

Gift of the statue

Tutor's top tips

Read the instructions carefully!

You are not asked to describe potentially exempt transfers in detail, just to state **why** this transfer will be a PET, and how this treatment could be avoided.

Potentially exempt transfer

As the transfer of the statue is a lifetime gift of a UK asset from one individual to another, it will be a potentially exempt transfer.

How to avoid this treatment

Sushi can only avoid this treatment if she is not UK domiciled (i.e. she has not acquired a domicile of choice in the UK), and if the statue is an overseas asset.

As long as the statue is transferred to Sushi's son whilst it is in Zakuskia, it will not be subject to UK inheritance tax.

Tutorial note

It may also be possible to avoid UK inheritance tax by varying Sushi's mother's will, within 2 years of her death, so that the statue was left directly to Sushi's son, although the will would be subject to Zakuskian law.

The examiner has stated that you would have been given credit if you had discussed this as a possibility.

(ii) **The Zakuskian income**

Tutor's top tips

Again, there are specific instructions to follow here, and you must try to address all of them.

Remittance basis

Under the remittance basis, overseas income is only taxed in the UK when it is remitted, or brought in, to the UK.

The remittance basis is only available to individuals who are not UK domiciled. Accordingly, it will only be available to Sushi if she has not chosen to acquire UK domicile.

Meaning of remittance

The most obvious example of a remittance is when income is brought directly into the UK.

However, the definition of remittance also includes:

- Using overseas income to settle debts in the UK
- Using overseas income to purchase goods and services which are subsequently bought into the UK with the exception of:
    - Personal items (e.g. clothes, shoes, jewellery)
    - Items brought to the UK for repair
    - Items costing no more than £1,000.

There are also exceptions for amounts remitted to the UK to:

- Acquire shares in or make a loan to an unquoted trading company or member of a trading group
- Pay the remittance basis charge.

Tutor's top tips

You would not have to list all the above examples of a remittance and the exceptions to gain full marks in the exam.

Increase in UK tax liability due to Zakuskian income

> **Tutor's top tips**
>
> You only need to calculate the increase in Sushi's UK tax liability, not her total tax liability. This can be achieved very quickly by working in the margin.
>
> The question states that Sushi is an additional rate taxpayer, so any additional UK tax will be levied at the rate of 45%.
>
> Make sure that you add brief footnotes to your calculations as these are specifically requested, and therefore will score marks.

Remittance basis not available

	£
Gross Zakuskian income	200,000
UK income tax (45% × £200,000)	90,000
Less: Double tax relief for Zakuskian tax (lower than UK tax) (£200,000 × 10%)	(20,000)
Additional UK tax payable	70,000

Remittance basis available and claimed (Note 1)

	£
Gross Zakuskian income remitted	100,000
UK income tax (45% × £100,000)	45,000
Less: Double tax relief for Zakuskian tax (lower than UK tax) (£100,000 × 10%)	(10,000)
	35,000
Plus: Remittance basis charge (Note 2)	60,000
Plus: Loss of capital gains tax annual exempt amount (Note 3) (£11,100 × 28%)	3,108
Additional UK tax payable	98,108

Notes

1. As Sushi's unremitted overseas income is more than £2,000, the remittance basis is not automatically available. She will have to elect to use it.

2. The remittance basis charge is due because Sushi is claiming the remittance basis, and she has been resident in the UK for 12 of the previous 14 tax years.

3. If Sushi claims the remittance basis, she will lose her entitlement to the capital gains tax annual exempt amount.

   She also loses her entitlement to the income tax personal allowance, but this will already have been reduced to £Nil due to the level of Sushi's income, and therefore has no effect on the additional tax payable as a result of making a remittance basis claim.

Tutorial note

The fact that Sushi is an additional rate taxpayer tells you that she must have taxable income of more than £150,000.

Once an individual's net income exceeds £121,200, the personal allowance is fully withdrawn.

Conclusion

If Sushi remits £100,000 to the UK, it would not be beneficial for her to claim the remittance basis, if it is available.

Her UK income tax liability will increase by £98,108 if the remittance basis is claimed, but by £70,000 if it is not.

Tutor's top tips

Make sure that you clearly show your conclusion, if required.

Even if your answer is wrong, you will still be given credit if your conclusion is consistent with your analysis.

Examiner's report

Part (i) concerned inheritance tax and, in particular, the relevance of domicile to an individual's tax position. The level of knowledge here was good with some very strong, thorough answers. However, many candidates who scored well for this part of the question often did so in an inefficient manner which may have left them short of time for the remainder of the exam. As always, there was a need to pause; this time in order to determine the best way to say what needed to be said. Weaker candidates simply kept writing, often repeating themselves, until they finally got to where they wanted to be. Stronger candidates wrote short, precise phrases which earned all of the marks despite using very few words. Candidates should practise explaining areas of taxation making sure that their explanations are concise and clear.

There was a need to address the position of both the mother and the daughter but many candidates simply addressed 'inheritance tax' rather than the situation of the individuals. Candidates will be more successful in the exam if they think in terms of providing advice to individuals and companies rather than addressing technical issues as this will help them to stick to the point and to satisfy the questions' requirements.

A substantial minority of candidates produced muddled explanations confusing the importance of domicile with residence. This confusion was also evident in answers to part (ii). The two factors of residence and domicile have various implications depending on the taxes concerned and candidates need to know where to start such that they can then avoid writing about all of the factors at once.

A somewhat surprising error made by a significant minority of candidates was to state that the inheritance tax position on the death of Sushi's mother depended on the domicile status of Sushi as opposed to that of her mother. It is, of course, the status of the person whose estate has fallen in value that is relevant.

A final thought on this part of the question is that many candidates wasted time calculating inheritance tax, despite not having sufficient information, whilst others provided a considerable amount of detail regarding the taxation implications of making a potentially exempt transfer, despite being specifically told not to in the question.

Part (ii) concerned overseas income and the remittance basis. The performance of candidates for this part was mixed. To begin with there was much confusion regarding the conditions that must be satisfied in order for the remittance basis to be available with candidates mixing up domicile and residence with the 7 out of 9 years/12 out of 14 years rule (and the 17 out of 20 years rule in respect of inheritance tax deemed domicile).

The application of the £2,000 rule was also misunderstood by many. There is no doubt that there is plenty to be confused about in this area but that is why candidates need to learn it rather than acquire a hopeful understanding of it.

Candidates were asked to explain the meaning of 'remittance' and the 'remittance basis'. Most candidates attempted to do this, which was very encouraging, but few had much knowledge beyond the absolute basics. Similarly, most candidates were aware of the remittance basis charge but a significant number were confused as to the situation in which the charge would be levied.

On the plus side, the vast majority of candidates provided a conclusion (as requested) and many produced neat and reasonably accurate calculations.

ACCA marking scheme		
		Marks
(i)	Assets subject to inheritance tax	1.5
	Mother's death	1.0
	Sushi's death	
	UK assets	0.5
	Foreign assets	0.5
	Domicile of origin	1.0
	Domicile of choice	1.0
	Deemed domicile	2.5
	UK IHT on land and buildings in Zakuskia	
	Valuation	1.5
	UK IHT and double tax relief	2.0
	The statue	2.5
		14.0
	Maximum	12.0

		Marks
(ii)	Meaning and availability of remittance basis	1.5
	Meaning of remittance	3.0
	Calculations	
	Remittance basis not available	2.0
	Remittance basis available	
	Remittance basis charge	1.0
	Loss of annual exempt amount	1.0
	Loss of personal allowance has no effect	1.0
	Tax on remitted income	1.0
	Explanatory notes (1 mark per sensible point) – maximum	3.0
	Conclusion	1.0
		14.5
	Maximum	**13.0**
Total		**25.0**

40 MIRTOON (ADAPTED)

  Online question assistance and Walk in the footsteps of a top tutor

Key answer tips

There are two separate parts to this question, which could be attempted in any order.

Part (a) requires calculation of how a disposal of assets, use of trading losses and departure from the UK will affect an individual's financial position. Although the calculations are generally straightforward, this part is challenging due to its size and the fact that there is no indication as to how the 16 marks available are split.

Part (b) asks for a letter that covers three totally separate issues, which could be dealt with in any order.

Part (b)(i) requires discussion of the VAT implications of cessation of a business, and is pure F6 level knowledge.

Part (b)(ii) covers the popular topic of overseas aspects of income tax and capital gains tax for an individual who is leaving the UK. This area is tested regularly, so you must ensure that you learn the complex rules that apply.

Part (b)(iii) asks for explanation of the associated operations rules relating to inheritance tax. These rules are not tested regularly, so you may not have been familiar with them.

The highlighted words in the written sections are key phrases that markers are looking for.

ANSWERS TO PRACTICE QUESTIONS: **SECTION 2**

Tutor's top tips

Again, the requirement at the end of the question just tells you how many marks are available for each section. The detailed requirements are all in the email from your manager.

You may find it useful to number these requirements so that you can tick them off as you attempt them.

There are four marks available for professional skills, such as preparing your answer in letter format in part (b). These are easy marks, so you should aim to get them.

(a) **Mirtoon's financial position**

Tutor's top tips

It is important that you answer the question here. You are asked to calculate **the total** of the after tax proceeds from the sale of the house and business assets, the tax saving from the trading losses and 'any other tax liabilities'.

A good approach to take would be to set out a pro forma working, fill in the easy figures such as the proceeds from the sale of the house and business, and then cross reference this to separate workings for the calculation of the other missing amounts.

Even if your individual workings are wrong, you will still gain a mark for satisfying the requirement and arriving at a total.

Total net proceeds

	£
Proceeds from sale of home	850,000
Less: Capital gains tax (W1)	(6,200)
Proceeds from sale of business assets	14,000
After tax proceeds from sale of home and business assets	857,800
Tax saving in respect of trading losses (W3)	21,840
Other tax liabilities	
Capital gains tax in respect of agricultural land (W1)	(16,184)
Total net proceeds	863,456

KAPLAN PUBLISHING

Workings

(W1) Capital gains tax

Tutor's top tips

Think about **all** of the gains that will arise before you calculate the capital gains tax payable.

There will be a gain on disposal of the house, as part of it was used for business purposes.

Less obviously, there will also be a held over gain that crystallises when Mirtoon leaves the country.

Remember that capital losses and the annual exempt amount can be set off against these gains in the most beneficial way, in order to minimise the tax payable.

	£	£
Gains qualifying for entrepreneurs' relief		
Sale of house (W2)		62,000
Not qualifying for entrepreneurs' relief		
Gain crystallising on agricultural land (Note 1)	72,000	
Less: Capital losses (Note 2)	(3,100)	
Less: Annual exempt amount (Note 2)	(11,100)	
Taxable gains	57,800	62,000
Capital gains tax:		
Qualifying gains (£62,000 × 10%) (Note 3)		6,200
Non-qualifying gains (£57,800 × 28%) (Note 4)	16,184	

Explanatory notes

Tutor's top tips

Although the requirement is to 'calculate', you are asked to include explanatory notes, particularly in relation to the availability of reliefs and allowances and the offset of the trading losses. There will be marks available for providing these notes, so try to remember to do this.

1   As Mirtoon emigrates from the UK within six years of the end of the tax year in which the gift of the agricultural land was made, the held over gain from the time of the gift crystallises and is chargeable on the day before emigration (i.e. January 2017), and will be taxed in 2016/17.

ANSWERS TO PRACTICE QUESTIONS: SECTION 2

Tutorial note

There is an exception to the rule regarding the emigration of the donee.

Where the donee goes overseas to take up full time employment abroad a chargeable gain will not crystallise on his departure from the UK provided:

(i) he resumes his status as UK resident within three years; and

(ii) he has not disposed of the asset whilst abroad.

However, as Mirtoon is leaving the UK for at least four years, this exception does not apply here.

2   The capital losses and the annual exempt amount can be set off in the most tax-efficient manner. Accordingly, they will be deducted from gains that would otherwise be taxed at 28%.

3   The gain in respect of the business use of the house will qualify for entrepreneurs' relief because the house was an asset:

- used in a business that has now ceased, and
- was sold within three years of cessation, and
- was held for at least 12 months before the disposal

Accordingly, the gain will be taxed at 10%.

4   Mirtoon's basic rate band is fully used by his income and qualifying gains. Accordingly, the non-qualifying gains will all fall into the higher rate band and will be taxed at 28%.

Tutorial note

Even though Mirtoon does have some of his basic rate band remaining after deducting his taxable income, this must be set against the gains qualifying for entrepreneurs' relief first. As these qualifying gains alone are greater than £31,785, there is clearly no basic rate band left. Had there had been, any non-qualifying gains in the basic band would be taxed at 18% instead of 28%.

Tutor's top tips

Don't worry if you missed the gain crystallising on the agricultural land. In that case, you would have been given credit for setting off the capital losses and the annual exempt amount against the gain on the house, and you would still be given the mark for summarising the net cash position based on your figures.

KAPLAN PUBLISHING

(W2) **Chargeable gain on sale of house**

	£
Sale proceeds	850,000
Less: Cost	(540,000)
	310,000
Less: Principal private residence relief (£310,000 × 80%) (Note)	(248,000)
Chargeable gain	62,000

Tutorial note

Alternatively, it would be perfectly acceptable to calculate the chargeable gain as the business percentage of the total gain (i.e. £310,000 × 20% = £62,000).

Explanatory note

Principal private residence relief is available to exempt the gain on the part of the house that was used as Mirtoon's main residence. However, relief is not available on the part that was used exclusively for business purposes.

(W3) **Tax saving in respect of trading losses**

Tutor's top tips

*The requirement specifically tells you to offset the loss against total income of the previous tax year (i.e. normal carry back relief) and **not** to consider any other loss reliefs.*

Accordingly, although terminal loss relief would be available here for the loss arising in the last 12 months of trading, there will be no marks for calculating the terminal loss or for discussing terminal loss relief.

Assessable trading loss for 2016/17

	£
Loss for year ended 30 June 2016	(20,000)
Loss for six months ending 31 December 2016	(17,000)
Less: Overlap profits	(7,600)
Loss for the tax year 2016/17 (Note 1)	(44,600)

Tutorial note

In the final tax year of trading the loss is matched to the tax year using the current year basis rules in exactly the same way as a profit, including the deduction of overlap profits from commencement, which will increase the loss available for relief.

There is no cap on the use of the trading loss against other income as the loss is less than £50,000.

Income tax liability for 2015/16

Tutor's top tips

Note that in this question, the examiner specifically tells you to prepare calculations of the income tax liability both before and after the offset of losses. This is unusual, as he normally likes you to work in the margin and not prepare full computations! However, you should always do as he tells you in order to maximise your marks.

Watch out for the personal allowance. Remember that this is reduced if adjusted net income is greater than £100,000, but will effectively be 'reinstated' after setting off the losses, as the adjusted net income then falls below the £100,000 limit.

	Before offset of losses £	After offset of losses £
Trading income	95,000	95,000
Bank interest (£22,600 × 100/80)	28,250	28,250
Total income	123,250	123,250
Less: Loss relief	(Nil)	(44,600)
Net income	123,250	78,650
Less: PA (Note 2)	(Nil)	(10,600)
Taxable income	123,250	68,050

Income tax

£	£			
31,785	31,785	× 20%	6,357	6,357
91,465	36,265	× 40%	36,586	14,506
123,250	68,050			

Income tax liability	42,943	20,863

Tax saving (£42,943 − £20,863)		22,080

Explanatory notes

1. As 2016/17 is Mirtoon's final tax year, the assessment will include any losses not yet assessed (i.e. both of the accounting periods ending in 2016/17, less the overlap profits from commencement).

2. The personal allowance is reduced by £1 for every £2 by which adjusted net income exceeds £100,000, and is reduced to £Nil where the adjusted net income is greater than £121,200.

Tutorial note

As the non-savings income is greater than £5,000, the interest income does not fall within the starting rate band. Accordingly, there is no need to separate out the non-savings income and the savings income when calculating the tax as the rates will be the same for both types of income.

It is possible to calculate the tax saving at the margin as follows:

	£
Benefit of loss (£44,600 × 40%)	17,840
Benefit of PA now available (£10,600 × 40%)	4,240
	22,080

However, the email from the manager specifically asked you to prepare calculations of Mirtoon's income tax liability before and after the offset of the losses, so that is the approach you should have adopted.

(b) **LETTER**

Firm's address

Mirtoon's address

9 December 2016

Dear Mirtoon

Tutor's top tips

There are marks available for using the correct format for your letter. Try to make sure that your answer looks like a letter. Remember to address Mirtoon as 'you' as you are writing the letter to him, and remember to sign off your letter with 'yours sincerely'.

Departure from the UK

Please find below the information you require regarding the various tax matters to be considered on the cessation of your business and departure from the UK.

(i) **VAT implications of the cessation of your business**

You must deregister from VAT when you cease to make taxable supplies and notify HM Revenue and Customs within 30 days of cessation (i.e. by 30 January 2017). Failure to do so could result in a penalty.

As you are not selling your business as a going concern, you will need to charge output VAT on any assets sold prior to deregistration.

If you still hold inventory and non-current assets (on which you have recovered input VAT) at the date of deregistration, you must account for output VAT on the replacement value of these assets. However, this charge will be waived if the output VAT is less than £1,000.

Tutorial note

If Mirtoon was to sell his business as a going concern, to a VAT registered person, the transfer would not be a taxable supply. This is not the case here, as the question specifically tells you that Mirtoon has not been able to find a buyer for his business and is, therefore, going to cease trading and then sell any remaining business assets.

(ii) **Liability to UK income tax and capital gains tax whilst living in Koro**

Tutor's top tips

Overseas aspects of income tax and capital gains tax are often tested in the P6 exam. In order to gain a good mark in this type of question, you must ensure that you apply your knowledge to the scenario and don't just talk generally about the tax implications of residence and domicile.

You should deal with income tax and capital gains tax separately, as the rules are not the same for the two taxes.

As you are going abroad to work full time, and are not planning to make any return trips, you will automatically be non-UK resident for the tax years that you are away.

The tax year that you leave will be split, as you will be leaving to work full time overseas and will not spend any time in the UK after departure, having been UK resident in the previous tax year, UK resident in the current year and not UK resident in the following year.

Therefore, you will lose your residency from the date that you leave the UK, and will regain it on the date you return.

Income tax

As you will not be UK resident, you will not be taxed in the UK on your overseas income.

Your UK income is still taxable, so you will be taxed on your UK bank interest. However, where you are non-UK resident for a complete tax year, the tax will be limited to the tax deducted at source.

Also, as you will be non-UK resident, it may also be possible to arrange to have your bank interest paid gross, by making a 'not resident' declaration to the bank.

Tutorial note

There are some slightly obscure points set out above, in relation to the UK bank interest.

The key points that you should have in your answer are that UK income is taxable, whereas overseas income is not taxable in the UK.

Capital gains tax

Generally, you will not be subject to UK capital gains tax if you are not resident in the UK unless you dispose of UK residential property.

However, as you have been resident in the UK for at least four of the seven years before leaving the UK, the temporary non-residence rules will apply.

According to these rules, you must remain outside the UK for five years to avoid capital gains tax on assets owned before your departure. If you sell such an asset while you are abroad, you will be taxed on the gain in the tax year of return to the UK.

Sale of agricultural land

If you sell the agricultural land in June 2018, while you are in Koro and return to the UK within five years (i.e. before January 2022), the gain will be taxed in the tax year of return. However, if you return after January 2022 the gain will not be taxed in the UK.

Sale of UK residential home

If you were to sell your UK home whilst you are in Koro, the gain will not be exempt. However, only gains accruing after 5 April 2015 are chargeable and even then, only to the extent that they are not covered by principal private residence (PPR) relief or the annual exempt amount.

As your home was purchased before 5 April 2015, there are three methods of calculating the gain accruing since 5 April 2015 before the consideration of reliefs:

1   rebasing the cost to market value at 5 April 2015
    (automatic treatment without an election)
2   electing for time apportionment of gain pre and post 5 April 2015
3   electing to be assessed on the whole gain or loss.

You should opt for the method that gives the smallest gain.

PPR relief will exempt any part of the gain that relates to periods of occupation since 5 April 2015, although relief is not available on the part of the house that was used for business purposes.

ANSWERS TO PRACTICE QUESTIONS: SECTION 2

For periods of non-occupation (once you have moved to Koro) the gain may be chargeable, although the last 18 months of ownership will be covered by PPR relief.

If there are any further periods of non-occupation, the whole tax year (not just the actual period of occupation) will be treated as a period of non-occupation, and thus not exempt, unless you have stayed in your house for a total of at least 90 nights in the tax year.

Any gain remaining after PPR relief and the annual exempt amount will be taxed at 18% or 28%, depending on the level of your UK taxable income and consequential remaining basic rate band in the normal way.

You should note that HMRC must be notified of the disposal of any UK residential property by a non-UK resident individual within 30 days of the conveyance of the property, even if there is no CGT liability.

(iii) **Inheritance tax planning**

Tutor's top tips

This part of the question asks you to write about a very specific area of inheritance tax: associated operations.

There will be no marks available for discussing other areas of inheritance tax or inheritance tax planning.

There are some inheritance tax anti-avoidance rules that you need to be aware of when we discuss your inheritance tax planning ideas.

Associated operations

Tutor's top tips

You may not have learnt the associated operations rules, as these have not previously been tested in the P6 exam.

There were only two marks available for writing about these rules, so you could still score a good pass mark even if you left out this part of the question.

The associated operations rule may apply where there are two or more transactions which affect the same property and as a result tax is avoided.

For example, if an asset is transferred piecemeal, so that the total value of the individual transactions is less than the value of the whole asset.

KAPLAN PUBLISHING

Where tax is avoided by making a series of transactions and the associated operations rule is applied:

- the associated operations are treated as one transaction, and
- any resulting transfer of value is treated as being made at the time of the last associated operation.

Please do not hesitate to contact me if you require any further information.

Yours sincerely

Tax manager

> **Examiner's report**
>
> In part (a), the sale of the house was handled well with almost all candidates identifying the availability of principal private residence relief and the need to restrict the relief to 80% of the gain arising. The crystallisation of the heldover gain in respect of the agricultural land (due to Mirtoon becoming non-resident), on the other hand, was spotted by only a small minority of candidates. However, this was an easy point to miss and it was possible to obtain a perfectly good mark without any reference to it.
>
> The treatment of the losses arising on the cessation of the business was not handled well due to a lack of knowledge of the closing year rules. This meant that many candidates struggled to determine the assessment for the final years of trading. There was also a considerable number of candidates who erroneously treated the overlap profits brought forward as taxable profits in the final tax year as opposed to being part of the allowable loss. The unincorporated trader is examined with great regularity and candidates are likely to benefit from knowing, in particular, the opening and closing years rules.
>
> A minority of candidates demonstrated a lack of precision when considering the tax due in respect of the sale of the house and the tax saving in respect of the offset of the trading losses. This lack of precision included a failure to take account of the capital losses brought forward and/or the annual exempt amount and the omission of the personal allowance from the income tax computations. It was important to consider the personal allowance as Mirtoon's income exceeded £100,000 such that the personal allowance was restricted.
>
> Part (b) was in three parts and produced a wide variety of answers.
>
> Part (i) concerned the VAT implications of Mirtoon ceasing to trade. This part was done reasonably well, although, perhaps not as well as expected. Some candidates made it hard for themselves by writing generally rather than addressing the facts of the question. In particular, many candidates wrote at length about the sale of a business as a going concern. However the question made it clear that the business was to cease with the assets then being sold. The vast majority of candidates identified the need to deregister. However, a considerably smaller number pointed out the possible need to account for output tax on business assets owned as at cessation.
>
> Part (ii) concerned Mirtoon's liability to income tax and capital gains tax whilst living overseas. There were some good answers to this part but also two particular areas of confusion.

> The first area of confusion related to the taxation of income where an individual is not resident in the UK. It needs to be recognised that where an individual is not resident in the UK, any foreign income will not be subject to UK income tax. Where many candidates went wrong was to imagine that the remittance basis was relevant here (perhaps because Mirtoon was not resident but continued to be domiciled in the UK). This led candidates to write at length about the remittance basis thus wasting time.
>
> The second area of confusion concerned the temporary non-resident rules. These rules relate to capital gains tax and cause gains that would otherwise not be taxable in the UK to be so taxable if the individual returns to the UK within five years of leaving. However, a minority of candidates incorrectly treated these rules as an extension of the residency rules as they relate to income tax.
>
> *The section concerning the sale of Mirtoon's UK home whilst non-UK resident is a new section added following the change in rules in FA2015.*
>
> Part (iii) concerned inheritance tax and the associated operations rules. Knowledge of associated operations was less common but this was to be expected.
>
> Many candidates did not restrict their answers to the area asked about but wrote at length about inheritance tax generally. Candidates must take care in identifying what has been asked and try to avoid addressing other areas.
>
> *The original question also contained a section on the gift with reservation rules which has been removed to enable the new overseas topic to be tested instead.*

ACCA marking scheme		
		Marks
(a)	Sale of home	
	Capital gain	0.5
	Principal private residence relief	1.0
	Capital gains tax	1.5
	Agricultural land	2.5
	Trading losses	
	Loss available for relief	2.0
	Tax relief	4.0
	Total proceeds net of tax adjustments	2.0
	Explanatory notes (one mark each – maximum four marks)	4.0
		17.5
	Maximum	16.0

				Marks
(b)	(i)	Requirement to deregister		1.5
		Output tax		2.0
				3.5
			Maximum	3.0
	(ii)	Status		2.5
		Income tax		1.5
		Capital gains tax		8.0
				12.0
			Maximum	10.0
	(iii)	Associated operations		2.5
			Maximum	2.0
		Approach to problem solving		1.0
		Appropriate style and presentation		1.0
		Effectiveness of communication		2.0
			Maximum	4.0
Total				35.0

41 SHUTTELLE (ADAPTED) *Walk in the footsteps of a top tutor*

Key answer tips

The question is divided into two distinct parts which are unrelated.

Part (a) is a question on personal pension contributions and you are required to calculate the income tax liability of an individual who has contributed to a personal pension scheme in excess of the annual allowance. Based on your calculation, you are then required to calculate the tax relief obtained as a result of the personal pension contribution.

Part (b) is a question regarding the remittance basis for three individuals. In addition you are required to state whether or not the remittance basis charge is applicable to the individuals and if so quantify it. The final part of (b) is a straight forward question asking for just two examples of actions that would be regarded as remittances. But the examiner does say 'other than bringing cash into the UK' so do not use this as an example!

The highlighted words in the written sections are key phrases that markers are looking for.

ANSWERS TO PRACTICE QUESTIONS: **SECTION 2**

(a) **Shuttelle**

Tutor's top tips

You should score some easy marks for a basic income tax computation which includes salary and an accommodation benefit.

The key was recognising that there would also be an excess pension contribution. You may not have realised that the contributions by the employer must be included in the excess pension contribution calculation. However, you would still score some marks for recognising that the excess pension contributions needed to be included as part of the tax calculation.

In order to calculate the annual allowance available you had to consider if there was any unused relief brought forward from the previous three years. Remember the annual allowance is £40,000 for 2015/16 but can be increased by any unused AA in the previous three years, starting with the earliest year first. Note that the AA was £40,000 in 2014/15, but £50,000 in the two previous tax years. These amounts are given in the tax rates and allowances in the exam.

The personal pension contributions also extend the basic and higher rate bands.

Note that the excess pension contribution tax liability is calculated using the taxpayer's marginal rate of tax.

(i) **Income tax liability – 2015/16**

		£
Salary		204,000
Accommodation (W1)		4,937
		———
		208,937
Annual allowance charge (W2)		59,000
		———
Total income		267,937
Less: Personal allowance (W4)		(10,600)
		———
Taxable income		257,337
		———

Analysis of income:
Excess pension contribution £59,000   Other income £198,337

£		£
151,785 × 20% (W5)		30,357
46,552 × 40%		18,621
———		
198,337		
59,000 × 40% (Annual allowance charge)		23,600
———		———
257,337		
———		
Income tax liability		72,578
		———

KAPLAN PUBLISHING

>
>
> *Tutorial note*
>
> The excess pension contribution is not part of the adjusted net income used to calculate the personal allowance.
>
> The basic rate and higher rate limits are extended due to the pension contributions. Accordingly, the excess pension contributions will be taxed at 40%.

Workings

(W1) Benefit in respect of accommodation

	£
Annual value	7,000
Expensive accommodation benefit ((£500,000 – £75,000) × 3%)	12,750
	19,750
Benefit in 2015/16 (£19,750 × 3/12)	4,937

(W2) Annual allowance charge

	£
Gross contributions by Shuttelle	120,000
Gross contributions by Din Ltd	4,000
Less: Annual allowance available in 2015/16 (W3)	(65,000)
Annual allowance charge	59,000

(W3) Annual allowance available – 2015/16

	£
Brought forward from 2013/14 (£50,000 – £19,000 – £4,000)	27,000
Used in 2014/15 (£40,000 – £38,000 – £4,000)	(2,000)
Current year available in 2015/16	40,000
	65,000

(W4) Personal allowance

	£
Total income (excluding AA charge) = Net income	208,937
Less: Gross PPCs	(120,000)
Adjusted net income	88,937

As ANI is < £100,000; the full personal allowance is available.

(W5) **Extended basic and higher rate bands**

	£	£
Current bands	31,785	150,000
Add: Gross PPCs	120,000	120,000
Revised bands	151,785	270,000

(ii) **Total tax relief in respect of the gross personal pension contributions**

Tutor's top tips

This is a comparison of the income tax liability without the pension contribution with your answer from part (i).

Don't forget

- *the tax relief at source as personal pension contributions are paid net of 20% tax, and*
- *without the PPC relief, there would be no personal allowance available.*

	£		£
31,785	× 20%		6,357
118,215	× 40%		47,286
150,000			
58,937	× 45%		26,522
208,937			

	£
Income tax liability – ignoring the gross PPCs	80,165
Income tax liability – reflecting the gross PPCs (part (i))	(72,578)
Pension contributions – tax relief at source (£120,000 × 20%)	24,000
Total tax relief in respect of pension contributions	31,587

KAPLAN PUBLISHING

Tutorial note

1   When calculating the liability ignoring the pension contributions, there would be no personal allowance due to the level of the net income.

2   By charging tax on the excess pension contributions, relief is effectively only given for £61,000 (£120,000 – £59,000), the balance of the contributions, as set out below:

	£	£
58,937 × 45% (additional rate)		26,522
2,063 × 40% (higher rate)		825
	61,000	
Tax saved in respect of personal allowance becoming available: (£10,600 × 40%)		4,240
Total tax relief in respect of pension contributions		31,587

(b)   **The three non-UK domiciled individuals**

Tutor's top tips

Overseas aspects for individuals is a popular syllabus area as it is a new topic in the P6 syllabus and the rules have changed significantly in recent years, so make sure you have learnt the rules.

(i)   **The availability of the remittance basis and the remittance basis charge**

The availability of the remittance basis

The remittance basis is available to UK resident individuals who are not domiciled in the UK.

Accordingly:

- the remittance basis is available to Lin and Yu.
- the remittance basis is not available to Nan as he is not UK resident.

The remittance basis charge

Tutor's top tips

Don't forget that if an individual is not domiciled in the UK then the level of unremitted overseas income and gains is significant.

If unremitted overseas income and gains is ≤ £2,000 then the remittance basis is automatic, otherwise it must be claimed.

The remittance basis charge is assessed on individuals who have claimed the remittance basis (not where the remittance basis is automatically applied) and differs depending upon the length of time they have been resident in the UK.

- *Resident for 7 out of 9 tax years the charge is £30,000*
- *Resident for 12 out of 14 tax years the charge is £60,000*
- *Resident for 17 out of 20 tax years the charge is £90,000.*

Lin has unremitted overseas income and gains of less than £2,000. Accordingly, the remittance basis will apply automatically, such that there will not be a remittance basis charge.

Nan has unremitted overseas income and gains of more than £2,000. If Nan were able to claim the remittance basis, the remittance basis charge would be £60,000 because he has been resident in the UK for 12 of the 14 tax years prior to 2015/16.

Yu has unremitted overseas income and gains of more than £2,000. The remittance basis charge would be £30,000 because Yu has been resident in the UK for 7 of the 9 tax years prior to 2015/16.

(ii) **Actions that would be regarded as remittances**

- Bringing property into the UK which was purchased out of overseas income/gains.
- Paying for services received in the UK out of overseas income/gains.
- The use of overseas income/gains to pay the interest/capital on a debt where the funds borrowed have been brought into the UK or used to acquire property or services in the UK.

Tutorial note

There are various actions that would be regarded as remittances, however the examiner was only looking for two in this question.

Examiner's report

Part (a) was a tricky question to get absolutely correct, and very few candidates did so, but there were plenty of marks available to candidates who knew how to put an income tax computation together and were aware of the rules relating to the determination of the annual allowance for a particular year. On the whole candidates scored reasonably well.

In particular, most candidates handled the accommodation benefit well and knew that the tax bands needed to be extended. Many candidates were also aware that there was a three-year rule in respect of the annual allowance, although many were not absolutely clear as to how the rule worked. Many candidates missed the fact that the personal allowance would be available in full possibly because they did not pause and think at that stage of the calculation. Tax calculations should be done as a series of small steps with thought at each step in order to ensure that important matters are not missed.

The second part of the question concerned the remittance basis and was not done particularly well. The problem here was that candidates did not have a clear set of rules. Instead, they had an awareness of a series of technical terms and time periods that were all confused. This made it very difficult to score well.

The first thing candidates had to do was to explain whether or not the remittance basis was available to each of three individuals. This required a statement of the availability of the remittance basis together with a reason. For those who did not know the rules there was a 50:50 chance as regards the availability of the remittance basis. However, the reason for its availability or non-availability caused a lot more problems.

Candidates must learn the rules and be able to apply them and state them clearly. In addition, the marks available for giving a reason are only awarded where the whole of the reason given is correct. For example, the remittance basis was available to Lin because he was UK resident but not UK domiciled. Candidates who stated this together with various time periods of residency could not score the mark for the reason as it was not clear from their answer whether it was his residence and domicile status that was relevant or the time periods.

The second thing candidates had to do was to state, with reasons, the remittance basis charge applicable to each of the individuals on the assumption that the remittance basis was available to all of them. Again, this was not done particularly well due to many candidates having a very confused knowledge of the rules. One particular area of confusion related to the automatic applicability of the remittance basis where unremitted income and gains are less than £2,000; many candidates thought the rule related to the level of remitted income and gains.

ANSWERS TO PRACTICE QUESTIONS: SECTION 2

ACCA marking scheme				Marks
(a)	(i)	Benefit in respect of accommodation		2.0
		Personal allowance		1.0
		Tax bands		1.5
		Relevance of employer's pension contributions		1.0
		Annual allowance		2.0
		Tax on excess pension contributions		1.5
				9.0
			Maximum	8.0
	(ii)	Comparison with original liability		2.5
		Tax relief at source on pension contributions		1.0
				3.5
			Maximum	3.0
(b)	(i)	Availability of remittance basis		
		General rule		1.5
		Application of the rule to the individuals		1.5
		The remittance basis charge		
		Lin		1.0
		Nan		1.5
		Yu		1.5
				7.0
	(ii)	Examples of remittances – one mark each		2.0
Total				**20.0**

42 KESME AND SOBA   *Walk in the footsteps of a top tutor*

Key answer tips

This question was a popular choice in the exam.

Part (a) requires the calculation of taxable income on the basis that rent-a-room relief is claimed and an explanation of the availability and operation of the relief so was relatively straightforward. Most students should have scored high marks on rent-a-room relief as it is pure F6 knowledge. This part of the question also included the accrued income scheme, which is not often tested.

Part (b) requires an explanation of the effect of renting out furnished rooms on the capital gain on disposal of a taxpayer's main residence. There were lots of easy marks available for basic knowledge of the principal private residence exemption and letting relief.

Part (c) requires a straightforward explanation of the UK domicile election on IHT payable and a calculation of the death estate residue. The computation of the death estate residue was technical as the gift needed to be grossed up.

The highlighted words in the written sections are key phrases that markers are looking for.

KAPLAN PUBLISHING

(a) **Income tax**

Tutor's top tips

You need to explain the availability and operation of rent-a-room relief as well as calculate the taxable income.

If the rent-a-room relief is claimed then £4,250 of the gross rents are exempt. This applies only when part of a main residence is rented out. If the rent-a-room relief is claimed then property expenses cannot be deducted.

Kesme and Sobia bought the house jointly so the rental income and any rent-a-room relief is shared between them.

Where gross rents exceed £4,250, the relief must be claimed so you should mention the time limit.

Availability and operation of rent-a-room relief

Rent-a-room relief is available because Kesme and Soba are letting furnished rooms in their main residence.

Claiming the relief will allow each of them to deduct £2,125 (£4,250 ÷ 2), rather than their share of the allowable expenses (a smaller figure), from their share of the gross rental income.

This relief must be claimed by 31 January 2018 (22 months after the end of the tax year 2015/16). The claim will then continue to apply until it is withdrawn.

Tutorial note

The election would also cease to apply in the unlikely event that the gross annual rent fell below £4,250.

It is beneficial to claim the rent-a-room relief exemption as this results in a lower assessment as shown below.

Option 1 Rent-a-room: (£14,400 – £4,250) = £10,150 ÷ 2 = £5,075

Option 2 Deduct expenses: (£14,400 – £1,600) = £12,800 ÷ 2 = £6,400

Kesme
Taxable income – 2015/16

	£
State retirement pension	7,900
Pension from former employer	24,100
Property business income ((£14,400 ÷ 2) – £2,125)	5,075
8% loan stock interest ((£18,000 × 8% × 6/12) + (£18,000 × 8% × 4/12))	1,200
	38,275
Less: Personal allowance	(10,600)
Taxable income	27,675

Tutorial note

Kesme has sold the loan stock cum interest. Under the accrued income scheme, Kesme will be treated as having received interest for the period from 1 June 2015 to 30 September 2015.

(b) **Effect of renting out rooms on the capital gain on sale of the family home**

Tutor's top tips

With regard to the principal private residence exemption, the last 18 months of ownership are always treated as deemed occupation so no capital gain can arise in relation to this.

With regard to the gain accruing in relation to the earlier period, 30% is taxable as a result of the rooms rented out.

After claiming the PPR exemption, the gain is also eligible for letting relief.

No capital gain arises on the sale of a house which has always been occupied by its owner due to the availability of the principal private residence (PPR) exemption.

Accordingly, if the rooms were not rented out, no capital gain would arise on the eventual sale of the family home.

However, following the renting out of the furnished rooms, part of the property (30%) is no longer occupied by Kesme and Soba, such that a taxable capital gain may arise on the eventual sale.

This taxable gain will be calculated as follows:

- The initial gain is the excess of the sales proceeds over the original cost. This will then be reduced by the PPR exemption and the letting exemption.
- The PPR exemption is calculated by assuming that the gain has accrued evenly over the period of ownership (i.e. from 1 July 1991 until the sale of the property).

It exempts the total of the following:

- The part of the gain which accrued from 1 July 1991 until 5 April 2015 (i.e. prior to the date on which the rooms were first rented out).

- 70% (the proportion of the property occupied by Kesme and Soba) of the gain which accrued during the period from 6 April 2015 until the date 18 months prior to the date of sale; and

- The part of the gain which accrued during the last 18 months of ownership.

- That part of the gain not covered by the PPR exemption (i.e. the 30% of the gain which accrued during the period from 6 April 2015 until the date 18 months prior to the date of sale) is then reduced by the letting exemption.

This is equal to the lowest of:

- The PPR exemption (as calculated above).

- The part of the gain not covered by the PPR exemption (which is attributable to the letting).

- £40,000.

- The deduction of the letting exemption cannot create a loss.

(c) **Soba**

Tutor's top tips

Kesme is UK domiciled while his wife Soba is non-UK domiciled. As a result, the inter-spouse exemption is restricted to £325,000. If Soba makes a UK domicile election then the inter-spouse exemption is not restricted.

The disadvantage of making a UK domicile election is Soba now becomes liable to IHT on her worldwide assets as opposed to just her UK assets.

Election to be treated as UK domiciled

This election will remove the limit of £325,000 on the 100% spouse exemption which would otherwise apply on transfers from Kesme to Soba. It will also mean that any overseas assets owned by Soba will be subject to UK inheritance tax in the future.

Tutorial note

The limit of £325,000 on the 100% spouse exemption only applies where the transferor spouse is UK domiciled and the transferee spouse is non-UK domiciled.

Value of the residue of the estate

Soba will receive the residue of the estate (i.e. the estate less the gift to the daughter and the inheritance tax on that gift).

Tutor's top tips

When computing the inheritance tax on the daughter's gift, you first allocate the NRB to the daughter's legacy of £370,000. The taxable amount of £45,000 is deemed to be net of 40% IHT so it is actually 60%. To find the IHT, you multiply £45,000 by 40/60 which is £30,000.

Even if you treated the £45,000 as a gross amount and computed IHT by multiplying this by 40%, you would have been able to earn most of the marks here as the calculation of the IHT was only worth 2 marks.

	£
Kesme's house, land and chattels	1,280,000
Less: Gross gift to daughter (W)	(400,000)
Residue of the estate received by Soba	880,000

Working: Single grossing up	£
Legacy to daughter	370,000
Less: Nil rate band	(325,000)
Net chargeable estate	45,000
Inheritance tax @ 40/60 (Note)	30,000
Gross chargeable estate (£370,000 + £30,000)	400,000

Tutorial notes

1 The inheritance tax due on the specific gift to the daughter will be paid out of the residue of the estate, such that it will be borne by Soba. Because the residue of the estate is exempt due to the spouse exemption, the gift must be grossed up.

2 Proof of Kesme's IHT liability:

	£
Kesme's estate	1,280,000
Less: Legacy to Soba (above – spouse exemption)	(880,000)
Gross chargeable estate	400,000
Less: Nil rate band	(325,000)
Taxable estate	75,000
Inheritance tax at 40%	30,000

Examiner's report

In part (a) the basics of rent-a-room relief were reasonably well-known by many candidates. However, a minority thought that the £4,250 could be deducted in addition to expenses incurred as opposed to instead of those expenses. Also, many candidates neglected to divide the £4,250 between the two owners of the property. Very few candidates mentioned the need to make an election for the relief to apply.

The calculation of the individual's taxable income was done well by the majority of candidates in relation to the pension income. The interest arising in respect of the loan stock was not handled particularly well with the majority of candidates failing to recognise that the accrued income scheme applied, such that 10 months of interest needed to be included.

Following on from a relatively straightforward part (a), part (b) was more challenging. Almost all candidates realised that this required them to consider the principal private residence exemption but many were not sufficiently methodical in their approach.

The main area of difficulty related to thinking about the whole of the period over which the property will have been owned as opposed to just the period during which the property will have been let. The period of ownership should be split into three parts: the period prior to letting (wholly exempt), the last 18 months of ownership (wholly exempt) and the period in between (70% exempt). Very few candidates addressed these three periods in a clear manner.

There was then the need to consider the letting exemption. Most candidates recognised the need to refer to this exemption and their knowledge of it was satisfactory. However, a minority of candidates did not mention the exemption at all. Candidates will always benefit from thinking before they start writing an answer to a question in order to ensure that they have identified the principal points that need to be made in the time available.

The final part of the question concerned inheritance tax and was done reasonably well. The explanation of the election to be treated as UK domiciled required two main points to be made: the effect on the spouse exemption and the fact that overseas assets would become subject to UK inheritance tax. Many candidates identified both of these points, although a minority wrote about the remittance basis, which did not have any relevance here.

The calculation aspect of the question was more challenging than the explanations and very few candidates did particularly well. The difficulty was that most candidates wanted to calculate an inheritance tax liability when what was required was a calculation of the residue.

The residue was calculated by deducting the legacy to the daughter and the inheritance tax liability from the estate. So a calculation of the inheritance tax liability was a necessary step on the way but was not an end in itself. The calculation of the inheritance tax liability also required the gift to the daughter to be grossed up because the residue of the estate was exempt. Very few candidates identified this point but it was possible to score a very good mark without it.

ANSWERS TO PRACTICE QUESTIONS: SECTION 2

ACCA marking scheme		
		Marks
(a)	Rent-a-room relief	
	Availability	1.0
	Operation	1.5
	Claim	1.5
	Pension income	1.0
	Property business income	1.0
	8% loan stock	2.0
	Personal allowance	0.5
		8.5
	Maximum	8.0
(b)	Situation prior to letting the rooms	1.0
	Principal private residence exemption	3.0
	Letting exemption	3.0
		7.0
	Maximum	6.0
(c)	Election to be treated as UK domiciled	2.5
	Value of assets	
	Calculation of amount received by Soba	1.5
	Inheritance tax liability	2.0
	Maximum	6.0
Total		20.0

43 JODIE *Walk in the footsteps of a top tutor*

Key answer tips

This question asks you to prepare the contents of a letter to a client covering overseas aspects of personal taxes (income tax, capital gains tax and inheritance tax), terminal loss relief for a sole trader and VAT on cessation of trade.

The four requirements in the question are not related so you can address them in any order so long as each section is clearly labelled.

The highlighted words in the written sections are key phrases that markers are looking for in your letter.

KAPLAN PUBLISHING

Tutor's top tips

Note that a full letter is not required so no marks are available for addresses etc. To gain the professional marks available you must ensure your language is formal and you should assume the client has no technical tax knowledge. You should also address Jodie as 'you' not 'she'.

PARAGRAPHS FOR INCLUSION IN A LETTER FROM MANAGER

Client   Jodie
Prepared by   Tax senior
Date   5 June 2016

Tax implications of emigration from the UK and related matters

(a)   **UK tax residence status and liability to UK income tax**

Tutor's top tips

You must always use the three step procedure outlined below to determine residence status. For the sufficient ties tests, note that there is relevant information about Jodie's current home at the beginning of the 'Other matters' section of her letter. The question strongly suggests that your conclusion should be that Jodie is non-UK resident.

Automatic residence tests

Using the automatic overseas tests, it has already been concluded that you will not be automatically regarded as non-UK resident in the tax year 2017/18.

It is therefore necessary to consider the automatic UK residence tests.

Applying these, you will also not be regarded as UK resident because you will not:

–   be in the UK for 183 days or more; or

–   have a home in the UK but no home overseas; or

–   work in the UK.

Sufficient ties tests

Since your residence status cannot be determined automatically, it will be determined by the number of ties you have with the UK.

Because you have been UK resident in one or more (actually all) of the three tax years preceding 2017/18 and you will be in the UK for between 46 and 90 days in the tax year 2017/18, you will be UK resident if you satisfy three or more UK ties.

I set out the ties below:

	Satisfied?
– In the UK for more than 90 days in either or both of the tax years 2015/16 and 2016/17	Yes
– Spouse or children under 18 who are resident in the UK	No
– Working in the UK for 40 days or more	No
– Accommodation available in the UK for a continuous period of more than 90 days	No
– In the UK for the same or more days than in any other country	No

You can see from this that, if you proceed in accordance with your plans, you will only satisfy one of the UK ties, such that you will not be UK resident in the tax year 2017/18.

However, if you were to change your plans (for example, the number of days which you spend in the UK in 2017/18), this may have an effect on your residence status.

Liability to UK income tax

As a non-UK resident you will have no liability to UK income tax as you will not be subject to UK income tax on your overseas income and I note that you will not have any sources of income in the UK.

(b) **Relief available in respect of the trading loss**

Tutor's top tips

The question only asks you to consider terminal loss relief so make sure you do not waste time referring to any other forms of loss relief.

The terminal trade loss for the final 12 months of trading is £22,750 (appendix A).

This loss can be offset against your taxable trading profits for the final tax year of trading (however, you have no trading profit in the tax year 2016/17) and the three previous tax years, relieving later years before earlier years.

The total tax which you will save by relieving the losses in this way will be £7,500 (appendix A).

(c) **Capital gains tax**

Tutor's top tips

Jodie's letter gives information relevant to the calculation of her capital gains tax in both the 'My unincorporated business' section and the 'Other matters' section.

The question asks for an explanation of the rates of capital gains tax that will be charged, which is a hint that entrepreneurs' relief will be relevant.

PAPER P6: ADVANCED TAXATION (FA2015)

> *Non-UK residents are not subject to UK CGT on asset disposals (including UK assets) with the exception of UK residential property. As Jodie sold her house in the UK on 30 April 2016 this is not a concern in this scenario.*

Becoming non-UK resident in the tax year 2017/18

As a non-UK resident, you will not be subject to UK capital gains tax on the disposal of any assets.

However, if you were to return to the UK within five years, any gains made whilst you were in Riviera in respect of assets owned when you left the UK (for example, the shares in Butterfly Ltd) would be subject to capital gains tax in the tax year you return.

This rule will apply because you have been UK resident for at least four of the seven years prior to the tax year 2017/18.

Crystallisation of gain held over

Because you will become non-UK resident within six tax years of receiving the shares in Butterfly Ltd from your mother, you will be treated as having made a chargeable gain equal to the gain held over at the time of the gift.

This gain will be chargeable immediately before you become non-UK resident (i.e. on 5 April 2017).

Accordingly, a chargeable gain of £23,000 (£60,000 – £37,000) will arise in the tax year 2016/17.

This gain will be taxed at 28% rather than 18% because the gain on the sale of your business premises (see below) will be regarded as having used the whole of your basic rate band.

Sale of your business assets

The chargeable gain of £55,000 (£190,000 – £135,000) on the sale of your business premises will be taxed at 10% due to the availability of entrepreneurs' relief.

This relief is available because you had owned the business for at least a year prior to 31 May 2016 and you have sold the premises within three years of ceasing to trade.

The computer equipment is not a chargeable asset as the cost and sales proceeds of each item did not exceed £6,000. There is no chargeable gain on the inventory because inventory is not a capital asset.

Sale of your home

Tax is not normally charged on a gain on the sale of a home if the owner has always lived in it.

However, where the land exceeds 0.5 hectares, this exemption does not apply to the excess land unless the land is necessary for the enjoyment of the property. This is a judgemental matter and will require further work before a conclusion can be reached.

Capital gains tax liability for 2016/17

Your total capital gains tax liability for 2016/17 will be at least £8,832 (appendix B).

(d) **Other matters**

Leaving the UK – inheritance tax implications

Tutor's top tips

Remember that domicile, not residence, determines a person's liability to inheritance tax.

You will become non-UK domiciled once you have left the UK and severed all ties with the UK. Since you may return to the UK within four years you will not immediately be non-UK domiciled.

However, even once you have ceased to be domiciled under the general law, for the purposes of UK inheritance tax, you will be deemed to be UK domiciled for a further three years.

Whilst you are UK domiciled, or deemed domiciled, your worldwide assets will be subject to UK inheritance tax, even after you have left the UK.

Once you are no longer UK domiciled or deemed UK domiciled, only your assets located in the UK will be subject to UK inheritance tax.

Value added tax (VAT)

Tutor's top tips

This part of the question tests VAT knowledge from F6 and illustrates the importance of retaining such knowledge.

You should notify HM Revenue and Customs that you have ceased trading by 30 June 2016. If you fail to do so, you may be required to pay a penalty.

On your final VAT return you are required to account for VAT on any business assets which you have retained and in respect of which you have claimed input tax (i.e. the inventory).

This is invariably calculated by reference to the market value of the assets at the cessation of trade. However, this VAT is not payable if it does not exceed £1,000. Accordingly, you will not need to account for VAT in respect of your inventory as it was only worth £3,500.

APPENDICES

A TERMINAL LOSS RELIEF

1 Calculation of the terminal trading loss

	£	£
2016/17 (6 April 2016 to 31 May 2016)		
Loss (£18,000 × 2/5)		7,200
Overlap relief		6,500
2015/16 (1 June 2015 to 5 April 2016)		
1 June 2015 to 31 December 2015		
Profit (£3,000 × 7/12)	(1,750)	
1 January 2016 to 5 April 2016		
Loss (£18,000 × 3/5)	10,800	
		9,050
Terminal loss		22,750

2 Tax saving available in respect of the terminal loss

	Note	2013/14 £	2014/15 £	2015/16 £	Total £
Trading income		67,000	2,000	3,000	
Offset of loss		17,750	2,000	3,000	22,750
Tax relief available:					
2015/16	1			× 0%	Nil
2014/15	2		× 20%		400
2013/14	3	× 40%			7,100
Tax saving					7,500

Tutor's top tips

The question specifically asks you to explain how you have determined the tax saved, so there will be marks for your explanatory notes.

Notes

1 Your income in the tax year 2015/16 was relieved in full by your personal allowance, such that no income tax will be saved in respect of the loss relieved against your trading income of that year.

2 In the tax year 2014/15, relief for the losses is available at 20% because you were a basic rate taxpayer.

3   In the tax year 2013/14, relief for the losses is available at 40% because you had at least £17,750 of income which was taxable at the higher rate of tax.

B   CAPITAL GAINS TAX LIABILITY FOR THE TAX YEAR 2016/17

	Qualifying for ER £	Not qualifying for ER £
Chargeable gains:		
Business premises (£190,000 – £135,000)	55,000	
Shares in Butterfly Ltd (£60,000 – £37,000)		23,000
Less: Annual exempt amount		(11,100)
Taxable gains	55,000	11,900
Capital gains tax @ 10%/28%	5,500	3,332
Total liability (£5,500 + £3,332)		8,832

Tutorial note

The annual exempt amount will be deducted from the gain on the shares in Butterfly Ltd as this gain is taxed at a higher rate than that applied to the business premises.

Examiner's comments

Part (a) concerned the individual's residence status and liability to income tax. It was generally answered well, with many candidates demonstrating a strong knowledge of these aspects of the syllabus. In particular, candidates knew how to determine the number of ties that needed to be satisfied and were able to describe the ties and relate them to the facts of the question.

Unfortunately, many candidates failed to consider the automatic UK residence tests and were unable to state clearly the income tax implications of being non-UK resident, i.e. not being subject to UK income tax on overseas income. This latter point was part of an overall lack of clarity among many candidates in relation to the overseas aspects of personal tax. Candidates were vague about the implications or wasted time providing significant amounts of information on the remittance basis.

Part (b) concerned terminal loss relief for an unincorporated sole trader, and was generally answered well. This was a marked change in the performance in this area when compared with that in recent exams.

In particular, many candidates were able to calculate the terminal loss reasonably accurately and to calculate the tax saving at the margin without preparing detailed income tax computations.

Those candidates who performed less strongly had two main problems. Firstly, they did not know the detailed process necessary to calculate a terminal loss, such that they simply used the loss of the final trading period. Secondly, they prepared various detailed income tax computations in the hope that this would eventually lead to the tax saving required by the question. The problem with this approach was that it was very time consuming and, on the whole, it did not produce an acceptable answer.

Well prepared candidates scored well in this part and were able to do so in a sensible amount of time.

Part (c) covered various aspects of capital gains tax. It was perhaps more challenging than part (b), but there were still plenty of very accessible marks, such that a well prepared candidate should have no issue achieving a reasonable number of marks.

This part of the question had two requirements.

The first requirement was for an explanation of the effect of Jodie's departure from the UK on her liability to UK capital gains tax. This was the more challenging aspect of this part of the question and required candidates to state the basic rule in relation to residency and capital gains tax and to highlight the possible issue of temporary non-residence. The temporary non-resident rule was relevant due to the statement in the question that Jodie would return to the UK after four years (i.e. within five years) if her children were not happy overseas. This was only answered well by a minority of candidates.

The main problem related to something which came up throughout this exam which was a lack of clarity as regards the overseas aspects of personal taxation. Some candidates thought that being non-resident was only relevant in relation to assets situated overseas whilst others wrote at length about the remittance basis and the importance of either remitting or not remitting gains made but did so by reference to Jodie's non-resident status as opposed to her domicile status.

The second requirement was for a calculation of Jodie's capital gains tax liability. There were a number of tasks to carry out in order to satisfy this requirement and those candidates who kept moving and tried to address all of the aspects of the question were able to score well.

The gains on the business assets and the availability of entrepreneurs' relief were tackled well by the majority of candidates. The availability of the relief in respect of the principal private residence was identified by most candidates but only a minority considered the relevance of the size of the plot of land on which the property stood.

The more challenging aspect of the question related to the charging of the heldover gain on the Butterfly Ltd shares as a result of Jodie leaving the UK within six years of the gift. This was, perhaps not surprisingly, missed by many candidates although it was picked up by some.

The final part of the question related to other aspects of Jodie leaving the UK and concerned inheritance tax and VAT.

The inheritance tax aspects were not done particularly well with only a minority of candidates stating clearly the implications of Jodie's departure from the point of view of inheritance tax. In particular, candidates should have stated the relevance of domicile to inheritance tax and referred to the relevance of deemed domicile.

The VAT aspects were handled better but still very few candidates were able to pick up all of the available marks here.

ANSWERS TO PRACTICE QUESTIONS: SECTION 2

	ACCA marking scheme		
			Marks
(a)	Automatic UK residence		2.0
	UK ties		
		Number of ties	1.0
		Consideration of each tie (1 mark each – maximum four marks)	4.0
		Conclusion	1.0
	Tax implications		1.0
			9.0
		Maximum	7.0
(b)	Calculation of terminal loss		4.0
	Relief available		
		Calculation	2.0
		Explanations	3.0
			9.0
		Maximum	8.0
(c)	Becoming non-UK resident		
		Future liability to capital gains tax	3.0
		Shares in Butterfly Ltd	3.0
	Disposals		
		Business assets	3.0
		Home	2.0
	Liability		2.0
			13.0
		Maximum	11.0
(d)	Inheritance tax		
		Cessation of UK domicile	1.0
		Deemed domicile	1.0
		Liability to UK inheritance tax	1.0
	Value added tax		
		Notify HM Revenue and Customs	1.0
		Business assets retained	2.0
			6.0
		Maximum	5.0
	Followed instructions		1.0
	Clarity of explanations and calculations		1.0
	Effectiveness of communication		1.0
	Overall presentation and style		1.0
Total			**35.0**

44 CATE AND RAVI *Walk in the footsteps of a top tutor*

Key answer tips

This question is about a husband, Ravi, who is UK resident but not domiciled and his wife, Cate who is a sole trader.

Part (a) requires calculation of the cost of Cate taking on an employee, and is similar to requirements seen in previous exam questions.

In part (b) Cate is planning to sell some items she inherited and you need to consider the badges of trade in relation to this new venture.

Part (c) covers the popular topic of arising versus remittance basis for a non-UK domiciled individual, but for CGT rather than income tax.

The highlighted words in parts (b) and (c) are key phrases that markers are looking for.

(a) **Cate – After-tax cost of taking on the part time employee**

Tutor's top tips

The first three headings from the scenario relate to this part of the question. Make sure you use all of the information given; in particular consider why you have been provided with Cate's dividend income.

The requirement is to 'calculate', so you do not need to provide written explanations, although you should show all of your workings.

You are calculating the after-tax cost for Cate, so you do not need to consider the tax payable by the employee.

	£
Salary	12,000
Childcare vouchers (£25 × 52 weeks)	1,300
Mileage allowance (£0.50 × 62 × 48 weeks)	1,488
Class 1 NICs (W1)	557
Total additional expenditure	15,345
Less: Income tax and class 4 NIC saving (£15,345 × 42%) (Note)	(6,445)
Income tax saving on personal allowance (£7,673 × 40%) (W2)	(3,069)
After-tax cost	5,831

ANSWERS TO PRACTICE QUESTIONS: SECTION 2

Tutorial note

The additional expenditure is deductible from Cate's taxable trading profit and will save income tax and class 4 NICs.

The income tax saving is at 40% as Cate is a higher rate taxpayer. Class 4 NICs are saved at 2% as Cate's taxable trading profits are above the upper limit for class 4.

Workings

(W1) Class 1 NICs: employer's contributions

	£
Salary: (£12,000 – £8,112) × 13.8%	536
Mileage allowance: ((£0.50 – 0.45) × 62 × 48 weeks) × 13.8%	21
	557

Tutorial notes

1. Only the excess mileage allowance over 45p per mile is liable to NICs.

2. Childcare vouchers up to £55 a week for a basic rate taxpayer are exempt from NICs.

3. The £2,000 employment allowance would already have been fully offset against the class 1 NICs payable in respect of D-Designs' existing employees.

(W2) Personal allowance

	Before taking on employee		After taking on employee	
	£	£	£	£
Basic PA		10,600		10,600
Less: Abatement				
ANI (W3)	120,000		104,655	
Less: Limit	(100,000)		(100,000)	
	20,000		4,655	
50% deduction		(10,000)		(2,327)
Revised PA		600		8,273
Increase in PA (£8,273 – £600)				7,673

KAPLAN PUBLISHING

Tutorial note

Before taking on the additional part time employee Cate's adjusted net income was £120,000, so her personal allowance would have been reduced to £600.

After taking on the employee, Cate's adjusted net income will be reduced by the total additional expenditure of £15,345. She will therefore be entitled to a reduced personal allowance for the year of £8,273.

(W3) **Adjusted net income**

	Before taking on employee £	After taking on employee £
Trading profit	90,000	90,000
Dividends (£27,000 × 100/90)	30,000	30,000
	120,000	120,000
Less: Additional allowable expenditure	–	(15,345)
Total income = Net income = ANI	120,000	104,655

(b) **Cate – Sale of second-hand books**

Tutor's top tips

To score the marks here you must apply the badges of trade to the scenario.

Make sure you structure your answer with headings, and give a conclusion for an easy mark.

Badges of trade

The tax treatment of the income from the sale of the second-hand books will depend on whether or not Cate is deemed to be carrying on a trade of selling books.

If she is, the income will be treated as trading income, and subject to income tax in the same way as her taxable profits from D-Designs.

If not, then the sales will be dealt with under the capital gains tax rules.

In determining how Cate should be taxed, HMRC will make reference to the 'badges of trade', a series of factors to be considered in order to determine whether or not an individual is trading.

Factors indicating that the sale of books does not constitute a trade

– Cate has inherited the books; she did not buy them for resale.

– Selling second-hand books is not related in any way to Cate's existing business, the running of a chain of dress shops.

– The frequency of transactions; this would appear to be a one-off batch of sales.

Factors indicating that the sale of books does constitute a trade

- Having some of the books rebound may be viewed as 'supplementary work' in order to generate increased profit.
- Taking steps to find purchasers by advertising the books on the internet could indicate a trading motive.

Conclusion

Based on the above factors, it is more likely that the capital gains tax treatment will apply.

For capital gains tax purposes books are chattels so, as no individual book is likely to have a value in excess of £6,000, if the capital gains tax treatment does apply, any gains made by Cate will be exempt from tax.

Tutorial note

Marks were available for discussion of any relevant factors and for reaching a sensible conclusion.

(c) Ravi – Capital gains tax on overseas property gain

Tutor's top tips

It is more efficient to perform your workings for the two options alongside one another. Remember to give a conclusion as you have been asked to advise.

Arising basis

Ravi is resident in the UK, so would normally be liable to pay UK capital gains tax on disposals of both his UK and overseas assets on an arising basis.

On this basis, the gain on the disposal of the overseas property is fully liable to UK capital gains tax, as his annual exempt amount for the tax year 2015/16 has already been used.

As Ravi is a higher rate taxpayer, capital gains tax will be charged at the rate of 28% and the capital gains tax payable will therefore be £19,600 (W).

Double tax relief will be available against this UK capital gains tax liability for any tax suffered on the same gain in Goland.

Remittance basis

However, as Ravi is not domiciled in the UK, he should consider making a claim for the remittance basis for the taxation of his overseas gain.

As he has not remitted any of the proceeds from the sale, if he makes such a claim, there will be no gain chargeable in the UK.

However, he will lose his entitlement to the annual exempt amount, which will generate an additional capital gains tax liability of £3,108 (W) on his UK asset gains.

Additionally, as Ravi has been resident in the UK since February 2008 (at least seven out of the last nine tax years), he will be liable to pay a remittance basis charge of £30,000.

The total amount payable as a result of claiming the remittance basis would therefore be £33,108 (W).

Conclusion

A remittance basis claim will not be worthwhile for the tax year 2015/16.

Working: Capital gains tax

	Arising basis £	Remittance basis £
Overseas gain	70,000	N/A
UK gains	11,100	11,100
Less: AEA	(11,100)	N/A
Taxable gains	70,000	11,100
Capital gains tax at 28%	19,600	3,108
Plus: Remittance basis charge	N/A	30,000
Total capital gains tax	19,600	33,108

Examiner's comments

Part (a) concerned an individual, Cate, running a successful unincorporated business that required an additional part-time employee. The requirement was to calculate the annual cost of employing the part-time employee.

The first thing candidates had to do was determine all of the costs that were going to be incurred. On the whole this was done reasonably well, although some candidates confused cost with tax deductibility, and some simply prepared tax computations for Cate, which was not what they had been asked to do. In addition, many candidates failed to consider the employer national insurance contributions aspects which were a key part of the question.

Once the costs had been determined, it was simply a case of recognising that Cate was a higher rate tax payer, such that she would save income tax at 40% and class 4 national insurance contributions at 2% as a result of the increased costs. This was not tackled well by the majority of candidates who tried to do before and after calculations rather than working at the margin. In addition, many failed to consider the class 4 national insurance contribution implications altogether.

There was a more subtle point in the question in relation to the income tax personal allowance. The reduction in Cate's taxable trading income due to the costs relating to the part-time employee meant that part of her personal allowance would be reinstated, thus reducing the after-tax cost to her of taking on the new employee.

ANSWERS TO PRACTICE QUESTIONS: SECTION 2

Part (b) required a discussion of the tax treatment of the profit derived from the sale of books on the internet. This required candidates to consider the badges of trade in relation to the specific transactions taking place. This part of the question was done well by many candidates. However, some candidates did not give themselves sufficient thinking time, such that they failed to realise what the question was testing.

It was important that candidates tried to reach a conclusion based on the information provided and that they thought about the capital gains tax implications as well as the income tax implications. There was no right answer as such, just a need to think about the relevant issues and to express the implications in a clear manner.

The final part of the question was arguably more challenging. It concerned the capital gains tax position of an individual, Ravi, who was resident in the UK but domiciled overseas and focussed principally on the remittance basis.

Although some candidates did reasonably well here, almost all candidates could have scored more marks if they had organised their thoughts before they began writing. There was a mark for making the point that Ravi was liable to UK capital gains tax because he was UK resident and a further mark for recognising that the remittance basis was available because he was domiciled overseas. In order to score these two marks, candidates had to make it clear that the liability to capital gains tax was due to his residence status and the remittance basis was due to his domicile status. Many candidates did not make these two points clearly, such that they only scored one of the two available marks.

Candidates were then expected to address the remittance basis charge and the loss of the annual exempt amount. This was done well by the majority of candidates.

	ACCA marking scheme		Marks
(a)	Total additional expenditure		5.0
	Income tax and class 4 NIC saving		2.0
	Saving due to personal allowance		2.5
			9.5
		Maximum	9.0
(b)	Trading income v capital gain issue		1.0
	Relevant badges of trade factors		3.0
	Any reasonable conclusion		1.0
	Chattels, so exempt CGT		1.0
			6.0
		Maximum	5.0
(c)	CGT on an arising basis as UK resident		2.0
	Optional remittance basis as not UK domiciled		1.0
	CGT effect if remittance basis used		2.0
	Remittance basis charge		1.5
	Conclusion		0.5
			7.0
		Maximum	6.0
Total			**20.0**

PERSONAL FINANCE, BUSINESS FINANCE AND INVESTMENTS

45　ADAM SNOOK (ADAPTED) *Walk in the footsteps of a top tutor*

Key answer tips

This question is all about an individual setting up in business as a sole trader, and covers virtually all the different taxes: capital gains tax, income tax, NICs, VAT and inheritance tax!

The first section requires you to calculate the external finance needed, which is a clever way of asking you to calculate the capital gains tax payable out of the proceeds from selling assets. You also need to recognise that, in order to find the appropriate rate of CGT, a computation of taxable income is required. There are some nice easy marks here.

There are also some straightforward NICs, and a simple explanation of inheritance tax on a PET.

The harder parts of this question are the section on VAT for land and buildings, the explanation of the income tax relief for the purchase and renovation of the theatre and the explanation of the effect of charitable bequests on IHT.

The highlighted words in the written sections are key phrases that markers are looking for.

Tutor's top tips

One of the hardest aspects of this question is that some of the information is scattered around, particularly the information about Adam's income. Once you have read the requirement and know which taxes you will be dealing with, run through the question and annotate it with 'IT', 'CGT' etc. so that you know which bits of information are relevant for each part of your answer.

Make sure you cover all the points raised in the email – this is the real requirement! The requirements at the end of the question are a less detailed summary, and just set out how many marks are available.

The question specifically asks you to note any assumptions made, so make sure you do this as you go along as there will be marks for anything sensible.

MEMORANDUM

To　　　Tax manager
From　　Tax assistant
Date　　3 December 2016
Subject　Adam Snook

This memorandum considers the external finance required by Adam Snook (AS) to start his new business together with a number of related matters.

(a) (i) **External finance required**

Tutor's top tips

The examiner does remind you that you need to take into account capital gains tax – you will need to calculate this first. In addition, before you can calculate the CGT payable you need to calculate Adam's taxable income to see how much basic rate band remains.

Once you have calculated the CGT, whether it is right or wrong, you will be given credit here for netting the tax off the proceeds and comparing this to the total cost of the project.

	£	£
Total cost of project		310,000
Sale proceeds of shares/loan stock (£104,370 + £29,900)	134,270	
CGT on sale of shares/loan stock (W1)	(7,775)	
		(126,495)
External finance required		183,505

Assumptions:

AS has made no other disposals for the purposes of capital gains tax in 2016/17.

AS has no capital losses brought forward.

Tutor's top tips

The capital gains tax calculation is hard, as the shares and loan stock were acquired as a result of a takeover.

You need to break the computation down into three stages:

Step 1 Calculate the 'cost' (W4)

Step 2 Calculate the gains on disposal (W2/W3)

Step 3 Calculate the tax after deducting the annual exempt amount (W1/W5).

Remember that you don't need to get this completely right to pass and if your income tax computation is incorrect, marks will be given here providing your answer is right using the income tax position you have calculated.

KAPLAN PUBLISHING

Workings: Capital gains tax

(W1) Capital gains tax on sale of shares/loan stock

	£
Gains realised (£36,114 (W2) + £8,616 (W3))	44,730
Less: Annual exempt amount	(11,100)
Taxable gains	33,630

Capital gains tax:	£	
Gains in BRB (£31,785 – £15,370 (W5))	16,415 × 18%	2,955
Balance of gains (£33,630 – £16,415)	17,215 × 28%	4,820
	33,630	7,775

Tutor's top tips

You should have considered but dismissed the possibility of entrepreneurs' relief being available on this disposal at this stage.

There is no entrepreneurs' relief available as Snapper plc is not Adam's personal trading company. It is a public limited company and it is assumed that Adam has a less than 5% interest. In addition, Adam does not work for the company and has held the shares and loan stock for less than 12 months.

(W2) Gain on sale of shares

	£
Sale proceeds	104,370
Less: Deemed cost (W4)	(68,256)
Capital gain	36,114

Tutorial note

There is no gain on the share for share exchange element at the time of the takeover.

However, the original cost of the shares in Brill plc is allocated between the shares and the loan stock received in Snapper plc in proportion to their market values the day after the takeover (see W4).

A gain arises on the subsequent disposal of the shares.

ANSWERS TO PRACTICE QUESTIONS: SECTION 2

(W3) **Gain crystallising on sale of loan stock**

	£
Market value of loan stock on 1 November 2016	28,400
Less: Deemed cost (W4)	(19,784)
Capital gain	8,616

Tutorial note

A capital gain is calculated when the shares in Brill plc are exchanged for the loan stock in Snapper plc. However, the gain is frozen and not charged until the loan stock is sold at a later date.

The increase in value of the loan stock from the time of the takeover to the disposal date does not give rise to a capital gain as the loan stock is a qualifying corporate bond and therefore an exempt asset for the purposes of capital gains tax.

(W4) **Deemed cost of shares and loan stock**

	Total consideration £	Allocation of cost £
Shares	97,980	
Deemed cost £88,040 × (£97,980/£126,380)		68,256
Loan stock	28,400	
Deemed cost £88,040 × (£28,400/£126,380)		19,784
	126,380	88,040

KAPLAN PUBLISHING

463

(W5) **Remainder of basic rate band**

Taxable income in 2016/17

Tutor's top tips

Make sure that you find all the different types of income from the information in the question, not just the salary and the car benefit. Watch the dates carefully!

	£
Salary: Full time (£25,200 × 9/12)	18,900
Part time (£1,050 × 3)	3,150
Car benefit (W6)	2,720
Trading income – period ended 31 March 2017 (£400 × 3)	1,200
	25,970
Less: Personal allowance	(10,600)
Taxable income	15,370

Assumptions:

No tax adjustments are required to AS's net profit of £400 per month.

AS has no other sources of income.

Tutor's top tips

You may have assumed that Adam received some interest on the loan stock before the sale in November 2016 – this would have been a valid assumption, and earned marks accordingly.

(W6) **Car benefit**

CO_2 emissions 142 g/km, available for 9 months in 2016/17

	%
Diesel	17
Plus: (140 – 95) × 1/5	9
Appropriate percentage	26
Car benefit (£13,950 × 26% × 9/12)	£2,720

(ii) **Proposal to increase the after tax proceeds from the sale of the loan stock**

AS should delay the sale of the loan stock until after 5 April 2017. The gain made at the time of the takeover would then crystallise in 2017/18 and would be covered by the annual exempt amount for that year. The net proceeds would be increased by the capital gains tax saved of £2,412 (£8,616 × 28%).

ANSWERS TO PRACTICE QUESTIONS: SECTION 2

Tutorial note

Delaying the sale is feasible as not all of the funding is required immediately. The theatre renovations (costing £45,000) will be carried out in April and May 2017.

Tutor's top tips

The other benefit of delaying the sale until after 5 April 2017 is that the CGT will not be payable until 31 January 2019. However, this question just asked for the increase in net proceeds.

More appropriate forms of external finance

A bank overdraft is not the most appropriate form of long term business finance. This is because the bank can demand repayment of the overdraft at any time and the rates of interest charged are fairly high.

AS should seek long term finance for his long term business needs, for example a bank loan secured on the theatre, and use a smaller bank overdraft to finance the working capital required on a day-to-day basis.

Tutor's top tips

Probably the easiest 2 marks in the whole question – you could probably just use your common sense!

(b) **Related matters**

(i) **National insurance contributions – 2016/17**

Tutor's top tips

The NIC rates are provided in the tables. Don't forget to apply them to the question – Adam's trading profit will be below the thresholds

The profit for the period ending 31 March 2017 is expected to be £1,200 (£400 × 3).

No class 2 contributions will be due as the profit is less than the small profits threshold of £5,965.

No class 4 contributions will be due as the profit is less than the lower profits limit of £8,060.

Tutorial note

Adam will have paid class 1 contributions in respect of his earnings from Rheims Ltd, thus preserving his entitlement to state benefits and pension, and therefore there is no disadvantage in claiming the small earnings exemption from class 2 contributions.

(ii) **Purchase and renovation of the theatre**

Tutor's top tips

Think carefully before answering this part of the question. It is all about capital versus revenue expenses. Remember that buildings do not qualify for capital allowances.

The theatre is a capital purchase that does not qualify for capital allowances as it is a building. Accordingly, the cost of purchasing the theatre will not give rise to a tax deduction for the purpose of computing AS's taxable trading income.

The tax treatment of the renovation costs may be summarised as follows:

- The costs will be disallowed if the renovations are necessary before the theatre can be used for business purposes. This is because they will be regarded as further capital costs of acquiring appropriate premises.
- Some of the costs may be allowable if the condition of the theatre is such that it can be used in its present state and the renovations are more in the nature of cosmetic improvements.

Tutorial note

Capital allowances will be available on any element of the purchase price which relates to fixtures and fittings or furniture, and on any renovations in relation to those items.

(iii) **VAT position**

Tutor's top tips

Make sure you learn the VAT treatment of land and buildings, as this has been tested several times recently.

The grant of a right to occupy the theatre in exchange for rent is an exempt supply. Accordingly, as all of AS's activities will be regarded as one for VAT purposes, AS will become partially exempt once he begins to rent out the theatre.

AS will be able to recover the input tax that is directly attributable to his standard rated supplies (i.e. those in connection with the supply of children's parties). He will also be able to recover a proportion of the input tax on his overheads; the proportion being that of his total supplies that are standard rated.

The remainder of his input tax will only be recoverable if it is de-minimis. There are 3 different tests to determine if the blocked VAT is de minimis.

1. The total input tax is not more than £625 per month (on average) and the value of the exempt supplies is no more than 50% of the value of all its supplies

2. The total input tax less input tax directly attributable to taxable supplies is no more than £625 per month (on average) and the value of exempt supplies is no more than 50% of the value of all supplies.

3. The irrecoverable input tax is less than or equal to £625 per month on average, and is less than or equal to 50% of total input tax.

AS only needs to meet one test to be de minimis, and able to recover all the VAT on the inputs.

If AS were to opt to tax the theatre, the right to occupy the theatre in exchange for rent would then be a standard rated supply. AS could then recover all of his input tax, regardless of the amount attributable to the rent, but would have to charge VAT on the rent and on any future sale of the building.

The decision as to whether or not to opt to tax the theatre will depend on:

- the amount of input tax at stake; and
- whether or not those who rent the theatre are in a position to recover any VAT charged.

Tutorial note

Most supplies of land and buildings are exempt for VAT purposes. This means that input VAT on any related expenses is not recoverable. However, the trader has the 'option to tax', which can also be referred to as an option to 'waive the exemption'. If he opts to tax, he must add output VAT at 20% to ALL supplies of the building (rent and subsequent sale), but can then reclaim all input VAT. When deciding whether or not to opt to tax, it is important to consider who the supply is made to. If the tenant/purchaser is not VAT registered, the VAT will represent an extra cost to them.

(c) **Inheritance tax payable by Adam**

Tutor's top tips

This section is fairly straightforward, but make sure you use the dates and figures from the question

The gift by AS's aunt was a potentially exempt transfer. No tax will be due if she lives until 1 June 2023 (i.e. seven years after the date of the gift).

The maximum possible liability, on the assumption that there are no annual exemptions or nil band available, is £35,216 (£88,040 × 40%). This will only arise if AS's aunt dies before 1 June 2019.

The maximum liability will be reduced by taper relief of 20% for every full year after 31 May 2019 for which AS's aunt lives.

The liability will also be reduced if the chargeable transfers made by the aunt in the seven years prior to 1 June 2016 are less than £325,000 or if the annual exemption for 2015/16 and/or 2016/17 is/are available.

Effect of charitable bequests

Any gifts to charity comprised within AS's will are exempt legacies and will reduce the amount of the estate subject to inheritance at 40%.

However, if the value of the charitable gifts are at least 10% of the baseline amount (chargeable estate after the nil rate band, but before the deduction of the exempt legacy) then inheritance tax on the death estate will be payable at 36% and not 40%.

> **Examiner's report**
>
> This question principally concerned a number of issues relating to the establishment of an unincorporated business. It was pleasing that most candidates produced a memorandum as required and structured their answer in an appropriate manner.
>
> In part (a)(i) candidates had to calculate the external finance required by the new business. This calculation had to be done in two stages.
>
> First, it was necessary to calculate the capital gains arising on the sale of shares and loan stock acquired as a result of a paper for paper transaction. Whilst many candidates were aware that particular rules applied in this situation (and many described them, unnecessarily, in great detail) only a well prepared minority were able to calculate the gains correctly.
>
> It was then necessary to use the information to determine the capital gains tax payable.
>
> Part (a)(ii) required candidates to identify a strategy to increase the after tax proceeds from the sale of the loan stock and to suggest a form of external finance more appropriate than a bank overdraft. The first task was not done well as many candidates were of the opinion, incorrectly, that the sale of the loan stock would not give rise to a tax liability and therefore the position could not be improved. The second task was done well.
>
> Part (b) required candidates to address various issues relating to the new business. This was not done particularly well. Candidates were happy to outline the national insurance position of unincorporated traders in general but, unfortunately, were less willing to apply their knowledge to the taxpayer's particular situation. The VAT implications of renting out the building were not well understood.
>
> The final part of the question concerning the potential inheritance tax liability in respect of a lifetime gift was done well.

ANSWERS TO PRACTICE QUESTIONS: SECTION 2

				Marks
(a)	(i)	Total costs less after tax sale proceeds		1.0
		Calculation of gains:		
		On shares		1.0
		Crystallisation of gain on loan stock		2.0
		Annual exempt amount		0.5
		No entrepreneurs' relief		0.5
		Remainder of basic rate band		
		Salary		1.5
		Car benefit		1.5
		Trading income		1.0
		Personal allowance		0.5
		Tax due		1.0
		Assumptions – 0.5 each – maximum 1.0		1.0
				11.5
			Maximum	10.0
	(ii)	Proposal to increase after tax sales proceeds:		
		Identification of strategy		1.0
		Tax saved		1.0
		More appropriate forms of finance:		
		Bank overdraft inappropriate with reason		1.0
		Longer term finance with reason		1.0
				4.0
			Maximum	3.0
(b)	(i)	National insurance contributions:		
		Class 2		1.0
		Class 4		1.0
	(ii)	Purchase and renovation of the theatre:		
		Purchase price		1.5
		Two possible treatments of renovations		2.0
	(iii)	VAT position:		
		Partial exemption with reason		1.5
		Recoverable input tax		1.5
		De minimis limits		1.0
		Effect of opting to tax		1.5
		Factors affecting decision – 1 each – maximum 2		2.0
				13.0
			Maximum	11.0
(c)		Gift is a PET, no tax if survives seven years		1.0
		Maximum possible liability		1.0
		Relevance of date of death/taper relief		1.5
		Annual exemption and nil rate band		1.0
		Charitable bequests exempt		1.0
		Possibility of 36% IHT rate		1.0
		Explanation of conditions		1.0
				7.5
			Maximum	7.0
		Appropriate style and presentation		2.0
		Effectiveness of communication		2.0
				4.0
Total				**35.0**

46 GAGARIN (ADAPTED)

Key answer tips

In part (a) it is very important to take note of the examiner's instructions. The question states that you can assume the company qualifies for EIS relief and you are not required to list any of the conditions. If you do then you will not earn any marks for them.

Part (b) requires knowledge of the capital goods scheme. Here the examiner asks for illustrative examples in your explanations. Even if you are not sure about the capital goods scheme, you should have picked up the marks for calculating the input tax recovery in the year of purchase

(a) (i) **The tax incentives immediately available**

Income tax

- The investor's income tax liability for 2016/17 will be reduced by 30% of the amount subscribed for the shares.
- The amount invested can be treated as if paid in 2015/16 rather than 2016/17. Relief can be claimed on a maximum of £1 million in any one tax year.
- This ability to carry back relief to the previous year is useful where the investor's income tax liability in 2016/17 is insufficient to absorb all of the relief available.

Tutorial note

There would be no change to the income tax liability of 2015/16 where an amount is treated as if paid in that year. This ensures that such a claim does not affect payments on account under the self-assessment system. Instead, the tax refund due is calculated by reference to 2015/16 but is deducted from the next payment of tax due from the taxpayer or is repaid to the taxpayer.

Capital gains tax deferral

- For every £1 invested in Vostok Ltd, an investor can defer £1 of capital gain and thus, potentially, 28 pence of capital gains tax.
- The gain deferred can be in respect of the disposal of any asset.
- The shares must be subscribed for within the four year period starting one year prior to the date on which the disposal giving rise to the gain took place.

ANSWERS TO PRACTICE QUESTIONS: SECTION 2

(ii) **Answers to questions from potential investors**

Maximum investment

- For the relief to be available, a shareholder (together with spouse and children) cannot own more than 30% of the company.
- Accordingly, the maximum investment by a single subscriber will be £315,000 (15,000 (W) × £21).

Borrowing to finance the purchase

- There would normally be tax relief for the interest paid on a loan taken out to acquire shares in a close company such as Vostok Ltd. However, this relief is not available when the shares qualify for relief under the enterprise investment scheme.

Implications of a subscriber selling the shares in Vostok Ltd

- The income tax relief will be withdrawn if the shares in Vostok Ltd are sold within three years of subscription.
- Any profit arising on the sale of the shares in Vostok Ltd on which income tax relief has been given will be exempt from capital gains tax provided the shares have been held for three years.
- Any capital loss arising on the sale of the shares will be allowable regardless of how long the shares have been held. However, the loss will be reduced by the amount of income tax relief obtained in respect of the investment.
- The loss may be used to reduce the investor's taxable income, and hence his income tax liability, for the tax year of loss and/or the preceding tax year.
- Any gain deferred at the time of subscription will become chargeable in the year in which the shares in Vostok Ltd are sold.

  If the asset qualified for entrepreneurs' relief (ER) at the time the gain was deferred, a claim can still be made for ER to apply to this gain when it crystallises on the disposal of the EIS shares. The claim must be made within 12 months of the 31 January following the end of the tax year in which the gain actually becomes chargeable.

Working: Maximum investment

As 20,000 represents a 40% interest in the company, a 30% interest will be 15,000 shares (20,000 × 30/40).

Tutorial note

The theoretical maximum investment is £1 million but it would not be possible for an investor to make this amount of investment. See the Examiner's report in respect of this answer.

(b) **Recoverable input tax in respect of new premises**

Vostok Ltd will recover £54,720 (£456,000 × 1/6 (or 20/120) × 72%) in the year ending 31 March 2017.

The capital goods scheme will apply to the purchase of the building because it is to cost more than £250,000. Under the scheme, the total amount of input tax recovered reflects the use of the building over the period of ownership, up to a maximum of ten years, rather than merely the year of purchase.

Further input tax will be recovered in future years as the percentage of exempt supplies falls. (If the percentage of exempt supplies were to rise, Vostok Ltd would have to repay input tax to HMRC.)

The additional recoverable input tax will be computed by reference to the percentage of taxable supplies in each year including the year of sale.

For example, if the percentage of taxable supplies in a particular subsequent year were to be 80%, the additional recoverable input tax would be computed as follows.

£456,000 × 1/6 × 1/10 × (80% – 72%) = £608 p.a. (or until another change)

Further input tax will be recovered in the year of sale as if Vostok Ltd's supplies in the remaining years of the ten-year period are fully VATable.

For example, if the building is sold in year seven, the additional recoverable amount for the remaining three years will be calculated as follows.

£456,000 × 1/6 × 1/10 × (100% – 72%) × 3 = £6,384.

Tutorial note

If Vostok Ltd waives the VAT exemption in respect of the building (often referred to as 'opting to tax'), then when the building is sold, VAT must be charged and the previously partially exempt use of the building becomes fully taxable.

Examiner's report

Part (a) of the question was in two parts

In the first part, although most candidates had a good knowledge of the income tax deduction available to investors, many of them did not identify the possibility of investors deferring capital gains. A minority of candidates included information regarding the conditions that needed to be satisfied by the company despite a specific instruction in the question not to do so.

When it came to addressing the possible questions from investors, candidates did well on the implications of a future sale of the shares. However, when addressing the maximum investment by a potential shareholder, candidates resorted to making general comments in relation to the maximum investment of £1 million, when they should have applied the specific rules to the facts of the question. This would have led them to the need to restrict any investment to no more than 30% of the company (i.e. £315,000).

ANSWERS TO PRACTICE QUESTIONS: SECTION 2

> Although this part of the question was answered well, many candidates would have done better if they had written less and spent some time relating their knowledge to the particular situation in the question.
>
> Part (b) concerned the recovery of VAT input tax in respect of a building acquired by a partially exempt company. It was not answered well with many candidates failing to identify the need to apply the capital goods scheme to the situation.

ACCA marking scheme			
			Marks
(a)	(i)	Income tax	
		Reduction in income tax	1.0
		Carry back	2.0
		Capital gains tax	
		Deferral	1.0
		Any asset	0.5
		Time period	1.0
			–––
			5.5
		Maximum	5.0
			–––
	(ii)	Maximum investment	1.5
		Borrowing to finance the purchase	1.0
		Sale of the shares	
		Importance of three-year period	1.0
		Withdrawal of income tax relief	1.0
		Treatment of gain arising	1.0
		Treatment of loss arising	
		Allowable	1.0
		Effect on loss of income tax relief	0.5
		Relief of loss against income	1.0
		Gain deferred at time of subscription	1.0
			–––
			9.0
			–––
(b)		Recoverable input tax in the year ending 31 March 2017	1.0
		Additional recoverable input tax	
		Capital goods scheme applies	1.0
		Explanatory rationale	1.0
		Input tax recoverable in future years	2.0
		Input tax recoverable following sale	2.0
			–––
			7.0
		Maximum	6.0
			–––
Total			**20.0**

47 CALISIA *Walk in the footsteps of a top tutor*

Key answer tips

This is really two separate questions.

Part (a) requires capital gains tax computations for a number of proposed disposals by a mother in order to generate extra income for her daughter. The technical content here is quite basic, but you will need to think carefully about the interaction between the income tax implications for the daughter and the amount of shares given by her mother. There are four options to deal with so try to keep moving and deal with all of them.

Part (b) is fairly straightforward and requires explanation of how Calisia's inheritance tax liability would be calculated on her death.

The highlighted words in the written sections are key phrases that markers are looking for.

Tutor's top tips

The requirement at the end of the question just tells you how many marks are available for each section. The detailed requirements are all in the schedule from the manager.

You may find it useful to number these requirements so that you can tick them off as you attempt them.

NOTES FOR MEETING WITH CALISIA

Prepared by   A. Taxadviser

Date   6 June 2016

Subject   Additional income for Farfisa and Calisia's Inheritance tax position

(a) **Farfisa – Additional income**

Tutor's top tips

The examiner tells you how to approach this part of the question, so make sure that you follow his instructions!

Start by calculating Farfisa's excess of expenditure over her salary. Don't forget to take into account the income tax and NICs that she will pay.

Additional income required

	£	£
Budgeted expenditure (£2,500 × 12)		30,000
Salary	28,000	
Less: Income tax ((£28,000 − £10,600) × 20%)	(3,480)	
Class 1 national insurance contributions ((£28,000 − £8,060) × 12%)	(2,393)	
Net salary		(22,127)
Additional income required		7,873

The interest-free loan from Jelmini Ltd will not result in a tax liability because it is for less than £10,000.

Tutorial note

Remember that beneficial loans to employees are exempt if the amount borrowed does not exceed £10,000 at any point during the tax year.

(i) **Gift of shares quoted on the UK stock exchange**

Tutor's top tips

You are required to calculate Calisia's capital gains tax liability for four different options, the first being a gift of shares.

You may have been confused, as the question does not actually say how many shares Calisia is giving away. That is because you are expected to work out the value of shares given, based on the amount of dividend income that Farfisa needs. This is a little tricky!

*Farfisa needs £7,873 income **after** tax, so the first step is to calculate the income **before** tax, which will represent 4% of the value of the shares, then gross this up by 100/4 to find the value of shares required.*

Remember that the amount of tax on the dividends will depend on whether they fall into the basic rate or higher rate band, so you need to check this first.

Market value of shares given

Farfisa currently has taxable income of £17,400 (£28,000 − £10,600), and therefore has £14,385 (£31,785 − £17,400) of her basic rate band remaining.

If Farfisa were to receive cash dividends of £7,873, this would give gross dividend income of £8,748 (£7,873 × 100/90), which would all fall into the basic rate band.

Dividends in the basic rate band are taxed at 10% with a 10% tax credit, leaving no further tax liability to pay.

Therefore, as there will be no tax payable on the dividends, Farfisa requires enough shares to generate £7,873 in dividend income.

At a rate of return of 4%, the market value of shares required to generate income of £7,873 would be £196,825 (£7,873 × 100/4).

Tutor's top tips

Even if you did not correctly calculate the income required by Farfisa and/or the value of the shares given, you could still score full marks for the calculation of capital gains tax based on your figures.

Capital gains tax payable on gift of shares

	£
Proceeds = market value	196,825
Chargeable gain (£196,825 × 25%)(Note)	49,206
Less: Annual exempt amount (used)	(Nil)
Taxable gain	49,206
Capital gains tax (£49,206 × 28%)	13,778

Gift relief is not available for shares in quoted companies, as Calisia does not own at least 5% of the shares before the disposal.

Tutorial note

Calisia has estimated that the gain on the shares will be a quarter (25%) of their market value.

Tutor's top tips

Watch out for the information given in the question: you are told that Calisia has used her annual exempt amount, and is a higher rate taxpayer. This means that her gains will be taxed at 28%.

Stamp duty

As there is no consideration payable for the gift of shares, there is no stamp duty.

Tutor's top tips

Don't forget to mention stamp duty as the examiner specifically asks for it.

These are generally easy marks gained and easily lost if you are not organised in your approach and attention to the detailed requirements.

(ii) **Sale of investment property followed by gift of proceeds**

Tutor's top tips

This option is more complicated than the first, and a logical approach is needed so that you don't get lost. You should approach this part as follows:

1 Calculate Calisia's capital gains tax on the sale of the investment property.

2 Calculate the cash proceeds after tax from the sale of the property.

3 Calculate the net interest received by Farfisa on the cash proceeds.

4 Deduct this net interest from the total additional income required by Farfisa, to give the net dividend income required.

5 Gross up the dividend by 100/4 to find the value of shares required, as for option (i).

6 Calculate the CGT on the disposal of the shares.

Capital gains tax payable on investment property

	£
Proceeds	260,000
Less: Disposal costs	(6,000)
Net proceeds	254,000
Less: Cost	(90,000)
Chargeable gain qualifying for entrepreneurs' relief	164,000
Less: Annual exempt amount (used)	(Nil)
Taxable gain	164,000
Capital gains tax (£164,000 × 10%)	16,400

Entrepreneurs' relief is available as the property qualifies as furnished holiday accommodation, so the gain will be taxed at 10%.

Net proceeds to be gifted to Farfisa

	£
Proceeds	260,000
Less: Disposal costs	(6,000)
Net proceeds	254,000
Less: CGT payable	(16,400)
Net cash proceeds for Farfisa	237,600

Market value of shares given

The shares to be gifted will need to generate enough dividend income to cover the shortfall in additional total income required of £7,873, after taking into account the net interest received on the cash proceeds.

	£
Gross interest received (3% × £237,600)	7,128
Less: Income tax at basic rate (20% × £7,128)	(1,426)
Net interest received	5,702
Dividend income required (£7,873 – £5,702)	2,171

The interest and the dividends will fall into the remaining basic rate band of £14,385, as described above. There will be 20% income tax to pay on the gross interest, but no extra tax on the dividends.

Market value of shares required to generate cash dividend of £2,171:

(£2,171 × 100/4)	£54,275

Capital gains tax payable on gift of shares

	£
Proceeds = market value	54,275
Chargeable gain (£54,275 × 25%)	13,569
Capital gains tax (£13,569 × 28%)	3,799

Stamp duty

Stamp duty land tax would be payable on the sale of the property, but by the purchaser, not by Calisia.

Again, as there is no consideration payable for the gift of shares, there is no stamp duty.

(iii) **Gift of investment property – rented out by Farfisa**

Tutor's top tips

This option is very similar to option (ii), except that the property is given to Farfisa instead of being sold.

Farfisa will receive rent from the property instead of interest on the cash proceeds.

Capital gains tax payable on investment property

	£
Chargeable gain (as for option (ii))	164,000
Less: Gift relief	(164,000)
Taxable gain	Nil

As the property qualifies as furnished holiday accommodation, it is a qualifying business asset for gift relief purposes. Therefore gift relief is available.

The gain can be deferred until Farfisa sells the property, and no immediate tax is payable.

Market value of shares given

The shares to be gifted will need to generate enough dividend income to cover the shortfall in the total additional income required of £7,873, after taking into account the net rent received from the investment property.

	£
Annual rental income	5,100
Less: Income tax at basic rate (20% × £5,100)	(1,020)
Net rent received	4,080
Dividend income required (£7,873 – £4,080)	3,793

The rental income and the dividends will fall into the remaining basic rate band of £14,385, as described above. There will be 20% income tax to pay on the rental income, but no extra tax on the dividends.

Market value of shares required to generate cash dividend of £3,793:

(£3,793 × 100/4)	£94,825

Capital gains tax payable on gift of shares

	£
Proceeds = market value	94,825
Chargeable gain (£94,825 × 25%)	23,706
Capital gains tax (£23,706 × 28%)	6,638

Stamp duty

As there is no consideration payable for the gift of property or the gift of shares, there is no stamp duty.

(iv) **Gift of investment property – lived in by Farfisa**

Tutor's top tips

This option is very similar to option (iii), except that Farfisa will live in the property instead of paying rent for a separate property, and will rent out a room in the property instead of receiving dividends from gifted shares.

As the capital gains tax position for Calisia is exactly the same as for option (iii), there is no need to duplicate the calculations.

Capital gains tax payable on investment property

As for option (iii), the gain can be deferred until Farfisa sells the property, and no immediate tax is payable.

Minimum monthly rent

	£
Additional income required	7,873
Less: Rental expenditure saved (£550 × 12)	(6,600)
Annual rent required	1,273
Minimum monthly rent required from second bedroom (£1,273 ÷ 12)	106

As long as the second bedroom is rented out furnished, and as long as the rent is less than £4,250, the rental income will be exempt under the rent-a-room scheme.

Stamp duty land tax

There would be no stamp duty land tax on the gift of the property.

Summary of capital gains tax payable

Capital gains tax payable by Calisia under each alternative:

	Option (i) £	Option (ii) £	Option (iii) £	Option (iv) £
Gift of shares	13,778	3,799	6,638	N/A
Sale/gift of property	N/A	16,400	Nil	Nil
	13,778	20,199	6,638	Nil

ANSWERS TO PRACTICE QUESTIONS: SECTION 2

Tutor's top tips

The examiner specifically asks for a summary of the capital gains tax payable for each of the four alternatives.

There are easy marks to be gained here. It doesn't matter if your figures are wrong, as long as you summarise them as requested!

(b) **Calisia – Inheritance tax**

Explanation of inheritance tax liability on death

Tutor's top tips

To score well here you must make sure that you answer the question set and don't just talk about inheritance tax in general terms.

You are asked to:

- *Explain how the IHT would be calculated if Calisia died today*
- *Identify all the issues that are relevant to Calisia's situation*
- *Identify any matters to be confirmed for reliefs/exemptions to be available*
- *Not perform any calculations.*

Use the information in the scenario and avoid discussing areas that are not directly relevant.

Death estate

Calisia will be subject to inheritance tax on her death estate.

The death estate will include all of the assets owned by Calisia at the date of her death, at their market values.

Any liabilities due can be deducted from the value of the estate, along with reasonable funeral costs and the cost of a tombstone.

Calisia's home

Calisia is wrong to assume that her home will not be taxed. It will be included in her estate at market value, less any outstanding mortgage.

Donation to political party

The political donation can be deducted from the value of the estate, but only if the Fairness for All party is a qualifying political party.

To be a qualifying political party, it must either have:

- two members elected to the House of Commons, or
- one member and received at least 150,000 votes at the last general election.

This should be confirmed.

KAPLAN PUBLISHING

Investment property in the country of Sakura

As Calisia is domiciled in the UK, she will be taxed on her overseas assets as well as her UK assets, so the property in Sakura will be subject to inheritance tax.

Administrative fees may be deducted from the value of the property, subject to a maximum of 5% of the value.

Tutor's top tips

There is no point in discussing the conditions for domicile or deemed domicile to apply, as the examiner states that Calisia **is** UK domiciled.

Share in Therson Partnership

The share in the Therson Partnership will be subject to 100% business property relief and will not be taxable as long as it is a trading partnership and Calisia has owned her share for at least two years.

If the partnership has any assets held for investment purposes, the relief will be restricted.

These matters require confirmation.

Building used by Therson Partnership

This will qualify for 50% business property relief, as long as it is used in a qualifying trade by the Therson Partnership and has been owned for at least two years.

This should be confirmed with Calisia.

Shares quoted on the UK stock exchange

These will not qualify for business property relief unless Calisia controls the company, which is highly unlikely.

Tutor's top tips

Try to be specific when you are talking about business property relief. You need to give details about the rates of relief available and the conditions to be satisfied for the relief to apply.

Calculation of tax

The first £325,000 of the total estate value will be covered by Calisia's nil rate band, as she has not made any lifetime gifts.

In addition, Calisia's husband's nil rate band will be available, as this was not used on his death.

The excess estate will be taxed at 40%.

There will be double tax relief available for any death tax paid in the country of Sakura. This will be a tax credit for the lower of the Sakuran tax or the UK tax on the Sakuran property, calculated at the average estate rate.

Examiner's report

Part (a) was for 21 marks. With a question part of this size it was important for candidates to be clear as to what they had been asked to do and how they were going to do it. It was very pleasing to see the majority of candidates taking a well-structured approach to this question and addressing all of the alternatives in a consistent manner. There were some very good answers to this question with some candidates scoring full marks.

The question centred on capital gains business reliefs and the taxation of various sources of income. The income tax elements were done well but candidates' knowledge of business reliefs was often not as good as it could have been. However, there was a clear indication that candidates were taking the right approach to capital gains tax in that they were considering the availability of reliefs every time a gain arose. This was very good to see and it now remains for candidates to improve their knowledge of the conditions that must be satisfied for the reliefs to be available.

The first task was to calculate the amount of additional income required by the client's daughter, Farfisa. This was a relatively simple task and many candidates scored full marks. Other candidates failed to identify that the proposed loan was for less than £10,000 such that it was an exempt benefit or were not careful enough in distinguishing taxable income (income less personal allowance) from post-tax income (income less tax).

Under the first alternative the income was to be provided via a transfer of quoted shares. The majority of candidates were happy calculating the number of shares to be transferred but many failed to consider how the dividends would be taxed in the hands of Farfisa.

Those who did address this point often considered the rate of tax but not the credit. The point that needed to be identified was that there would be no tax to pay on the dividend income because, as Farfisa would be a basic rate taxpayer, the tax liability would be covered by the tax credit.

Under the first alternative candidates then had to calculate the capital gain on the proposed gift of the shares. This is where some candidates began to have problems as they thought that gift relief would be available.

However, the relief was not available because the shares were quoted and Calisia did not own at least 5% of the voting rights.

Under the second alternative candidates had to calculate the capital gains on the proposed sale of a building that was rented out as qualifying furnished holiday accommodation.

Calculating the gain was simple; but again there was the need to consider the availability of business reliefs. Many candidates failed to realise that entrepreneurs' relief would be available such that tax would only be taxed at 10%. A minority of candidates also had the problem here of distinguishing a taxable gain (proceeds less cost) from post-tax proceeds (proceeds less tax).

Under the third and fourth alternatives the rental property was to be gifted rather than sold. Candidates had to identify that gift relief would be available under both alternatives. It was then necessary to consider how the rental income received by Farfisa in respect of the property would be taxed.

Under the third alternative the income would simply be taxed at 20%. But under the fourth alternative rent-a-room relief would be available. These points were identified by the vast majority of candidates.

Candidates were also asked to consider stamp duty and stamp duty land tax and to prepare a summary of the capital gains tax liabilities under each of the alternatives. A minority of candidates did not carry out one or both of these tasks thus sacrificing some fairly easy marks.

Part (b) required candidates to prepare a comprehensive explanation of how Calisia's inheritance tax liability would be calculated; this was done well by many candidates.

This question was fairly unstructured such that candidates had to think and impose their own structure in order to maximise their marks. Candidates who failed to do this often repeated themselves, did not cover sufficient aspects of the question and included material in their answers which was irrelevant.

In particular, some candidates wasted time by writing about inheritance tax in general terms, including giving general advice on inheritance tax planning, or by preparing computations when they were told not to.

Candidates' knowledge of inheritance tax was often very good. The link between domicile and the taxation of overseas assets, the transfer of the husband's nil rate band, the treatment of the donation to the political party and the taxation of the client's home were identified and understood by the majority of candidates.

Business property relief was often explained well although, as always, there was a small minority of candidates who confused reliefs available in respect of capital gains tax with those available in respect of inheritance tax.

It was important to provide some detail here (the requirement was for a comprehensive explanation) so a statement that 'business property relief would be available' was, despite being true, insufficient to score. Candidates needed to address the assets that would qualify for the relief, the qualifying ownership period and the rate of relief; many candidates did not address as much as they could have.

In respect of the property situated overseas, the marks available for explaining the relief in respect of tax suffered overseas were missed by many candidates.

Other marks that were often missed included the deduction available for the costs of administering the property situated overseas, the treatment of Calisia's home, the deduction available in respect of funeral costs and the need for the political party to qualify in order for the donation to be exempt.

ANSWERS TO PRACTICE QUESTIONS: SECTION 2

ACCA marking scheme		
		Marks
(a)	Calculation of additional income required	3.5
	Gift of shares	
	Tax on dividends	1.5
	Capital gains tax	3.5
	Sale of investment property followed by gift of proceeds	
	Capital gains tax on investment property	2.5
	Farfisa's income position	3.5
	Capital gains tax on transfer of shares	1.5
	Gift of investment property – rented out by Farfisa	
	Gift relief available	1.0
	Farfisa's income position	2.0
	Capital gains tax on transfer of shares	1.0
	Gift of investment property – to be lived in by Farfisa	2.5
	Summary of capital gains tax payable	1.0
	Stamp duty and stamp duty land tax	2.0
		25.5
	Maximum	21.0
(b)	Relevance of domicile	1.0
	Calisia's home subject to tax	0.5
	Business property relief	4.0
	Cost of administering the property in Sakura	1.0
	Political party	1.5
	Funeral costs	0.5
	Nil rate bands	1.5
	Tax and double tax relief	2.0
		12.0
	Maximum	10.0
	Appropriate style and presentation	2.0
	Effectiveness of communication	1.0
	Approach to problem solving	1.0
	Maximum	4.0
Total		**35.0**

KAPLAN PUBLISHING

48 TETRA   *Walk in the footsteps of a top tutor*

Key answer tips

This question covers a variety of different areas including redundancy payments, venture capital trust investment, personal pension contributions and computing class 4 NICs on partnership profits.

Redundancy payments are a popular area in the exam and easy marks are available here.

Computing the partnership profits requires some detailed calculations due to the change in profit sharing arrangements part way through the accounting period ending on 31 December 2016.

The final part of the question requires you to compare the effect on the income tax liability of making an investment in either a VCT or a personal pension and easy marks are available for discussion on the risk and timing of the alternative investments.

The highlighted words in the written sections are key phrases that markers are looking for.

(a) **Income tax implications of the redundancy payments made by Ivy Ltd**

Tutor's top tips

This part of the question is purely a test of knowledge, and should have been easy to score well on. Note that there are only three marks available, so you should keep your answer brief and concise.

The statutory redundancy of £4,200 falls within the £30,000 exemption such that it is not subject to income tax.

The first £25,800 (£30,000 – £4,200) of the non-contractual payment is also exempt from income tax, provided it relates solely to redundancy and is not simply a terminal bonus. The remainder of the payment is subject to income tax in full.

The payment in consideration of Tetra agreeing not to work for any competitor of Ivy Ltd for 12 months is subject to income tax.

ANSWERS TO PRACTICE QUESTIONS: SECTION 2

Tutor's top tips

The first £30,000 of an ex gratia redundancy payment is tax free as long as it is non-contractual and does not coincide with retirement.

Statutory redundancy is also tax free but reduces the £30,000 exemption limit for ex gratia payments.

Taxable termination payments are treated as the top slice of the individual's taxable income and therefore taxed at their highest marginal rate. This point was not included in the examiner's model answer but would have earned credit.

Reward for services whether past, present or future is fully taxable. Accordingly, the £7,000 'golden handcuffs' payment is taxable.

(b) **Class 4 national insurance contributions – 2016/17**

Tutor's top tips

Although this part of the question requires class 4 NICs computations, most of the marks are for calculating taxable profits for a partner commencing in partnership.

The opening rules for sole traders and partnerships are tricky, but they often get tested in the P6 exam. It is crucial that you retain your F6 knowledge of these rules.

Make sure that you approach the calculations in the correct order:

(i) Apportion the partnership profits between the partners for each accounting period, based on their profit sharing agreement. Don't forget to time apportion the profits where the agreement changes mid-year.

(ii) Apply the opening year assessment rules to Tetra to determine the profits matched to the tax year 2016/17.

(iii) Calculate class 4 NICs based on the taxable profits for 2016/17.

Allocation of partnership profits:

Year ended 31 December 2016

	Total £	Zia £	Fore £	Tetra £
1.1.16 – 31.5.16				
(£300,000 × 5/12) (60:40)	125,000	75,000	50,000	–
1.6.16 – 31.12.16				
Salaries (7/12)	24,500	–	14,000	10,500
Balance (40:30:30)	150,500	60,200	45,150	45,150
(Profits £300,000 × 7/12)	175,000			
	300,000	135,200	109,150	55,650

KAPLAN PUBLISHING

Year ended 31 December 2017

	Total £	Zia £	Fore £	Tetra £
Salaries	42,000	–	24,000	18,000
Balance (40:30:30)	338,000	135,200	101,400	101,400
	380,000	135,200	125,400	119,400

Tutor's top tips

You could have just calculated the profits apportioned to Tetra to save time, rather than showing the full allocation between all of the partners.

If you do it this way, you need to be careful and must still remember to deduct the salaries allocated to the other partners before calculating the balance to be given to Tetra in each period.

Tetra's taxable trading profit – 2016/17

Period from 1 June 2016 to 5 April 2017

	£
1 June 2016 to 31 December 2016	55,650
1 January 2017 to 5 April 2017 (£119,400 × 3/12)	29,850
	85,500

Class 4 NICs

	£
(£42,385 – £8,060) × 9%	3,089
(£85,500 – £42,385) × 2%	862
	3,951

Tutorial note

Tetra starts trading on 1 June 2016 which falls in the tax year 2016/17. As this is the first tax year of trading, Tetra will be assessed on his actual profits from commencement to the 5 April in this first tax year, which will be 10 months of profits.

(c) **The alternative investments: effect on income tax liability**

Tutor's top tips

Don't waste time writing about the conditions and rules for VCT relief and pension contributions. All you are asked to do is consider the effect on Tetra's income tax liability.

Watch out for the personal allowance. This is reduced if adjusted net income (ANI) is more than £100,000 (which it currently is) so you need to consider whether either of the investments will affect Tetra's ANI.

Venture capital trust

In the absence of any pension contributions, Tetra's net income would exceed £121,200 (£100,000 + (2 × £10,600)) such that he would not receive any amount of personal allowance.

If Tetra subscribes for the shares in the venture capital trust, his income tax liability would be as follows:

	£
Net income	130,000
Less: Personal allowance	(Nil)
Taxable income	130,000

£		
31,785	× 20%	6,357
98,215	× 40%	39,286
130,000		
		45,643
Less: Relief for investment in VCT (£32,000 × 30%)		(9,600)
Income tax liability		36,043

Tutorial note

A VCT investment will not reduce the net income, and so will not affect the personal allowance. An income tax reducer of 30% is available.

Personal pension contribution

If Tetra were to make pension contributions of £32,000, the pension fund would receive a further £8,000 (£32,000 × 20/80) from HMRC as the contributions would be deemed to be made net of basic rate tax.

Tetra's basic rate band would be extended by £40,000 (£32,000 × 100/80) and his adjusted net income for the purposes of determining his personal allowance would be reduced by the same amount. He would therefore receive the whole of the personal allowance as his adjusted net income would be less than £100,000 ((£130,000 − £40,000) = £90,000).

His income tax liability would be as follows:

	£
Net income	130,000
Less: Personal allowance	(10,600)
Taxable income	119,400

£		£
71,785	× 20% (W)	14,357
47,615	× 40%	19,046
119,400		
Income tax liability		33,403

Tutorial note

Personal pension contributions are made net of 20% income tax so the gross pension investment is £40,000 (£32,000 × 100/80).

*The personal pension contribution **does** affect the adjusted net income and thus the personal allowance. As the gross contribution of £40,000 reduces the net income to less than £100,000, the full personal allowance of £10,600 is available.*

The £40,000 will also extend the basic rate band from £31,785 to £71,785, causing a further income tax reduction.

By making pension contributions, Tetra would save income tax of £2,640 (£36,043 − £33,403).

This, together with the additional contributions into the pension fund of £8,000 from HMRC, would result in an overall financial advantage of £10,640 (£2,640 + £8,000).

Working: Extended basic rate band

	£
Basic rate band	31,785
Plus: Gross PPCs (£32,000 × 100/80)	40,000
	71,785

ANSWERS TO PRACTICE QUESTIONS: SECTION 2

Tutorial note

Alternative approach to calculation of tax saving

The net income tax saving could have been calculated at the margin as follows:

	£
Pension contribution:	
Tax saved by personal allowance (£10,600 × 40%)	4,240
Tax saved by extension of BRB (£40,000 × (40% − 20%))	8,000
Income tax reduction from pension contribution	12,240
Less: Income tax reduction with VCT investment	(9,600)
Income tax saving from pension contribution	2,640

Non-tax matters

Tutor's top tips

Easy marks are available for discussing the risk level and length of time the investments have to be retained.

*However, to score well here you must **compare** the two alternative investments.*

VCTs are high risk investments as the fund manager must invest in unquoted companies and the VCT shares should be retained for at least 5 years.

Pension investments are relatively low risk investment funds that can be invested in low risk investments such as cash and government securities, but pension benefits are only available after age 55.

Risk

A VCT is a relatively high-risk investment in that it must hold at least 70% of its investments in unquoted trading companies.

A personal pension fund is permitted to hold a very wide range of investments such that the level of risk can be varied to suit the preferences of Tetra.

Timing

A VCT is a medium-term investment; the tax relief will be withdrawn if Tetra holds the shares for less than five years.

A pension fund is a long-term investment; Tetra cannot withdraw benefits from the scheme until he is 55 years old (unless he is incapacitated due to ill health).

KAPLAN PUBLISHING

Examiner's report

The first part concerned the tax treatment of statutory redundancy, compensation for loss of office and a payment for agreeing not to work for a competitor. It was a test of knowledge and was done well by the majority of candidates with many scoring full marks. The only problem that some candidates had was a tendency to write too much. There were only three marks available so only three points were required. Some candidates wrote significantly more than this and used time that they should have been using elsewhere.

Part (b) required candidates to calculate the class 4 national insurance contributions in respect of a partner's first year of trading. It required knowledge of the opening year rules, the allocation of profits between partners and the calculation of national insurance. It was done well. Common errors included the treatment of the partner's salary as employment income rather than trading income and the failure to adjust the profit for the partners' salaries before splitting the remainder between the partners.

The final part of the question concerned the tax implications of investing in a venture capital trust and of making pension contributions; it was not done as well as expected. Candidates were required to 'compare the effect of the two alternative investments on Tetra's income tax liability'. This meant that calculations were required.

However, many candidates simply treated the question as being about venture capital trusts and pension contributions and explained all the rules they could remember that related to these two areas of the syllabus.

Marks are only awarded in the exam for relevant points that address the requirements and much time was wasted here that could have been spent earning marks.

There were, however, many knowledgeable answers to this part of the question. Many candidates successfully identified the effect of making pension contributions on Tetra's personal allowance situation. In addition, the majority of candidates were able to explain the effect on the basic rate band of making pension contributions and the tax relief available in respect of the investment in a venture capital trust.

ANSWERS TO PRACTICE QUESTIONS: **SECTION 2**

ACCA marking scheme		Marks
(a) Statutory redundancy		1.0
£30,000 exemption		1.5
Restrictive covenant		1.0
		3.5
	Maximum	3.0
(b) Tetra's share of the adjusted trading profit		3.5
Tetra's taxable trading profit		2.0
Class 4 National Insurance contributions		1.5
		7.0
(c) Income tax		
Venture capital trust		
Personal allowance		1.5
Tax liability with VCT credit		1.5
Pension contributions		
Basic rate band		1.0
Tax liability with pension contributions		1.0
Tax relief at source		1.0
Risk		1.5
Timing		1.5
		9.0
	Maximum	8.0
Total		**18.0**

49 MONISHA AND HORNER *Walk in the footsteps of a top tutor*

Key answer tips

The first part of (a) concerns various aspects of income tax and capital gains tax in relation to tax planning for a married couple and in particular deals with furnished holiday accommodation.

The second part of (a) was the more difficult part of the question. It required a calculation of the total tax saving on the transfer of a 20% interest in a rental property from one spouse (Monisha) to the other (Asmat) together with the property being let as furnished holiday accommodation in the future. It is necessary to think very clearly about the taxes that would be saved and the impact on the computations of both husband and wife.

Part (b) covers the personal service company (IR35) rules and required an outline of the circumstances in which the rules apply, and clear explanations were needed to score highly. Then a calculation of the deemed employment income under the personal service company (IR35) rules was required.

The highlighted words in the written sections are key phrases that markers are looking for.

Tutor's top tips

The definition of furnished holiday accommodation should supply easy marks provided the conditions had been learnt.

(a) **Monisha**

(i) **Furnished holiday accommodation in the UK – conditions**

- The property must be available for commercial letting to the public as holiday accommodation for at least 210 days in the tax year.
- The property must be commercially let as holiday accommodation for at least 105 days in the tax year, excluding any periods of longer term occupation.
- There must be no more than 155 days of longer term occupation in the tax year.

Longer term occupation occurs where there is a continuous period of occupation by the same person for more than 31 days.

(ii) **The total tax saving for the six years ending 5 April 2023**

Tutor's top tips

With the time allocation for this part, it is important to pause, think about which taxes are involved (i.e. income tax and capital gains tax) and then perform the calculations at the margin.

There is insufficient time to do full blown income tax computations before and after, and there is no need to do computations for multiple years as the levels of income and gains are the same for the first five years.

Once the situation is defined, the calculations are very straightforward. However, time needs to be spent making sure the requirement is fully understood before any calculations are performed; to avoid time wasted doing unnecessary calculations.

Furnished holiday accommodation has several tax benefits. For income tax, capital allowances are available instead of the wear and tear allowance and the income is relevant earnings for pension relief purposes. From a CGT point of view, the gain is eligible for entrepreneurs' relief, rollover relief and gift relief.

Income tax

	£
Income tax saved in the first five tax years (£6,660 (W) × 40% × 5 years) (Note)	13,320
Income tax saved in the final tax year (£6,660 (W) × (40% – 20%))	1,332
Total income tax saved	14,652

Tutorial note

In the first five years, Monisha is a higher rate taxpayer but as Asmat has no other income his share of property income will be covered by his personal allowance (PA) and he will pay no tax on that income. The income tax saving will therefore be 40%.

Note that with or without the proposals, Asmat would not be able to transfer £1,060 of his unused PA to Monisha as she is a higher rate taxpayer. Therefore all of his PA remains with him. Without the proposal to transfer income to him, his PA would be wasted.

In the final year (2022/23), Asmat will be earning £18,000 p.a. and therefore he will utilise all of his PA, even without the proposal, and he will be a basic rate taxpayer. The income tax saving from moving income from Monisha into his computation is therefore 20% (40% − 20%).

Working: Taxable property income

	£
Rental income	20,000
Less: Allowable expenses (£1,600 + £1,200 + £2,000)	(4,800)
Capital allowances equal to wear and tear allowance ((£20,000 − £1,200) × 10%)	(1,880)
Total property income	13,320
Amount subject to income tax in the hands of Asmat (£13,320 × 50%) (tutorial note)	6,660

For the first five tax years, Asmat will not have any other income, such that his share of the property income will be covered by his personal allowance.

Tutorial note

Despite the fact that Monisha gifts only a 20% interest in the investment property to Asmat, the income of a jointly held asset is automatically split equally between a married couple, regardless of their actual interests in the property.

Monisha and Asmat could elect to split the income between them in the ratio 80:20, but to do so would not be beneficial in their particular circumstances.

Accordingly, property income of £6,660 (W) will be subject to income tax in the hands of Asmat, rather than being taxed at 40% in the hands of Monisha, in each of the six tax years.

Capital gains tax

Tutor's top tips

Once the scenario is understood, this part follows on easily. However, remember that part of Monisha's annual exempt amount is still available.

Asmat will have a full annual exempt amount available and entrepreneurs' relief will be available if the property is treated as furnished holiday accommodation.

Inter spouse transfer

The gift of the 20% interest in the property will take place at no gain, no loss because Monisha and Asmat are married.

Capital gains tax saving on the disposal of the property

If the proposals are not carried out:

Monisha

	£
Total gain	100,000
Less: Annual exempt amount available	
(£11,100 – £6,000 other chargeable gains)	(5,100)
Taxable gain	94,900
CGT at 28%	26,572

If the proposals are carried out:
Monisha

	£	£
Share of gain (£100,000 × 80%)		80,000
Less: Annual exempt amount available		
(£11,100 – £6,000 other chargeable gains)		(5,100)
Taxable gain		74,900
Asmat		
Share of gain (£100,000 × 20%)	20,000	
Less: Annual exempt amount available	(11,100)	
Taxable gain		8,900
Total taxable gains		83,800
CGT at 10%		8,380
Capital gains tax saved (£26,572 – £8,380)		18,192
Total tax saved (£14,652 + £18,192)		32,844

Tutorial note

1   The gain on the sale of the property will be allocated between Monisha and Asmat in the ratio 80:20.

2   A gain on the sale of furnished holiday accommodation qualifies for entrepreneurs' relief.

3   To be advantageous for capital gains tax purposes, it was not necessary for Monisha to transfer 50% of the interest in the property to Asmat. It was only necessary to utilise Asmat's annual exempt amount. The excess gain above the annual exempt amount is taxed at 10% regardless of who it accrues to.

(b)   **Horner**

Tutor's top tips

Clear explanations of when the rules apply are needed to score highly on this part.

As there are only three marks available, there is no need to go into great detail about the factors used to determine an employed or self-employed type relationship.

(i)   **The circumstances in which the personal service company (IR35) rules apply**

1   A company enters into a contract to provide services to a client.

2   The services are carried out by an individual.

3   If the services were provided under a contract between the individual and the client, the individual would be regarded as an employee of the client.

4   The individual has an interest of at least 5% in the company or an entitlement to receive payments from the company, other than salary, in respect of the services provided to the client.

In respect of condition 3, when determining whether or not the individual would be regarded as an employee of the client, the rules used to distinguish between employees and the self-employed are used.

Tutorial note

It is possible for a partnership, rather than a company, to enter into the contract with the client.

(ii) **Deemed employment income for the year ending 5 April 2017**

Tutor's top tips

A straightforward calculation is required here which should supply easy marks provided the pro forma computation had been learnt.

Do not forget to calculate the employer's NICs on the annual salary paid in the year, as well as on the deemed employment income.

		£
Otmar Ltd – income from relevant engagements		85,000
Less: 5% deduction (Note 1)		(4,250)
Salary paid to Horner		(50,000)
Pension contributions		(2,000)
Employer's NIC		
((£50,000 – £8,112) × 13.8%)	5,781	
Less: Employment allowance (Note 2)	(2,000)	
		(3,781)
		24,969
Less: Employer's NIC on deemed employment income		
(£24,969 × 13.8/113.8)		(3,028)
Deemed employment income		21,941

Tutorial note

1 A flat rate 5% allowance is given to cover allowable general expenses incurred in running a personal service company, therefore the actual cost of administering the company is ignored.

2 As Horner is the only employee, the £2,000 employer allowance is available to set against the class 1 secondary contributions of £5,781 on the actual salary paid to Horner in the tax year.

Note however that if the employer's secondary contributions on the actual salary paid to Horner were less than £2,000, any remaining employer's allowance could not be set against the additional employer's NICs payable on the deemed payment.

3 The £15,000 dividends paid to Horner are treated as being part of the deemed employment income of £21,941 and are not treated separately as dividends in his income tax computation. The deemed employment income is taxed instead.

Examiner's report

Part (a)(i) was answered very well by the majority of candidates. The only difficulty related to confusion over the meaning of 'longer term accommodation' and the maximum number of days of such occupation permitted in a tax year.

Part (a)(ii) was done poorly by many candidates who either did not have a thorough attempt at it or worked very hard but did not pause to think about how to approach the problem.

The key was to first calculate the taxable property income in order to identify the amount of taxable income that would be taxed in the hands of Asmat rather than Monisha.

It was then necessary to recognise that for the first five years under consideration, Monisha would be a higher rate taxpayer whereas Asmat's income would be covered by his personal allowance, such that no tax would be payable. Accordingly, by working at the margin, it was easy to see that for the first five years the saving would be 40% of the income transferred. In the sixth year, Asmat was expected to be employed, such that the income transferred would be taxed at 20% and the saving would therefore be 20% (40% – 20%) of the income transferred.

The problem was that very few candidates chose to work at the margin. Instead, many chose to prepare income tax computations for the two individuals before and after the transfer of the interest in the property in order to quantify the difference in the total liability. This was very time consuming. Some candidates even prepared calculations for each of the five years despite the fact that the figures were the same in each year.

Calculating tax liabilities can be very time consuming. Candidates should always stop and think about the most efficient way of approaching a set of calculations before they start writing.

The capital gains tax element of this part of the question was not handled particularly well. This was perhaps due to a shortage of time. It required candidates to recognise that an additional annual exempt amount would be available and that tax would be charged at 10%, due to the availability of entrepreneurs' relief, rather than at 28%. Only a minority of candidates were able to quantify the effect of these points.

The majority of candidates struggled to satisfy the requirement in part (b)(i) despite a reasonable knowledge of the rules. It was generally recognised that the rules were in place in order to prevent the avoidance of tax but there was some confusion as to exactly where tax was being avoided. Very few candidates were able to state the commercial relationship between the taxpayer, the personal service company and the client in a clear manner.

Part (b)(ii) was done well or very well by the majority of candidates. The only common error was a failure to calculate employer's national insurance contributions in respect of the salary paid.

		ACCA marking scheme	
			Marks
(a)	(i)	The conditions – one mark each	3.0
		Meaning of longer term occupation	1.0
			4.0
		Maximum	3.0
	(ii)	Income tax	
		Taxable property income	2.0
		Allocated equally	1.0
		First five tax years	1.5
		Final tax year	1.0
		Capital gains tax	
		Gift of 20% interest is at no gain, no loss	1.0
		Capital gains tax if the proposals are not carried out	1.5
		Capital gains tax if the proposals are carried out	2.5
		Total saving	0.5
			11.0
		Maximum	10.0
(b)	(i)	The conditions – one mark each	3.0
		Reference to rules used to determine employer, employee relationship	1.0
			4.0
		Maximum	3.0
	(ii)	Income less 5%	1.5
		Deductions for:	
		Salary and pension contributions	1.0
		Employer's NICs on salary	1.0
		Employer's NICs on deemed employment income	1.0
			4.5
		Maximum	4.0
Total			**20.0**

ANSWERS TO PRACTICE QUESTIONS: SECTION 2

50 STELLA AND MARIS (ADAPTED) *Walk in the footsteps of a top tutor*

Key answer tips

This is really two separate questions. The first covers income tax and relief for pension contributions; the second covers pension benefits and inheritance tax exemptions.

Given the heavy emphasis on pensions, this may not have been the most popular question choice in the exam.

Part (a) is similar to questions seen in other P6 exams and tests the pensions annual allowance charge.

Part (b)(i) tests the application of the lifetime allowance for pensions, which had not been examined before this exam.

Part (b)(ii) is a much more straightforward section covering the small gifts exemption and normal expenditure from income.

The highlighted words in the written sections are key phrases that markers are looking for.

(a) **Stella – Income after tax and pension contributions 2016/17**

Tutor's top tips

There are easy marks here for basic income tax computations and for calculating income after tax.

The key to scoring well was recognising that there would also be an excess pension contribution. In order to calculate the annual allowance available you had to consider if there was any unused relief brought forward from the previous three years. Remember the annual allowance is £40,000 for 2016/17 but can be increased by any unused AA in the previous three years, starting with the earliest year first. Note that the AA was £40,000 in 2015/16 and 2014/15, but £50,000 in 2013/14. These amounts are given in the tax rates and allowances in the exam.

The personal pension contributions also extend the basic and higher rate bands.

Note that the excess pension contribution tax liability is calculated using the taxpayer's marginal rate of tax.

There is a tricky technical point to deal with: the pension contribution exceeds the individual's relevant earnings as well as exceeding the annual allowance. However, if you missed this issue you could still score follow through marks and obtain a pass.

KAPLAN PUBLISHING

Income tax liability

	£
Employment income	80,000
Property income	92,000
Net income	172,000
Excess pension contribution (AA charge) (W1)	30,000
Total income	202,000
Less: Personal allowance (W2)	(10,600)
Taxable income	191,400

Analysis of income:
Excess pension contribution £30,000   Other income £161,400

	£
111,785 × 20% (W3)	22,357
49,615 × 40%	19,846
30,000 × 40% (Annual allowance charge)	12,000
191,400	
Income tax liability	54,203

Income after tax and pension contributions

	£
Income received	172,000
Less: Income tax liability	(54,203)
Less: Pension contributions paid (W4)	(74,000)
Income after tax and pension contributions	43,797

Tutorial note

The P6 examining team has stated that credit was also awarded to candidates who calculated the class 1 national insurance contributions on Stella's employment income

ANSWERS TO PRACTICE QUESTIONS: SECTION 2

Workings

(W1) Excess pension contribution

	£
Annual allowance for 2016/17	40,000
Unused annual allowance for three previous tax years:	
2013/14 (£50,000 – £40,000)	10,000
2014/15 (£40,000 – £40,000)	0
2015/16 (£40,000 – £40,000)	0
Maximum gross pension contribution in 2016/17	50,000

Excess pension contribution is £30,000 (£80,000 – £50,000).

(W2) Personal allowance

The pension contributions qualifying for tax relief cannot exceed Stella's net relevant earnings, which are £80,000.

	£
Net income	172,000
Less: Gross PPCs qualifying for tax relief	(80,000)
Adjusted net income	92,000

As ANI is < £100,000; the full personal allowance is available.

(W3) Extended basic and higher rate bands

	£	£
Current bands	31,785	150,000
Add: Gross PPCs qualifying for tax relief	80,000	80,000
Revised bands	111,785	230,000

(W4) Pension contributions paid

The amount actually paid in respect of the pension contribution by Stella is £74,000 (£64,000 (£80,000 × 80%) + £ 10, 000).

(b) (i) Maris – Maximum receivable as a lump sum

Tutor's top tips

You should be aware of the basic rule that 25% of the pension fund can be taken tax free, and you are given the lifetime allowance in the tax rates and allowances. There are easy marks for discussing and applying these.

The value of Maris's pension fund exceeds the lifetime allowance of £1,250,000.

Accordingly, the maximum lump sum which she can take tax-free is restricted to £312,500 (25% × £1,250,000).

The excess of the fund over the lifetime allowance may be taken as a lump sum, subject to an income tax charge at 55% on the value of this excess.

Any withdrawals from the balance of the lifetime allowance will be treated as taxable 'other' income. As Maris is a higher rate taxpayer, these would be taxed at 40%, or possibly 45% if her total income increases above the higher rate limit of £150,000.

(ii) **Inheritance tax – Lifetime exemptions available**

Tutor's top tips

This section should offer easy marks as long as you write down the conditions for the exemptions to apply and refer to the information given in the question wherever possible.

There are 6 marks available, so try to make 6 separately identifiable points in your answer.

Small gift exemption

Maris can make exempt gifts valued at up to £250 each tax year to any number of recipients. If the total value of the gifts to any one recipient exceeds £250, the full value of the gifts will be taxable. The gifts can comprise either cash or shares.

Exemption for normal expenditure out of income

The following conditions must be satisfied for the gifts to be exempt:

– The gift is made as part of Maris's normal expenditure. As she is intending to make regular gifts to her family on their birthdays, she should be able to establish a regular pattern of giving.

– The gift is made out of income, not capital. Maris must therefore give cash, not part of her shareholdings.

– Maris is left with sufficient income to maintain her usual standard of living. As she appears to have fairly significant pension and savings income this condition should be satisfied.

There is no monetary limit on the amount of this exemption.

ANSWERS TO PRACTICE QUESTIONS: SECTION 2

ACCA marking scheme			
			Marks
(a)		Qualifying pension contributions	1.5
		Taxable income	2.0
		Excess pension contribution	3.0
		Income tax liability	2.5
		Net income after tax and pension contributions	2.0
			11.0
		Maximum	10.0
(b)	(i)	Tax free amount	1.5
		Taxed amount	2.5
			4.0
	(ii)	Small gift exemption	3.0
		Exemption for normal expenditure out of income	4.0
			7.0
		Maximum	6.0
Total			20.0

TAXATION OF CORPORATE BUSINESSES

FAMILY COMPANY ISSUES

51 BANDA ROSS (ADAPTED) *Walk in the footsteps of a top tutor*

Key answer tips

Parts (a) and (b) of this question are based on the scenario of an individual setting up a new business either as a sole trader or through a company, with the added twist that the company could be set up as a subsidiary of another company owned by the individual. There are lots of marks here for loss reliefs and calculation of the tax saved.

Part (c) is completely separate and much more straightforward, requiring discussion of a loan to a participator of a close company and the ethical issues related to the non-disclosure of this loan.

The highlighted words in the written sections are key phrases that markers are looking for.

Tutor's top tips

Parts (a) and (b) of this question are very tough, and it would be easy to get bogged down here and not have time to do part (c), which is actually very easy if you have learned the close company rules! There will be up to 5 marks on every exam for ethical issues, and these marks should always be easy to score.

The best approach would be to do part (c) first, and then move on to the opening sections.

The requirement specifically asks for 3 schedules, so make sure you label them as such. You can use the wording from the requirement as headings.

(a) **Banda Ross**

Tax adjusted profit/(loss) of the Aral business

Tutor's top tips

Don't forget to calculate the capital allowances for each accounting period on the equipment and the car, and note that the first accounting period is only 6 months long.

As there is no private use of any of the assets, the capital allowances and adjusted profits for the accounting periods will be exactly the same whether Banda sets up the business as a sole trader or a company.

	Period ending 30 June 2017 £	Year ending 30 June 2018 £	Year ending 30 June 2019 £
Budgeted profit/(loss)	(25,000)	(13,000)	77,000
Pre trading expenditure (£6,000 × 1/2) (Note 1)	(3,000)		
Capital allowances:			
Equipment (Note 2)	(13,479)	(1,781)	(1,461)
Tax adjusted profit/(loss)	(41,479)	(14,781)	75,539

Notes

(1) Expenditure incurred in the seven years prior to the start of trading is treated as tax allowable as if incurred on the first day of trading if it would normally be allowable if incurred whilst trading. Entertaining expenditure however is not allowable whether incurred pre or post trading.

Tutor's top tips

The examiner informed us that candidates who stated as an assumption that the tax adjusted figure has already taken into account the pre-trading expenditure would be given appropriate credit.

(2) **Capital allowances on equipment**

	General pool £	Allowances £
6 months ending 30 June 2017		
Additions: no AIA		
Car	10,875	
Additions qualifying for AIA:		
Cost in January 2017 — 12,500		
Less: AIA (see tutorial note) — (12,500)		12,500
	Nil	
	10,875	
Less: WDA (£10,875 × 18% × 6/12)	(979)	979
TWDV c/f	9,896	
Total allowances		**13,479**
Year ending 30 June 2018		
WDA (18%)	(1,781)	1,781
	8,115	
Year ending 30 June 2019		
WDA (18%)	(1,461)	1,461
TWDV c/f	6,654	

Tutorial note

1   Companies or businesses that are owned by the same person and are 'related' will only be entitled to one AIA which can be allocated between the businesses in whatever proportion the taxpayer chooses.

   'Related' means that the business or companies share premises and/or have similar activities.

2   It is assumed in this answer that of the £250,000, maximum AIA available (£500,000 × 6/12 as it is only a 6 month accounting period), Banda will choose to allocate £12,500 to the Aral business.

3   The car qualifies for an 18% WDA as it has CO_2 emissions of between 76 and 130 g/km.

(b) **Banda Ross**

Tax relief available in respect of the anticipated trading losses.

Tutor's top tips

You need to think very carefully before attempting this section.

If Banda sets up the business as a sole trader, the losses must be matched to tax years before you start thinking about how to relieve them. As this is a new business, you will need to apply the opening year rules.

However, if the business is set up through a company, the loss reliefs will be for chargeable accounting periods, so no further adjustments will be needed.

It is vital that you clearly label your answer so that the marker can see which option you are dealing with.

(i) **Business run as a sole trader**

The anticipated allowable losses for the business are set out below.

	Trading income £	Allowable loss £
2016/17 (1 January 2017 to 5 April 2017) Allowable loss (− £41,479 loss × 3/6)	Nil	(20,740)
2017/18 (1 January to 31 December 2017) Allowable loss (− £41,479 loss + £20,740 used) + (− £14,781 loss × 6/12)	Nil	(28,130)
2018/19 (Year ending 30 June 2018) Allowable loss (− £14,781 loss + (£14,781 × 6/12) used)	Nil	(7,390)

Tutorial note

Remember that when you apply the opening year rules to losses, there is no overlap! Losses can only be relieved once, and if they are matched with two tax years in the assessments, they must be removed from the later year.

Banda can offset the losses against her total income of:

- The year of loss and/or the previous year.
- The three years preceding the year of loss starting with the earliest year.

All of the losses can be used in this way and therefore the possibility of carrying the losses forward has not been considered.

Tutor's top tips

Don't just list all the loss reliefs you know for a sole trader, pick out the ones that are actually going to be useful.

There is no loss relief cap as the trading loss is less than £50,000.

Banda's income throughout the years in which the losses can be relieved (2013/14 to 2018/19) consists of her salary and dividends from Flores Ltd. In any year in which she claims loss relief, she will save the income tax on her employment income only. There will be no saving in respect of her dividend income because the 10% tax credit is not repayable.

The potential tax saving in a particular year is calculated below:

	£
Salary	15,635
Dividend income (£20,250 × 100/90)	22,500
Total income	38,135
Less Personal allowance	(10,600)
Taxable income (basic rate taxpayer)	27,535

Income tax on employment income of £5,035 (£15,635 – £10,600) at 20% is £1,007. This will have been collected under the PAYE system.

The tax refunded if a claim is made against total income is therefore £1,007.

Any loss relieved must be set off before the application of the personal allowance. Accordingly, in order to maximise the tax saved, Banda could claim to offset the losses of the first three tax years in each of three different tax years.

The total tax saved would be £3,021 (£1,007 × 3) as the losses would be set off against 'other income' in preference to dividend income.

Tutor's top tips

The examiner did not require any more detailed computation to prove that the tax saving would be £1,007 each year. He expected you to appreciate that dividend tax credits are non-repayable and therefore the tax saving would only be in respect of 'other non-savings income'.

To prove this is true, consider the carry back of the 2016/17 loss of £20,740 to the tax year 2013/14 as follows:

	Total £	Other £	Dividends £
Salary	15,635	15,635	
Dividends	22,500		22,500
Total income	38,135		
Less: Losses	(20,740)	(15,635)	(5,105)
Net income	17,395	Nil	17,395
Less: Personal allowance	(10,600)		(10,600)
Taxable income	6,795	Nil	6,795
Income tax liability (£6,795 × 10%)			680
Tax credits			
On dividends (£22,500 × 10%) (restricted)			(680)
PAYE			(1,007)
Income tax repayable			(1,007)

(ii) **Business run as a company – Aral Ltd**

Tutor's top tips

There are two possibilities here: the company could either be owned by Banda directly, or could be set up as a 100% subsidiary of Flores Ltd.

The difference is that if it is owned directly by Banda, the losses will only be available for relief against Aral Ltd's profits, as an individual cannot link companies to form a 75% losses group.

However, if Aral Ltd is set up as a subsidiary of Flores Ltd, they would form a 75% group and the losses could be surrendered to Flores Ltd

The anticipated allowable losses for Aral Ltd are set out below.

	Trading income £	Allowable Loss £
6 months ending 30 June 2017	Nil	(41,479)
Year ending 30 June 2018	Nil	(14,781)

Aral Ltd owned by Banda

The losses would have to be carried forward and deducted from the trading profits of the year ending 30 June 2019. Aral Ltd cannot offset the loss in the current period or carry it back as it has no other income or gains.

Aral Ltd owned by Flores Ltd

The two companies will form a group relief group if Flores Ltd owns at least 75% of the ordinary share capital of Aral Ltd. The trading losses could be surrendered to Flores Ltd in the year ending 30 June 2017 and the year ending 30 June 2018. The total tax saved would be £11,252 ((£41,479 + £14,781) × 20%).

Tutor's top tips

Don't forget to include your recommendation. As always, marks will be given if this is consistent with your analysis, even if you have come to the wrong conclusion!

Recommended structure

The Aral business should be established in a company owned by Flores Ltd.

This will maximise the relief available in respect of the trading losses and enable relief to be obtained in the period in which the losses are incurred.

Tutorial note

The whole of the loss for the period ending 30 June 2017 can be surrendered to Flores Ltd as it is less than that company's profit for the corresponding period (i.e. £60,000 (£120,000 × 6/12)).

(c) **Tax implications of there being a loan from Flores Ltd to Banda**

Tutor's top tips

You should have spotted that Flores is a close company, as it is wholly owned by Banda. Note that a close company is one that is controlled either by its directors, or up to five participators

Flores Ltd should have paid tax to HMRC equal to 25% of the loan (i.e. £5,250 (25% × £21,000)). The tax should have been paid on the company's normal due date for corporation tax in respect of the accounting period in which the loan was made (i.e. 1 April following the end of the accounting period).

The tax is due because Flores Ltd is a close company that has made a loan to a participator and that loan is not in the ordinary course of the company's business.

HMRC will repay the tax when the loan is either repaid or written off.

Flores Ltd should have included the loan on Banda's Form P11D in order to report it to HMRC.

Assuming that Banda is not paying interest on the loan, she should have paid income tax on an annual benefit equal to 3% of the amount of loan outstanding during each tax year. Accordingly, for each full year for which the loan was outstanding, Banda should have paid income tax of £126 (£21,000 × 3% × 20%).

Flores Ltd should have paid class 1A NICs in respect of this benefit each year of £87 (£21,000 × 3% × 13.8%).

Interest and penalties may be charged in respect of the tax underpaid by both Flores Ltd and Banda and in respect of the incorrect returns made to HMRC.

Willingness to act for Banda

We would not wish to be associated with a client who has engaged in deliberate tax evasion as this poses a threat to the fundamental principles of integrity and professional behaviour. Accordingly, we should refuse to act for Banda unless she is willing to disclose the details regarding the loan to HMRC and pay the ensuing tax liabilities. Even if full disclosure is made, we should consider whether the loan was deliberately hidden from HMRC or Banda's previous tax adviser.

In addition, companies are prohibited from making loans to directors under the Companies Act unless the transaction has been approved by a resolution of the members of the company. We should advise Banda to seek legal advice on her own position and that of Flores Ltd.

ANSWERS TO PRACTICE QUESTIONS: SECTION 2

Examiner's report

This question concerned a business venture where losses were anticipated. Candidates were asked to produce three distinct schedules, which should have had appropriate headings taken from the requirement; sadly, many failed to do so.

In part (a) candidates were required to calculate the tax adjusted trading profit/loss of the new business.

Part (b), representing almost half of the question, required candidates to determine the tax relief available in respect of the anticipated trading losses depending on the legal structure of the venture. This necessitated some clear thinking, ideally communicated to the examiner via the use of subheadings, such that a distinction was drawn between operating as an unincorporated trader and operating as a company. In many cases there was little evidence of such thinking taking place.

The majority of candidates either ignored the opening year rules for the unincorporated trader or failed to apply them to the situation. To be fair this was a relatively tricky situation due to the presence of the losses but it did seem as though many candidates had forgotten the basic rules governing the taxation of an unincorporated trader.

In order to calculate the potential tax relief it was necessary to determine the taxpayer's income tax liability for the years in which loss relief was available. Candidates had no problems calculating the income but were unsure how to proceed from there. In particular there was a lack of thought with many candidates performing calculations for all years rather than recognising that the income was the same in each year such that only one calculation was necessary.

Answers improved when considering the position of a company but there was a lack of precision when describing the loss reliefs available. There was also some confusion as to whether group relief would be available if the two companies were owned personally by the individual taxpayer (it wouldn't). Finally, there was a general unwillingness to satisfy the requirement and calculate the 'tax relief available'.

The final part of the question concerned a loan from a close company to a participator. Candidates did well in identifying the tax implications of the loan but many ignored the ethical considerations inherent within the question.

PAPER P6: ADVANCED TAXATION (FA2015)

ACCA marking scheme		
		Marks
(a)	Three trading periods	0.5
	Capital allowances on equipment	3.0
	Pre-trading expenditure	1.5
		―――
		5.0
		―――
(b)	Business run as a sole trader:	
	Basis periods	1.5
	Losses	1.5
	Exclusion of overlap losses	1.0
	The reliefs available	2.5
	Total income	1.0
	Dividend credit not repayable	1.0
	Saving in any particular year	2.0
	Total potential tax saving	1.5
	Business run as a company:	
	Allowable losses	1.5
	Aral Ltd owned by Banda	1.5
	Aral Ltd owned by Flores Ltd:	
	Group relief	2.0
	Potential tax saving	1.5
	Recommendation	1.0
		―――
		19.5
	Maximum	18.0
		―――
(c)	Tax implications:	
	Tax payable to HMRC	1.0
	Due date	0.5
	Reasons for tax being due	1.5
	Repayment of tax by HMRC	1.0
	Report on Form P11D	1.0
	Income tax due	1.5
	Interest and penalties	1.0
	Class 1A NICs	1.0
	Willingness to act for Banda:	
	Threat to fundamental principles	1.0
	Require full disclosure	1.0
	Full disclosure may not be enough	0.5
	Legal issue	0.5
		―――
		11.5
	Maximum	8.0
		―――
	Appropriate style and presentation	2.0
	Effectiveness of communication	1.0
	Logical structure	1.0
		―――
		4.0
		―――
Total		**35.0**
		―――

52 SPICA (ADAPTED)

Key answer tips

This question is an exam favourite with the purchase of own shares comparing income and capital treatment.

Since Spica has no other income, her personal allowance and basic rate band are available. This means you cannot use the shortcut method applicable to higher rate taxpayers of saying that tax on a dividend is 25% of the net dividend.

With the capital route you must be careful not to use the entire annual exempt amount as Spica has other gains.

In (a)(ii) you must focus on points to be confirmed.

(a) (i) **The most beneficial tax treatment of the payment received**

The payment received by Spica will be treated as either an income distribution or as capital.

Income treatment

	£
Payment received (8,000 × £8)	64,000
Less: Original subscription price (8,000 × £1.25)	(10,000)
Distribution (Note 1)	54,000
Taxable dividend income (£54,000 × 100/90)	60,000
Less: Personal allowance	(10,600)
Taxable income	49,400

Income tax
£
31,785 × 10%   3,178
17,615 × 32.5%   5,725
─────
49,400

Income tax liability	8,903
Less: Income tax credit (£49,400 × 10%) (Note 2)	(4,940)
Income tax payable	3,963

KAPLAN PUBLISHING   515

Tutorial notes

1   Remember that to calculate the dividend income, you must deduct the original subscription price from the payment irrespective of who subscribed for the shares.

2   The tax credit on the dividend is restricted to that on the dividend actually brought into the charge to tax. In this case, £10,600 of dividend income is covered by the personal allowance, therefore the tax credit is only available on £49,400, not £60,000. However, as this is a rather rare situation, you would still have gained full marks if you had shown the tax credit as £6,000 (£60,000 × 10%).

3   A capital loss of £21,600 [8,000 × (£3.95 − £1.25)] will also arise. Spica cannot claim to offset this capital loss against income as she did not subscribe for the shares. £2,800 of the loss will be offset against her gains in 2016/17 (wasting the annual exempt amount) and the remaining £18,800 will be carried forward.

Capital treatment

	£
Gain qualifying for entrepreneurs' relief	
Sales proceeds (8,000 × £8)	64,000
Less: Cost (8,000 × £3.95)	(31,600)
	32,400
Less: Remainder of the annual exempt amount (£11,100 − £2,800)	(8,300)
Taxable gain	24,100
Capital gains tax (£24,100 × 10%)	2,410

Tutorial note

Entrepreneurs' relief is available as the shares are shares in Spica's personal trading company. Spica has a holding of more than 5%, held for over a year, is an employee of the company and Acrux Ltd is a trading company.

Conclusion

The capital treatment gives rise to the lower tax liability.

(ii) **Ensuring capital treatment**

For the capital treatment to apply, a number of conditions need to be satisfied such that the following points need to be confirmed:

- Spica is UK resident despite living in both the UK and Solaris.
- The transaction is being carried out for the purpose of the company's trade and is not part of a scheme intended to avoid tax.

  This is likely to be the case as HMRC accepts that a management disagreement over the running of the company has an adverse effect on the running of the business.

In addition, Spica must have owned the shares for at least five years so the transaction must not take place until 1 October 2016.

Key answer tips

The question asks for points that must be confirmed.

Since Spica is selling back all her shares, the conditions for substantial reduction of her shareholding, and ceasing to be connected with the company, will automatically be met and will therefore not attract marks.

(b) (i) **Immediate tax implications of accepting employee shareholder shares**

There will be an income tax charge on receipt of the shares.

As Mimosa will own less than 25% of the voting rights in Acrux Ltd, she will be deemed to have paid £2,000 for the shares, and will be subject to tax on the excess.

The income tax charge will be = (£25,000 – £2,000) × 40% = £9,200.

There will be no class 1 national insurance contributions as Acrux Ltd is not a quoted company, therefore the shares are not readily convertible assets.

(ii) **Capital gains tax implications of future disposal**

As the shares are worth less than £50,000, any gain on future disposal will be exempt from capital gains tax.

However, if a loss arises on disposal of the shares, this loss will not be allowable.

Tutorial notes

As Mimosa will own more than 5% of the shares and will be an employee of the company, the shares would qualify for entrepreneurs' relief if they were owned for more than 12 months.

However, this is irrelevant as the gain on disposal will be exempt.

KAPLAN PUBLISHING

(iii) **Other factors to be considered**

Mimosa should also consider the employment rights that she will have to give up as a result of entering the employee shareholder agreement.

She may have to give up rights in relation to statutory redundancy pay, for example.

> **Examiner's report**
>
> The first part on the tax treatment of the purchase of own shares was done well by the majority of candidates. The only common error was the general failure to recognise that, under the income distribution route, the distribution is the amount received less the amount *originally subscribed* for the shares (as opposed to the cost to the shareholder). A minority of candidates did not pick up easy marks by failing to include the personal allowance and/or the annual exemption or by using incorrect rates of tax.
>
> Performance in the second part concerning the conditions for the capital treatment was not as good with many candidates simply listing all of the conditions they could think of as opposed to thinking and identifying the particular conditions that were relevant in these particular circumstances. This meant that time was wasted and that irrelevant conditions were provided at the expense of some that would have earned marks.
>
> *The comments above relate to part (a) of this question. Part (b) replaces the original part (b), which covered areas that are no longer in the syllabus.*

ACCA marking scheme				
				Marks
(a)	(i)	Income treatment		
		Calculation of distribution		1.0
		Gross up by 100/90		0.5
		Personal allowance		0.5
		Income tax liability		1.0
		Income tax credit		0.5
		Capital treatment		
		Capital gain		1.0
		Entrepreneurs' relief		1.5
		Annual exempt amount		1.0
		Capital gains tax liability		0.5
		Conclusion		0.5
				8.0
			Maximum	7.0
	(ii)	Spica UK resident		1.0
		Benefit of company's trade		2.0
		Five Year ownership period		1.0
				4.0
(b)	(i)	Income Tax charge		1.0
		Owns less than 25%: deemed paid £2,000		1.0
		Income tax calculation		1.0
		No NIC as unquoted company		1.0
				4.0

ANSWERS TO PRACTICE QUESTIONS: SECTION 2

			Marks
(ii)	Shares worth less than £50,000		1.0
	Gain exempt		1.0
	Capital losses not allowable		1.0
			3.0
(iii)	Employment rights given up		1.0
	Example		1.0
			2.0
Total			**20.0**

53 JAMES (ADAPTED) *Walk in the footsteps of a top tutor*

Key answer tips

There are three main topic areas covered by this question: share incentive plans, redundancy payments, and the IR35 legislation.

When choosing which optional questions to attempt, you should always look at the number of marks available for each specific area of tax and gauge your knowledge to the level of detail you think the question requires.

In this question, 13 of the 20 marks available are for IR35. Therefore, if you have not studied IR35 in detail, you may find this question hard to pass!

The highlighted words in the written sections are key phrases that markers are looking for.

(a) **Taxation of shares in Quark Ltd and redundancy payment**

Shares in Quark Ltd

Tutor's top tips

Make sure you apply your knowledge to the specific scenario. James will have had some of the shares for more than three years, and some for less than three years, but will not have had any of the shares for more than five years.

There is, therefore, no need to consider or comment on the situation where the shares have been in the plan for five years or more as the first award was less than five years prior to the date on which they will be withdrawn.

No marks would have been given for such comments and time would have been wasted in doing so.

KAPLAN PUBLISHING

Withdrawal of shares

- If the shares have been within the plan for less than three years, income tax and national insurance contributions will be charged on their market value at the time of withdrawal.
- If the shares have been within the plan for more than three years, income tax and national insurance contributions will be charged on the lower of
    (i)   their value at the time they were awarded to James, and
    (ii) their value at the time of withdrawal.

Sale of shares

- The shares will have a base cost for the purposes of capital gains tax equal to their market value at the time of their withdrawal from the plan.

   Accordingly, no capital gain will have arisen on their immediate sale.

Redundancy payment

Any amount of statutory redundancy included within the payment is not subject to income tax or to national insurance contributions.

The first £30,000 of the balance of the payment, as reduced by any amount of tax-free statutory redundancy, will be exempt from income tax and national insurance contributions provided it relates solely to redundancy and is not simply a terminal bonus.

The remainder of the payment will be subject to income tax in full, but not to national insurance contributions.

The payment in lieu of notice will be subject to both income tax and national insurance contributions on the full amount, as it is the normal custom of Quark Ltd to make such payments.

(b) (i) **The effect on James's annual after tax income of working for Proton Ltd rather than Quark Ltd**

Tutor's top tips

The examining team expected you to identify that James would be a higher rate taxpayer regardless of whether he was working for Quark Ltd or Proton Ltd.

Accordingly, he hoped that you would carry out your calculations of the effect on his income after deduction of all taxes 'at the margin'. Using the margin for calculations is a common theme in many P6 questions.

The examining team also said that candidates who prepared full income tax computations were able to score full marks but may have spent more time on them than was necessary and possibly at the expense of time that should be spent on other questions.

	£
Reduction in salary (£70,000 – £48,000)	(22,000)
Reduction in income tax on salary (£22,000 × 40%)	8,800
Reduction in national insurance contributions (£22,000 × 2%)	440
Additional dividend	18,000
Tax on dividend (Note 1)	–
Tax on deemed employment income (£20,207 (W) × 40%)	(8,083)
National insurance on deemed employment income (£20,207 × 2%)	(404)
Fall in James's annual income after all taxes	(3,247)

Working: Deemed employment income

	£	£
Income of Proton Ltd in respect of relevant engagements		80,000
Less: 5% deduction		(4,000)
Reimbursed travel expenses		(1,500)
Salary paid to James		(48,000)
Employer's NIC ((£48,000 – £8,112) × 13.8%)	5,505	
Less: Employment allowance (Note 2)	(2,000)	
		(3,505)
		22,995
Less: Employer's NIC on deemed employment income (£22,995 × 13.8/113.8)		(2,788)
Deemed employment income		20,207

Tutorial note

1   A claim can be made by Proton Ltd for the dividend to be regarded as having been paid out of the deemed employment income and therefore not be subject to income tax in the hands of James.

2   As James is the only employee of Proton Ltd, the £2,000 employment allowance against class 1 secondary NICs is available to reduce the contributions payable by Proton Ltd.

Tutor top tips

If you find it difficult to calculate the effect at the margin in this way, you could compare James' after tax income for each option as shown below.

Alternative approach

	Working for Quark Ltd £	Working for Proton Ltd £
Income tax:		
Salary	70,000	48,000
Dividend	N/A	*Nil
Deemed salary (W)	Nil	20,207
Total income	70,000	68,207
Less: Personal allowance	(10,600)	(10,600)
Taxable income	59,400	57,607

* Dividend excluded as replaced by deemed salary.

£	£			
31,785	31,785	× 20%	6,357	6,357
27,615	25,822	× 40%	11,046	10,329
59,400	57,607			

Income tax liability	17,403	16,686
National insurance:		
(£42,385 – £8,060) × 12%	4,119	4,119
(£70,000 – £42,385) × 2%	552	
(£48,000 – £42,385) × 2%		112
£20,207 × 2%		404
NIC liability	4,671	4,635
Net income (after all taxes):		
Salary	70,000	48,000
Dividend	Nil	18,000
Less: Income tax	(17,403)	(16,686)
Less: NIC	(4,671)	(4,635)
Net income	47,926	44,679
Difference: as above (£47,926 – £44,679)	£3,247	

Tutorial note:

Clearly this approach involves significantly more work for the same number of marks, although it does give the same answer!

(ii) **The effect on James's annual after tax income, if the income of Proton Ltd were not regarded as being in respect of relevant engagements**

	£
Anticipated fall in annual income per part (b)(i)	(3,247)
Income tax and NICs on deemed employment income no longer payable (£8,083 + £404)	8,487
Income tax on dividends (£18,000 × 25%) (see tutorial note)	(4,500)
Increase in James's annual income after all taxes	740

Tutorial note

The effective rate of tax on dividend income that falls within the higher rate band is 25% ((32.5% – 10%) × 100/90).

Tutorial note

It is quite acceptable to use the effective rate of tax on a net dividend in this kind of calculation, provided you make it clear where your figures are coming from.

However, as in part (b)(i), if you find it difficult to calculate the effect at the margin in this way, you could calculate James' net income working for Proton Ltd and compare to his net income as an employee, as shown below.

Alternative approach:

Working for Quark Ltd

	£
Net income after all taxes (as above)	47,926

Working for Proton Ltd

	£
Income tax:	
Salary	48,000
Dividend (£18,000 × 100/90)	20,000
Deemed salary (not applicable)	Nil
Total income	68,000
Less: Personal allowance	(10,600)
Taxable income	57,400

Analysed as: Dividends £20,000, Other income (balance) £37,400

Income tax				£
£				
31,785	× 20%	(Other income)		6,357
5,615	× 40%	(Other income)		2,246
37,400				
20,000	× 32.5%	(Dividend income)		6,500
57,400				

	£
Income tax liability	15,103
Less: Tax credit on dividends (£20,000 × 10%)	(2,000)
Income tax payable	13,103
National insurance:	
(£42,385 – £8,060) × 12%	4,119
(£48,000 – £42,385) × 2%	112
Total national insurance	4,231
Net income after all taxes:	
Salary	48,000
Dividend	18,000
	66,000
Less: Income tax	(13,103)
Less: NIC	(4,231)
Net income	48,666
Increase in net income (£48,666 – £47,926)	740

Tutorial note

Again, this gives the same answer but involves a great deal more work for the same number of marks.

(c) **Specific contractual arrangements**

Tutor's top tips

The arguments to justify that the relationship between Proton Ltd and its customers do not count as 'relevant engagements' per IR35 are the same as the arguments that would be used to justify self-employment as opposed to employment status. Therefore the usual factors that HMRC would look for need to be considered.

However, be careful!

'Having more than one customer' would not score marks here, as it is not something that could be built into a contract. The requirement specifically asks for 'contractual arrangements' that would assist in the argument.

Any THREE of the following:

- Any necessary equipment or tools should be provided by Proton Ltd rather than its customers.
- The degree of the customers' control over when and how the work is carried out by James should be kept to a minimum.
- If James is unable to complete the work he would provide a mutually acceptable substitute.
- Proton Ltd should bear a degree of financial risk, e.g. by quoting fixed contract prices.
- Payments should be made under the contracts by reference to the work done rather than periods of time.
- Proton Ltd should be obliged to correct any unsatisfactory work at its own expense, and to insure against such matters.
- Payments should be made under the contracts in respect of the work carried out. The contracts should not include any provisions whereby payments will be made in respect of illness or holidays.
- Each contract should only come to an end when the work is completed or the contract has been breached in some way.

Tutorial note

The relationships between Proton Ltd and each of its customers will each have to be considered separately.

A contract may be regarded as a relevant engagement if it would have been an employer/employee relationship had it been between the customer and James.

Examiner's report

In part (a), on the whole, candidates had a better knowledge of redundancy payments than they did of share incentive plans. However, candidates with less than perfect knowledge were still able to do well provided they kept going and addressed every aspect of the question. Weaker candidates wasted time by either writing too much or preparing unnecessary calculations of tax liabilities.

The model answer in part (b) shows how the difference between working for Proton Ltd as opposed to Quark Ltd can be calculated in one step but full marks were available to candidates who prepared separate calculations of the two situations and then found the difference between them. Those candidates who had memorised the pro forma used to calculate the deemed employment payment from a personal services company were able to score well. Weaker candidates either did not know the pro forma or failed to take sufficient time in order to understand the scenario and thus produced irrelevant corporation tax computations or incorrect income tax computations.

In the final part of the question candidates had a good knowledge of the features that distinguish an employer/employee relationship from other relationships where services are provided. However, many did not score as well as they could because they referred to the general situation, for example the bearing of financial risk, rather than specific contractual arrangements.

		ACCA marking scheme	
			Marks
(a)		Shares in Quark Ltd	
		Income tax where shares in plan for less than three years	1.0
		Income tax where shares in plan for three years or more	1.5
		Also subject to NICs	0.5
		Capital gains tax on sale	1.0
		Redundancy payment	
		Statutory redundancy	1.0
		£30,000 exemption	1.5
		Not subject to NICs	0.5
		Payment in lieu of notice	1.0
			8.0
		Maximum	7.0
(b)	(i)	Effect of fall in salary net of all taxes	2.5
		Dividend income	0.5
		No tax on dividend income	1.0
		Tax and NICs on deemed employment income	1.0
		Deemed employment income	
		Income	0.5
		5% deduction, travel expenses, salary (0.5 each)	1.5
		Employer's NICs on salary	1.0
		Employer's NICs on deemed payment	1.0
			9.0
		Maximum	8.0
	(ii)	Income tax and NICs no longer payable	1.0
		Income tax on dividends	1.0
			2.0
(c)		One mark for each contractual arrangement	3.0
Total			**20.0**

ANSWERS TO PRACTICE QUESTIONS: SECTION 2

54 FEDORA AND SMOKE LTD (ADAPTED) *Walk in the footsteps of a top tutor*

Key answer tips

There are three separate parts to this question, all covering fairly mainstream areas.

Part (a) covers close company loans to participators.

Part (b) is a typical calculation of the net effect of employing someone. Marginal rates of tax can be used to save time here.

Part (c) requires calculation of a chargeable gain for a part disposal, with a detailed explanation of rollover relief (depreciating assets).

The highlighted words in the written sections are key phrases that markers are looking for.

(a) Repayment of loan

Tutor's top tips

Remember that a company controlled by five or fewer participators (shareholders) is a close company. There are special tax implications for loans to participators.

Even if you failed to spot that Smoke Ltd is a close company, you could still obtain the two and a half marks needed to pass this section by talking about the tax saved on the employment benefit for Fedora, and the class 1A NIC saving for Smoke Ltd.

Smoke Ltd is a close company (as it is controlled by Fedora), that has made a loan to a participator (Fedora).

Accordingly, Smoke Ltd will have paid HM Revenue and Customs £4,600 (25% × £18,400) on 1 January 2012 (i.e. nine months after the end of the year ended 31 March 2011, the year in which the loan was made) (Note 1).

HM Revenue and Customs will repay the £4,600 to the company nine months after the end of the accounting period in which the loan is repaid.

The loan also gives rise to an annual employment income benefit for Fedora of £552 (£18,400 × 3%). This benefit will no longer be charged to income tax once the loan is repaid, saving Fedora £221 (£552 × 40%) each year.

In addition, Smoke Ltd will no longer have to pay class 1A national insurance contributions in respect of the loan benefit. This will save the company £61 (£552 × 13.8% × 80%) (Note 2).

KAPLAN PUBLISHING

Tutorial note

1   The 25% tax charge is due by the normal due date for the CAP in which the loan is made.

2   Class 1A NIC is tax deductible, so would have saved corporation tax at 20%.

    If this NIC is no longer payable, the NIC saving is offset by the corporation tax saving lost, giving a net saving of 80% (100% – 20%).

(b)   **Annual net effect of Smoke Ltd employing Wanda**

Tutor's top tips

Label your answer clearly here: you need to consider the effect on

- Fedora
- Wanda
- Smoke Ltd

You are calculating the net effect on **tax liabilities** (not net income) – so think about how these are going to change.

Fedora is a higher rate taxpayer and is above the NIC upper limit, so a reduction in salary will save income tax at 40% and Class 1 NIC at 2%.

Wanda, however, still has part of her personal allowance available, so marginal rates cannot be used.

	Cost £	Saving £
Fedora		
Reduction in income tax liability (£20,000 × 40%)		8,000
Reduction in national insurance liability (£20,000 × 2%)		400
Wanda		
Increase in income tax liability (W)	1,974	
National insurance liability ((£20,000 – £8,060) × 12%)	1,433	
Smoke Ltd		
Employer national insurance contributions		
Reduction in salary to Fedora (£20,000 × 13.8%)		2,760
Salary to Wanda ((£20,000 – £8,112) × 13.8%)(Note 1)	1,641	
Corporation tax effect (£1,641/£2,760 × 20%) (Note 2)	(328)	(552)
	4,720	10,608
Annual net saving (£10,608 – £4,720)		5,888

ANSWERS TO PRACTICE QUESTIONS: SECTION 2

Tutorial note

1   The employment allowance of £2,000 will have already been deducted from the total class 1 secondary liability of the company and therefore there is no employment allowance deduction against the class 1 secondary contributions in respect of employing Wanda.

2   Note that there is no 20% corporation tax saving in respect of paying the £20,000 to Wanda.

   This is because previously this amount was paid to Fedora and so the total salary paid to Wanda and Fedora (£60,000 + £20,000) is the same as the total salary previously paid to Fedora (£80,000). As the total tax deductible amount in Smoke's corporation tax computation is the same, there is no saving.

   The corporation tax saving is therefore only in respect of the increase and decrease in the class 1 secondary NICs.

Tutor's top tips

Make sure that you highlight the total annual net effect. Even if you have made mistakes, you will still be given credit for consistency and for trying to answer the specific question asked!

Working: Wanda – Increase in income tax liability

	£
Employment income	20,000
Bank interest (Note 1)	470
Less: Personal allowance (Note 2)	(10,600)
Taxable income	9,870
Income tax (£9,870 × 20%)	1,974

Tutorial note

1   Before employment, this was Wanda's only source of income which was covered by her personal allowance and therefore she was a non-taxpayer.

   As a non-taxpayer, Wanda will have been receiving the bank interest gross, therefore the £470 quoted in the question must be the gross amount.

2   Before employment, Wanda did not utilise all of her PA, however she could not transfer any unused allowance to Fedora as he is a higher rate taxpayer.

KAPLAN PUBLISHING

(c) **The sale of the land**

Taxable gain arising on the sale of the land

Tutor's top tips

This is a straightforward F6 level calculation of a chargeable gain on the part disposal of land, with rollover relief following partial reinvestment of the proceeds.

	£
Proceeds	22,000
Less: Cost	
£174,000 × (£22,000 ÷ (£22,000 + £491,000))	(7,462)
Less: Indexation allowance	
((279.5 – 162.6)/162.6)) = 0.719 × £7,462	(5,365)
	9,173
Less: Rollover relief	
Proceeds not spent = (£22,000 – £19,000) = £3,000	
Relief available = balance of the gain = (£9,173 – £3,000)	(6,173)
Taxable gain = chargeable gain (Note)	3,000

Tutorial note

Note that for a company the taxable gain = chargeable gain as there is no annual exempt amount available for companies.

The relief available

Tutor's top tips

Note the requirement here to explain 'in detail'. There are 8 marks available for part (c), so you will need to make your answer as full as possible.

The examiner also asks you to explain how the deferred part of the gain will be charged in the future – a clue that this is rollover relief for a depreciating asset, rather than a non-depreciating asset.

Rollover relief is available in respect of the gain because it has arisen on the disposal of a qualifying asset (land) that has been used for business purposes.

The gain can be rolled over if qualifying assets are purchased for use in the business in the four-year period commencing 1 February 2016.

Plant and machinery only qualifies for rollover relief if it is fixed rather than movable.

On the assumption that the engineering machinery is fixed, and that Smoke Ltd will not purchase any other qualifying assets during the four-year period, the gain that will be charged will be equal to the amount of the proceeds from the sale of the land that has not been used to purchase qualifying assets (i.e. £3,000), with the balance of the gain of £6,173 (£9,173 – £3,000) being deferred.

Machinery has a statutory useful life of less than 50 years and is therefore a depreciating asset for the purposes of rollover relief (tutorial note).

Accordingly, the deferred gain of £6,173 will become chargeable on the earliest of:

- the date on which the machinery is sold
- the date on which the machinery is no longer used in the business; and
- ten years from the date the machinery is purchased (i.e. in March 2027).

Tutorial note

Technically, the definition of a depreciating asset is 'a wasting asset or one which will become a wasting asset in the next ten years'. A wasting asset has a life of 50 years.

Therefore, a depreciating asset is one which has a life of less than 60 years.

Machinery has a statutory life of less than 50 years so it is clearly a depreciating asset for rollover relief purposes.

Examiner's report

In part (a) most candidates identified Smoke Ltd as a close company and went on to point out that the 25% charge paid when the loan was made would be refunded once the loan had been repaid. However, for many candidates that was the end of the story. Stronger candidates pointed out that there would no longer be an income tax liability for Fedora in respect of the employment benefit and the best candidates went on to point out that, consequently, there would no longer be a class 1A liability for Smoke Ltd.

Identifying all of these points was not difficult; most of the candidates in the exam were fully aware of them. However, you will only pick up all of these points if you think about the issues before you start writing.

Although many candidates scored well in part (b), a little bit of thought would have made things much easier. In particular, it was clear that Fedora was a higher rate tax payer and therefore, the tax saved if his salary was reduced by £20,000 would be £8,000 together with national insurance of £400 (at 2%). Many candidates prepared a page or more of calculations of the income tax and national insurance due on the both the old and the new salaries in order to arrive at the difference of £8,400. This represented a lack of thought and a waste of valuable time as the figure of £8,400 was only worth one mark.

In the final part the calculation was done well. However, although the majority of candidates recognised that the relief available was rollover relief, the majority of explanations were not detailed and did not consider a sufficient number of the relevant rules. In particular, many candidates failed to identify that the engineering machinery would be a depreciating asset for the purposes of rollover relief. This may be explained in part by the fact that this was, for many candidates, their final question and time was running out.

PAPER P6: ADVANCED TAXATION (FA2015)

ACCA marking scheme		
		Marks
(a)	Close company loan to participator	1.0
	Payment made to HMRC will be repaid	1.5
	Annual benefit will cease	3.0
		5.5
	Maximum	5.0
(b)	Fedora	
	Income tax	0.5
	National insurance	0.5
	Wanda	
	Income tax	2.0
	National insurance	1.0
	Smoke Ltd	
	National insurance	1.5
	Corporation tax	1.0
	Annual net saving	0.5
		7.0
(c)	Calculation of gain before rollover relief	2.0
	Calculation of gain after rollover relief	1.0
	Land is a qualifying business asset	1.0
	Qualifying period	1.0
	Fixed plant and machinery is a qualifying asset	1.0
	Assumptions	1.0
	Plant and machinery is a depreciating asset	1.0
	Taxation of deferred gain	1.5
		9.5
	Maximum	8.0
Total		**20.0**

55 TRIFLES LTD, VICTORIA AND MELBA (ADAPTED) *Walk in the footsteps of a top tutor*

Key answer tips

This question covers two different areas: purchase of own shares by a company, and the tax implications of a close company. Whilst these areas tend not to appear in every exam, they are tested every few sittings.

Part (a) requires a discussion of the conditions for purchase of own shares, but focuses on just two conditions.

Part (b) requires the calculation of after tax proceeds for both the income and the capital treatment but for the purchase of Victoria's shares only. This section should provide some easy marks.

Part (c) is trickier. It appears to cover loans to participators due to the wording of the information in the question (i.e. 'loan of a motorcycle'), but actually covers the provision of benefits to participators (i.e. 'use of asset' benefit).

The highlighted words in the written sections are key phrases that markers are looking for.

(a) **Purchase of own shares: Conditions for capital treatment**

Tutor's top tips

Read the requirement carefully. You are not required to consider all of the conditions for capital treatment, just the period of ownership and reduction in shareholding.

There will be no marks available for discussing any other conditions.

*To score marks here you must **apply** these conditions to Victoria and to Melba.*

Victoria

Ownership period

As Victoria inherited the shares from her husband, the required ownership period is reduced from five years to three years.

Victoria can include her husband's ownership as well as her own, giving a total ownership period from 1 February 2013 to 28 February 2017.

This is more than three years, therefore Victoria satisfies this condition.

Tutorial note

Even if you did not know that the ownership period was reduced to three years for inherited shares, you could still score some marks here for applying the condition to the facts.

Reduction in level of shareholding

Victoria sells all her shares, and therefore satisfies the 'substantial reduction' in her shareholding test as she disposes of all of her shares.

Tutorial note

Victoria also has a lack of 'connection' to the company after the disposal as she no longer holds any shares in the company. However, the requirement was only to discuss the reduction in holding condition.

Melba

Ownership period

Melba has owned her shares since 1 February 2009. This is longer than the required five years, therefore Melba satisfies this condition.

Reduction in level of shareholding

Tutor's top tips

This is tricky! Remember that once shares are sold back to the company, they will be cancelled, so the total number of shares will be reduced.

Victoria will sell her shares back to the company **before** Melba, so these shares will have already been cancelled.

Before the buy back

Melba will have 1,700 shares from a total of 8,500 (10,000 – 1,500).

This represents a 20% share (1,700/8,500) in the company.

After the buy back

Melba will have 1,250 shares (1,700 – 450) from a total of 8,050 (8,500 – 450).

This represents a 15.5% share (1,250/8,050) in the company.

Melba's new percentage share in the company must be no more than 75% of her old share (i.e. no more than 15% (75% × 20%)).

15.5% is more than 15%, therefore this test is **not** satisfied.

ANSWERS TO PRACTICE QUESTIONS: SECTION 2

Tutorial note

*The 75% (or 25% substantial reduction) test must be applied to the **percentage** shareholding, not the number of shares.*

If you got this wrong, or if you missed the fact that Victoria's shares had already been cancelled, you could still score follow-through marks here for applying the 75% test and for coming to a conclusion.

As well as the 75% test, Melba must also own no more than 30% of the remaining shares after the repurchase. There were no marks for discussing this, as the requirement was only to discuss the reduction in holding condition.

(b) **Victoria: after tax proceeds from purchase of shares**

Capital treatment

Gain qualifying for entrepreneurs' relief (Note 1)

	£
Proceeds (1,500 × £30)	45,000
Less: Cost (probate value) (Note 2)	(16,000)
	29,000
Less: Capital loss brought forward	(4,100)
	24,900
Less: Annual exempt amount	(11,100)
Taxable gains	13,800
Capital gains tax (£13,800 × 10%)	1,380
After tax proceeds (£45,000 – £1,380)	43,620

Tutorial note

1. *Victoria will have been a director of the company and held at least 5% of the shares for the 12 months prior to the disposal, and will therefore qualify for entrepreneurs' relief.*

2. *Where shares are inherited from a spouse, the deemed cost to the recipient for capital gains tax purposes is the probate value.*

   If the shares were transferred during lifetime, the transfer would be at no gain, no loss and the recipient would take over the original cost.

Income treatment

	£
Proceeds (1,500 × £30)	45,000
Less: Original subscription price (1,500 × £2)	(3,000)
Distribution (Note 1)	42,000
Income tax (£42,000 × 25%) (Note 2)	10,500
After tax proceeds (£45,000 – £10,500)	34,500

Tutorial note

1   Remember that to calculate the deemed dividend income (i.e. distribution), you must deduct the original subscription price from the payment irrespective of who subscribed for the shares, and regardless of any price actually paid for the shares.

2   As Victoria is a higher rate taxpayer, the effective rate of tax suffered on the deemed dividend (i.e. distribution) is 25% (i.e. 100/90 × (32.5% – 10%)).

There would be no withdrawal of the personal allowance, as Victoria's total taxable income would be less than £100,000 (£50,000 + (£42,000 × 100/90) = £96,667).

3   A capital loss of £13,000 (£3,000 – £16,000) will also arise. Victoria cannot claim to offset this capital loss against income as she did not subscribe for the shares. This loss therefore has no effect on the current period's after tax proceeds but may reduce tax on a future capital gain.

(c)   **Tax implications of the loan of the motorcycle**

Tutor's top tips

The key to success here was to spot that Trifles Ltd is a close company.

Look out for this as many 'Ltd' companies are owned by only a few shareholders and are therefore close companies.

Remember that there are special rules governing the provision of loans and benefits to participators in a close company.

Trifles Ltd is controlled 5 or fewer shareholders (participators), and is therefore a close company.

Implications for Melba

The provision of the motorcycle to Melba will be treated as a distribution, as Melba will not be an employee of Trifles Ltd after the sale of her shares.

The value of the benefit, calculated using the income tax rules, will be treated as a net dividend:

	£
Use of asset (£9,000 × 20%) (Note 1)	1,800
Less: Contribution (£30 × 12)	(360)
Distribution	1,440
Income tax (£1,440 × 25%) (Note 2)	360

Tutorial notes

1   The loan of the motorcycle will be treated as a 'use of asset' benefit each year Melba has the use of the motorcycle.

2   As Melba is a higher rate taxpayer, the effective rate of tax suffered on the deemed dividend (i.e. distribution) is 25% (i.e. 100/90 × (32.5% – 10%)).

If Melba was still an employee, the motorcycle would be treated as a normal employment benefit, and would be taxed at 40% in the normal way.

Implications for Trifles Ltd

Tutor's top tips

You will be given marks here for consistency!

Remember that dividends are not allowable expenses for companies, so it follows that if the loan of the motorcycle is to be treated as a dividend, none of the associated expenses are deductible.

However, if you missed the fact that Trifles Ltd is a close company and that Melba will no longer be an employee, you may have treated the motorcycle as a normal employment benefit. In this case, you will be given marks here for saying that costs will be allowable and employer's class 1A NIC will be due.

Trifles Ltd will not be able to claim capital allowances on the motorcycle, and there will be no allowable deduction for any running costs.

Examiner's report

Many candidates answered part (a) well but others, with similar knowledge levels, did not perform well because they failed to answer the question. Rather than addressing the two particular conditions set out in the question, this latter group attempted to address all of the conditions despite the majority of them being irrelevant.

Candidates had a good knowledge of the five-year rule and the 30% rule but were much less comfortable with the condition relating to the shareholder's interest in the company following the purchase. The rules require the shareholder's interest to be no more than 75% of the interest prior to the purchase – this is not the same as the shareholder selling 25% of his shares because the shares sold are cancelled thus reducing the number of issued shares.

Only a minority of candidates were aware that the ownership period of the husband could be added to that of the wife. Even fewer knew that the usual five-year ownership period is reduced to three where the shares are inherited.

Part (b) was answered well by the vast majority of candidates. The only point that many candidates missed was the availability of entrepreneurs' relief. It was particularly pleasing to see the majority of candidates correctly identify the after tax proceeds as the amount received less the tax liability (as opposed to the taxable amount less the tax liability).

The final part of the question was more difficult and, unsurprisingly, caused more problems. The question concerned the loan of a motorcycle to a shareholder in a close company who was not an employee. Candidates had no problem recognising that the company was a close company but many then decided that this was a loan to a participator as opposed to the loan of an asset.

Another relatively common error was to state, correctly, that the benefit would be treated as a distribution but to then give an incorrect tax rate of 40%. Candidates would benefit from slowing down and ensuring that they apply their basic tax knowledge correctly in the exam.

ACCA marking scheme		
		Marks
(a)	Victoria	
	Period of ownership	2.5
	Reduction in level of shareholding	0.5
	Melba	
	Period of ownership	1.0
	Reduction in level of shareholding	3.0
		7.0
(b)	Capital receipt	4.0
	Income receipt	3.0
		7.0
(c)	Close company	1.5
	Melba	
	Recognition of distribution	1.5
	Supporting calculations	2.0
	Trifles Ltd	1.0
		6.0
Total		**20.0**

56 SANK LTD AND KURT LTD (ADAPTED) *Walk in the footsteps of a top tutor*

Key answer tips

This question covers several different areas including instalment payments for large companies, validity of a compliance enquiry, claiming AIA on machinery and the enhanced relief available for research and development expenditure.

Part (a) requires an explanation and computation of the instalment payments and detailed knowledge of HMRC compliance check rules.

Part (b) examines two popular areas in the P6 exam: the annual investment allowance for plant and machinery and the tax relief for R&D expenditure.

The highlighted words in the written sections are key phrases that markers are looking for.

(a) **Sank Ltd**

Tutor's top tips

The term 'related 51% group company' has been introduced in FA2015.

The requirement to this part is to explain the meaning (i.e. give the definition) of a related 51% group company and then to explain the significance of there being a large number of such companies in a group.

(i) **Related 51% group companies**

Definition

Two companies are related 51% group companies if:

- one is a 51% subsidiary of the other, or
- both are 51% subsidiaries of a third company.

A 51% subsidiary is one where more than 50% of the ordinary share capital is directly or indirectly owned.

Significance

- To determine the due date of payment of corporation tax, it is important to determine whether or not a company is large.
  A company is large if its augmented profits (taxable total profits (TTP) plus franked investment income (FII)) exceed the statutory threshold.
  The threshold is £1,500,000 divided by the number of related 51% companies in the group at the end of the previous chargeable accounting period.
- Accordingly, if Sank Ltd has a large number of related 51% companies, it will be more likely to pay corporation tax by quarterly instalments.

Tutorial note

Note that if two companies are over 50% owned by an individual they are not related 51% group companies. Companies can only be linked through a corporate parent company..

You could also mention that dividends received from related 51% group companies are ignored in the calculation of FII – but this is not directly relevant to answering the question of the significance of there being a large number of related 51% companies in a group.

Tutor's top tips

The examining team like to test the detail of the quarterly instalment system for payment of corporation tax.

Note that the requirement in the next part is to **explain** with supporting calculations. This means that there will be marks for written explanations as well as dates and figures.

There are really three aspects to deal with here:

- Why quarterly payments are required.
- How the quarterly instalment system works for a short CAP, with dates.
- The effect of an increase in expected profits and, consequently, the expected liability, meaning that the company has underpaid its corporation tax.

(ii) **Increase in the budgeted corporation tax liability**

– 11 m/e 30 September 2016

Sank Ltd's corporation tax liability for the period is expected to be £150,000 (£750,000 × 20%).

Sank Ltd will be a 'large' company (per the question, its augmented profits for the period will exceed the threshold and it has a large number of related 51% group companies).

It is required to pay its corporation tax liability for the period in instalments because it was also large in the previous accounting period.

The payments required are:

14 May 2016	3/11 of the final liability for the period
14 August 2016	3/11 of the final liability for the period
14 November 2016	3/11 of the final liability for the period
14 January 2017	2/11 of the final liability for the period

A payment should have been made on 14 May 2016 of £34,909 (£640,000 × 20% × 3/11), based on the budget prepared on 31 March 2016.

However, if the new figure of taxable total profits is correct, the payment required on that day was £40,909 (£750,000 × 20% × 3/11), and so the company has underpaid.

Interest will be charged from 14 May 2016 until the additional £6,000 (£40,909 – £34,909) is paid. The total interest due will be calculated by HM Revenue and Customs, once the corporation tax return has been submitted.

Future payments (i.e. from 14 August 2016 onwards) should be based on the latest budgeted figures in order to minimise interest charges.

Tutorial note

Large companies have to pay tax quarterly if the company was large in the previous chargeable accounting period (CAP) as well.

If the CAP is less than 12 months the instalments are computed using the formula:

3/n × estimated corporation tax liability

where n = the number of months in the accounting period.

Here, the accounting period is 11 months in length so the payments would be:

3/11, 3/11, 3/11 and finally the balance 2/11.

The first payment is always paid on the 14th day of the seventh month following the start of the CAP which would be 14 May 2016.

The next two payments are made three months after the previous payment and the last payment is due 2 months after the penultimate payment.

Note that the final payment is always due on the 14th day of the fourth month after the end of the CAP.

However, you do not need to learn all of this as long as you remember the first payment date and that:

- *if the following payment is paying a full three months of tax, the pay day is three months after the previous payment date*
- *if it is paying less than three months worth of tax (i.e. two or one months worth), the pay day is the appropriate number of months later (i.e. two or one month after the previous payment date).*

(iii) **Circumstances necessary for a compliance check enquiry to be valid**

Tutor's top tips

This part of the question covers an area that is not often tested in the exam: HMRC compliance checks.

There are only three marks available here, so it is still possible to score a good pass on the question as a whole even if you haven't learnt the rules regarding compliance checks.

The deadline for raising a notice of intention to carry out a compliance check depends on when the corporation tax return was filed.

KAPLAN PUBLISHING

Where the return was filed on time (i.e. by 31 October 2014), the notice must be raised by 31 October 2015.

Where the return was submitted late, the notice must be raised by the first quarter day following the first anniversary of the date on which the return was submitted.

The quarter days are: 31 January, 30 April, 31 July and 31 October.

Accordingly, an notice dated 31 May 2016 will only be valid if the corporation tax return was submitted after 30 April 2015.

Tutorial note

Companies must submit their tax return 12 months after the end of the CAP and HMRC must usually raise a notice of intention to carry out a compliance check within 1 year of that date.

However, if a tax return is submitted late then the notice must be raised by the first quarter date following the anniversary of the late return.

(b) **Kurt Ltd**

Tutor's top tips

Think carefully before you answer this part of the question.

It is tempting to focus on the relief available for research and development expenditure, but half of the marks available are for discussing capital allowances for plant and machinery.

Machinery

A 100% annual investment allowance is available for expenditure on machinery up to a maximum of £500,000 for a 12-month period.

The maximum amount available to Kurt Ltd for the period ended 31 March 2016 is therefore £333,333 (£500,000 × 8/12).

However, only one annual investment allowance is available to companies that are related to each other. The other companies controlled by Mr Quinn will be regarded as related to Kurt Ltd for the purposes of AIA if they share premises or carry on similar activities.

Mr Quinn can choose to allocate the allowance available to related companies in the most tax efficient manner.

The excess of the expenditure over the available annual investment allowance will be eligible for a writing down allowance of 12% (18% × 8/12) in the period to 31 March 2016.

ANSWERS TO PRACTICE QUESTIONS: SECTION 2

Tutorial note

An AIA of £500,000 is assumed to be available each year but this must be time apportioned as the accounting period is only 8 months in length.

The AIA is shared between related businesses (51% groups, or businesses under common control that share the same premises or have the same activities).

The WDA of 18% must also be time apportioned.

Scientific research

Tutor's top tips

As well as explaining the relief available for research and development expenditure, you were asked to 'comment on any choices available to the company'.

Remember that the surrender of R&D losses for an immediate tax credit is optional, so you need to explain what will happen if the company chooses not to claim this relief and advise on the factors that must be considered in making that choice (i.e. timing of relief vs. tax saving).

Kurt Ltd is a small enterprise for the purposes of research and development. Accordingly, the expenditure of £28,000 will result in tax deductions of £64,400 (£28,000 × 230%).

Kurt Ltd can choose to claim a repayment of 14.5% of the lower of its trading loss and £64,400. This relief is an alternative to carrying the loss forward against future profits of the same trade.

Kurt Ltd should consider claiming the 14.5% repayment if cash flow is its main priority. Alternatively, if the company wishes to maximise the tax saved in respect of the expenditure, it should carry the loss forward; it will then save tax at a rate of 20% (provided it succeeds in becoming profitable).

Tutorial note

SMEs can claim a total allowable deduction of 230% on qualifying research and development. This can include staff costs, materials and software.

Where the enhanced deduction for R&D produces a trading loss it is possible to exchange the loss for an immediate cash repayment of just 14.5%.

This relief is only beneficial for companies that have cash flow problems, as it is more tax efficient to carry forward the loss against future profits to achieve a corporation tax saving of 20%.

KAPLAN PUBLISHING

> **Examiner's report**
>
> Part (a) concerned the payment of corporation tax by Sank Ltd and compliance checks. The payment of corporation tax appeared to be fairly straightforward but care was needed if sufficient marks were to be earned.
>
> The majority of candidates did not realise that interest would be charged on any quarterly payment that was less than a quarter of the company's final tax liability of the period. Weaker candidates confused quarterly accounting with the payments of income tax by individuals and thought that the payments were paid on account by reference to the liability for the previous year.
>
> *Note that this part of the question has been adapted since the question was originally set.*
>
> Part (a)(ii) related to compliance checks into a corporation tax return. It required candidates to explain the validity of the compliance check enquiry 'in relation to the date on which (it)...... was raised'. Many candidates simply wrote about compliance check enquiries generally such that this part of the question was not answered well.
>
> Part (b) related to capital allowances and scientific research. Most candidates produced reasonable answers but many would have done better if they had simply read the question more carefully and identified the relevance of all of the information and slowed down. In particular, many candidates wrote about the basic rules at some length rather than thinking about the particular situation of the question.
>
> The owner of the company concerned owned three other companies. This information was intended to elicit a discussion of the need to split the annual investment allowance between the companies. However, many candidates wrote instead about the unavailability of group relief. The question also pointed out that the relevant accounting period was only eight months. This meant that the annual investment allowance and the writing down allowance needed to be multiplied by 8/12. However, this point was missed by many candidates.
>
> A significant number of candidates were of the opinion that, because the company was loss-making, it should not claim all of its capital allowances. It should be remembered that, where the annual investment allowance is concerned, failing to claim allowances in full will considerably slow down the time it takes for a tax deduction to be obtained for the cost incurred as, in the future, there will only be a 18% writing down allowance on a reducing balance basis. Accordingly, there needs to be a strong reason not to claim allowances in full. Such a reason might include the situation where there are insufficient profits in the group to relieve a company's losses in the current year and any losses carried forward are likely to be locked inside the company for a considerable period of time. In such a situation it may be worthwhile claiming reduced capital allowances in the current year in order to have increased capital allowances in future years that can then be group relieved.
>
> The tax treatment of the expenditure on scientific research was explained well by the majority of candidates, many of whom were aware that there was a possibility of claiming a 14.5% repayment. However, very few candidates attempted to evaluate whether or not the repayment should be claimed.

ANSWERS TO PRACTICE QUESTIONS: **SECTION 2**

ACCA marking scheme			
			Marks
(a)	(i)	Definition of 51% related group company	1.5
		Significance of a large number	1.5
			3.0
	(ii)	Corporation tax	
		Payments required	3.0
		Payment already made	1.5
		Interest	1.0
		Future payments	0.5
			6.0
	(iii)	Deadlines	2.5
		Conclusion	1.0
			3.5
		Maximum	3.0
(b)		Equipment	
		Annual investment allowance	3.0
		Writing down allowance	1.0
		Scientific research	
		Tax deduction	1.0
		Repayment	2.0
		Evaluation	2.0
			9.0
		Maximum	8.0
Total			**20.0**

KAPLAN PUBLISHING

57 BANGER LTD AND CANDLE LTD (ADAPTED) *Walk in the footsteps of a top tutor*

>
>
> **Key answer tips**
>
> This question has two unrelated parts. However, both parts deal with the rules for close companies.
>
> In part (a)(i) the focus is on a benefit to a shareholder who is not an employee and should not have posed any problems.
>
> Part (a)(ii) is trickier and covers the effect of making distributions before or after the appointment of a liquidator.
>
> Part (a)(iii) requires knowledge of disincorporation relief and application to the scenario.
>
> Part (b) requires a corporation tax computation for a close investment-holding company which has overseas gains and has received shares and cash as part of a takeover of one of its investments. There are some tricky points to deal with here but there are also a number of easy marks for corporation tax basics.
>
> The highlighted words in the written sections are key phrases that markers are looking for.

(a) **Banger Ltd**

   (i) **Minority shareholder's taxable income in respect of the use of the motor car**

   >
   >
   > *Tutor's top tips*
   >
   > *It is important to start by identifying Banger Ltd as a close company. Students often lose marks for not stating what seems obvious to them!*

   The minority shareholder is not employed by Banger Ltd. Accordingly, because Banger Ltd is a close company (it is controlled by Katherine), the use of the motor car will be treated as a distribution.

   The distribution will equal the amount that would have been taxable as employment income in respect of the motor car as set out below:

   (£22,900 × 18%) = £4,122.

   The taxable income to include in the shareholder's income tax computation will be the distribution multiplied by 100/90 (i.e. £4,122 × 100/90 = £4,580).

   >
   >
   > *Tutorial note*
   >
   > *If the minority shareholder was employed by Banger Ltd then the car benefit would be taxed on them using the normal employment income rules.*

Working: Appropriate percentage

CO_2 emissions = 117 g/km, petrol car

Appropriate percentage = 14% + (115 − 95) × 1/5 = 18%

(ii) **The tax implications of the distributions being considered**

Tutor's top tips

Note that the requirement is to explain the tax implications for:

(1) The minority shareholders

(2) Katherine.

To maximise your chances of success, you need to write about both of these and you must make sure that your answer is clearly labelled.

- **The distribution of cash to minority shareholders**

    The distribution of cash is to be made prior to the appointment of the liquidator and will therefore be taxed as a normal dividend.

    It will be grossed up at 100/90 and subject to income tax at 10%, 32.5% and 37.5%, depending on the tax position of the individual shareholders.

    A 10% tax credit will be available.

Tutorial note

There is no difference in the way that minority and majority shareholders are taxed on their dividends. The only difference is the amount they receive.

- **The distribution of the building to Katherine**

    The distribution is to be made after the appointment of the liquidator and will therefore be taxed as a capital receipt.

    The market value of the building will be treated as the sales proceeds received for Katherine's shares in Banger Ltd from which the base cost of the shares (or part of the base cost if there are to be further distributions to Katherine) will be deducted in order to calculate the capital gain.

    The gain will be taxable at 18% and/or 28% depending on Katherine's tax position or, alternatively, at 10% where entrepreneurs' relief is available.

    Banger Ltd is a trading company. Accordingly, entrepreneurs' relief will be available, provided Katherine has both owned at least 5% of the shares and been employed by Banger Ltd for a period of at least a year ending with the date of disposal (i.e. the date of the distribution).

(iii) **The tax implications of the distribution of the building for Banger Ltd**

Tutorial note

The distribution of cash will be a normal dividend with no tax implications for Banger Ltd. However, the requirement just asks you to write about the transfer of the building.

A dividend paid in the form of an asset other than cash is known as a 'dividend in specie'.

Such dividends are treated as a normal dividend in the hands of the recipient and the company if they occur before the appointment of the liquidator.

However, if the distribution occurs after the appointment of the liquidator, it is treated as a capital receipt in the hands of the recipient and a capital disposal in the hands of the company distributing the asset.

The distribution of the building (a dividend in specie) will give rise to a deemed disposal of the building by Banger Ltd at market value.

This will result in a chargeable gain or allowable loss equal to the market value of the building less its cost. Indexation allowance will be deducted from any chargeable gain arising.

Availability of disincorporation relief

Disincorporation relief will not be available as:

- The business is not being transferred as a going concern, and
- The total market value of the building is more than £100,000.

Tutorial note

To qualify for disincorporation relief, the following conditions must be satisfied:

- The business must be transferred as a going concern.
- All of the assets of the business (apart from cash) must be transferred to the shareholders.
- The total market value of land and buildings and goodwill must not exceed £100,000.
- All of the shareholders to whom the business is transferred must be individuals who have held their shares in the company for the 12 months prior to the date of transfer.

If available, disincorporation relief must be claimed within two years of the date on which the business is transferred. The claim must be made jointly by the shareholders and the company.

The relief operates by deeming the sale proceeds received by the company to be equal to the lower of cost and market value. This means that no gain would arise within the company on the disposal of the building, and therefore no tax would be payable.

(b) **Candle Ltd**

Corporation tax liability – year ended 31 March 2016

Tutorial note

A close investment-holding company has no trade so Candle Ltd's taxable profits will come from its worldwide rents (none here), non-trading loan relationship income and capital gains.

Management expenses can be deducted from total profits.

Tutor's top tips

Even if you were not sure how to deal with the shares in Rockette, there are some easy marks here for grossing up the overseas gains and calculating the deficit on the non-trading loan relationships.

You could present the computation in one column as shown below or with separate columns for the Total, UK and overseas profits.

	£
Chargeable gains realised in Sisaria (£15,580 × 100/82)	19,000
Chargeable gains realised in the UK	83,700
Sale of shares in Rockette plc (Explanation 1)	Nil
	102,700
Less: Deficit on non-trading loan relationships (W)	(25,800)
General expenses of management	(38,300)
Taxable total profits	38,600
Corporation tax at 20% (Explanation 2)	7,720
Less: Double tax relief	
Lower of	
(i) UK tax on overseas gain = (£19,000 × 20%) = £3,800	
(ii) Overseas tax = (£19,000 × 18%) = £3,420	(3,420)
Corporation tax liability	4,300

Working: Deficit on non-trading loan relationships

	£
Interest receivable	41,100
Interest payable	(52,900)
Fees charged by financial institution	(14,000)
	(25,800)

It has been assumed that the company has chosen to offset the deficit against its current period profits.

Tutor's top tips

The examining team asks you to state your assumptions, so you will be given credit for doing this.

Tutorial note

Candle Ltd will choose to offset the expenses of management and the deficit on the non-trading loan relationship against profits other than the chargeable gains realised in Sisaria in order to maximise double tax relief.

Explanation: Disposal of shares in Rockette plc

The disposal of the shares in Rockette plc was a qualifying share for share disposal because Piro plc acquired more than 25% of Rockette plc and the acquisition was a commercial transaction that did not have the avoidance of tax as one of its main purposes. Accordingly, no gain arose in respect of the shares received.

In addition, no gain arose in respect of the cash received because the cash represented less than 5% of the value of the total consideration received as set out below:

	£
Value of shares received in Piro plc	147,100
Cash received	7,200
	154,300

Cash received represents 4.67% of the total consideration.

Tutorial note

Where cash is received on a takeover, there is a deemed part disposal.

However, where the cash proceeds received are small, there is no chargeable gain arising at that time.

> *The definition of small in this context is that the cash proceeds are:*
>
> *(i)   ≤ 5% of the of the total consideration received for the original shares, or*
>
> *(ii)   ≤ £3,000.*

Tutor's top tips

Most of the marks here are for identifying that this is a share for share exchange and explaining the reasons for this.

If you did not spot that the cash consideration was less than 5% of the total consideration then you would have wasted some time calculating a gain but lost practically no marks.

Examiner's report

In part (a)(i), almost all candidates were able to calculate the benefit in respect of the use of the car but not all of them realised that this would be taxed as a distribution rather than employment income. Many of those who knew this point still failed to earn full marks because they did not state the reasons for this treatment; those reasons being that the company is a close company and that the individual is not an employee.

Performance in part (a)(ii) of the question was mixed. Those candidates who did not do well either did not know the rules or were not careful enough in addressing the requirements. A lack of knowledge of the rules was unfortunate and not something that could easily be rectified in the exam room. Failure to address the requirements carefully was a greater shame as potentially easy marks were lost. The requirement asked for the tax implications for 'Banger Ltd, the minority shareholders and Katherine'. Most candidates dealt with the minority shareholders and Katherine but many omitted the implications for Banger Ltd.

Candidates should always read the requirement carefully and identify all of the tasks. It would have been helpful then to use sub-headings for each of the three aspects of the requirement to ensure that all of the aspects of the requirement were addressed.

Note that this part of the question has been adapted since the question was originally set.

On the whole, part (b) was done quite well by many candidates.

The two more difficult areas of this part of the question concerned loan relationships and a share for share disposal. The loan relationships issue was not done well. The vast majority of candidates failed to apply the basic rules such that they did not offset the amounts in order to arrive at a deficit on non-trading loan relationships.

This was not a difficult or obscure matter; it simply felt as though candidates were not giving themselves the time to think before answering the question.

The share for share disposal was identified by the vast majority of candidates who went on to point out that no chargeable gain would arise in respect of the shares. There was then a further mark for recognising that there would also be no gain in respect of the cash received as it amounted to less than 5% of the total consideration received. This point was picked up by only a small number of candidates.

PAPER P6: ADVANCED TAXATION (FA2015)

ACCA marking scheme					
					Marks
(a)	(i)	Explanation			2.0
		Calculations			1.5
					3.5
				Maximum	3.0
	(ii)	Shareholders – distribution of cash			1.5
		Katherine			
			Capital gain		1.5
			Taxation		2.5
					5.5
				Maximum	4.0
	(ii)	Banger Ltd – capital gain			1.5
		Disincorporation relief			2.0
					3.5
				Maximum	3.0
(b)		Taxable total profits			
		Loan relationships			3.5
		Chargeable gains			1.5
		Sale of shares in Rockette plc			0.5
		Expenses of management			0.5
		Corporation tax liability			
		Corporation tax			0.5
		Double tax relief			1.0
		Explanation of treatment of shares			3.0
					10.5
				Maximum	10.0
Total					**20.0**

58 BAMBURG LTD *Walk in the footsteps of a top tutor*

Key answer tips

This question was the least popular of the optional questions when it was set, yet was the easiest.

Part (a) requires explanation of the conditions for joining the flat rate scheme and the advantages and disadvantages of doing so. This is very straightforward and the VAT schemes for small businesses such as the cash accounting, annual accounting and flat rate schemes are regularly examined.

Part (b) requires an explanation of the tax and financial implications of selling a machine. Once again there are lots of easy marks available if you understand capital allowances and holdover relief.

Finally, in part (c) the examining team expects you to calculate the after tax proceeds of a payment of £14,000 as either a bonus or a dividend. This is very straightforward as long as you realise that Charlotte is a higher rate taxpayer and use the marginal rates of tax.

The question also asks you to explain the tax implications of a close company making an interest free loan to a shareholder. Close companies are regularly examined and this was very straightforward with most well prepared students scoring full marks here.

The highlighted words in the written sections are key phrases that markers are looking for.

Tutor's top tips

The question is broken down into 4 parts with each part worth 5 marks so it is important to manage your time effectively so that you attempt all parts of the question.

Where there are 5 marks available in a written question, try and make sure you have at least 5 distinct points to earn all the marks.

Avoid spending too long on the computations.

(a) **Value added tax (VAT) – Flat rate scheme**

Tutor's top tips

The flat rate scheme is available to small businesses with a good VAT record whose taxable supplies do not exceed £150,000 per year. It works by simply multiplying VAT inclusive sales by a fixed % given by HMRC.

Benefits include simplicity, no requirement to keep detailed purchase records and a reduced VAT liability.

However, before Bamburg Ltd joins the scheme, it is necessary to do two VAT calculations: one based on the normal calculation (output VAT less input VAT) and one based on the liability under the flat rate scheme.

Bamburg Ltd should only join the flat rate scheme if this results in a lower VAT liability.

Bamburg Ltd will be permitted to join the flat rate scheme provided its taxable supplies for the next year are not expected to exceed £150,000.

On the basis that its budgeted taxable supplies for the year ending 31 March 2017are expected to be £114,000 (£120,000 – £6,000), it is likely that this condition will be satisfied.

Bamburg Ltd currently pays VAT to HM Revenue and Customs (HMRC) equal to the output tax on its standard rated sales less its recoverable input tax.

Under the flat rate scheme, the company would pay HMRC a fixed percentage of the total of its VAT inclusive sales. Exempt supplies are included in sales for this purpose. The percentage will depend on the particular business sector in which Bamburg Ltd operates.

Whether or not it is financially beneficial for Bamburg Ltd to join the flat rate scheme will depend on the percentage which it is required to use. However, the scheme is mainly intended to reduce administration and any financial benefit is unlikely to be significant.

(b) **Implications of selling the 'Cara' machine**

Tutor's top tips

The 'Cara' machine satisfies the functional test and would be eligible for capital allowances, all of which have been claimed in the past. Now, when the machine is sold a balancing adjustment will arise based on the difference between the tax written down value and the sale proceeds.

As capital allowances have been claimed on the machine, HMRC do not permit the capital loss to be claimed as well. However, if a capital gain arises the gain is taxable.

Remember that as the machine is a depreciating asset the deferred gain is held over separately and does not reduce the cost of the depreciating asset.

The tax written down value on the main pool of Bamburg Ltd is £Nil. Accordingly, the sale of the machine will result in a balancing charge equal to the sales proceeds received of £80,000. This will increase the taxable trade profit of Bamburg Ltd.

The 'Cara' machine is a depreciating asset for the purposes of rollover relief. Accordingly, the chargeable gain of £13,000 which was deferred in respect of the purchase of the 'Cara' machine will become chargeable when the machine is sold. This will increase the taxable total profit of Bamburg Ltd in the year of sale.

No capital loss will arise on the sale of the machine because it will have qualified for capital allowances.

Even if a capital loss were to arise in respect of the sale, it could only be offset against chargeable gains and not against profits generally.

In summary, Bamburg Ltd will receive proceeds of £80,000 but will have to pay additional corporation tax of £18,600 ((£80,000 + £13,000) × 20%).

Once the machine has been sold, Bamburg Ltd will have to pay rent in respect of the replacement machine. This represents an outflow of cash for the company, although it will be an allowable deduction when computing the company's taxable trading profit.

Tutorial note

When a capital gain is held over against a depreciating asset, the gain is postponed until the earliest of three events.

(1) Sale of replacement asset.

(2) Replacement asset ceases to be used in the trade.

(3) 10 years after the replacement asset is bought.

(c) (i) **Bamburg Ltd – Additional payment to Charlotte of £14,000**

Tutor's top tips

As Charlotte is a higher rate taxpayer, the bonus is subject to 40% income tax and 2% employee class 1 NIC which is a total of 42%. So, in order to receive £14,000 net, Bamburg must actually pay her £24,138 (£14,000 × 100/58).

The bonus is an allowable expense in computing the taxable profit of Bamburg Ltd and will result in a corporation tax saving.

On the other hand, the dividend is subject to income tax of 25% (100/90 × (32·5% − 10%)). So, in order to receive £14,000 net, Bamburg must actually pay her £18,667 (£14,000 × 100/75).

Dividends are an appropriation of profit and cannot be deducted from taxable profit.

Payment of bonus

	£
Bonus required (£14,000 ÷ 58%) (Note)	24,138
Employer's NICs (£24,138 × 13·8%)	3,331
	27,469
Less: Reduction in corporation tax (£27,469 × 20%)	(5,494)
Total cost to Bamburg Ltd	21,975

Payment of dividend

	£
Cash dividend required (£14,000 ÷ 75%) (Note)	18,667
Total cost to Bamburg Ltd	18,667

(ii) **Tax implications of Bamburg Ltd making a loan of £14,000 to Charlotte**

Tutor's top tips

The loan benefit is subject to income tax for Charlotte but not employee's class 1 NIC.

On the other hand, Bamberg Ltd will have to pay employer's class 1A NIC at 13.8% on the loan benefit.

Bamburg Ltd is a close company as it is controlled by no more than 5 participators. As a result, the loan is subject to tax of 25%.

This tax is not payable if ALL 3 of the following conditions are satisfied:

(1) Loan does not exceed £15,000

(2) Individual works full time for the company.

(3) Individual owns less than 5% of the ordinary share capital.

As Charlotte owns 100% of Bamburg Ltd, the final condition is not satisfied and tax of 25% is payable.

Charlotte

The interest-free loan will result in an annual employment income benefit for Charlotte because she is an employee of Bamburg Ltd.

The benefit will be £420 (£14,000 × 3%) on which Charlotte will have to pay income tax at 40%.

Bamburg Ltd

Bamburg Ltd is a close company as it is wholly owned and controlled by Charlotte.

When a close company makes a loan to a participator (e.g. a shareholder), it must pay HMRC an amount equal to 25% of the loan (i.e. £3,500).

This will be payable at the same time as Bamburg Ltd's corporation tax liability on 1 January 2018.

The payment to HMRC will be required even though the loan will be for less than £15,000. This is because Charlotte owns more than 5% of the company.

Bamburg Ltd will also have to pay class 1A national insurance contributions of £58 (£420 × 13.8%) in respect of the loan benefit. These contributions will be allowable when computing the company's taxable trading profits.

> **Examiner's report**
>
> In part (a) almost all candidates realised that the ability of the company to join the scheme depended on its taxable supplies being below the limit of £150,000. However, a small minority did not apply their knowledge to the facts of the question where there was sufficient information to reach a conclusion in respect of the company concerned.
>
> The matters that needed to be considered in relation to the financial implications of joining the scheme were not handled particularly well with many candidates appearing to be somewhat confused as to the implications of joining the scheme. This was partly due to mixing up the flat rate scheme with other VAT special schemes and also due to a lack of methodical thought. In particular, candidates should have slowed down and tried to explain the payments made to HMRC under the existing arrangements and the payments that would be made under the flat rate scheme so that a comparison could be made.
>
> In part (b), candidates were required to explain 'the tax and financial implications' of proposals to sell a machine and rent a replacement. When candidates read the model answer to this question they will realise that this was not a challenging requirement.
>
> However, very few candidates scored well. The problem here was that candidates started writing before they had identified the issues. As a consequence of this, most candidates addressed the chargeable gain point and very little else. This was unfortunate as the chargeable gain point was not as easy as it appeared, such that many candidates got it wrong.
>
> Other points that most candidates should have been well-equipped to tackle if they had thought to do so included: a balancing charge would arise, the inability to offset capital losses against trading profits and the rent representing a cost to the company that would reduce its taxable profits.
>
> The first part of the final part of the question was relatively challenging and was not done particularly well.
>
> Candidates needed to identify that Charlotte was a higher rate taxpayer and paying national insurance contributions at the margin at the rate of 2% in order to gross up the amount required at the appropriate rate. They then had to identify that the company would have to pay employer's national insurance contributions and that this would be a tax deductible expense for the purposes of corporation tax.
>
> A minority of candidates did not read the question carefully enough, such that they calculated the cost to Charlotte of being paid a bonus or a dividend of £14,000.
>
> The second part of (c) required an explanation of the immediate tax implications for the company and Charlotte of the company making an interest-free loan to Charlotte. The use of the word 'immediate' was important here as no marks were available for explaining what would happen when the loan was either repaid or written off in the future.
>
> It was important here to identify the implications for **both** the company and Charlotte, otherwise not all of the marks were available to be earned.

Most candidates stated (correctly) that an amount equal to 25% of the loan would have to be paid to HMRC but very few explained that this was because it was a loan by a close company to a participator. Also, quite a few candidates did not state that the loan would be a taxable employment income benefit for Charlotte. This meant that they also failed to identify the class 1A national insurance contributions that would be payable by the company.

In both parts of (c) a little more thought from some candidates would have been of great benefit.

ACCA marking scheme			
			Marks
(a)		Eligibility	1.5
		VAT due normally	1.0
		VAT due under the flat rate scheme	2.5
		Conclusion	1.0
			6.0
		Maximum	5.0
(b)		One mark for each relevant point – maximum five marks	5.0
(c)	(i)	Payment of bonus	3.5
		Payment of dividend	2.0
			5.5
		Maximum	5.0
	(ii)	Charlotte	1.5
		Bamburg Ltd	
		Close company loan to participator	2.5
		Class 1A national insurance contributions	1.0
		Exemption not applicable	1.0
			6.0
		Maximum	5.0
Total			20.0

ANSWERS TO PRACTICE QUESTIONS: SECTION 2

59 NOCTURNE LTD *Walk in the footsteps of a top tutor*

Key answer tips

This question has three separate requirements which can be attempted in any order.

The first two parts relate to Nocturne being a close company:

(a) is about the gift of an asset to a participator who is not an employee or a director;

(b) is about a loan made to the company by a participator who is also a director.

Part (c) is about the partial exemption for VAT.

The highlighted words in the written sections are key phrases that markers are looking for.

(a) **Provision of a laptop computer for Jed**

Tutor's top tips

Read the question carefully: you are only asked to consider the after-tax cost for the company, Nocturne Ltd, not the impact on Jed.

Option 1: Purchase of a new laptop computer

Nocturne Ltd is a close company as it is controlled by any three of its four shareholders. As Jed is not a director or employee of Nocturne Ltd, the provision of the laptop computer will not be treated as a taxable benefit, but as a distribution.

Nocturne Ltd will not be able to claim capital allowances in respect of the new laptop computer and there will be no national insurance contribution implications.

No further capital allowances are available to Nocturne Ltd in respect of the existing laptop computer as its tax written down value is already £nil.

Option 2: Transfer of an existing laptop computer

The disposal of the laptop computer to Jed will give rise to a balancing charge in Nocturne Ltd (W). The laptop computer is an exempt asset for capital gains tax purposes, as it is a chattel which cost and is worth no more than £6,000.

The new laptop computer to be used in the business will be eligible for capital allowances. The annual investment allowance is available for the full amount of the expenditure.

The corporation tax relief in the year ending 31 March 2017 due to capital allowances will be £330 (20% × £1,650 (W)).

KAPLAN PUBLISHING

Working: Capital allowances for year ended 31 March 2017

	Main pool £	Allowances £
TWDV b/f	Nil	
Additions qualifying for AIA – laptop	1,800	
Less: AIA	(1,800)	1,800
	Nil	
Disposal	(150)	
	(150)	
Balancing charge	150	(150)
TWDV c/f	Nil	
Total allowances		1,650

Summary of after tax costs

Tutor's top tips

When considering two possible courses of action it is useful to summarise the tax implications of the two options in a table.

To calculate the after tax costs, take account of all costs to the company and any corporation tax relief available for that expenditure.

	Option 1 £	Option 2 £
Amount paid for new laptop	1,800	1,800
Less: Corporation tax saving (above)	Nil	(330)
After-tax cost	1,800	1,470

Conclusion

Option 2 is therefore the preferable option for Nocturne Ltd.

(b) **Provision of loan finance by Siglio**

Tutor's top tips

Make sure you are clear about the situation being described in the scenario: this is a loan **from** a participator, not **to** a participator.

Explaining how savings income is taxed on an individual and the tax relief available for eligible interest on qualifying loans draws on pure F6 knowledge and should have provided easy marks.

Interest received by Siglio

Siglio will receive interest on the loan from Nocturne Ltd net of a 20% income tax deduction. It will be taxed as savings income in Siglio's income tax computation at his marginal rate of tax, but with credit given for the tax deducted at source.

Interest paid by Siglio

As Siglio has taken out a loan to provide the loan finance to Nocturne Ltd, he will be able to obtain tax relief on the interest paid on the loan because the following conditions are satisfied:

– Nocturne Ltd is a close company; and

– Siglio owns at least 5% of the shares in Nocturne Ltd.

Also, as he is the company's managing director, it is highly likely that he works full time for Nocturne Ltd. Therefore, Siglio will be able to deduct the interest paid on the bank loan in calculating his taxable income each year.

(c) (i) **Recoverable input VAT for the year ended 31 March 2016**

Tutor's top tips

All input tax (including that relating wholly or partly to exempt supplies) may be recovered if a business is below the de minimis limits. There are three tests to see whether a business is de minimis; the business need only meet one of them.

Test 1

Total input tax ≤ £625 per month on average, and value of exempt supplies ≤ 50% of value of total supplies.

Test 2

Total input tax less input tax directly attributable to taxable supplies ≤ £625 per month on average, and value of exempt supplies ≤ 50% of value of total supplies.

Test 3

Input tax relating to exempt supplies ≤ £625 per month on average, and input tax relating to exempt supplies ≤ 50% of total input VAT.

In this question you are only required to consider tests 1 and 2.

Applying the de minimis tests to the annual figures provided:

Test 1

Although the value of the exempt supplies is less than 50% of the total supplies, the total input VAT of £13,132 (£7,920 + £1,062 + £4,150) is above the de minimis limit of £7,500 (£625 × 12) so test 1 is not satisfied.

Test 2

Total input VAT less input VAT directly attributed to taxable supplies is £5,212 (£13,132 – £7,920).

This is below the de minimis limit of £7,500 and the value of exempt supplies is less than 50% of the total supplies so test 2 is satisfied and all the input VAT incurred of £13,132 is reclaimable.

Tutorial note

As test 2 is satisfied and all of the input tax is reclaimable, there is no need to apportion the unattributable input VAT.

Had both tests 1 and 2 been failed, the following working would have been required in order to carry out test 3:

Recoverable input VAT for the year ended 31 March 2016:

	Total	Recover	Disallow
	£	£	£
Wholly attributable to taxable supplies	7,920	7,920	
Wholly attributable to exempt supplies	1,062		1,062
Unattributable (£4,150 × 86%/14%)	4,150	3,569	581
Total	13,132	11,489	1,643

(ii) **Annual test**

Tutor's top tips

This part of the question covers the annual test for partially exempt businesses, and has nothing to do with the annual accounting scheme for VAT!

Nocturne Ltd's eligibility for the annual test

The annual test allows a business to apply the de minimis tests once a year instead of for every VAT return period.

The conditions to be satisfied are:

1   The business must have been de minimis in the previous partial exemption year

2   The business will consistently apply the annual test throughout any given partial exemption year; and

3   There are reasonable grounds to expect that the input tax incurred by the business in the current partial exemption year will not exceed £1 million.

Nocturne Ltd satisfied the de minimis condition in respect of the partial exemption year ended 31 March 2016 (condition (1)) and there is no reason to believe that conditions (2) and (3) will not be met in relation to the partial exemption year ending 31 March 2017.

Potential benefits to be gained from use of the annual test

The benefits for Nocturne Ltd result from a provisional recovery of all input tax during the partial exemption year ending 31 March 2017 as the company can recover the full amount of input tax suffered in each return period without performing calculations to see if the de minimis tests are satisfied each time.

This will provide a cash flow benefit and an administrative time saving. This administrative time saving is particularly useful as Nocturne Ltd's turnover and associated costs are expected to increase in the year ended 31 March 2017, such that the simplified de minimis tests 1 and 2 may not be satisfied and the more complicated de minimis test 3 might otherwise be required.

Notwithstanding these benefits, an annual adjustment will have to be performed at the end of the year using the de minimis limits for the year as a whole, which may result in the need to repay part of the VAT previously recovered in full.

Examiner's comments

The first part concerned two alternative ways in which a computer was to be provided to a shareholder who was not employed by the company. Despite knowing the relevant rules, candidates did not perform as well as they could have done in this part for two reasons. Firstly, they failed to consider all of the aspects of the situation and secondly, they did not answer the question set.

Most candidates appreciated that the provision of the computer would give rise to a distribution but many failed to address the capital allowances position of the company. This was important because it differed in the two alternative situations. Similarly, many candidates failed to address the tax treatment of the loss on the transfer of the existing computer in the second alternative. Candidates will benefit if they think before they write and identify all the different aspects of the transaction. They should then address each of the aspects in a concise manner.

The failure to answer the question set related to the need to determine the after-tax cost for the company. Most candidates focussed on the tax treatment for the individual, which meant that they missed out on some of the available marks.

Part (b) concerned Siglio, the company's managing director, who was going to borrow money from a bank and then lend it to the company. Many candidates provided unsatisfactory answers to this question part because they wanted the question to deal with a loan from a close company to a participator in that company – but it wasn't. It was also important to deal with the two loans separately.

The loan to the company was a normal commercial loan. The company would obtain a tax deduction for the interest paid and Siglio would pay income tax on the interest income in the normal way. It was no more complicated than that.

The loan from the bank to Siglio was more interesting in that in that it would be a qualifying loan, such that the interest paid by Siglio would be tax deductible. Some candidates were aware of this point but very few stated the detailed reasons for the tax deduction being available.

> The final part of the question concerned VAT and was in two parts.
>
> Part (i) concerned the partial exemption de minimis tests. It was a straight forward test of the rules and was done well by those candidates who knew them. As always, it was important to read the question carefully and to address the requirement and nothing more; some candidates wasted time by addressing other aspects of VAT that were not required. Candidates should recognise that VAT is tested at every sitting and that the partial exemption rules are tested regularly.
>
> Part (ii) concerned the annual test for computing recoverable input tax and was not done well. The problem here was that the majority of candidates addressed the annual accounting scheme rather than the subject of the question. This was unfortunate and meant that very few candidates did well on this part of the question. Candidates should always try to be sure as to what the question is about; both parts of part (b) related to partial exemption.

		ACCA marking scheme	Marks
(a)		Close company	1.0
		Purchase of new computer for Jed	2.5
		Transfer of existing computer to Jed	3.5
		Conclusion	0.5
			7.5
		Maximum	7.0
(b)		Treatment of interest received	1.5
		Conditions for income tax deduction	2.5
		Conclusion re Siglio	0.5
			4.5
		Maximum	4.0
(c)	(i)	De minimis test 1	2.0
		De minimis test 2	2.0
		Conclusion	0.5
			4.5
		Maximum	4.0
	(ii)	Annual test – conditions	2.0
		– Application to Nocturne	1.0
		– Implications	3.0
			6.0
		Maximum	5.0
Total			20.0

GROUPS, CONSORTIA AND OVERSEAS COMPANY ASPECTS

60 PALM PLC (ADAPTED)

Key answer tips

This is a question that needs a lot of reading to make sure you are clear about what is going on. Drawing diagrams of the group structure and timelines of events often helps in this process.

It is important for part (a) to note the relatively high mark allocation and to write enough detail to achieve the marks. Research and development relief is important for UK companies. Make sure you explain why the expenditure on Project Sabal will qualify. There is a tricky point regarding the degrouping charge in (a)(ii) but you should be able to pick up the marks for the treatment of the Date Inc dividends and the fact Nikau Ltd will suffer further tax on their share of the Date Inc profits.

Part (b) has a few marks for overseas VAT which should have been straightforward.

(a) **Nikau Ltd and Palm plc**

Effect on corporation tax payable for the year ending 31 March 2017

(i) **Project Sabal**

Research and development expenditure

The expenditure incurred in respect of research and development will give rise to additional relief in the form of a taxable 'above the line' tax credit of 11% of the qualifying expenditure, as Nikau Ltd is a large enterprise for this purpose.

The net effect of this is as follows:

	£	£
Tax credit received (11% × £70,000)		7,700
Net deduction in accounts:		
Allowable expense	70,000	
Taxable R&D credit	(7,700)	
Net deduction	62,300	
Corporation tax saving (20% × £62,300)		12,460
Total cash benefit		20,160

Tutorial note

Alternatively, Nikau Ltd could claim an enhanced deduction of 130% of the qualifying expenditure, with no tax credit. The expenditure would reduce the taxable total profits of Nikau Ltd by £91,000 (£70,000 × 130%) giving a corporation tax saving of £18,200 (£91,000 × 20%) compared to £20,160 with the tax credit. This is clearly not beneficial.

The budgeted expenditure will qualify for the enhanced relief because it appears to satisfy the following conditions:

- It is likely to qualify as research and development expenditure within generally accepted accounting principles as it will result in new technical knowledge and a significant advance in technology for the industry.
- It relates to staff costs, consumable items or other qualifying expenditure as opposed to capital items.
- It will result in further trading activities for Nikau Ltd.

Use of brought forward trading losses

The development of products for the North American market and also for VAT registered customers in the European Union (EU) is likely to represent a major change in the nature and conduct of the trade of Nikau Ltd. This is because the company is developing new products and intends to sell them in new markets. It is a major change as sales to North America and in the EU are expected to generate significant additional profits.

Because this change will occur within three years of the change in the ownership of Nikau Ltd on 1 November 2016, any trading losses arising prior to that date cannot be carried forward beyond that date.

Accordingly, the trading losses brought forward may only be offset against £173,658 ((£360,000 – £62,300) × 7/12) of the company's trading profits for the year. The remainder of the trading losses £22,042 (£195,700 – £173,658) will be lost resulting in lost tax relief of £4,408 (£22,042 × 20%).

Tutorial note

The profits for the year ending 31 March 2017 will be apportioned to the periods pre and post 1 November 2016 on either a time basis or some other basis that is just and reasonable.

However, it could be argued that the net research and development costs of £62,300 do not arise until after the change in ownership, as Project Sabal does not commence until after the purchase of Nikau Ltd.

Therefore profits of £210,000 (£360,000 × 7/12) would be treated as accruing before the change in ownership. This would enable full relief for the brought forward losses and none of the losses would be lost. This point would need to be clearly argued to receive full credit.

(ii) **Date Inc**

Controlled foreign company

Date Inc is caught by the controlled foreign company rules. The profits of such a company are attributed to its UK resident shareholders such that they are subject to UK corporation tax.

Nikau Ltd will therefore be subject to corporation tax on its share of the profits of Date Inc, i.e. £420,000 (£1,200,000 × 35%). This will give a tax charge of £84,000 (£420,000 × 20%).

There will be double tax relief available for the 4% overseas withholding tax suffered on the dividend received, i.e. £15,917 (£382,000 × 4/96) leaving tax payable of £68,083 (£84,000 − £15,917).

Tutorial note

There are ways of avoiding attribution of the profits of the CFC, for example: accounting or taxable profits less than £500,000, or genuine trading activities. However, the information clearly states that this is a CFC and that the chargeable profits are caught by the legislation, so there are no exemptions available here.

(iii) **Sale of shares in Olive Ltd by Palm plc**

Degrouping charge

There will be a degrouping charge in the year ending 31 March 2017 in respect of the sale of the shares in Olive Ltd. This is because Olive Ltd has left the Palm Group within six years of the no gain, no loss transfer of the property from Spring Ltd whilst still owning the property.

The degrouping charge is calculated by treating the original no gain no loss transfer from Spring Ltd to Olive Ltd as a market value disposal. This will give rise to a gain, ignoring indexation allowance, of £520,000 (£900,000 − £380,000).

The gain is added to the sales proceeds of the Olive Ltd shares in order to calculate any gain arising in Palm plc on the disposal.

Disposal of shares in Olive Ltd

The disposal of the shares in Olive Ltd will not qualify for the substantial shareholding exemption as Olive Ltd is not a trading company.

The gain will be calculated as follows:

	£
Proceeds of share disposal	1,400,000
Add: Degrouping charge	520,000
	1,920,000
Less: Cost (ignoring IA per question)	(338,000)
Gain	1,582,000

This gain will give rise to additional corporation tax of £316,400 (£1,582,000 × 20%) in Palm plc.

Tutorial note

A property was transferred between two Palm plc group companies and then the company owning the property leaves the group within 6 years.

A degrouping charge therefore arises on 1 November 2016 when Palm plc sells the shares in Olive Ltd.

The degrouping charge is added to the proceeds of the sale of shares when calculating the gain on the disposal of those shares.

The substantial shareholding exemption does not apply to these shares as Olive Ltd is not a trading company.

(b) **Recoverability of input tax**

Sales by Nikau Ltd of its existing products are subject to UK VAT at 20% because it is selling to domestic customers who will not be registered for VAT. Accordingly, at present, Nikau Ltd can recover all of its input tax.

Sales to customers in North America will be zero rated because the goods are being exported from the EU to a non-EU resident country. Sales to VAT registered customers in the European Union will also be zero rated.

Zero rated supplies are classified as taxable for the purposes of VAT and therefore Nikau Ltd will continue to be able to recover all of its input tax.

Tutorial note

Overseas VAT issues are important. You must remember that exports outside the EU and to VAT registered customers within the EU are zero rated, not exempt. Making zero rated supplies has no effect on input tax recovery.

Sales to non-VAT registered customers within the EU would be standard rated, and so would also have no effect on input tax recovery.

ANSWERS TO PRACTICE QUESTIONS: SECTION 2

> **Examiner's report**
>
> This question was the least popular of the optional questions and was not done particularly well by those who attempted it.
>
> Part (a) was in three parts. All parts required candidates to identify the implications of the proposed transactions and to apply their knowledge to the facts.
>
> Part (i) concerned research and development and the use of brought forward losses. Whilst these issues were often successfully identified by candidates, the detail requested in the requirement was missing as was the effect of the issues on the amount of corporation tax payable. Some candidates thought, erroneously, that the restriction on the use of losses brought forward following the change in ownership and the major change in the nature of the trade related to group relief.
>
> Parts (ii) and (iii) concerned the identification of a degrouping charge and the treatment of the profits of a controlled foreign company. Again, the issues were successfully identified by many candidates but there was a lack of precise knowledge of the rules and a tendency to describe the rules in general terms rather than to simply apply them to the facts.
>
> Part (b) required candidates to understand the VAT implications of sales to domestic customers within and outside the European Union (standard rated and zero rated respectively). This was a straightforward test of important VAT rules but the majority of answers were poor and many confused the terms exempt and zero rated.

ACCA marking scheme			
			Marks
(a)	(i)	Research and development	
		Additional relief available	0.5
		11% tax credit	1.0
		Effect on tax liability	1.5
		Conditions 0.5 each – maximum 1.5	1.5
		Use of brought forward trading losses	
		Project Sabal will represent a major change in the nature and conduct of the trade with reasons	2.0
		Within three years of change of ownership	1.0
		Losses cannot be carried forward beyond date of change of ownership	1.0
		Tax effect of losses used/lost	2.0
			10.5
			10.0
	(ii)	Controlled foreign company	
		Profits of CFC are attributed to UK resident shareholders	0.5
		Calculation of share of profits	0.5
		Corporation tax at 20% less double tax relief	1.5
			2.5
		Maximum	2.0

KAPLAN PUBLISHING

			Marks
	(iii)	Sale of shares	
		Identification of degrouping charge	0.5
		Reason for charge and calculation	1.0
		No substantial shareholding exemption	0.5
		Gain on shares	1.5
			3.5
		Maximum	3.0
(b)		Current position	1.5
		Position in the future	3.5
			5.0
Total			20.0

61 PARTICLE LTD GROUP (ADAPTED) *Walk in the footsteps of a top tutor*

Key answer tips

This is a tough question on corporation tax for a group of companies. The largest single section covers a classic scenario encountered in practice; the sale of shares versus sale of assets. Not an easy topic and one you may find tricky if you have not seen it before.

There are, however, some easier marks in part (iii) of the question requiring detail about corporation tax payment dates and in part (iv) relating to the taxation of patent profits.

The highlighted words in the written sections are key phrases that markers are looking for.

Tutor's top tips

Having read the whole question, you should have realised that the requirement at the end of the question does not give the complete detail of all that is required – more detail regarding what you need to do is given in the body of the question itself, mainly under the headings 'Report' and 'Advice required'.

Before you start writing, you should spend time identifying the relationship between the parties involved, perhaps annotating the group diagram so that you know where assets have been transferred, which companies have losses, which are overseas and so on.

Note also that there are four marks in this question for format and style. To get these marks, you need to set up your answer as a report, make sure that you use headings, write in short sentences, and have a logical flow to your answer.

Report

To	The management of Particle Ltd
From	Tax advisers
Date	1 December 2016
Subject	Particle Ltd Group – Various group issues

(i) **Sale of Kaon Ltd**

Tutor's top tips

The two alternatives for the sale of the business are very different.

Either Particle Ltd disposes of its shares in Kaon Ltd, so that the company Kaon Ltd leaves the group; or Kaon Ltd sells all of its individual assets but the company remains within the group as a dormant company.

The split of marks in the requirement should give you a clue that there is much more to consider for the sale of individual assets than the sale of shares!

Sale of share capital

A sale by Particle Ltd of the share capital of Kaon Ltd will not result in a tax liability due to the availability of the substantial shareholdings exemption.

This exemption is available because Particle Ltd is selling a trading company of which it has owned at least 10% for a year.

Accordingly, the after tax proceeds resulting from the sale will be £650,000.

Tutorial note

There will not be a degrouping charge arising in respect of Atom House, as Kaon Ltd is leaving the group more than six years after the no gain, no loss inter-group transfer.

Had there been a degrouping charge, this would be added to the proceeds from the sale of shares for Particle Ltd and would be exempt due to the availability of the substantial shareholdings exemption.

Sale of the trade and assets of the business

The sales proceeds of £770,000 will be reduced by the corporation tax payable on the sale as set out below.

Tutor's top tips

This is not a single disposal for tax purposes, so you need to consider each asset separately. Think about all the possible tax implications: capital gains for chargeable assets; capital allowances for plant and machinery; possibly VAT.

	Note	£
Chargeable gain on sale of Atom House (W1)	1	260,976
Balancing allowance (£65,000 – £46,000)	2	(19,000)
Profit on sale of goodwill	3	120,000
Additional taxable total profits		361,976
Corporation tax (£361,976 × 20%)		72,395

The after tax proceeds resulting from the sale will be £697,605 (£770,000 – £72,395).

Tutor's top tips

As always, as long as your after tax proceeds is consistent with your calculations, you will pick up the marks here.

This figure must then be reduced by £25,000 in respect of the payment of the company's net liabilities in order for it to be comparable with the net proceeds on the sale of shares.

Accordingly, the net after tax proceeds are £672,605 (£697,605 – £25,000).

Notes

1 **Atom House**

The purchase of Atom House from Baryon Ltd in March 2009 was a no gain, no loss transfer. Accordingly, Kaon Ltd's base cost for the building is its original cost to the group, as reduced by the claim for rollover relief, plus indexation allowance up to the date of transfer.

The gain arising on the sale by Kaon Ltd can be reduced by the capital loss of £37,100 in Baryon Ltd, as the two companies are in a capital gains group. This will require a claim to be submitted to HM Revenue and Customs (HMRC) by 31 March 2019 (i.e. two years from the end of the accounting period).

The claim will be to treat £37,100 of the capital gain as arising in Baryon Ltd in order to match the gain with the brought forward capital loss.

2   **Machinery and equipment**

It has been assumed that no item of machinery or equipment will be sold for more than cost. The excess of the tax written down value over the sales proceeds will give rise to a tax allowable balancing adjustment.

3   **Goodwill**

The profit on the sale of goodwill is taxed as a trading profit.

VAT on the sale of the business

The sale of the business of Kaon Ltd will not be a taxable supply, such that no VAT should be charged, provided the following conditions are satisfied.

- The business is transferred as a going concern.
- The purchaser intends to use the assets to carry on the same kind of business as Kaon Ltd.
- The purchaser is VAT registered or will become registered as a result of the purchase.

As Kaon Ltd will cease making taxable supplies, the company will need to deregister for VAT and cannot remain in the VAT group.

Workings

(W1) **Tax on gain on sale of Atom House**

Tutor's top tips

Be very careful here!

Before you can work out Kaon Ltd's gain, you need to calculate the cost of Atom House. There has been a rollover relief claim, but only part of the original proceeds were reinvested, so only part of the gain on Bohr Square will have been rolled over.

	£
Proceeds	604,000
Less: Deemed cost (W2)	(242,220)
Unindexed gain	361,780
Less: Indexation allowance (March 2009 to January 2017)	
(£242,220 × 0.263)	(63,704)
Chargeable gain	298,076
Less: Reallocated to Baryon Ltd to use capital loss	(37,100)
Net chargeable gain	260,976

(W2) **Deemed cost of Atom House**

	£
Original cost to Baryon Ltd	272,000
Less: Rollover relief (W3)	(51,600)
	220,400
Plus: Indexation allowance (July 2005 to March 2009) (£220,400 × 0.099)	21,820
Deemed cost	242,220

(W3) **Rollover relief in respect of Atom House**

	£
Gain on sale of Bohr Square	89,000
Less: Sales proceeds not reinvested in Atom House (£309,400 – £272,000)	(37,400)
Rollover relief claimed	51,600

Tutorial note

There is no degrouping charge if the assets are sold, as Kaon Ltd is still part of the original gains group.

Instead, Kaon Ltd will be taxed on the disposal as if they have always owned the asset.

Strictly, you should calculate two indexation allowances: one to the date of the intra-group transfer, then another from that date to the date of sale. However, if you simply indexed the base cost from July 2005 to January 2017 you would score most of the marks.

(ii) **Muon Inc**

VAT

Tutor's top tips

You must learn the definitions of the different types of groups for corporation tax purposes and in particular, which types of group an overseas resident company can, and cannot, be a part of.

It will not be possible for Muon Inc to join the Particle Ltd group registration unless it has an established place of business in the UK.

This is not a problem, however, as there will be no VAT on the sales of components to Muon Inc; exports to countries outside the European Union (EU) are zero rated.

Tutor's top tips

Watch your terminology when you are writing about VAT. 'Zero rated' is very different from 'exempt'!

Interest on the loan from Particle Ltd

The profit or loss arising on transactions between Particle Ltd and Muon Inc must be determined as if the two companies are independent of each other because Particle Ltd controls Muon Inc.

This rule applies regardless of the size of Particle Ltd because Muon Inc is resident in a country that does not have a double tax treaty with the UK.

Accordingly, the taxable profit of Particle Ltd must be increased in order to reflect a market rate of interest on the loan.

(iii) **Payment of corporation tax**

Tutor's top tips

The examining team did not specify which accounting periods they wanted you to discuss here, but the fact that there are eight marks available should make it obvious that you needed to consider all periods affected by the acquisitions, not just one year.

Year ended 31 March 2016

The threshold for determining whether the company is large for the purposes of paying corporation tax by instalment is divided by the number of related 51% group companies at the end of the previous accounting period.

Accordingly, in the year ended 31 March 2016, the threshold would have been divided by three (namely Particle Ltd, Baryon Ltd and Kaon Ltd).

This is the year of acquisition of the additional 51% group companies Hadron Ltd, Electron Ltd and Muon Inc. However, these companies will not be taken into account in determining the need to pay by quarterly instalments until the next year.

The taxable profit of each of the three companies (Particle Ltd, Baryon Ltd and Kaon Ltd) was less than £500,000 (£1,500,000 × 1/3) such that no company will have to pay tax by instalment.

Therefore, the tax is due on 1 January 2017, nine months and one day after the end of the accounting period.

Year ended 31 March 2017

In the year ended 31 March 2017 the threshold will be divided by six due to the additional 51% group companies acquired in the previous year.

Note that this is also the year of disposal of Kaon Ltd, however Kaon Ltd is still included as it was a related 51% group company at the end of the previous year.

Some of the companies in the group will have taxable profits that exceed £250,000 (£1,500,000 × 1/6).

However, this will not affect the date on which corporation tax is payable provided it is the first year in which it has occurred.

Corporation tax will therefore be payable on 1 January 2018.

Year ended 31 March 2018

In the year ended 31 March 2018 there will be five companies in the group as Kaon Ltd was not a related 51% group company at the **end** of the previous year.

Those companies with taxable profits in excess of £300,000 (£1,500,000 x 1/5) will have to pay their corporation tax liability in four equal instalments (if they were large in the year ending 31 March 2017).

The instalments will be due on 14 October 2017, 14 January 2018, 14 April 2018 and 14 July 2018.

Quarterly payments

It should be noted that, under the instalment system, a company's tax liability has to be estimated because the first three payments are due during and shortly after the end of the accounting period.

Once the final liability is known, interest will be charged by HMRC on any amounts paid late and will be paid to the company on any amounts paid early or overpaid (albeit at a lower rate of interest).

Interest paid is allowable for tax purposes and interest received is taxable.

Group payment arrangement

In view of the difficulties involved in estimating the tax due, a system exists for groups of companies whereby a nominated company can pay instalments on behalf of the group and allocate them between the group members once the liabilities are known.

This enables underpayments and overpayments of tax that might have otherwise arisen in separate companies to be offset thus mitigating the effect of the differential between the interest charged and paid by HMRC.

The group for this purpose can include any of the companies in the Particle Ltd group required to pay tax in instalments.

Tutorial note

Under a group payment arrangement, it is only the instalments that can be paid as a group. Each company must still prepare a separate tax return to send to HMRC.

(iv) **Taxation of patents**

The 'patent box' scheme, as it is known, allows companies that hold patents for the purposes of their trade to elect for profits relating to those patents to be taxed at a lower rate of corporation tax.

ANSWERS TO PRACTICE QUESTIONS: SECTION 2

The scheme is optional and, if claimed, applies to all profits derived from patents:

- royalty income, and
- a proportion of the profits made on goods or services where a patent has been used in the underlying production process.

A reduced rate of tax is then established by deducting an amount (see below) from the profits in the 'patent box', such that when the corporation tax rate is applied to this reduced figure, the effective rate of tax is 10%.

As the scheme is being phased in over a number of years, currently only 80% of the net patent profit is subject to the reduced rate.

To calculate the deduction the following formula will be applied:

80% × net patent profit × (20% − 10%)/20%

Tutorial note

For FA2015 the deduction from total profits in the corporation tax computation is effectively 40% of the net patent profits (i.e. 80% x ((20% − 10%) ÷ 20%)).

Examiner's report

The majority of answers were well structured and logical such that many of the relevant issues were addressed.

Many candidates identified that the sale of the shares would be an exempt disposal due to the availability of the substantial shareholding exemption.

A number of aspects of the sale of the business was also handled well including the profit on the goodwill and the capital allowances.

The capital gain on the sale of the property was more difficult and was not dealt with particularly well. Candidates were inclined to charge the held over gain as a separate item rather than simply deducting it from the base cost of the building.

Credit was given for simply identifying the possibility of a degrouping charge with further credit for correct relevant statements. There was evidence of some confusion here with candidates referring to degrouping charges arising on a sale of assets whereas, of course, they can only arise on a sale of shares.

There was similar confusion concerning the VAT implications of the sale with a significant minority of candidates incorrectly describing a sale of shares as a transfer of a going concern.

The second part of the report concerned VAT and the interest being charged on a loan from the parent company to a subsidiary. Candidates needed to identify the issues, have precise knowledge of particular rules and to express that knowledge briefly as per the instructions in the tax manager's email.

The majority of candidates identified the need to charge a market rate of interest under the transfer pricing rules.

KAPLAN PUBLISHING

PAPER P6: ADVANCED TAXATION (FA2015)

However, the performance in respect of VAT was not as good. This was due in part to a lack of knowledge but also to candidates writing too much and not giving themselves time to think. Weaker candidates provided detailed, but irrelevant, explanations of the advantages and disadvantages of VAT groups. There was also a significant minority who thought, incorrectly, that exports outside the European Union are exempt as opposed to being zero rated.

The final part of the report required candidates to consider the dates on which corporation tax would be payable by the group companies. This was not a difficult requirement, as most candidates will have a good knowledge of the rules. However, many candidates failed to maximise their marks because they wrote about the general rules concerning payment dates and failed to take a logical approach that addressed the specifics of the companies in the question.

Candidates who thought about the circumstances surrounding the group identified the fact that the change in the number of related 51% group companies would affect the date on which the corporation tax would be payable.

The 'patent box' taxation treatment has been added to the legislation since this question was written, hence the question is longer than the original question set by the examiner.

	ACCA marking scheme	
		Marks
(i)	Sale of share capital:	
	Availability of substantial shareholding exemption	1.0
	Reason for availability	1.0
	After tax proceeds	0.5
	Sale of business:	
	Atom House	
	Cost of Atom House	
	Use of original cost to Baryon Ltd	0.5
	Rollover relief	1.5
	IA to March 2009	1.0
	Gain on sale by Kaon Ltd	0.5
	Use of capital loss from Baryon Ltd	1.0
	Claim required	1.0
	Machinery and equipment	1.0
	Goodwill	1.0
	Corporation tax	0.5
	Payment of net liabilities	1.0
	After tax proceeds	0.5
	Explanatory notes – 1 mark each – max 3 marks	3.0
	VAT	2.0
		17.0
	Maximum	14.0
(ii)	VAT group	1.0
	Zero rated	1.0
	Transfer pricing :	
	Identification of issue	1.0
	Why rules apply	2.0
	Effect	1.0
		6.0
	Maximum	5.0

			Marks
(iii)	Year ended 31 March 2016		1.5
	Year ended 31 March 2017		2.5
	Year ended 31 March 2018		
	Reason for instalment basis		1.0
	Due dates		1.0
	Interest and need to estimate liabilities		1.5
	Group payment		
	Operation		1.0
	Why possibly beneficial		1.0
			9.5
		Maximum	7.0
(iv)	Lower rate of corporation tax		1.0
	Optional		1.0
	Applies to all profits from patents		1.0
	Effective rate 10%		1.0
	Phased in – 80% of net patent profit		1.0
	Formula		1.0
			6.0
		Maximum	5.0
	Appropriate style and presentation		1.0
	Effectiveness of communication		2.0
	Logical structure		1.0
			4.0
Total			35.0

62 CACAO LTD GROUP (ADAPTED) *Walk in the footsteps of a top tutor*

Key answer tips

This question is really three independent short questions, which could be addressed in any order.

As is usual for Section A questions, the requirement at the end of the question really just tells you how many marks are available for each section. The real requirements can mainly be found in the emails in the question.

There are some easy marks available for basic corporation tax computations in part (i), and you should be able to score highly here.

Part (ii) requires detailed discussion of the CFC rules. If you have not revised these rules, you will find this part of the question difficult. There are also some marks here for discussing the treatment of interest under the loan relationship rules.

Part (iii) covers the capital goods scheme for VAT. As this is an area that the examiner has specifically mentioned as being important, you should make sure that you are able to explain how the scheme operates.

The highlighted words in the written sections are key phrases that markers are looking for.

PAPER P6: ADVANCED TAXATION (FA2015)

Tutor's top tips

As you read through the information in the question, highlight any requirements and instructions that you find. Most of the requirements are in the email from the manager, but there are some additional requirements in Maya's email.

Keep looking back at these as you attempt each part of the question to ensure that you address all of them in your answer.

Make sure that you set out your answer as a memorandum, as there are marks available for this.

To   The files

From   Tax senior

Date   7 June 2016

Subject Cacao Ltd group of companies

(i) **The corporation tax liability for the year ending 30 September 2017**

Tutor's top tips

There are two steps here:

(i) Calculate the total corporation tax liability for Ganache Ltd, Truffle Ltd and Fondant Ltd **without** the additional expenditure.

(ii) Explain, with calculations, the effects of the additional expenditure on the tax liabilities. This means that you need to quantify any extra tax due or saved.

Note also the clue given in the question that you should 'take advantage of any opportunities available to reduce the total corporation tax liability'. This clearly means that there are some opportunities!

Based on the original budget

The corporation tax liabilities based on the original budget for the year ending 30 September 2017 are set out below.

These calculations do not reflect the projected scientific research costs or the capital expenditure.

ANSWERS TO PRACTICE QUESTIONS: SECTION 2

	Ganache Ltd £	Truffle Ltd £	Fondant Ltd £
Taxable trading profit	45,000	168,000	55,000
Chargeable gain	–	42,000	–
Transfer of chargeable gain (Note)	–	(23,000)	23,000
Less: Capital loss brought forward			(23,000)
Taxable total profits	45,000	187,000	55,000
Corporation tax at 20%	9,000	37,400	11,000

Subsidiaries' total corporation tax liability = (£9,000 + £37,400 + £11,000) = £57,400

Transfer of chargeable gain

An election can be made to transfer £23,000 of Truffle Ltd's chargeable gain to Fondant Ltd in order to take advantage of that company's capital losses.

Tutorial notes

1 *If you transferred all of the gain to Fondant Ltd, the total corporation tax liability would be the same and you would still score full marks.*

2 *It may also be possible to reduce the taxable profits of one or more of the subsidiaries by surrendering the non-trading loan relationships deficit that will arise in Cacao Ltd.*

However, there was no requirement to consider this issue in this part of the question.

Try to keep your answer simple and succinct and do not try to confuse your answer by interlinking ideas before you have stated the key obvious points on ideas in isolation

Tutor's top tips

Don't worry if your taxable total profits were not correct.

You could still score full marks for the calculation of the corporation tax, and for stating the total liability based on your figures.

Research costs

The research costs will be tax deductible resulting in a corporation tax saving for Ganache Ltd of up to £2,200 (£11,000 × 20%).

A further tax deduction of 130% of the cost incurred will be available as staff costs are qualifying revenue expenses.

Accordingly, qualifying expenditure of £11,000 would give rise to an additional reduction in the company's tax liability of £2,860 (£11,000 × 130% × 20%).

Capital expenditure

The group is entitled to a 100% tax deduction for up to £500,000 of expenditure on manufacturing equipment. The balance will receive an 18% writing down allowance in the year ending 30 September 2017.

Cacao Ltd will be using £400,000 of the AIA, leaving £100,000 (£500,000 – £400,000), which can be allocated between the companies in the group in the most tax efficient manner. As Truffle Ltd and Ganache Ltd are both profitable, it makes no difference which of these companies uses the remaining AIA.

The excess expenditure will qualify for the 18% WDA.

The allowances available will be:

	£	Allowances £
Total expenditure (£86,000 + £29,000)	115,000	
AIA	(100,000)	100,000
	15,000	
WDA (18% × £15,000)		2,700
Total allowances for capital expenditure		102,700

Corporation tax liability – incorporating research costs and capital expenditure

	£
Total liability based on original budget	57,400
Tax relief for capital expenditure (above):	
(£102,700 × 20%)	(20,540)
Tax relief for research costs	
Deduction for expenditure (£11,000 × 20%)	(2,200)
Possible additional deduction (£11,000 × 130% × 20%)	(2,860)
Revised total corporation tax liability	31,800

(ii) **Praline Inc**

Tutor's top tips

There are 13 marks available for this section, which indicates roughly how many points are required. Generally, there will be half to one mark available per relevant point.

Most of the marks here are for discussing CFCs. A good approach to such a question is to state the conditions and exemptions, then apply each one to the scenario. If you do not refer to the scenario, you are unlikely to pass.

Break your answer down into short paragraphs to make it easier to mark.

Make sure that you discuss the implications of Praline Inc being a CFC and provide a summary of your findings, as requested. Remember also to discuss what would happen if Praline Inc was not a CFC.

Consideration of whether or not Praline Inc is a controlled foreign company (CFC)

A company is a CFC if it satisfies both of the following conditions.

- It is resident outside the UK.
- It is controlled by UK resident persons.

Condition 1:

Although Praline Inc is incorporated in Noka it may not be resident there. For example, it will be resident in the UK if it is managed and controlled here.

Accordingly, we will need to consider where the main decisions are made in connection with the management of the company, the rules concerning residency in Noka and the terms of any double tax treaty between Noka and the UK in order to determine its residence status.

Condition 2:

The second condition will be satisfied as, following its purchase, Praline Inc will be controlled by Cacao Ltd, a UK resident person.

The implications of Praline Inc being a CFC

If Praline Inc is a controlled foreign company, Cacao Ltd may have to self-assess UK corporation tax on Praline Inc's chargeable profits unless Praline Inc can satisfy one of the following exemptions.

(1) Exempt Period

If Praline is a CFC, it will be exempt for the first 12 months of the company coming under the control of UK residents. For this exemption to be available, the company must continue to be a CFC for the accounting period following the exempt period **and** not be subject to a CFC charge in that subsequent period.

(2) Excluded territories

HMRC provide a list of approved territories where rates of tax are sufficiently high to avoid a CFC charge arising. However, the low rate of tax in Nokia suggests that it is unlikely to be an excluded territory.

(3) Low profits

Its accounting or taxable profits do not exceed £500,000 in a 12-month period, of which no more than £50,000 comprises non-trading profits.

Praline Inc currently satisfies these conditions but may not do so in the future.

(4) Low profit margin

The foreign company's accounting profits are no more than 10% of relevant operating expenditure.

More information would be required to say whether or not Praline Inc satisfied this exemption.

(5) Tax exemption

The tax paid in the overseas country is at least 75% of the UK corporation tax which would be due if it were a UK resident company.

This exemption is unlikely to be satisfied as the rate of corporation tax in Noka (12%) is considerably less than 75% of the rate that would be payable in the UK (20%).

However, it is not the tax rate that is relevant but rather the amount of tax payable.

Accordingly, it will be necessary to compare the tax payable in Noka (under Noka rules) with the amount that would be payable in the UK had the company been UK resident.

If none of the exemptions are satisfied, the profits of Praline Inc still may not be subject to tax in the UK, if it is regarded as having no chargeable profits, i.e. income profits that have been artificially diverted from the UK. This will be the case if one of the following conditions is satisfied:

- the CFC does not hold any assets or bear any risks under any arrangements or tax planning schemes intended to reduce UK tax
- the CFC does not hold any assets or bear any risks that are managed in the UK
- the CFC would continue in business if the UK management of its assets and risks were to cease.

However, given Maya's intention to take advantage of the tax rate in Noka by transferring additional investment properties to Praline Inc, it appears that these profits would only be arising in the CFC for the purpose of avoiding UK tax. In this case, they probably would be subject to tax in the UK.

Conclusion

If Praline Inc is UK resident it will not be a CFC. However, Praline Inc would then be subject to UK corporation tax on its world-wide income such that the advantage of the low rate of tax in Noka would be lost.

If Praline Inc is not UK resident we will need to prepare the tax computations and acquire the additional information described above in order to determine whether or not it will be caught by the CFC rules.

If Praline Inc is caught by the rules, Cacao Ltd may have to pay corporation tax on Praline Inc's chargeable profits once the non-trade profits exceed £50,000 (or once its total profits exceed £500,000). A credit would be available to Cacao Ltd for the corporation tax suffered by Praline Inc in Noka.

Relief for interest on loan to acquire Praline Inc

Tutor's top tips

It would be easy to overlook this part of the question, as the requirement was in Maya's email, not the email from your manager. This reinforces the importance of highlighting all the requirements as you read through the question.

The loan is for the purpose of acquiring Praline Inc and not for the purposes of the trade of Cacao Ltd.

Accordingly, the interest on the loan, together with any fees incurred by Cacao Ltd in order to obtain the loan, represent non-trading debits under the loan relationship rules, which will be offset against any non-trading loan relationship credits of Cacao Ltd, for example, interest income.

There is likely to be a net debit, or deficit, as Cacao Ltd's taxable profits are very small. This deficit represents a form of loss that can be offset against the profits of Cacao Ltd or surrendered to Cacao Ltd's UK resident subsidiaries as group relief.

The subsidiary will deduct the amount surrendered from its taxable profits for the year in which the costs were incurred.

Tutorial note

Under the loan relationship rules, a loan to purchase an investment in a subsidiary is treated as a non-trade loan.

(iii) **Fondant Ltd**

Tutor's top tips

There are two requirements to address here:

(i) *Outline the capital goods scheme and explain what would happen if Fondant Ltd purchased the building.*

(ii) *Consider whether it would be advantageous to use last year's partial exemption percentage rather than the percentage for each quarter.*

VAT on purchase of office premises

Purchasing the building would not solve the problem of irrecoverable VAT.

The landlord would be obliged to charge VAT on the purchase price because it is charging VAT on the rent.

Fondant Ltd would be able to recover a percentage of the VAT charged in the normal way by reference to its partial exemption percentage.

The capital goods scheme will apply because the cost of the building will be more than £250,000. Under the capital goods scheme, the total amount of input tax recovered reflects the use of the building over the period of ownership, up to a maximum of ten years, rather than merely the year of purchase.

In future years, as the percentage of exempt supplies increases, Fondant Ltd will have to repay HM Revenue and Customs some of the input tax recovered.

For example, if Fondant Ltd recovers 62% of the input tax in the year of purchase and the percentage of taxable supplies in a particular subsequent year were to be 52%, the input tax repayable to HM Revenue and Customs would be calculated as follows.

VAT charged × 1/10 × (62% – 52%)

Similarly, if the percentage of exempt supplies were to fall, Fondant Ltd would be able to recover additional input tax from HM Revenue and Customs.

Tutor's top tips

It is easier to explain the effect of the capital goods scheme using some figures, but you do not have to do this to score the marks.

Partial exemption percentage

If Fondant Ltd is preparing its VAT returns by reference to its supplies in each quarter it should consider using the percentage for the previous year instead.

This would simplify its administration and, whilst its percentage of exempt supplies is increasing, improve its cash flow position, as it would recover a greater percentage of VAT in each quarter.

There would be no change to the total VAT recovered as the annual adjustment would ensure that the amount of VAT recovered reflects the actual supplies made in the year.

Examiner's report

The corporation tax computations in part (i) were the straightforward marks and were prepared well. However, many candidates let themselves down by failing to satisfy the precise details of the requirement. The question asked for a calculation of the total of the liabilities of the three subsidiaries before taking account of the additional expenditure set out in the e-mail from the client, together with an explanation of the effects of that expenditure on the total of the liabilities. Unfortunately, many candidates simply calculated three corporation tax liabilities.

The manager's instructions required candidates to 'take advantage of any opportunities available to reduce the total corporation tax liability'. One of the companies, Truffle Ltd, had a chargeable gain. Candidates were expected to propose that some of that gain should be transferred to Fondant Ltd to take advantage of that company's capital loss. Many candidates did not spot this opportunity and would perhaps have benefited from pausing for a moment in order to give themselves a chance to think about the situation presented to them.

Candidates demonstrated an excellent knowledge of the relief available in respect of expenditure on research and development and the rules concerning the annual investment allowance.

The second part of the question required a 'detailed analysis' of whether or not a proposed acquisition would be a controlled foreign company together with the implications of it being such a company. This was a chance for candidates to present detailed knowledge of this area in a structured manner and many answers were very good. Candidates who did not score well either did not know this area of the syllabus well enough or did not pick up on the instructions to provide a 'detailed analysis' such that their answers were too brief and superficial. Many candidates would have benefited from pausing and thinking before they started writing in order to ensure that they approached the question in a logical manner and thus identified more of the points that needed to be made.

ANSWERS TO PRACTICE QUESTIONS: SECTION 2

> Candidates need to ensure that they identify all of the elements of the requirements in each question. In part (ii) of this question the client questioned the tax treatment of the arrangement fees and interest relating to the loan taken out to purchase the overseas subsidiary. This was not a difficult point but it was not addressed by many candidates.
>
> The final part of the question concerned a partially exempt company considering the purchase of a building and the workings of the capital goods scheme. This was reasonably straightforward and was done reasonably well. A small minority of candidates wasted time by providing detailed descriptions of partial exemption and other aspects of VAT and many candidates were confused about who was going to be charging VAT to whom. However, having said that, a good proportion of candidates understood the operation of the capital goods scheme and explained it well. Only a minority of candidates addressed the possible advantages of using the company's partial exemption percentage for the previous year.

ACCA marking scheme

		Marks
(i)	Reallocation of capital gain	1.0
	Use of capital loss brought forward	0.5
	Corporation tax liabilities	1.0
	Research and development	
	Tax deduction for cost incurred	0.5
	Further deduction	2.0
	Capital allowances	
	Annual investment allowance and writing down allowance	1.0
	Tax savings	1.5
	Budgeted liability for the subsidiaries	1.0
		8.5
	Maximum	8.0
(ii)	Consideration of whether or not Praline Inc is a CFC	
	Definition of CFC	1.5
	Consideration of the rules	
	Resident	1.0
	Control	0.5
	Implications of Praline Inc being a CFC	
	Apportionment of profits	1.0
	Unless exemption applies	0.5
	Exemptions	
	Identification of exemptions (0.5 mark each, maximum 2)	2.0
	Consideration of exemptions (1 mark each, maximum 3 marks)	3.0
	No chargeable profits	1.0
	Conclusions	2.0
	Double tax relief	1.0
	Loan to acquire Praline Inc	
	Non-trading deficit	1.0
	Availability of group relief	1.0
		15.5
	Maximum	13.0

KAPLAN PUBLISHING

		Marks
(iii) Purchase of office premises		
VAT charged and initial recovery		2.0
Outline of capital goods scheme		3.0
Partial exemption percentage		2.0
		7.0
	Maximum	6.0
Appropriate style and presentation		2.0
Effectiveness of communication		2.0
		4.0
Total		**31.0**

63 DAUBE GROUP (ADAPTED) *Walk in the footsteps of a top tutor*

Key answer tips

Part (a) is a typical corporation tax groups question covering: trading losses, capital gains aspects, VAT and stamp duty land tax.

The key to success is applying your knowledge to the scenario given and making sure that your answer only deals with the required issues; otherwise you are likely to run out of time.

You may not be familiar with the rules on pre-entry capital losses, as these have not been regularly tested in the past. However, there was a clue in the question.

Part (b) is a totally separate stand-alone section on the professional and ethical issues to consider before taking on a new client. Remember there will always be up to 5 marks in each exam on ethics.

There are easy marks available here, and it may therefore be a good idea to start with this part of the question just in case you run out of time on part (a).

The highlighted words in the written sections are key phrases that markers are looking for.

Tutor's top tips

As is usual for Section A questions, the requirement at the end of the question really just tells you how many marks are available for each section. The real requirements can all be found in the information provided in the question.

As you read through, highlight any requirements and instructions that you find. The requirements in this question are all in the email from the manager.

You may find it useful to number these requirements so that you can tick them off as you attempt them.

Make sure that you set out your answer to part (a) as a report, as there are marks available for this. You need to write in full sentences, but don't waste time preparing a lengthy introduction.

(a) **Report**

To   Mr Daube
From   Tax advisers
Date   6 December 2016
Subject Various corporate matters

(i) **Sale of Shank Ltd**

Use of trading losses

Tutor's top tips

There are two different trading losses to consider here:

- *The loss brought forward from the year ended 31 March 2016*
- *The current year loss for the year ended 31 March 2017.*

You will need to deal with each of these separately in your answer, and clearly label them.

The examining team asks you to consider all possibilities, so make sure that you do that. However, you must ensure that you apply your knowledge to the scenario: there is no point in spending time discussing reliefs that are not actually possible.

Loss brought forward

The loss brought forward of £35,000 can only be set against future trading profits of the same trade within Shank Ltd.

However, there is a possible restriction on the use of this loss as Shank Ltd will change its owners when it is sold to Raymond Ltd on 1 February 2017.

If there is a major change in the nature or conduct of trade within three years of this change in ownership, the loss will not be allowed to be carried forward past 1 February 2017.

A major change would include a change in products or services offered, markets or customers.

As Mr Daube is of the opinion that the company will only become profitable if there are fundamental changes to its commercial operations, it seems likely that the restriction will apply.

Tutor's top tips

Look for clues in the question – you are specifically asked to consider any anti-avoidance legislation that may restrict the use of the losses. This is a big hint that there is some relevant anti-avoidance legislation here!

Make sure that you apply the rules to the scenario: there will be 'fundamental changes' to the company's commercial operations.

Tutorial note

A 'change in ownership' occurs when more than 50% of the share capital in the company changes ownership. As Hock Ltd is disposing of all of the share capital in Shank Ltd, there clearly is a change in ownership.

*However, for the restriction in use of losses to apply, there must be **both** a change in ownership and a major change in the nature and conduct of trade.*

Current year loss

Tutor's top tips

Read the question carefully. The statement that Shank Ltd has surrendered the maximum possible losses to group companies applies to the losses in the past pre-31 March 2016, not the loss for the year ended 31 March 2017.

Therefore you need to include group relief as a key option available in your answer for the use of the loss in the year ended 31 March 2017.

The loss for the year ended 31 March 2017 cannot be set against current year profits or previous year profits of Shank Ltd, as there are none available. Shank Ltd has no other source of income.

All or part of this loss could be surrendered to other companies within Shank Ltd's 75% losses group. This group contains Hock Ltd, Shank Ltd, Rump Ltd and Brisket Ltd, but **not** Knuckle Ltd.

The loss available for surrender must be time apportioned, as Shank Ltd will only be part of the losses group for part of the year. For the purposes of group relief, Shank Ltd is deemed to leave the group once 'arrangements' for sale are in place. The contract for sale will represent such an 'arrangement', therefore Shank Ltd can only surrender losses up to 1 November 2016.

The maximum loss available for surrender to Hock Ltd and Rump Ltd is therefore £31,500 (7/12 × £54,000) from 1 April 2016 to 31 October 2016.

Brisket Ltd has only been part of the losses group since 1 May 2016, therefore the maximum loss available for surrender to Brisket Ltd is £27,000 (6/12 × £54,000), from 1 May 2016 to 31 October 2016.

The maximum loss that can be claimed by group companies will be limited to their taxable total profits for the corresponding period.

Any remaining losses will be carried forward by Shank Ltd along with its £35,000 brought forward loss and the loss incurred between 1 November 2016 and 31 January 2017, as described above.

Tutor's top tips

This part of the question is all about explaining the reliefs available, not about giving advice on which relief might be best.

There is no information given about the profits of the other group companies for you to offer such advice.

Tutorial note

The requirement is to give advice to Mr Daube about the options for the use of the trading loss within his group of companies, and so marks in the answer are going for advising on the loss incurred up to 31 January 2017 only, when Shank Ltd leaves the group.

There are therefore no marks for commenting on what can happen with the loss after Shank Ltd left Mr Daube's control.

However, were this a requirement, the loss for the year ended 31 March 2017 is actually divided into three parts:

- 1 April 2016 to 31 October 2016 (7 months loss = £31,500):
  group relief possible within Hock Ltd group
- 1 November 2016 to 31 January 2017 (3 months loss = £13,500):
  can only be used within Shank Ltd and as it has no other income, will be carried forward
- 1 February 2017 to 31 March 2017 (2 months loss = £9,000):
  can be group relieved within the new group

Loss on sale of Shank Ltd

The sale of Shank Ltd will be covered by the substantial shareholding exemption, as Hock Ltd is disposing of shares and has held at least 10% of the shares in Shank Ltd for 12 months in the two years before the sale, and both companies are trading companies.

Accordingly, there will be no relief for the capital loss on the disposal of the shares.

Tutorial note

You are probably aware that gains on the sale of shares are covered by the substantial shareholding exemption. However, remember that the 'exemption' means that not only are there no chargeable gains, there are no allowable losses either!

Threshold for payment of corporation tax by instalment

Tutor's top tips

Make sure that you read the verb in the question. You are asked to 'explain' the threshold for **all** of the companies. Just calculating the threshold is not enough here.

Also, remember that not all companies will necessarily have the same limits. Check the dates carefully to see which companies have joined or left during the year, as these may be related to old or new groups too.

Companies are related 51% group companies where one company controls another, or where companies are under the common control of another company.

Companies that join during the accounting period are deemed to be part of the group from the beginning of the following accounting period. Companies that leave during the accounting period are deemed to still be part of the group until the end of the current chargeable accounting period.

Knuckle Ltd has no related 51% group companies, so the threshold for Knuckle Ltd will be £1,500,000.

All of the Hock Ltd group companies except Brisket Ltd are related 51% group companies for the year ended 31 March 2017.

Accordingly the threshold for Hock Ltd and Rump Ltd for the year ended 31 March 2017 is £500,000 (£1,500,000 ÷ 3).

Brisket Ltd will be related to its previous owner and any other companies related to its previous owner. The threshold for Brisket Ltd could therefore be different from that shown above.

Tutorial note

A company is a related 51% group company in the year that it leaves a group, but not in the year that it joins.

Shank Ltd will not be related to its new owner until the following year.

Brisket Ltd, however, will be related to its previous owners, and if applicable, other related companies in that group.

There is not enough information in the question, to specifically calculate the number of related 51% group companies and therefore the threshold for Brisket Ltd.

(ii) **Sales of buildings**

Gains/losses on sale

Gar building

The sale of the Gar building to Hock Ltd will be at no gain, no loss, as Shank Ltd and Hock Ltd are part of the same 75% capital gains group.

Tutor's top tips

There is no need to do a calculation here, it is enough to just state that the transfer will be at no gain, no loss.

There were no extra marks available for any calculations of the base cost of the deemed transfer.

Tutorial note

Although Shank Ltd is deemed to leave the 75% group losses group on 1 November 2016, it is still part of the 75% capital gains group until the sale is completed on 1 February 2017.

Had the base cost been requested, the transfer would have occurred at the base cost of £283,500 (£210,000 + IA (£210,000 × 0.350)). The estimated proceeds given in the question are irrelevant.

There will be no degrouping charge in respect of the Gar building when Shank Ltd leaves the group. A degrouping charge only arises if the **recipient** company leaves the group less than 6 years after a no gain, no loss transfer, with the asset acquired.

Cray building

	£
Proceeds	420,000
Less: Cost	(240,000)
Unindexed gain	180,000
Less: Indexation allowance (£240,000 × 0.250)	(60,000)
Chargeable gain	120,000

Monk building

	£
Proceeds	290,000
Less: Cost	(380,000)
Capital loss	(90,000)

Indexation allowance is not available to increase the capital loss.

Sword building

Tutor's top tips

Be very careful here!

Before you can work out the gain on the Sword building, you need to calculate the allowable cost. There has been a rollover relief claim, but only part of the proceeds were reinvested, so only part of the gain on the Pilot building will have been rolled over.

	£
Proceeds	460,000
Less: Deemed cost (W1)	(210,000)
Unindexed gain	250,000
Less: Indexation allowance (£210,000 × 0.480)	(100,800)
Chargeable gain	149,200

Workings

(W1) **Deemed cost of Sword building**

	£
Original cost	255,000
Less: Rollover relief (W2)	(45,000)
Deemed cost	210,000

(W2) **Rollover relief in respect of Sword building**

	£
Gain on sale of the Pilot building	60,000
Less: Sale proceeds not reinvested in the Sword building (£270,000 – £255,000)	(15,000)
Rollover relief claimed	45,000

Tutorial note

The chargeable gains will arise in the company that made the disposal.

The chargeable gain arising in Knuckle Ltd's corporation tax computation cannot be moved to any other company.

However, the chargeable gain arising in Rump Ltd can be moved within the capital gains group, for example to utilise capital losses brought forward.

Explaining this, however, is not mark earning as it is not specifically required in the question.

Use of capital losses

Tutor's top tips

Make sure that you provide the detailed explanations requested, and remember that capital losses are more restricted than trading losses.

The examining team is kind here, and tells you to watch out for the pre-entry loss on the Monk building. Even if you were unsure about the rules regarding pre-entry capital losses, you could still score some marks for a sensible attempt at describing its possible use.

Pre-entry loss

The Monk building was sold by Brisket Ltd before it joined the Hock Ltd group. Accordingly, the capital loss that arose before 1 May 2016 when Brisket Ltd joined the group is a restricted pre-entry loss.

It can only be set-off against gains on disposals made by Brisket Ltd on assets that it owned before it joined the group, or bought subsequently from unconnected persons for use in its own business.

Tutorial note

The question asks for the options available for the use of the loss only.

It does not ask for discussions re tax planning.

Therefore, no marks would be allocated to making such comments.

VAT on sale of buildings

Tutor's top tips

VAT on land and buildings and the option to tax are regularly tested in the exam. You must make sure that you learn the rules!

Inter-group transfer

Provided Hock Ltd and Shank Ltd are members of a VAT group, VAT should not be charged on the inter-group sale of the Gar building.

Other sales

VAT should only be charged on the sale of commercial buildings if:

- they are less than three years old; or
- the owner has opted to tax the building.

Stamp duty land tax

Tutor's top tips

The stamp duty rates and thresholds are given in the tax tables provided in the examination. To score marks here, you must make sure that you apply these rates to the buildings in the question.

Inter group transfer

There will be no stamp duty land tax payable on the transfer of the Gar building, as Shank Ltd and Hock Ltd are within the same 75% group.

Other sales

Stamp duty land tax will be payable at 3% on the sale price of other buildings, and will be payable by the purchaser.

Tutorial note

Even though Shank Ltd leaves the 75% group within three years of the transfer of the Gar building, there is still no stamp duty payable.

Stamp duty is only payable where the **transferee** company leaves the group within three years.

(iii) **Sales by Knuckle Ltd to overseas customers**

VAT implications

Tutor's top tips

Consideration of the VAT implications of imports and exports is another popular area in the exam.

Note that the examining team does not state whether the exports by Knuckle Ltd will be within the EU or outside the EU; so you must discuss both possibilities.

There are four marks available here, so you should try to make at least four separate points in your answer.

Sales outside the EU

Sales to customers outside the EU are zero rated.

Sales within the EU

Sales to VAT registered customers within the EU are also zero rated, provided the customer's VAT number is known.

Sales to customers who are not VAT registered will be standard rated.

If the level of sales to non-VAT registered customers in another EU country are above the relevant threshold limit in that country, Knuckle Ltd may have to register for VAT in that country.

The exports (whether zero rated or standard rated) will not affect Knuckle Ltd's ability to reclaim input VAT, as all sales will still be taxable sales.

Knuckle Ltd must retain evidence of the exports.

(b) **Before agreeing to become tax advisers to Mr Daube and his companies**

Tutor's top tips

There are 5 marks available for this section, so try to make sure that you have at least 5 separately identifiable points available and address each of the requirements: information needed and actions to take!

Information needed:

- Proof of identity for Mr Daube (e.g. passport), and proof of address (e.g. utility bill)
- Proof of incorporation, primary business address and registered office for each company
- The structure, directors and shareholders of the companies
- The identities of those persons instructing the firm on behalf of the company and those persons that are authorised to do so.

Action to take:

Consider whether becoming tax advisers to Mr Daube and his companies would create any threats to compliance with the fundamental principles of professional ethics, for example integrity and professional competence.

Where such threats exist, we should not accept the appointment unless the threats can be reduced to an acceptable level via the implementation of safeguards.

Contact the existing tax adviser in order to ensure that there has been no action by Mr Daube or his companies that would, on ethical grounds, preclude us from accepting appointment.

Examiner's report

Part (a) was in three parts and, on the whole, was done well by many candidates. The vast majority of candidates prepared their answer in the correct report format although a minority wasted time producing a long and unnecessary introduction.

Candidates' knowledge of the reliefs available in respect of trading losses was often very good but many let themselves down by addressing the issue in the abstract rather than in relation to the companies in the question.

This resulted in detailed explanations of reliefs that were simply not applicable (in particular the offset of losses against current and previous years' profits) such that candidates then had too little time to explain the relevant points properly.

As always, candidates benefited if they paused to allow themselves to identify the issues within the question.

There was to be a change of ownership of the loss making company and an apparent major change in the manner in which it would carry on its activities going forward. Accordingly, it is likely that it would be unable to carry forward its losses beyond the date of the change of ownership. There were also arrangements in force for the company to be sold such that it would leave the group relief group prior to the legal transfer of the shares.

Many candidates spotted both of these points but those that did not need to think about how they would do things differently such that they would spot them in the future. Finally, a surprising number of candidates thought, incorrectly, that Knuckle Ltd was a member of the group relief group.

The capital loss on the sale of the company was not available for offset due to the substantial shareholding exemption. Somewhat surprisingly, many candidates missed this and, of those that spotted the point, many thought that whilst a gain would not be subject to tax, a loss would still be allowable.

For the final element of this part of the question candidates were asked to explain the corporation tax threshold of the companies. Many candidates simply stated the number of related 51% group companies and the consequent thresholds; but that was not an explanation. What was needed were the reasons for the limits being what they were including references to the companies being controlled by the same company and the effect of companies joining and leaving the group. The threshold was not the same for each of the companies. Candidates needed to consider each of the companies and apply their knowledge of the rules to that company's particular circumstances.

Note that this part of the question has been amended since it was originally set.

Part (ii) concerned the planned disposal of a number of buildings. The capital gains were reasonably straightforward with just an added complication of a gain rolled over into the cost of one of the buildings.

However, many candidates missed the fact that one of the buildings would be transferred at no gain, no loss as the vendor and the purchaser were in a capital gains group. Others made errors in connection with the indexation allowance (increasing a capital loss with indexation or applying the indexation factor to the unindexed gain rather than the cost) and the treatment of the held over gain. There was a sense here that some candidates had switched off in that some of the errors were very basic and were perhaps an indication of not paying sufficient attention as opposed to a lack of knowledge.

Candidates were told in the question that there was a pre-entry capital loss arising on the sale of one of the buildings. Only a small minority had a clear understanding of the manner in which the pre-entry loss could be used.

A minority of candidates wasted time on this part of the question explaining, often in some detail, how the gains and losses should be offset. This was not part of the requirements and there was insufficient information in the question to arrive at sensible conclusions. Candidates will always benefit from taking the time to read each requirement carefully and then taking care not to deviate from the tasks set.

The VAT and stamp duty land tax elements were handled well by many candidates. Those who did not do so well need to apply their knowledge to the facts as opposed to simply writing what they know. For example, the prices at which the buildings were to be sold meant that, where duty was payable, the rate would be 3%. Yet some candidates answered in the abstract and gave the various rates of duty for all possible prices that could be charged. Only a small number of candidates considered the possibility of there being a VAT group; slightly more identified that there would be no stamp duty land tax on the property transferred within the group.

ANSWERS TO PRACTICE QUESTIONS: SECTION 2

Part (iii) concerned the VAT implications of selling goods overseas. There were many excellent answers to this part that, whilst being brief, often scored almost full marks. Weaker candidates either had not learned the rules or confused their terminology using the phrase 'no VAT will be charged' as opposed to 'zero rated'; the two terms do not mean the same thing.

The majority of candidates scored well in part (b). Many took the sensible approach of starting the question with this part in order to ensure that they had sufficient time available to prepare an appropriate answer. A minority had not taken the time to learn this area of the syllabus with the result that they were unable to obtain some very straightforward marks.

ACCA marking scheme			
			Marks
(a)	(i)	Use of trading losses	
		Losses carried forward	3.5
		Current year loss	5.5
		Loss on sale of Shank Ltd	2.0
		Corporation tax threshold	3.5
			14.5
		Maximum	12.0
	(ii)	Gar building	2.0
		Cray building	1.0
		Sword building	2.5
		Monk building	
		Capital loss	1.0
		Use of pre-entry loss	2.0
		VAT	3.0
		Stamp duty land tax	2.0
			13.5
		Maximum	10.0
	(iii)	Customers situated outside the EU	1.0
		Customers situated within the EU	2.5
		Possibility of need to register in other countries	1.0
		Recoverability of input tax	1.0
			5.5
		Maximum	4.0
		Appropriate style and presentation	2.0
		Effectiveness of communication	2.0
			4.0
(b)		Information needed	3.0
		Action to take	3.0
			6.0
		Maximum	5.0
Total			**35.0**

64 LORIOD PLC GROUP *Walk in the footsteps of a top tutor*

Key answer tips

This question is all about overseas aspects of corporation tax. Question 5 in the exam often covers overseas aspects of tax, either for an individual or a company.

Part (a) covers branch versus subsidiary for a business making losses, and should have offered some easy marks.

Part (b) is tricky, and requires calculation of the maximum group relief claim to avoid wasting DTR.

Part (c) is a written section on transfer pricing, which again should have offered some easy marks.

The highlighted words in the written sections are key phrases that markers are looking for.

(a) **Relief available for expected loss of Frager business**

Tutor's top tips

You may be tempted to write everything you know about branch versus subsidiary here, but the question just requires you to discuss the relief available for losses. There will be no marks for discussing other aspects.

The examining team asks for a 'detailed explanation'. Take note of the number of marks available: 7 marks means that you need to aim to write at least 7 separate points.

Make sure that your answer is clearly labelled so that the marker knows whether you are talking about Strategy A or Strategy B.

Strategy A – Overseas branch

If Elivar Ltd purchases the trade and assets, the Fragar business will be an overseas branch and treated as extension of Elivar Ltd for tax purposes.

As it is controlled from the UK, its results will be part of Elivar Ltd's results. The loss will automatically be offset against Elivar Ltd's trading profits. It would be inadvisable to elect for the branch results to be exempt from UK tax, as this would result in the denial of loss relief.

If this leads to an overall trading loss in Elivar Ltd, this may be surrendered to other 75% group companies.

Any excess losses will be carried forward in Elivar Ltd to set against future trading profits from the same trade.

The losses will save UK corporation tax at 20%.

Strategy B – Overseas subsidiary

If Elivar Ltd purchases the shares, Syme Inc will remain as a separate legal entity and will be an overseas subsidiary.

As Syme Inc is resident overseas, the losses cannot be surrendered to the Loriod plc group.

Instead, the losses will be subject to the rules in Kuwata. It may be possible to carry back the losses in Syme Inc and obtain immediate relief, otherwise they are likely to be carried forward.

The losses will only save tax in Kuwata at 14%, as opposed to 20% if Strategy A is adopted, although relief may be obtained earlier under Strategy B if carry back of the loss is possible.

(b) **Maximum loss surrendered to Elivar Ltd**

Tutor's top tips

The calculations here are quite challenging. Remember that DTR is restricted to the UK tax due on the foreign profits, so the UK tax on the foreign profits needs to be exactly the same as the overseas tax to avoid wasting DTR.

Even if you did not manage to calculate the correct answer, you could still score marks for explaining the principles involved.

The double tax relief available for the tax suffered in Kuwata will be given as a tax credit for the lower of:

(i) the overseas tax suffered, or

(ii) the UK tax on the overseas profits.

To avoid wasting relief, the UK tax should be the same as the tax suffered in Kuwata, i.e. £18,200 (14% × £130,000).

Tutor's top tips

Once you have established what the UK tax needs to be, work backwards to find the level of profit needed.

As the UK tax is at 20%, to achieve UK tax on overseas income of £18,200, the taxable profit remaining after loss relief should be £91,000 (£18,200 ÷ 20%).

In order to maximise DTR, the qualifying charitable donation and group relief are set off against UK profits in priority to overseas profits.

The maximum loss to be surrendered is therefore £127,000, calculated as follows:

Elivar Ltd – corporation tax computation

	Total £	UK profits £	Overseas profits £
Taxable UK profits	90,000	90,000	
Taxable overseas profits	130,000		130,000
Less: Qualifying charitable donation	(2,000)	(2,000)	
Total profits before group relief	218,000	88,000	130,000
Less: Group relief (balancing figure)	(127,000)	(88,000)	(39,000)
Taxable total profits required (see above)	91,000	Nil	91,000

Tutorial note

Proof that this amount of group relief does not waste DTR:

	£
UK corporation tax on overseas profits (20% × £91,000)	18,200
Less: DTR = lower of	
(i) Overseas tax = (£130,000 × 14%) = £18,200	
(ii) UK tax = £18,200	(18,200)
Corporation tax payable	Nil

(c) **Impact of prices on total tax paid by group**

Tutor's top tips

This part of the question is about transfer pricing. To score well you need to make sure that you apply your knowledge to the specific scenario set, and think about the rates of tax that each company is paying.

Transfer pricing

The subsidiary in Kuwata will pay tax at 14%, whereas the UK group companies will be taxed at 20%. Profits could be shifted from the UK group to the overseas subsidiary by charging higher prices in the subsidiary, and thus save tax.

However, the transfer pricing rules state that where transactions between connected parties are not at market value, and this results in less tax payable in the UK, the UK company gaining the advantage must adjust its profits to reflect the arm's length price.

The rules will apply as Elivar Ltd controls Syme Inc. There is no exemption in this case, whether or not the group is large, as there is no double tax treaty with Kuwata.

It is possible to obtain HMRC approval of group pricing arrangements in advance.

Tutorial note

Usually, small and medium sized enterprises are not subject to the transfer pricing legislation. However, where one of the parties is overseas and there is no double tax treaty, the rules will apply.

Examiner's report

Part (a) required candidates to explain the relief available in respect of the expected loss to be made by the business depending on whether it was established as a branch or a subsidiary of the UK company. This was an area where candidates had a certain amount of knowledge but, on the whole, did not score as well as they could have done because they wrote generally about branch versus subsidiary as opposed to addressing the particular facts and requirements of this question.

In particular, despite being asked to address loss relief, many candidates wrote about the taxation of profits. Many of those who did address losses did not address them as precisely as they could have done in the context of the question such that they did not consider the relevance of the tax rates provided.

Part (b) was carried out elegantly by a minority of candidates but the majority struggled with the problem. Credit was available for approaching the question by reference to double tax relief but many candidates simply stated that group relief was restricted to the lower of the losses available and the profits subject to tax.

The final part of the question concerned transfer pricing and was done reasonably well by many candidates who had a good knowledge of the transfer pricing rules. However, only a small minority made reference to the relevance of the size of the companies in determining whether or not the rules would apply or to the possibility of reaching an agreement with HM Revenue and Customs.

The question also required candidates to explain how the prices charged between the group companies would affect the total tax paid by the group. In order to do this, candidates had to focus on the difference between the tax rate in the UK and that in Kuwata and the possibility of group profits being taxed at the lower rate. It was important here to address the situation from a group perspective rather than that of a particular company. However, the majority of candidates did not address this element of the question.

PAPER P6: ADVANCED TAXATION (FA2015)

ACCA marking scheme		Marks
(a)	Use of permanent establishment	4.0
	Use of subsidiary	3.0
	Comparison	1.0
		8.0
	Maximum	7.0
(b)	Explanations	
	Double tax relief	2.0
	UK tax on overseas profits	2.0
	Calculations	2.0
		6.0
	Maximum	5.0
(c)	Impact of prices on total tax paid by group	2.0
	Transfer pricing	
	Why the rules apply	2.0
	Application of the rules	1.5
	HMRC confirmation of pricing arrangements	1.0
		6.5
	Maximum	6.0
Total		18.0

65 DRENCH, HAIL LTD AND RAIN LTD (ADAPTED) Online question assistance

 Walk in the footsteps of a top tutor

Key answer tips

This is really four separate questions.

Part (a)(i) covers the acquisition of a subsidiary, with or without losses, by either an individual or a company, and is the hardest part of the question.

Part (a)(ii) is really two written questions: one on close company loans to participators and one on the cash accounting scheme for VAT. These questions should have been very straightforward if you have learnt the rules, and could be attempted before (a)(i).

Part (b) deals with the ethical issue of confidentiality. Again, this part is very straightforward and could be attempted before the other parts of the question, in order to gain some easy marks.

The highlighted words in the written sections are key phrases that markers are looking for.

ANSWERS TO PRACTICE QUESTIONS: SECTION 2

Tutor's top tips

The requirement at the end of the question just tells you how many marks are available for each section. The detailed requirements are all in the email from your manager.

You may find it useful to number these requirements so that you can tick them off as you attempt them.

(a)

MEMORANDUM

To   The files
From   Tax assistant
Date   9 December 2016
Subject   Acquisition of Rain Ltd and other matters

(i) **Acquisition of Rain Ltd**

Tutor's top tips

There are four alternatives to consider here:

*1   Drench acquires Rain Ltd personally and Rain Ltd **does not** obtain the new contracts.*

*2   Drench acquires Rain Ltd personally and Rain Ltd **does** obtain the new contracts.*

*3   Hail Ltd acquires Rain Ltd and Rain Ltd **does not** obtain the new contracts.*

*4   Hail Ltd acquires Rain Ltd and Rain Ltd **does** obtain the new contracts.*

In order to score well on this part of the question, you must consider all four options. It is very important that you label your answer clearly, so that the marker can see which option you are dealing with.

Rain Ltd acquired by Drench personally

Tutor's top tips

Think carefully about the group relationships that exist here.

Drench is an individual, not a company.

Companies controlled by the same individual will not be related 51% group companies for corporation tax purposes and cannot form a 75% group relief group.

Therefore, the companies cannot transfer losses and will not affect the payment dates for corporation tax purposes.

KAPLAN PUBLISHING   605

Rain Ltd does not obtain the new contracts

The only option available for relief of the £110,000 trading loss will be to set it against Rain Ltd's own profits.

An amount of £50,750 can be set against taxable total profits (i.e. the chargeable gain) for the period ending 30 June 2017.

The remaining loss of £59,250 (£110,000 − £50,750) will then be carried forward for offset against Rain Ltd's first available future trading profits of the same trade.

There is no possibility of carrying back the remaining loss, as Rain Ltd had no taxable income or gains in the previous accounting period.

Tutor's top tips

*Be very specific when writing about loss reliefs. For example, just saying that the remaining loss will be carried forward is not enough. You must also state that it will be set against future trading profits from the **same trade**.*

Rain Ltd does obtain the new contracts

The corporation tax liability of Rain Ltd will be as follows:

Corporation tax – 9 months ending 30 June 2017

	£
Trading profit	285,000
Chargeable gain	50,750
Taxable total profits	335,750
Corporation tax at 20%	67,150

Corporation tax payment date

If Rain Ltd is acquired by Drench personally, Rain Ltd will not be related to Hail Ltd as both companies will not be under common control of the same company.

Rain Ltd, Flake Ltd and Mist Ltd will be related 51% group companies for the period ending 30 June 2017, giving three related companies in total.

As Rain Ltd prepares accounts for a nine month period, the threshold must also be time apportioned.

Rain Ltd's threshold for corporation tax purposes for the nine months ending 30 June 2017 is, therefore £375,000 (£1,500,000 × 1/3 × 9/12).

ANSWERS TO PRACTICE QUESTIONS: SECTION 2

Tutorial note

Remember that when a company leaves a group part way through the accounting period, it is taken into account in determining the payment dates of the old group and its payment date is affected by the other companies in the old group, as it was a related 51% group company at the end of the previous CAP.

Rain Ltd will not need to pay its corporation tax in quarterly instalments, as it does not have profits above this threshold.

The corporation tax will be due by 1 April 2018 (i.e. nine months and one day after the end of the chargeable accounting period).

Rain Ltd acquired by Hail Ltd

Tutor's top tips

Again, think carefully about the group relationships that exist here.

Hail Ltd is a company, so this time, Rain Ltd and Hail Ltd can form a 75% group relief group, and therefore can transfer losses.

Rain Ltd does not obtain the new contracts

This time, there are several options for relief of the £110,000 loss, and Rain Ltd should choose the option that gives the earliest tax saving, as all options will save tax at the same rate of 20%.

Rain Ltd could again claim relief for the loss against its own profits, as set out above where Drench acquires Rain Ltd.

Group relief

Hail Ltd and Rain Ltd will form a 75% group relief group.

Rain Ltd could, therefore, surrender its current period loss against Hail Ltd's taxable total profits for the same period.

As Rain Ltd only joins the Hail Ltd group on 1 January 2017, the maximum loss available for surrender must be time apportioned as follows:

(£110,000 × 6/9) = £73,333 available

The maximum loss claimed by Hail Ltd would be restricted to its taxable total profits for the corresponding period:

(£100,000 × 6/12) = £50,000

As the available loss is more than the maximum claim, the maximum group relief would be restricted to £50,000.

Accordingly, in order to obtain relief as early as possible, the loss should be utilised as follows:

	Loss used £	Tax saved £
Set against Rain Ltd taxable total profits	50,750	
Surrender to Hail Ltd	50,000	
	100,750	
Total tax saved (£100,750 × 20%)		20,150

Payment for group relief

Amounts paid for group relief are ignored for corporation tax purposes, as long as the amount paid is no more than the amount of loss surrendered.

Rain Ltd does obtain the new contracts

Rain Ltd will still have the same corporation tax as when acquired by Drench (i.e. £67,150).

As Rain Ltd will now be controlled by Hail Ltd, Hail Ltd will be a related 51% group company. However, this will not affect the threshold for payment of corporation tax by instalment until the following accounting period.

Therefore the payment date will be exactly the same as before (i.e. 1 April 2018).

Tutorial note

Remember that when a company joins a group part way through the accounting period, it is not taken into account in determining the payment dates of the new group and the new group companies are not taken into account in determining its payment date, as it was not a related 51% company at the end of the previous CAP. It will be related in the following CAP.

This means that when a company moves from one group to another, it is related to the old group in the year of change and the new group in the following CAP.

Tax treatment of Rain Ltd's building

Potential tax liabilities: Degrouping charge

The transfer of the building from Mist Ltd to Rain Ltd would have been at no gain, no loss, as Mist Ltd and Rain Ltd were part of a 75% gains group at the time.

Whether Rain Ltd is purchased by Drench or Hail Ltd, it will be leaving the Flake Ltd group within six years of the no gain, no loss transfer whilst still owning the building.

This will result in a degrouping charge in the nine months ending 30 June 2017 as set out below.

	£
Market value on 1 July 2013 (date of the no gain/no loss transfer)	260,000
Less: Cost to Mist Ltd	(170,000)
Less: Indexation allowance	
((249.7 – 183.1)/183.1) = 0.364 × £170,000	(61,880)
Degrouping charge	28,120

The degrouping charge will be added to Flake Ltd's proceeds for the sale of the shares in Rain Ltd, and may increase the gain on disposal of the shares.

However, it is likely that the disposal of shares will be covered by the substantial shareholding exemption, assuming that Flake Ltd is a trading company, as it will have held at least 10% of the shares for at least 12 months in the two years before the disposal.

Base cost of the building

The base cost of the building for Rain Ltd will now be £260,000 as at 1 July 2013 (i.e. the market value at the date of the no gain, no loss transfer).

Tutorial note

If Rain Ltd did not leave the Flake Ltd group, the base cost of the building would be the original cost to the group of £170,000 plus indexation allowance to the date of the transfer on 1 July 2013.

(ii) **Loan to Drench and value added tax (VAT) cash accounting scheme**

Loan from Hail Ltd to Drench

Tutor's top tips

The requirement asks for the tax implications for Hail Ltd (i.e. the employer) only, so don't waste time writing at length about the implications for Drench.

However, you do need to consider the taxable benefit for Drench, as employer's class 1A national insurance contributions will be based on this.

Hail Ltd is a close company, as it is controlled by one shareholder (participator): Drench.

Accordingly, this will be a loan from a close company to a participator, and Hail Ltd must pay a tax charge to HMRC of £4,500 (25% × £18,000).

This tax charge should be paid with the corporation tax liability, by 1 April 2018.

When the loan is repaid by Drench, HMRC will repay the £4,500 tax charge to Hail Ltd within nine months and one day from the end of the accounting period of repayment.

Tutorial note

Watch out for close companies in the exam, as they regularly feature in questions.

A company is close if it is controlled by its directors (any number), or if it is controlled by 5 or fewer shareholders.

Hail Ltd must also pay employer's class 1A national insurance contributions, as the loan will give rise to a taxable employment benefit for Drench.

The benefit will be based on the official rate of interest of 3%, and the NICs payable will be calculated at 13.8% as follows:

(£18,000 × 3%) = £540 × 13.8% = £75.

The NICs will be deductible when computing the company's taxable trading profits.

Hail Ltd should include the loan on Drench's Form P11D in order to report it to HMRC.

VAT cash accounting scheme

Tutor's top tips

The cash accounting scheme for VAT is a topic that was tested at F6.

It is important that you retain your F6 knowledge, as the examiner frequently tests F6 topics in the P6 exam.

There are two specific aspects to write about here:

1   The advantages of the scheme

2   Whether it will be possible for Rain Ltd to operate the scheme.

Advantages

The advantages of the scheme are:

- Improved cash flow, as output VAT in respect of credit sales is only paid to HMRC when cash is received from the customer.
- Automatic relief for irrecoverable debts. If the customer does not pay, no output VAT is paid to HMRC.

Tutor's top tips

*Don't just describe how the scheme works. You need to say **why** it is advantageous for VAT to be accounted for when cash is received from a customer.*

ANSWERS TO PRACTICE QUESTIONS: SECTION 2

Availability to Rain Ltd

A business can only join the cash accounting scheme if it has annual taxable sales revenue of no more than £1,350,000.

If Rain Ltd acquires the new contracts, it will have sales revenue of £1,425,000 for the nine months ending 30 June 2017, and so will not be able to join the scheme.

If Rain Ltd does not acquire the new contracts, it will be able to join the scheme, as long as its VAT returns and payments are up to date and it has had no convictions for VAT offences or penalties for dishonest conduct.

Tutor's top tips

Even if you could not remember the limits applicable to the scheme, you could still score marks here for knowing that there were limits, and for attempting to apply the rules to the scenario.

(b) **Briefing note – use of knowledge**

Tutor's top tips

Ethical issues appear in every P6 exam, for up to five marks. It is worth learning the key principles, as these are often easy marks that can be scored very quickly.

However, you must make sure that you apply the principles to the scenario and don't just list them.

Try to make sure that you have at least five separate points in your answer, as you will probably score one mark per relevant point.

- As members of the ACCA, we must comply with the ACCA Professional Code of Ethics.
- One of the fundamental principles of this code is confidentiality.
- We must not disclose confidential information to other parties without our client's permission.
- This restriction continues to apply even if we no longer act for the client.
- Accordingly, we should not use confidential information acquired from our ex-client to assist Rain Ltd.
- However, it is acceptable to use our general experience and expertise gained from advising our ex-client.

KAPLAN PUBLISHING

Examiner's report

In part (a)(i) there were four possibilities to consider.

The question asked for the tax implications to be compared such that numbers should have been produced for each of the four possible situations. The question also stated that Drench was aware of the general implications of forming a group and that the comparison should focus on certain specific issues. It was important for candidates to be clear as to what they had been asked to do and also what they had been asked not to do. The answers to this question were not as good as expected.

The following general mistakes were made by many candidates:

- Many candidates did not structure their answers to this part particularly well such that it was not always clear which of the four possible situations was being addressed.

- Despite the question instructing candidates to focus on specific issues, many candidates wasted time by addressing general issues. Accordingly, a considerable amount of unnecessary information was provided in connection with groups generally and the extraction of profits from companies.

- A minority of candidates reached an initial conclusion that Rain Ltd should be acquired by Hail Ltd such that numbers were only prepared for that eventuality.

- When addressing the purchase of Rain Ltd by Drench, a minority of candidates erroneously relieved the company's losses against the income of Drench.

In addition to the general mistakes set out above, many candidates stated that the losses of Rain Ltd would have to be carried forward if the company were purchased by Drench due to the unavailability of group relief. This omitted the possibility of a current year offset against the chargeable gains in Rain Ltd. The other specific common error related to the effect of the acquisition on the accounting periods of Rain Ltd with many candidates confusing the need to time apportion losses for the purposes of group relief with the need to prepare tax computations for separate accounting periods.

Matters done well included the identification of the degrouping charge, the corporation tax payment dates and the calculations of the maximum possible group relief.

Part (a)(ii) concerned a loan from Hail Ltd to Drench and the VAT cash accounting scheme. This part was done reasonably well with many candidates demonstrating a good knowledge of the technical areas.

The question asked for the tax implications **for Hail Ltd** of the loan. Almost all candidates recognised that Hail Ltd was a close company such that a 25% charge would be payable to H M Revenue and Customs. However, very few candidates identified that Hail Ltd would have to pay class 1A national insurance contributions in respect of the benefit relating to the loan. This is not an obscure point and would have been known to almost all candidates. It may be candidates need to think about the requirement and identify all of the possible issues before commencing writing in order to identify as many relevant points as possible.

The majority of candidates were able to identify the advantages of using the VAT cash accounting scheme and to link the facts in the question to the scheme's limit in respect of annual taxable supplies; this part of the question was answered well.

The final part of the question concerned the ethical considerations relating to confidentiality and was done well by the majority of candidates.

ANSWERS TO PRACTICE QUESTIONS: SECTION 2

		ACCA marking scheme	
			Marks
(a)	(i)	Rain Ltd acquired by Drench personally	
		Rain Ltd makes tax adjusted loss	
		Use of losses	2.5
		Rain Ltd makes tax adjusted profit	
		Corporation tax liability	1.0
		Corporation tax threshold	1.5
		Corporation tax payment date	2.0
		Rain Ltd acquired by Hail Ltd	
		Rain Ltd makes tax adjusted loss	3.5
		Rain Ltd makes tax adjusted profit	1.5
		Rain Ltd building	
		Degrouping charge and tax treatment	3.5
		Base cost to Rain Ltd	1.0
			16.5
		Maximum	15.0
	(ii)	Loan to Drench	
		Close company loan to participator	1.0
		Payment to HMRC	2.0
		Employment income benefit	2.5
		Cash accounting scheme	
		Advantages	2.0
		Conditions	2.0
			9.5
		Maximum	8.0
		Appropriate style and presentation	1.0
		Effectiveness of communication	1.0
			2.0
(b)		Confidentiality, 1 mark per relevant point	5.0
Total			**30.0**

KAPLAN PUBLISHING

66 JANUS PLC GROUP (ADAPTED)   *Walk in the footsteps of a top tutor*

Key answer tips

This question mainly covers corporation tax groups but also examines the capital goods scheme, intangible assets (patent rights), VAT on the import of services, the substantial shareholding exemption and the responsibilities of senior accounting officers.

The groups section tests whether you understand the different types of groups that exist for corporation tax purposes. If you were not able to distinguish between the different groups you would struggle to score high marks here.

The highlighted words in the written sections are key phrases that markers are looking for.

Tutor's top tips

Before answering the groups part of the question you should take some time to decide which companies form a group relief group and identify the consortium. It is also important to realise which companies have joined or left the group in the year as this will affect the loss claims.

Remember that Castor Ltd is not a consortium owned company because the remaining 30% is owned by individuals.

(a) **Use of the trading loss of Janus plc**

(i) **Alternative reliefs available**

Tutor's top tips

To score the marks available for explaining the reliefs you need to apply your knowledge to the facts in the scenario. Don't just list all of the possible option; be specific.

Janus Ltd can use the trading loss itself and/or surrender the loss as group/consortium relief. Make sure that you state clearly:

- *which profits the loss can be set against, and*
- *for which period.*

Utilising the loss themselves

Janus plc can relieve the trading loss against its chargeable gain of £44,500 in the year ended 31 March 2016. Once this current period claim has been made, the loss can then be relieved against the company's total profits of the previous chargeable accounting period of £95,000.

Group relief

Janus plc can surrender trading losses to its 75% subsidiaries. For a company to be a 75% subsidiary, Janus plc must have an effective 75% interest in the company's ordinary share capital, its distributable income and its net assets were it to be wound up. Accordingly, Janus plc is in a group relief group with Seb Ltd and Viola Ltd only (Tutorial note).

Any amount of losses can be surrendered up to the level of the group member's taxable total profits for the corresponding accounting period. Seb Ltd and Viola Ltd did not become members of the group until 1 December 2015. Accordingly, only 4/12 of each of these companies' taxable total profits can be relieved via group relief.

Tutorial note

Castor Ltd (and therefore Pollux Ltd also) is not in a group relief group with Janus plc as Janus plc owns < 75% in Castor Ltd. There is no need to mention this specifically in the answer as once the definition is given, it is sufficient to demonstrate the application of the rules by just concluding which companies are in the group relief group.

Similarly Duet Ltd is not in a group relief group with Janus plc as Janus plc owns < 75%, but it is a consortia company as explained below.

Consortium relief

Duet Ltd is a consortium company as at least 75% of its share capital is owned by companies, each of which own at least 5%. Accordingly, £110,000 (£200,000 × 55%) of its taxable total profits can be relieved via consortium relief.

Tutorial note

The maximum consortium relief is always based on the % share of the results in the consortium company.

If the consortium company makes a loss, the members can each claim their % of that loss.

If the consortium company makes a profit (as is the case here), the members can each surrender losses against their % of the consortia company's profit.

Castor Ltd is not a consortium company as the minority interest shareholding is owned by an individual rather than a company.

(ii) **Strategy in order to maximise the loss utilised**

Tutor's top tips

Having set out the reliefs available in (a) (i) you then need to apply those reliefs in this part of the question.

The trading loss of Janus plc should therefore be relieved as follows:

	Loss utilised £	Loss available £
Total loss		330,000
Janus plc: Current year	44,500	
Prior year	95,000	
Seb Ltd (maximum = 4/12 × £37,000)	12,333	
Viola Ltd (maximum = 4/12 × £86,000)	28,667	
Duet Ltd (maximum = 55% × £200,000)	110,000	
		(290,500)
Loss carried forward		39,500

(b) **Assets to be sold**

(i) **P HQ**

Tutor's Top Tips

Castor Ltd owns 80% of Pollux Ltd which is at least 75% thus the two companies are in the same capital gains group, so when P Ltd acquired the building from C Ltd the transfer took place at nil gain/nil loss.

The transfer value of the building would be original cost plus indexation allowance to date.

However, Janus only owns 70% of Castor Ltd which is less than 75% so when P Ltd sells the building to J Ltd the transfer must take place at market value which will result in a capital gain arising.

The examining team has asked you to **explain** how to compute this.

Pollux Ltd and Janus plc are not in a capital gains group as Castor Ltd is not a 75% subsidiary of Janus plc.

The sale of the building will result in a chargeable gain equal to the excess of the proceeds, £285,000, over the building's base cost.

Tutorial note

There is no degrouping charge here, as such a charge can only occur when a company leaves a capital gains group (i.e. when there is a sale of shares).

This question involved the sale of a building, not a sale of shares.

Pollux Ltd acquired the building from Castor Ltd. The two companies are in a capital gains group as Pollux Ltd is a 75% subsidiary of Castor Ltd.

Accordingly, the building would have been transferred at no gain, no loss.

The base cost of the building to Pollux Ltd is the original cost when it was acquired by Castor Ltd (assuming Castor Ltd did not acquire it via a no gain, no loss transfer), together with indexation allowance from the date the building was acquired by Castor Ltd until the date it was sold to Pollux Ltd.

Further indexation allowance will then be available from the date of the no gain, no loss transfer until the date of sale by Pollux Ltd.

The indexation allowance reflects the movement in the retail prices index for the relevant period (rounded to three decimal places) multiplied by the relevant cost of the building.

Information required – the date the building was acquired by Castor Ltd and the price paid.

(ii) **Warehouse**

Tutor's Top Tips

A good knowledge of the capital goods scheme for VAT is required in order to answer this part of the question.

The requirement is to 'calculate', so there is no need to provide any explanation.

Year ended 31 March 2015
£64,000 × 70%   £44,800 recoverable from HMRC

Year ended 31 March 2016
£64,000 × 15% (70% – 55%) × 1/10   £960 repayable to HMRC

Year ended 31 March 2017
£64,000 × 20% (70% – 50%) × 1/10   £1,280 repayable to HMRC
£64,000 × 30% (100% – 70%) × 7/10   £13,440 recoverable from HMRC

Tutorial note

The capital goods scheme is relevant where a partially exempt business buys a building for more than £250,000 and there is a change in the partial exemption % during the 10 year adjustment period.

Here the recoverable input VAT drops from 70% to 55% then 50%, so Viola Ltd has to pay back some of the input VAT initially reclaimed.

There is also a final adjustment in the year of disposal for the remainder of the 10 year adjustment period.

The % used for the final adjustment on the sale of the building will always be either:

- *100% taxable (if the sale of the building is subject to VAT, as it is here), or*
- *0% taxable (if the sale of the building is an exempt supply).*

(iii) **Patent rights**

Tutor's top tips

Patent rights are an intangible non-current asset.

For intangibles other than goodwill, the tax treatment generally follows the accounting treatment with the effect that:

- amortisation of an intangible asset is an allowable expense (or, if preferred, a writing down allowance of 4% straight line can be claimed instead of amortisation)
- the taxable profit on disposal is calculated as the sale proceeds less the net book value (i.e. amortised cost) if no election has been made (or, if the election is made, the sale proceeds less the tax written down value).

As the patent rights relate to the company's trade, both the amortisation and the profit on disposal are included in taxable trading profits.

If Castor Ltd elected for the patent box rules to apply, a reduced rate of corporation tax would be applied to the profit on sale of the patent. The question, however, clearly states the election has not, and will not, be made.

The patent rights are an intangible non-current asset. On a disposal of the rights, the sales proceeds will be compared with the amortised cost.

	£	£
Proceeds		41,000
Cost	45,000	
Less: Amortisation (£45,000 × 10% × 4)	(18,000)	
Amortised cost		(27,000)
Profit on sale		14,000

The profit on sale will be included as part of Castor Ltd's trading income because the patent rights were purchased for the purposes of the trade. As the patent box rules have not been enacted, the profit will be taxed at Castor Limited's marginal rate of corporation tax.

(c) **Investment in Kupple Inc**

(i) **Value added tax (VAT) on the import of consultancy services**

Tutor's top tips

The VAT implications for purchasing consultancy services from overseas are very similar to the implications for importing goods.

The VAT treatment of imports and exports is regularly tested in the P6 exam.

When services are provided to a business, the place of supply is the place where the customer's business is established.

Accordingly, the consultancy services provided by Kupple Inc to Janus plc will be treated as being made in the UK.

Janus plc will be required to account for output tax in respect of the supply under the reverse charge procedure. It will then be able to recover the output tax as input tax in the normal way.

(ii) **Sale of the shares**

Tutor's top tips

Knowledge of the substantial shareholding exemption for companies – particularly the 12 month ownership requirement – is the key to success in this part.

The examining team deliberately leaves the disposal date vague, and does not say whether the shares will be sold at a profit or loss.

This means that you need to consider all possibilities:

- *Sale within 12 months at a gain*
- *Sale within 12 months at a loss*
- *Sale after more than 12 months at a gain*
- *Sale after more than 12 months at a loss.*

The tax treatment of the profit or loss on the sale of the shares will depend on when the sale occurs.

Sale within 12 months

If the shares are sold during the first 12 months of ownership, the sale will result in a chargeable gain (proceeds less cost less indexation allowance) or an allowable loss (proceeds less cost).

An allowable loss could be offset against the chargeable gains of Janus plc or of the other companies in its chargeable gains group (Seb Ltd and Viola Ltd).

Sale after more than 12 months

However, as Janus plc will hold at least 10% of Kupple Inc's shares, once the shares have been held for 12 months, the substantial shareholding exemption will apply.

As a result of this exemption, any profit would not be taxable and any loss would not be allowable.

(d) **Janus plc group senior accounting officer**

Tutor's top tips

There are easy marks here for simply stating the statutory responsibilities of senior accounting officers – if you have learnt these rules.

To gain full marks you also need to state whether you think these rules will apply to Mrs Pairz.

The senior accounting officer of Janus plc is the director or officer with overall responsibility for the company's financial accounting arrangements. In relation to the Janus plc group of companies, this is likely to be Mrs Pairz, as she is the Group Finance Director.

The rules will only impose responsibilities if the Janus plc group of companies has a turnover of more than £200 million and/or a statement of financial position total of more than £2 billion.

Where the rules apply, the senior accounting officer is required to:

- Establish and monitor accounting systems that are adequate for the purposes of accurate tax reporting.
- Certify to HM Revenue and Customs that such accounting systems exist for each financial year; or notify HM Revenue and Customs of any inadequacies in the accounting systems.

Penalties apply for non-compliance with the rules.

> **Examiner's report**
>
> Some candidates spent too long on part (a) and provided very detailed explanations of group relief and consortium relief; the amount of detail provided must relate to the number of marks on offer. Also, there was a tendency to repeat things, for example stating that Janus plc is in a loss group with Seb Ltd and Viola Ltd followed by a statement that it was not in a loss group with Castor Ltd. Candidates should identify the points they intend to make and then make them as concisely as possible. They will find this more efficient than making it up as they go along.
>
> *Note that this part of the question has been adapted since the question was originally set.*
>
> For part (b)(i) those candidates, who knew their stuff, slowed down, thought more and wrote less did well. This question demanded a clear understanding of the conditions necessary for a chargeable gains group to exist.
>
> Unfortunately many candidates thought that Janus plc and Pollux Ltd were members of a chargeable gains group; this was not the case because Janus plc does not own at least 75% of Castor Ltd. Other candidates failed to notice that Castor Ltd and Pollux Ltd were members of such a group.
>
> The other technical problem that candidates had with this question was that many thought it included a degrouping charge. However, a degrouping charge can only occur when a company leaves a chargeable gains group, i.e. there needs to be a sale of shares, and this question involved the sale of a building. Accordingly, time spent writing about degrouping charges was wasted.
>
> In part (b)(ii) applying the capital goods scheme to the purchase, use and subsequent sale of a building was done well by those candidates who both knew what to do and had practised applying the rules prior to the exam. Weaker candidates had a vague, confused knowledge of the rules or simply tried to describe them as opposed to apply them to the specific circumstances of the question. Very few candidates knew how to handle the adjustment following the sale of the building.
>
> Part (b)(iii) the sale of an intangible asset and was done reasonably well by the majority of candidates.

> In part (c)(i) the purchase of services from overseas to which the reverse charge applied was not answered particularly well; very few candidates had a clear understanding of the VAT treatment of the transaction.
>
> Part (c)(ii) concerned the sale of shares in a company and was answered well. It required candidates to recognise that the substantial shareholding exemption might apply to the sale provided the conditions were satisfied. This question illustrated the need for candidates to be methodical as, if maximum marks were to be obtained, candidates needed to consider four situations; sale at a profit and sale at a loss with the substantial shareholding exemption either applying or not applying in each case.
>
> In part (d) only a minority of candidates knew the rules concerned the responsibilities of a senior accounting officer, but those who did answered the question well.

		ACCA marking scheme		
				Marks
(a)	(i)	Alternative reliefs		
		Against total profits of Janus plc		1.5
		Group relief		
		Identification of group		1.5
		Amount of loss		1.0
		Consortium relief		2.0
	(ii)	Advice and summary		2.5
				8.5
			Maximum	8.0
(b)	(i)	Administrative premises		
		There will be a gain on the disposal		1.5
		Indexed base cost		4.5
		Information required		0.5
				6.5
			Maximum	5.0
	(ii)	Warehouse		4.0
	(iii)	Patent rights		
		Calculation		1.5
		Explanation		1.5
				3.0
(c)	(i)	VAT on consultancy services		2.5
			Maximum	2.0
	(ii)	Sale of shares		4.0
(d)		Responsibilities of senior accounting officer		4.5
			Maximum	4.0
Total				**30.0**

67 FLAME PLC GROUP *Walk in the footsteps of a top tutor*

Key answer tips

Part (a) asks for a report which addresses three unrelated issues.

Issue (i) asks for a comparison of the tax cost of selling either the shares of a company or its trade and assets. It is important that you read the question carefully and include the concise explanations requested by the examining team.

Part (ii) deals with company share option plans (CSOPs). Even if you could not remember the details of the CSOP rules you should have been able to state the advantages of the scheme as they are similar across all approved plans.

Part (iii) is a short section dealing with VAT implications of opting to tax a building prior to granting a lease. VAT on property is an important issue at this level but there were only a few marks available here.

Part (b) deals with ethical issues surrounding an unexpected refund of corporation tax. This area has been tested before and you should be able to pick up some easy marks here.

The highlighted words in the written sections are key phrases that markers are looking for.

Tutor's top tips

As is usual for Section A questions, the actual requirements at the end of the question only tell you how many marks are available for each section. The real requirements can be found in the information provided in the question.

As you read through highlight any requirements and instructions that you find. The requirements in this question are all in the email from the manager.

In part (a) the question has asked for a report which addresses certain issues and you may find it useful to number these requirements so that you can tick them off as you attempt them.

Make sure you set out your answer in the required format. For a report you need a suitable heading which will identify to whom the report is addressed. Numbered headings which agree to the numbered points in the manager's email will make your answer easier to mark Question 1 will always have 4 professional marks to cover presentation, relevant advice and quality of communication.

(a) **REPORT TO THE GROUP FINANCE DIRECTOR OF FLAME PLC**

To: Group Finance Director of Flame plc
From: Tax advisors
Date: 7 December 2016
Subject: Various tax issues

(i) **Flame plc – Sale of Inferno Ltd**

Sale by Flame plc of the whole of the ordinary share capital of Inferno Ltd

Tutor's top tips

The examining team has said that the substantial shareholding exemption is not available so you need to calculate the gain on the sale of the shares.

By itself this is not too difficult but you must remember that whenever a company is being sold out of a 75% gains group you add to the sales proceeds any degrouping charges that arise as a result of the company leaving the group.

A sale of the share capital will result in a liability to corporation tax as follows:

	£
Sale proceeds	1,000,000
Plus: Degrouping charge (W1)	24,480
	1,024,480
Less: Cost of shares (March 2012)	(600,000)
Indexation allowance from purchase (March 2012) to sale of shares (January 2017) (£600,000 × 0.108)	(64,800)
Chargeable gain	359,680
Corporation tax (£359,680 × 20%)	71,936

Working: Degrouping charge

	£
Market value of the premises at date of inter group transfer (15 March 2012)	300,000
Less: Cost of building to Flame plc (January 2008)	(240,000)
Indexation allowance from purchase (January 2008) to inter group transfer (March 2012) (£240,000 × 0.148)	(35,520)
Degrouping charge	24,480

Due to the unavailability of the substantial shareholding exemption, the sale of Inferno Ltd will result in a gain chargeable to corporation tax.

Tutor's top tips

The question tells you that there are approximately equal marks for calculations and for explanations in part (i). Accordingly, calculations on their own will not be enough to pick up a decent mark.

The question also tells you that the substantial shareholding exemption is not available and you must explain the effect of this – it may be obvious to you but you need to spell it out to your reader.

A degrouping charge will arise in respect of the building because it was transferred at no gain, no loss (Flame plc and Inferno Ltd are members of a capital gains group) within the six years prior to the sale of Inferno Ltd.

Inferno Ltd will be regarded as having sold the building at the time of the no gain, no loss transfer for its market value at that time.

Inferno Ltd's base cost in the building, resulting from the no gain, no loss transfer, is the original cost to Flame plc plus indexation allowance up to 15 March 2012, the date Inferno Ltd purchased the building.

The degrouping charge will increase the sales proceeds on the disposal of Inferno Ltd.

Tutor's top tips

The question asks you for the tax cost of the two different methods. This means that any gains or profits you calculate must be multiplied by the appropriate tax rate to arrive at the tax cost.

Sale by Inferno Ltd of its trade and assets for their market value

Tutor's top tips

For the sale of trade and assets you need to think about three possible areas which will increase taxable total profits.

(i)   Any balancing adjustments for capital allowance purposes

(ii) Profits/losses on disposal of intangibles (e.g. goodwill)

(iii) Capital gains on disposal of chargeable assets.

A sale of the trade and assets will result in a liability to corporation tax as follows:

	£
Balancing charge on sale of equipment and milling machine (W1)	140,000
Trading profit on the sale of goodwill	530,000
Additional trading profits	670,000
Crystallisation of deferred gain on the milling machine (Note)	8,500
Chargeable gain on the sale of the premises (W3)	184,724
Taxable profits	863,224
Corporation tax (£863,224 × 20%)	172,645

Tutorial note

A chargeable gain of £8,500 was deferred against the purchase of the milling machine.

As this is a depreciating asset the gain was not deducted from the base cost of the milling machine. Instead, the deferred gain is 'frozen' and a record kept in the tax files until the later disposal of the machine. When the machine is sold, the frozen gain becomes chargeable.

Workings

(W1) Balancing charge on sale of equipment and milling machine

		£
Market value –	equipment	60,000
–	milling machine	80,000
		140,000
Less: Tax written down value		(Nil)
Balancing charge		140,000

(W2) Inter group transfer – March 2012

	£
Deemed proceeds = Base cost to Inferno Ltd	275,520
Less: Cost (Jan 2008)	(240,000)
IA up to March 2012 (£240,000 × 0.148)	(35,520)
Chargeable gain	Nil

Tutorial note

The inter group transfer is a nil gain/nil loss transaction (NGNL).

The deemed proceeds will be the base cost to the receiving company and will be the original cost of the asset plus indexation allowance from the date of purchase to the date of the inter group transfer.

(W3) **Chargeable gain on sale of premises**

	£
Sale proceeds	490,000
Less: Base cost (March 2012) (W2)	(275,520)
IA up to January 2017 (£275,520 × 0.108)	(29,756)
Chargeable gain	184,724

Tutorial note

As a shortcut, the chargeable gain on the sale of the premises could have been calculated by treating the property as if Inferno Ltd had always owned it.

This alternative calculation would give the following result:

	£
Proceeds	490,000
Less: Cost of building (January 2008)	(240,000)
IA (Jan 2008 – Jan 2017) (£240,000 × 0.272)	(65,280)
Chargeable gain	184,720

The result is slightly different due to rounding the indexation factor only once, whereas the correct piecemeal calculation rounds the indexation factor twice; up to the intra-group transfer and then to the date of sale.

If you use the shortcut in the exam, you might not score full marks but you should score enough to pass.

Tutor's top tips

Remember that to get full marks you need to include concise explanations of matters where the calculations are not self-explanatory.

The excess of the sales proceeds (market value) of the equipment and the milling machine over the balance on the main pool will result in a taxable balancing charge.

Where goodwill is sold at a profit, the profit on its sale will be additional trading income.

Tutorial note

If a loss is made on the disposal of goodwill, this loss will be treated as a non-trading debit and can be set against total profits of the current year, group relieved or carried forward, but not carried back.

When a rollover relief claim has been made in respect of the purchase of a depreciating asset, as in the case of the milling machine, the deferred gain crystallises on the sale of that replacement asset.

The equipment and the milling machine are to be sold for less than cost. However, no capital loss will arise because capital allowances have been claimed.

As noted above, Inferno Ltd's base cost in the building is the original price paid by Flame plc plus indexation allowance up to March 2012.

Inferno Ltd will cease trading when it sells its business on 1 January 2017. This will bring about the end of a chargeable accounting period.

(ii) **Flame plc – employee share scheme**

Tutor's top tips

The examining team has given you a structure for this part of your answer so it is best to follow it.

- *Tax advantages for **employees** of CSOP compared to unapproved schemes*
- *Why a CSOP is a suitable choice*
- *Restrictions on the number of share options and the issue price.*

Tax advantages of an approved company share option plan (CSOP) over an unapproved scheme

- With a CSOP, there would be no income tax or national insurance contributions liability on the grant or exercise of the option, provided it is exercised between three and ten years after it is granted.

  Whereas with an unapproved scheme, there would be a liability when the option is exercised.

- With a CSOP, the whole of the employee's profit on the shares will be subject to capital gains tax when the shares are sold.

Whereas with an unapproved scheme, the excess of the market value of the shares at the time the option is exercised over the amount paid by the employee for the shares will be subject to income tax and national insurance contributions in the year the option is exercised; any subsequent increase in the value of the shares will be subject to capital gains tax when the shares are sold.

The advantages of capital gains tax over income tax and national insurance contributions are the availability of the annual exempt amount and the lower tax rates.

Tutor's top tips

Note that it is not enough to say that under an approved scheme the profit is taxed as a gain not as income. You need to add the advantages of gains (i.e. a higher annual exempt amount than the personal allowance and lower tax rates).

Suitability of a CSOP

Gordon wants to use the scheme to reward the company's senior managers as opposed to all of the company's staff. Accordingly, he needs to use a scheme that allows him to choose which employees are able to join. The two approved schemes that allow this are the CSOP and the Enterprise Management Incentive (EMI) scheme.

Restrictions

- The value of shares in respect of which an employee holds options cannot exceed £30,000.
- The exercise price of the shares must not be manifestly less than the value of the shares at the time of the grant of the option.

(iii) **Bon Ltd – the grant of a lease**

Tutor's top tips

*The question asks for the implications for the **lessee**. These depend on whether the lessee is VAT registered or not. Since we do not know the status of the lessee you should write about both registered and non registered businesses.*

There are 3 marks available for this section so you should try to write 3 good points.

If Bon Ltd were to opt to tax the building, the proposed granting of the lease would be a standard rated supply rather than an exempt supply, such that Bon Ltd would have to charge value added tax (VAT) on the rent.

A lessee that was registered for VAT and making wholly taxable supplies would be able to recover all of the VAT charged. However, some or all of the VAT would be a cost for a lessee that was not registered or one that was partially exempt and not within the *de minimis* limits.

ANSWERS TO PRACTICE QUESTIONS: SECTION 2

(b) **Refund of corporation tax**

We should review the tax affairs of Bon Ltd in order to identify the reason for the tax refund.

If, as would appear likely, it is an error on the part of HM Revenue and Customs (HMRC), we should inform Bon Ltd that it should be repaid immediately. Failure to return the money in these circumstances may well be a civil and/or a criminal offence.

We should advise Bon Ltd to disclose the matter to HMRC immediately in order to minimise any interest and penalties that may otherwise become payable.

In addition, unless the money is returned, we would have to consider ceasing to act as advisers to Bon Ltd. In these circumstances, we are required to notify the tax authorities that we no longer act for the company, although we would not provide them with any reason for our action. We should also consider whether or not we are required to make a report under the money laundering rules.

Tutor's top tips

Ethical issues appear in every P6 exam, for up to five marks. It is important to learn the key principles as these are often easy marks that can be scored quickly.

Make sure you apply the principles to the scenario and do not just list them.

Try to have at least five separate points in your answer as you will probably score one mark per relevant point.

Note that it is important to investigate the circumstances surrounding the refund before taking further action. The refund may be justified and an adviser should determine this first.

Examiner's report

Answers to part (a)(i) varied in quality quite considerably. There were many candidates who clearly understood the two alternatives and the related tax implications whilst weaker candidates were unsure of the precise nature of the transactions and the related tax implications, such that they produced confused answers. This was also one of the questions referred to in the general comments above where a small minority of candidates treated the companies as individuals.

The sale of Inferno Ltd had two main implications; a chargeable gain on the sale of the shares and a degrouping charge. The chargeable gain was worth one mark. However, it took some candidates half a page or more to calculate and write about this gain in order to score that mark. This was most likely because it was the first thing they did in the exam and there were still almost three hours to go, such that the pressure was not yet on.

Candidates must approach every mark in the exam in the same way and get on with it. There is no time to dither when there is so much to do.

Frustratingly, it was not uncommon for some candidates to only score half a mark for this gain because they based the indexation allowance on the unindexed gain rather than the cost. I suspect that this was a lack of concentration rather than a lack of knowledge but the half mark was still lost.

KAPLAN PUBLISHING

It was stated in the question that the substantial shareholding exemption was not available. Many candidates simply included a statement to that effect in their report and earned a mark. However, a small minority of candidates wasted time writing at length about the exemption rather than getting on with the question.

The degrouping charge was done well on the whole. Those candidates who did not do so well were divided into two groups. The first group missed the degrouping charge altogether. This was perhaps due to a lack of knowledge but, in view of the fact that degrouping charges are examined regularly, was more likely due to a lack of thought. Candidates must give themselves time in the exam to think about issues before they start writing; it is difficult to successfully think of one issue whilst writing about a different one.

The second group of candidates knew that there would be a degrouping charge somewhere in the answer and earned most of the marks available for saying why and for calculating it. However, they did not know which of the two possible transactions would give rise to the charge and either put it into the wrong section of the report or put it into both sections.

This was not particularly costly, but would have been in a different question which was only concerned with one of these two transactions. Candidates must know their stuff; degrouping charges only occur on the sale of a company, i.e. on the sale of shares, and not on the sale of assets.

The sale by Inferno Ltd of its trade and assets was not done particularly well. A small minority of candidates treated the disposal as the disposal of a single asset by adding up all of the proceeds and then deducting the total cost. Even those candidates who knew that each asset had to be handled separately failed to apply basic rules concerning capital allowances and chargeable gains.

Capital allowances were handled particularly poorly with very few candidates identifying that where the tax written down value is zero, any sale of machinery must result in a balancing charge. In addition, most candidates calculated capital losses on the sale of the machinery, thus failing to recognise that, due to the claiming of capital allowances, no capital losses would be available. Finally, only a minority of candidates identified that the deferred gain of £8,500 would crystallise on the sale of the milling machine; most candidates thought, incorrectly, that the gain would be deducted from the asset's base cost.

A final thought on part (a)(i) relates to the narrative provided by candidates in their reports. The question required candidates to include concise explanations of matters where the calculations were not self-explanatory. On the whole this was done well. Most candidates kept their answers brief and very few fell into trap of writing down everything they knew about the broad technical areas relating to the question.

Part (a)(ii) was a straightforward question that tested candidates' knowledge of a particular share scheme. In order to do well, candidates needed to slow down for a moment and make sure that they were about to write about the correct scheme. They then needed to ensure that they addressed all of the issues set out in the question. The majority of candidates did both of these things and therefore scored well.

Part (a)(iii) concerned the VAT implications of the granting of a lease and was done reasonably well by most candidates.

ANSWERS TO PRACTICE QUESTIONS: SECTION 2

> Part (b) of question 1 concerned a refund of corporation tax. Candidates needed to realise that this refund had been received some time ago and that, if it had been paid in error, it had to be returned to HM Revenue and Customs. Most candidates recognised this situation and were able to list the actions that the firm needed to take and the matters that needed to be drawn to the attention of Bon Ltd.
>
> Marks were available for professional skills in question 1. In order to earn these marks candidates had to use the information provided in the question correctly and then provide specific advice, clear explanations and coherent calculations in an appropriately formatted report. On the whole, the performance of candidates in this area was good with the majority of candidates producing a report in a style that was easy to follow.

ACCA marking scheme		
		Marks
(a) (i) Sale of share capital		
Calculations		
Degrouping charge		2.0
Other matters		1.5
Narrative – one mark for each relevant point		5.0
Sale of trade and assets		
Calculations		
Equipment and milling machine		2.0
Goodwill		0.5
Premises		1.5
Liability		0.5
Narrative – one mark for each relevant point		4.0
		17.0
	Maximum	15.0
(ii) Advantages		
Timing		2.5
Taxes		3.5
Suitability of company share option plan		1.0
Restrictions		2.0
		9.0
	Maximum	8.0
(iii) Nature of supply		1.0
Recoverable input tax		2.0
		3.0
Format and presentation		1.0
Analysis		2.0
Quality of calculations and explanations		1.0
		4.0
(b) The need to repay the tax		3.0
Ceasing to act		3.0
		6.0
	Maximum	5.0
Total		**35.0**

KAPLAN PUBLISHING

68 LIZA   *Walk in the footsteps of a top tutor*

Key answer tips

The question asks for answers that address three unrelated issues.

Part (a)(i) requires a calculation of the chargeable gain on the sale of the building and the correct treatment of the various expenses incurred in acquiring, enhancing and maintaining the property. This is a straightforward part of the question.

Part (a)(ii) requires the identification of which companies in the group can or cannot purchase qualifying replacement assets for group rollover relief purposes **and** the period within which the assets can be required. Make sure you discuss why a company may not be able to purchase replacement assets.

Part (a)(iii) is a tricky part of the question as it requires you to calculate the additional expenditure required such that the chargeable gain calculated in (a)(i) can be fully deferred. The complication is that the asset owned by Bar Ltd was not used in the trade for the entire period of ownership and the new asset acquired is only partly used for the trade.

Part (b) is a straight forward part of the question and is essentially from the F6 syllabus. The question is about capital allowances on integral features of a building.

Part (c) is again a straight forward part of the question and is essentially from the F6 syllabus. The question requires an explanation of which companies can join a VAT group and the advantages and disadvantages of registering companies as a single VAT group.

The highlighted words in the written sections are key phrases that markers are looking for.

(a) (i) **Chargeable gain – Sale of Building 1**

Tutor's top tips

Don't forget that expenditure on an asset in order to make it fit for use is capital expenditure and as such is allowable expenditure for chargeable gains purposes.

	£	£
Net sales proceeds		860,000
Less: Purchase price	315,000	
Legal fees	9,000	
Work on roof to make fit for use	38,000	
		(362,000)
Unindexed gain		498,000
Less: Indexation allowance		
(262.7 – 224.1)/224.1 = 0.172 × £362,000		(62,264)
Chargeable gain		435,736

ANSWERS TO PRACTICE QUESTIONS: SECTION 2

Tutorial note

A deduction is available for the legal fees incurred in acquiring the building and the costs incurred shortly afterwards in order to make the building fit for use.

The cost of repainting the building would have been an allowable deduction in calculating the company's trading profits and thus would not be allowable when computing the chargeable gain.

(ii) **Acquisition of qualifying assets for the purposes of rollover relief**

Tutor's top tips

You need to explain why a company is or is not part of a 75% group for chargeable gains and therefore can purchase replacement assets for rollover relief purposes.

The assets can be purchased by companies within the Bar Ltd chargeable gains group.

A chargeable gains group consists of a principal company, Bar Ltd, its 75% subsidiaries, the 75% subsidiaries of those subsidiaries and so on.

Bar Ltd must have an effective interest of more than 50% in all of the companies in the group.

Accordingly, the only companies able to purchase qualifying replacement assets are Bar Ltd and Pommel Ltd.

Ring Ltd is not a 75% subsidiary of Bar Ltd, such that it and Vault Ltd cannot be members of the Bar Ltd chargeable gains group.

The Hoop Ltd group is a separate group.

The qualifying replacement assets must be purchased in the period from 1 June 2015 to 31 May 2019.

(iii) **The additional amount that would need to be spent on qualifying assets**

Tutor's top tips

Don't forget that rollover relief is only available if the asset has been used in the trade.

Bar Ltd owned the building from 1 June 2010 to 31 May 2016, a period of 72 months. The building was not used for trading purposes from 1 January 2012 to 30 June 2013, a period of 18 months.

Accordingly, the building was used for the purposes of the trade for a period of 54 (72 – 18) months, such that only 54/72 of the gain can be relieved via rollover relief.

Therefore, qualifying business assets costing £645,000 (£860,000 × 54/72) will need to be acquired in order to relieve the whole of the gain qualifying for rollover relief.

Only two-thirds of the new building is to be used for trading purposes, such that only £480,000 (£720,000 × 2/3) of its cost will be a qualifying acquisition for the purposes of rollover relief.

Accordingly, the additional amount that would need to be spent on qualifying acquisitions in order to relieve the whole of the gain that qualifies for rollover relief would be £165,000 (£645,000 − £480,000).

(b) **Capital allowances available in respect of the new building**

Tutor's top tips

Don't forget that the P6 exam frequently tests material from the F6 syllabus.

Capital allowances at 8% p.a. are available on integral features of a building which form part of the special rate pool.

Electrical, water and heating systems qualify for plant and machinery capital allowances.

They are classified as integral features, such that they are included in the special rate pool where the writing down allowance is only 8%.

The annual investment allowance available to the Bar Ltd group should be set against these additions in priority to those assets which qualify for the 18% writing down allowance.

(c) **Group registration for the purposes of Value Added Tax (VAT)**

Tutor's top tips

This section also covers material from the F6 syllabus.

VAT groups are frequently tested so make sure you can demonstrate a good knowledge of VAT groups and be specific to the question.

Note that zero rated companies should not be included in the VAT group as they can reclaim any VAT charged by the other group companies on a monthly basis. The companies that charge VAT will only pay quarterly. This is a cash flow advantage to the group.

The companies able to register as a group

Two or more companies may register as a group provided they are established in the UK, or have a fixed establishment in the UK, and they are controlled by the same person. The person can be an individual, a company, or a partnership.

Accordingly, all of the companies in the Bar Ltd and Hoop Ltd groups can register as a single group for the purposes of VAT.

The potential advantages and disadvantages of registering as a group

The advantage of a group registration would be that there would be no need to charge VAT on the transactions between the group companies. This would reduce administration and improve the group's cash flow.

The group would have to appoint a representative member which would account for the group's VAT liability as if the group were a single entity. Consequently, there would be a need to collate information from all of the members of the group and to present it in a single VAT return. This may not be straightforward, depending on the accounting systems and procedures used by the various companies within the two separate groups.

Vault Ltd makes zero rated supplies and will therefore be in a repayment position, such that it can improve its cash flow by accounting for VAT on a monthly basis. However, if it were registered as part of a VAT group, it would not be able to do this as the group, as a single entity, is very unlikely to be in a regular repayment position. Accordingly, if a group registration is to be entered into, consideration should be given to excluding Vault Ltd from that registration.

Finally, it should be recognised that all of the companies within the group registration would have joint and several liability for the VAT due from the representative member. Liza, and the minority shareholders, should give careful consideration to the possible dangers of linking the two groups in such a manner.

Examiner's report

Part (a)(i) was a gentle introduction to the question and was done well.

Part (a)(ii) was done well by those candidates who knew the rules for group rollover relief and who expressed themselves carefully.

This part required candidates to know three things: that rollover relief can be claimed where one company in a gains group sells a qualifying business asset and another company in the group buys one, the definition of a gains group, and the time period in which a replacement asset needs to be purchased in order for rollover relief to be available.

The majority of candidates knew the first and third points although a small minority failed to address the third point despite, probably, knowing the rule. The difficulty came in dealing with the second point and the definition of a gains group where a minority of candidates revealed a level of confusion. This stemmed from a problem in distinguishing the 75% aspect of the rule from the 51% aspect and led to some candidates concluding erroneously that Vault Ltd and Bar Ltd were in a gains group. For there to be a chargeable gains group, the direct holding between each company in the chain must be at least 75%; if it isn't, the two companies cannot be in a group regardless of the level of the indirect holding.

The final part of part (a) was the hardest part of the question and was not done particularly well.

It required candidates to know the basic rule whereby the whole of the relevant proceeds has to be spent on replacement assets in order for the maximum gain to be rolled over, whilst recognising the relevance of the non-business use of both the asset sold and the asset acquired. Almost all candidates knew the basic rule but the majority struggled to apply it in these particular circumstances.

Part (b) concerned the availability of capital allowances in respect of electrical, water and heating systems acquired as part of a building and was done well.

In the final part of the question the majority of candidates made a reasonable job of discussing the advantages and disadvantages of registering as a VAT group and made a series of concise points. However, the definition of a group for the purposes of VAT was not handled particularly well. In particular, a sizable minority of candidates thought that the required holding was 75% as opposed to control. In addition, many candidates did not appreciate that control could be exercised by an individual (i.e. Liza), as well as by a company, such that all of the companies in the question were able to register as a single group.

As always, a minority of candidates wrote in general terms, for example, about partial exemption, rather than addressing the specifics of the question, such that they wasted time.

ACCA marking scheme

				Marks
(a)	(i)	Chargeable gain		3.5
			Maximum	3.0
	(ii)	Chargeable gains group		2.0
		Identification of relevant companies		1.5
		Qualifying period		1.0
				4.5
			Maximum	4.0
	(iii)	Amount relievable via rollover relief		2.0
		Total acquisitions necessary		1.0
		Further acquisitions necessary		1.5
				4.5
			Maximum	4.0
(b)		Plant and machinery as integral feature		1.0
		Special rate pool		0.5
		Use of AIA		1.0
				2.5
			Maximum	2.0
(c)		Ability to register as a group		2.0
		Discussion		6.0
				8.0
			Maximum	7.0
Total				20.0

ANSWERS TO PRACTICE QUESTIONS: SECTION 2

69 SPETZ LTD GROUP *Walk in the footsteps of a top tutor*

Key answer tips

The question concerns VAT and overseas issues in relation to corporation tax and income tax, and was the least popular of the optional questions in Section B in this paper. This is probably because it requires detailed knowledge of some smaller topics in the syllabus and involved some overseas aspects!

Part (a) requires a calculation of the VAT partial exemption annual adjustment in respect of a company and should have been straightforward, although remembering all the detail of the three de minimis tests is demanding.

The first part of (b) requires an explanation of how to determine whether or not the company was resident in the UK which is worth only 3 marks. It is testing F6 knowledge which should be easy if you have learnt the rules, but difficult if you have not.

The second part of (b) requires an explanation of the company's corporation tax liability together with the advantages and disadvantages of making an election to exempt the profits of an overseas permanent establishment (branch) from UK tax.

Finally, part (c) covers the travel and subsistence costs of an employee seconded to work overseas. It is difficult in that it required knowledge of some detailed rules, but a decent mark could be scored by applying general principles.

The highlighted words in the written sections are key phrases that markers are looking for.

Tutor's top tips

The VAT requirement is a standalone part and asks for a calculation, a due date and an explanation of reasons as to whether the de minimis limits apply.

Make sure that you address all three elements of the requirement.

Note that partial exemption is regularly examined in the P6 exam.

When a business sells both taxable and exempt sales it is necessary to apportion input VAT on overheads between taxable sales and exempt sales. If the input VAT attributable to exempt sales exceeds the de minimis amount then it cannot be claimed back.

KAPLAN PUBLISHING

(a) **Novak Ltd**

Value added tax – partial exemption annual adjustment

	Total £	Recoverable £	Irrecoverable £
Input tax			
– attributed to taxable supplies	12,200	12,200	
– attributed to exempt supplies	4,900		4,900
Unattributed input tax (W1)	16,100	11,914	4,186
	33,200	24,114	9,086

To determine whether or not the £9,086 irrecoverable input VAT is in fact recoverable, the three de minimis tests must be considered:

- De minimis test 1 is not satisfied, as the total input tax (£33,200) exceeds an average of £625 per month (£625 × 12 = £7,500).

- De minimis test 2 is not satisfied, as the total input tax less that directly attributed to taxable supplies (£33,200 – £12,200 = £21,000) exceeds an average of £625 per month (£21,000 ÷ 12 = £1,750).

- De minimis test 3 is also not satisfied, as exempt input tax of £9,086 exceeds the de minimis limit of £625 per month.

Accordingly, in total for the year, only £24,114 is recoverable.

The £9,086 input VAT is not de minimis and is therefore irrecoverable.

	£
Recoverable input VAT for the year	24,114
Less: Input tax recovered on quarterly returns	(23,200)
Annual adjustment = Additional input tax recoverable	914

The annual adjustment must be made on:

- the final VAT return of the year

    (i.e. the return for the period ended 30 September 2016), or

- the first VAT return after the end of the year.

Working: Recoverable unattributed input tax

(Taxable supplies/Total supplies) × 100

= (£1,190,000 ÷ (£1,190,000 + £430,000)) × 100 = 73.4%

This is rounded up to 74%.

ANSWERS TO PRACTICE QUESTIONS: SECTION 2

(b) (i) **Residence status of Kraus Co**

Tutor's top tips

With only three marks available, three short succinct points need to be made and applied to the scenario given.

The key point to make is that overseas incorporated companies such as Kraus Co are treated as UK resident if they are controlled and managed from the UK.

- A company is regarded as resident in the UK if it is incorporated in the UK or if its central management and control is exercised in the UK.
- Kraus Co was incorporated in the country of Mersano. Accordingly, it will only be resident in the UK if its central management and control is exercised in the UK.
- The central management and control of a company is usually regarded as being exercised in the place where the key operational and financial decisions are made (e.g. where meetings of the board of directors are held).

(ii) **Kraus Co**

Tutor's top tips

The calculation required is very simple as Kraus Co has no other income or gains other than trading income.

However, the majority of the marks are available for explaining the branch profits exemption and consequences.

UK resident companies are subject to corporation tax on their worldwide income, with DTR available if applicable.

	£
Corporation tax at the main rate (£520,000 × 20%)	104,000
Less: Unilateral double tax relief	
Lower of UK rate and overseas rate	
(£520,000 × 18%)	(93,600)
UK corporation tax liability	10,400

KAPLAN PUBLISHING

Tutorial note

The profits will be subject to tax because no election has been made to exempt the profits and losses of the overseas permanent establishment from UK corporation tax.

Note that the branch election is irrevocable and applies to all overseas branches, including those making losses and those wishing to claim capital allowances. It is therefore important to make the right decision.

Election to exempt the overseas profits from UK tax

The advantage of making such an election would be that the profits made in Mersano would not be subject to UK corporation tax. Based on the current rates of corporation tax in the two countries, this would save corporation tax at the rate of 2% (20% – 18%).

When considering this election, it should be recognised that it is irrevocable and would apply to all future overseas permanent establishments of Kraus Co. Accordingly, there would be no relief in the UK for any losses incurred in the trade in Mersano in the future or for any other losses incurred in any additional overseas trades operated by Kraus Co.

(c) **Meyer's secondment to Kraus Co**

Tutor's top tips

Reasonable marks could be obtained here even if you did not know the detailed rules and applied general principles such as wholly, exclusively and necessarily and general travel expense rules.

The reimbursement of expenses by an employer represents taxable income for an employee. Accordingly, the cost of the flights at the start and end of the contract represents taxable income for Meyer.

However, a deduction of an equal amount will be available because:

- it is necessary for Meyer to travel to Mersano in order to perform the duties of his employment; and
- the workplace in Mersano is a temporary workplace (the secondment is for less than 24 months), such that the travelling does not constitute ordinary commuting.

The cost of the return journey to the UK in February 2017 has no UK tax implications. Meyer will not be able to claim a tax deduction for the costs incurred because the journey is for a private purpose and he, rather than Spetz Ltd, will bear the cost.

The reimbursement of the cost of laundry and telephone calls home will be exempt from tax if the average cost is less than £10 per day. However, if this limit is exceeded, the whole of the amount reimbursed will be subject to UK income tax.

Tutorial note

Credit was also available to candidates who focused their answers on the special rules relating to travel costs where duties are performed abroad.

Note that an employee working abroad will always be allowed the first trip out at the beginning of the contract and the last trip back at the end of the contract as tax deductible.

An unlimited amount of other trips to any place in the UK are also allowed, but only provided the expenses are borne by the employer.

The cost of the trip back to the UK for a holiday in February 2017 was paid for by the employee himself and would therefore have no tax implications.

Examiner's report

Part (a) was done reasonably well by those candidates who had a working knowledge of the de minimis rules. A minority of candidates had very little awareness of the rules, such that their performance was poor. Candidates who did not have a precise knowledge of the rules were able to score reasonably well provided they satisfied the requirement and attempted to address all three de minimis tests.

Part (b)(i) simply required a statement of the rules regarding country of incorporation and place of management and control but the majority of candidates were unable to state these fundamental rules.

Part (b)(ii) was done well. The majority of candidates prepared a short accurate calculation and were able to state the particular disadvantages of making such an election.

Part (c) was relatively tricky but was done reasonably well by those candidates who were methodical in their approach. In particular, candidates who did not necessarily know all of the detailed rules were still able to score an acceptable mark if they applied basic principles to all three elements of the question.

Very few candidates identified that the overseas workplace would be a temporary workplace. In addition, a minority of candidates discussed the tax implications for the company rather than for the employee. Candidates must read the requirement for each question carefully and ensure that their answer is always focussed on satisfying that requirement.

PAPER P6: ADVANCED TAXATION (FA2015)

ACCA marking scheme		Marks
(a) Input tax attributed to taxable supplies and unattributed input tax		1.5
Test 1		1.0
Test 2		1.5
Test 3		1.5
Adjustment and date		1.5
		7.0
(b) (i) Not incorporated in the UK		1.0
Central management and control		2.0
		3.0
(ii) Calculation of liability		1.5
Taxation of worldwide profits		1.0
Discussion of election		
Advantage		1.5
Disadvantages		2.0
		6.0
	Maximum	5.0
(c) Flights at the start and end of the contract		3.0
Return journey in February		1.5
Laundry and telephone calls		2.0
		6.5
	Maximum	5.0
Total		20.0

70 OPUS LTD GROUP Walk in the footsteps of a top tutor

Key answer tips

This question features a group of companies which is a regular feature in section A of the P6 exam.

Part (a) of the question deals with the surrender of losses via group relief and requires a sound knowledge of both the computation of profits available for group relief and the identification of which losses can be surrendered.

You need to take advantage of the tax benefits of having a capital gains group which allows capital gains to be transferred between members by making an election within two years from the end of the accounting period in which the disposal is made.

There are easy marks available for identifying the losses carried forward and further information required.

Part (b) examines the sale of shares in Venere Ltd and requires understanding of the substantial shareholding exemption, which has regularly featured in the exam. As long as you mastered the conditions there were easy marks to be earned.

ANSWERS TO PRACTICE QUESTIONS: SECTION 2

It is important to note that in order for the substantial shareholding exemption to apply, the company must have owned 10% of the ordinary share capital for at least 12 months out of the previous 24 months, it does not have to be the PREVIOUS 12 months.

Part (c) examines how interest on underpaid tax is computed and requires knowledge of quarterly instalment payments for large companies.

There are then 5 easy marks on ethics focusing on the actions tax advisors should take when dealing with clients that may be guilty of tax evasion. This is a popular examination topic. Well prepared students could easily earn full marks on this section, and it may be a good idea to answer this part of the question first.

The highlighted words in the written sections are key phrases that markers are looking for.

Tutor's top tips

The best way to approach the question is to start by identifying all the different groups that will be relevant to your answer.

A capital gains group is a 75% group but the indirect shareholding only has to be 51%.

However, with trading loss groups although they are also 75% groups the indirect shareholding has to be 75% as well.

*Opus Ltd owns (80% x 85%) in Lido Ltd which means that the indirect shareholding is 68%. As a result, Lido Ltd would be included in the gains group but **not** in the trading loss group.*

It is important to focus on the need to relieve the losses as soon as possible.

Akia Ltd cannot surrender trading losses to Lido Ltd.

However, Lido Ltd can allocate its capital gain of £21,000 to the other companies in the gains group, thus enabling group losses to be set against this gain.

It was tempting to think that Venere Ltd was a consortium company but this is impossible as Jarrah Ltd owns 75% of Venere Ltd. This means that the two companies would form a trading loss group in priority to Opus Ltd and Jarrah Ltd forming a consortium.

(a) **Trading losses of Akia Ltd and Ribe Ltd**

Tutor's top tips

Akia Ltd can surrender its loss via group relief to Opus Ltd, Ribe Ltd and Binni Ltd. However, as all the companies in the group pay tax at 20% this would not result in a higher tax saving. Consequently, Akia Ltd would first use up the loss itself in the current period before surrendering group relief.

With regard to Binni Ltd, it joined the group on the 1 December 2015 so the group relief would be restricted to the 4 month common period (1.12.2015 – 31.3.2016).

KAPLAN PUBLISHING

> Ribe Ltd has a trading loss brought forward of £68,000 and this loss can only be offset against its own trading profits of £41,000. Brought forward losses cannot be surrendered as group relief.
>
> Remember that profits available for group relief include chargeable gains so it is possible for the group relief claim to be made against gains as well.

	Notes	£	£
Akia Ltd			
Trading loss – y/e 31 March 2016			93,000
Offset of losses in Akia Ltd:			
y/e 31 March 2016			(6,000)
y/e 31 March 2015	1		Unknown
Group relief:	2		
Opus Ltd			
Trading profit		10,000	
Property income		8,000	
Chargeable gain – sale of the shares in Venere Ltd	3	Nil	
Chargeable gain – transferred from Lido Ltd	4	21,000	
			(39,000)
Binni Ltd	5		(31,000)
Ribe Ltd	6		–
Amount unrelieved	7		17,000
Ribe Ltd			
Trading loss b/f – 1 April 2015			68,000
Offset against trading profit – y/e 31 March 2016	6		(41,000)
Trading loss c/f – 31 March 2016			27,000

Notes

1. Akia Ltd can offset its trading loss against its total income and chargeable gains of the loss-making period and those of the previous 12 months. Accordingly, we need to know the amounts (if any) of the company's unrelieved income and chargeable gains for the year ended 31 March 2015.

2. Akia Ltd is in a 75% group relief group with Opus Ltd, Ribe Ltd and Binni Ltd. Lido Ltd is not in the group, as the effective interest of Opus Ltd in Lido Ltd of 68% (80% x 85%) is less than 75%.

   Venere Ltd is a 75% subsidiary of Jarrah Ltd, such that it cannot be a consortium company.

3. The chargeable gain on the sale of the shares will be exempt under the substantial shareholding exemption. This is because Opus Ltd and Venere Ltd are trading companies and Opus Ltd had owned at least 10% of the shares in Venere Ltd for a 12 month period during the two years prior to the sale.

ANSWERS TO PRACTICE QUESTIONS: SECTION 2

4   Lido Ltd is in a chargeable gains group with Opus Ltd. This is because Opus Ltd has a direct interest of at least 75% in Ribe Ltd which, in turn, has a direct interest of at least 75% in Lido Ltd, and Opus Ltd has an effective interest in Lido Ltd of more than 50% (80% x 85% = 68%).

The chargeable gain of Lido Ltd can therefore be transferred to Opus Ltd and can then be relieved via group relief from Akia Ltd.

5   Binni Ltd joined the Opus Ltd group on 1 December 2015, such that it is in a group relief group with Akia Ltd for the four months from 1 December 2015 to 31 March 2016.

The maximum loss which can be surrendered by Akia Ltd to Binni Ltd

= Lower of:

(i)   Available loss of Akia Ltd for the overlapping period

(£93,000 × 4/12)   £31,000

(ii) Available profits of Binni Ltd for the overlapping period

(£78,000 × 4/10)   £31,200

6   The trading losses brought forward in Ribe Ltd must be offset against the first available trading profits of the same trade. Accordingly, the company has no profits which can be relieved via group relief.

The remaining losses cannot be surrendered as group relief to Lido Ltd as only current period losses can be group relieved.

7   The use of losses carried forward in Akia Ltd can only be against future profits from the same trade, hence their use will be delayed because the company is not expected to be profitable for some time. Akia Ltd could reduce its current year loss and create greater losses arising in future (available for immediate relief via group relief) by not claiming capital allowances equal to its unrelieved current period trading loss.

Reducing the capital allowances would increase the tax written down value of the main pool and consequently the capital allowances and trading loss in future periods. The increased trading loss in future years could then be group relieved.

However, reducing the capital allowances would reduce the trading loss of Akia Ltd for the year ended 31 March 2016, which would in turn reduce the maximum loss which could be surrendered to Binni Ltd.

Tutorial note

The chargeable gain of Lido Ltd could be transferred to Akia Ltd or Ribe Ltd, rather than Opus Ltd, and be relieved via Akia Ltd's losses in a similar way to that set out above. It would not be beneficial to transfer the gain to Binni Ltd, due to the restriction on the surrender of losses to that company.

You may not have picked up the point regarding not claiming capital allowances. You would still have scored well on this part of the question even if you had not picked up on this point.

KAPLAN PUBLISHING

(b) **Sale of shares in Venere Ltd**

Tutor's top tips

In order for the substantial shareholding exemption to apply, the disposing company must own at least 10% of the ordinary share capital for at least **12 months out of the previous 24 months** preceding the date of disposal.

With regard to the earlier disposal of 120,000 shares on 1 October 2015, Opus Ltd owned 17% for 24 months out of the previous 24 months so the gain was exempt. After this disposal, Opus Ltd only owns 5% of the shares, which is no longer a 'substantial share'. However, they can still qualify for the SSE on any disposals of Venere Ltd shares in the following 12 months.

With the sale of 50,000 shares on 30 June 2016, Opus Ltd will have owned at least 10% for 15 out of the last 24 months so the gain is exempt.

If the sale of the 50,000 shares is postponed to 30 April 2017, Opus Ltd will have owned at least 10% for just 5 out of the last 24 months so the exemption no longer applies and the gain is now taxable.

This part of the question is quite tricky and the best way to approach this is to start with each date of disposal and then go back 24 months. It is then easy to count the number of months to the earlier disposal (when the 10% ownership ceased) which took place on 1 October 2015.

Easy marks were available for mentioning the cash flow benefit of receiving the money sooner and the uncertainty over the amount of proceeds if the sale was delayed.

If the shares are sold on 30 June 2016

If the shares are sold on 30 June 2016, the chargeable gain arising will be exempt under the substantial shareholding exemption.

This is because Opus Ltd would have owned at least 10% of the shares in Venere Ltd for a 12 month period during the two years prior to the sale. In fact they owned 17% for the 15 months from 1 July 2014 to 30 September 2015 which falls within the 24 months prior to sale.

Accordingly, the post-tax proceeds will be equal to the gross proceeds of £80,000.

If the shares are sold on 30 April 2017

If the shares are sold on 30 April 2017, there will not be a 12 month period in the previous two years where Opus Ltd has owned at least 10% of the shares in Venere Ltd.

Accordingly, on the assumption that the shares are sold for £100,000, there will be a chargeable gain of £72,183 (W). This gain will be subject to corporation tax of £14,437 (£72,183 × 20%).

The post-tax proceeds will be £85,563 (£100,000 – £14,437).

Delaying sale

Therefore, while there may be a marginal increase in the post-tax proceeds of £5,563 (£85,563 – £80,000) from delaying the sale until after the results for the year ending 31 March 2017 are known, there is no guarantee that a higher level of sales proceeds will be achieved and there will be a significant delay in obtaining the sales proceeds.

Also, these figures assume that any costs of sale will be the same at both dates, which may not be the case.

Working: Chargeable gain

	£
Proceeds	100,000
Less: Cost (£65,000 × (50,000/170,000))	(19,118)
Less: Indexation allowance (£19,118 × 0·455)	(8,699)
Chargeable gain	72,183

(c) **Error in the corporation tax return of Binni Ltd**

Tutor's top tips

*In the first part of this section you were asked to **explain** how interest would be calculated.*

Interest is always calculated from the date tax was due, so you needed to spot that as Binni Ltd is a large company, the corporation tax would have been payable in quarterly instalments with the first payment due on the 14th of month 7 in the CAP. This was the 14 December 2014. Subsequent instalments are made at quarterly intervals.

You were not asked to actually calculate interest or discuss penalties and there are no marks available for doing this. It is important to limit your answer to the requirements of the question in order to avoid wasting time.

There are 5 easy marks on ethics, so try to make sure that you have 5 separately identifiable points in your answer.

When discussing tax evasion it is important to also consider any money laundering obligations.

Interest on underpaid tax

Binni Ltd will be regarded as having underpaid corporation tax on each of the four payment dates for the year ended 31 May 2015. Accordingly, interest may be charged from 14 December 2014, 14 March 2015, 14 June 2015 and 14 September 2015 on any amounts of underpaid corporation tax.

Disclosure of the error

The error must be disclosed to HM Revenue and Customs (HMRC). It is not acceptable for our firm to continue to act for the company unless this disclosure is made.

Binni Ltd can disclose the information or it can authorise us to do so. However, we must not disclose the error unless we have permission from the company.

We should notify the company of the following consequences of not informing HMRC of the error:

- If the company refuses to disclose the error, we will advise HMRC that we no longer act for the company. We would not, however, give any reason for our actions.
- Non-disclosure of the errors would also represent tax evasion by the company. This could result in criminal proceedings under both the tax and money laundering legislation.

> **Examiner's report**
>
> Part (a) concerned relief for trading losses within the group. As is often the case, some thought was required before starting because the question did not have as its objective the relief of losses in order to maximise the tax saved as all companies pay tax at the same rate. Instead, the question stated that all of the companies were large and therefore the objective was simply to relieve the losses as soon as possible. However, many candidates ignored this point and focussed on tax rates and tax computations. This was not necessarily that costly in terms of marks but, as the question did not require tax computations to be prepared, was potentially costly in terms of time.
>
> The question was all about identifying various individual points in respect of each of the companies. That's why the email from the manager suggested 'you should think carefully about the tax position of each company'.
>
> Akia Ltd, the loss-making company, had realised a chargeable gain against which the loss could be offset. There was also the possibility of carrying the loss back 12 months, although very few candidates identified this point.
>
> Once the position of Akia Ltd, the loss-making company, had been considered it was then necessary to consider the group and consortium position. The group position was handled well but many candidates failed to spot that because Venere Ltd was a 75% subsidiary of Jarrah Ltd, it could not be a consortium company.
>
> Ribe Ltd had trading losses brought forward. These could not be group relieved (because only current period losses can be group relieved) and therefore could only be used against that company's trading profits. However, a minority of candidates simply added the losses of Ribe Ltd to those of Akia Ltd and then addressed the total losses together.
>
> Finally, Binni Ltd was not a member of the group for the whole of the period so it was necessary to determine the maximum loss that could be surrendered to it by Akia Ltd. This is a straightforward point but it was missed by many candidates.
>
> There were plenty of relatively straightforward marks to be earned in this part of the question but candidates needed to slow down slightly, think and, in particular, make a real effort to answer the question set as opposed to the question that they might have been expecting.
>
> The second part of the question concerned the sale of shares by one of the group companies and the availability of the substantial shareholding exemption (SSE). This was not done well for two main reasons.
>
> First, many candidates failed to consider the SSE despite it being an important exemption at P6. There were follow through marks available for those who found themselves in this predicament but only if they answered the question set. Unfortunately, many candidates failed to do so.
>
> Two lessons may be learned from what happened here.

ANSWERS TO PRACTICE QUESTIONS: SECTION 2

> Firstly, it is always worth thinking about how to do a calculation in an efficient manner rather than to just immediately start it. Those candidates who thought it was necessary to calculate a chargeable gain on each of the possible disposal dates should have realised that the only difference was an increase in sales proceeds of £20,000. This would, of course, increase the gain by £20,000; there was no need to repeat the whole calculation to determine this.
>
> The second lesson is that you must answer the question set. Candidates were asked to consider on which of the two dates it would be more financially advantageous to sell the shares. This required candidates to consider the post-tax proceeds on each of the potential disposal dates, but the majority of candidates simply focussed on the amount of the chargeable gain.
>
> Part (c) was a standard question and an opportunity for all candidates to earn some straightforward marks.
>
> Unfortunately, a minority of candidates decided to address the penalties aspect of the question in great detail without thinking about the other relevant issues. Stronger candidates recognised the need to consider the importance of disclosing the error from the point of view of tax evasion, money laundering and the acceptability of continuing to act for the company. These stronger candidates were able to score well on this part of the question.

	ACCA marking scheme	
		Marks
(a)	Loss of Akia Ltd	
	Offset against total profits of Akia Ltd	2.0
	Group relief	
	Members of group and consortium	2.0
	Opus Ltd	2.5
	Binni Ltd	1.5
	Ribe Ltd	1.0
	Lido Ltd chargeable gain	2.0
	Loss carried forward	2.0
	Loss of Ribe Ltd	1.0
	Capital allowances	2.0
		16.0
	Maximum	14.0
(b)	Sale on 30 June 2016	1.5
	Sale on 30 April 2017	3.0
	Comparison	1.0
		5.5
	Maximum	5.0
(c)	Interest on underpaid tax	2.0
	Action required	
	Necessary to disclose	2.0
	Implications of failing to disclose	3.5
		7.5
	Maximum	6.0
Total		25.0

KAPLAN PUBLISHING

71 BOND LTD *Walk in the footsteps of a top tutor*

Key answer tips

This is a corporation tax question with some minor group elements. Topics covered include capital allowances and rollover relief (both F6 level topics), restriction of trading losses brought forward, patent box relief and the capital goods scheme for VAT.

Part (a) requires a corporation tax computation for a short chargeable accounting period with adjustments to capital allowances, rollover relief with partial reinvestment, and a simple corporation tax computation – none of which should have caused too many problems. However, two-thirds of the marks in this section are for written notes, so calculations alone would not score a pass.

There are also marks for discussing the restriction of trading losses following a change in ownership, which is hinted at in the information provided.

Part (b) requires a brief description of the relatively new patent box regime, which has not been tested before. You must keep up to date with changes in the tax rules, as the examining team likes to test new areas.

Part (c) covers the recovery of VAT for a partially exempt business, and the capital goods scheme. These elements of VAT have been tested several times before, so you should make sure that you know the rules and are able to explain them.

The highlighted words in the written sections are key phrases that markers are looking for.

Tutor's top tips

The requirements at the end of the question serve only to highlight the number of marks available for each section. The real requirements are in the email from your manager.

Highlight the requirements as you come across them, and don't forget to keep looking back at them to make sure your answer is focused.

As this question involves a group of companies, you may find it useful to draw a group structure diagram before you start, and identify the group relationships that exist. Think about how these will impact on your answer.

Watch the dates: Madison was not acquired until 1 October 2016.

ANSWERS TO PRACTICE QUESTIONS: SECTION 2

(a) **Corporation tax liability of Bond Ltd – six months ended 30 September 2016**

> ***Tutor's top tips***
>
> *You are asked to calculate corporation tax for a six month accounting period, so you need to think about how that will impact on your computation.*
>
> *Capital allowances will be affected: the AIA and WDA should be time apportioned.*
>
> *Only one third of the marks (approximately 6 marks) are available for calculations; the remaining 11 marks are for written notes.*
>
> *The email from your manager also asks you to make a note of any assumptions you have made, so there will be marks available for doing this.*

	Notes	£
Tax adjusted trading income		470,000
Add: Reduction in capital allowances (£285,000 – £253,150)	1	31,850
		501,850
Less: Trading losses brought forward	2	Nil
		501,850
Chargeable gain	3	40,000
Taxable total profits		541,850
Corporation tax at 20%		108,370

Notes

1 Capital allowances

The maximum annual investment allowance (AIA) for the six-month period ended 30 September 2016 is £250,000 (£500,000 × 6/12).

This is the maximum AIA for Bond Ltd and Ungar Ltd together because they belong to a group of companies. It will be necessary to consider the most beneficial way of allocating this maximum AIA between the two companies. However, if they both make capital purchases, as they both pay tax at 20%, the group is indifferent as to which company receives the AIA.

As Bond Ltd has a substantial purchase, it is assumed that the whole of the AIA is allocated to Bond Ltd.

The capital allowances for the period will therefore be calculated as follows.

	Main pool £	Allowances £
Additions qualifying for AIA	285,000	
Less: AIA	(250,000)	250,000
	35,000	
Less: WDA (18% × 6/12)	(3,150)	3,150
TWDV c/f	31,850	
Maximum capital allowances		253,150

2 Trading losses brought forward

Tutor's top tips

There is a clue in the email from your manager that there will be a restriction on the use of the trading losses brought forward, where it says 'bearing in mind that Mr Stone only recently acquired the company'.

Remember that losses are restricted if a company has both a change in ownership and a major change in the nature or conduct of trade within three years.

Try to relate your answer to the scenario: there is information about a 'new range' of bread and cakes.

Trading losses brought forward can only be offset against future profits of the same trade. Although Bond Ltd has made some significant changes to the way in which it carries on its trade, it has not changed its trade; the trade continues to consist of baking and selling bread and other baked products.

However, the changes made by Bond Ltd to its products and customers are likely to amount to a major change in the nature or conduct of its trade.

This change has occurred within three years of the change in ownership of the company on 1 April 2014.

Accordingly, it is likely that the trading losses brought forward cannot be carried forward beyond 1 April 2014, the date of the change of ownership, such that there are no trading losses brought forward for relief in the period ended 30 September 2016.

Tutorial note

If there has been a major change in the nature or conduct of its trade, the company's corporation tax liabilities for the two previous accounting periods will need to be recalculated because the trading losses brought forward and deducted during those periods will no longer be available for offset.

ANSWERS TO PRACTICE QUESTIONS: SECTION 2

3 Rollover relief

Tutor's top tips

Rollover relief is very popular in corporation tax questions, as it is the only capital gains relief available to companies.

There are several elements that you need to consider when deciding if relief is available:

1. *Qualifying business assets: must be sold and purchased*
2. *Qualifying time period: reinvestment within 1 year before to 3 years after disposal*
3. *Gains groups: reinvestment can be by other companies within a 75% gains group*
4. *Proceeds reinvested: relief is restricted if proceeds are only partially reinvested.*

Rollover relief will be available in respect of the chargeable gain on the land by reference to the qualifying business assets purchased in the four year period commencing one year prior to the sale of the land. Qualifying business assets consist of land, buildings and fixed plant, purchased for use in a trade.

A capital gains group is treated as a single entity for the purposes of rollover relief. Accordingly, qualifying assets can be purchased by Ungar Ltd whilst it is a member of the Bond Ltd capital gains group, as well as by Bond Ltd. Madison Ltd is not a member of the Bond Ltd capital gains group, as it is not a 75% subsidiary of Bond Ltd.

The whole of Bond Ltd's gain can be rolled over if qualifying assets costing at least £350,000 (the proceeds in respect of the sale of the land) are acquired. Otherwise, there will be a chargeable gain equal to the amount of proceeds not reinvested up to a maximum of the gain of £180,000.

Based on the information we have, the only qualifying purchase is the building acquired by Ungar Ltd. Accordingly, the chargeable gain after rollover relief will be equal to the proceeds not reinvested of £40,000 (£350,000 – £310,000).

It will be possible to defer the whole of the gain if there are further acquisitions of qualifying assets costing at least £40,000, for example, items of fixed plant within the purchases of plant and machinery made by Bond Ltd.

(b) **Ungar Ltd – Patent box regime**

Tutor's top tips

*You need to describe the **effect** of the relief, and also refer to the scenario to decide whether or not it is available to Ungar Ltd.*

The formula for calculating patent box relief is given in the tax tables in the exam, and you will not score marks if you simply copy the formula, although you would be given credit if you used some illustrative figures.

KAPLAN PUBLISHING

> There are four marks available here, so try to make sure that you have four separately identifiable points in your answer.
>
> This is a standalone section, so you could attempt it before part (a).

The patent box regime is likely to be available to Ungar Ltd as it holds patents as a result of having developed new baking processes (the patented inventions).

Ungar Ltd would need to submit an election to HM Revenue and Customs in order for the patent box regime to apply.

Under the patent box regime, Ungar Ltd's patent profits would be subject to an effective reduced rate of corporation tax of 10%. The company's patent profits consist of its royalty income in respect of its patents and a proportion of its profits in respect of the sale of products incorporating the use of those patents.

In the early years of the regime, only a proportion of a company's patent profits will benefit from the reduced rate of corporation tax. This proportion will increase gradually over a number of years until the whole of a company's patent profits are included.

Tutorial note

For computations in FA2015, patent box relief will apply to 80% of the company's profits.

If calculations are required in the exam, the appropriate percentage will be provided in the question.

(c) **Recovery of value added tax (VAT) in respect of the assets acquired by Madison Ltd**

Tutor's top tips

The capital goods scheme for VAT is a popular area in the exam. Make sure that you are able to explain how it works, as well as performing calculations.

Madison Ltd will be able to recover 80% of the VAT incurred in respect of both the building and the machinery in the year ending 30 September 2017:

((£400,000 + £300,000) × 20% × 80%) = £112,000

The building will be subject to the capital goods scheme because it cost more than £250,000. This means that an adjustment will be made in each of the next nine years to reflect any change in the VAT recovery percentage.

For example, if the VAT recovery percentage in the year ending 30 September 2018 is 75%, Madison Ltd will have to repay VAT to HM Revenue and Customs as follows:

(£400,000 × 20%) × 1/10 × (80% − 75%) = £400.

The capital goods scheme does not apply to machinery and therefore the initial recovery of input tax of £48,000 (£300,000 × 20% × 80%) is final.

Tutorial note

The capital goods scheme applies to land and buildings costing £250,000 or more and computer equipment costing £50,000 or more. It does not apply to other machinery.

Examiner's comments

In part (a) almost all candidates identified that they were dealing with a six-month accounting period, but many of them did not recognise all of the areas where this point was relevant (i.e. the annual investment allowance, and the rate of writing down allowance).

Other than that, the corporation tax computation was done well.

It was stated in the question that the required notes represented approximately two thirds of the marks available and it was pleasing that most candidates picked up on this guidance and addressed all three areas on which notes were required in various levels of detail.

The capital allowances were handled reasonably well with most candidates recognising the mistake the client had made. However, many candidates did not recognise that the expenditure that did not qualify for the additional investment allowance would qualify for writing down allowances. Of those that did, many forgot to reduce the rate of the writing down allowance by 6/12 to reflect the length of the accounting period.

The use of the company's brought forward trading losses required candidates to consider two matters. First, had the company changed its trade? If it had, the losses brought forward could not be used in the future. Secondly, because there had been a change in ownership of the company, it was necessary to consider if there had been a major change in the nature or conduct of the trade. The company's trade continued to be the baking and selling of bread and baked products. However, the changes made to its products and customers were likely to represent a major change in the nature or conduct of the trade, such that the losses could not be carried forward beyond the date of the change of ownership of the company.

The third area of explanatory notes concerned rollover relief. In order to score well here, candidates had to first be aware of the meaning of a qualifying business asset for the purposes of rollover relief and the qualifying period for reinvestment. Qualifying business assets include land and buildings and **fixed** plant and machinery used in the business. Most candidates were not sufficiently clear on these rules. The qualifying time period was identified by the majority of candidates.

Candidates then had to consider the chargeable gains group aspects of rollover relief. A sizable minority of candidates did not consider this aspect and, of those who did, a minority thought that Madison Ltd, a 65% subsidiary, was a member of the gains group because the holding was more than 50%. However, the direct holding between each company in the group has to be at least 75%; it is any indirect holding between the principal company and a non-directly held subsidiary that has to be more than 50%.

Finally, candidates had to point out that only part of the gain can be rolled over if only part of the sales proceeds are reinvested in qualifying replacement assets. Although many candidates were aware of this point, not all of them were able to calculate the amount of gain that could be rolled over given a specific level of reinvestment in the question.

Part (b) was mainly knowledge-based. A minority of candidates were not aware of the regime and consequently did not score well. Those who knew about the patent regime scored well provided they took care to address the requirement and made separately identifiable points rather than repeating themselves. As always, time spent identifying relevant points before putting pen to paper was time well spent.

Part (c) concerned the VAT capital goods scheme. Despite this being examined regularly, it was not tackled particularly well. Many candidates thought, incorrectly, that the scheme applies to plant and machinery generally. The way in which the scheme operates was also misunderstood by many candidates who were unable to explain the adjustments that would be made in future years. This aspect of VAT is not part of the Paper F6 (UK) syllabus and thus is new knowledge at P6 (UK). It should be regarded as an area that is likely to continue to be examined regularly in future Paper P6 (UK) exams.

	ACCA marking scheme	
		Marks
(a)	Corporation tax computation	
	Taxable total profits	2.0
	Corporation tax liability	1.5
	Capital allowances	
	Maximum AIA	1.0
	Calculation of adjustment to capital allowances	1.5
	Group aspect	1.0
	Losses brought forward	
	Offset against future profits of the same trade	2.0
	Major change in the nature or conduct of the trade	3.0
	Rollover relief	5.0
	Assumption	1.0
		18.0
	Maximum	17.0
(b)	Identification of each relevant point – one mark	
	Possible points include:	
	Availability of scheme	
	Meaning of patent profits	
	10% tax rate on patent profits	
	Example	
	Phasing in of the scheme	
	Election required	
	Maximum	4.0
(c)	Initial recovery of input tax	1.0
	Capital goods scheme	2.0
	Example	2.0
		5.0
	Maximum	4.0
Total		25.0

72 KLUBB PLC *Walk in the footsteps of a top tutor*

Key answer tips

This question covers three areas: corporation tax administration; a comparison of share schemes: SIP versus CSOP, and the CFC rules.

Part (a) is F6 revision of filing dates for a long accounting period and basic corporation tax penalties. This should offer easy marks for those who remember the rules.

Part (b) requires very detailed knowledge of the conditions for both SIPs and CSOP schemes. You may want to revise the rules before attempting this part of the question.

Part (c) also requires detailed knowledge of a specific area: CFCs. Again, if you have not learnt the detailed rules you may struggle with this part of the question.

The highlighted words in the written sections are key phrases that markers are looking for.

Tutor's top tips

This is really three separate, standalone questions and you can attempt them in any order as long as you clearly label your answer.

(a) Late submission of corporation tax returns

Tutor's top tips

You are not asked to identify corporation tax payment dates or the penalties for late payment of tax, so there would be no marks for doing so.

Corporation tax returns are required for the two accounting periods within the long period of account: the 12 months ended 30 November 2014 and the four months ended 31 March 2015.

The returns should have been filed by 31 March 2016 (12 months after the end of the 16 month period of account).

There will be a late filing penalty of £100 in respect of each of the returns because they were filed within three months of the filing date.

However, this £100 penalty is increased to £500 where the returns for the two preceding accounting periods were also submitted late.

Tutorial note

It has been assumed that HM Revenue and Customs issued notices prior to 1 January 2016 requiring the returns to be made.

(b) **Comparison of a share incentive plan (SIP) with a company share option plan (CSOP)**

Tutor's top tips

This part of the question does not ask you to write everything you know about SIPs and CSOPs. The client is specifically interested in the flexibility each scheme offers and the tax implications.

It requires a comparison of three specific areas:

- Employees who can/must be included in the scheme
- Number or value of shares which can be acquired
- Income tax and CGT implications of acquiring and selling shares.

Use these as headings in your answer to help you to focus, and make sure that you clearly state which scheme you are referring to and which tax: income tax or CGT.

Employees who must be included in the plan

A CSOP is significantly more flexible than a SIP.

Klubb plc would be able to select particular employees to join a CSOP whereas, under the rules for SIPs, Klubb plc would be required to offer shares to all of its full time and part time employees, although a minimum qualifying period of employment may be specified.

The number or value of shares which can be acquired by each plan member

Again, a CSOP is more flexible than a SIP.

Klubb plc can choose to award options to purchase different numbers of shares to each member of a CSOP. The options awarded are simply at the discretion of Klubb plc. However, the award is subject to a maximum whereby a member is only allowed to hold options to purchase shares with a maximum value (at the time the options were granted) of £30,000.

Under the rules for SIPs, free shares up to a maximum value of £3,600 can be given to each member of the plan each tax year. These free shares must be awarded on similar terms to all of the plan members. This means that any variation in the number of free shares awarded must be by reference to objective criteria, for example, length of service or performance targets.

In addition, a member of a SIP can purchase partnership shares (at market value) up to a maximum value of the lower of £1,800 and 10% of salary each tax year. Klubb plc could then give the plan members up to two further free shares (known as matching shares), in respect of each partnership share purchased. This represents additional free shares with a maximum value of £3,600.

Tax implications of acquiring and selling the shares

Under the rules for SIPs, there are no income tax implications when free shares or matching shares are awarded to scheme members. Similarly, there are no income tax implications when shares are withdrawn from the plan if they have been held within the plan for five years. There will be no capital gains tax on the immediate sale of the shares because their base cost is equal to their market value at the time they are withdrawn from the SIP.

The rules for a CSOP are not as generous as those for a SIP.

There would be no tax charged on the grant and exercise of the options.

However, there would be a chargeable gain on the sale of the shares equal to the proceeds received less the amount paid for them.

Tutorial note

It was not necessary to make all of the above points in order to score full marks for this question.

(c) (i) **Status of Hartz Co and availability of the low profits exemption**

Tutor's top tips

The controlled foreign company rules are complex, and there are several exemptions that could apply.

However, this part of the question just requires you to know – and apply:

- *the definition, and*
- *the low profits exemption.*

There are no marks available for discussing other aspects of CFCs.

Hartz Co is a non-UK resident company.

It will be a controlled foreign company (CFC) if it is controlled by UK resident persons.

Accordingly, its status depends on the residency of Mr Deck. If he is a UK resident, Hartz Co will be a CFC.

Hartz Co is not expected to satisfy either of the conditions for the low profits exemption. This is because:

- its profits are expected to exceed £50,000; and
- although its profits are expected to be less than £500,000, it will have chargeable gains (non-trading profits) of more than £50,000.

(ii) **CFC charge**

	£
Chargeable profits of Hartz Co	330,000
Chargeable profits apportioned to Klubb plc (30% × £330,000)	99,000
Corporation tax at 20%	19,800
Less: Creditable tax (£330,000 × 11% × 30%)	(10,890)
CFC charge	8,910

Tutorial note

Chargeable gains are not part of chargeable profits and thus are not included in the calculation of the CFC charge.

Examiner's comments

In part (a) the first thing candidates had to point out was the need to split the long period of account into two accounting periods. Unfortunately, many candidates failed to identify this point. Candidates then had to know the filing dates and the penalty rules. However, many candidates wrote about the dates on which corporation tax has to be paid as opposed to the filing dates of the returns, such that they did not answer the requirement set.

Part (b) of the question was more substantial. It was very important to identify clearly the particular areas that needed to be addressed, and to stick to them. Failure to do this could result in irrelevant parts of an answer that would score no marks, despite being technically accurate. Unfortunately many candidates were insufficiently disciplined in their approach and regarded the question as being about the two share schemes generally as opposed to being about certain aspects of the two schemes.

Generally, candidates' knowledge of this area was good with many candidates providing satisfactory answers. The candidates who did best were those who structured their answer in a very clear manner so that it was always clear which aspect of which scheme was being addressed. This clear structure enabled candidates to keep their answers relatively brief whilst addressing all of the precise requirements of the question.

However, a minority of candidates appeared to be making up their answer as they went along, such that they were setting out each thought as it occurred to them. The problem with this approach was that some points were repeated, other points were made which were not relevant and some aspects of the requirement were omitted altogether.

Most candidates knew that under a share incentive plan, shares need to be offered to, broadly, all employees whereas, under a company share option plan, the employer can choose certain employees to join the scheme. Candidates' knowledge of the number or value of shares that could be offered under each scheme was also satisfactory notwithstanding that some candidates confused the two schemes or confused the different categories of shares that can be offered under a share incentive plan.

When it came to the tax implications of acquiring and selling the shares it was important for candidates to stick to the facts of the question. It was clear from the question how long the shares would be held for and when they would be sold. Accordingly, there was no need to address all of the different tax implications that could occur if the shares were sold at other times. Candidates who failed to realise this wasted time writing lengthy answers that were not addressing the requirements of the question.

When explaining the tax implications, stronger candidates were clear as to which scheme they were writing about and which tax (income tax or capital gains tax) they were addressing. The answers of other candidates were more confused and used the general term 'tax' as opposed to the specific tax concerned.

Part (c)(i) was done reasonably well by many candidates.

Candidates had two main problems when answering this first part of the question. First, they confused the definition of a controlled foreign company with the exemptions that are available. Secondly, there was a tendency to write about all of the available exemptions as opposed to the particular one in the question requirement; this resulted in irrelevant parts of answers.

For part (c)(ii) candidates had to remember to exclude the gains from the calculation of a CFC charge, bring in only 30% of the trading profits, and deduct an appropriate amount of creditable tax. Answers here were generally not as accurate as might have been hoped.

ACCA marking scheme

			Marks
(a)		Two accounting periods	1.0
		Filing date	1.0
		Penalty	2.0
			4.0
(b)		Employees	2.0
		Value	
		SIP	4.0
		CSOP	2.0
		Tax on realisation of value	
		SIP	2.0
		CSOP	2.0
			12.0
		Maximum	9.0
(c)	(i)	Status of Hartz Co	2.5
		Low profits exemption	2.0
			4.5
		Maximum	4.0
	(ii)	Profits apportioned	1.5
		Calculation of charge	1.5
			3.0
Total			20.0

73 HELM LTD GROUP *Walk in the footsteps of a top tutor*

Key answer tips

This question asks you to prepare some work for a manager in preparation for his meeting with a potential new client, the 100% owner of a group of companies.

Before you consider the tax issues raised in parts (a) – (c) you could attempt part (d), which asks for a list of the information and documentation your firm should obtain before taking on a new client, and the ethical issues you should consider.

The highlighted words in the written sections are key phrases that markers are looking for.

(a) **Sale of Bar Ltd**

Tutor's top tips

You are asked to explain any significant matter(s) which affect the calculation of the chargeable gain resulting from the sale of Bar Ltd. The significant matter is the degrouping charge that will arise.

Chargeable gain on the sale of Bar Ltd

On 1 December 2014, Aero Ltd and Bar Ltd were members of a capital gains group because they were both 75% subsidiaries of Helm Ltd.

Accordingly, the building was deemed to have been transferred for consideration which gave Aero Ltd neither a gain nor a loss ('no gain, no loss') on this date.

However, a degrouping charge equal to the gain which would have arisen if the building had been sold at its market value as at 1 December 2014 arises because:

– The sale of Bar Ltd on 30 April 2015 was within six years of the no gain, no loss transfer; and

– Bar Ltd owned the building at the time it left the Helm Ltd group.

The degrouping charge is added to the sales proceeds received by Helm Ltd in respect of the sale of Bar Ltd.

	£
Sale proceeds	1,200,000
Degrouping charge (below)	82,000
	1,282,000
Less: Cost	(1,000,000)
Less: Indexation allowance (October 2014 to April 2015) ((255.7 – 251.9)/251.9) × £1,000,000	(15,085)
Chargeable gain on the sale of Bar Ltd	266,915

Tutorial note

The indexation factor should not be rounded to three decimal places because the disposal relates to shares in the share pool.

Degrouping charge in respect of the building

	£
Deemed proceeds of market value as at 1 December 2014	830,000
Less: Cost to Aero Ltd	(425,000)
Less: Indexation allowance (July 1994 to December 2014) ((253.4 − 144.0)/144.0) = 0.760 × £425,000	(323,000)
Degrouping charge	82,000

Substantial shareholding exemption (SSE)

The SSE is automatically available where a trading company sells shares in another trading company out of a shareholding of at least 10% of that company's ordinary share capital.

The SSE is not available unless the substantial shareholding has been owned for a continuous period of at least 12 months in the two years prior to the sale.

However, this 12 month period can include a period where the assets used in the trade of the company being sold were used in the trade of another company in the capital gains group.

Accordingly, because the assets owned by Bar Ltd were used in the trade of Aero Ltd (which has itself been part of the capital gains group for 12 months), the SSE will be available on the sale of the shareholding in Bar Ltd even though Helm Ltd had not owned these shares for 12 months.

Stamp duty land tax (SDLT)

No SDLT was due on the purchase of the building by Bar Ltd from Aero Ltd because Helm Ltd owned at least 75% of the ordinary share capital of both companies at the time of the purchase.

However, because Helm Ltd has sold Bar Ltd within three years of the transfer of the building, the relief from SDLT will be withdrawn and Bar Ltd will have to pay SDLT of £33,200 (£830,000 × 4%).

(b) **Drill Ltd**

Tutor's top tips

This part of the question requires you to apply your knowledge of the loan relationship rules. Remember that the rules apply to all expenses relating to loans, not just interest.

There are easy marks here for stating the reliefs available for non-trade loan relationship deficits, but you must make sure that your answer is precise in order to score the marks.

Any amounts charged in the accounts in relation to the loan (i.e. both the interest and the loan arrangement fee) will be relieved in accordance with the loan relationship rules. The tax treatment of these amounts depends on whether the loan is for trading or non-trading purposes.

One quarter of the building will initially be rented out to a third party, such that £300,000 (1/4 × £1,200,000) of the loan is for non-trading purposes.

Accordingly, 22.2% (£300,000/£1,350,000) of the loan is for non-trading purposes, and the balance of 77.8% is for trading purposes.

The amounts charged for trading purposes are allowable when calculating taxable trading profits.

The amounts charged for non-trading purposes are deducted from any income or other credits relating to non-trade loan relationships (i.e. the small amount of interest income received by Drill Ltd).

Given the amounts involved, this will result in a non-trade loan relationship deficit, which can be utilised as follows:

– deducted from total profits of the accounting period

– surrendered as group relief

– carried back and offset against credits in respect of non-trading loan relationships in the previous 12 months

– carried forward for offset against future non-trading income and chargeable gains.

(c) **Cog Ltd – chargeable gain on the sale of the warehouse**

Tutor's top tips

This part of the question requires no calculations, just application of your knowledge of the conditions for rollover relief and for the use of pre-entry capital losses.

Rollover relief

Rollover relief will not be available to relieve the chargeable gain arising on the sale of Cog Ltd's warehouse. This is because the warehouse was not a qualifying business asset for the purposes of this relief, as it had never been used by the company for the purposes of its trade.

Drill Ltd's capital losses

Drill Ltd's capital losses are pre-entry capital losses because they were realised before Drill Ltd became a member of the Helm Ltd group.

As such, the losses can only be offset against chargeable gains on:

– assets sold by Drill Ltd before it became a member of the Helm Ltd capital gains group

– assets already owned by Drill Ltd at the time it became a member of the Helm Ltd capital gains group

– assets purchased by Drill Ltd for use in its trade after it became a member of the Helm Ltd capital gains group (excluding any assets purchased from members of the Helm Ltd group).

Accordingly, Drill Ltd's capital losses cannot be used to relieve the chargeable gain on the sale of the warehouse by Cog Ltd.

(d) **Becoming tax advisers to Gomez and the Helm Ltd group of companies**

Tutor's top tips

Professional ethics is an essential attribute required in practice and a topic which will appear for roughly 5 marks in Section A of every examination.

Information required:

- Evidence of the identity of Gomez (for example, his passport) and his address.
- The primary business address and registered office of each of the companies.
- Proof of incorporation of each of the companies.
- Details of the directors and shareholders of the companies and the identities of those persons instructing the firm on behalf of the companies.

Actions to take:

- We must have regard to the fundamental principles of professional ethics, for example, integrity and professional competence. This requires us to consider whether becoming tax advisers to Gomez and the Helm Ltd group of companies would create any threats to compliance with these principles. If any such threats are identified, we should not accept the appointment unless the threats can be reduced to an acceptable level via the implementation of safeguards.
- We should contact the existing tax adviser(s) in order to ensure that there has been no action by Gomez or the companies which would preclude the acceptance of the appointment on ethical grounds.

Examiner's comments

Part (a) was for 11 marks and was the largest part of the question. It consisted of various aspects of corporation tax with some easy and some more challenging marks. Candidates who did well had a good knowledge of the subject and addressed all of the issues briefly rather than writing about a small number of issues in great detail.

When calculating the gain on the sale of the shares in Bar Ltd, the majority of candidates recognised that here would be a degrouping charge and most candidates explained the reasons for the charge arising. However, a minority of candidates were unable to calculate the indexation allowance correctly and so failed to gain some of the available marks.

Candidates who performed less well often confused the sale of shares with the sale of assets and calculated gains on the individual assets owned by the company. Candidates must take the time to ensure that they understand the transactions that have taken place in a scenario.

It was then necessary to consider the availability of the substantial shareholding exemption. Most candidates knew that at least 10% of the company's shares needed to be owned for 12 months in the two years prior to the sale. However, fewer candidates pointed out that the companies needed to be trading companies. The final element, which was only picked up by a small number of candidates, was the fact that the ownership period was satisfied in this particular situation due to the trade of Bar Ltd having been owned by another group company, Aero Ltd, previously.

The stamp duty land tax aspects of the question were not handled well with very few candidates recognising that the inter group exemption that was available when the trade and assets of Aero Ltd were transferred to Bar Ltd would be withdrawn due to the sale of Bar Ltd within three years.

Part (b) concerned the loan relationships rules and produced a great variety of answers. Those candidates with a good knowledge of the rules were able to present a brief, methodical answer that scored very well. Candidates who were less confident in this area did not pursue the question to its conclusion and therefore did not address the detail of the offset of non-trading loan relationship deficits. This made it difficult to pick up many marks.

Part (c) concerned rollover relief and the offset of capital losses within a capital gains group. Most candidates identified the fact that rollover relief was not available because the building had never been used in the company's trade. The problem was that many candidates described all of the rules relating to rollover relief in addition to making the one relevant point that was worth a mark.

Performance in respect of capital losses was mixed. The majority of candidates knew that, in certain circumstances, capital losses can effectively be transferred between companies in capital gains groups.

The problem was that this could not occur in this question because the capital losses concerned were pre-entry capital losses, such that their use was restricted. Many candidates did not identify this point but I suspect that they would have done if they had simply paused and thought before they started writing.

The final part of the question concerned the information required and the actions to be taken before becoming tax advisers to a new client. Many candidates did well here. Those who did not either did not have the necessary knowledge or did not make a sufficient number of points briefly, but instead wrote at length about a small number of matters.

ACCA marking scheme		
		Marks
(a)	Chargeable gain on the sale of Bar Ltd	
	Calculations	
	Degrouping charge	2.0
	Chargeable gain on the sale of Bar Ltd	2.5
	Explanations	2.0
	Substantial shareholding exemption	3.0
	Stamp duty land tax	3.0
		12.5
	Maximum	11.0
(b)	Loan arrangement fee	1.0
	Split of loan	1.5
	Tax treatment of costs	4.0
		6.5
	Maximum	5.0
(c)	Rollover relief	1.0
	Capital losses	3.0
		4.0
(d)	Information needed	3.0
	Action to take	3.0
		6.0
	Maximum	5.0
Total		25.0

74 SPRINT LTD AND IRON LTD (ADAPTED) *Walk in the footsteps of a top tutor*

Key answer tips

This question covers three separate areas: corporation tax for a long period of account, the differences between purchase of shares by an individual or by another company and registration for VAT.

Part (a) requires calculation of tax for a 16 month period of account, which is mainly revision of F6. Once again, this reinforces the importance of retaining basic F6 knowledge.

Part (b) is a written section that requires clear understanding of the differences between individuals and companies. Think carefully before answering this section.

Part (c) covers registration for VAT – another F6 topic that should have offered easy marks. You could have answered this part of the question first.

The highlighted words in the written sections are key phrases that markers are looking for.

(a) **Iron Ltd – corporation tax payable for the period ending 30 June 2017**

Tutor's top tips

Remember that a long accounting period must be split into the first 12 months and the balance, with two corporation tax computations prepared.

The RPIs provided in the requirement should have given a hint that there were some gains to calculate here.

Rollover relief is often tested in P6 corporation tax questions, so you should try to learn the rules. Watch out for depreciating assets, as they are treated differently for rollover relief purposes.

There are easy marks available for stating the due dates for payment of the corporation tax.

Year ending	Year ending 28 February 2017 £	4 months ending 30 June 2017 £
Trading income		
£30,000 × 12/16	22,500	
£30,000 × 4/16		7,500
Chargeable gains (below)		
Industrial building	87,435	
Fixed machinery	0	
Crystallisation of deferred gain re sale of fixed machinery	3,200	
	———	———
Taxable total profits	113,135	7,500
	———	———
Corporation tax payable		
£113,135/£7,500 × 20%	22,627	1,500
	———	———
Due date (W)	1 December 2017	1 April 2018

Chargeable gains

	Industrial building £	Fixed machinery £
Proceeds	160,000	14,000
Less: Cost (£100,000 – £31,800)	(68,200)	(13,500)
Indexation allowance (June 2013 to December 2016)		
(0.064 ((265.7 – 249.7)/249.7) × £68,200)	(4,365)	
(0.064 × £13,500 – but restricted because indexation allowance cannot create a loss)		(500)
	———	———
Chargeable gain	87,435	0
	———	———

Working: Due date

The threshold for payment of corporation tax by instalment is as follows:

Year ending 28 February 2017	£1,500,000
4 months ending 30 June 2017 (£1,500,000 × 4/12)	£500,000

As Iron Ltd's taxable total profits are below the threshold, quarterly instalment payments are not required.

Tutorial note

Iron Ltd is not related to Sprint Ltd (or Olympic Ltd) for the purposes of establishing the corporation tax threshold, as they are not 51% subsidiaries of a third company. Christine is an individual, not a company.

(b) **Ownership of Iron Ltd**

Tutor's top tips

There are four different aspects to consider in this part of the question: ownership of shares by the company (with group implications); ownership of shares by the individual; sale of shares by the company (with substantial shareholding exemption); sale of shares by the individual (with entrepreneurs' relief).

A logical structure and use of headings to deal with each aspect in turn is important here.

Where possible, try to refer to facts from the scenario such as the potential trading loss in Iron Ltd. This will gain more marks than simply writing about general tax implications.

Ongoing ownership of Iron Ltd

Corporation tax

It would be advantageous for Sprint Ltd, rather than Christina, to purchase Iron Ltd for the following reasons.

- It is possible that Iron Ltd will make a trade loss for the period ending 30 June 2017. If this were to occur, a proportion of the loss could be surrendered by way of group relief to Sprint Ltd and/or Olympic Ltd and be deducted in arriving at the taxable total profits of the recipient company. Whilst all three companies remain in the group, group relief would also be available between them in respect of any losses in future periods.

- Iron Ltd will join Sprint Ltd's capital gains group on 1 November 2016. The capital loss to be made by Sprint Ltd on the sale of the warehouse could therefore be relieved against the chargeable gains to be realised by Iron Ltd on the sale of the industrial building and the fixed machinery. This would reduce the corporation tax liability of Iron Ltd by £7,600 (£22,627 − ((£113,135 − £38,000) × 20%)).

- A gain made by one of the companies in the group on the disposal of a qualifying business asset (land, buildings or fixed machinery used in the business) could be deferred if a qualifying business asset is purchased by any other company in the group during the qualifying period.

– Any future transfers of assets from one group company to another would take place on a no gain, no loss basis.

There is a possible disadvantage in Iron Ltd joining the Sprint Ltd group of companies in relation to capital allowances. The annual investment allowance will be split between the three companies if they are members of a group, whereas an additional full annual investment allowance would be available to Iron Ltd if Christina were to own Iron Ltd personally (unless Iron Ltd were to share premises or carry on activities similar to those of Sprint Ltd or Olympic Ltd).

Another disadvantage in Iron Ltd being purchased by Sprint Ltd is that Iron Ltd will be a related 51% group company with Sprint Ltd (and consequently Olympic Ltd) for the purposes of determining the threshold for payment of corporation tax by instalment. Accordingly, the corporation threshold will be divided by three, making it more likely that one or all of the companies may have to pay tax by quarterly instalment.

Value added tax (VAT)

It may be beneficial for Sprint Ltd and Iron Ltd (and possibly Olympic Ltd) to register as a group for the purposes of VAT. This is because it would remove the need for Iron Ltd to charge VAT on the sales it makes to Sprint Ltd. This will, however, be possible regardless of who owns Iron Ltd because Christina will have effective control of all three companies in both situations.

Sale of Iron Ltd

Sprint Ltd owns Iron Ltd

Any chargeable gain (or loss) on the sale of the shares will be exempt due to the substantial shareholding exemption (SSE). This exemption will be available because Sprint Ltd will have owned at least 10% of the ordinary share capital of Iron Ltd for more than a year and both companies are trading companies.

Although the existence of the SSE would appear to be a significant advantage, it should be recognised that the proceeds of sale will then need to be transferred to Christina. This could be carried out via, for example, the payment of a dividend to Christina. As Christina is a higher rate taxpayer, she would have an income tax liability of 25% or even 30.55% of the dividend received.

Tutorial notes

1 The rate of income tax payable by a higher rate taxpayer on dividend income is 25% (100/90 × (32.5% – 10%)). However, the dividend could cause Christina to become an additional rate taxpayer; the rate of income tax payable by an additional rate taxpayer on dividend income is 30.55% (100/90 × (37.5% – 10%)).

2 Credit was also available for reference to other ways in which the proceeds of sale could be transferred to Christina, for example, via the payment of a bonus.

Christina owns Iron Ltd personally

On a sale by Christina of the shares in Iron Ltd, there will be a chargeable gain equal to the excess of the sales proceeds over the price paid for the shares. This gain, after the deduction of any annual exempt amount not used against any other gains, will be subject to capital gains tax at 10% due to the availability of entrepreneurs' relief.

Entrepreneurs' relief will be available because Iron Ltd is a trading company and Christina will have owned at least 5% of its shares for more than a year, and Christina will be a director of Iron Ltd.

Tutorial note

It can be seen from the marking guide that it was not necessary to make all of the above points in order to score full marks.

(c) **VAT registration**

Tutor's top tips

This looks like a fairly standard section on VAT registration and penalties. The twist here was to spot that the client should be monitoring taxable sales, not cash receipts.

Iron Ltd should be monitoring the level of its taxable supplies (excluding sales of capital assets), as opposed to its cash receipts, in order to determine when it needs to register for VAT.

The implications of registering late are:

– Iron Ltd will be required to account for output tax on the sales it has made after the date on which it should have been registered. This will be a cost to Iron Ltd unless it is able to recover the VAT from its customers.

– A penalty may be charged for failing to register by the appropriate date. This penalty would be a percentage of the potential lost revenue where the percentage depends on the reason for the late registration.

– Interest may be charged in respect of the VAT paid late.

Examiner's comments

Part (a) required a calculation of the corporation tax payable for a company in respect of a 16-month set of accounts, including consideration of two asset disposals where rollover relief had been claimed previously. It was surprising, and indeed disappointing, to see that the majority of candidates calculated the corporation tax payable for the 16-month period as a whole, rather than recognising the need to split this into two separate accounting periods, the first covering the first 12 months and the second covering the remaining four months. This led to the loss of a number of what should have been easy marks. Candidates are reminded that a good level of familiarity with the F6 (UK) syllabus is required for P6; it is not enough to just focus on the new areas, candidates must ensure that they are also confident in dealing with more basic issues.

The majority of candidates recognised that the sale of the two business assets would cause the gain rolled over on the acquisition of these assets to become chargeable. However, the different treatments in respect of the depreciating asset (fixed machinery) and non-depreciating asset (building) was identified by only a small number of candidates.

Part (b) was for 13 marks and was the largest part of the question. It required a comparison of the tax implications of a company being acquired by an individual as opposed to by another company. Candidates who did well had a good knowledge of the subject, adopted a sensible, logical approach and addressed all of the issues briefly, as instructed in the question. Weaker candidates fell down in at least one of these areas.

The adoption of a logical approach in this sort of question requiring a comparison of two alternatives can save considerable confusion and avoid wasting time due to needless repetition. Candidates should pause and think before they start writing. Dealing fully with the implications of one of the alternatives first, and then the other, tended to provide a much clearer answer than those who adopted a less logical approach, apparently writing points as they occurred to them, without making it clear which alternative they were dealing with, constantly swapping between the two, and leading to a confusing answer.

Candidates should avoid repetition, including making the same point from different angles. An example in this case would be where a candidate has stated that if the company is acquired by another company, they would form a group for group relief purposes. Stating separately at a later point that if acquired by an individual there will not be a group for group relief purposes, scored no additional marks.

Part (c) concerned the often-tested area of registration for VAT, an area which the vast majority of candidates are very technically comfortable with. However, all but a handful failed to read the question in sufficient detail, and provided a very detailed account of the tests applied to determine whether compulsory registration is required, but this did not address the question and wasted a good deal of time. Where the subject coverage is very familiar it is particularly important to understand the context in which it is being tested. In this case, the key issue was recognition that monitoring the level of cash receipts is not relevant, it is the level of taxable supplies, i.e. the invoiced value of taxable sales which is relevant.

PAPER P6: ADVANCED TAXATION (FA2015)

ACCA marking scheme		
		Marks
(a)	Trading income	1.0
	Chargeable gains	
	Industrial building	2.0
	Machinery	1.5
	Crystallisation of deferred gain	1.0
	Chargeable gains in correct period	0.5
	Corporation tax payable	1.0
	Due dates	2.5
		9.5
	Maximum	9.0
(b)	Ongoing	
	Group relief	2.0
	Relief for capital losses	2.0
	Rollover relief	1.0
	No gain, no loss transfers	1.0
	Annual investment allowance	1.0
	Related 51% group companies	1.0
	VAT group registration	2.0
	Sale of Iron Ltd	
	Sprint Ltd owns Iron Ltd	3.5
	Christina owns Iron Ltd	2.0
		15.5
	Maximum	13.0
(c)	Taxable supplies as monitoring basis	1.0
	Implications of late registration	2.5
		3.5
	Maximum	3.0
Total		**25.0**

75 CINNABAR LTD *Walk in the footsteps of a top tutor*

Key answer tips

This question has three separate requirements which can be attempted in any order.

Part (a) covers research and development and intangible assets, which are popular topics in the P6 exam.

Part (b) requires detailed knowledge of the substantial shareholding exemption rules. These rules should be learnt as they are regularly tested.

Part (c) requires explanation of loss relief for two different group structures: a 75% group relief group and a consortium.

The highlighted words in the written sections are key phrases that markers are looking for.

(a) (i) **Research and development expenditure**

Tutor's top tips

This is a reasonably straightforward section on research and development relief for a small company. Note that the rates of relief for research and development are not provided in the tax rates and allowances in the exam and must be learnt.

There is a slightly tricky point regarding subcontracted costs, but a good pass could be obtained without this.

The computer hardware qualifies for a 100% capital allowance as capital expenditure on an asset related to research and development.

As Cinnabar Ltd is a small enterprise for research and development purposes, the revenue expenditure which is directly related to undertaking research and development activities qualifies for an additional 130% deduction in calculating its taxable trading income. This additional deduction applies to the software and consumables and the staff costs. However, as the external contractor is provided by an unconnected company, only £6,500 (65% of the £10,000 fee) will qualify for this additional deduction.

The rent payable is not a qualifying category of expense, so is not eligible for the additional deduction.

The total deduction from taxable trading profit for the year ended 31 March 2016 is therefore £423,650 (£228,000 + 130% × (£18,000 + £126,000 + £6,500)).

(ii) **Intra-group transfer of an intangible asset**

Tutor's top tips

There are just two marks available for setting out the tax implications of the transfer of an intangible asset within a 75% group, but these should have been an easy two marks to score.

As Cinnabar Ltd owns more than 75% of Lapis Ltd, the intangible asset will be treated for corporation tax purposes as having been transferred intra group at its tax written down value, thereby giving rise to neither profit nor loss in Cinnabar Ltd's corporation tax computation.

(b) **Disposal of Garnet Ltd shares**

Tutor's top tips

There are easy marks in this section for basic gains computations.

Don't forget to calculate the after-tax proceeds. Even if your tax calculation is wrong, you will still score marks for following through.

Watch out for the substantial shareholding exemption in questions involving companies disposing of shares.

A chargeable gain will arise on the proposed disposal in November 2016, calculated as follows:

	£
Sale proceeds	148,000
Less: Cost £120,000 × 2/3	(80,000)
Indexation allowance 0.1903 × £80,000	(15,224)
Chargeable gain	52,776
Corporation tax payable (£52,776 × 20%)	10,555
After-tax proceeds (£148,000 – £10,555)	137,445

The substantial shareholding exemption would not be available in respect of a disposal in November 2016. This is because Cinnabar Ltd's shareholding was reduced to 8% following the disposal on 20 October 2015 and consequently it has not held at least 10% of the shares in Garnet Ltd for a continuous 12-month period in the two years prior to disposal.

As Cinnabar Ltd held 12% of the shares prior to the first disposal on 20 October 2015, the sale should be brought forward to a date prior to 20 October 2016 in order for the substantial shareholding exemption to apply to the sale. In this case, Cinnabar Ltd's corporation tax liability in relation to the disposal of these shares will be reduced to nil.

Tutorial note

The shares in Garnet Ltd are in the share pool. Accordingly, the indexation factor is not rounded to three decimal places.

(c) **Loss relief implications of the alternative structures**

Tutor's top tips

You may find it useful to draw the two alternative group structures to help you to visualise the groups that exist for tax purposes.

This section really tests your knowledge of the definition of a consortium. Remember that there is no consortium where a single company owns at least 75% of the shares.

Structure 1:

Under this structure, Amber Ltd will own more than 75% of the shares in Beryl Ltd, so Beryl Ltd will be in a group with Amber Ltd for the purposes of group relief for trading losses. Accordingly, none of Beryl Ltd's trading loss will be available for surrender to Cinnabar Ltd.

Structure 2:

Under this structure, Beryl Ltd will be a consortium-owned company, with Amber Ltd and Cinnabar Ltd as the consortium members. This is because each of the companies owns at least 5% of the shares in Beryl Ltd, and together they hold at least 75% of the shares.

Beryl Ltd's trading loss for the year ending 31 December 2017 may be surrendered to the consortium members according to their respective shareholdings. Cinnabar Ltd may therefore claim a maximum of £19,200 (24% of Beryl Ltd's loss of £80,000) in respect of this year. Relief will be taken against Cinnabar Ltd's taxable total profits for the corresponding accounting period(s).

As Cinnabar Ltd prepares accounts to 31 March annually, the maximum loss which can be claimed for relief in the year ending 31 March 2017 will be the lower of £4,800 (3/12ths of the available loss of £19,200) and 3/12ths of Cinnabar Ltd's taxable total profit for the year ending 31 March 2017. Similarly, the maximum loss which can be claimed for relief in the year ending 31 March 2018 is the lower of £14,400 (9/12ths of £19,200) and 9/12ths of Cinnabar Ltd's taxable total profit for the year ending 31 March 2018.

PAPER P6: ADVANCED TAXATION (FA2015)

ACCA marking scheme				Marks
(a)	(i)	Computer hardware – 100% capital allowance		1.0
		Revenue expenditure qualifying for additional deduction		3.5
		Calculation of total deduction		1.0
				5.5
			Maximum	5.0
	(ii)	Intra-group disposal of intangible asset		2.0
(b)		After-tax proceeds		2.0
		Advantage of disposal in October		3.0
				5.0
(c)		Structure 1		2.0
		Structure 2 – Consortium		2.0
		Relief available		4.5
				8.5
			Maximum	8.0
Total				**20.0**

Examiner's comments

The first part required an explanation of the tax relief available for a small company in respect of expenditure on research and development. The majority of students were aware that directly related revenue expenditure qualifies for an additional 130% deduction, but were rather vague in their explanations as to why items were or were not included. A small minority wasted time by discussing the tax credit which could be obtained in respect of a loss created by the enhanced deduction, despite there being no mention of a loss in the question, nor sufficient information to be able to calculate one.

The first of the two assets sold was an intangible asset, which was sold to a wholly-owned subsidiary. Intangible assets are examined fairly frequently at P6, so candidates need to be aware of their tax treatment as trading assets, rather than capital assets, for companies, which will give rise to a balancing charge or allowance on sale, rather than a capital gain or loss. In the case of a transfer between two companies in a 75% group, the asset will be transferred at its written down value, thereby giving rise to neither profit nor loss. Interestingly, the majority of candidates identified one or other of these points, but very few identified both.

The second asset disposal related to shares in an unquoted trading company. This was the sale of an 8% shareholding in a company following a sale of 4% the previous year. In any question regarding the sale of shares in one company by another, candidates should automatically consider the application of the substantial shareholding exemption (SSE). This is an area where it is very important to know the precise conditions, to be able to state definitively whether or not the exemption applies, and the reasons why, or why not. In this case the timing of the disposal was critical; bringing the date of disposal forward would mean that the requirement to hold at least 10% of the shares for a continuous 12 month period in the two years prior to sale would be satisfied, whereas this would not be the case if the disposal was delayed. An ability to advise on the timing of transactions in respect of all taxes is an important skill at P6.

ANSWERS TO PRACTICE QUESTIONS: SECTION 2

> The final part of this question concerned a proposed joint venture between two companies, where two alternative group structures were being considered. The new company to be set up would be loss-making initially. The key issue here was to be able to differentiate between a group for group relief purposes (which requires one company to have a minimum 75% holding in another) and a consortium (which is formed where two or more companies hold a minimum of 75% between them in a third company, each with at least 5%, but none holding 75% or more on their own). It was disappointing to see that a good number of candidates were unclear on these definitions, thereby producing incorrect answers and scoring few marks. However, well-prepared candidates who were able to make this distinction tended to go on and score well in respect of the way in which the new company's trading losses could be relieved.

Section 3

PILOT PAPER EXAM QUESTIONS

Note: This pilot paper is not in the current exam format, but still provides useful practice.

SECTION A – BOTH QUESTIONS ARE COMPULSORY AND MUST BE ATTEMPTED

1   Hutt plc has owned the whole of the ordinary share capital of Rainbow Ltd and Coronet Ltd since 2003. All three companies are resident in the UK.

Their results for the year ended 31 March 2016 are as follows:

	Hutt plc £	Rainbow Ltd £	Coronet Ltd £
Taxable trading profit/(loss)	(309,000)	800,000	63,000
Capital gain	144,000	–	–
Rental income	65,000	–	–
UK bank interest receivable	2,000	57,000	18,000
Qualifying charitable donations	(15,000)		

Hutt plc's rental income of £65,000 per annum arises in respect of Hutt Tower, an office building acquired on 1 April 2015.

In the year ended 31 March 2015 Hutt plc had a trading profit of £735,000, UK bank interest receivable of £2,000 and a capital loss of £98,000, which was carried forward as at 31 March 2015.

Hutt plc and Coronet Ltd both carry on trades in the UK. Rainbow Ltd conducts both its manufacturing and trading activities wholly in the country of Prismovia. The system of corporation tax in Prismovia is mainly the same as that in the UK although the rate of corporation tax is 18%. There is no double taxation agreement between the UK and Prismovia.

Hutt plc has agreed that it will purchase the whole of the share capital of Lucia Ltd, a UK resident engineering component manufacturing company, on 1 July 2016 for £130,000.

Hutt plc will need to take out a loan to finance the purchase of Lucia Ltd. The company intends to borrow £190,000 from BHC Bank Ltd on 1 July 2016. BHC Bank Ltd will charge Hutt plc a £1,400 loan arrangement fee and interest at 7.25% per annum. Hutt plc only needs £130,000 of the loan to buy the share capital of Lucia Ltd and intends to use the balance of the loan as follows: £45,000 to carry out repairs to Hutt Tower; and the remainder to help fund the company's ongoing working capital requirements.

Lucia Ltd is a UK resident company. The scale of its activities in the last few years has been very small and it has made tax adjusted trading losses. As at 31 March 2016 Lucia Ltd has trading losses carried forward of £186,000. The company's activities from 1 April 2016 to 30 June 2016 are expected to be negligible and any profit or loss in that period can be ignored.

Because of the small scale of its activities Lucia Ltd has not been registered for value added tax (VAT) since March 2015. In arriving at the purchase price for the company, the owners of Lucia Ltd have valued the company's trading losses at £37,200 (£186,000 at 20%).

On the purchase of Lucia Ltd, Hutt plc has plans to return the company to profitability and the budgeted turnover of Lucia Ltd for the nine months ended 31 March 2017 is as set out below. All amounts relate to the sales of engineering components and are stated exclusive of VAT. It can be assumed that all categories of turnover will accrue evenly over the period.

		£
UK customers:	– VAT registered	85,000
	– non-VAT registered	25,000
European Union customers:	– VAT registered	382,500
	– non-VAT registered	70,000
Other non-UK customers		180,000
		742,500

Lucia Ltd will incur input VAT of £7,800 per month from 1 July 2016 in respect of purchases from UK businesses. It will also purchase raw materials from Dabet Gmbh for £17,000 in November 2016. Dabet Gmbh is resident and registered for VAT in Germany.

Lucia Ltd owns a number of properties but due to the reduced demand for its products has sold one property in Leeds in January 2016 realising a capital loss of £56,000. A second property in Manchester will be sold on 1 December 2016, and it is anticipated that a loss of £60,000 will arise on this disposal. It is proposed that an office building owned by Coronet Ltd be sold to Lucia Ltd in May 2017 at its market value. This building will then be sold on by Lucia Ltd, to Vac Ltd, an unconnected third party in June 2017, giving rise to a capital gain of £92,000. The intention is that this gain will be reduced by the capital losses arising on the sale of the properties.

Required:

(a) Describe and evaluate the options available in respect of the trading losses of Hutt plc for the year ended 31 March 2016. Assume today's date is 1 June 2016.

Your answer should include a recommendation on the most tax efficient use of these losses, together with details of and time limits for any elections or claims that would need to be submitted, assuming that the losses are to be used as soon as possible and are not to be carried forward. **(13 marks)**

(b) Prepare a report for the management of Hutt plc concerning the acquisition of Lucia Ltd.

The report should be in three sections, addressing the three sets of issues set out below, and should, where appropriate, include supporting calculations.

(i) **The purchase price**

Comment on the valuation placed on Lucia Ltd's trading losses, by the owners of Lucia Ltd.

Provide an explanation of the tax treatment of the loan arrangement fee and the interest payable on the loan of £190,000, assuming that Hutt plc continues to have bank interest receivable, in the year ended 31 March 2017, of £2,000. **(9 marks)**

(ii) **VAT issues**

Provide an explanation of the date by which Lucia Ltd will be required to register for VAT in the UK and any other relevant points in respect of registration.

Provide a calculation of the VAT payable by, or repayable to, Lucia Ltd in respect of the period from registration to 31 March 2017.

With reference only to the facts in the question, suggest ONE disadvantage of Lucia Ltd entering into a group VAT registration with Hutt plc. **(6 marks)**

(iii) **The office building**

Advise on the tax implications of the proposed sale of the office building by Coronet Ltd to Lucia Ltd in May 2017.

Your answer should consider all relevant taxes.

Evaluate the proposed strategy to reduce the capital gain arising on the sale of the office building by offsetting the capital losses on the sale of the properties in Leeds and Manchester. **(9 marks)**

Appropriateness of the format and presentation of the report and the effectiveness with which its advice is communicated. **(2 marks)**

You may assume that the tax rates and allowances for the financial year to 31 March 2016 and for the tax year 2015/16 will continue to apply for the foreseeable future.

(Total: 39 marks)

2 Your manager has had a meeting with Pilar Mareno, a self-employed consultant, and has sent you a copy of the following memorandum.

To:	The files
From:	Tax manager
Date:	31 May 2016
Subject:	Pilar Mareno – Business expansion

Pilar Mareno (PM) has been offered a contract with DWM plc, initially for two years, which will result in fees of £80,000 plus VAT per annum.

In order to service this contract, PM would have to take on additional help in the form of either a part-time employee for two days a week or the services of a self-employed contractor for 100 days per year. She would also have to acquire a van, which would be used wholly for business purposes. PM has decided that she will only enter into the contract if it generates at least an additional £15,000 per annum, on average, for the family after all costs and taxes.

PM's annual profitability and the profit generated by the contract (before taking into account the costs of the part-time employee/contractor and the van) are summarised below.

	Existing business	New contract
	£	£
Sales revenue	180,000	80,000
Less: Materials, wages and overheads	(120,000)	(33,000)
Profit per accounts and taxable profit	60,000	47,000

Supplies made under the contract will be 65% standard rated and 35% exempt for value added tax (VAT) purposes; this is the same as for PM's existing business. £31,500 of the costs incurred in relation to the contract will be subject to VAT at the standard rate. The equivalent figure for PM's existing business is £100,000.

PM has identified Max Wallen (MW) as a possible self-employed contractor. MW would charge £75 per day plus VAT for a contract of 100 days per year, with a rate of £25 per day plus VAT in respect of any days when he is ill (up to a maximum of 8 days per year). PM has a spare copy of the specialist software that MW would need but MW would use his own laptop computer.

Alternatively, PM could employ her husband, Alec (AM), paying him a gross annual salary of £8,600. AM would have to give up his current full time job, but would expect to do other part-time employed work earning a further £10,000 (gross) per annum.

PM estimates that a second hand van will cost £7,800 plus VAT or alternatively, a van could be leased for £300 plus VAT per month. We can assume that if the van is purchased, it will be sold at the end of the two year contract for £2,500 plus VAT.

Tax manager

An extract from an email from your manager is set out below.

Please prepare a memorandum for me, incorporating the following:

1 Calculations to demonstrate whether or not Pilar's desired annual after tax income from the new contract will be achievable depending on

 – whether she leases or buys the van; and
 – whether she employs Alec or uses Max Wallen.

 You may find it easier to:

 (i) work out the after tax cost of buying or leasing the van. When calculating the annual cost of the van, assume that the total cost can be averaged over the two years of the contract.

 and then to consider:

 (ii) the after tax income depending on whether Alec is employed or the self-employed contractor, Max, is used.

2 A rationale for the approach you have taken and a summary of your findings.

3 Any other issues we should be considering in respect of Pilar employing Alec, including any alternative to employment.

> 4 It seems to me that HM Revenue and Customs may be able to successfully contend that Max Wallen would be an employee, rather than a self-employed contractor.
>
> Prepare your figures on the basis that he is self-employed but include a list of factors in your memorandum, based on the information we have, that would indicate either employed or self-employed status.
>
> Take some time to think about your approach to this before you start. Also, as always when working on Pilar's affairs, watch out for the VAT as it can get quite tricky. I suspect the VAT will affect the costs incurred so you'll need to address VAT first. Pilar's estimate of the profit on the contract will have ignored these complications.
>
> Tax manager

You have extracted the following further information from Pilar Mareno's client file.

- None of Pilar's VAT inputs is directly attributable to either standard rated or exempt supplies.
- Alec has worked for a UK bank for many years and is currently paid an annual salary of £17,000.
- The couple have no sources of income other than those set out above.

Required:

Prepare the memorandum requested by your manager.

Marks are available for the four components of the memorandum as follows:

1	Relevant calculations.	(16 marks)
2	Rationale for the approach taken and summary of findings.	(2 marks)
3	Other issues in respect of Pilar employing Alec, together with any suggestions as to an alternative to employment.	(2 marks)
4	The employment status of Max Wallen.	(3 marks)

Appropriateness of the format and presentation of the memorandum and the effectiveness with which the information is communicated. **(2 marks)**

You may assume that the rates and allowances for the tax year 2015/16 will continue to apply for the foreseeable future.

(Total: 25 marks)

PAPER P6: ADVANCED TAXATION (FA2015)

SECTION B – TWO QUESTIONS ONLY TO BE ATTEMPTED

3 Stanley Beech, a self-employed landscape gardener, intends to transfer his business to Landscape Ltd, a company formed for this purpose.

The following information has been extracted from client files and from meetings with Stanley.

Stanley:

- Acquired a storage building for £46,000 on 1 July 2006 and began trading.
- Has no other sources of income.
- Has capital losses brought forward from 2013/14 of £10,900.

The whole of the business is to be transferred to Landscape Ltd on 1 September 2016:

- The market value of the assets to be transferred is £118,000.
- The assets include the storage building and goodwill, valued at £87,000 and £24,000 respectively, and various small pieces of equipment and consumable stores.
- Landscape Ltd will issue 5,000 £1 ordinary shares as consideration for the transfer.

Advice given to Stanley in respect of the sale of the business:

- "No capital gains tax will arise on the transfer of your business to the company."
- "You should take approximately 65% of the payment from Landscape Ltd in shares with the balance left on a loan account payable to you by the company, such that you can receive a cash payment in the future."

Advice given to Stanley in respect of his annual remuneration from Landscape Ltd:

- "The payment of a dividend of £21,000 is more tax efficient than paying a salary bonus of £21,000 as you will pay income tax at only 25% on the dividend received, whereas you would pay income tax at 40% on a salary bonus. The dividend also avoids the need to pay national insurance contributions."
- "There is no tax in respect of an interest free loan from an employer of less than £10,000."
- "The provision of a company car is tax neutral as the cost of providing it is deductible in the corporation tax computation."

Stanley's proposed remuneration package from Landscape Ltd:

- An annual salary of £50,000 and an annual dividend of approximately £21,000.
- On 1 December 2016 an interest free loan of £3,600, which he intends to repay in two years' time.
- A company car with CO_2 emissions of 122 g/km. The only costs incurred by the company in respect of this car will be lease rentals of £300 per month and business fuel of £100 per month.
- The annual employment income benefit in respect of the car is to be taken as £3,420.

Landscape Ltd:

- Will prepare accounts to 31 March each year.

PILOT PAPER EXAM QUESTIONS: SECTION 3

Required:

(a) (i) Explain why there would be no capital gains tax liability on the transfer of Stanley's business to Landscape Ltd in exchange for shares.

Calculate the maximum loan account balance that Stanley could receive without giving rise to a capital gains tax liability and state the resulting capital gains tax base cost of the shares. **(8 marks)**

(ii) Explain the benefit to Stanley of taking part of the payment for the sale of his business in the form of a loan account, which is to be paid out in cash at some time in the future. **(1 mark)**

(b) Comment on the accuracy and completeness of the advice received by Stanley in respect of his remuneration package.

Supporting calculations are only required in respect of the company car. **(9 marks)**

Ignore value added tax (VAT) in answering this question.

You may assume that the rates and allowances for the financial year to 31 March 2016 and the tax year 2015/16 will continue to apply for the foreseeable future.

(Total: 18 marks)

4 Mahia Ltd is an unquoted, UK resident trading company formed in May 2008. One of its shareholders, Claus Rowen, intends to sell his shares back to Mahia Ltd on 31 July 2016. Another shareholder, Maude Brooke, intends to give some of her shares to her daughter, Tessa.

The following information has been extracted from client files and from meetings with the shareholders.

Mahia Ltd:

– In May 2008 the company issued 40,000 shares at £3.40 per share as follows:

Claus Rowen	16,000
Charlotte Forde	12,000
Olaf Berne	12,000

– Olaf sold his 12,000 shares to Maude Brooke on 1 October 2014 when they were worth £154,000.

Claus and Charlotte:

– Have always lived in the UK.
– Are higher rate taxpayers who use their capital gains tax annual exempt amount every year.

Maude:

– Was born in the UK, but moved to Canada on 1 April 2012 with her daughter, Tessa.
– Has not visited the UK since leaving for Canada, but will return to the UK permanently in December 2021.
– Is employed in Canada with an annual salary equivalent to £70,000.

Sale of shares by Claus:

- Charlotte and Maude want to expand the company's activities in the UK but Claus does not. The shareholders have been arguing over this matter for almost a year.
- In order to enable the company to prosper, Claus has agreed to sell his shares to the company on 31 July 2016.

Gift of shares by Maude:

- Maude will gift 4,000 shares in Mahia Ltd to her daughter, Tessa, on either 1 August 2016 or 1 June 2017.
- She will delay the gift until 1 June 2017 (Tessa's wedding day) if this reduces the total tax due.
- The tax due in Canada will be the same regardless of the date of the gift.
- She has made no previous transfers of value for UK inheritance tax purposes.
- For the purposes of this gift, you should assume that Maude will die on 31 December 2020.

Market values of shares in Mahia Ltd on all relevant dates are to be taken as:

Size of shareholding %	Market value per share £
< 25	10.20
25 – 35	14.40
> 35	38.60

Market values of the assets of Mahia Ltd on all relevant dates are to be taken as:

	£
Land and buildings used within the trade	1,400,000
Three machines of equal value used within the trade	15,000
Motor cars used by employees	45,000
Quoted shares	42,000
Inventory, trade receivables and cash	145,000

Required:

(a) Advise Claus on the tax treatment of the proceeds he will receive in respect of the sale of his shares to Mahia Ltd.

Prepare a calculation of the net (after tax) proceeds from the sale based on your conclusions. **(8 marks)**

(b) Advise Maude on the UK tax consequences of gifting the shares to Tessa and prepare computations to determine on which of the two dates the gift should be made, if the total UK tax due on the gift is to be minimised.

Your answer should consider all relevant taxes. **(10 marks)**

You may assume that the rates and allowances for the tax year 2015/16 will continue to apply for the foreseeable future.

(Total: 18 marks)

PILOT PAPER EXAM QUESTIONS: SECTION 3

5 Vikram Bridge has been made redundant by Bart Industries Ltd, a company based in Birmingham. He intends to move to Scotland to start a new job with Dreamz Technology Ltd.

The following information has been extracted from client files and from meetings with Vikram.

Vikram Bridge:

- Is unmarried, but has been living with Alice Tate since 2002. The couple have four young children.
- Receives dividends of approximately £7,800 each year and makes annual capital gains of approximately £2,600 in respect of shares inherited from his mother.
- The couple have no sources of income other than Vikram's employment income and the £7,800 of dividends.

Made redundant by Bart Industries Ltd on 28 February 2016:

- Vikram's employment contract entitled him to two months' notice or two months' salary in lieu of notice. On 28 February 2016 the company paid him his salary for the two-month period of £4,700, and asked him to leave immediately.
- On 30 April 2016 the company paid him a further £1,300 in respect of statutory redundancy, together with a non-contractual lump sum of £14,500, as a gesture of goodwill.

Job with Dreamz Technology Ltd:

- Starts on 1 October 2016 with an annual salary of £45,480.
- The company will contribute £9,400 in October 2016 towards Vikram's costs of moving to Scotland.
- In November 2017, the company will issue free shares to all of its employees. Vikram will be issued with 200 shares, expected to be worth approximately £2,750.

Moving house:

- Vikram's house in Birmingham is fairly small; he intends to buy a much larger one in Glasgow.
- The cost of moving to Glasgow, including the stamp duty land tax in respect of the purchase of his new house, will be approximately £12,500.
- To finance the purchase of the house in Glasgow Vikram will sell a house he owns in Wales, in August 2016.

House in Wales:

- Was given to Vikram by his mother on 1 September 2007, when it was worth £145,000.
- Vikram's mother continued to live in the house until her death on 1 May 2016, when she left the whole of her estate to Vikram.
- At the time of her death the house had severe structural problems and was valued at £140,000.
- Vikram has subsequently spent £18,000 improving the property and expects to be able to sell it for £195,000.
- Vikram is keen to reduce the tax payable on the sale of the house and is willing to transfer the house, or part of it, to Alice prior to the sale if that would help.

Required:

Prepare explanations, including supporting calculations where appropriate, of the following issues suitable for inclusion in a letter to Vikram.

(a) The taxable gain on the sale of the house in Wales in August 2016, together with the potential effect of transferring the house, or part of it, to Alice prior to the sale, and any other advice you consider helpful. **(3 marks)**

(b) The inheritance tax implications in respect of the house in Wales on the death of Vikram's mother. **(2 marks)**

(c) The income tax treatment of redundancy payments received from Bart Industries Ltd and Vikram's taxable income in 2016/17. **(4 marks)**

(d) The income tax treatment of the receipt by Vikram of the shares in Dreamz Technology Ltd. **(3 marks)**

(e) How Vikram's job with Dreamz Technology Ltd will affect the amount and date of payment of the income tax due on his dividend income for 2018/19 and future years. **(6 marks)**

Ignore national insurance contributions in answering this question.

You may assume that the rates and allowances for the tax year 2015/16 will continue to apply for the foreseeable future.

(Total 18 marks)

Section 4

ANSWERS TO PILOT PAPER EXAM QUESTIONS

SECTION A

1 HUTT PLC

>
>
> **Key answer tips**
>
> The first part of the question covers standard use of losses within a group to achieve the 'most tax efficient' result. However, you must be careful of the complication, which is that Rainbow has most of its profits taxed abroad, so any group relief claim must not prejudice the double tax relief available.
>
> In the report section, the question has set out the structure and you need to stick with this. Use the headings given with sub headings for each separate issue.
>
> In discussing Lucia's losses for (b)(i) the examining team has given you a clue to the fact that the losses brought forward will be disallowed by telling you that the company's activities immediately before the sale are negligible.
>
> In discussing VAT registration in part (ii) it is always necessary to consider whether the future test may be applicable – students often miss this. VAT on exports is an important exam topic.
>
> Finally in part (iii) note the instruction to consider all relevant taxes, which for a building transfer will always include stamp duty land tax and VAT.

(a) **Options available in respect of the trading losses of Hutt plc of £309,000**

  (i) **Within Hutt plc**

   The loss can be offset against the total profits before qualifying charitable donations of Hutt plc for the year ended 31 March 2016.

	£
Capital gain	144,000
Less: Capital loss brought forward	(98,000)
	46,000
Rental income	65,000
Interest income	2,000
Total profits	113,000

KAPLAN PUBLISHING 691

This claim is an 'all or nothing' claim, and would reduce the profits of Hutt plc to £Nil, which would result in the £15,000 qualifying charitable donations becoming unrelieved and wasted.

However, Hutt plc could surrender part of its loss as group relief (see below) and could ensure that the losses retained would reduce its total profits to exactly £15,000, to preserve the relief for the qualifying charitable donations.

Hutt plc could also make a claim to carry back the losses to the previous twelve months. However, a current period offset has to be made before losses can be carried back to the previous twelve months, which would again waste the qualifying charitable donations in the current year.

(ii) **Group relief**

Hutt plc, Rainbow Ltd and Coronet Ltd are in a group for group relief purposes as Hutt plc controls at least 75% of the other two companies. Any amount of the £309,000 loss can be surrendered to each of the two subsidiary companies in order to reduce their taxable total profits. However, the maximum surrender is restricted to the taxable total profits of the recipient company.

Coronet Ltd has taxable total profits of £81,000 (£63,000 + £18,000), and could claim £81,000 of Hutt plc's loss.

Rainbow Ltd has taxable total profits of £857,000 (£800,000 + £57,000), and could possibly claim all of Hutt plc's loss.

However, Rainbow Ltd has a permanent establishment in Prismovia as it manufactures and trades in that country. The profits arising in Prismovia will be taxed in that country at 18%. Double tax relief will be available in the UK in respect of the Prismovian tax suffered, up to a maximum of the UK tax on the Prismovian profits; any surrender to Rainbow Ltd must ensure that relief for the foreign tax suffered is not lost.

The maximum surrender that can be made to Rainbow Ltd whilst preserving relief for the foreign tax is calculated as follows.

	£
Trading profit ((£800,000 × 2%)/20%)	80,000
Interest income	57,000
Maximum surrender	137,000

Tutorial note

The differential in tax rates in the UK and Prismovia is 2% (20% − 18%).

All of the interest income is taxable at 20% and trading profits left to be charged to tax after loss relief will be taxable at an effective rate of 2%.

Therefore the trading profits that need to be included in taxable total profits to cover DTR will be 2/20 of the trading profit for the year (see proof below).

(iii) **Recommendations**

In order to maximise the tax saved, the losses should be offset against the profits of Hutt plc, Coronet Ltd and Rainbow Ltd whilst preserving the relief for the qualifying charitable donations in Hutt plc and the foreign tax suffered in Rainbow Ltd.

Accordingly, £98,000 of the losses should be offset against the total profits in Hutt plc to leave £15,000 (£113,000 – £98,000) profit to be offset by the qualifying charitable donations. Losses of £81,000 should be surrendered to Coronet Ltd, with the balance of £130,000 (£309,000 – £81,000 – £98,000) surrendered to Rainbow Ltd. This is less than £137,000, and therefore, preserves relief for all of the foreign tax.

Tax will be saved within all companies at 20%.

Tutorial note

Alternatively, the surrender of £137,000 to Rainbow Ltd and £74,000 (£309,000 – £137,000 – £98,000) to Coronet Ltd would achieve the same result, and would gain full marks.

When making a claim to offset a company's trading loss against its total profits, it is not possible to specify the amount to be offset; all of the losses available will be offset subject to the level of taxable profits. Accordingly, in order to achieve the desired result, the claims must be made in the following order.

1. Elections to surrender losses of £130,000 to Rainbow Ltd and £81,000 to Coronet Ltd. These must be made by 31 March 2018 (i.e. within one year of the filing date of the claimant company's tax return). Both Rainbow Ltd/Coronet Ltd and Hutt plc must elect.

2. An election to offset the remaining losses (£98,000) against the total profits of Hutt plc should be submitted by the same date (i.e. within two years of the end of the period in which the loss was made).

Tutorial note

The tax computation of Rainbow Ltd for the year ended 31 March 2016 following the group relief claim is set out below. Group relief of £57,000 is offset against the interest income with the balance of £73,000 (£130,000 – £57,000) being offset against the trading profit in order to maximise the double tax relief:

	£
Trading profit (£800,000 – £73,000)	727,000
Interest income (£57,000 – £57,000)	–
Taxable total profits	727,000
Corporation tax @ 20%	145,400
Less: Double tax relief (£800,000 × 18%)	(144,000)
Corporation tax payable	1,400

If more than £130,000 was surrendered to Rainbow Ltd, the maximum group relief claim that should be made to preserve DTR would be only £137,000 as shown below:

	£
Trading profit (£800,000 – £80,000)	720,000
Interest income (£57,000 – £57,000)	–
Taxable total profits	720,000
Corporation tax @ 20%	144,000
Less: Double tax relief (£800,000 × 18%)	(144,000)
Corporation tax payable	Nil

(b) **Report to the management of Hutt plc**

To: The management of Hutt plc

From: Tax advisers

Date: 1 June 2016

Subject: The acquisition of Lucia Ltd

(i) **The purchase price**

Valuation of the trading losses in Lucia Ltd

Lucia Ltd has no profits in the year ended 31 March 2016 or the previous year against which to offset the losses.

The trading losses arose before Lucia Ltd joined the Hutt plc group, and therefore, they cannot be surrendered to any of the group members.

The losses cannot be carried forward as there will be a change of ownership of Lucia Ltd after its activities have become negligible. Losses arising prior to the change of ownership cannot be offset against profits arising once the trade has been revived.

The losses cannot be used, and therefore, they have no value to Hutt plc.

Loan from BHC Bank

Hutt plc is to enter into a loan relationship with BHC Bank. Any amounts charged to the company's statement of profit or loss in respect of the relationship are allowable deductions for tax purposes. Accordingly, a tax deduction is available for the interest and the loan arrangement fee on the accruals basis.

On the assumption that the loan arrangement fee is charged to the statement of profit or loss in full in the year ended 31 March 2017, the total amount charged in the accounts will be £11,731 (£1,400 + (£190,000 × 7.25% × 9/12)).

The income from which this amount can be deducted in the corporation tax computation depends on the use made of the finance obtained.

	Finance £		Allowable cost £
For the purpose of investments:			
Acquisition of Lucia Ltd	130,000		
Repairs to Hutt Tower	45,000		
	175,000	175/190 × £11,731	10,805
For the purpose of the trade:			
Working capital requirements	15,000	15/190 × £11,731	926
Total finance obtained	190,000		11,731

Where the finance has been used for trading purposes, the cost of £926 is deductible in arriving at Hutt plc's taxable trading income.

Where the finance has been used for non-trading purposes, the cost of £10,805 is deductible from Hutt plc's interest income in respect of loan relationships. This results in a deficit, or loss, of £8,805 (£10,805 – £2,000) in the year ended 31 March 2017.

The deficit can be:

- Offset against other income and gains of Hutt plc of the same accounting period.
- Offset against the interest income of Hutt plc of the previous 12 months.
- Surrendered as group relief to companies within the group relief group.
- Carried forward and offset against future non-trading income and gains.

The most tax efficient use of the deficit will depend on the level of profits in Hutt plc and the other group companies in the year ended 31 March 2017.

(ii) **VAT issues**

Registration

All the supplies made by Lucia Ltd are taxable supplies for the purposes of VAT. The company must register for VAT if its taxable supplies:

- in the previous 12 months exceed £82,000; or
- in the next 30 days are expected to exceed £82,000.

It is anticipated that the company's supplies in the nine months ended 31 March 2017 will be £742,500 and that these supplies will accrue evenly over the period. This amounts to supplies of £82,500 per month. Accordingly, Lucia Ltd must register with effect from 1 July 2016 and must notify HMRC by 30 July 2016.

Lucia Ltd intends to make supplies to non-VAT registered customers in the European Union (EU). If Lucia Ltd is responsible for the delivery of the goods it should be aware that once its supplies in any one particular member state exceed that state's 'distance selling' threshold, it may be required to register for VAT in that state.

VAT in respect of the nine months ended 31 March 2017

	£
Output tax	
UK customers – VAT registered (£85,000 × 20%)	17,000
UK customers – non-VAT registered (£25,000 × 20%)	5,000
EU customers – VAT registered – zero-rated	–
EU customers – non-VAT registered (£70,000 × 20%)	14,000
Other non-UK customers – zero-rated	–
Acquisition from Dabet Gmbh (£17,000 × 20%)	3,400
	39,400
Input tax	
In respect of purchases from UK businesses (9 × £7,800)	70,200
Acquisition from Dabet Gmbh	3,400
	73,600
Repayment of VAT due (£73,600 – £39,400)	34,200

Tutorial note

VAT must be charged on supplies to all UK customers, whether or not they are registered for VAT.

Supplies to EU customers are zero-rated in the country of origin, unless the customer is not registered. In this case, VAT is charged at the point of origin at the appropriate rate. Therefore Lucia Ltd must charge 20% VAT in the normal way (i.e. the origin system).

All supplies to non-EU customers are zero-rated, regardless of whether or not the customer is registered.

An acquisition from a VAT registered EU supplier will be treated as zero-rated in the country of origin, however is chargeable at the appropriate rate in force in the country of destination. Therefore Lucia Ltd must account for output VAT at 20% on the purchase from Dabet Gmbh, but can reclaim the equivalent amount of input VAT in the same quarter (i.e. the destination system).

Disadvantage of entering into a group VAT registration

Lucia Ltd makes mainly zero-rated supplies and is in a VAT repayment position. It can improve its cash flow position by accounting for VAT monthly and receiving monthly repayments of VAT. It would not be in a position to do this if it were to register in a VAT group.

Under a group registration, the group's representative member will account for VAT payable to HMRC on behalf of all group companies. It may be some time before Lucia Ltd's accounting system is aligned with that of Hutt plc. The existence of two different systems may create administrative difficulties in preparing a group VAT return.

Note: Only one of the above disadvantages was required

(iii) **Sale of the office building from Coronet Ltd to Lucia Ltd**

Tax implications:

Corporation tax

At the time of the transfer, Coronet Ltd and Lucia Ltd will be in a capital gains group as they will both be 75% subsidiaries of Hutt plc. Therefore the transfer of the office building will be deemed to occur at no gain, no loss. Lucia Ltd will have a capital gains tax base cost in the building equal to the cost to Coronet Ltd plus indexation allowance up to the date of the transfer

Value added tax (VAT)

The transfer will be outside the scope of VAT if the two companies are in a VAT group.

If the two companies are registered separately, the treatment depends on whether the building is less than three years old or if Coronet Ltd has opted to tax the building. If so, then the transfer to Lucia Ltd will be standard rated and VAT must be charged. If not, the transfer will be an exempt supply.

Stamp duty land tax

There will be no stamp duty land tax on the transfer as both companies are 75% subsidiaries of Hutt plc.

Relief of the gain on the sale of the office building to Vac Ltd

Lucia Ltd has made two capital disposals at a loss.

The first property in Leeds was sold before Lucia Ltd became a member of the Hutt plc group. As a result, the capital loss can only be deducted from capital gains made by Lucia Ltd on assets it owned when it joined the group, or ones bought after from unconnected parties and used for the purposes of their own business.

The loss on the Manchester property will be realised after the company joined the group and can therefore be set-off against any gains made by Lucia Ltd or other group companies, including the gain on the sale of the office building to Vac Ltd.

It is not necessary to transfer the office building to Lucia Ltd before the sale as Lucia Ltd and Coronet Ltd can make a joint election to reallocate the gain to Lucia Ltd. The election must be submitted by 31 March 2020 (i.e. within two years of the end of the accounting period in which the disposal of the office building occurs).

Alternatively the loss on the Manchester property could be transferred to Coronet Ltd leaving the gain chargeable in their computation. The election to transfer the loss must be submitted by 31 March 2019, as the loss arises in the year ended 31 March 2017.

Either would produce the same tax cost for the group.

The tax saving would be £12,000 (£60,000 × 20%).

ACCA marking scheme		
		Marks
(a) Hutt plc trading losses		
Within Hutt plc		
Current year offset		0.5
Available profits		1.0
Avoid wasting QCDs		1.0
Carry back opportunity		0.5
Group relief		
Relevant companies		0.5
Available relief		0.5
Coronet Ltd available profits		0.5
Rainbow Ltd		
Available profits		0.5
Tax position in Prismovia		1.0
Effect of DTR		2.0
Recommendation		
Identify sensible objective		1.0
Hutt plc – restrict to preserve QCDs		0.5
Surrender to Coronet		0.5
Surrender to Rainbow Ltd		0.5
Order of elections		1.0
Group relief election – both companies/time limit		1.0
Current year offset election/time limit		1.0
		13.5
	Maximum	13.0
(b) (i) The purchase price		
Trading losses:		
No current relief in Lucia Ltd		0.5
No group relief with reason		1.0
No carry forward with reasons		1.5
Conclusion		0.5
Loan from BHC Bank		
Tax deduction per accounts treatment		1.0
Total amount allowable in the period		0.5
Amount relating to trading purpose		1.0
Amount relating to non-trading purpose		2.0
Uses of deficit		2.0
Recommendation		0.5
		10.5
	Maximum	9.0

ANSWERS TO PILOT PAPER EXAM QUESTIONS: SECTION 4

	Marks
(ii) VAT issues	
Registration	
Historic and future limits	1.0
Registration and notification dates	1.0
Distance selling thresholds	0.5
Calculation	
Output tax	2.5
Input tax	1.0
Disadvantage of group VAT registration	
– either of Lucia Ltd in repayment position; or administrative difficulties	1.0
	7.0
Maximum	6.0
(iii) The office building	
Sale from Coronet Ltd to Lucia Ltd	
Capital gain	
CGT group	0.5
Consequences	1.0
VAT	
If group registration	0.5
If no group registration	1.5
Stamp duty land tax	1.0
Sale of building to Vac Ltd	
Pre-entry losses	
Identify	0.5
Consequences	1.0
Loss on Manchester property	1.0
Election re notional transfer – availability	1.0
Impact of tax rates on transfer	0.5
Both companies and time limit	1.0
	9.5
Maximum	9.0
Format and style	
Appropriate style and presentation	1.0
Effectiveness of communication	1.0
	2.0
Total	**39.0**

2 PILAR MARENO

Key answer tips

This is a tricky question asking for a decision on whether a self-employed consultant should take on a new contract and how the contract should be carried out.

The question requires quite careful calculations of the net of tax cost of each option and it is important to consider all relevant taxes – in this case NIC and VAT as well as income tax.

Note also that the question gives marks for recognising the relevant issues as well as for calculations, so it is important to state relevant points even if you cannot see exactly how to calculate the tax implications.

To: The files

From: Tax assistant

Date: 1 June 2016

Subject: Pilar Mareno – Business expansion

This memorandum considers the implications of Pilar Mareno (PM) accepting the DWM plc contract.

Rationale and approach

PM has decided to accept the contract if it generates at least £15,000 per annum on average for the family after all costs and taxes.

PM will either employ her husband, Alec, or use the services of Max Wallen, and will either buy or lease a van. However, it can be seen from workings 3 and 4 that it is cheaper to buy rather than lease the van, and therefore, there are only two options to consider.

- Employ Alec and buy a van – Appendix 1
- Use Max Wallen and buy a van – Appendix 2.

Summary of findings

The contract generates sufficient income after tax and costs for the family under both of these options (see Appendices) and a higher income after tax and costs is achieved if PM employs Alec.

However, the issues raised below in relation to PM employing Alec should be considered before a decision is made.

Issues in respect of PM employing Alec

1   Alec has worked for a UK bank for many years. It is risky to give up an apparently secure job in exchange for a two year contract requiring two days' work a week and other, as yet unidentified, part-time work.

   Accordingly, Alec should obtain advice as regards his personal situation. If we are asked to provide this advice we must recognise that PM and Alec would be two separate clients. The work would have to be managed in such a way as to ensure that we do not allow the interests of PM to adversely affect those of Alec or vice versa.

2   PM and Alec should consider forming a partnership. This would reduce national insurance contributions as Alec would only pay 9% on his share of the profit plus class 2 at £2.80 per week whereas the cost of employer and employee class 1 contributions where Alec is an employee is 13.8% and 12% respectively.

Alec's profit share could be more than £8,600. This would enable income currently taxed at 40% in PM's hands to be taxed at 20% in Alec's hands.

However, this saving in income tax would be offset by increased national insurance costs as the national insurance on PM's marginal income is only 2% whereas Alec would pay 9%.

Employment status of Max Wallen

Max's employment status will be determined by reference to all of the facts surrounding his agreement with PM.

Factors indicating employee status

1   It appears that Max has to do the work himself and cannot use a substitute.

2   Max is to be paid by the day rather than by reference to the performance of particular tasks.

3   Max is to be paid for the days when he is sick.

4   Max is to be provided with the specialist software he needs to do the work.

Factors indicating self-employed status

1   Max provides his own laptop computer.

Tutorial note:

Remember that no one factor is conclusive. HMRC will look at all of the facts to decide Max's status.

There is insufficient information provided regarding other factors, such as the level of control over Max's work, to justify their inclusion within the terms of the brief provided.

Without further information a conclusion cannot be drawn.

APPENDIX 1 – EMPLOY ALEC AND BUY A VAN

	£
Profit on contract	47,000
Irrecoverable VAT due to partial exemption (W1)	(9,205)
Salary paid to Alec	(8,600)
Class 1 secondary NICs re Alec ((£8,600 – £8,112) × 13.8% = £67) Reduced to nil by employment allowance of £2,000	Nil
	29,195
Income tax and class 4 NICs due (£29,195 × (40% + 2%))	(12,262)
	16,933
Increase in Alec's income (W2)	1,088
Purchase of van (less than cost of leasing van) (W3 and W4)	(1,696)
Income of family after all taxes	16,325

Tutorial note:

Pilar requires additional income for the family of £15,000 before agreeing to enter into the contract. Consideration is therefore needed of the effect on both Pilar's and Alec's position.

The salary paid to Alec is a cost as far as Pilar is concerned and therefore tax allowable. The effect of the salary on Alec's income is calculated in (W2) below.

APPENDIX 2 – USE MAX WALLEN AND BUY A VAN

	£
Profit on contract	47,000
Irrecoverable VAT due to partial exemption (W1)	(9,205)
Fees paid to Max Wallen (100 × £75)	(7,500)
Irrecoverable VAT on fees (£7,500 × 20% × 35%)	(525)
	29,770
Income tax and class 4 NICs due (£29,770 × (40% + 2%))	(12,503)
	17,267
Purchase of van (less than cost of leasing van) (W3 and W4)	(1,696)
Income of family after all taxes	15,571

Tutorial note:

There are no NICs payable by Pilar on Max's fees if she uses Max on a self-employed contract basis.

Workings

(W1) Irrecoverable VAT due to partial exemption

	£
Without the new contract:	
In respect of the existing business (£100,000 × 20% × 35%)	7,000

This is below the annual de minimis limit of £7,500 (£625 × 12) and is therefore fully recoverable.

	£
With the new contract:	
In respect of the existing business (as above)	7,000
In respect of the costs of the DWM contract (£31,500 × 20% × 35%)	2,205
	9,205

This exceeds the annual de minimis limit and is irrecoverable.

Tutorial note:

Pilar's taxable turnover is not affected by the sale of the van as it is a capital asset.

Neither of the other two de minimis tests are relevant here as they require either the total input tax to be not more than £625 per month on average, or the difference between the total input tax and the input tax on directly attributable taxable supplies to be not more than £625 per month on average.

(W2) Increase in Alec's income

	£
Increase in gross salary ((£8,600 + £10,000) – £17,000)	1,600
Less: Income tax and NICs on additional salary (£1,600 × (20% + 12%))	(512)
Increase in after tax income	1,088

Tutorial note:

At the margin, Alec pays income tax at the basic rate of 20% and NIC at 12%.

Alec will also be better off because he now has two jobs, and class 1 NICs are calculated independently for each employment (unless they are related). So in each job the first £8,060 of salary has no NICs and he would save £967 (£8,060 × 12%). This point has not been included in the calculation as the details of his other employment are not known.

(W3) Cost of purchasing van

	£
Net cost (£7,800 – £2,500) for two year period	5,300
Income tax and class 4 NICs saved (£5,300 × (40% + 2%))	(2,226)
Irrecoverable VAT (£7,800 × 20% × 35%)	546
Income tax and class 4 NICs saved (£546 × (40% + 2%))	(229)
	3,391
Average cost per year (£3,391 × ½)	1,696

Tutorial note:

The net cost of the van will be tax allowable through the capital allowances system and therefore income tax and class 4 NICs will be saved.

There will be irrecoverable VAT of 35% of the cost of the van as the business is partially exempt, but this will also be tax allowable and save both income tax and NICs.

(W4) Cost of leasing van (per year)

	£
Lease rentals (£300 × 12)	3,600
Income tax and class 4 NICs saved (£3,600 × (40% + 2%))	(1,512)
Irrecoverable VAT (£3,600 × 20% × 35%)	252
Income tax and class 4 NICs saved (£252 × (40% + 2%))	(106)
	2,234

As the annual cost of purchasing the van (W3) is less than the costs of leasing, all further calculations in the Appendices are based on the decision that PM will purchase the van.

ANSWERS TO PILOT PAPER EXAM QUESTIONS: SECTION 4

ACCA marking scheme	
	Marks
(1) Calculations	
Employ Alec:	
Net profit of contract	0.5
Alec's salary and class 1 secondary NICs	1.5
Irrecoverable VAT/purchase of van	0.5
Tax and NICs saved	0.5
Increase in Alec's income:	
Identification of issue	1.0
Calculation	1.5
Use Max:	
Fees paid	0.5
Irrecoverable VAT on fees	0.5
Tax and NICs saved	0.5
Supporting calculations	
Irrecoverable VAT:	
Identification of issue	1.0
Current partial exemption position	1.0
Application of de minimis	1.0
Irrecoverable amount with new contract	1.0
Purchase of van:	
Net cost	0.5
Irrecoverable VAT	1.0
Tax and NICs saved	1.0
Cost per year	0.5
Leasing van	
Rentals	0.5
Irrecoverable VAT	1.0
Tax and NICs saved	1.0
	16.5
Maximum	**16.0**
(2) Rationale and summary	
Reference to Pilar's income criterion	1.0
Conclusion re van and implications	1.0
Summary of findings	1.0
	3.0
Maximum	**2.0**
(3) Employment of Alec	
Secure job, short term contract	1.5
Use of partnership	2.0
Alec would be a separate client from Pilar	1.0
	4.5
Maximum	**2.0**
(4) Employment status of Max	
Depends on all of the facts	0.5
Each valid factor – 0.5 mark (max 5 factors)	2.5
	3.0
Format and style	
Appropriate style and presentation	1.0
Effectiveness of communication	1.0
Maximum	**2.0**
Total	**25.0**

3 STANLEY BEECH

Key answer tips

The key to success in part (a) is understanding that Stanley can afford to have some chargeable gains after incorporation relief, because these can be covered by his capital losses and the annual exempt amount.

In part (b) it is important to answer the question set and not do unnecessary calculations. Also remember that an owner managed company like this will always be a close company and look out for any close company implications.

(a) **Transfer of the business to Landscape Ltd**

(i) **Capital gains tax liability**

Where all of the assets of Stanley's business are transferred to Landscape Ltd as a going concern wholly in exchange for shares, any capital gains arising are relieved via incorporation relief such that no capital gains tax liability arises.

However, where part of the payment received from the company is in the form of a loan account, Stanley will have chargeable gains as set out below.

For Stanley to have no liability to capital gains tax in 2016/17, assuming he has no other capital gains in the year, his chargeable gains must be covered by his capital losses brought forward (£10,900) and the annual exempt amount of £11,100.

	£
Gain on building (£87,000 – £46,000)	41,000
Gain on goodwill	24,000
Total capital gains before reliefs	65,000

Incorporation relief should therefore be:
(£65,000 – £10,900 – £11,100) 43,000

Therefore the MV of the shares to be accepted should be:

$$£43,000 = £65,000 \times \frac{\text{MV of shares}}{£118,000}$$

MV of shares = £78,062

Therefore the loan account to accept as part of the consideration can be up to the value of £39,938 (£118,000 – £78,062) and there will be no capital gains tax arising on the transfer.

The shares will have a capital gains tax base cost of £35,062 computed as:

	£
MV of shares (see above)	78,062
Less: Incorporation relief	(43,000)
Base cost of shares	35,062

Tutorial note:

Proof that incorporation relief of £43,000 will avoid a CGT liability is as follows:

	£
Total capital gains	65,000
Less: Incorporation relief $£65,000 \times \dfrac{£78,062}{£118,000}$	(43,000)
	22,000
Less: Capital losses	(10,900)
	11,100
Less: Annual exempt amount	(11,100)
Taxable gains	Nil

No entrepreneurs' relief is used as there is no chargeable gain arising on incorporation.

A chargeable gain will arise on the disposal of shares and entrepreneurs' relief may then be available subject to the normal conditions based on the ownership of the shares.

This should not be an issue providing Stanley retains the shares in the company for at least 12 months before he disposes of them.

(ii) **The benefit of using a loan account**

The loan account crystallises capital gains at the time of incorporation without giving rise to a tax liability due to the availability of capital losses, and the annual exempt amount.

This reduces the gains deferred against the base cost of the shares in Landscape Ltd from £65,000 to £43,000 such that any future gains on the disposal of the shares will be smaller.

Stanley can extract the loan account of £39,938 from Landscape Ltd in the future with no 'tax cost', by having the loan repaid.

Tutorial note:

The subsequent disposal of the shares will be eligible for entrepreneurs' relief provided the conditions are satisfied, as none of Stanley's lifetime allowance of £10,000,000 has been utilised.

(b) **Advice on Stanley's remuneration package**

(i) **Dividend**

The advice in respect of the dividend is accurate but not complete as it ignores the cost to Landscape Ltd. Because Stanley owns Landscape Ltd, he must consider the effect on the company's position as well as his own.

Dividends are not tax deductible. The profits paid out as a dividend to Stanley will have been subject to corporation tax at 20%. On the other hand, Landscape Ltd will obtain a tax deduction at 20% for a salary bonus together with the related national insurance contributions.

There will be an overall tax saving from paying a dividend as opposed to a salary bonus. However the benefit will not be as great as suggested by the advice that Stanley has received due to the different treatment of the two payments in hands of the company.

(ii) **Interest free loan**

The advice in respect of the loan is again accurate but not complete. The loan will not give rise to an employment income benefit as it is for not more than £10,000, but the advice again ignores the position of the company.

As the company is controlled by Stanley, Landscape Ltd will be a close company. Accordingly, the loan to Stanley is a loan to a participator in a close company, and as Stanley owns more than 5% of the company's share capital there is no de minimis in this case.

Thus, Landscape Ltd must pay an amount equal to 25% of the loan (£900) to HMRC. The payment will be due on 1 January 2018 (i.e. nine months and one day after the end of the accounting period in which the loan is made).

When the loan is repaid by Stanley, Landscape Ltd may reclaim the £900. The repayment by HMRC will be made nine months and one day after the end of the accounting period in which the loan is repaid.

(iii) **Company car**

The advice in respect of the company car is not correct because of the difference in the tax rates applying to the company and to Stanley, and the liability to class 1A national insurance contributions.

Tax cost of providing car:	£
Class 1A national insurance contributions (£3,420 × 13.8%)	472
Income tax on benefit (£3,420 × 40%)	1,368
	1,840

ANSWERS TO PILOT PAPER EXAM QUESTIONS: SECTION 4

	£
Tax saved:	
Cost of providing car (£400 × 12)	4,800
Class 1A national insurance contributions	472
	5,272
Corporation tax @ 20%	1,054
Net tax cost (£1,840 – £1,054)	786

ACCA marking scheme

			Marks
(a)	(i)	Split of consideration	
		Incorporation relief – 3 conditions	1.5
		Amount of future cash payment:	
		Rationale – gains to equal capital losses and annual exempt amount	1.5
		Gains on transfer of business	1.0
		Gains after incorporation relief:	
		Incorporation relief	1.0
		Calculation of gains after incorporation relief	0.5
		Solving to find value of the loan account	1.0
		Entrepreneurs' relief	1.0
		CGT base cost of shares:	
		Value of assets transferred for shares	0.5
		Incorporation relief	1.0
	(ii)	Benefit of using a loan account	
		Capital gains	1.0
		Extract funds with no tax cost	0.5
			10.5
		Maximum	**9.0**
(b)		Advice on remuneration package	
		Dividend	
		Advice is correct but incomplete with reason	1.0
		CT position re dividend	0.5
		CT position re bonus	0.5
		Conclusion with reason	1.0
		Interest free loan	
		Advice is correct but incomplete with reason	1.0
		Close company	0.5
		Loan to a participator and reason	1.0
		Tax due/when	1.0
		Repayment position	0.5
		Company car	
		The advice is not correct with reason	1.0
		Calculation	
		Tax cost	1.0
		Tax saving	1.0
			10.0
		Maximum	**9.0**
Total			**18.0**

4 MAHIA LTD

Key answer tips

It is important when dealing with purchase of own shares to state all the factors that make a transaction either income or capital. Most of the marks for part (a) are available for this with only a few for the calculation of the after tax proceeds.

In part (b), even if you missed the tricky point that the percentage holdings of the remaining shareholders increase after the cancellation of Claus's shares, you could still pick up most of the marks for this section.

(a) **Sale of shares in Mahia Ltd**

The proceeds received on a purchase by a company of its own shares are subject to either income tax or capital gains tax depending on the circumstances.

The normal assumption on a purchase of own shares by a company is that any payment you receive for the shares, over and above the amount originally subscribed for them, would be an income distribution, and treated in the same way as a payment of a dividend. The net amount received, less the amount originally subscribed, would be grossed up by 100/90 and included in your taxable income.

Alternatively, where the transaction satisfies the conditions set out below, the proceeds are treated as capital proceeds giving rise to a capital gain.

Your proposed sale of shares to Mahia Ltd satisfies these conditions and will therefore give rise to a capital gain.

- Mahia Ltd is an unquoted trading company.
- The purchase of shares is for the benefit of the company's trade as the disagreement between you and your sisters is having an adverse effect on the company's trade.
- You are resident in the UK.
- You have owned the shares for more than five years.
- You are selling all of your shares such that your holding is reduced by at least 25% and you will own less than 30% of Mahia Ltd following the sale.
- The purchase is not part of a scheme designed to avoid tax.

Advance clearance can be obtained from HM Revenue and Customs, to confirm that the capital treatment applies to a purchase of own shares.

The capital gains tax arising on the sale and the net cash proceeds after tax will be:

Number of shares sold (16,000/40,000)	40%

Gain qualifying for entrepreneurs' relief

	£
Proceeds (16,000 × £38.60)	617,600
Less: Cost (16,000 × £3.40)	(54,400)
Chargeable gain	563,200
Capital gains tax (£563,200 × 10%)	56,320
Proceeds after tax (£617,600 – £56,320)	561,280

Tutorial note:

Entrepreneurs' relief is available as Claus is disposing of shares in his personal trading company (i.e. he has more than a 5% holding) and he is an employee of the company.

Claus has already used his CGT annual exempt amount, therefore all of the remaining gain is taxed at 10%.

Following the purchase of its own shares from Claus, Mahia Ltd will cancel the shares. The company will therefore have 24,000 issued shares with effect from 1 August 2016.

(b) **Gift to Tessa**

Capital gains tax (CGT)

Maude lives in Canada and is non-UK resident. In addition, she is not a temporary non-resident for the purposes of capital gains tax as her stay in Canada will be for more than five years.

Accordingly, there will be no UK CGT on the gift of the shares to Tessa.

Even if Maude were a temporary non-resident, there would be no capital gains tax on the gift of the shares as she acquired them after she left the UK.

Inheritance tax (IHT)

As the shares are situated in the UK, UK IHT will be due on any transfers of value concerning them, regardless of the domicile of the transferor. Therefore, we do not need to consider Maude's domicile.

The gift by Maude to Tessa will be a potentially exempt transfer (PET) and no IHT will be payable. In addition, if Maude were to survive seven years from the date of the gift, there would be no IHT to pay on death.

However, the question asks us to assume that Maude will die on 31 December 2020. As this date is within seven years of the proposed dates of the gift, there would be a potential liability to IHT on death for each proposed date as follows:

Gift on 1 August 2016

	£
Value of shares before gift (12,000 × £38.60 (50% holding)) (Note 1)	463,200
Value of shares after gift (8,000 × £14.40 (33.3% holding))	(115,200)
Transfer of value	348,000
Less: BPR (Note 2)	(Nil)
Less: Annual exemptions for 2016/17 and 2015/16	(6,000)
Taxable amount	342,000
IHT (40% × (£342,000 – £325,000 NRB available))	6,800
Less: Taper relief (4 to 5 years) (£6,800 × 40%)	(2,720)
Potential IHT payable (Note 3)	4,080

Tutorial note:

1. On 1 August 2016 Mahia Ltd will have 24,000 issued shares as the shares sold by Claus to the company will have been cancelled, therefore Maude's holding before the gift will be a 50% holding.

2. BPR is not available as Maude acquired the shares on 1 October 2014 and therefore has not owned the shares for two years.

3. Double tax relief may be available to reduce this UK liability, in respect of any inheritance taxes payable in Canada.

Gift on 1 June 2017

	£
Transfer of value (as above)	348,000
Less: BPR (W) £348,000 × £1,605,000 / £1,647,000	(339,126)
	8,874
Less: Marriage exemption	(5,000)
Less: Annual exemptions for 2017/18 and 2016/17 (part only)	(3,874)
Taxable amount	Nil

Conclusion

Maude should therefore make the gift on 1 June 2017 as there would be no potential IHT liability due to the availability of BPR.

However, this presupposes that Tessa will continue to own the shares or replacement business property up to the date of Maude's death on 31 December 2020, and so preserve the entitlement to BPR.

If these conditions are not satisfied BPR is denied and a potential liability would arise. This would still be lower than potential liability if the gift were in August 2016, due to the availability of the marriage exemption.

Stamp duty

As the transfer of shares is made by way of gift (i.e. for no consideration), no stamp duty is payable.

Working: Restriction of BPR due to excepted assets in the company

	£
MV of assets (£1,400,000 + £15,000 + £45,000 + £145,000 + £42,000)	1,647,000
Less: MV of excepted assets (Quoted shares)	(42,000)
MV of assets excluding excepted assets	1,605,000

ACCA marking scheme		
		Marks
(a)	Sale of shares by Claus	
	Purchase of own shares	
	Identify and distinguish between the two possible treatments	1.0
	CGT treatment applies	1.0
	Reasons why:	
	Unquoted trading company	0.5
	Resident	0.5
	Owned for more than 5 years	0.5
	Not part of a scheme to avoid tax	0.5
	For benefit of company's trade with	1.0
	Reduction in holding criteria	1.0
	Availability of advance clearance	1.0
	Calculation	
	Gain	1.0
	Effect of entrepreneurs' relief on tax charge	1.0
	Net of tax proceeds	0.5
		9.5
	Maximum	**8.0**

		Marks
(b)	**Gift to Tessa**	
	CGT	
	No CGT due	0.5
	Reasons why:	
	Not resident	0.5
	Asset acquired after becoming resident abroad	0.5
	Not temporarily non-resident	0.5
	IHT	
	IHT applies, shares are UK property	0.5
	Gift on 1 August 2016	
	Transfer of value	1.0
	No BPR with reason	1.0
	Chargeable transfer (2 × annual exemptions)	0.5
	Taper relief available	0.5
	Calculation of tax due	0.5
	Reference to DTR	0.5
	Gift on 1 June 2017	
	Assumption re Tessa's continued ownership	1.0
	BPR	1.0
	Marriage and annual exemptions	1.0
	Advice	1.0
	Stamp duty	
	Not applicable, gift	0.5
		11.0
	Maximum	10.0
Total		**18.0**

5 VIKRAM BRIDGE

Key answer tips

The question requires you to prepare explanations, with supporting calculations, suitable for inclusion in a letter to Vikram.

The answer should therefore adopt the appropriate language and style you would expect to use when writing to a client.

(a) **Taxable gain on the sale of the house in Wales**

Your taxable capital gain on the sale of the Welsh property will be computed as follows:

	£
Proceeds in August 2016	195,000
Less: Base cost (Note 1)	(145,000)
Enhancement expenditure	(18,000)
Chargeable gain (Note 2)	32,000
Less: Annual exempt amount (£11,100 – £2,600)	(8,500)
Taxable gain	23,500

Tutorial note:

1 The base cost is the market value as at 1 September 2007. The fact that his mother continued to live in it and it declined in value up to the date of her death is not relevant for capital gains tax.

2 Principal private residence relief is not available as Vikram never lived in the house, and entrepreneurs' relief is not available as the house is not a qualifying business disposal. The gain would not, therefore, benefit from the 10% tax rate.

Proposal to gift part of the house to Alice prior to disposal

Giving the house, or part of it, to Alice prior to the sale will not reduce the taxable gain. As you and Alice are not married, the inter spouse exemption is not available.

Therefore, if you make a gift to Alice, a capital gain will arise by reference to the market value of the property in exactly the same way as if you had sold the property to an unconnected third party.

The gain on such a gift cannot be deferred with a gift relief claim as the house is not a business asset for gift relief purposes.

(b) Inheritance tax due in respect of the house in Wales

Usually, where a gift is made to an individual more than seven years prior to the donor's death, as in the case of your mother's gift of the house to you, there are no inheritance tax (IHT) implications on the death of the donor.

However, because your mother continued to live in the house after she gave it to you, the gift will be taxed under the rules applying to 'gifts with reservation of benefit'.

In these circumstances, HM Revenue and Customs will ignore the original gift as, although the asset was gifted, your mother continued to use it as if it were her own. Therefore, the house will be included in your mother's death estate for IHT purposes at its market value at the date of her death (i.e. £140,000).

(c) Income tax treatment of redundancy payments

The payments you received on being made redundant from Bart Industries in 2016/17 are taxed as follows:

- The payment in lieu of notice of £4,700 is taxed in 2015/16, the year of receipt.
- Statutory redundancy pay is not taxable.
- A non-contractual lump sum up to a maximum of £28,700 (£30,000 – £1,300) is not subject to income tax. As the amount is £14,500, it will be exempt.

The relocation costs paid by Dreamz Technology Ltd are exempt from income tax up to a maximum of £8,000.

Taxable income – 2016/17

	£
Salary (£45,480 × 6/12)	22,740
Removal costs (£9,400 – £8,000)	1,400
Employment income – Dreamz Technology Ltd	24,140
Dividend income (£7,800 × 100/90)	8,667
Total income	32,807
Less: Personal allowance	(10,600)
Taxable income	22,207

(d) **Shares in Dreamz Technology Ltd**

The income tax treatment of the issue to you of shares in Dreamz Technology Ltd depends on whether or not the shares are issued via an approved share incentive plan.

Where there is no share incentive plan, the market value of the shares received (£2,750) will be taxable as employment income in 2017/18 (i.e. the year in which you receive them).

If there is a share incentive plan (SIP) approved by HM Revenue and Customs then an employer can give shares to its employees, up to a maximum value of £3,600 per employee per year, with no income tax consequences. However, the shares must be kept within the plan for a stipulated period and income tax will be charged if they are withdrawn within five years.

If you withdraw the shares from the plan within three years, income tax will be charged on their value at the time of withdrawal. If you withdraw them more than three years but within five years, income tax will be charged on the lower of their value when you acquired them and their value at the time of withdrawal.

(e) **Amount of income tax on dividend income**

When you worked for Bart Industries Ltd you were not a higher rate taxpayer as your taxable income was less than £31,785, as set out below. Accordingly, your dividend income was taxed at 10%, with a 10% tax credit such that there was no income tax payable.

	£
Employment income (£4,700 × ½ × 12)	28,200
Dividend income (£7,800 × 100/90)	8,667
Total income	36,867
Less: Personal allowance	(10,600)
Taxable income	26,267

In 2018/19 your annual salary from Dreamz Technology Ltd less the personal allowance is £34,880 (£45,480 – £10,600). As this exceeds £31,785, all of your dividend income will fall into the higher rate tax band such that it is taxed at 32.5% less a 10% tax credit. This gives rise to income tax payable on the dividend income of £1,950 (£8,667 × 22.5%).

Tutor's top tips

Knowing that Vikram is a higher rate taxpayer you could calculate the income tax payable using the marginal rate of tax for dividends of 25% (i.e. income tax payable = (25% x £7,500) = £1,950).

Date of payment of income tax on dividend income

The tax due in respect of your dividend income must be paid on 31 January after the end of the tax year (i.e. on 31 January 2020 for 2018/19) under self-assessment.

You do not have to pay the tax earlier than this by instalments as the amount due is less than 20% of your total annual income tax liability as set out below.

The income tax on your employment income from Dreamz Technology Ltd will continue to be collected under the PAYE system.

	£
Taxable employment income (£45,480 – £10,600)	34,880

Income tax:

£	
31,785 @ 20%	6,357
3,095 @ 40%	1,238
34,880	

	£
Income tax liability on employment income	7,595
Income tax liability on dividend income (£8,667 × 32.5%)	2,817
Total annual income tax liability	10,412
Less: PAYE (equal to liability on employment income)	(7,595)
Tax credit on dividend income (£8,667 × 10%)	(867)
Income tax payable via self-assessment	1,950
Threshold for payments by instalments (£10,412 × 20%)	2,082

Tutorial note

The important thing in this working is to determine the total income tax liability, and then assume that only the higher rate tax on the dividend will be payable by self-assessment (i.e. £1,950).

It could have been set out as a standard income tax computation.

PAPER P6: ADVANCED TAXATION (FA2015)

	ACCA marking scheme	
		Marks
(a)	**Taxable capital gain on the sale of the house**	
	Computation of capital gain	
	Capital gain	0.5
	Annual exempt amount	0.5
	Effect of gift to Alice	1.0
	Style	1.0
		3.0
(b)	**Inheritance tax due in respect of the house**	
	Gift more than seven years prior to death	0.5
	Gift with reservation rules apply	0.5
	Consequences	1.0
		2.0
(c)	**Income tax**	
	Treatment of redundancy payments	2.0
	Computation of taxable income	2.0
		4.0
(d)	**Shares in Dreamz Technology Ltd**	
	Identify two possible treatments	0.5
	Treatment if no share incentive plan	1.0
	Exemption under share incentive plan	1.0
	Withdrawal from plan within five year	1.0
		3.5
	Maximum	3.0
(e)	**Amount of income tax on dividend income**	
	Tax position whilst working for Bart Industries Ltd	
	No tax payable on dividends	1.0
	Computation	1.0
	Tax position whilst working for Dreamz Technology Ltd	1.5
	Date of payment of income tax on dividend income	
	Due date with reason	1.5
	Computation	2.5
		7.5
	Maximum	6.0
Total		**18.0**